MSC/NASTRAN Primer

Static and Normal Modes Analysis

MSC/NASTRAN Primer

Static and Normal Modes Analysis

Harry G. Schaeffer

Schaeffer Analysis, Inc.

Schaeffer Analysis, Inc.
Kendall Hill Road
Mont Vernon, New Hampshire 03057

Library of Congress Number 79-63973

MSC/NASTRAN Primer: Static and Normal Modes Analysis

© 1979 by Schaeffer Analysis, Inc. All rights reserved. No part of this book may be reproduced, stored in a retrieval system, or transmitted in any form or by any means without prior written permission of Schaeffer Analysis, Inc.

Printed in the United States of America

Third Printing (with substantial revisions)
   January, 1982

Produced by Wallace Press, Inc.
   Milford, New Hampshire

Technical illustrations — Leah Rideout

Jacket Design — Jill Weber

Table of Contents

Appendices

Preface

The field of linear structural analysis has matured to the point where useful technology has been coded and is available as computer programs. This state of affairs could well be called computerized technology.

The computer programs which support structural analysis represent the cutting edge of technology in structural mechanics as well as the fields of computer science and numerical analysis. It is an unfortunate fact of life that the structural engineer must be aware of the technological content of the large analysis programs such as MSC/NASTRAN in order to use them efficiently and effectively.

It has been my observation that the typical user of general purpose programs based on the finite element analysis has a marginal background in structural analysis with little or none in numerical analysis or computer science. The task of confronting the user is thus staggering. The user must master the vocabulary of the program sufficiently well to cause it to execute, and meet delivery and cost schedules.

The resulting state of affairs is truly dangerous. The user will be frustrated by poor documentation, a limited background and a series of fatal error messages from the program. When the program finally accepts the data and produces results the user may be mesmerized into believing that just because the program ran, the results are correct. Nothing could be further from the truth. In fact, the engineers' job has just begun since the computer results must be validated.

The purpose of this book is twofold. The first goal is to provide the user with a description of the technological content of a current general purpose finite element program using MSC/NASTRAN as a model. The second goal is to describe the MSC/NASTRAN vocabulary and capability for static and normal modes analysis.

The material presented in this text is not new or original, but its organization is a departure from finite element text books and the MSC/NASTRAN manuals. The material is organized functionally rather than in alphabetic order. Thus all of the input data associated with specifying degrees of freedom or in modifying the stiffness matrix are described in Chapter 7. Similarly, the finite elements are described in Chapter 9, material properties in Chapter 10 and static loads in Chapter 11.

The organization of the MSC/NASTRAN program is described in Chapter 1 which includes a discussion of the various data decks in MSC/NASTRAN. Chapter 2 provides a review of matrix and index notation and Chapter 3 is included to try to motivate the reader to learn more about the MSC/NASTRAN language called DMAP.

The theoretical foundation for the finite element method is presented in Chapters 4 through 6, and the behavioral functions used to approximate element behavior are presented in Chapter 8.

Chapters 12 and 13 describe the use of MSC/NASTRAN for static and normal modes analysis, respectively. Chapter 13 includes the formulation of real eigenvalue problems and a discussion of the eigenvalue extraction routines.

The material in this book describes MSC/NASTRAN as it appeared in the Spring of 1979. Since the software/hardware environment is continually changing it is inevitable that the program will change over a period of time to the point where the descriptive material contained herein is out of date.

The material presented in this book has been used to support intensive short courses on the finite element method and static and normal modes analysis using MSC/NASTRAN. In the university environment the material could be adequately covered in two semesters. Students should be encouraged to use the program during the course since the program provides a source of example problems and is the ultimate learning tool.

This book is similar to the *NASTRAN Primer: Statics and Normal Modes Analysis* which was printed in 1977 and which reflected Level 15.5 COSMIC NASTRAN. In order to reflect the current version of MSC/NASTRAN it was necessary to essentially rewrite those portions of the original text that described the program capability. A close comparison of the two books will show that Chapters 2, 4, 5, 6, and 8, which present the technological content of the program, are basically unchanged. The remainder of the book, while organized similarly to the original, has been rewritten.

I would like to acknowledge the cooperation of the MacNeal-Schwendler Corp. in preparing this book. In particular, Dr. Richard MacNeal who encouraged me to undertake the project and who later spent long hours at the Boulder Patch proofreading the copy; and Steve Wall, Jerry Joseph, Mike Gockel, Dean Bellinger, and C. W. McCormick for their technical assistance.

It is also a personal pleasure to acknowledge the day-to-day assistance and support from my close friend, business associate, and wife, Judith Ann. This book is truly a joint venture and would not have been written in any other way.

Finally, this book is dedicated to you, the reader and the soon-to-be MSC/NASTRAN expert. If you really want to understand and master the technique for using the program you have a long journey ahead of you. Bon Voyage!

Harry G. Schaeffer   March, 1979
Schaeffer Analysis, Inc.
Kendall Hill Road
Mont Vernon, N. H. 03057

PREFACE — to 3rd Edition

The field of engineering analysis is a dynamic one. More efficient matrix methods are developed, new capability is defined and the user/program interface must be modified to reflect these changes. Any book such as this one, which attempts to describe current computerized technology, always runs the risk of becoming obsolete since the program is an almost living entity that will change with time.

Fortunately, in the restricted area of static analysis the technology appears to be stabilizing. The element technology and the analysis algorithm have not changed significantly, and in these areas the 3rd edition differs from the 2nd only in eliminating typographical errors as well as an occasional error in substance.

However, the recommended algorithm for normal modes analysis have been completely rewritten to include a powerful technique for reduction of dynamic degrees of freedom which is termed generalized dynamic reduction. Chapter 13 on normal modes analysis has thus been extensively rewritten to reflect the new recommended rigid format as well as the deletion of the determinate method for eigenvalue extraction.

I have also enhanced the material on the MSC/NASTRAN language which is called DMAP and which is described in Chapter 3. My goal is to provide a sufficiently detailed explanation of the language so that it can be used in later sections to describe the algorithms and the concept of changing existing rigid formats.

List of Symbols

The following is a list of the principal symbols used in this text. Other symbols are defined where they appear.

Matrices are denoted by a boldface symbol. Subscripts, if they appear, are generally used to denote the MSC/NASTRAN displacement set associated with the matrix. The order of the matrix is then indicated by the number of subscripts with the first indicating the row set and the second the column set. For example $\mathbf{M}_{ao}$ is a partition of the mass matrix which has "a" rows and "o" columns.

Overbars and tildas ($\sim$) are used to denote special quantities. The dot notation is used to represent derivatives with respect to time.

Matrices and Sets

$\mathbf{a}$	Set of polynomial coefficients (eq. 8.1) or acceleration vector
a_{ij}	Direction cosines (Sec. 4.1.5)
$\mathbf{B}$	Boolian transformation matrix (eq. 7.2)
$\mathbf{b}$	Defined by (eq. 6.33)
$\mathbf{C}$	Compliance matrix (eq. 4.72)
$\mathbf{c}$	Forces of constraint
c_i	Number of active columns in i^{th} row of a matrix (Sec. 7.3.5)
$\mathbf{D}$	Matrix of differential operators (eq. 6.29) or rigid body transformation matrix
$\mathbf{E}$	Elasticity matrix (eq. 4.64)
$\mathbf{E}_f$	Bending rigidity matrix (eq. 4.93)
E_{ijkl}	Elasticity tensor (Sec. 4.3.1)
$\mathbf{e}$	Physical components of strain (eq. 4.66)
$\mathbf{e}_I$	Initial strain (Sec. 4.3.6)
$\mathbf{e}^o$	Reference surface strains (eq. 4.79)
$\mathbf{F}$	Force or Flexibility matrix (Sec. 7.9)
$\mathbf{G}$	Transformation matrix
$\mathbf{G}_1, \mathbf{G}_2, \mathbf{G}_3, \mathbf{G}_4$	Material matrices associated with membrane, bending, shear, and membrane-bending coupling, respectively (eq. 9.57)
$\mathbf{I}$	Unit matrix or inertia tensor
$\mathbf{i}_1, \mathbf{i}_2, \mathbf{i}_3$	Unit vectors in coordinate directions
$\mathbf{J}$	Jacobian of transformation (Sec. 8.6.2) or transformed matrix in the standard form of the eigenvalue problem (eq. 13.30)
$\mathbf{k}$	Element Stiffness matrix (Sec. 6.2)
$\mathbf{K}$	Assembled Stiffness matrix
$\mathbf{L}$	Lower triangular matrix (Sec. 2.2.2.5)
L_{ij}	Lagrangian large strain tensor (eq. 4.14)
ℓ_{ij}	Lagrangian small strain tensor (eq. 4.14)
$\mathbf{M}$	Assembled mass matrix (eq. 13.5) or moment resultants (eq. 4.82)
$\mathbf{m}$	Element mass matrix (eq. 6.72)
$\mathbf{N}$	Shape functions (Sec. 8.2), force resultants (eq. 4.83), or defining direction of force (eq. 11.2)
$\mathbf{n}$	Unit normal to surface, matrix representation
n_i	Unit normal to surface, indicial representation
$\mathbf{P}$	Set of node point forces
$\mathbf{p}(m)$	Set of polynomial functions up to m^{th} order (eq. 8.1)
$\mathbf{Q}$	Shear resultant vector
$\mathbf{R}$	Position of material point in deformed body (Sec. 4.1), or coefficient matrices in MPC relation (Sec. 7.5.1)
$\mathbf{r}$	Position of material point in undeformed body (Sec. 4.1)

S	Element rigid body transformation matrix (Sec. 7.8) or compliance matrix (Eq. 10.17)
T	Set of surface tractions (Sec. 6.5)
U	Upper triangular matrix (Sec. 2.2.4)
u	Set of node point displacements
v	Displacement vector or orientation vector used to define local coordinate system for finite elements
v_i	Displacement vector, indicial representation
v*	Prescribed displacement on the boundary (eq. 5.30)
X	Body force
Y	Prescribed displacement values

Special Symbols

M	Modal mass matrix (13.26)
K	Modal stiffness matrix (13.27)

Scalars

A	Area
C	Degree of freedom code
D	Bending rigidity (eq. 4.94)
E	Modulus of elasticity
G	Grid or scalar point identification number, or shear modulus
I	Moment of inertia
I_{yy}, I_{zz}, I_{zy}	Area moments of inertia about local bending axes
J	Torsional constant
K_y, K_z	Shear coefficients
L	Length
M	Moment or experimentally determined multiply and add time (Sec. 7.3.5)
m	Mass
Q_x, Q_y	Shear resultants
q	Distributed surface pressure
t	Time or thickness
U	Internal strain energy (eq. 4.19)
U_o	Internal strain energy density (eq. 5.17)
U*	Complementary internal strain energy (eq. 5.31)
V	Potential, or beam forces shear resultant, or volume
(u, v, w)	Scalar components of displacement (eq. 4.76)
W	Work or solution wavefront (Sec. 7.3.5)
W_e	Work of external forces
W_i	Work of internal forces

Greek Symbols

α	Coefficients of thermal expansion (Sec. 4.3.6)
δ_{ij}	Kronecker delta
σ	Stress vector (eq. 4.37) or components of stress (eq. 4.66)
σ_i	Stress vector, indicial representation
σ_{ij}	Components of stress, indicial representation
σ*	Prescribed stress vector on boundary (eq. 5.21)
λ	Lamé coefficient (eq. 4.70), eigenvalue, or transformation matrix
ν	Poissons' ratio
μ	Lamé coefficient (eq. 4.70)
κ^o	Curvatures of reference surface (eq. 4.81)
θ	Rotation or angular coordinate
ρ	Density
ϵ	Error

(ξ, η, ζ)	Intrinsic coordinates
ϕ	Eigenvector
ω	Circular frequency or Angular velocity vector
ω_i	Components of rotation vector (eq. 4.24)

Subscripts

a	Analysis set
e	Denotes e^{th} element
f	Set of free displacements
g	Set of all degrees of freedom
h	Set of modal coordinates in solution set
i	Denotes i^{th} node
ℓ	Set left over
m	Set removed by use of multipoint constraint equations
n	Set not removed by multipoint constraints
o	Set omitted by static condensation
q	Set of generalized coordinates in the solution set
r	Set which removes rigid body motion
s	Set specified by single point constraint
t	Set of physical degrees of freedom in the solution set
w	Partition of a-set that has null columns
x	Partition of a-set that has non zero matrix coefficients
(x, y, z)	Denote component in coordinate sense

1

Structural Analysis Using NASTRAN

1.1. Introduction

NASTRAN (NAsa STRuctural ANalysis) was conceived and developed by the National Aeronautics and Space Administration (NASA) to fill a need for a universally available finite element program. The program was originally to be machine independent to facilitate its dissemination, but differences in word length, overlay structure, and system input/output routines made this goal impractical and led to the development of NASTRAN versions for the three most widely used computers.

NASTRAN was initially released into the public domain in 1969 through the Computer Software management and information center (COSMIC). The program originally was available on a purchase basis until the COSMIC release of Level 16.0. This and all subsequent COSMIC releases have been available only on a restricted lease basis.

In addition to the NASA-supported version of NASTRAN which is commonly called COSMIC/NASTRAN there are several proprietary versions of NASTRAN. The most widely known of these propriety versions is called MSC/NASTRAN which is developed and maintained by the MacNeal-Schwendler Corporation.

MSC/NASTRAN and COSMIC/NASTRAN have common origins in Level 15.5 NASTRAN. Both versions have been developed by separate organizations and although the programs bear a superficial resemblance they are different programs.

The MSC/NASTRAN version is taken to be the standard for NASTRAN for several reasons including:

1. Its wide usage
2. Advanced features
3. Responsiveness to user needs

MSC/NASTRAN is used throughout the world. These installations include many of the world's largest corporations and most of the large commercial data centers in the United States, Europe and Japan.

MSC/NASTRAN has been continually maintained and developed. The program includes a consistent set of isoparametric two and three dimensional elements, rigid elements, superelements for substructural analysis, and improved cyclic symmetry as well as numerical analysis and computer science enhancements.

Although MSC/NASTRAN is significantly different from COSMIC/NASTRAN in terms of relative efficiency and program capability it still retains downward compatibility to Level 15.5. Thus, the data decks for static and normal modes analyses will generally be the same or similar for both versions. Data decks that have been developed using COSMIC/NASTRAN can be executed with few if any changes on MSC/NASTRAN. Data decks which have been developed on MSC/NASTRAN and use unique MSC/NASTRAN capability cannot generally be executed using COSMIC/NASTRAN.

MSC/NASTRAN is also available from various data centers throughout the United States and the world. MSC/NASTRAN, thus, is becoming the de facto standard for structural analysis. Because of MSC/NASTRAN's wide-spread use and ready availability, this book will present the theory of matrix structural analysis and the finite element method in terms of the MSC/NASTRAN program.

1.2. Overview of MSC/NASTRAN

MSC/NASTRAN is a system that will create and manipulate a data base to solve problems using matrix structural analysis. The program acronym is now out of date since MSC/NASTRAN has been used to formulate and solve problems in all fields of continuum mechanics.

The system, shown schematically in Fig. 1-1, is composed of a data base, an executive system, and modules that perform modeling, data base manipulation, and program I/O. The data base can be created directly from the input stream by the I/O modules, or it can be created by modeling modules. The data base is then manipulated by the functional modules (addition, subtraction, equation solving, etc.) to obtain a solution data set that is then selectively displayed by the user. The whole process is controlled by the MSC/NASTRAN executive, which is, in turn, under user control by means of the MSC/NASTRAN language that is called DMAP (Direct Matrix Abstraction Programming). The MSC/NASTRAN executive is always controlled by a sequence of DMAP statements, but sets of pre-coded DMAP sequences, called rigid formats, have been included in the program. The user can then incorporate the entire set of DMAP instructions associated with a particular rigid format by a single directive in the MSC/NASTRAN data deck.

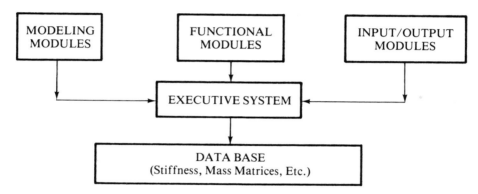

Figure 1-1. Schematic of NASTRAN Functional Organization

A specific analysis capability is thus an ordered execution of a set of DMAP instructions. MSC/NASTRAN includes rigid formats for performing a large number of analyses types including

- Static Analysis
- Static Analysis with Inertia Relief
- Normal Modes Analysis
- Static Analysis with Differential Stiffness
- Buckling Analysis
- Direct Complex Eigenvalue Analysis
- Direct Frequency and Random Response
- Direct Transient Analysis
- Modal Complex Eigenvalue Analysis
- Modal Frequency and Random Response
- Modal Transient Analysis
- Static Analysis with Cyclic Symmetry
- Normal Modes with Cyclic Symmetry

Only those rigid formats that perform linear static and normal modes analysis will be described in this Primer.

There is a natural aversion to learning a new programming language, and these rigid formats allow one to use certain MSC/NASTRAN capability without having to learn the MSC/NASTRAN DMAP language. However, the user's ability to utilize DMAP will increase the scope of the problems that can be solved. In addition, the user can bypass unnecessary steps in a rigid format and selectively stop, start, and print intermediate results. Finally, an understanding of DMAP will increase the user's understanding of MSC/NASTRAN.

The DMAP language allows the user to specify symbolic names for matrices in much the same sense that any higher level programming language uses a variable name without considering where in the system the data will be stored. The executive, under DMAP control, will write data blocks on a checkpoint tape and a corresponding restart instruction, which contains sufficient information to identify the data block on the system punch file. The user is thus provided with a checkpoint/restart capability that is desirable for large problems or when a change of rigid format is required.

There is some rationale for studying MSC/NASTRAN without actually implementing it. First, the mnemonics used to describe the various subsets of input data are gaining wide acceptance within the structural mechanics community. It is conceivable that the language will become rather universal, and that independent of one's specialty field, we will understand what is meant by CBAR, CQUAD4, MPC, SPC, etc. Second the program documentation is rather good and moderately complete. Third, MSC/NASTRAN is available in a data center environment on a variety of computers so that the program can be evaluated (and used) without making a sizeable investment. In this book the program is described from the point of view of a general purpose finite element program, i.e., we are interested in the capability represented by the rigid formats for static and normal modes analysis of structures.

1.3. NASTRAN Documentation

The MSC/NASTRAN documentation is both one of the program's principal assets and one of its principal liabilities. The completeness of the documentation is an asset, while its magnitude is a liability to the new MSC/NASTRAN user. The principal MSC/NASTRAN documents are described by Table 1-1.

TITLE	SOURCE
MSC/NASTRAN User's Manual	MSC*
MSC/NASTRAN Programmer's Manual	MSC
MSC/NASTRAN Applications Manual	MSC
MSC/NASTRAN Theoretical Manual	MSC
MSC/NASTRAN Handbook for Linear Static Analysis	MSC
MSC/NASTRAN Demonstration Manual	MSC
MSC/NASTRAN MSGMESH Analyst's Guide	MSC

Table 1-1. MSC/NASTRAN Source Documentation

The definition of the physical model for even small prototype problems can be a nontrivial task. The user will thus find data generation processors to be of great value. These data generation processors include

- Stand-alone proprietary interactive graphic-oriented systems such as MSC/GRASP, PATRAN-G®, SUPERTAB®, FASTDRAW®, or UNISTRUC®.
- CAD/CAM systems with finite element modeling software such as ComputerVision, Applicon, CALMA, Auto-trol, or Intergraph.
- Batch-oriented capability incorporated into MSC/NASTRAN.

The batch-oriented capability which is an optional feature in MSC/NASTRAN includes a sophisticated three dimensional solid modeling processor which is called MSGMESH as well as simple

* Available from the MacNeal-Schwendler Corporation, 7442 North Figueroa Street, Los Angeles, CA 90041

PATRAN-G® is a registered trademark of PDA Engineering
SUPERTAB® is a registered trademark of Structural Dynamics Research Corporation
FASTDRAW® is a registered trademark of McDonnell Douglas Automation
UNISTRUC® is a registered trademark of Control Data Corporation

data replication commands. Brief descriptions of MSGMESH features which are useful in defining simple prototype example problems are included in appropriate sections of the MSC/NASTRAN Primer.

The theoretical manual describes the sparse-matrix and finite element technology that has been incorporated in the program, the user's manual describes the MSC/NASTRAN input data, and the programmer's manual describes the MSC/NASTRAN program. In order to use and understand the program it has been necessary in the past for the user to have all three manuals.

A principal motivation for the present text was that of incorporating all the information required to use MSC/NASTRAN to solve static and normal modes problems in a single volume. The MSC/NASTRAN Primer provides the user with a complete description of the MSC/NASTRAN technology for this subset of MSC/NASTRAN capability. The material presented in this text is thus adequate for those who intend to utilize the program without making modifications. The ambitious MSC/NASTRAN user will find use for all the documentation described by Table 1-1.

1.4.   The MSC/NASTRAN Data Deck

The MSC/NASTRAN program is completely controlled by user-specified input data. The functions of the MSC/NASTRAN input can be logically described as

1.   Defining the physical problems or the system of equations to be solved.

2.   Providing user control over MSC/NASTRAN I/O

3.   Providing user control over the MSC/NASTRAN executive functions.

The MSC/NASTRAN data deck is thus logically composed of three subdecks each of which performs one of the functions described above. The complete data deck is shown schematically in Fig. 1-2 and consists of

1.   The EXECUTIVE CONTROL DECK performs function 3 above and is physically the first subdeck. (Section 1.9)

2.   The CASE CONTROL DECK performs function 2 above and is physically the second subdeck. (Section 1.8)

3.   The BULK DATA DECK performs function 1 above and is physically the third subdeck. (Section 1.7)

These subdecks will be discussed in what appears to be reverse order since the user typically defines the problem first by Bulk Data, then considers I/O control by Case Control, and then defines the executive control necessary to accomplish a specific task. The delimiter cards shown in Fig. 1-2 are required in every MSC/NASTRAN data deck even if the corresponding subdeck is an empty set. These delimiter cards are

ID   The first physical card (There is an exception, the user may override default values for executive parameters by using a NASTRAN card).

CEND   Terminates the Executive Control deck.

BEGIN BULK   Terminates the Case Control deck

ENDDATA   Terminates the Bulk Data deck

4

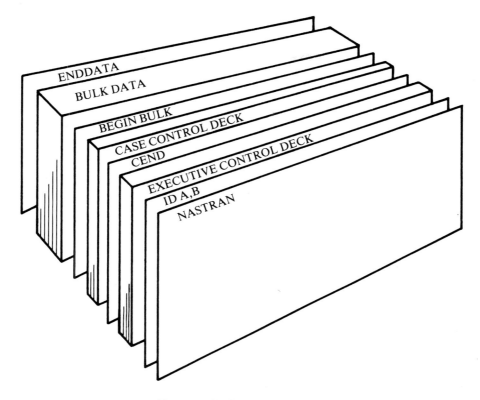

Figure 1-2. NASTRAN Data Deck

1.5. Getting Started with MSC/NASTRAN

The new user can be overwhelmed by NASTRAN's size and the many volumes of documentation. The fact is that while MSC/NASTRAN does have an internal language and while there are literally hundreds of subroutines these are not a concern to the user because MSC/NASTRAN *appears* to be a general purpose finite element program based on the displacement approach.

Let us suppose that you, the user, have a background in matrix structural analysis and the finite element method and have, perhaps, used another general purpose finite element program. The question then isn't so much "what does the program do" as much as "how do I pose my problem so that MSC/NASTRAN will understand it."

A reasonable approach is to first define the physical problem then worry about the rest of the MSC/NASTRAN input deck. It thus seems to make sense to think first about that portion of the data deck called Bulk Data in Fig. 1-2. This is the section of the input deck that is used to define

- The grid point locations
- The element connectivity
- The element properties
- The material properties
- The constraints
- The loads
- Eigenvalue extraction routines
- etc.

After defining the problem (Bulk Data) it is reasonable to think about selecting data items that are defined in Bulk Data that are also to be included in the present analysis and, in addition, about specifying the behavioral variables to be printed. The concept of sets of input data items is important in NASTRAN since this concept allows the user to define any number of logical sets of loads or constraints in the input and then, by using appropriate Case Control directives, to specify which of the logical sets are to be included at execution time. We will see that loads and constraints are given a numerical tag (the set identification number) which is specified by an appropriate Case Control directive. For example, suppose that a set of forces has been given the set identification number 101. Then this set of loads would be specified in static analysis by the following Case Control directive

$$LOAD = 101$$

In addition to selecting input data sets from Bulk Data the Case Control can be used to

- Echo the Bulk Data

- Display element behavioral variables such as element forces, stresses, and strain energy

- Display point functions such as displacements, velocities, accelerations, forces of constraint, etc.

- Define Subcases

- Add the results of subcases

Finally, after completely defining the problem we must tell MSC/NASTRAN what type of analysis we have in mind, i.e., is it a static analysis or normal modes and frequencies. This is done by means of Executive Control directives in the Executive Control Deck which

- Define the rigid format

- Specify MSC/NASTRAN Time

- Request the display of certain executive tables such as displacement set membership

This text includes a description of all of the MSC/NASTRAN capability associated with statics and normal modes analyses. The organization of the Primer is as follows:

- Description of the physical format of Bulk Data in Sec. 1.6

- Summary of all structurally-oriented Bulk Data by function with section references to detailed description in the text in Sec. 1.7

- Description of Case Control deck in Sec. 1.8

- Description of Executive Control deck in Sec. 1.9

Examples of static and normal modes solutions using MSC/NASTRAN are included in Chapters 12 and 13, respectively. In addition the MSC/NASTRAN Demonstration Manual includes examples of the use of all the rigid formats and most, if not all, of the MSC/NASTRAN modeling capability.

After preparing the complete data deck the user may still have a dilemma . . . how to interface with the computer in order to execute MSC/NASTRAN. The execution of MSC/NASTRAN on any one of the computer systems on which it is installed is controlled by machine-dependent operating system commands. The computer command structure required for a particular installation is described in the MSC/NASTRAN Application Manual for that particular computer but the best course of action for a new user is to ask a colleague who is familiar with the system.

The new user should run small example problems, the examples in the Primer for instance, to make sure that the program actually runs and gives the right answers. Then the user can start to think about the problems associated with defining the model of a real-life structure.

After mastering the MSC/NASTRAN capability described in the Primer the user is ready to move on to new and better things. At that time it is appropriate to become familiar with the full set of MSC/NASTRAN documentation. A selected menu of the documentation that will be of interest is as follows:

MSC/NASTRAN User's Manual	**Section**
Complete Description of MSC/NASTRAN Data Deck	2.0
Description of all Rigid Formats	3.0
Description of the MSC/NASTRAN Plot package	4.0
Description of DMAP	5.0

MSC/NASTRAN Applications Manual	**Section**
Postprocessors for Plotting	2.3
Variance Analysis	2.8
Geometric Nonlinearities	2.9
Rigid Elements and Multipoint Constraints	2.10
Viscoelasticity	2.11
Response Spectrum Analysis	2.15
Automatic Generation of SPCs	2.19
Plotting Stresses, MSGSTRESS	2.21
Cyclic Symmetry	3.2
DMAP Alter Library	4.0
Calculation of Time and Storage Requirements	7.2
Using MSC/NASTRAN on Specific Types of Computers	7.6

MSC/NASTRAN MSGMESH Analyst's Guide
Describes an optional batch-oriented system for generating MSC/NASTRAN input

7

1.6.   The Bulk Data Deck

1.6.1.   General Format of Bulk Data

The Bulk Data is the subset of the entire MSC/NASTRAN input data deck that provides the user with the means of generating a system of equations which governs the behavior of a physical system. The analyst may choose to provide the MSC/NASTRAN program with certain descriptive information about the structural system and let the MSC/NASTRAN modeling modules generate the equations, or the user may specify matrix coefficients directly in the input stream.

A large proportion of the MSC/NASTRAN Bulk Data deck is applicable to all problems in structural mechanics, independent of whether the analysis is to be static or dynamic. All the Bulk Data that are independent of analysis type as well as applicable to static and normal modes analysis will be considered in this book.

The Bulk Data deck defines the structural model, specifies sets of constraints and/or loads, and the values of parameters used in the rigid formats. The concept of data sets is of importance because it allows the user to define several load or constraint conditions in one Bulk Data deck. The particular set of loads and constraints to be utilized at execution time is specified by a Case Control Directive in the Case Control deck.

Each logical Bulk Data card may consist of one or more physical cards. Each physical card must be either prepared according to formats that are described in Appendix A or using a free field format described below. Independent of the card formats, the Bulk Data cards have the following important attributes or restrictions:

1. Each logical input data card is given a tag that defines its attributes. This tag is a mnemonic that must appear in the first field of each logical card. The use of a mnemonic field for each card allows MSC/NASTRAN to read the Bulk Data in any order. The Bulk Data is then sorted alphanumerically by MSC/NASTRAN before interpreting the data fields. The sort algorithm favors decks that are physically close to alphanumeric sort. For large Bulk Data decks the sort time for out-of-sort decks can become a significant cost factor.

2. Each card type is described in alphanumerical order in the MSC/NASTRAN User's Manual (Table 1-1). The Bulk Data cards that are appropriate for static structural analysis are summarized by function in Section 1.6 of the present text, and a detailed description of the card and the associated capability is presented in an appropriate section of the book. The user should note that there are restrictions on the format (i.e., real or integer) and range that the data elements must satisfy.

3. The datum may be placed anywhere within the appropriate fields. The user may find it convenient to left- or right-justify the datum within each field from a coding point of view, but this is not required by MSC/NASTRAN. The MSC/NASTRAN input interpreter assumes that a blank is a termination character; thus, imbedded blanks within the field are not allowed.

4. Each logical card may consist of one or more physical cards so that continuation of physical cards is allowed. A continuation is effected by a unique continuation mnemonic in the last field of the "parent" card and the same mnemonic is preceded by a continuation character in the first field of the "child" card. The construction of continuations is discussed in more detail in Appendix A, but it should be emphasized at this point that the continuation mnemonic must be unique among all card mnemonics in the entire Bulk Data deck. The use of card mnemonics allows the Bulk Data cards to be placed in any order. The MSC/NASTRAN program then sorts the Bulk Data using the card mnemonics. During the sort process, the existence of a special continuation character in the mnemonic field implies that a "child"/"parent" relation exists, and MSC/NASTRAN then searches for a "parent" with the same continuation mnemonic as that found on the continuation card.

1.6.2.   Free Field Bulk Data

MSC/NASTRAN provides the user with an alternative to the Bulk Data card format which is described in Appendix A. The alternate form allows the user to separate field entries for small field cards by a comma (,) thereby greatly simplifying the task of preparing Bulk Data input. The form of the free field Bulk Data card is

$$f_1, f_2, f_3, f_4, f_5, f_6, f_7, f_8, f_9, f_{10}$$

where the fields, f_i, are separated by commas. Successive commas define blank fields so that the free field Bulk Data card

$$TABLED1,,,,,,,, + T1$$

would be interpreted by MSC/NASTRAN as TABLED1 in field one, blanks in fields two through nine and + T1 in field ten.

1.6.3.   Replication and Field Generation

A simple, but useful, set of duplication and generation commands can be imbedded in the Bulk Data deck. These commands are
1. Duplication of field from previous card is defined by an equal sign, (=), in the associated field.
2. Duplication of all remaining fields from previous card is defined by two equal signs, (==), in the first of the fields to be repeated.
3. Generation of an incremented value of a field from a previous card is defined by the construct, *(w), in the associated field where w is the real or integer value of the increment.
4. Repeated duplication and incrementation is defined by including a duplication control card after the last card definition that has the form =(n), where n is the number of additional cards to generate.

The rules which govern these features are as follows:
1. Only small-field cards can be generated
2. Continuation cards cannot be generated
3. Data items must be separated with one or more blanks or a comma

Examples of the use of this feature are included in later sections (see, Sec. 7.3.3 which uses this feature to generate GRID Bulk Data Cards).

1.7.   Summary of Structurally Oriented Bulk Data Cards

The Bulk Data cards of interest for static and normal modes analyses of structures are grouped by function and are described below.

CARD MNEMONIC	DESCRIPTION	SECTION

1.7.1.   Specification of Scalar Degrees of Freedom

SPOINT	Scalar degree of freedom	7.3.1

1.7.2.   Specification of Geometric Grid Points

CORD1C	Cylindrical Coordinate System	7.3.2
CORD1R	Rectangular Coordinate System	7.3.2

1.7   Summary of Structurally Oriented Bulk Data Cards

1.7.11.   Material Specification

MAT1	Isotropic material coefficients	10.1
MAT2	Anisotropic coefficients for two-dimensional elements	10.2
MAT8	Orthotropic material coefficients	10.3
MAT9	Anisotropic material for three-dimensional stress state	10.4
MATT1	Specifies temperature dependence of material coefficients on MAT1	10.5
MATT2	Specifies temperature dependence of coefficients specified on MAT2	10.5
MATT9	Specifies temperature dependence of material coefficients on MAT9	10.5

1.7.12.   Specification of Static Loads

FORCE	Specification of concentrated forces at geometric grid point	11.1.1
FORCE1		11.1.2
FORCE2		11.1.3
MOMENT	Specification of concentrated moments at geometric grid points	11.1.1
MOMENT1		11.1.2
MOMENT2		11.1.3
SLOAD	Load applied to scalar point	11.2
PLOAD1	Defines load distribution along length of BAR or BEAM elements	11.3
PLOAD2	Defines a normal pressure load on two-dimensional elements	11.4
PLOAD4	Defines a surface load on two and three dimensional isoparametric elements	11.4
GRAV	Specifies gravity vector for entire structure	11.5
RFORCE	Specifies rotational velocity vector for calculating centrifugal forces	11.6
LOAD	Load combination	11.7
SPCD	Specify an enforced displacement for static analysis which is treated as a load rather than as a constraint	11.8
DEFORM	Initial misfit of lineal elements	11.9
TEMP	Grid point temperature	11.10
TEMPD		

TEMPRB	Specify temperature distribution for truss and beam elements	11.11
TEMPP1	Specify temperature distribution in plate and membrane elements	11.12

1.7.13. Mass Elements

CMASS1	Scalar mass connection	13.4.4
CMASS2	Scalar mass connection	13.4.4
CMASS3	Scalar mass connection	13.4.4
CMASS4	Scalar mass connection	13.4.4
PMASS	Scalar mass property	13.4.4
CONM1	Concentrated mass at (or optionally offset from) GRID	13.4.4
CONM2	point	13.4.4

1.7.14. Eigenvalue Extraction

EIGR(INV)	Eigenvalue extraction using inverse power method	13.5.1
EIGR(GIV)	Eigenvalue extraction using Givens' method	13.5.2
EIGR(MGIV)	Eigenvalue extraction using modified Givens' method	13.5.2
DYNRED	Dynamic reduction for reduced number of dynamic degrees of freedom	13.6

1.7.15. Miscellaneous Cards

DMI, DMIG	Direct input of matrix coefficients	3.4, 12.1.1
CNGRNT	Specifies identical element	9.12
PARAM	Specifies parametric input data	Appendix B
$	Comment card	

1.8. Case Control Deck

The Case Control Directives perform the following functions:

1. Specify set of Bulk Data input that are to be included in the analysis at execution time.

2. Select solution techniques as appropriate.

3. Control the calculation and display of derived quantities.

4. Control subcases.

The Case Control Directives are free-field. The directive is separated from the specification by one or more blanks or by an equal sign.

1.8.1. Data Selection

The concept of data sets in the Bulk Data deck allows the user to define any number of different load and constraint sets. The particular set to be used at execution time is then specified by an appropriate Case Control Directive. The form of the data selection cards is

<name> = SID

13

1.8   Case Control Deck

where <name> indicates the particular type of data to be included in the analysis and SID is the set identification number associated with the data in the Bulk Data deck. In this book, the following convention is to be used for variable names or quantities to be filled in by the user. The name or quantity will be lowercase, preceded by a <, and succeeded by a >. The angle brackets (< and >) are not part of the name or quantity to be added by the user. All Case Control directives may be shortened to the first four characters provided they are unique.

1.8.1.1.   Load Selection

The following Case Control Directives are used to select sets of load-type Bulk Data:

DEFORM   Selects initial element deformations specified by a set of DEFORM Bulk Data.

LOAD   Selects a set of static loads defined by LOAD, PLOAD, PLOAD1, PLOAD2, PLOAD4, FORCE, MOMENT, FORCE1, MOMENT1, FORCE2, MOMENT2, GRAV, RFORCE, or SPCD Bulk Data.

1.8.1.1.1.   Example: Load Specification

The Case Control Directives

```
DEFORM = 2
LOAD = 13
```

specify that the set of initial deformations defined by DEFORM Bulk Data with set identification number 12 and the set of static loads defined by appropriate Bulk Data having set identification number 13 are to be combined to define the set of grid point loads.

1.8.1.2.   Thermal Field Selection

The following Case Control Directives are used to specify thermal fields defined by temperature-type Bulk Data:

TEMP(LOAD)   Selects a temperature set defined by TEMP, TEMPD, TEMPRB, TEMPP1 Bulk Data to be used for calculating equivalent thermal loads.

TEMP(MATERIAL)   Selects a temperature set defined in Bulk Data to be used only for determining temperature-dependent material properties.

TEMPERATURE   Selects a temperature set from Bulk Data for calculation of thermal loads and temperature-dependent properties.

1.8.1.2.1.   Example: Thermal Field Specification

The Case Control Directive

$$TEMP = 25$$

specifies that the temperatures defined by suitable Bulk Data with set identification 25 are to be used to calculate both thermal loads and temperature-dependent properties.

1.8.1.3.   Selection of Constraints

MPC   Selects a multipoint constraint set defined by MPC or MPCADD Bulk Data.

SPC   Selects a single point constraint set defined by SPC, SPC1, or SPCADD Bulk Data.

1.8.1.3.1.   Example: Specification of Constraints

The directives

$$MPC = 10$$
$$SPC = 10$$

specify that multipoint constraints defined by MPC Bulk Data with set identification number 10 and single point constraints defined by SPC Bulk Data with set identification number 10 are to be used to define constraints.

1.8.1.4.   Specification of Eigenvalue Method

The user specifies an eigenvalue extraction algorithm for normal modes analysis with the following Case Control Directive:

METHOD   Selects a real eigenvalue extraction method defined by an EIGR Bulk Data card.

1.8.1.4.1.   Example: Specification of Eigenvalue Routine

The Case Control Directive

$$METHOD = 10$$

specifies that the EIGR Bulk Data with set identification number 10 defines the real eigenvalue extraction algorithm to be used.

1.8.2.   Output Control

Printer output requests may be placed anywhere in the Case Control deck ahead of any structure plotter or curve plotter requests. The description of plotter requests is beyond the scope of the present text and the reader should consult Ref. 1-1. The Case Control Directives that are used for output control are listed below in functional groups.

1.8.2.1.   Titling Directives

TITLE   Defines text to be printed on first line of each page of output.

SUBTITLE   Defines text to be printed on second line of each page of output.

LABEL   Defines text to be printed on third line of each page of output.

1.8.2.2.   Output Line Control

LINE   Defines the number of data lines per printed page, default is 50 lines for 11-inch paper.

MAXLINES   Defines the maximum number of output lines, default is 100,000.

1.8.2.3.   Bulk Data Echo

ECHO   Selects echo options for Bulk Data. The options are

SORT	Prints only sorted Bulk Data (default)
UNSORT	Prints only the unsorted Bulk Data
BOTH	Prints both unsorted and sorted Bulk Data
NONE	Prints neither
PUNCH	Writes the sorted Bulk Data on the system punch file

NOSORT	Prints only Bulk Data cards which were changed on a "check-pointed" run (see Sec. 1.9.3)
SORT(t1, t2)	Prints sorted echo of only card types t1, t2, . . . along with their line numbers.

The user can selectively control the echo of selected portions of the unsorted Bulk Data deck by requesting

$$ECHO = UNSORT$$

and including the desired Bulk Data between pairs of ECHOON and ECHOOFF cards in Bulk Data.

1.8.2.4. Set Specification

SET   Defines set of point numbers, element numbers, times, or frequencies for use in point and element output directives.

1.8.2.5. Element Output Requests

ELFORCE   Requests forces in a set of structural elements.
STRESS   Requests the stresses in a set of structural elements.
ESE   Requests strain energy for set of elements (see associated PARAMeter "TINY" in Appendix B).

1.8.2.6. Grid and Scalar Point Requests

SPCFORCES   Requests single point constraint forces at a set of points.

OLOAD   Selects applied loads at a set of grid or scalar points.

ACCELERATION   Requests accelerations for a selected set of grid or scalar points.

DISPLACEMENT   Requests displacements for a selected set of grid or scalar points.

VELOCITY   Requests velocities for a selected set of grid or scalar points.

VECTOR   Equivalent to DISPLACEMENT.

GPFORCE   Requests grid point force balance for a selected set of physical points.

The form of the output directives is

$$<request> = N$$

where $<request>$ is one of the output directives and N is the number of a SET that defines the elements or grid points for which the calculated quantity is to be displayed. If N is ALL, then the calculated quantity will be displayed for ALL elements or ALL points. A subset of ALL must be defined before it can be referenced by an output control directive. For example, the specification

$$ELFORCE = ALL$$

specifies that the element forces in all the elements in the finite element model are to be printed. The specification

$$SET 5 = 5, 6, 10$$
$$ELFORCE = 5$$

specifies that element forces are to be printed for set five which consists of elements five, six, and ten. The specification

SET 10 = 1 THRU 25, EXCEPT 10
DISP = 10

specifies that the displacements be printed at grid or scalar point 1 through 25, except for point 10.

1.8.3. Subcase Definition

In general, a separate subcase may be defined for each loading condition. In static analysis, separate subcases are also allowed for each set of constraints. Subcases may be used in connection with output directives, such as requesting different output for each mode in a real eigenvalue solution.

The Case Control deck is structured so that a minimum amount of repetition is required when using subcases. Only one level of subcase definition is provided and all items placed above the subcase level (ahead of the first subcase) will be used for all following subcases, unless overridden within the individual subcase.

In static problems, provision has been made for the combination of the results of several subcases. This capability is convenient for combinations of individual loading conditions and for superposition of solutions for symmetrical and antisymmetrical boundary conditions.

Typical examples of subcase definition are given, following a brief description of the subcase Case Control Directives.

SUBCASE Defines the beginning of a subcase that is terminated by the next SUBCASE Case Directive.

SUBCOM Defines a combination of two or more immediately preceding subcases in statics problems. Output requests above the subcase level are used.

SUBSEQ Must appear in a subcase defined by SUBCOM to give coefficients for making the linear combination of the preceding subcases.

SYM Defines a subcase in statics problems for which only output requests within the subcase will be honored. Primarily for use with symmetry problems where the individual parts of the solution may not be of interest.

SYMCOM Defines a combination of two or more immediately preceding SYM subcases in static problems. Output requests above the subcase level are used.

SYMSEQ May appear in a subcase defined by SYMCOM to give the coefficient for making the linear combination of the preceding SYM subcases. A default value of 1.0 is used if no SYMSEQ card appears.

REPCASE Defines a subcase in statics problems that is used to make additional output requests for the previously run subcases. This capability is required because multiple output requests for the same item are not permitted in the same subcase. Output requests above the subcase level are still used.

MODES Repeats the subcase in which it appears MODES times for eigenvalue problems. Used to repeat the same output request for several consecutive modes.

The following examples of the use of subcases in the Case Control deck have been included:

1. Static Analysis and Multiple Loads

DISPLACEMENT = ALL
MPC = 3

17

```
SUBCASE 1
    SPC = 2
    TEMP(LOAD) = 101
    LOAD = 11
SUBCASE 2
    SPC = 2
    DEFORM = 52
    LOAD = 12
SUBCASE 3
    SPC = 4
    LOAD = 12
SUBCASE 4
    MPC = 4
    SPC = 4
```

Four subcases are defined by this example. The output request for displacements will be honored for all subcases and MPC set three will be used for all subcases except subcase four where MPC = 4 overrides the specification above the subcase level.

Since subcase one and two have the same constraint sets the solutions will be performed simultaneously. The thermal load set 101 and external load set 11 will be combined for subcase one, and the external load set 12 will be combined with deformation set 52 for subcase two. Since there is no load set specified in subcase four, the SPC set four must include enforced grid point displacements.

   2. Linear Combination of Subcases

```
SPC = 2
OUTPUT
    SET 1 = 1 THRU 10, 20, 30
    DISP = ALL
    STRESS = 1
SUBCASE 1
    LOAD = 101
    OLOAD = ALL
SUBCASE 2
    LOAD = 201
    OLOAD = ALL
SUBCOM 51
    SUBSEQ = 1.0, 1.0
SUBCOM 52
    SUBSEQ = 2.5, 1.5
```

Two static load cases are defined. SPC = 2 is used for each subcase because the specification is made above the subcase level. The subcase combination SUBCOM = 51 is a linear combination of one times the result of subcase one and one times the result of subcase two. The subcase combination SUBCOM = 52 consists of 2.5 times subcase 1 plus 1.5 times the result of subcase 2. The displacements at all grid points and the stresses in the elements defined by set one will be printed.

   3. Statics Problem with One Plane of Symmetry

```
SET 1 = 1, 11, 21, 31, 41
SET 2 = 1 THRU 50
DISP = 1
```

```
        ELFORCE = 2
SYM 1
    SPC = 11
    LOAD = 21
    OLOAD = ALL
SYM 2
    SPC = 12
    LOAD = 22
SYMCOM 3
    SYMSEQ 1., 1.
SYMCOM 4
    SYMSEQ 1., − 1.
```

Two symmetry subcases are defined by subcases one and two. The symmetric subcase combination SYMCOM 3 defines the sum of the previous subcases while SYMCOM 4 define the difference. The nonzero components of static load will be printed for subcase one; and the displacements associated with set one and the element forces for set two will be printed for symmetric combination three and four. Note that only output requests defined within the symmetric subcase are honored while output requests above the subcase level are honored by SYMCOM.

4. Use of REPCASE in Statics:

```
SET 1 = 1 THRU 10
SET 2 = 11 THRU 20
SET 3 =  21 THRU 30
            SUBCASE 1
    LOAD = 100
    SPC = 101
    DISP = ALL
    SPCF = ALL
    ELFO = 1
            REPCASE 2
    ELFO = 2
            REPCASE 3
    ELFO = 3
```

One subcase is requested for solution and with two additional subcases defined for output. The displacements and SPC forces at all grid points and the element forces in SET 1 will be displayed for subcase one. The element forces in SET 2 will be printed for REPCASE 2 and those in SET 3 will be printed for REPCASE 3.

5. Use of MODES in Eigenvalue Problem

```
METHOD = 12
            SUBCASE 1
    MODES = 5
    STRESS = ALL
            SUBCASE 6
    DISPLACEMENT = ALL
```

The METHOD Case Control Directive points to an EIGR Bulk Data card that defines the real eigenvalue method to be used and associated parameters. The MODES Case Control Directive causes the results for each eigenvalue to be considered as a separate subcase starting with the subcase number containing the MODES request. The stress will be printed in all elements for the first five modes, and the displacements will then be printed for all additional modes.

If the MODES request is not included in a subcase, the output requests will apply to all eigenvalues starting with the subcase number. The following output request could then be used to print the displacements associated with the first three modes.

```
METHOD = 12
          SUBCASE 1
     MODES = 3
     DISP = ALL
          SUBCASE 4
     DISP = NONE
```

1.8.4.   Case Control Examples

The following examples illustrate the use of Case Control Directives for static and normal modes analysis.

1.8.4.1.   Static Analysis

The following tasks
1. Print both sorted and unsorted bulk data.

2. Specify maximum number of output lines to be 75000.

3. Specify 35 lines of output per page.

4. Two sets of loads have been defined; a temperature set five, and a force set six. Print the results for each and then combine the results by multiplying thermal loads by a factor of one and the external loads by two.

5. Multipoint constraints for both load sets are defined by MPC set 14.

6. Single point constraints for both load sets are defined by SPC set 12.

7. Print external loads, displacements, and forces of reaction at all grid points.

8. Print element type output for elements 100 through 200, except for element 151.

could be performed by this Case Control deck:

```
TITLE = STATIC ANALYSIS OF TRUSS
SUBTITLE = NASTRAN EXAMPLE
ECHO = BOTH
MAXLINES = 75000
LINES = 35
SET 100 = 100 THRU 200, EXCEPT 151
MPC = 14
SPC = 12
     SPCFORCE = ALL
     OLOAD = ALL
     DISPLACEMENT = ALL
     STRESS = 100
     ELFORCE = 100
SUBCASE 1
     LABEL = THERMAL STRESSES
```

```
                    TEMP(LOAD) = 5
          SUBCASE 2
                    LABEL = STRESSES DUE TO EXTERNAL LOADS
                    LOAD = 6
                    OLOAD = ALL
          SUBCOM 12
                    LABEL = COMBINED OUTPUT
                    SUBSEQ 1.0, 2.0
                    TEMP(LOAD) = 5
          BEGIN BULK
```

It should be noted that the TEMP(LOAD) = 5 must be included under the SUBCOM Case Control directive in order to properly account for thermal strains when element stresses and element forces are calculated for the combined loading condition. (See Ref.1-3)

1.8.4.2. Normal Modes Analysis

The following tasks
1. Print out sorted and unsorted Bulk Data.

2. Specify maximum number of output lines to be 125,000.

3. Specify 35 lines of output per page.

4. Print nodal displacements for all degrees of freedom for all nodes. (10 eigenmodes are expected)

5. Print stress output for elements 2, 5, and 10 for eigenmodes four and five.

could be performed by this Case Control deck:

```
          TITLE = NORMAL MODE ANALYSIS OF TRUSS
          SUBTITLE = NASTRAN EXAMPLE
          ECHO = BOTH
          METHOD = 12
          MAXLINES = 125000
          LINES = 35
          SET 5 = 2, 5, 10
                    DISP = ALL
          SUBCASE 1
                    LABEL = OUTPUT FOR MODES 1 THRU 3
                    MODES = 3
          SUBCASE 4
                    LABEL = OUTPUT FOR MODES 4 AND 5
                    STRESS = 5
                    MODES = 2
          SUBCASE 6
                    LABEL = OUTPUT FOR MODES 6 THRU 10
                    MODES = 5
          SUBCASE 11
                    DISP = NONE
                    VELO = NONE
                    ACCEL = NONE
          BEGIN BULK
```

1.9. Executive Control Deck

The Executive Control deck is the first of the three subdecks that comprise the NASTRAN data deck. The Executive Control Directives perform the following functions:

1. Provides user control over the NASTRAN interface with the computer operating system by an optional NASTRAN card.

2. Specifies the rigid format DMAP sequence by the SOL card.

3. Provides a means of modifying the DMAP for a rigid format by means of ALTER Card.

4. Provides a means of specifying that intermediate results are to be saved (CHKPNT card) or that previously saved data are to be used (RESTART).

5. Provides a means of printing internal data sets.

The Executive Control Directives that accomplish these functions are freeform, which means that the directive may start at any place on the data card. The directive is separated from the specification by one or more blanks.

The Executive Control deck begins with an optional NASTRAN card. If the NASTRAN card is not present, then the first card is the required ID card. The Executive Control deck then includes as few as one additional card (SOL) and is terminated by CEND. The Executive Control cards are described as follows:

1.9.1. NASTRAN card

NASTRAN keyword = value, keyword = value (Optional)
The keywords of interest to the structural analyst are

1. HICORE   Defines core size on Univac, Default is 60,000 words.

2. DAYLIMIT   Defines number of entries allowed in CDC dayfile.

3. REAL   Specifies amount of open core on IBM virtual memory machines to prevent "thrashing". Must be equal or less than real address space available to user.

4. FILES   Specifies that NASTRAN internal files are to be assigned to permanent file on CDC machines. Allowable MSC/NASTRAN file names are as follows:

NASTRAN FILE NAME	FILE DESCRIPTION
OPTP	Old problem tape
NPTP	New problem tape
PLT1, PLT2	Plot Files
INTP	Input tape
INP1 - INP9	Input tapes 1 thru 9
DB01-DB16	Data Base Files

A set of files is indicated by including the file names, separated by commas, within parentheses. For example

NASTRAN FILES = (OPTP,NPTP,PLT2)

1.9.2. ID card

The ID Executive Directive will be the first card of the MSC/NASTRAN data deck if the optional NASTRAN card is not present. The form of the ID card is

ID A1, A2 (required)

> where A1 and A2 are any legal alphanumeric fields chosen by the user for problem identification, where legal fields must start with alpha character and be eight or less characters long.

1.9.3. Checkpoint Specification

CHKPNT A1 (Optional)

> A1 YES if problem is to be checkpointed NO if problem is not checkpointed (default is NO).

The MSC/NASTRAN program saves selected data blocks during the execution of a DMAP sequence on a file called NPTP, an acronym that stands for **N**ew **P**roblem Ta**P**e. Thus, when the user specifies that a checkpoint is desired, the file NPTP must be defined to the computer's operating system by a suitable job stream command.

During the generation of the New Problem Tape MSC/NASTRAN writes a restart dictionary that is directed to the computer system punch file. A restart thus requires both the checkpoint tape and the restart dictionary. If the restart dictionary is not redirected to a tape or disc file, the system will punch a set of cards. In this case the user must inform the computer system that punched output is expected.

1.9.4. Restarts

The first card of the restart dictionary that is punched during a checkpoint run is

RESTART A1,A2,K1/K2/K3,K4 (Required for RESTART)

where

A1,A2 are fields from the ID card of checkpointed run

K1/K2/K3 Month/Day/Year that the checkpoint tape was generated

K4 Number of seconds after midnight at which check point starts

The cards that follow the RESTART card identify the data blocks which are written on the checkpoint tape.

MSC/NASTRAN expects to find the checkpointed data blocks on a file named OPTP, an acronym for **O**ld **P**roblem Ta**P**e. During restart a system file of this name must be specified by suitable job control cards. The restart is accomplished by defining OPTP and by physically incorporating the restart dictionary in the Executive Control deck.

The form of the MSC/NASTRAN data deck depends on which type of restart is specified:

1. Unmodified

2. Pseudo modified

3. Modified

4. Rigid Format Switch

The MSC/NASTRAN data deck for the restarted run includes complete Executive and Case Control decks. However, only those items of the Bulk Data deck that have been changed from the checkpointed run are included in the data deck for the restarted run.

For an unmodified restart the job is resubmitted with no changes to the original Bulk Data.

23

Since Bulk Data is a data block on the checkpoint tape, this means that the Bulk Data in the MSC/NASTRAN Data deck from the previous run must be removed before submission for the unmodified restart. The MSC/NASTRAN data deck includes the previous Executive Control deck including the RESTART dictionary, the unmodified Case Control deck, and a null Bulk Data deck, terminated with the ENDDATA card. The unmodified restart is used to continue the solution from the last successful checkpoint. In practice, it is usually more effective to duplicate the Executive and Case Control and maintain a separate restart deck.

A Pseudo Modified Restart is used to calculate additional output. The Output specifications in Case Control are thus changed to request the additional output items.

A modified restart includes changes in Bulk Data that require recalculation of data blocks. The restart dictionary is searched for usable data blocks. Data blocks that must be recalculated are flagged, and the appropriate MSC/NASTRAN modules are re-executed.

For a switch in rigid formats, any changes to Bulk Data are included. MSC/NASTRAN must then determine which data blocks are usable in the new rigid format and the associated calculations are bypassed.

1.9.5. Specification of Rigid Format

SOL K_n $(,K_i)$ where the allowable rigid format numbers, K_n, are defined in Table 1-2. The rigid format subset number K_i, may be used for the static rigid format. Its function is to remove specific features from the DMAP instructions as defined in Table 1-3. The subset specification is not required but it is recommended that $K_i = 1$ be used to eliminate DMAP looping when only a single set of constraints is specified for static analysis.

MSC/NASTRAN RIGID FORMAT K_n	Type of Analysis
24	STATICS
3	NORMAL MODES

Table 1-2. Recommended Rigid Formats for Statics and Normal Modes Analysis

Subset No. K_i	Functional Capability Removed from Rigid Format
1	DMAP loop control instructions
2	Mode acceleration data recovery
3	Structural plot operation
4	Recovery of grid point force and element force data
6	Updating structural matrices
7	Generation and assembly of structural matrices

Table 1-3. Rigid Format Subsets

1.9.6. Specification of Rigid Format Alters

ALTER K1, K2 (Optional)

    K1, K2 First and last DMAP instructions of series to be deleted and replaced with any user-supplied DMAP instructions. The ALTER is terminated by an ENDALTER, RESTART, or CEND.

ALTER K (Optional)

    K Input any user-supplied DMAP instructions after statement number K

24

ENDALTER   Optional if followed by RESTART or CEND

1.9.7.   Rigid Format Alter Library

The ALTER capability provides the user with the capability of modifying the DMAP sequences for any of the Rigid Formats. MSC/NASTRAN provides a library of useful pre-defined DMAP alter sequences which are called RFALTERs.

The RFALTERs which are useful for static analysis are described in Chapter 12 and those for normal modes analysis are described in Chapter 13. The RFALTERs are identified by the following code

$$RF <no> D <libno>$$

where

    <no>   is the rigid format number

    <libno>   is the RFALTER library number

The RFALTERs for rigid format 24 thus have the form RF24D <libno> while those for rigid format 3 have the form RF3D <libno>.

The user must merge RFALTERs into the Executive Control deck by using a machine-dependent operating system utility for merging files. The user should consult Ref. 1-4 for the procedures which are appropriate for the computer system being used.

1.9.8.   Specification of NASTRAN Execution Time

TIME K (Default), 1 minute

      K   Maximum allowable cpu execution time in minutes.

The time specified in Executive Control deck is MSC/NASTRAN time and is used in conjunction with timing algorithms for each of the computer models to lessen the possibility of running out of time during the matrix operations. The system estimates the time required for a matrix operation and then checks to see if there is sufficient time remaining, based on the current time used and the MSC/NASTRAN time estimated. If sufficient time remains, MSC/NASTRAN will terminate normally, including checkpointing if CHKPNT = YES is specified.

1.9.9.   Diagnostic Print Requests

The DIAG Executive request provides the user with a means of requesting printout of MSC/NASTRAN executive tables or for requesting override of certain MSC/NASTRAN defaults. The form of the request is

$$DIAG <K>$$

The DIAGs of general interest to the structural analyst are described below. Complete tabulation of all DIAGs can be found in Ref. 1-5.

K	Meaning
1	Dump memory when non-preface fatal error is detected
4	Print cross reference table which is produced during DMAP compilation
5,6	Print BEGIN and END time for each DMAP module
8	Print matrix summary data as it is generated
9	Print echo of checkpoint dictionary
13	Print length of open core
14	Print the DMAP source compilation

16 Provide values of pivotal eigenvalues used in inverse power method
17 Punch the compiled DMAP sequence
19 Print data for multiply-add (MPYAD) and forward-backward substitution selection
23 Request strain rather than stress output for isoparametric shell elements
26 Print material coordinate systems for thin shell elements
33 Calculate Hencky-von Mises Stresses
35 Turn off automatic RFL on CDC and MORECORE on UNIVAC
36 Calculate stresses for elements which use composite material
48 Do not calculate stresses in elements which use composite materials

Multiple options may be selected by using multiple integers separated by commas. Other options and other rules associated with the DIAG card that primarily concern the programmer can be found in Ref. 1-6.

1.9.10.   DMAP Compiler Control

The DMAP statements which comprise the solution algorithm are always compiled, in the same sense that FORTRAN statements are compiled, by the DMAP compiler. The following executive control statement provides an alternative to the use of DIAGs 4, 14, and 17.

COMPILER A1, A2, A3, A4

A1 — LIST if DMAP statements are to be printed, default is NOLIST
A2 — DECK if Compiled DMAP is to be punched. Default is NODECK
A3 — REF if cross-reference table is to be printed. Default is NOREF
A4 — NOGO if the job is to be terminated after compilation even if no errors are detected. Default is GO.

1.9.11.   Termination Card

CEND (Required)
Indicates end of Executive Control deck.

The ID Card must appear first and CEND must be the last card of the Executive Control deck. Otherwise, the Executive Control card groups (RESTART dictionary, DMAP sequence, ALTER packet) can be in any order.

1.9.12.   Executive Control Examples

1.9.12.1.   Static Analysis, No Checkpoint

```
ID   NASTRAN, PRIMER
TIME   3
SOL   24
CEND
```

The SOL 24 card then specifies that the static rigid format is to be used. The TIME card specifies that the total NASTRAN execution time is expected to be three minutes or less.

1.9.12.2.   Static Analysis, Optional Output

```
ID   NASTRAN, PRIMER
TIME   3
SOL   24
DIAG   13,14
CEND
```

The Executive Control deck is the same as the previous case except for the inclusion of the DIAG card. As a result of the optional requests on this card, NASTRAN will

1. Print length of open core. This is the amount of high speed core that is available for storing data in each module (DIAG 13).

2. Print the DMAP listing for the rigid format. Recommended practice if DMAP ALTERS or user-supplied DMAP program is used (DIAG 14).

1.9.12.3.   Static Analysis with Checkpoint to Tape
```
<Inform the system that punched card output is expected>
<Inform the system that NPTP is to be a tape>
ID NASTRAN, PRIMER
SOL   24
TIME   2
CHKPNT YES
CEND
```

The NASTRAN program will write the checkpoint file on tape and punch the restart deck. The computer system will inform the user of the tape number of the checkpoint tape, and the output will include both printed and punched data.

1.9.12.4.   Restart of Static Analysis with Checkpoint
Assume that the checkpoint tape from the previous run is N532. We suppose that the termination in the previous run was a scheduled exit before decomposing the stiffness matrix. The run is then restarted by

1. Merging the RESTART deck into the Executive Control deck

2. Removing all Bulk Data, leaving only ENDDATA card.
```
<Inform system that punched output is expected>
<Inform system that OPTP is tape number N532>
<Inform system that NPTP is to be on tape >
ID NASTRAN, PRIMER
SOL   24
TIME   10
CHKPNT YES
$RESTART DICTIONARY FROM CHECKPOINTED RUN
RESTART NASTRAN,PRIMER MO/DAY/YEAR
   .
   .
   .
$END OF CHECKPOINT DICTIONARY
CEND
```

1.9.12.5.   Normal Modes Analysis
The previous examples are applicable to the normal modes analysis as well as static analysis. The only change is that the SOL card is changed to specify rigid format three:

27

SOL   3

1.10.   References

1-1   MSC/NASTRAN User's Manual, Vol. II, Sec. 4.
1-2   MSC/NASTRAN Programmer's Manual, Vol. I, pp. 2.4-13, - 13d.
1-3   MSC/NASTRAN Application Manual, Vol. II, Sec. 2.13.
1-4   MSC/NASTRAN Application Manual, Vol. II, Sec. 7.6.3.6.
1-5   MSC/NASTRAN User's Manual, Vol. IV, pp. 6.3-1.
1-6   MSC/NASTRAN Programmer's Manual, Vol. IV, pp. 6.3-1.

2

Matrix and Index Notation

2.0. Introduction

It is important that we understand the differences between equation generation and equation solving. In computational structural analysis a set of algebraic equations which represents the behavior of a system is generated using a technique which has been termed the finite element method. Given a set of equations we then use the techniques of matrix algebra to provide a complete mathematical description of the constrained structure and to obtain a solution.

While general purpose finite element programs such as MSC/NASTRAN automate the generation and solution phases it is important that the analyst understand matrix algebra and set notation as well as the concepts of finite elements. We will describe the development of the system of field equations that governs the behavior of elastic bodies and the finite element technique in later Chapters. In this section we are interested in considering the use of index notation to represent a set of equations, the terminology and rules of matrix algebra, and finally a discussion of a technique which is termed Gauss elimination for the solution of a set of matrix equations.

2.1. Index Notation

The representation of a structural model involves sets of one to several thousand algebraic equations that relate the behavioral variables. This representation would be impossible without the compact notation given by matrix notation. Let us consider the set of equations

$$a_1 x + b_1 y + c_1 z = f_1$$
$$a_2 x + b_2 y + c_2 z = f_2 \qquad (2.1)$$
$$a_3 x + b_3 y + c_3 z = f_3$$

where the x, y, and z are independent variables. The coefficients of the independent variables are a, b, and c, respectively, and f is the inhomogenous term. The subscript on the coefficients indicates the appropriate equation number.

The set of equations (2.1) can be represented in a more concise fashion by defining a set of independent variables to be x_i and an associated range convention. The range convention that we will use is that x_i stands for the set of variables x_1, x_2,..., x_n where n is the range of the index. Thus to represent the set of independent variables in equations (2.1), we would define

$$x_1 = x, \qquad x_2 = y, \qquad x_3 = z \qquad (2.2)$$

The set x_i (i = 1,2,3) would then represent the independent variables by the equivalence defined by equations (2.2). The set of equations (2.1) can then be written as

$$a_1 x_1 + b_1 x_2 + c_1 x_3 = f_1$$
$$a_2 x_1 + b_2 x_2 + c_2 x_3 = f_2 \qquad (2.3)$$
$$a_3 x_1 + b_3 x_2 + c_3 x_3 = f_3$$

2.1 Index Notation

At this point the form of (2.3) is certainly no improvement over the original form. We can simplify the representation by extending the index notation for the representation of sets to include more than one index. In (2.3) for example, we can define a set of coefficients a_{ij} and f_i (i,j = 1,2,3) where

a_{ij} is the coefficient of the jth independent variable in the ith equation

f_i is the nonhomogenous term in the ith equation.

Equation (2.3) can then be represented as

$$\sum_{j=1}^{3} a_{ij}\, x_j = f_i \qquad (i = 1, 2, 3) \qquad\qquad (2.4)$$

The form of (2.4) includes a summation of the repeated index over the range of the index. The inclusion of the summation symbol is cumbersome so we define a summation convention: a repeated index in a term implies a summation over the range of the index. Finally, the set (2.1) can be represented in the following compact form using index notation:

$$a_{ij}\, x_j = f_i \qquad\qquad (2.5)$$

The number of algebraic equations represented by (2.5) is implied by range of the free index i, which takes on the values one, two, and three. The first step in expanding equations (2.5) is to write a separate equation for each value of the free index:

$$\sum_{j=1}^{3} a_{1j}\, x_j = f_1$$
$$\sum_{j=1}^{3} a_{2j}\, x_j = f_2 \qquad\qquad (2.6)$$
$$\sum_{j=1}^{3} a_{3j}\, x_j = f_3$$

where the implied summation over the range of the repeated index has been explicitly expressed for emphasis. Finally, expanding the summation gives

$$a_{11}x_1 + a_{12}x_2 + a_{13}x_3 = f_1$$
$$a_{21}x_1 + a_{22}x_2 + a_{23}x_3 = f_2 \qquad\qquad (2.7)$$
$$a_{31}x_1 + a_{32}x_2 + a_{33}x_3 = f_3$$

The form of the set of index equations is the same independent of the range of the indices so that

$$a_{ij}\, x_j = f_i \qquad\qquad \begin{array}{l} i = 1, 2 \ldots, M \\ j = 1, 2 \ldots, N \end{array} \qquad (2.8)$$

represents a set of M equations that relate N independent variables. We also note that the subscript itself has no meaning. It is the concept of the range and summation conventions that is of importance, thus

$$a_{mn}\, x_n = f_m$$
$$a_{rs}\, x_s = f_r$$
$$a_{kp}\, x_p = f_k$$

are equivalent representations, where (m,r,k = 1,2...M) and (n,s,p = 1,2...N)

2.1.1.   Representation of a Vector

A vector is a quantity with magnitude and direction. The position of point B relative to point A as shown by Fig. 2-1 can be represented by the vector **a** which is the directed line segment between points A and B. The definition of the vector is conceptual and is not based on any particular frame of reference. We do find it convenient to define the positions on points A and B relative to a coordinate system and then to describe the vector **a** in terms of components in specified coordinate directions. Consider points A and B defined relative to a rectangular cartesian coordinate (rcc) system (x_1, x_2, x_3) shown by Fig. 2-1.

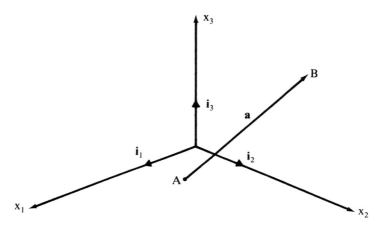

Figure 2-1. Rectangular Coordinate System

The vector **a** can then be expressed as

$$\mathbf{a} = a_1 \, \mathbf{i}_1 + a_2 \, \mathbf{i}_2 + a_3 \, \mathbf{i}_3 \tag{2.9}$$

where $\mathbf{i}_m$ (m = 1,2,3) are unit vectors in the directions of the x_m (m = 1,2,3) coordinate axes and where a_m (m = 1,2,3) are the components of **a** in the x_m-directions. The representation of the vector in component form can be simplified by using the summation convention:

$$\mathbf{a} = a_m \, \mathbf{i}_m \tag{2.10}$$

Finally, since we are representing the vector **a** in terms of its components referred to the x_m coordinate system, it can be represented as the set a_m where

$$a_m \Rightarrow (a_1, a_2, a_3) \tag{2.11}$$

2.1.2.   Transformation of Vector Components

The concept of a vector is independent of the coordinate system used to determine its components. Thus, if we have two coordinate systems x_j and x'_j, the vector is the same in each coordinate system, but the components of the vector are different so that

$$\mathbf{a}' = \mathbf{a} \tag{2.12}$$

we can express (2.12) in component form as

$$a'_1 \, \mathbf{i}'_1 + a'_2 \, \mathbf{i}'_2 + a'_3 \, \mathbf{i}'_3 = a_1 \, \mathbf{i}_1 + a_2 \, \mathbf{i}_2 + a_3 \, \mathbf{i}_3 \tag{2.13}$$

31

where i_m' are unit vectors in the directions of the x_m'-coordinates, and a_m' are components of **a** in the x_m' system. If we take the scalar vector product of each side of (2.13) with respect to i_1' we find

$$a_1' = a_1 \ (i_1' \cdot i_1) \ + a_2 \ (i_1' \cdot i_2) + \ a_3 \ (i_1' \cdot i_3)$$

and similarly   (2.14)

$$a_2' = a_1 \ (i_2' \cdot i_1) \ + a_2 \ (i_2' \cdot i_2) \ + \ a_3 \ (i_2' \cdot i_3)$$
$$a_3' = a_1 \ (i_3' \cdot i_1) \ + a_2 \ (i_3' \cdot i_2) \ + \ a_3 \ (i_3' \cdot i_3)$$

where the unit vectors satisfy the orthonormal relations.

$$i_m \cdot i_n \ = \delta_{mn} = \quad \begin{cases} 1 & m=n \\ 0 & m \neq n \end{cases}$$ (2.15)

The scalar products between the unit vectors appearing on the right-hand side of equation (2.14) are seen to be direction cosines, i.e.,

$$i_j' \cdot i_k \ = \ \cos(x_j', x_k)$$

A set of direction cosines a_{mn} is therefore defined as

$$a_{mn} \ = \ i_m' \cdot i_n$$ (2.16)

where a_{mn} is the direction cosine between x_m' and x_n. The components of **a** in the x_j' coordinates are then given by

$$a_1' = a_{11} a_1 + a_{12} a_2 + a_{13} a_3$$
$$a_2' = a_{21} a_1 + a_{22} a_2 + a_{23} a_3$$
$$a_3' = a_{31} a_1 + a_{32} a_2 + a_{33} a_3$$

or, using index notation,

$$a_m' \ = \ a_{mn} a_n$$ (2.17)

Equation (2.17) is the general transformation law for the components of a vector referred to rectangular cartesian coordinates. The inverse relationship can be shown to be

$$a_i = a_{ij} \ a_j'$$ (2.18)

so that

$$a_{im} a_{jm} = \delta_{ij}$$ (2.19)

2.2.   Matrix Notation

Index notation is extremely useful in representing sets of field equations in the theory of elasticity; it will be used extensively in Chapter Four. In the representation and manipulation of the algebraic equations governing structural behavior we will find it useful to specify a set of equations such as (2.7) in matrix form as

$$\mathbf{Ax} = \mathbf{f}$$ (2.20)

The notation used in (2.20) eliminates the use of a set of indices to represent a set of equations. The matrix representation implies both a structure in the sets **A**, **x**, and **f** and a rule for multiplying **A** by **x**. The set structure and the rule for multiplication can be defined by considering equations (2.7). The matrices **A**, **x**, and **f** are defined to be

$$A = \begin{bmatrix} a_{11} & a_{12} & a_{13} \\ a_{21} & a_{22} & a_{23} \\ a_{31} & a_{32} & a_{33} \end{bmatrix} \quad ; \quad x = \begin{Bmatrix} x_1 \\ x_2 \\ x_3 \end{Bmatrix} \quad ; \quad f = \begin{Bmatrix} f_1 \\ f_2 \\ f_3 \end{Bmatrix} \qquad (2.21)$$

So that (2.20) is written using the definitions (2.21) as

$$\begin{bmatrix} a_{11} & a_{12} & a_{13} \\ a_{21} & a_{22} & a_{23} \\ a_{31} & a_{32} & a_{33} \end{bmatrix} \begin{Bmatrix} x_1 \\ x_2 \\ x_3 \end{Bmatrix} = \begin{Bmatrix} f_1 \\ f_2 \\ f_3 \end{Bmatrix} \qquad (2.22)$$

2.2.1. Basic Definitions

A matrix is an ordered array with m rows and n columns:

$$A = \begin{bmatrix} a_{11} & a_{12} & a_{13} & \cdots & a_{1n} \\ a_{21} & a_{22} & a_{23} & \cdots & a_{2n} \\ \vdots & \vdots & \vdots & & \vdots \\ a_{m1} & a_{m2} & a_{m3} & \cdots & a_{mn} \end{bmatrix} \qquad (2.23)$$

The matrix **A** is then said to be of order m-by-n; i.e., it is a matrix with m rows and n columns. Three useful subcases of the general m by n matrix is described below.

2.2.1.1. Row Matrix (1-by-n)-matrix

$$A = \begin{bmatrix} a_{11} & a_{12} & a_{13} & \cdots & a_{1n} \end{bmatrix} \qquad (2.24)$$

2.2.1.2. Column Matrix (m-by-1)-matrix

$$A = \begin{Bmatrix} a_{11} \\ a_{21} \\ a_{31} \\ \vdots \\ a_{m1} \end{Bmatrix} \qquad (2.25)$$

2.2.1.3. Square Matrix (n-by-n)-matrix

$$A = \begin{bmatrix} a_{11} & a_{12} & a_{13} & \cdots & a_{1n} \\ a_{21} & a_{22} & a_{23} & \cdots & a_{2n} \\ \vdots & \vdots & \vdots & & \vdots \\ a_{n1} & a_{n2} & a_{n3} & \cdots & a_{nn} \end{bmatrix} \qquad (2.26)$$

2.2.2. Special Matrices

There are several special matrix forms that are useful in matrix algebra. These special matrices are discussed in the following sections.

2.2.2.1. Unit Matrix

The unit matrix, which is generally denoted by **I**, is a square matrix with the ones on the diagonal and with zeros for all other elements.

$$I = \begin{bmatrix} 1 & 0 & 0 & 0 \\ 0 & 1 & 0 & 0 \\ 0 & 0 & 1 & 0 \\ 0 & 0 & 0 & 1 \end{bmatrix} \qquad (2.27)$$

2.2.2.2. Symmetric Matrix
A symmetrical matrix is a square matrix whose elements satisfy the equality

$$a_{ij} = a_{ji} \qquad (2.28)$$

2.2.2.3. Antisymmetric Matrix
An antisymmetrical matrix is a square matrix whose elements satisfy the equality

$$a_{ij} = {}^-a_{ji} \qquad (2.29)$$

Since $a_{ii} = -a_{ii}$ for diagonal elements it follows that $a_{ii} = 0$. The terms on the diagonal are therefore all equal to zero.

2.2.2.4. Banded Matrix
A matrix is termed a *band matrix* if all nonzero entries lie within a region of the matrix which parallel to the main diagonal as shown schematically by Fig. 2.2.

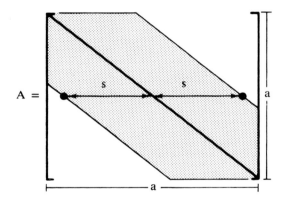

Figure 2.2. A band matrix

The half-bandwidth, s, is defined to be the number of columns, including the diagonal, beyond which all coefficients are zero. The total bandwidth, b, is then given as

$$b = 2s - 1 \qquad (2.31)$$

which accounts for the diagonal and $s - 1$ terms on each side of the diagonal. If we define m to be the number of columns beyond the diagonal to the last column which contains a nonzero element then we can represent the semi-bandwidth as

$$s = m + 1 \qquad (2.32)$$

Many of the matrices that govern the behavior of discretized continuum problems are characterized by being sparse and banded, where sparse means that the number of nonzero terms in the matrix is a fraction (typically 1 percent or less) of the total number of terms in the matrix. General-purpose computer programs take advantage of the matrix topology (symmetric and banded) and sparseness for efficient storage and matrix manipulations.

2.2.2.5. Triangular Matrices
A triangular matrix is a square matrix that has all entries either above or below the diagonal equal to zero:

34

$$L = \begin{bmatrix} \ell_{11} & 0 & 0 \\ \ell_{21} & \ell_{22} & 0 \\ \ell_{31} & \ell_{32} & \ell_{33} \end{bmatrix} \quad , \quad U = \begin{bmatrix} u_{11} & u_{12} & u_{13} \\ 0 & u_{22} & u_{23} \\ 0 & 0 & u_{33} \end{bmatrix}$$

L is a lower triangular matrix, and U is an upper triangular matrix. Note that any of the ℓ_{ij} or u_{ij} terms may also be equal to zero.

2.2.3.   Matrix Operations

We have already identified the concept of matrix multiplication by defining the matrix representation of the set of equations given by (2.7). There are a number of primitive operators with which we are familiar. Our interest here is to extend the basic concepts of the operations of equality, addition, and multiplication and to define the matrix operations of inversion and transposition.

2.2.3.1.   Matrix Equality

Two matrices A and B can be equal if and only if A and B are of the same order.

$$a_{ij} = b_{ij} \qquad \begin{aligned} & i = 1, 2, ..., m \\ & j = 1, 2, ..., n \end{aligned} \qquad (2.33)$$

2.2.3.2.   Addition and Subtraction

Two matrices A and B can be added only if they are of the same order; then their sum is

$$C = A + B$$

where

$$c_{ij} = a_{ij} + b_{ij} \qquad \begin{aligned} & i = 1, 2, ..., m \\ & j = 1, 2, ..., n \end{aligned} \qquad (2.34)$$

2.2.3.3.   Matrix Multiplication

The concept of matrix multiplication associated with the matrix representation of (2.7) can be generalized for the case where we have the product

$$C = AB \qquad (2.35)$$

where A is of order (m-by-n) and B is of order (n-by-r). The rule for matrix multiplication given by (2.5) then holds for each column of B and defines an element in the associated column of C. The product of two rectangular matrices is defined as

$$c_{ij} = \sum_{k=1}^{n} a_{ik} b_{kj} \qquad (2.36)$$

where c_{ij} is the general element of C. In order to perform the operation defined by (2.36) A and B must be conformable; i.e., the number of columns of A must be equal to the number of rows of B. It follows that the product AB is not equal to the product BA and, except for the case where A and B are square matrices, the product BA will not be defined because the matrices are not conformable.

Example:

Let A and B be defined as

$$A = \begin{bmatrix} 1 & 3 & 5 & 6 \\ 3 & 7 & 3 & 5 \\ 7 & 3 & 2 & 1 \end{bmatrix}_{3 \times 4} , \quad B = \begin{bmatrix} 2 & 3 \\ 4 & 5 \\ 6 & 7 \\ 8 & 9 \end{bmatrix}_{4 \times 2}$$

2.2   Matrix Notation

Then the product is given by

$$
\begin{bmatrix} 1 & 3 & 5 & 6 \\ 3 & 7 & 3 & 5 \\ 7 & 3 & 2 & 1 \end{bmatrix}_{3\times4} \begin{bmatrix} 2 & 3 \\ 4 & 5 \\ 6 & 7 \\ 8 & 9 \end{bmatrix}_{4\times2} = \begin{bmatrix} (2+12+30+48) & (3+15+35+54) \\ (6+28+18+40) & (9+35+21+45) \\ (14+12+12+8) & (21+15+14+9) \end{bmatrix}_{3\times2}
$$

where **C** is a (3-by-2) matrix. Note that **BA** is not defined in this case, since the matrices are not conformable.

2.2.3.4.   Matrix Transposition

The transpose of a matrix **A** is obtained by interchanging the rows and columns of **A**. Denoting the transpose by $\mathbf{A}^T$, we have

$$a_{ij}^T = a_{ji} \tag{2.37}$$

If **A** is of order m-by-n, then the transpose will be of order n-by-m.
The transpose of the product of two matrices **C = AB** is given by

$$c_{ij}^T = c_{ji} = \sum_{k=1}^{m} a_{jk} \, b_{ki} = \sum_{k=1}^{m} b_{ik}^T \, a_{kj}^T \tag{2.38}$$

so that the transpose of the product is

$$\mathbf{C}^T = \mathbf{B}^T \mathbf{A}^T \tag{2.39}$$

The rule for transposition of a product is to take the transpose of the individual matrices and then reverse the order of multiplication.

Example:

Let the matrix **A** be given as

$$\mathbf{A} = \begin{bmatrix} 1 & 3 & 5 & 6 \\ 3 & 7 & 3 & 5 \\ 7 & 3 & 2 & 1 \end{bmatrix}$$

The the transpose, $\mathbf{A}^T$ is given by

$$\mathbf{A}^T = \begin{bmatrix} 1 & 3 & 7 \\ 3 & 7 & 3 \\ 5 & 3 & 2 \\ 6 & 5 & 1 \end{bmatrix}$$

2.2.3.5.   Matrix Inversion

In order to solve the matrix equation

$$\mathbf{A}\,\mathbf{x} = \mathbf{b} \tag{2.40}$$

an operation similar to division is required. The operation is called matrix inversion where the inverse of **A**, designated by $\mathbf{A}^{-1}$, is defined by

$$\mathbf{A}^{-1}\,\mathbf{A} = \mathbf{I} \tag{2.41}$$

36

The definition (2.41) allows us to evaluate A^{-1} since there are n^2 equations for the n^2 unknown elements in the A^{-1} matrix. Once the inverse has been found, (2.40) can be solved by premultiplying both sides of the equation A^{-1} to give

$$x = A^{-1} b \tag{2.42}$$

The inverse exists if and only if A is square, and then only if the determinant of the coefficients of A is not zero.

The determinant is a number given by

$$\det A = \sum_{j=1}^{n} (-1)^{j+1} \, a_{1j} \, \det A_{1j} \tag{2.43}$$

The term a_{1j} is the jth element of the first row and it is multiplied by plus or minus one depending on whether j is even or odd; plus one if j is odd and minus one if j is even. The quantity $\det A_{1j}$ is the determinant of the $(n-1)$ by $(n-1)$ matrix that remains after eliminating the first row and jth column. The $\det A_{1j}$ can be expanded using (2.43) until A_{ij} is a two-by-two matrix whose determinant is given by

$$\tag{2.44}$$

$$\det \begin{bmatrix} a_{11} & a_{12} \\ a_{21} & a_{22} \end{bmatrix} = (a_{11}a_{22} - a_{12}a_{21})$$

Example:

Let the matrix A be given by

$$A = \begin{bmatrix} 5 & -4 & 2 \\ -4 & 6 & -4 \\ 2 & -4 & 1 \end{bmatrix}$$

Then the determinant is found to be

$$\det A = 5(6-16) + 4(-4+8) + 2(16-12) = -26$$

Now that the determinant has been defined, we can return to the evaluation of inverse of the matrix A. Consider the set of equations

$$\begin{aligned} a_{11} x_1 + a_{12} x_2 &= b_1 \\ a_{12} x_1 + a_{22} x_2 &= b_2 \end{aligned} \tag{2.45}$$

where the A matrix is

$$A = \begin{bmatrix} a_{11} & a_{12} \\ a_{21} & a_{22} \end{bmatrix}$$

Let the inverse of A be defined as G so that

$$G A = I$$

Then

$$\begin{bmatrix} g_{11} & g_{12} \\ g_{21} & g_{22} \end{bmatrix} \begin{bmatrix} a_{11} & a_{12} \\ a_{21} & a_{22} \end{bmatrix} = \begin{bmatrix} 1 & 0 \\ 0 & 1 \end{bmatrix} \tag{2.46}$$

2.2 Matrix Notation

By performing the matrix multiplication indicated in equation (2.46), we obtain the following equations in terms of the elements of $\mathbf{G}$ and $\mathbf{A}$

$$
\begin{aligned}
g_{11}\,a_{11} + g_{12}\,a_{21} &= 1 \\
g_{11}\,a_{12} + g_{12}\,a_{22} &= 0 \\
g_{21}\,a_{11} + g_{22}\,a_{21} &= 0 \\
g_{21}\,a_{12} + g_{22}\,a_{22} &= 1
\end{aligned}
$$

Solving for the elements of $\mathbf{G}$, we find

$$
\mathbf{G} = \mathbf{A}^{-1} = \frac{1}{\det \mathbf{A}} \begin{bmatrix} a_{22} & -a_{12} \\ -a_{21} & a_{11} \end{bmatrix}
\tag{2.47}
$$

In actual practice the inverse of the coefficient matrix is not formed in order to solve for the unknowns in a set of equations. The techniques that are used are based on Gaussian elimination and take advantage of the matrix sparseness and topology. There is a tremendous computational saving in taking advantage of matrix topology since it requires approximately $\tfrac{1}{3}n^3$ multiplications to formally evaluate $\mathbf{A}^{-1}$. Those techniques that take advantage of the topology of the matrix and utilize Gaussian elimination require on the order of nW_{rms}^2 multiplications where W_{rms} is a topological parameter called the root-mean-square wavefront which is defined in Sec. 7.3.5. The time required to evaluate the inverse of matrix can be reduced by factors of hundreds or thousands by using sparse matrix techniques. A general discussion of Gaussian elimination is presented in Sec. 2.2.4.

2.2.3.6. Matrix Partitioning and Reduction

It may be useful to consider subsets of the solution vector $\mathbf{x}$ in the matrix equation

$$
\mathbf{A}\,\mathbf{x} = \mathbf{b}
$$

The set $\mathbf{x}$ is therefore partitioned into the two subsets

$$
\mathbf{x} = \left\{ \begin{matrix} x_a \\ x_b \end{matrix} \right\}
\tag{2.48}
$$

Then the partitioned set of equations can be represented by the matrix equations

$$
\begin{bmatrix} A_{aa} & A_{ab} \\ A_{ba} & A_{bb} \end{bmatrix} \left\{ \begin{matrix} x_a \\ x_b \end{matrix} \right\} = \left\{ \begin{matrix} b_a \\ b_b \end{matrix} \right\}
\tag{2.49}
$$

where (2.49) represents the two matrix equations

$$
\begin{aligned}
A_{aa}\,x_a + A_{ab}\,x_b &= b_a \\
A_{ba}\,x_a + A_{bb}\,x_b &= b_b
\end{aligned}
\tag{2.50}
$$

Example:

Let the matrix $\mathbf{x}$ be represented by the partitioned sets

$$
\mathbf{x} = \lfloor x_1\ x_2\ x_3\ x_4\ x_5 \rfloor^T \quad ; \quad x_a = \left\{ \begin{matrix} x_3 \\ x_5 \end{matrix} \right\} \quad ; \quad x_b = \left\{ \begin{matrix} x_1 \\ x_2 \\ x_4 \end{matrix} \right\}
$$

The partitions of $\mathbf{A}$ are then given as

$$\mathbf{A}_{aa} = \begin{bmatrix} a_{33} & a_{35} \\ a_{53} & a_{55} \end{bmatrix} \quad ; \quad \mathbf{A}_{ab} = \begin{bmatrix} a_{31} & a_{32} & a_{34} \\ a_{51} & a_{52} & a_{54} \end{bmatrix}$$

$$\mathbf{A}_{ba} = \begin{bmatrix} a_{13} & a_{15} \\ a_{23} & a_{25} \\ a_{43} & a_{45} \end{bmatrix} \quad ; \quad \mathbf{A}_{bb} = \begin{bmatrix} a_{11} & a_{12} & a_{14} \\ a_{21} & a_{22} & a_{24} \\ a_{41} & a_{42} & a_{44} \end{bmatrix}$$

By using matrix partitioning we can reduce the order of the number of equations that are to be solved at one time. We proceed to solve for x_b from the second of equation (2.50), which gives

$$x_b = \mathbf{A}_{bb}^{-1} \ [b_b - \mathbf{A}_{ba} \ x_a] \tag{2.51}$$

Then the substitution of (2.51) into the first of (2.50) gives

$$\mathbf{A}_{aa} \ x_a + \mathbf{A}_{ab} \ [\mathbf{A}_{bb}^{-1} \ (b_b - \mathbf{A}_{ba} \ x_a)] = b_a$$

or

$$[\mathbf{A}_{aa} - \mathbf{A}_{ab} \ \mathbf{A}_{bb}^{-1} \ \mathbf{A}_{ba}] \ x_a = b_a - \mathbf{A}_{ab} \mathbf{A}_{bb}^{-1} \ b_b \tag{2.52}$$

The matrix

$$\mathbf{A}_{aa}' = [\mathbf{A}_{aa} - \mathbf{A}_{ab} \ \mathbf{A}_{bb}^{-1} \ \mathbf{A}_{ba}] \tag{2.53}$$

is called the reduced stiffness matrix and is of order (a-by-a) rather than (n-by-n).

2.2.4.   Solutions Based on Gaussian Elimination

2.2.4.1.   Triangular Factorization

While the formal operations associated with forming the inverse of a matrix are straight forward, in actual practice this technique is not used. Instead we solve sets of equations by using a technique which was invented by Gauss. In order to understand this method we begin by considering a set of three equations written in matrix form as

$$\begin{bmatrix} 2 & 4 & 6 \\ 6 & 3 & 0 \\ -1 & 2 & 3 \end{bmatrix} \begin{Bmatrix} x_1 \\ x_2 \\ x_3 \end{Bmatrix} = \begin{Bmatrix} 4 \\ -6 \\ 7 \end{Bmatrix} \tag{2.54}$$

The objective of the method is to operate on (2.54) in such a way that it is transformed to triangular form. We thus proceed by
   a) Subtracting three times the first equation from the second equation.
   b) Adding 1/2 times the first equation from the third equation
Which results in

$$\begin{bmatrix} 2 & 4 & 6 \\ 0 & -9 & -18 \\ 0 & 4 & 6 \end{bmatrix} \begin{Bmatrix} x_1 \\ x_2 \\ x_3 \end{Bmatrix} = \begin{Bmatrix} 4 \\ -18 \\ 9 \end{Bmatrix} \tag{2.55}$$

2.2.4.2 Forward Backward Substitution

Then, to complete the triangularization, we operate on (2.55) by adding 4/9 of the second equation to the third giving

$$\mathbf{U x} = \begin{bmatrix} 2 & 4 & 6 \\ 0 & -9 & -18 \\ 0 & 0 & -2 \end{bmatrix} \begin{Bmatrix} x_1 \\ x_2 \\ x_3 \end{Bmatrix} = \begin{Bmatrix} 4 \\ -18 \\ 1 \end{Bmatrix} \qquad (2.56)$$

The original equation has thus been transformed by the elimination procedure in a "forward sweep" such that the coefficient matrix, $\mathbf{U}$, is an upper triangular matrix. We then see that there is an obvious order in which to solve the set of equations.

For the process we have described above we see that three operations are required which correspond to the steps in the elimination process. The first operation, i.e. subtracting three times the first equation from the second can be defined by the matrix product $\mathbf{C}_{12}\mathbf{A}$ where

$$\mathbf{C}_{12} = \begin{bmatrix} 1 & 0 & 0 \\ -3 & 1 & 0 \\ 0 & 0 & 1 \end{bmatrix}$$

and where the first subscript identifies the row which is to scaled and the second defines the row to which the scaled numbers are to be added. The total reduction process, then, can be viewed as a repeated set of matrix multiplications such that

$$\mathbf{C}_{23}\mathbf{C}_{13}\mathbf{C}_{12}\mathbf{A} = \mathbf{U} \qquad (2.57)$$

where $\mathbf{U}$ is given by (2.56) and the transformations are $\mathbf{C}_{13}$ and $\mathbf{C}_{23}$ are

$$\mathbf{C}_{13} = \begin{bmatrix} 1 & 0 & 0 \\ 0 & 1 & 0 \\ 1/2 & 0 & 1 \end{bmatrix} \text{ and } \mathbf{C}_{23} = \begin{bmatrix} 1 & 0 & 0 \\ 0 & 1 & 0 \\ 0 & 9/4 & 1 \end{bmatrix}$$

We could further write (2.57) as

$$\mathbf{C A} = \mathbf{U} \qquad (2.58)$$

where the matrix $\mathbf{C}$ is given by the repeated product of transformation matrices and is, by inspection, a lower triangular matrix. Since we know (or could determine) the coefficient matrix $\mathbf{C}$ we could form $\mathbf{C}^{-1}$ and find $\mathbf{A}$ to be

$$\mathbf{A} = \mathbf{L U} \qquad (2.59)$$

where $\mathbf{L} = \mathbf{C}^{-1}$ which is also a lower triangular matrix. The bottom line of this little exercise is that under certain conditions a general square matrix $\mathbf{A}$ can be represented as the product of a lower and upper triangular matrix. This operation is called *decomposition* because the matrix is decomposed into the two triangular factors.

2.2.4.2. Forward-Backward Substitution

Now that decomposition has been defined we might ask why anyone would want to go to the extra work involved with finding $\mathbf{L}$ since, according to (2.56), only the upper triangular factor is involved in the solution. The answer is twofold.

1. We did something more than forming $\mathbf{U}$ in the reduction process — we also modified the right hand side.

2. The formation of $\mathbf{L}$ is required to allow solution for multiple load cases — and it's free.

In order to gain some insight to both of these points let's consider a set of linear algebraic equations written in matrix form as follows

$$\mathbf{A}\,\mathbf{x} = \mathbf{b} \qquad (2.60)$$

where **b** contains one or more columns and may thus represent several load cases. The matrix **A** is now decomposed into its **L** and **U** factors so that (2.60) becomes

$$\mathbf{L}\,\mathbf{U}\,\mathbf{x} = \mathbf{b} \qquad (2.61)$$

At this point we take note of the special form of the **L** and **U** factors and proceed by defining a transformation of the form

$$\mathbf{U}\,\mathbf{x} = \mathbf{w} \qquad (2.62)$$

the substitution of (2.62) into (2.61) then gives

$$\mathbf{L}\,\mathbf{w} = \mathbf{b} \qquad (2.63)$$

Since **L** is a lower triangular form and since both **L** and **b** are known the **w** can be determined starting with $\mathbf{w}_1$, in a forward sweep. The **w** then becomes the right hand side of (2.62) so that solution, **x**, can be recovered starting with the last one in a backward substitution. We thus see that the determination of the **L U** factors allows us to solve for multiple load cases.

2.2.4.3. Numerical Error in Solution

We note, in the simple example which we described in Sec. 2.2.4.1., that the division of all terms in a "pivotal row" by the value of the diagonal which is called the pivot is one of the principal operations in Gauss elimination. A fairly obvious question arises then concerning what to do if we find a zero, or a very very small term, on the diagonal. A work-around solution is called partial-pivoting which is a procedure in which the column containing the zero pivot is searched for the largest value and then the corresponding rows are exchanged to make this largest value the pivot. If all terms on a below the pivot in a given column are zero then the matrix is singular and we cannot proceed with the decomposition routine.

This all suggests that the values of the pivots tell us something about the characteristic of the results of the decomposition process, if indeed the decomposition process can be completed. Small values of the diagonal terms of the upper triangular factor, which are in turn the values of the pivots, might be indicative of an ill-conditioned matrix. These diagonal values can thus be used to calculate a "conditioning number" which tells the analyst something about the original system of equations.

A possible conditioning number, and one that can be calculated by MSC/NASTRAN, is the conditioning number, c_i, as

$$c_i = \frac{a_{ii}}{u_{ii}} \qquad (2.69)$$

where the index i refers to the ith equation in the system of equations, a_{ii} in (2.60), and u_{ii} is the diagonal term in the upper triangular factor.

In structural analysis solutions generally accepted guidelines for conditioning numbers (see Ref 2-1 for example) are

$c_i > 10^{10}$ indicates the pivot is approaching zero and that the matrix is, for all intents, singular

$10^8 \le c_i \le 10^7$ indicates possible modeling problem

$10^0 \le c_i \le 10^2$ indicates a well-conditioned solution.

2.3   References

MSC/NASTRAN prints the largest conditioning number for each matrix decomposition and the associates equation number which the analyst can use to make some judgment on the accuracy of the solution.

Another "goodness" number which has a physical interpretation for continuum mechanics problems is the product (2.70) which is the virtual work done by the calculated displacements.

$$\delta W = \frac{\tilde{X}^T (A \tilde{X} - b)}{\tilde{X}^T b} \tag{2.70}$$

where $\tilde{X}$ is the approximate numerical solution. This number should be zero, which indicates that the virtual work for an arbitrary virtual displacement $\tilde{X}$ is zero, as it should be for a system which is in equilibrium. A significant value of δW, greater than 10^{-5}, is cause for some consternation and a review of the finite element model which was used to generate the set of equations is in order.

2.3.   References

2-1   Haggenmacher, G. W., and Lahey, R. S., "Diagnostics in Finite Element Analysis," *Proceedings of The First Chautauqua on Finite Element Modeling*, Edited by J. H. Conaway, Schaeffer Analysis, Inc., 1980, pp. 193-213.

3

Solution of Matrix Equations Using MSC/NASTRAN

3.1.   Direct Matrix Abstraction Programming (DMAP)

Conceptually, a set of algebraic equations can be generated by employing a technique called the finite element method and this set of equations can be modified and solved by using the techniques of matrix algebra. The set of operations which leads to the solution can then be reduced to a procedure, or an algorithm, that will produce results of interest.

A procedure for the analysis of a structure, for example, may incorporate a number of steps, each of which can be expressed in terms of matrix operations. The procedure can thus be coded for a digital computer by writing a suitable computer program which defines the set of computer instructions which, when executed, will represent the matrix operations and their order of execution.

MSC/NASTRAN provides a high-level language for defining algorithms which are represented as a sequence of matrix operations. A high-level language is one that allows the user to define operations and data in a symbolic way without having to worry about where matrices are stored, what machine instructions represent the algorithm, the size of system matrices, etc. This NASTRAN language is called **D**irect **M**atrix **A**bstraction **P**rogramming (DMAP). For example, suppose we want to form the sum of two matrices, **A** and **B** (which are defined somehow) to give **C**. The associated DMAP instruction is then

$$\text{ADD} \quad \text{A, B/C} \quad \$$$

where the mnemonic name ADD is called the *module name* and defines the operation to be performed, **A** and **B** are the *input data blocks* and **C**, the result is called the *output data block*. The construction of the instruction is such that the list of input data blocks (i.e. matrices) and output data blocks are separated by a slash (/). The dollar sign ($) is used to terminate the instruction.

MSC/NASTRAN can be viewed as a computational workshop where the DMAP modules are a set of tools and where the NASTRAN Executive provides the framework for the correct sequence of DMAP operations and for the storage and retrieval of all the data which is associated with each DMAP instruction.

Workshops are used to produce finished products and, in a sense, the product produced by the NASTRAN workshop is a solution algorithm such as that which represents the procedure for the static analysis of a structure. This procedure is then simply a collection of DMAP instruction which, when executed, performs the operational steps involved with a specific type of solution. Several DMAP procedures have been predefined by the MSC/NASTRAN developers and can be requested by including a "SOL" Executive Control request (see sec. 1.9.5.) where the solution number is associated with a specific solution algorithm.

A complete description of the DMAP language and all of the DMAP modules is beyond the scope of this book. Our purpose here is to describe the construct of the language and provide an understanding of the capability that will allow us to

• Understand the solution sequences.

• Change rigid formats.

• Use MSC/NASTRAN as a powerful workshop for the development of algorithms which involve sparse matrix operations.

43

For additional information the reader is referred to Refs. 3-1 and 3-2.

3.2.   Form of the DMAP Instruction

The MSC/NASTRAN program consists of modules for matrix manipulation, executive functions, input and output, and generating systems of equations using a user-supplied finite element model. Each of these modules has a name, accepts a specific number of inputs, produces a specified number of outputs and may be controlled by or manipulate a set of scalar numbers called parameters. The form of the MSC/NASTRAN DMAP instruction is

(MODULE NAME)   (INPUT DATA BLOCKS)/(OUTPUT DATA BLOCKS)/(PARAMETER LIST)$

where

MODULE NAME   Name of a MSC/NASTRAN module

INPUT   List of data block names whose number is specified for the module and that are
DATA BLOCKS   separated by commas

OUTPUT   List of data block names that are output by the module whose number is
DATA BLOCKS   specified for the module and that are separated by a comma

PARAMETER   List of parameters that is utilized to control the module and to provide
LIST   parametric input or output

The slash (/) is used as a delimiter between data groups and the dollar sign ($) is used to terminate the DMAP instruction. The ($) is only required if the instruction ends with a (/).

The construction of the statement seems to be more complex than a FORTRAN statement and indeed it is because the operations defined by a DMAP statement involve matrices or data blocks rather than numbers. There is nothing formidable about the DMAP language, it is simply another language that the user must master in order to take advantage of the richness of the MSC/NASTRAN program.

3.3.   Matrix Operations Modules

In order to perform matrix operations on sets of data, we need to be able to define matrix data in the input queue, operate on the data, and print the results. We will proceed by describing the operational modules followed by a discussion of how the data is specified and printed.

The matrix operation modules are shown by Table 3-1. Each of the DMAP modules is described in either Ref. 3-1 or Ref. 3-2. All the modules that comprise the MSC/NASTRAN system are summarized in Ref. 3-1, which also directs the user to the appropriate section of the MSC/NASTRAN documentation to obtain a detailed description of the module.

The DMAP module description includes

1. DMAP module name

2. The purpose of the module

3. The form of the DMAP module and the number of input data blocks, output data blocks, and parameters is specified

4. Description of input data blocks

5. Description of output data blocks

6. Description of parameters

7. Remarks appropriate to the use of the module

MODULE NAME	MATRIX OPERATION
ADD	$X = aA + bB$
ADD5	$X = aA + bB + cC + dD + eE$
CEAD	Solves for p and u in $(Mp^2 + Bp + K) u = 0$
DECOMP	$A = LU$
DIAGONAL	Creates a diagonal matrix raising each diagonal element to a power
FBS	$X = (LU)^{-1} B$
MERGE	$A \Leftarrow \begin{bmatrix} A_{11} & A_{12} \\ A_{21} & A_{22} \end{bmatrix}$
MPYAD	$X = AB + C$
NORM	Normalizes a matrix so that the maximum element in each row is equal to 1
PARTN	$A \Rightarrow \begin{bmatrix} A_{11} & A_{12} \\ A_{21} & A_{22} \end{bmatrix}$
READ	Solves for λ and u in $(K - \lambda M)u = 0$
SMPYAD	$X = ABCDE + F$
SOLVE	$X = A^{-1} B$
TRNSP	$X = A^T$
UMERGE	Merge using displacement sets
UPARTN	Partition using displacement sets

Table 3-1. Matrix Operation Modules

3.4. DMAP Rules

Now that we have seen some of the MSC/NASTRAN modules it is appropriate to consider the rules for using the language.

45

3.4 DMAP Rules

3.4.1. Form of Instruction

The DMAP statement must conform to the form of the DMAP instruction as specified by the corresponding module description. This includes

1. The module name

2. The number of input data blocks

3. The number of output data blocks

4. The number and type of each parameter

3.4.2. Input Data Blocks

It is a MSC/NASTRAN rule that an input data block must be either output by a previous DMAP statement, input by an appropriate Bulk Data specification using DMI (see Sec. 3.5) for matrix input or DTI (see Ref. 3-1) for tabular input, or defined on a checkpoint tape (OPTP). Input data blocks are referenced by a user-specified name and are separated by commas. Data blocks need not exist, but the appropriate number of commas must exist. Consider the module ADD5 which allows the addition of five matrices and thus has five input data blocks for example. If only one data block existed, then the calling sequence could be

$$ADD5 \quad A,,,, / X / (parameter\ list) \qquad \$$$

where we note that four null data blocks are specified by the commas following data block A.

3.4.3. Output Data Blocks

A data block name may appear as output only once. Since the number of output data blocks is prescribed for each module, the number of separating commas must be one less than the number of blocks. As in the case of input data blocks, consecutive commas indicate presence of null data blocks.

3.4.4. Parameters

Module parameters serve many purposes, including

1. Flags that control computational algorithm used by module

2. Convey data values to and/or from the module

The use of parameters is complicated by the fact that the user must specify

1. Whether the parameter is a constant or a variable

2. Whether the parameter value may be specified on a PARAM Bulk Data Card

3. The value of the parameters, either directly or by reference to a parameter name

The parameter specification thus reflects these three requirements and is constructed using the following three fields:

(Constant or Variable), (Yes or No), (Value)

or, more succinctly,

CVS, YN, V

where

46

$$CVS = \begin{cases} C & \text{if parameter is a prescribed constant} \\ V & \text{if the parameter value may be changed in the module} \\ S & \text{if the parameter is variable and is to be saved} \end{cases}$$

$$YN = \begin{cases} Y & \text{if the initial parameter values may be specified on a PARAM card} \\ N & \text{otherwise} \end{cases}$$

$$V = \begin{cases} P \\ PNAME \\ PNAME = P \end{cases}$$ where P is the value of the parameter, which must be of the correct type (integer, real, or BCD as specified by the module description and where PNAME is the name of a parameter

The first two parts of the parameter specification would seem to be straightforward, but the available forms for specifying the value of the parameter call for some additional clarification.

During the compilation of the DMAP sequence, each parameter is assigned an initial value. The parameters may be assigned a default value in the module or, if there is no default value, an initial value must be prescribed. The value used at execution time may differ from the initial value only if the parameter is declared to be variable, the parameter value is changed by a previous module, and the parameter value is saved by declaring the CVS field to be S. The various forms of the parameter specification are described below:

null A null parameter is defined by a double slash (//) and indicates that the default value for the parameter is to be taken from an internal table called the Module Properties List (MPL). The MPL defines, among other things, the number, the type, and default values for all parameters. The entire parameter list can be assigned by its omission including the slash (/) following the output data blocks.

C, N, v A constant parameter with the value v.

v Entirely equivalent to C, N, v

C, Y, PNAME A constant parameter with the name PNAME. The value specified by a PARAM Bulk Data card is used if present, otherwise the module default value is used. An error will be detected if there is no PARAM or default values.

C, Y, PNAME = v A constant parameter with the name PNAME. The value v is used unless a PARAM card exists in Bulk Data.

V, Y, PNAME
or
V, Y, PNAME = v
A variable parameter that may be input, output, or both. The initial value is defined in the following order:

1. Value from most recent executed SAVE

2. Value from PARAM Bulk Data card

3. v if present in a DMAP instruction

4. Default if any

5. Zero

47

V, N, PNAME   Same as above except that the parameter cannot be specified on a PARAM Bulk
      or   Data card.
V, N, PNAME = v

The values of variable parameters are stored in a special place in MSC/NASTRAN that is called the variable parameter table. However, the parameter table *is not* automatically updated to reflect the current value of a variable parameter during the execution of the DMAP program unless the DMAP programmer has declared the parameter to be an S-type parameter. The form of the parameter definition in this case would be the same as the V-type parameters described above, but the specification

S, Y, PNAME

would imply that the parameter table would always reflect the current value of the parameter with the initial value being the same, in all instances, as the associated V-type parameter.

The parameter may be one of several possible types, where the types are described below. The parameters must be of the type prescribed in the module description.

1. Integer number

2. Real number

3. Literal string (also called Binary Coded Decimal, BCD)

4. Double precision

5. Complex, single precision

6. Complex, double precision

3.5.   User/Program Communication

The DMAP language not only gives us a set of tools which we can use to solve matrix equations, it also provides a set of utilities for reading and writing matrices and PARAMeters. These utilities are absolutely necessary if we intend to use DMAP to solve general matrix equations and they provide us with a powerful capability for modifying the built-in solution algorithms which generate matrix coefficients by means of the finite element method.

In order to clarify these ideas let's take a simple example where we are given two matrices, which we will call **R** and **T** which we want to add together by means of the DMAP ADD module to produce the result **W**. The matrices **R** and **T** are given as

$$\mathbf{R} = \begin{bmatrix} 3. & 5. & 6. \\ 5. & 7. & 4. \\ 6. & 4. & 21. \end{bmatrix} \qquad \mathbf{T} = \begin{bmatrix} 2. & -4. & -0. \\ -4. & 8. & -4. \\ 0. & -4. & 6. \end{bmatrix}$$

Because we know about the ADD module we are in a position to define the desired matrix operation as

ADD   R, T / W $

but just how are the matrices **R** and **T** defined and how do we print the resulting matrix **W**? The answer to this question comes in two parts: first, matrix data can be defined on a special DMI Bulk Data card which is described in Sec. 3.5.1.; and, second, several DMAP utilities exist which can be used to print matrix data that are described in Sec. 3.5.2. After describing these capabilities for getting data into and from the computer we will return to our example problem and describe the MSC/NASTRAN data deck which will lead to its solution in Sec. 3.5.3.

3.5.1. User-Specified Matrix Data

The user can specify the elements of matrices by the DMI Bulk Data card, which is shown in Card Image 3-1, where the matrix form and types are specified by numerical codes, as indicated in Tables 3-2 and 3-3, respectively. The term Card Image is used in this text to indicate a description of one or more related Bulk Data cards. The form of the card image always includes the numbers from 1 to 10 across the top of the card image to define the 10 data fields of the card. The data entries are then defined below the appropriate field entry. The entries in the first and last fields are shown as left-justified, while the remaining fields are shown centered. The user can place the data entries anywhere in the fields, as described in Appendix A.

*Header Card

1	2	3	4	5	6	7	8	9	10
DMI	\<name\>	0	FORM	TIN	TOUT		M	N	

*Column Specification

DMI	\<name\>	J	I	AI, J	AI + 1, J	AI + 2, J	K	AK, J	+ D1
+ D1	L	AL, J	AL + 1, J	etc.					

where

    \<name\> Name of a matrix that appears in the input data block of a DMAP statement (BCD string, first character must be alphabetic).

    FORM Matrix form (see Table 3-2) (integer, >0)

    TIN Type of input matrix (see Table 3-3) (integer, >0)

    TOUT Type of output matrix (see Table 3-3) (integer, ≥ 0)

    M, N Number of rows and columns of matrix (integer, >0)

    J A column number of matrix (integer, >0)

    I, K, L Row numbers in column J (integer, >0)

    AI, J Element of matrix of the type specified by TIN. If TIN ≥ 3, then two fields are used.

Card Image 3-1. Direct Matrix Input Using DMI Bulk Data

3.5.1 User-Specified Matrix Data

The DMI Bulk Data can only be used with user-written DMAP or DMAP Alters to a rigid format. There are a number of predefined internal data block names which are reserved to the MSC/NASTRAN system and are thus not available to the user. These include POOL, NPTP, OPTP, UMF, NUMF, PLT1, PLT2, INPT, GEOM1, GEOM2, GEOM3, GEOM4, GEOM5, EDT, MPT, EPT, DIT, DYNAMICS, IFPFILE, AXIC, FORCE, MATPOOL, PCDB, XYCDB, CASECC, DTI names, and SCRATCH1 thru SCRATCH9.

The number of fields used to define a value for a matrix element depends on the type of matrix being defined, i.e. TIN. If the type of matrix is real single or double precision then only one field is used. If the matrix type is complex single or double precision then two fields are required. In either case the non-zero coefficients for the entire matrix must be entered even for the case where the matrix is defined to be symmetric.

A coefficient value which is identical for several rows in a given column can be defined by specifying the starting row number and value followed by the literal 'THRU'. The integer value of the next field then defines the number of rows to be repeated. For example the DMI Bulk Data

1	2	3	4	5	6	7	8	9	10
DMI	PRIMER	1	2	1.	THRU	10	12	2.	+ 1

would define elements 2 thru 11 in Col. 1 of a matrix called PRIMER to be 1. with element 12 having the value of 2.

FORM CODE	MATRIX FORM
1	Square but not Symmetric
2	General Rectangular
3	Diagonal (N = 1, M = no. of rows)
4	Upper Triangular Factor
5	Lower Triangular Factor
6	Symmetric
7	Row (M = no. of Columns, N = 1)
8	Unit (M = no. of rows, N = 1)

Table 3-2. Form Codes for NASTRAN Matrices

TYPE CODE	NUMERICAL REPRESENTATION OF MATRIX
0	Pick best for machine configuration
1	Real, single precision
2	Real, double precision
3	Complex, single precision
4	Complex, double precision

Table 3-3. Type Codes for Numerical Representation of Matrices

3.5.2. Example: Use of DMI Bulk Data

The **R** and **T** matrices for the example in Sec. 3.5 can now be defined by means of Bulk Data. In defining these matrices we note that both are symmetric so that FORM = 6 in field 4 of the header card, they are to be defined as single precision numbers, TIN = 1, and we will let MSC/NASTRAN select the correct internal representation of the matrix, TOUT = 0. Finally both matrices are 3-by-3 so M = 3 and N = 3. With this in mind we can define the matrices **R** and **T** by means of the following Bulk Data cards

1	2	3	4	5	6	7	8	9	10
$DEFINE MATRIX R									
DMI	R	0	6	1	0		3	3	
DMI	R	1	1	3.	5.	6.			
DMI	R	2	1	5.	7.	4.			
DMI	R	3	1	6.	4.	21.			
$DEFINE MATRIX T									
DMI	T	0	6	1	0		3	3	
DMI	T	1	1	2.	− 4.				
DMI	T	2	1	− 4.	8.	− 4.			
DMI	T	3	2	− 4.	6.				

The reader should note that we have defined all non-zero matrix coefficients even though the matrices are symmetric. The reason for this requirement is that NASTRAN does not take advantage of symmetry when matrices are stored; all nonzero elements are stored even for a symmetric matrix. It will be left as an exercise for the reader to devise a DMAP algothrim which allows the user to define only the diagonal and the upper off-diagonal elements, and which then generates the full symmetric matrix.

3.5.3. Printing Matrix Data

Several modules are available for printing matrix data. The choice of a particular print module depends on the form of the matrix data to be printed. The following matrix print modules are available and are described in Ref. 3-1:

MODULE NAME	DESCRIPTION
MATGPR	Prints matrices generated by rigid formats
MATPRN	Prints general matrix data blocks
MATPRT	Prints matrices associated with grid points

In performing matrix operations with NASTRAN, the general matrix printer MATPRN is appropriate. The general calling sequence is

MATPRN   M1, M2, M3, M4, M5 / / $

where the form indicates that up to five matrices may be printed by one DMAP instruction and that there are no output data blocks.

The result of the ADD module in our example is called **W**. The following DMAP instruction will then print a matrix having this name

MATPRN   W   // $

3.5.4. Example of MSC/NASTRAN Data Deck

We are now in a position to use MSC/NASTRAN to solve our simple matrix algebra problem of adding two matrices together. The MSC/NASTRAN data deck which would solve this problem is as follows:

```
ID      DMAP,EXAMPLE
DIAG   8           $ PRINT MATRIX TRAILERS
TIME   2           $ ALLOW TWO MINUTES OF CPU-TIME
BEGIN              $ START THE DMAP PROGRAM
ADD R, T/W         $ R AND T DEFINED BY DMI
MATPRN W //        $ PRINT THE RESULTS
END                $ END OF ALGORITHM
CEND               $ LAST CARD OF EXECUTIVE DECK
BEGIN BULK         $ NO CASE CONTROL FOR THIS SOLUTION
```

	1	2	3	4	5	6	7	8	9	10
$DEFINE MATRIX R										
DMI	R	0	6	1	0		3	3		
DMI	R	1	1	3.	5.	6.				
DMI	R	2	1	5.	7.	4.				
DMI	R	3	1	6.	4.	21.				
$DEFINE MATRIX T										
DMI	T	0	6	1	0		3	3		
DMI	T	1	1	2.	− 4.					
DMI	T	2	1	− 4.	8.	4.				
DMI	T	3	2	− 4.	6.					

ENDDATA $ LAST CARD OF NASTRAN DATA DECK

A DMAP program such as this provides the analyst with algorithm for adding two matrices of any size. The actual matrix data including the size of the matrices is defined at execution time in the Bulk Data section of the MSC/NASTRAN data deck.

3.6. Printing Matrices in Rigid Formats

The matrices generated in the rigid formats based on the displacement approach can be printed using any of the modules for matrix printing. It is convenient to use the displacement approach matrix printer, MATGPR, because the matrix elements are defined with respect to the external degrees of freedom numbers rather than internal degrees of freedom. The disadvantage of its use is that the module MATGPR cannot be scheduled until all the input data blocks have been output by previous modules. The calling sequence for the MATGPR module in rigid format 24 is

MATGPR   GPL,USET,SIL,M / / C,N,c / C,N,r $

where the input data blocks and parameters are

GPL   Grid point list

USET   List of displacement set memberships

SIL   Scalar index list

M   Any matrix to be printed

c,r   literal values for parameters that define the matrix order by reference to a displacement set name.

If the rigid format for static analysis is considered, we would find that

1. The data blocks GPL and SIL are output from module GP1

2. The data block USET is output by module GP4

The matrix printer cannot be scheduled until after module GPSP1 has been executed. In order to use MATGPR to print a structurally-oriented module the user must first execute MSC/NASTRAN to obtain a listing of the rigid format. This could be accomplished by the following MSC/NASTRAN input data deck

ID PRINT,DMAP

SOL 24

DIAG 14

CEND

BEGIN BULK

ENDDATA

Then after locating the GPSP1 module the stiffness matrix associated with the g-set of displacements could be printed by using the following DMAP alter in a subsequent execution of rigid format 24

ALTER < stmt >

MATGPR GPL,USET,SIL,KGG/ /C,N,G/C,N,G $

where the PARAMeter value of 'G' for c and r defines KGG to be a square matrix of g-size.

3.7.   Parametric Data Definition, Modification, and Output

We described the need for and the form of scalar numbers which are called parameters in NASTRAN in Sec. 3.4.4. In this section we are interested in ways in which parameters are defined, modified, and displayed by the DMAP programmer

3.7.1.   Defining Values of Parameters

There are two general techniques for defining the values of parameters. These are

1. By using the PARAMeter list of a DMAP statement

2. By using appropriate DMAP utilities for this purpose

3.7.1.1.   Use of PARAMeter List

As an example of the use of the parameter list of a DMAP statement consider the full form of the ADD instruction

$$\text{ADD A, B / C / P1 / P2 / P3 \$}$$

where as before the first field, the input data section, contains the matrices **A** and **B**, the output data block section following the first slash contains the matrix **C**, and where the remaining fields P1, P2, and P3 define parameters using the construction which was described in Sec. 3.4.4. These parameters allow the user to define a general binary operation on two matrices as

$$\mathbf{C} = \alpha\,\mathbf{A} \oplus \beta\,\mathbf{C}$$

where

P1   defines a complex scalar value α
P2   defines a complex scalar value β
P3   defines the binary operation $\oplus$

Each of these parameters has a default value which NASTRAN will use if we chose not to list the parameters on the DMAP statement. The default values are

$$\alpha = (1., 0.)$$

$$\beta = (1., 0.)$$

$$\oplus \quad \text{is addition}$$

where the form of the complex number is (Real, Complex).

If we want a value of the parameter other than the default value we must include its definition on the DMAP statement using one of the forms described in Sec. 3.4.4.

Suppose, for example, that we will always use addition (P3 can thus be defaulted, i.e. not defined on the DMAP statement) but that we would like to be able to override default values of $\alpha = (-1., 3.)$ and $\beta = (5., -6.)$ with other values which, if they exist, are defined using the PARAM Bulk Data card as shown by Card Image 3-2.

1	2	3	4	5	6	7	8	9	10
PARAM	N	V1	V2						

where:

N   Parameter name (Literal)

V1, V2   Parameter value depending on the parameter type as follows:

TYPE	V1	V2
Integer	Integer	Blank
Real, single-precision	Real	Blank
Literal	Literal	Blank
Real, double-precision	D.P.	Blank
Complex, single-precision	Real	Real
Complex, double-precision	D.P.	D.P.

Card Image 3-2. PARAM Bulk Data

We could then write the ADD modules

ADD   A, B / C / V, Y, ALPHA = (− 1.,3.) / V, Y, BETA = (5., − 6.) $

where we note that the parameters are variable (V), they can be defined on PARAM Bulk Data (Y), and that we have explicitly defined the default value which these parameters are to take if no PARAM Bulk Data cards exist.

We now suppose that the ADD DMAP statement as defined above exists in our DMAP program but that we now want parameters to be defined as $\alpha = (6., − 3.)$ and $\beta = (7., − 1.)$. We could, of course, modify the DMAP statement, to redefine the defaults to the new values, but another more general way is to leave the present ADD statement unchanged and to include the following PARAM cards in Bulk Data.

1	2	3	4	5	6	7	8	9	10
PARAM	ALPHA	6.	− 3.						
PARAM	BETA	7.	− 1.						

3.7.2.   Parameter DMAP Utilities

Parameters are used not only in DMAP modules to define scalar coefficients and options but they are also used in DMAP programs as counters and logical variables. For this and other reasons we need PARAMeter-oriented DMAP utilities for defining, modifying, and performing logical tests on parameters. The appropriate DMAP utilities are shown in Table 3-4. A full description of each of these modules is beyond the scope of this summary and the user, as usual, is directed to Ref. 3-1.

   PARAM   Performs arithmetic and logical operations on integer parameters

   PARAMR   Performs FORTRAN-like functional operations on real and complex parameters

   PARAML   Selects data from matrix or tabular input

   SETVAL   Sets an equivalence between parameter variables and constants

Table 3-4. DMAP Modules Associated with Parameters

We will, however, make use of the parameter modules here to show how they can be included in a DMAP program. Suppose, for example, that we wanted to set the value of a logical parameter (i.e. integer) to a default value, let's say zero for true. If the parameter is true we want to add two matrices but if it is false (− 1), which is to be defined by PARAM Bulk Data, we want to branch to bypass the ADD and EXIT from the procedure.

Before describing the SETVAL module, which will be used to define a logical variable which we will call TEST, we need to say something about logical branches which are defined by a pair of DMAP statements of the following form

COND   LOOP,TEST

.
.
.

LABEL   LOOP

where the jump to the LABEL whose name is LOOP, in this case, is made if the value of the parameter, TEST, is false (− 1). If TEST is equal to or greater than zero then the next DMAP statement following COND is executed.

With that out of the way we now use the SETVAL module to define the default value of TEST

55

which is to be equal to zero. The form of the instruction is

SETVAL   // V, N, TEST / V, Y, NOADD = 0 $

which sets the first PARAMeter, TEST equal to the second PARAMeter, NOADD which has a default value of zero, but which is a Y-type PARAMeter which can be defined by a PARAM Bulk Data card. The DMAP program for our example problem is then

```
BEGIN        $

SETVAL   // V, N, TEST / V, Y, NOADD = 0   $

COND   LOOP, TEST  $

ADD   A, B / C   $

LABEL   LOOP  $

END  $
```

The user can selectively cause the ADD to be skipped by including a PARAM Bulk Data card of the form (in free format)

PARAM, NOADD, − 1

3.7.3. Manipulating Parameters

The DMAP modules PARAM, and PARAMR provide capability for performing arithmetic and logical operations on parameters. The PARAMR DMAP instruction could, for example, be used to add two real parameters, ALPHA and BETA to obtain GAMMA

PARAMR   // C,N,ADD / V,N,GAMMA / V,Y,ALPHA / V,Y,BETA $

The PARAM module would be used if the PARAMeters were integer rather than real. The PARAM module can also be used as a utility to

- Obtain the current CPU time from start of job
- Obtain the CPU time to go
- Define the precision of floating point operations
- Turn DIAG requests on and off dynamically in the DMAP program
- Dynamically retrieve and store data which controls system functions and attributes.

3.7.4. Printing Contents of Parameter Table — PRTPARM

The contents of the variable parameter table which defines the current value of all variable parameter can be printed under user control by means of the PRTPARM DMAP module. The form of the DMAP statement which will print the parameters is:

PRTPARM   // $

If the user desires to have the parameters sorted alphabetically the form of the command is

PRTPARM   / / / /1 $

3.8.   Executive Operation Modules

The executive operation modules include those that allow looping, those that save data blocks on external files, and those that control the DMAP compiler. The executive operation modules that are available to the user include those shown by Table 3-5.

BEGIN   Always first statement in DMAP

CHKPNT   Write data blocks on checkpoint tape

COND   Conditional forward jump

END   Always last statement in DMAP

EQUIV   Assign another name to data block

EXIT   Conditional DMAP termination

JUMP   Unconditional forward jump

LABEL   Specifies tag for DMAP statement

PURGE   Conditional data block elimination

REPT   Repeat a series of DMAP instructions

Table 3-5. Executive Operation Modules

We have already used some of these executive DMAP statements in our previous examples, particularly: the BEGIN and END statements to delimit the user-supplied DMAP program; and, the COND and LABEL to define a conditional jump and EXIT to provide a termination of the program.

3.8.1.   EXIT

The form of the EXIT command is

EXIT, N $

where N is a fixed integer number whose default value is zero which specifies the number of times the EXIT is to be ignored. This command can be altered into a DMAP Rigid Format to allow the analyst to stop program execution at a key point in the solution algorithm (after obtaining undeformed plots of the structure, for example). By using the CHECKPOINT and RESTART features (Secs. 1.9.3. and 1.9.4.) the user can then restart the analysis and proceed after removing the ALTERed-in EXIT.

3.8.2.   Unconditional Jump — JUMP

The unconditional jump can be used to produce a forward branch in the DMAP program. The form of the instruction is

JUMP   P $

where P is the name of a LABEL to which the jump is to be made. This command provides us with the capability of constructing DMAP programs with several logical branches.

3.8.3.   Looping

The COND and JUMP statements are restricted to forward branches, i.e. a branch to a subsequent DMAP statement. The REPT command together with LABEL provides the means for defining DMAP loops. The form of the REPT statement is

REPT   LBL,N $

where LBL is the name of a previous label and N is the number of times that the set of DMAP instructions between LBL and REPT is to be executed (i.e. N = 1 implies that the instructions are executed two times; once in reaching the REPT instruction and once more in response to the REPT). For example, in order to execute a set of instructions four times we could use the following DMAP construction.

```
BEGIN $
.
.

.
LABEL    TOPLOOP $
MOD1
MOD2
MOD3
REPT    TOPLOOP,3   $
END $
```

3.8.4.   Equivalencing Data Blocks

Often during the execution of a DMAP sequence we would like to create a new matrix (data block) whose data attributes are the same as another matrix which has already been generated. That is, we would like to give an existing set of data an alias name. In DMAP programming this is both useful and sometimes necessary because the DMAP compiler insists that a data block be defined as output (i.e. created by) a previous executable DMAP statement and furthermore that a data block can only occur as output once.

With those rules in mind, suppose now that we want to perform the matrix operation $A = B^n$ which implies a repeated multiplication of a matrix B. The matrix multiplication can be performed by the MPYAD module which as the form

MPYAD A,B,C   /   X $

and which defines the matrix operation

$$X = AB + C$$

where A and B can be the same matrix. However, because of the DMAP rule which states that the output data block X can only be defined once we would have to define MPYAD N times in order to calculate B^n. The equivalence statement will allow us to define the algorithm without multiple MPYADs where the form of the EQUIV is

EQUIV PDB, SDB/PARAM $

where PDB is a primary data block, i.e. a data block which exists as output from a previous executable DMAP module, SDB is the alias name that we want to append to the primary data block and PARAM is a parameter which controls the action of the EQUIV as follows

PARAM EQUIV
VALUE ACTION
   < 0 The data blocks are equivalenced.
   ≥ 0 If data blocks are equivalenced, the equivalence is broken. If data blocks are not
         equivalenced then there is no action.

Now that we know that the DMAP compiler enforces certain restrictions on the DMAP programmer, and that the EQUIV statement exists, let's get back to our task of writing a compact DMAP program which will find B^n.

We assume that the user has specified B by means of DMI Bulk Data and the power N by means of a PARAM Bulk Data Card of the form

$$PARAM, N, <value>$$

where $<value>$ is the integer power of B. The following MSC/NASTRAN data deck will define the algorithm to find B^n.

```
ID        MATRIXTO  NTHPOWER
DIAG      8       $ PRINT MATRIX TRAILERS
COMPILER  LIST,REF      $PRINT AND CROSS REF DMAP
BEGIN        $DMAP TO RAISE MATRIX B TO N-TH POWER
MATPRN      B/ /      $PRINT THE INPUT MATRIX
PARAM      / /SUB  /  V,N,NN  /  V,Y,N=− 1/2   $ COMPUTE NN=N − 2
$DEFAULT FOR N=− 1
COND      ERROR1,NN     $ERROR OUT IF N.LE.1
ADD      B,  /  BB        $MAKES A NEW DATA BLOCK BB
LABEL    TOP       $THIS IS THE TOP OF THE LOOP
EQUIV    BB,X  /   NEVER  $BREAK EQUIVALENCE AT TOP OF LOOP
MPYAD    B,BB,  /  X        $X is B∗B
EQUIV    X,BB  /  ALWAYS   $X IS NOW CALLED BB
PARAM / /SUB  /  NN  /  NN  /  1  $DECREMENT NN BY 1
COND    STOP,NN      $WERE DONE IF NN IS − 1.
REPT    TOP,100       $GO BACK TO TOP A MAXIMUM OF 100 TIMES
JUMP    ERROR2         $SHOULD NOT BE HERE
$BRANCH POINTS
LABEL    STOP   $NORMAL TERMINATION
MATPRN X   / /   $THIS IS THE ANSWER
EXIT       $
LABEL    ERROR1  $FORGOT TO SPECIFY N
PRTPARM / /  $PRINT THE VARIABLE PARAMETER TABLE
EXIT       $
LABEL    ERROR2   $PROGRAM LOOPED 100 TIMES
PRTPARM   / /   $
END        $
CEND
TITLE=SOLUTION OF B∗∗N USING DMAP
BEGIN BULK
```

1	2	3	4	5	6	7	8	9	10
DMI	B	0	6	1	0		4	4	
DMI	B	1	1	2.	− 1.				
DMI	B	2	1	− 1.	2.	− 1.			
DMI	B	3	2	− 1.	2.	− 1.			
DMI	B	4	3	− 1.	2.				
PARAM	N	4							
ENDDATA									

The need for equivalencing arises often in the Rigid Formats when we want to give an alias name to a data block if a specific action is not taken. For example, the stiffness matrix KNN is to be equivalenced to the matrix KGG if no multipoint constraints exist. Otherwise the constraints are to be applied and KNN will be defined as the output, in this case, of the MCE2 module. This alternative action is defined by the following DMAP sequence

        ADD   KGG1, KGG2/KGG $

        EQUIV   KGG, KNN/MCPF1 $

        COND   NOMPC, MCPF1 $

        MCE2   USET, KGG, GM,,,/KNN,,,/ $

        LABEL   NOMPC

        MATPRN   KNN// $

where we assume that the parameter MCPF1 is − 1 if there are no multipoint constraints. Then as a result of this DMAP sequence the MATPRN module will print the contents of KGG if there are no constraints or it will print the output data block from MCE2 if constraints are present.

3.9. References

3-1 MSC/NASTRAN User's Manual, Vol. II, Sec. 5.
3-2 MSC/NASTRAN Programmer's Manual, Vols. II & III, Sec. 4.

3.10. Problems

3.1   The DMAP module SOLVE which is used to solve a matrix equation $\mathbf{A} \, x = \mathbf{B}$ has the form

$$\text{SOLVE A, B / X} \quad \$$$

Write the complete MSC/NASTRAN data deck which the solution of the set of matrix equations where $\mathbf{A}$ and $\mathbf{B}$ are defined as follows

$$\mathbf{A} = \begin{bmatrix} 7. & -4. & 1. & 0. & 0. \\ -4. & 6. & -4. & 1. & 0. \\ 1. & -4. & 6. & -4. & 1. \\ 0. & 1. & -4. & 5. & -2. \\ 0. & 0. & 1. & -2. & 1. \end{bmatrix} ; \quad \mathbf{B} = \begin{bmatrix} 1. \\ 1. \\ 1. \\ 1. \\ .5 \end{bmatrix}$$

3.2   A set of linear equations can also be solved by using the DECOMP and FBS modules which are described in Ref. 3-1. Rewrite the algorithm for solving the set of equations defined in problem 3.1 using the DECOMP and FBS modules. Use the PRTPARM module to print out the values of all variable parameters which have been created by the DECOMP module.

3.3   The DMAP utility module DIAGONAL can be used to create a square matrix $\mathbf{B}$ whose only non zero terms are its diagonal, which is equal to the diagonal terms of $\mathbf{A}$ (i.e. it strips the diagonal from a matrix). The form of the DIAGONAL DMAP statement which performs this operation is

DIAGONAL   A / B / C, N, SQUARE $

Using this DMAP utility write a set of DMAP instructions which will create a full symmetric $\mathbf{B}$ from a matrix $\mathbf{A}$ which is defined by means of DMI which includes only the diagonal and the upper triangular half.

#

Basic Relations from the Theory of Elasticity

The matrix equations that govern the behavior of a structural system are obtained from the field equations which govern the behavior of solids. These relationships may be categorized as

1. Those that specify kinematic constraints

2. Those that govern the equilibrium of forces

3. Those that specify the constitutive relations between internal forces and displacements.

These relationships generally lead to a set of nonlinear partial differential equations that relate the behavioral variables. Since the NASTRAN program includes a certain class of nonlinear behavior, we will develop the complete nonlinear geometric strain-displacement relations and then indicate which terms are neglected in linear static analysis and in differential stiffness analysis.

4.1.   Kinematic Relations

The internal forces that are of interest in solid mechanics are associated with relative displacements between nearby points in the body. If a body moves as a rigid body, there is no relative motion between nearby points in the structure and the body is then said to be unstrained. In order to detect the presence of relative motion we consider the change in the distance between two nearby points A and B as shown by Fig. 4-1 in the body before and after deformation.

The position of points in the undeformed body is defined by the label (x_1, x_2, x_3) with reference to a fixed rectangular coordinate system (X_1, X_2, X_3). After deformation, the point that was originally at A in the undeformed body has moved to point A′, which has the coordinates (y_1, y_2, y_3) relative to the fixed system. The positions of the point A and A′ are related by the displacement vector $\mathbf{v}$, which has components (v_1, v_2, v_3) relative to the fixed system. Points in the undeformed body are mapped onto points in the deformed body according to the following transformation:

4.1 Kinematic Relations

$$\begin{aligned} y_1 &= x_1 + v_1 \\ y_2 &= x_2 + v_2 \\ y_3 &= x_3 + v_3 \end{aligned} \tag{4.1}$$

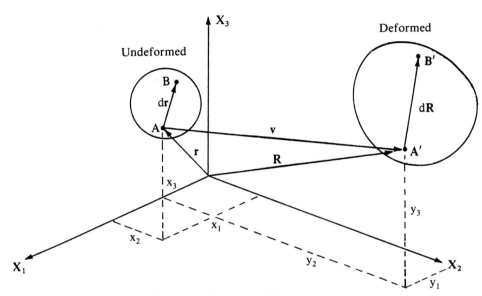

Figure 4-1. Geometry of Deformation

Now consider a point B in the undeformed body, which is in the neighborhood of A. As a result of the deformation, point B moves to B′, which is in the neighborhood of A′. The criteria for the existence of relative motion can be stated in terms of the change in the distance between the nearby points A and B. A quantity that indicates the presence of strain can then be called a strain indicator and which is defined as

$$\text{S.I.} = d\mathbf{R} \cdot d\mathbf{R} - d\mathbf{r} \cdot d\mathbf{r} \tag{4.2}$$

Where $\mathbf{r}$ is the position vector of a point before deformation and $\mathbf{R}$ is the position of the point after deformation. These position vectors are defined in terms of the undeformed and the deformed coordinates of the material point:

$$\mathbf{r} = x_1\, \mathbf{i}_1 + x_2\, \mathbf{i}_2 + x_3\, \mathbf{i}_3 \tag{4.3}$$

and

$$\mathbf{R} = y_1\, \mathbf{i}_1 + y_2\, \mathbf{i}_2 + y_3\, \mathbf{i}_3 \tag{4.4}$$

where $(\mathbf{i}_1, \mathbf{i}_2, \mathbf{i}_3)$ are unit vectors in the (X_1, X_2, X_3) directions. The positions of a point in the undeformed and deformed body are then related by

$$\mathbf{R} = \mathbf{r} + \mathbf{v} \tag{4.5}$$

The differentials $d\mathbf{R}$ and $d\mathbf{r}$ that appear in the strain indicator (4.2) can now be expressed in terms of derivatives taken with respect to the undeformed coordinates as

$$dR = \frac{\partial R}{\partial x_1} dx_1 + \frac{\partial R}{\partial x_2} dx_2 + \frac{\partial R}{\partial x_3} dx_3$$

and

$$dr = \frac{\partial r}{\partial x_1} dx_1 + \frac{\partial r}{\partial x_2} dx_2 + \frac{\partial r}{\partial x_3} dx_3$$

(4.6)

or, in terms of derivatives taken with respect to the coordinates of the deformed point by

$$dR = \frac{\partial R}{\partial y_1} dy_1 + \frac{\partial R}{\partial y_2} dy_2 + \frac{\partial R}{\partial y_3} dy_3$$

and

$$dr = \frac{\partial r}{\partial y_1} dy_1 + \frac{\partial r}{\partial y_2} dy_2 + \frac{\partial r}{\partial y_3} dy_3$$

(4.7)

where dx_i and dy_i are obtained by differentiating the expressions given by (4.1) and are

$$dy_1 = (1 + v_{1,1}) dx_1 + v_{1,2} dx_2 + v_{1,3} dx_3$$

(4.8)

$$dy_2 = v_{2,1} dx_1 + (1 + v_{2,2}) dx_2 + v_{2,3} dx_3$$

(4.9)

$$dy_3 = v_{3,1} dx_1 + v_{3,2} dx_2 + (1 + v_{3,3}) dx_3$$

(4.10)

The notation $(\ )_{,i}$ that is introduced in these equations means that the quantity preceding the comma is differentiated with respect to the coordinate x_i where i takes on the successive values one, two, three.

The differentials dR and dr as represented by (4.6) and (4.7) are thus equivalent since the transformations (4.8) through (4.10) must hold. If we choose to use (4.6), then the derivatives are taken with respect to the coordinates of the undeformed body. If (4.7) is used the derivatives are taken with respect to coordinates of the deformed body. These two equivalent approaches for the representation of the conditions that govern the displacement of material points are called the Lagrangian and Eulerian formulations, respectively. It is convenient to use the Lagrangian formulation in structural mechanics since the position of points in the undeformed body is known.

4.1.1. Lagrangian Large Strain Tensor

The strain indicator can be expressed in terms of the displacement gradients taken with respect to the undeformed coordinates by

$$S.I. = (v_{i,j} + v_{j,i} + v_{k,i} v_{k,j}) dx_i dx_j = 2L_{ij} dx_i dx_j$$

(4.11)

where the repeated indices imply a summation over the range of both subscripts. The set of coefficients L_{ij} is called the Green-St. Venant or the Lagrangian large displacement strain tensor, and the elements of the set are defined in terms of the displacement gradients:

$$L_{ij} = \tfrac{1}{2} (v_{i,j} + v_{j,i} + v_{k,i} v_{k,j})$$

(4.12)

The components of the Lagrangian large strain tensor are symmetric with respect to interchange of the subscripts. There are six independent components of strain that are expressed in extended notation as

4.1.2 Lagrangian Small Strain and Small Rotation Tensors

$$L_{11} = v_{1,1} + \tfrac{1}{2}\,(v_{1,1}^2 + v_{2,1}^2 + v_{3,1}^2)$$

$$L_{22} = v_{2,2} + \tfrac{1}{2}\,(v_{1,2}^2 + v_{2,2}^2 + v_{3,2}^2)$$

$$L_{33} = v_{3,3} + \tfrac{1}{2}\,(v_{1,3}^2 + v_{2,3}^2 + v_{3,3}^2)$$

and
(4.13)

$$L_{12} = \tfrac{1}{2}\,[v_{1,2} + v_{2,1} + v_{1,1}\,v_{1,2} + v_{2,1}\,v_{2,2} + v_{3,1}\,v_{3,2}]$$

$$L_{23} = \tfrac{1}{2}\,[v_{2,3} + v_{3,2} + v_{1,2}\,v_{1,3} + v_{2,2}\,v_{2,3} + v_{3,2}\,v_{3,3}]$$

$$L_{31} = \tfrac{1}{2}\,[v_{3,1} + v_{1,3} + v_{1,3}\,v_{1,1} + v_{2,3}\,v_{2,1} + v_{3,3}\,v_{3,1}]$$

4.1.2. Lagrangian Small Strain and Small Rotation Tensors.

The Lagrangian small strain tensor ℓ_{ij} and the rotation tensor r_{ij} are defined as

$$\ell_{ij} = \tfrac{1}{2}\,(v_{i,j} + v_{j,i}) \tag{4.14}$$

and

$$r_{ij} = \tfrac{1}{2}\,(v_{i,j} - v_{j,i}) \tag{4.15}$$

The strain gradient can then be expressed in terms of the small strain and rotation tensors by

$$v_{i,j} = \ell_{ij} + r_{ij} \tag{4.16}$$

The components of the Lagrangian large strain tensor can then be expressed in terms of the small strain and rotation tensor by

$$L_{ij} = \ell_{ij} + \tfrac{1}{2}\,[\,\ell_{ki}\,\ell_{kj} + \ell_{ki}\,r_{kj} + \ell_{kj}\,r_{ki} + r_{ki}\,r_{kj}\,] \tag{4.17}$$

The terms in the bracket in (4.17) involve products of the small strain and the rotation tensors that can be neglected if they are sufficiently small. In this case the components of the large strain and small strain tensors are the same and it follows that

$$L_{ij} = \ell_{ij} \tag{4.18}$$

The assumption that the strains and rotations are infinitesimal thus implies that there is no distinction between the undeformed and the deformed coordinates of points in the body.

4.1.3. Physical Strains

The set of kinematic relations (4.12) has the property that the vanishing of all the strain components defines a rigid body motion, and conversely, that a nonzero value of a component of the strain indicates that there is a relative displacement. In engineering practice physical components of stress are related to the physical components of strain so that we must relate the components of the strain tensor to the definition of physical strains. Two types of physical strain can be defined:

1. An extensional strain that is the change in length per unit of original length.

2. A shear strain that is the change in the angle between two lines which were originally orthogonal in the undeformed medium.

66

It is shown in Ref. 4-1 that a one-to-one relationship exists between the tensor components of strain and a set of kinematic relationships that are obtained from the definition of physical strain. These relationships are

$$e_{11} = \sqrt{1 + 2L_{11}} - 1$$
$$e_{22} = \sqrt{1 + 2L_{22}} - 1 \qquad (4.19)$$
$$e_{33} = \sqrt{1 + 2L_{33}} - 1$$

where e_{11}, e_{22}, e_{33} are physical extensional strains in the x_1, x_2, and x_3 directions. Further, if e_{ij} is defined to be the change in the angle between the x_i- and x_j-axes at a point in the body, then the following relationship exists between the tensor components of strain and the shear strain:

$$\sin e_{12} = \frac{2L_{12}}{(1+e_{11})(1+e_{22})}$$
$$\sin e_{23} = \frac{2L_{23}}{(1+e_{22})(1+e_{33})} \qquad (4.20)$$
$$\sin e_{31} = \frac{2L_{31}}{(1+e_{33})(1+e_{11})}$$

The tensor components L_{11}, L_{22}, and L_{33} thus characterize the extensional behavior, and the components L_{12}, L_{23}, and L_{31} characterize the shear behavior. The vanishing of the tensor components implies that the physical components also vanish.

For the case of small displacement gradients, the small strain tensor is equal to the large strain tensor, giving

$$L_{ij} = \ell_{ij}$$

The relationship between components of the small strain tensor and the extensional strain is obtained by retaining only the linear terms in a Taylor series expansion of the radicals in (4.19). The linearized equations are

$$e_{11} = \ell_{11}$$
$$e_{22} = \ell_{22} \qquad (4.21)$$
$$e_{33} = \ell_{33}$$

which shows that the physical extensional strains are equal to the associated component of the infinitesimal strain tensor. The linearized relationships between the components of the small strain tensor and the physical shears then follows directly from (4.20),

$$e_{12} = 2\ell_{12}$$
$$e_{23} = 2\ell_{23} \qquad (4.22)$$
$$e_{31} = 2\ell_{31}$$

which shows that the physical components of shear are equal to twice the value of the corresponding component of the infinitesimal strain tensor.

The strain-displacement relations for the physical components of strain are then obtained by substituting (4.14) into (4.21) and (4.22) to obtain

4.1.4 Small Deformation and Angles of Rotation

$$e_{11} = \frac{\partial v_1}{\partial x_1} \;, \qquad\qquad e_{22} = \frac{\partial v_2}{\partial x_2} \;, \qquad\qquad e_{33} = \frac{\partial v_3}{\partial x_3}$$

$$e_{12} = \frac{\partial v_1}{\partial x_2} + \frac{\partial v_2}{\partial x_1} \;, \qquad e_{23} = \frac{\partial v_2}{\partial x_3} + \frac{\partial v_3}{\partial x_2} \;, \qquad e_{31} = \frac{\partial v_3}{\partial x_1} + \frac{\partial v_1}{\partial x_3}$$

$$(4.23)$$

The yield strains are typically on the order of 0.2 percent for structural materials so that the physical strains in a large class of problems are extremely small. The set of linear strain-displacement equations (4.23) thus provides an accurate representation of the kinematic conditions in the elastic strain range. There are problems of practical interest where some or all the nonlinear terms in the large strain tensor must be retained. In these cases the linear relationships (4.23) are not adequate.

4.1.4. Small Strains and Small Angles of Rotation

As a first order approximation of the effect of the nonlinear terms, we will consider the case of small strains and small angles of rotation. The strain-displacement relations that result are utilized by NASTRAN and other finite element programs in the development of the geometric differential stiffness method, which is described in Ref. 4-2. Before proceeding it is convenient to define the components of the rotation vector as

$$\omega_1 = r_{32} \;, \quad \omega_2 = -r_{13} \;, \quad \omega_3 = r_{21}$$

$$(4.24)$$

The substitution of (4.24) into (4.17) then gives the following expression a typical extensional strain component L_{11}:

$$L_{11} = \ell_{11} + \tfrac{1}{2}\{\ell_{11}^2 + (\ell_{21} + \omega_3)^2 + (\ell_{31} - \omega_2)^2\}$$

$$(4.25)$$

If the strains are small, products of the infinitesimal strain tensor are small compared to linear terms so that (4.25) becomes

$$L_{11} \cong \ell_{11} + \ell_{21}\,\omega_3 - \ell_{31}\,\omega_2 + \tfrac{1}{2}\,(\omega_2^2 + \omega_3^2)$$

$$(4.26)$$

It is also shown in Ref. 4-3 that, when the components of the rotation vector are also small, terms which include the product of strain and rotation components such as $\ell_{21}\omega_3$ are an order smaller than the squares of the components of the rotation vector. Therefore, if both the strains and the rotation are small, (4.17) may be approximated by

$$L_{11} \cong e_{11} + \tfrac{1}{2}\,(\omega_2^2 + \omega_3^2)$$

$$L_{22} \cong e_{22} + \tfrac{1}{2}\,(\omega_1^2 + \omega_3^2)$$

$$L_{33} \cong e_{33} + \tfrac{1}{2}\,(\omega_1^2 + \omega_2^2)$$

$$(4.27)$$

and

$$2L_{12} = e_{12} - \omega_1\omega_2$$
$$2L_{23} = e_{23} - \omega_2\omega_3$$
$$2L_{31} = e_{31} - \omega_3\omega_1$$

$$(4.28)$$

4.1.5.   Transformation of Strain

The motivation for defining the kinematic relations in terms of the Lagrangian large and small strain tensors and the Lagrangian infinitesimal tensor is the ease with which the tensor components can be transformed to other coordinate systems. Let us suppose that the x_i'-coordinates are related to the x_i-coordinates as

$$x_i' = a_{ij}\ x_j \tag{4.29}$$

where the coefficient a_{ij} is the direction cosine between the ith-axis in the x_i' system and the jth-axis in the x_j system. The differentials are then related by

$$dx_i' = a_{ij}\ dx_j \tag{4.30}$$

The inverse relationship is obtained by noting that the set of direction cosines satisfy a set of orthonormal conditions so that

$$dx_i = a_{ji}\ dx_j' \tag{4.31}$$

The strain indicator is a scalar quantity that is the same, independent of the coordinate system, so that

$$L_{ij}'\ dx_i'\ dx_j' \ =\ L_{ij}\ dx_i\ dx_j \tag{4.32}$$

The substitution of (4.31) into (4.32) then gives

$$(\ L_{ij}' - a_{im}\ a_{jn}\ L_{mn})\ dx_i'\ dx_j' = 0$$

Since the strain tensor is symmetric and the differential distances are not equal to zero, we obtain the following transformation equation for the tensor components of strain:

$$L_{ij}' \ =\ a_{im}\ a_{jn}\ L_{mn} \tag{4.33}$$

As an application of these transformation equations, consider the rotation of coordinates about the x_3-axis as shown by Fig. 4-2.

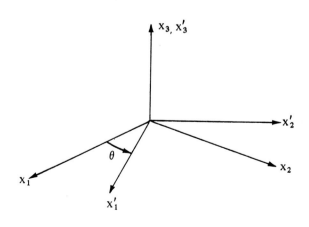

Figure 4-2. Rotation of Coordinate Axes

69

4.1.6   Summary of NASTRAN Strain-Displacement Formulation

The set of direction cosines is given by

$$a_{ij} \Rightarrow \begin{pmatrix} \cos\theta & \sin\theta & 0 \\ -\sin\theta & \cos\theta & 0 \\ 0 & 0 & 1 \end{pmatrix} \tag{4.34}$$

The transformed strain components L'_{11}, L'_{22}, and L'_{12} are then obtained by using (4.33) and are

$$L'_{11} = \cos^2\theta\, L_{11} + 2\sin\theta\,\cos\theta\, L_{12} + \sin^2\theta\, L_{22}$$

$$L'_{22} = \sin^2\theta\, L_{11} + 2\sin\theta\,\cos\theta\, L_{12} + \cos^2\theta\, L_{22} \tag{4.35}$$

$$L'_{12} = (L_{22} - L_{11})\sin\theta\,\cos\theta + L_{12}\,(\cos^2\theta - \sin^2\theta)$$

By using well-known trigonometric identities, (4.35) can also be expressed as

$$L'_{11} = \tfrac{1}{2}(L_{11} + L_{22}) + \tfrac{1}{2}(L_{11} - L_{22})\cos 2\theta + L_{12}\sin 2\theta$$

$$L'_{22} = \tfrac{1}{2}(L_{11} + L_{22}) + \tfrac{1}{2}(L_{22} - L_{11})\cos 2\theta - L_{12}\sin 2\theta \tag{4.36}$$

$$L'_{12} = \tfrac{1}{2}(L_{22} - L_{11})\sin 2\theta + L_{12}\cos 2\theta$$

The development of the transformation equations could not have been formulated in the elegant manner utilized for the tensor components if we had chosen to transform the physical components of strain. However, we can utilize (4.33) to transform the physical components by first using the relations developed in Section 4.1.3 to express the physical components in terms of tensor components. The tensor components are then transformed using (4.33), and the resulting tensor components are then converted to physical components.

4.1.6.   Summary of NASTRAN Strain-Displacement Formulation

The NASTRAN element formulations for linear static and dynamic analysis are based on the infinitesimal strain-displacement relationships given by (4.23). NASTRAN also includes first-order nonlinear geometric effects of small rotations in the differential stiffness approach where the strain-displacement relationships are given by (4.27) and (4.28).

It should be noted that the differential stiffness approach is only applicable if the structural response can be characterized by small strains and small rotations. The structural response including differential stiffness effects can be formulated as a linear analysis.

The inclusion of the full set of nonlinear strain-displacement equations would result in a set of nonlinear equations and an associated order-of-magnitude increase in the cost of obtaining a solution to the set of equations. The formulation of the equations governing nonlinear elasticity problems is given by Refs. 4-3 and 4-4. Techniques for solving sets of nonlinear equations are discussed in Ref. 4-5 and pages 262-267 of Ref. 4-4.

4.2.   Kinetic Relations

The kinetic requirements result in a set of equilibrium equations that must be satisfied by the internal forces in a continuum. Before discussing the equilibrium equations themselves it is appropriate to express the internal forces in terms of a force intensity that is called the stress.

70

4.2.1.   Definition of Stress Vector

The stress vector is defined as the force intensity per unit of area that has an outward unit normal n. Consider the element of the body that is shown by Fig. 4-3.

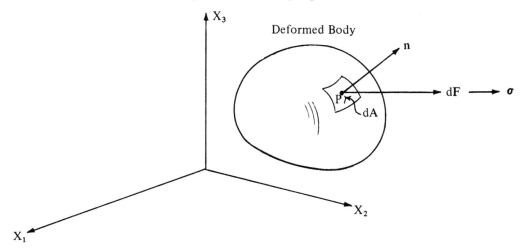

Figure 4-3. Definition of Stress Vector

The force vector dF acts at the point P in the body. The stress vector at a point P is then defined in terms of the element of area dA, which has an outward normal **n**, as

$$\sigma = \frac{dF}{dA} \tag{4.37}$$

4.2.2.   The Components of Stress

The internal forces vary from point-to-point in the structure so that the stress vector is a point function whose components depend on the orientation of the differential area at the point. In the development of the equilibrium equations it is convenient to consider the forces that act on a differential element of volume with the form of a rectangular parallelepiped whose faces have normals in the sense of the coordinate axes. The stress vectors that act on these faces are shown in their positive sense by Fig. 4-4, where the subscript on the stress vector identifies the direction of the normal to the area on which the stress vector acts.

Considering Fig. 4-4, we note that

1. The stress vector is positive when the normal component is in the direction of the outward normal to the surface.

2. The stress vector is a function of position. The stress vectors thus change by an amount $d\sigma_i$ in proceeding in a positive coordinate direction from a face with a normal in the negative coordinate sense to the face with a positive normal.

The stress vector is expressed in terms of its components in the coordinate directions as

4.2.2 The Components of Stress

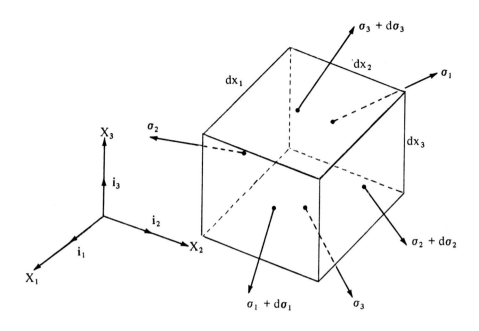

Figure 4-4. Stress Acting on A Parallelepiped

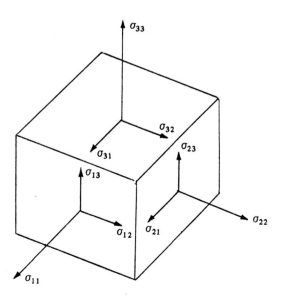

Figure 4-5. Components of Stress

$$\sigma_1 = \sigma_{11} \, i_1 + \sigma_{12} \, i_2 + \sigma_{13} \, i_3$$

$$\sigma_2 = \sigma_{21} \, i_1 + \sigma_{22} \, i_2 + \sigma_{23} \, i_3 \qquad (4.38)$$

$$\sigma_3 = \sigma_{31} \, i_1 + \sigma_{32} \, i_2 + \sigma_{33} \, i_3$$

where the vector components are called the components of stress. The set of relations expressed by (4.38) can be put in the following compact form by using index notation:

$$\sigma_i \;=\; \sigma_{ij} \, i_j \qquad (4.39)$$

where i and j take on the successive values 1, 2 and 3 and the repeated index implies summation over the range of the index. The components of stress acting on the faces with positive normals are shown in their positive sense on Fig. 4-5. The components of stress are seen to be positive when directed in the positive coordinate sense on faces with positive normals. Conversely, components of stress are positive on faces with negative normals when directed in the negative coordinate sense.

The stress components that are normal to the faces are called normal stresses, while those components of stress that are parallel to the faces are called shear stresses. A normal stress component is called a tensile stress if it acts in the positive direction and a compressive stress if it acts in the negative direction.

4.2.3.   Equilibrium Equations

The forces that act on an element of volume must be in equilibrium at all points in the body. If we consider the body shown by Fig. 4-4 and specify that body force **X** may exist at each point in the body, then moment equilibrium leads to the result

$$\sigma_{ij} = \sigma_{ji} \qquad (4.40)$$

The stress tensor is thus symmetric so that there are only six independent components of stress.
Equilibrium of forces then leads to

$$\frac{\partial \sigma_1}{\partial x_1} + \frac{\partial \sigma_2}{\partial x_2} + \frac{\partial \sigma_3}{\partial x_3} + \; X = 0 \qquad (4.41)$$

which can be expressed in terms of stress components by using (4.38) as

$$\frac{\partial \sigma_{11}}{\partial x_1} + \frac{\partial \sigma_{21}}{\partial x_2} + \frac{\partial \sigma_{31}}{\partial x_3} + X_1 \; = \; 0$$

$$\frac{\partial \sigma_{12}}{\partial x_1} + \frac{\partial \sigma_{22}}{\partial x_2} + \frac{\partial \sigma_{32}}{\partial x_3} + X_2 \; = \; 0 \qquad (4.42)$$

$$\frac{\partial \sigma_{13}}{\partial x_1} + \frac{\partial \sigma_{23}}{\partial x_2} + \frac{\partial \sigma_{33}}{\partial x_3} + X_3 \; = \; 0$$

Where the body forces can be expressed in terms of components as

$$X = X_1 \, i_1 + X_2 \, i_2 + X_3 \, i_3 \qquad (4.43)$$

The set (4.42) can be expressed in compact indicial notation as

$$\frac{\partial \sigma_{ij}}{\partial x_i} + X_j \; = \; 0 \qquad (4.44)$$

73

4.2.4. Stress Vector-Stress Component Transformation

Let us suppose that the components of stress are given at a point. We can then find the components of the stress vector defined in terms of the areas with normals in the orthogonal coordinate directions by using equations (4.38). In order to specify the stress vector defined relative to an area with a normal **n**, we must determine a relation between the components of the stress vector acting on the face d**A** and the components of stress as shown by Fig. 4-6.

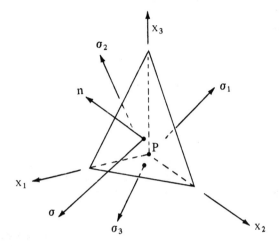

Figure 4-6. Stress Vector Acting on Tetrahedral Face

Let d**A** be the area of the face with normal **n**, and dA_i be the area of the faces with normals in the negative coordinate directions. The following equilibrium must then be satisfied:

$$\sigma \, d\mathbf{A} - \sigma_1 \, dA_1 - \sigma_2 \, dA_2 - \sigma_3 \, dA_3 = 0 \tag{4.45}$$

or

$$\sigma = \sigma_1 \, n_1 + \sigma_2 \, n_2 + \sigma_3 \, n_3 \tag{4.46}$$

where

$$n_i = \frac{dA_i}{dA} \tag{4.47}$$

The stress vector can then be represented by using indicial notation as

$$\sigma_i \, i_i = \sigma_i \, n_i \tag{4.48}$$

or, by using (4.39), as

$$\sigma_i = \sigma_{ji} \, n_j \tag{4.49}$$

The components of the stress vector are therefore related to the components of stress at a point and the components of the normal to the surface on which the stress vector acts. The relationships between the components of the stress vector and the components of stress are given in extended notation as

$$\begin{aligned}
\sigma_1 &= \sigma_{11}\, n_1 + \sigma_{21}\, n_2 + \sigma_{31}\, n_3 \\
\sigma_2 &= \sigma_{12}\, n_1 + \sigma_{22}\, n_2 + \sigma_{32}\, n_3 \\
\sigma_3 &= \sigma_{13}\, n_1 + \sigma_{23}\, n_2 + \sigma_{33}\, n_3
\end{aligned} \qquad (4.50)$$

4.2.5.   Stress Transformation

It is a simple matter to show that the stress components satisfy a transformation equation of the form (4.33) by noting that the component of stress normal to the surface is a scalar quantity and is thus unchanged by a transformation of coordinates. The normal components of the stress vector are thus equal so that

$$t' = t \qquad (4.51)$$

where $t = \sigma \cdot \mathbf{n}$

which leads to

$$\sigma' \cdot \mathbf{n}' = \sigma \cdot \mathbf{n} \qquad (4.52)$$

Then (4.52) can be expressed in terms of components of stress by using (4.49) to obtain

$$\sigma'_{ji}\, n'_j\, \mathbf{i}'_i \cdot n'_m\, \mathbf{i}'_m = \sigma_{ji}\, n_j\, \mathbf{i}_i \cdot n_m\, \mathbf{i}_m \qquad (4.53)$$

where the prime means that the quantities are defined relative to the transformed coordinate system. The unit vectors in the two coordinate systems are related by

$$\mathbf{i}'_m = a_{mn}\, \mathbf{i}_n \qquad (4.54)$$

where a_{mn} is the direction cosine between the axes of the two systems. The components of the unit normals then are transformed to

$$n_i = a_{ji}\, n'_j \qquad (4.55)$$

The use of (4.52) and some algebraic manipulation then leads to

$$\sigma'_{ij} = a_{im}\, a_{jn}\, \sigma_{mn} \qquad (4.56)$$

The stress transformation equations are given in extended notation as

$$\sigma'_{11} = \sigma_{11}\, a_{11}^2 + \sigma_{22}\, a_{12}^2 + \sigma_{33}\, a_{13}^2 + 2(\sigma_{12}\, a_{11}\, a_{12} + \sigma_{23}\, a_{12}\, a_{13} + \sigma_{31}\, a_{13}\, a_{11})$$

$$\sigma'_{22} = \sigma_{11}\, a_{21}^2 + \sigma_{22}\, a_{22}^2 + \sigma_{33}\, a_{23}^2 + 2(\sigma_{12}\, a_{21}\, a_{22} + \sigma_{23}\, a_{22}\, a_{23} + \sigma_{31}\, a_{23}\, a_{21})$$

$$\sigma'_{33} = \sigma_{11}\, a_{31}^2 + \sigma_{22}\, a_{32}^2 + \sigma_{33}\, a_{33}^2 + 2(\sigma_{12}\, a_{31}\, a_{32} + \sigma_{23}\, a_{32}\, a_{33} + \sigma_{31}\, a_{33}\, a_{31})$$

and $\qquad\qquad\qquad\qquad\qquad\qquad\qquad\qquad\qquad\qquad\qquad\qquad\qquad$ (4.57)

$$\sigma'_{12} = \sigma_{11}\, a_{11}\, a_{21} + \sigma_{22}\, a_{12}\, a_{22} + \sigma_{33}\, a_{13}\, a_{23} + \sigma_{12}\,(a_{11}\, a_{22} + a_{12}\, a_{21}) + \sigma_{23}\,(a_{12}\, a_{23} + a_{13}\, a_{22}) + \sigma_{31}\,(a_{13}\, a_{21} + a_{11}\, a_{23})$$

$$\sigma'_{23} = \sigma_{11}\, a_{21}\, a_{31} + \sigma_{22}\, a_{32}\, a_{22} + \sigma_{33}\, a_{23}\, a_{33} + \sigma_{12}\,(a_{21}\, a_{32} + a_{22}\, a_{31}) + \sigma_{23}\,(a_{22}\, a_{33} + a_{23}\, a_{32}) + \sigma_{31}\,(a_{23}\, a_{31} + a_{21}\, a_{33})$$

$$\sigma'_{31} = \sigma_{11}\, a_{31}\, a_{11} + \sigma_{22}\, a_{32}\, a_{12} + \sigma_{33}\, a_{33}\, a_{13} + \sigma_{12}\,(a_{31}\, a_{12} + a_{32}\, a_{11}) + \sigma_{23}\,(a_{32}\, a_{13} + a_{33}\, a_{12}) + \sigma_{31}\,(a_{33}\, a_{11} + a_{31}\, a_{13})$$

4.2.6. Principal Stress and Principal Stress Directions

The components of stress at a point are seen to be dependent on the orientation of the reference axes as shown by (4.57). It would appear that a direction $\mathbf{n}$ can be found such that the stress vector is in the direction of $\mathbf{n}$, i.e.,

$$\sigma = \sigma \mathbf{n} \tag{4.58}$$

The directions that satisfy (4.58) are called the principal directions, and the magnitude of the stress in this direction is called the principal stress.

It can be shown that the magnitude and directions must satisfy the set of homogenous equations

$$(\sigma_{ij} - \sigma \delta_{ij})\, n_j = 0 \tag{4.59}$$

The determination of principal stresses and directions is an eigenvalue problem. The principal stresses are the eigenvalues and the associated directions are the eigenvectors.

When stress output is requested for the three-dimensional elements in NASTRAN, the principal stresses and directions are recovered at several points in the element. The amount of calculation required may be significant so that the user should exercise judgement in requesting stress output.

4.3. Constitutive Relations

The constitutive equations represent the experimentally determined equations that relate the stress and the strain. Material tests have shown that the stress-strain relation for a typical material is as shown by Fig. 4-7.

Most engineering materials exhibit a linear relation between stress and strain up to some critical value of the stress, which is called the yield stress. Structural materials that exhibit a linear stress-strain relationship are called Hookian and the relationship between stress and strain, for the one-dimensional case, is given by

$$\sigma = E\, e$$

where E is called the modulus of elasticity.

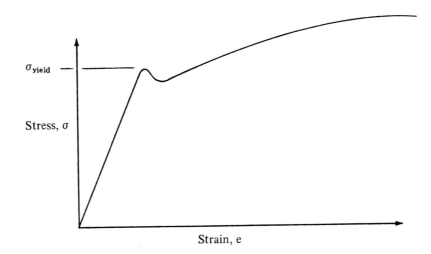

Figure 4-7. Stress-Strain Diagram for a Typical Structural Material

A large number of structural design problems are formulated using the yield stress as a constraint on the maximum value of stress. For this class of problems it is appropriate to use a set of linear constitutive relations. These relations together with the linear strain-displacement equations are the basis of the linear theory of elasticity and are, therefore, the basis of linear structural analysis.

There are many meaningful analysis problems that cannot be formulated on the basis of the linear constitutive relations, and for this class of problems the constitutive relations are formulated on the basis of theory of plasticity. The incorporation of nonlinear material effects is beyond the scope of the present text. Nonlinear constitutive relations in matrix structural analysis are discussed in Refs. 4-6 through 4-8.

4.3.1. Generalized Hookes Law

A general linear relation between the tensor components of stress and strain is given by

$$\sigma_{ij} = E_{ijkl}\, \ell_{kl} \tag{4.60}$$

Since each index can take on the values 1, 2, and 3 and since there are four indices, it would appear that there are 81 elastic constants. However, since both the stress and strain tensors are symmetric the following relations must hold when the indices (i, j) and (k, l) are interchanged so that

$$E_{ijkl} = E_{jikl}$$

and

$$E_{ijkl} = E_{ijlk} \tag{4.61}$$

Since there are only six independent combinations of the pairs (i, j) and (k, l), it follows that there are at most 36 independent elastic constants. Energy considerations further show that the elasticity tensor is also symmetric with respect to the interchange of the pairs of indices so that

$$E_{ijkl} = E_{klij}$$

The practical result of all these symmetry relations is that a material can have at most 21 independent elastic coefficients. A material that is characterized by this general relation is called an anisotropic material. Generally, materials of interest to structural engineers have a great deal of material symmetry, which means that they can be described by fewer than 21 elastic constants. If the material is isotropic, then the material behavior is completely defined by two elastic constants.

For the generalized Hookes law, the constitutive relations in expanded form become

$$\sigma_{11} = E_{1111}\,\ell_{11} + E_{1122}\,\ell_{22} + E_{1133}\,\ell_{33} + 2\,(E_{1112}\,\ell_{12} + E_{1123}\,\ell_{23} + E_{1131}\,\ell_{31})$$

$$\sigma_{22} = E_{2211}\,\ell_{11} + E_{2222}\,\ell_{22} + E_{2233}\,\ell_{33} + 2\,(E_{2212}\,\ell_{12} + E_{2223}\,\ell_{23} + E_{2231}\,\ell_{31})$$

$$\sigma_{33} = E_{3311}\,\ell_{11} + E_{3322}\,\ell_{22} + E_{3333}\,\ell_{33} + 2\,(E_{3312}\,\ell_{12} + E_{3323}\,\ell_{23} + E_{3331}\,\ell_{31})$$

$$\sigma_{12} = E_{1211}\,\ell_{11} + E_{1222}\,\ell_{22} + E_{1233}\,\ell_{33} + 2\,(E_{1212}\,\ell_{12} + E_{1223}\,\ell_{23} + E_{1231}\,\ell_{31})$$

$$\sigma_{23} = E_{2311}\,\ell_{11} + E_{2322}\,\ell_{22} + E_{2333}\,\ell_{33} + 2\,(E_{2312}\,\ell_{12} + E_{2323}\,\ell_{23} + E_{2331}\,\ell_{31})$$

$$\sigma_{31} = E_{3111}\,\ell_{11} + E_{3122}\,\ell_{22} + E_{3133}\,\ell_{33} + 2\,(E_{3112}\,\ell_{12} + E_{3123}\,\ell_{23} + E_{3131}\,\ell_{31})$$

$$\tag{4.62}$$

4.3.2. Transformation of Elastic Constants

The set of elastic constants appearing in (4.60) relate two sets of behavioral variables that transform according to (4.33) and (4.56) for strains and stresses, respectively. The elastic coefficients can thus be shown to satisfy the transformation rule

$$E'_{ijkl} = a_{im}a_{jn}a_{ko}a_{lp}E_{mnop} \qquad (4.63)$$

where the prime indicates the value of the coefficient defined with respect to the transformed coordinate system and where the coordinate transformation is defined by (4.29).

4.3.3. Matrix Representation of Constitutive Relation

Since there are six independent stresses and strains it is convenient to represent (4.62) in matrix form as

$$
\begin{Bmatrix} \sigma_1 \\ \sigma_2 \\ \sigma_3 \\ \sigma_4 \\ \sigma_5 \\ \sigma_6 \end{Bmatrix}
=
\begin{bmatrix}
E_{11} & E_{12} & E_{13} & E_{14} & E_{15} & E_{16} \\
E_{21} & E_{22} & E_{23} & E_{24} & E_{25} & E_{26} \\
E_{31} & E_{32} & E_{33} & E_{34} & E_{35} & E_{36} \\
E_{41} & E_{42} & E_{43} & E_{44} & E_{45} & E_{46} \\
E_{51} & E_{52} & E_{53} & E_{54} & E_{55} & E_{56} \\
E_{61} & E_{62} & E_{63} & E_{64} & E_{65} & E_{66}
\end{bmatrix}
\begin{Bmatrix} e_1 \\ e_2 \\ e_3 \\ e_4 \\ e_5 \\ e_6 \end{Bmatrix}
\qquad (4.64)
$$

or more compactly, as

$$\sigma = E\,e \qquad (4.65)$$

where E is the matrix of elastic constants given by (4.64) and where the elements of the stress and physical strain sets are defined to be

$$
\sigma =
\begin{Bmatrix} \sigma_{11} \\ \sigma_{22} \\ \sigma_{33} \\ \sigma_{12} \\ \sigma_{23} \\ \sigma_{31} \end{Bmatrix},
\qquad
e =
\begin{Bmatrix} e_{11} \\ e_{22} \\ e_{33} \\ e_{12} \\ e_{23} \\ e_{31} \end{Bmatrix}
\qquad (4.66)
$$

The constitutive equations (4.62) relate the tensor components of stress and strain while (4.64) is expressed in terms of the physical strain components. The relationship between elements of the matrix of elastic constants given in (4.64) and the elements of the elasticity tensor can be obtained by using (4.21) and (4.22). The form of the constitutive equations given by (4.65) is a convenient way of expressing the relations between stress and physical strain components. However, since these equations have no tensor character they are not convenient for defining the transformation characteristics of the elastic coefficients.

4.3.4. Orthotropic Materials

An orthotropic material exhibits material symmetry with respect to two orthogonal planes. This means that the material coefficients must be invariant for reflective symmetry through two orthogonal planes. This requirement together with the transformation equations lead to a reduction from 21 constants to the following nine constants:

$$
E =
\begin{bmatrix}
E_{11} & E_{12} & E_{13} & 0 & 0 & 0 \\
E_{21} & E_{22} & E_{23} & 0 & 0 & 0 \\
E_{31} & E_{32} & E_{33} & 0 & 0 & 0 \\
0 & 0 & 0 & E_{44} & 0 & 0 \\
0 & 0 & 0 & 0 & E_{55} & 0 \\
0 & 0 & 0 & 0 & 0 & E_{66}
\end{bmatrix}
\qquad (4.67)
$$

Several materials that are used in structural design can be characterized as being orthotropic including reinforced concrete, wood, and composite materials. For the case of plane stress, the relations (4.67) become

$$\begin{Bmatrix} \sigma_{11} \\ \sigma_{22} \\ \sigma_{12} \end{Bmatrix} = \begin{bmatrix} E_{11} & E_{12} & 0 \\ E_{12} & E_{22} & 0 \\ 0 & 0 & E_{44} \end{bmatrix} \begin{Bmatrix} e_{11} \\ e_{22} \\ e_{12} \end{Bmatrix} \tag{4.68}$$

4.3.5. Isotropic Properties

A material whose elastic constants are independent of the orientation of the material axes at a point is called isotropic. The elastic properties of an isotropic material can be completely characterized by two elastic constants. In this case the elasticity matrix can be written as

$$E = \begin{bmatrix} \lambda+2\mu & \lambda & \lambda & 0 & 0 & 0 \\ \lambda & (\lambda+2\mu) & \lambda & 0 & 0 & 0 \\ \lambda & \lambda & (\lambda+2\mu) & 0 & 0 & 0 \\ 0 & 0 & 0 & \mu & 0 & 0 \\ 0 & 0 & 0 & 0 & \mu & 0 \\ 0 & 0 & 0 & 0 & 0 & \mu \end{bmatrix} \tag{4.69}$$

where the parameters are called the Lamé coefficients. These coefficients are related to the modulus of elasticity E and Poissons' ratio ν by

$$\lambda = \frac{\nu E}{(1+\nu)(1-2\nu)}$$
$$\mu = \frac{E}{2(1+\nu)} \tag{4.70}$$

4.3.6. Initial Strains

The elastic body may be subject to an environment such as a temperature gradient or radiation that causes an initial strain state. The total strain is the sum of the elastic strains (i.e., those strains that are related to stress by Hookes law) and the initial strains e_I:

$$e = C \sigma + e_I \tag{4.71}$$

where

$$C = E^{-1} \tag{4.72}$$

The set of elastic coefficients C is called the compliance matrix and has the same symmetry properties as E. The stress-strain relation is then found from (4.71) to be

$$\sigma = E (e - e_I) \tag{4.73}$$

If the initial strains are due to thermal effects, then they can be expressed in terms of thermal expansion coefficients and the change of temperature T as

$$e_I = \alpha T \tag{4.74}$$

Since thermal expansion is a phenomenon that results in only extensional behavior, the set of thermal expansion coefficients has the following form for an anisotropic material:

$$\alpha = \begin{Bmatrix} \alpha_1 \\ \alpha_2 \\ \alpha_3 \\ 0 \\ 0 \\ 0 \end{Bmatrix} \qquad (4.75)$$

If the material is anisotropic orthotropic, then the coefficients of thermal expansion may be significantly different in the three materials directions. However, if the material is isotropic, then the coefficient of thermal expansion is the same in all directions. It is interesting to note in passing that the coefficient of thermal expansion for structures composed of carbon composites may be made close to zero for certain material configurations. This property makes these materials especially attractive for applications where very low thermal distortions are allowed. (see Ref. 4-9, for example).

4.4.   Plate Theory

In the development of plate theory we consider a body that is thin compared to other characteristic dimensions. The displacements at any point in the cross-section of the plate shown by Fig. 4-8 can then be represented entirely in terms of the displacement of the middle surface as

$$u\,(x,\,y,\,z) = v_x\,(x,\,y) + z\,\alpha\,(x,\,y)$$

$$v\,(x,\,y,\,z) = v_y\,(x,\,y) - z\,\beta\,(x,\,y) \qquad (4.76)$$

$$w\,(x,\,y,\,z) = v_z\,(x,\,y)$$

where we have identified the components of the displacement vector at any point in the cross-section as $(u,\,v,\,w)$. The components $(v_x,\,v_y,\,v_z)$ are then taken to be displacements of the neutral surface, and $(\alpha,\,\beta)$ are the slopes where

$$\alpha\,(x,\,y) = -\frac{\partial v_z}{\partial x} \qquad\qquad \beta\,(x,\,y) = \frac{\partial v_z}{\partial y} \qquad (4.77)$$

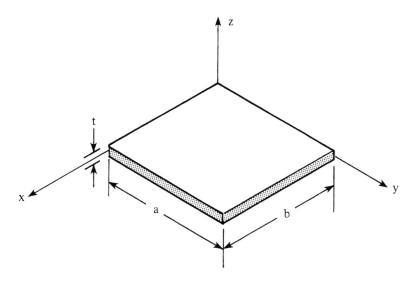

Figure 4-8. Plate Bending Element

The strain displacement equations (4.23) that result from the assumed displacements (4.76) are

$$e_{xx} = \frac{\partial v_x}{\partial x} - z \frac{\partial^2 v_z}{\partial x^2}$$

$$e_{yy} = \frac{\partial v_y}{\partial y} - z \frac{\partial^2 v_z}{\partial y^2} \tag{4.78}$$

$$e_{xy} = \frac{\partial v_x}{\partial y} + \frac{\partial v_y}{\partial x} - 2z \frac{\partial^2 v_z}{\partial x \partial y}$$

where all other strain components identically vanish. The strains can then be expressed in matrix form as

$$\mathbf{e} = \mathbf{e}^\circ - z \boldsymbol{\kappa}^\circ \tag{4.79}$$

where $\mathbf{e}^\circ$ and $\boldsymbol{\kappa}^\circ$ are the strains and curvatures of the neutral surface defined to be

$$\mathbf{e}^\circ = \begin{Bmatrix} e_{xx}^\circ \\ e_{yy}^\circ \\ e_{xy}^\circ \end{Bmatrix} = \begin{Bmatrix} \dfrac{\partial v_x}{\partial x} \\[2mm] \dfrac{\partial v_y}{\partial y} \\[2mm] \dfrac{\partial v_x}{\partial y} + \dfrac{\partial v_y}{\partial x} \end{Bmatrix} \tag{4.80}$$

and

$$\boldsymbol{\kappa}^\circ = \begin{Bmatrix} \kappa_{xx}^\circ \\ \kappa_{yy}^\circ \\ \kappa_{xy}^\circ \end{Bmatrix} = \begin{Bmatrix} \dfrac{\partial^2 v_z}{\partial x^2} \\[2mm] \dfrac{\partial^2 v_z}{\partial y^2} \\[2mm] 2 \dfrac{\partial^2 v_z}{\partial x \partial y} \end{Bmatrix} \tag{4.81}$$

In plate theory the stresses are replaced by moment and force resultants that are defined as

$$\mathbf{M} = -\int_{-\frac{t}{2}}^{\frac{t}{2}} z \, \boldsymbol{\sigma} \, dz \tag{4.82}$$

$$\mathbf{N} = \int_{-\frac{t}{2}}^{\frac{t}{2}} \boldsymbol{\sigma} \, dz \tag{4.83}$$

where

81

4.4.1 Plate Equilibrium Equations

$$M = \begin{Bmatrix} M_x \\ M_y \\ M_{xy} \end{Bmatrix}, \qquad N = \begin{Bmatrix} N_x \\ N_y \\ N_{xy} \end{Bmatrix}, \quad \text{and} \quad \sigma = \begin{Bmatrix} \sigma_{xx} \\ \sigma_{yy} \\ \sigma_{xy} \end{Bmatrix} \qquad (4.84)$$

The positive sign convention for the moment and force resultants follows from the sign convention for stresses and the definitions of (4.82) and (4.83). The positive force and moment resultants are shown by Fig. 4-9a and 4-9b, respectively.

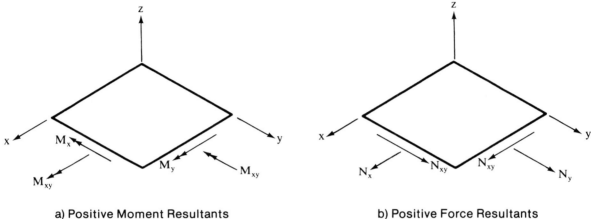

a) Positive Moment Resultants   b) Positive Force Resultants

Figure 4-9. Positive Force and Moment Resultants

4.4.1. Plate Equilibrium Equations

The equilibrium equations governing inplane behavior are obtained by considering an element of volume subject to inplane body forces. The resulting equations are

$$\frac{\partial N_x}{\partial x} + \frac{\partial N_{xy}}{\partial y} + t\, X_x = 0$$

$$\frac{\partial N_y}{\partial y} + \frac{\partial N_{xy}}{\partial x} + t\, X_y = 0 \qquad (4.85)$$

where t is the plate thickness and X_x and X_y are components of the body force acting in the neutral surface.

In order to obtain the equilibrium equations governing equilibrium normal to neutral surface, it is necessary to assume the presence of transverse shear resultants as shown by Fig. 4-10. The equilibrium equation governing transverse forces is then given by

$$\frac{\partial Q_x}{\partial x} + \frac{\partial Q_y}{\partial y} + q\,(x, y) = 0 \qquad (4.86)$$

82

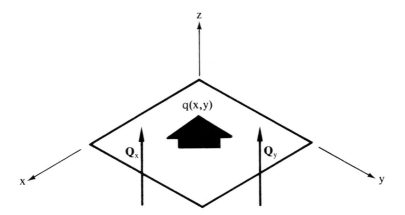

Figure 4-10. Transverse Load and Shear Resultants

where Q_x and Q_y are transverse shear resultants and $q(x, y)$ is the transverse load.

The transverse shears are then related to the moment resultants by considering moment equilibrium about the x- and y-axes. The moment equilibrium equations are

$$\frac{\partial M_x}{\partial x} + \frac{\partial M_{xy}}{\partial y} + Q_x = 0 \tag{4.87}$$

$$\frac{\partial M_y}{\partial y} + \frac{\partial M_{xy}}{\partial x} + Q_y = 0 \tag{4.88}$$

The equilibrium equation (4.86) can then be written in terms of moment resultants by substituting (4.87) and (4.88) into (4.86) to obtain

$$\frac{\partial^2 M_x}{\partial x^2} + \frac{2\partial^2 M_{xy}}{\partial x \partial y} + \frac{\partial^2 M_y}{\partial y^2} + q(x, y) = 0 \tag{4.89}$$

4.4.2.   Moment-Curvature Relations

The moment resultants are related to the curvatures by noting that the stresses are related to the strains by

$$\sigma = E\,(e^\circ + z\kappa^\circ) \tag{4.90}$$

The substitution of (4.90) into the definition for moment resultants (4.82) then leads to

$$\mathbf{M} = \frac{t^3}{12}\,\mathbf{E}\kappa^\circ \tag{4.91}$$

These relations are generally written in terms of the bending rigidity $\mathbf{E}_f$ as

$$\mathbf{M} = \mathbf{E}_f\,\kappa^\circ \tag{4.92}$$

4.5 References

where E_f, for an isotropic material, is defined as

$$E_f = D \begin{bmatrix} 1 & -\nu & 0 \\ -\nu & 1 & 0 \\ 0 & 0 & \dfrac{(1-\nu)}{2} \end{bmatrix} \quad (4.93)$$

where

$$D = \frac{Et^3}{12(1-\nu^2)} \quad (4.94)$$

4.5. References

4-1 Bishplinghoff, R. L., et al., *Statics of Deformable Solids*, Addison-Wesley, 1965, pp. 98-100.

4-2 *NASTRAN Theoretical Manual*, NASA SP-221(03), Sec. 7.

4-3 Novozhilov, V. V., *Foundations of Nonlinear Theory of Elasticity*, Graylock Press, 1953, pp. 47-53.

4-4 Oden, J. T., *Finite Elements of Nonlinear Continua*, McGraw-Hill, 1972, pp. 5-20.

4-5 Tillerson, J. R., Stricklin, J. A., and Haisler, W. E., "Numerical Methods for the Solution of Nonlinear Problems in Structural Analysis," *Numerical Solutions of Nonlinear Structural Problems*, ASME AMD-Vol. 6, 1973, pp. 67-101.

4-6 "Plastic Analysis of Structures," *Grumman Research Department Report*, RE-380J, April 1970.

4-7 *Nonlinear Analysis of Structures*, NASA CR-2351, March 1974.

4-8 "Selecting Solution Procedures for Nonlinear Structural Dynamics," *Shock and Vibration Digest*, Vol. 7, April 1975.

4-9 Jones, R. M., *Mechanics of Composite Materials*, McGraw-Hill, 1975, pp. 195-196.

5

Variational Principles

Variational principles are based as much in the philosophy of science as the methods of Newtonian mechanics are based in the physics of forces and displacements. The variational principles are the backbone of mathematical analysis and are the foundation upon which the modern concepts of the finite element are based.

Variational principles are based on work considerations and the concept of admissible behavioral functions. Admissible displacements are those that satisfy the kinematic constraints, and admissible forces are those that satisfy the equilibrium conditions. These two sets of behavioral variables are related by constitutive relations.

In order to develop an appreciation for the implications of the variational principle we will proceed by formulating a variational principle associated with admissible displacements and admissible forces by using a simple system as a prototype. These variational principles will then be generalized to hold for a structural body and a generalized variational principle will be defined. In the following we will use the heuristic approach taken by Crandall et al. in Ref. 5-1.

5.1.   Variational Principle Based on Admissible Displacements

Consider the structural system shown by Fig. 5-1, which is composed of two structural elements identified as k_1 and k_2 and a movable element on which an external force is applied. The ends of the springs are identified by points A_1 and A_2, which have displacements u_1 and u_2, respectively. The final configuration is obtained by attaching the structural elements to the movable body so that the ends of the elements are attached at B_1 and B_2.

The resulting equilibrium configuration will then include a set of self-equilibrating forces in the elements due to the difference in the free lengths of the two springs. The system configuration is defined by the displacement x as well as the spring displacements u_1 and u_2. These displacements are not independent so that among the infinity of possible values for each element in the system there is one set that actually represents the actual configuration. This set of displacements satisfies

1. The geometric constraints

2. The equilibrium conditions

3. The constitutive relations

5.1 Variational Principles Based on Admissible Displacements

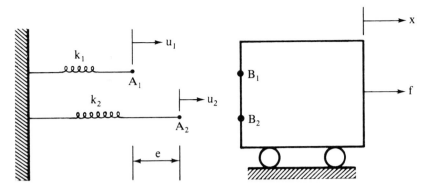

Figure 5-1. Discrete Structural System

In order to identify the displacement configuration that satisfies these requirements, we will consider the system with the ends of the structural elements attached to the movable element. Any displaced configuration will then satisfy the kinematic constraint

$$u_1 - u_2 - e = 0 \tag{5.1}$$

The forces in the springs can now be calculated by constitutive relations of the form

$$f_1 = f_1 (u_1)$$
$$f_2 = f_2 (u_2) \tag{5.2}$$

where the spring displacements are given by

$$u_2 = x$$
$$u_1 = u_2 + e \tag{5.3}$$

The forces in the springs determined by using the constitutive relations will not satisfy the equilibrium equations so that the summation of forces

$$\Sigma F = f - f_1 - f_2 \tag{5.4}$$

will not be equal to zero, in general, even though the kinematic constraints are satisfied.

We now consider changes to the system configuration such that the kinematic constraints are satisfied and define a variational indicator V.I. for the system,

$$V. I. = (f - f_1 - f_2) \, \delta x \tag{5.5}$$

where the notation δx is used to indicate an admissible variation of the displacements.

The variational indicator is interpreted as follows. The system configuration may be represented by any kinematically admissible displacement x. The associated element forces can be obtained by using the constitutive relations so that, in general, the variational indicator has some value different from zero. If we find a system configuration such that the variational indicator is zero, then the equilibrium condition must be satisfied because the variation in displacement is arbitrary. On the basis of these observations, the following variational principle can be stated:

If the variational indicator is equal to zero for any admissible variation in the displacement, then the system is in equilibrium.

5.1.1.   Generalization of Principle — Virtual work

The variational principle stated in the previous section can be generalized to hold for any structural system by expressing the variational indicator defined by (5.5) in a slightly different form. The admissible variations in displacement must satisfy the geometric constraints specified by (5.3) so that

$$\delta u_1 = \delta u_2 = \delta x \tag{5.6}$$

The variational indicator can now be expressed as

$$V.I. = f\delta x - (f_1\ \delta u_1 + f_2\ \delta u_2) \tag{5.7}$$

or

$$V.I. = \delta W_e + \delta W_i \tag{5.8}$$

where δW_e and δW_i represent the work done by the external and internal forces during an admissible variation of the displacements.

The variational indicator expressed in terms of external and internal work applies to any structural system. A variational principle, called the principle of virtual displacements, can then be stated for a general configuration:

If the work of the external forces equals the work of the internal forces for any admissible displacement, then the system is in equilibrium.

5.1.2.   Principle of Stationary Potential

The internal forces and displacements are related by a set of constitutive relations whose functional form is as shown by Fig. 5-2.

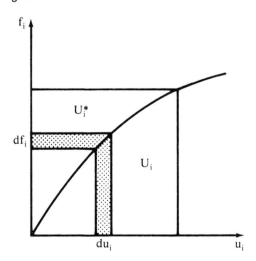

Figure 5-2. Force Displacement Relation

The energy stored in the structural element is given by

$$U_m = \int_0^{u_m} f_m\ du_m \tag{5.9}$$

87

5.1.3 Internal Strain Energy

The change in the internal energy for the entire structural system due to an admissible variation of displacement is then given by

$$\delta U = \sum_{m=1}^{M} f_m \, \delta u_m \tag{5.10}$$

where M is the total number of structural elements.

The work of the internal forces is thus seen to be related to the change of the internal energy by

$$\delta W_i = -\delta U \tag{5.11}$$

so that the variational indicator can be written as

$$V. \ I. = \delta W_e - \delta U \tag{5.12}$$

If the external forces are derivable from a potential function, then

$$f = -\frac{dV}{du} \tag{5.13}$$

and the work of the external forces is given by

$$\delta W_e = -\delta V \tag{5.14}$$

where the variation of the potential of the external forces is given by

$$\delta V = \frac{dV}{du} \, \delta u \tag{5.15}$$

If the internal and external forces are derivable from potential functions U and V, respectively, then the variational indicator can be expressed as

$$V. \ I. = \delta U + \delta V \tag{5.16}$$

The associated variational principle, called the principle of stationary total potential energy, is then stated as

If the total potential energy assumes a stationary value for any admissible variation of the displacement state, the system is in equilibrium.

5.1.3. Internal Strain Energy

The components of stress are related to the components of strain by a set of constitutive relations. The strain energy per unit volume can be expressed in terms of the stress and strain components as

$$dU_0 = \int_0^e \sigma^T d\mathbf{e} \tag{5.17}$$

where the integration is taken over the values of the strain from zero to their final values.

If the material is Hookian, the relationship between stress and strain is given by (4.73). The expression for the strain energy density then becomes

$$U_0 = \tfrac{1}{2} \left\{ (e^T - e_I^T) \, E \, e \right\} \tag{5.18}$$

The total strain energy in the body is then obtained by integrating the strain energy density over the entire volume to give

$$U = \int_{V_{o\ell}} U_o \; dV_{o\ell} \tag{5.19}$$

The internal strain energy for an isotropic material is found by substituting the expressions for the isotropic elastic constants (4.69) into (5.19) to give

$$U = \tfrac{1}{2} \int_{V_{o\ell}} \left\{ \frac{\nu E}{(1+\nu)(1-2\nu)} \, (e_{11} + e_{22} + e_{33})^2 + \frac{E}{(1+\nu)} \, (e_{11}^2 + e_{22}^2 + e_{33}^2) \right.$$

$$\left. + \frac{E}{2(1+\nu)} \, (e_{12}^2 + e_{23}^2 + e_{31}^2) - \frac{\alpha E T}{(1-2\nu)} \, (e_{11} + e_{22} + e_{33}) + \frac{3E}{2(1-2\nu)} \, (\alpha T)^2 \right\} dV_{o\ell} \tag{5.20}$$

5.1.4. Work of External Forces

The external forces acting on the body can be of two types:

1. Forces defined per unit volume that act throughout the body. Body forces are defined as force per unit volume.

2. Forces defined per unit area that act on the surface (boundary) of the body.

The work done by these external forces acting through variations of the admissible displacements is then given by

$$\delta W_e = \int_{V_{o\ell}} X^T \cdot \delta v \, dV_{o\ell} + \int_{A_f} \delta^{*T} \cdot \delta v \, dA \quad + \quad P^T \delta u \tag{5.21}$$

where

$\mathbf{X}$ Body force

σ^* Prescribed stress vector acting on the surface, defined with respect to the area dA, which has a normal n to the surface.

A_f Portion of the surface on which external forces are prescribed.

$\mathbf{P}$ Set of all concentrated loads acting on the structure

$\mathbf{u}$ Set of displacements at and in the direction of the applied concentrated load and where δu and δv are variations of the associated displacements.

5.1.5. Variational Form for Structural Body

The variational principle for admissible variations in the displacements and (5.19) and (5.21) can be used to express the internal and external work:

5.2. Variational Principles Based on Admissible Forces

$$-\int_{V_{o\ell}} \sigma^T \, \delta e \, dV_{o\ell} \; + \; \int_{V_{o\ell}} X^T \, \delta v \, dV_{o\ell} \; + \; \int_{A_f} \sigma^T \, \delta e \, dA + P^T \, \delta u = 0 \qquad (5.22)$$

where the stresses are given in terms of the displacements by the constitutive relations and where δe is the variation of the strain field which is produced by the virtual displacement δv. The associated variational principle, which is called the principle of virtual work, then states

> If the work expression given by (5.22) vanishes for any admissible variation in the displacements, then the system is in equilibrium.

5.2. Variational Principles Based on Admissible Forces

We return once more to the simple structural system shown by Fig. 5.1 and study the system behavior by first attaching the end of element k_2 to the movable body. For any displaced configuration, there will then be a gap between the end of the spring k_1 and the body. This gap is given by

$$g = u_2 + e - u_1 \qquad (5.23)$$

where the desired configuration is that for which the gap is equal to zero.

In order to develop the variational principle for admissible variations of internal force we consider the system to be in equilibrium under the action of the external forces such that the equilibrium equations are satisfied. Now we consider variations in the admissible internal forces where admissible variations must satisfy the equilibrium equations (5.4) so that

$$\delta f_1 \; + \; \delta f_2 \; = \; 0 \qquad (5.24)$$

A variational indicator is now defined as

$$V.\,I. = g \, \delta f_1 \qquad (5.25)$$

where we note that the variational indicator will be equal to zero for any admissible variation of the internal forces when the gap is equal to zero. Since the closing of the gap implies that the geometric constraint given by (5.1) is satisfied, we have the following variational statement for the simple system:

> The variational indicator given by equation (5.25) vanishes for any admissible variation in the internal forces when the geometric constraints are satisfied.

The variational indicator can be put into a form suitable for making generalizations by substituting the geometric constraint (5.23):

$$V.I. = (u_2 + e - u_1) \, \delta f_1 \qquad (5.26)$$

Since the variations of the internal force must satisfy equilibrium, equation (5.26) becomes

$$V.\,I. = e \delta f_1 - u_2 \delta f_2 - u_1 \delta f_1$$

We now define the complementary potential as the area U_i^* shown on Fig. 5-2 to be

$$U_i^* = \int_0^{f_i} u_i \, df_i \tag{5.27}$$

The variation of the complementary potential is given by

$$\delta U_i^* = u_i \, \delta f_i \tag{5.28}$$

so that the variational indicator can be expressed as

$$V.\,I. = e\delta f_1 \; - \; \delta U^* \tag{5.29}$$

where U^* is the complementary potential for the entire system.

The variational indicator for the simple system can be generalized by identifying e as the prescribed displacement on the surface of the body. The variational indicator can then be written as

$$V.\,I. = \int_{A_v} v^{*^T} \cdot \, \delta\sigma \; dA - \int_{V_{o\ell}} \delta U^* \, dV_{o\ell} \tag{5.30}$$

where A_v is that part of the surface on which displacements are prescribed.

The variational principle based on admissible variations in the internal forces is called the principle of virtual complementary work and is stated as

If the variational indicator vanishes for an arbitrary variation in the admissible forces, then the forces satisfy the kinematic constraints.

5.2.1. Complementary Strain Energy

The complementary strain energy density is given by

$$U_o^* = \int_0^{\sigma} e^T \, d\sigma \tag{5.31}$$

where the integration is taken over the values of stress from zero to their final values. If the material is Hookian, we can express the strain in terms of the stress by (4.71) so that the complementary strain energy can be written as

$$U_o^* = \tfrac{1}{2} \sigma^T \, C \, \sigma \; + \; e_I^T \, \sigma \tag{5.32}$$

The total complementary strain energy is then obtained by integrating the complementary strain density over the entire volume to give

$$U^* = \int_{V_{o\ell}} U_o^* \, dV_{o\ell} \tag{5.33}$$

The complementary strain energy for an isotropic material is given by

$$
\begin{aligned}
U^* = \tfrac{1}{2} \int_{V_{o\ell}} \Big\{ \frac{1}{E} \Big[(\sigma_{11}^2 + \sigma_{22}^2 + \sigma_{33}^2) + 2(1+\nu)(\sigma_{12}^2 + \sigma_{23}^2 + \sigma_{31}^2) \\
- 2\nu(\sigma_{11}\sigma_{22} + \sigma_{22}\sigma_{33} + \sigma_{33}\sigma_{11}) \Big] + \alpha T(\sigma_{11} + \sigma_{22} + \sigma_{33}) \Big\} \, dV_{o\ell}
\end{aligned}
\tag{5.34}
$$

5.3.   References

5-1   Crandall, S. H., Karnopp, D. C., E. F. Kurtz, Jr., Pridmore-Brown, D. C., *Dynamics of Mechanical and Electromechanical Systems*, McGraw-Hill, 1968.

6

Finite Element Formulations Based on Stiffness

The concept underlying the finite element method is the representation of a complex structural system by an assemblage of small but finite elements that are connected at a finite number of discrete points. We thus consider a typical finite element that is formed by overlaying the structure with a system of grid lines, as shown in Fig. 6-1.

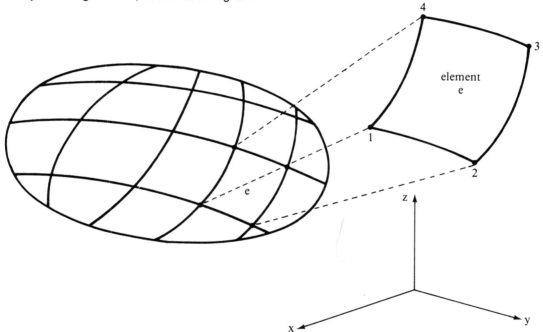

Figure 6-1. Discretization of the Structure

A general element identified as e on the figure will have n nodes. Each of the nodes can be associated with a geometric point that is located at the intersection of two grid lines or three grid planes. We now seek to express the behavior of the element entirely in terms of generalized displacement degrees of freedom and generalized forces defined only at the node points of the element.

6.1. Node Point Displacements and Forces

The finite elements that are used to model structural systems include those that exhibit bending behavior. For this class of elements, it is convenient to define both translational and rotational displacement degrees of freedom. For this reason six degrees of freedom are associated with each node point, as shown in Fig. 6-2a. These degrees of freedom include translations in the three coordinate directions, positive in the sense of the positive coordinate direction, and rotations about the three coordinate axes that are positive using the right-hand rule.

The node point can thus be considered to be a spherical ball joint with six rigid body degrees of freedom. The degrees of freedom at the nodes are then connected by an element, as shown in Fig. 6-1. An element can connect as few as one or as many as six of the degrees of freedom. If elements connect fewer than six degrees of freedom at a node, then the unconnected degrees of freedom do not exist in the formulation and must be purged using techniques discussed in Section 7.5.2.5.

A set of generalized forces is associated with the nodal displacements, as shown in Fig. 6-2b. These generalized forces include three linear forces that act in the sense of the three positive translational displacements and three moments that are positive in the sense of the three angular rotations.

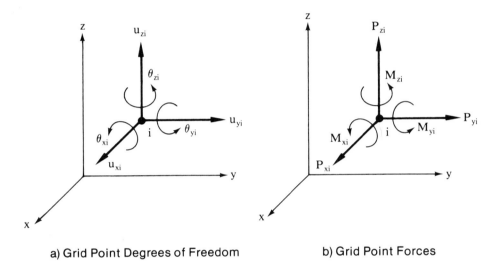

a) Grid Point Degrees of Freedom   b) Grid Point Forces

Figure 6-2. Node Point Displacements and Forces.

6.2.   Displacement Set Notation

The symbol **u** will be used to represent several different sets of displacements. It is always tempting to assume that the meaning of the specific set can be inferred in the context the symbol is being used. This approach has its disadvantages especially when the author is, in the estimation of the reader, being a little obtuse. The NASTRAN notation for sets will therefore be used, where the meaning of the base symbol is defined by a subscript.

The set $\mathbf{u}_i$ is identified as the set of all displacement degrees of freedom at node i where $i = 1, 2,...,N$ and where N is the total number of node points. NASTRAN always assumes six degrees of freedom at a node so that $\mathbf{u}_i$ is a column matrix whose six components are related to the physical degrees of freedom by

$$\mathbf{u}_i = \left\{ \begin{array}{c} u_1 \\ u_2 \\ u_3 \\ u_4 \\ u_5 \\ u_6 \end{array} \right\}_i = \left\{ \begin{array}{c} u_x \\ u_y \\ u_z \\ \theta_x \\ \theta_y \\ \theta_z \end{array} \right\}_i \qquad (6.1)$$

It is convenient to refer to node point degrees of freedom by the numbers one through six at a geometric grid point. Degrees of freedom one through three are taken to be the three linear displacements in the sense of coordinates, and four through six to be angular displacements, positive in the sense of the right-hand rule, in the three coordinate directions.

The set $\mathbf{u}_e$ is the union of all node point displacements for the element e so that

$$\mathbf{u}_e = \begin{Bmatrix} u_1 \\ u_2 \\ \cdot \\ \cdot \\ \cdot \\ u_i \\ \cdot \end{Bmatrix} \tag{6.2}$$

The stiffness formulation of the element behavior is based on a linear relation between node point displacements and node point forces of the form

$$\mathbf{k}_{ee}\,\mathbf{u}_e = \mathbf{P}_e \tag{6.3}$$

where $\mathbf{P}_e$ is the set of all element node point forces. The set of coefficients $\mathbf{k}_{ee}$ is called the elemental stiffness matrix and is defined with respect to a set of local element coordinates.

6.3. Physical Interpretation of Elemental Stiffness

The stiffness coefficients that relate the node point displacements and forces have a physical interpretation which we can establish by considering the beam element shown in Fig. 6-3.

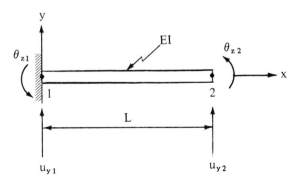

Figure 6-3. Planar Bending Element

The bending behavior of the planar beam element subjected to concentrated forces and moments at the ends is defined by the transverse displacement and rotation of each end of the element. The set of all element degrees of freedom is given by

$$\mathbf{u}_e = \begin{Bmatrix} u_{y1} \\ \theta_{z1} \\ u_{y2} \\ \theta_{z2} \end{Bmatrix} \tag{6.4}$$

95

The stiffness equation (6.3) for the beam element can be written in terms of the nodal forces and displacements as

$$
\begin{bmatrix}
k_{11} & k_{12} & k_{13} & k_{14} \\
k_{21} & k_{22} & k_{23} & k_{24} \\
k_{31} & k_{32} & k_{33} & k_{34} \\
k_{41} & k_{42} & k_{43} & k_{44}
\end{bmatrix}
\begin{Bmatrix}
u_{y1} \\
\theta_{z1} \\
u_{y2} \\
\theta_{z2}
\end{Bmatrix}
=
\begin{Bmatrix}
P_{y1} \\
M_{z1} \\
P_{y2} \\
M_{z2}
\end{Bmatrix}
\tag{6.5}
$$

We now prescribe a set of values for the element displacements such that the transverse displacement at node 1 is equal to unity and all other node point displacement degrees of freedom are set equal to zero. Equation (6.5) then becomes

$$
\begin{bmatrix}
k_{11} & k_{12} & k_{13} & k_{14} \\
k_{21} & k_{22} & k_{23} & k_{24} \\
k_{31} & k_{32} & k_{33} & k_{34} \\
k_{41} & k_{42} & k_{43} & k_{44}
\end{bmatrix}
\begin{Bmatrix}
1 \\
0 \\
0 \\
0
\end{Bmatrix}
=
\begin{Bmatrix}
P_{y1} \\
M_{z1} \\
P_{y2} \\
M_{z2}
\end{Bmatrix}
\tag{6.6}
$$

and we see that the stiffness coefficients in the first column of the stiffness matrix k_{j1} are the forces of constraint associated with the specified set of displacements. The deflected beam shape associated with this set of nodal displacements together with other possible unit displacements are shown in Fig. 6-4, where the forces required to hold the enforced displacement for each case are identified as the stiffness coefficients.

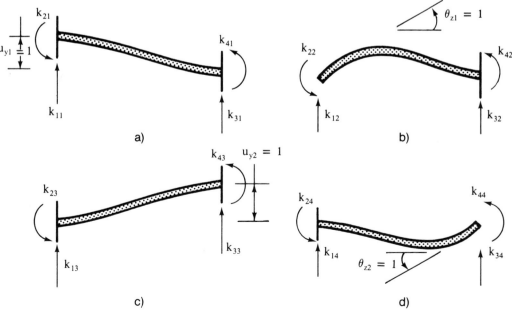

Figure 6-4. Physical Definition of Beam Stiffness Coefficients

The definition of the stiffness coefficient can thus be generalized as

> The stiffness coefficient k_{ij} is the force at and in the direction of degree of freedom i due to a unit displacement of degree of freedom j, with all other displacement degrees of freedom equal to zero.

Stiffness matrices can therefore be obtained for some elements such as the axial rod and the beam by direct methods (Ref. 6-1). While these techniques are not generally applicable to two- and three-dimensional elements, they are based on physical rather than mathematical concepts and thus may be of assistance in understanding the physical concepts involved in the stiffness approach. We will therefore use the direct methods to formulate the element stiffness relation for simple elements in the following sections. We will then describe in succeeding sections a technique that is applicable to all classes of finite elements based on the principle of virtual work.

6.4.   Direct Determination of Element Stiffness

The stiffness coefficients for simple one- and two-dimensional elements can be obtained by direct methods. While the direct methods are generally not applicable to the formulation of two- and three-dimensional elements, it is worthwhile to consider the direct formulation of the widely used axial rod and beam bending elements to show that the stiffness coefficients which are obtained by using the variational approach are the same as those that result from a more direct method.

6.4.1.   The Axial Rod

The axial rod is a one-dimensional element that connects a single degree of freedom at two node points, as shown in Fig. 6-5,

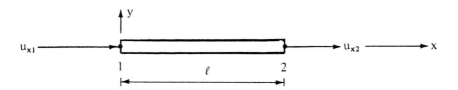

Figure 6-5. Axial Rod Element

The stiffness coefficients for the rod elements are obtained by a direct application of the equations of elasticity. The stress is related to the node point forces at nodes one and two by

$$\sigma_1 \; = \; - \, \frac{P_{x1}}{A} \qquad \sigma_2 \; = \; \frac{P_{x2}}{A} \tag{6.7}$$

where the negative sign in the first of (6.7) is required since a positive stress at end 1 of the rod is in the negative x-direction

The extensional strain in the element is related to node point displacements as

$$e_x \; = \; \frac{(u_{x2} - u_{x1})}{\ell} \tag{6.8}$$

97

6.4.2 The Beam Bending Element

Finally, the stress and strain are related by Hookes law so that

$$\sigma_1 = E\,e_x$$
$$\sigma_2 = E\,e_x$$

(6.9)

The substitution of (6.7) into (6.9) then gives

$$-P_{x1} = \frac{EA}{\ell}\,(u_{x2} - u_{x1})$$
$$P_{x2} = \frac{EA}{\ell}\,(u_{x2} - u_{x1})$$

(6.10)

The set of equations (6.10) can be put into the form of the elemental stiffness relation

$$\frac{AE}{\ell}\begin{bmatrix} 1 & -1 \\ -1 & 1 \end{bmatrix}\begin{Bmatrix} u_{x1} \\ u_{x2} \end{Bmatrix} = \begin{Bmatrix} P_{x1} \\ P_{x2} \end{Bmatrix}$$

(6.11)

6.4.2. The Beam Bending Element

The stiffness coefficients for the beam element shown by Fig. 6-3 can be obtained by direct solution of the differential equation that governs beam bending behavior

$$EI\,\frac{d^4 v}{dx^4} = p(x)$$

(6.12)

where

I   Moment of inertia of the cross-section

$v(x)$ Transverse displacement of the beam neutral axis in the y-direction

$p(x)$ Distributed load along the beam.

The stiffness coefficients for the beam element where shown to be the forces associated with the sets of deflection shapes shown by Fig. 6-4. This set of node point displacements can also be interpreted as boundary conditions for (6.12). The stiffness coefficients can then be obtained by

1. Solving (6.12) with each of the four sets of boundary conditions with $p(x) = 0$ to obtain an appropriate deflection function

2. Determining the moment and shear as

$$M = EI \frac{d^2 v}{dx^2} \tag{6.13}$$

$$V = -\frac{dM}{dx} \tag{6.14}$$

3. Evaluating M and V at the ends of the beam

4. Relating the beam moment and shear to the generalized node point forces.

To illustrate the implementation of this technique, we will obtain the set of stiffness coefficients associated with the deflection function shown in Fig. 6-4a. The general solution to the homogeneous beam equation (6.12) is a cubic polynomial

$$v(x) = a + bx + cx^2 + dx^3 \tag{6.15}$$

The polynomial coefficients can be determined from the four boundary conditions that can be expressed in functional form as

$$v(0) = 1$$
$$v(\ell) = 0$$
$$\frac{dv}{dx}(0) = 0 \tag{6.16}$$
$$\frac{dv}{dx}(\ell) = 0$$

that leads to the deflection function for the set of boundary conditions

$$v(x) = 1 - \frac{3x^2}{\ell^2} + \frac{2x^3}{\ell^3} \tag{6.17}$$

The moment and shear are then obtained by substituting (6.17) into (6.13) and (6.14) to give

6.4.2 The Beam Bending Element

$$M(x) = \left[-\frac{6}{\ell^2} + \frac{12x}{\ell^3} \right] EI \qquad (6.18)$$

$$V(x) = -\frac{12}{\ell^3} EI \qquad (6.19)$$

The shears and moments at the ends of the beam are then found to be

$$M_1 = M(0) = -\frac{6}{\ell^2} EI$$

$$M_2 = M(\ell) = \frac{6}{\ell^2} EI$$

$$V_1 = V_2 = \frac{12}{\ell^3} EI$$

These shears and moments are the element forces that result from the specified set of boundary conditions and are related to node point forces by

$$M_{z1} = -M_1 \qquad\qquad P_{y1} = -V_1$$

$$M_{z2} = M_2 \qquad\qquad P_{y2} = V_1$$

so that the associated stiffness coefficients are

$$k_{11} = \frac{12}{\ell^3} , \qquad k_{13} = -\frac{12}{\ell^3} , \qquad k_{12} = \frac{6}{\ell^2} , \qquad k_{14} = \frac{6}{\ell^2}$$

The entire set of stiffness coefficients could then be determined by considering the remaining three sets of boundary conditions. The resulting stiffness equation for the beam element is then found to be

$$\mathbf{k}_{ee} = \frac{2EI}{\ell^3} \begin{bmatrix} 6 & 3\ell & -6 & 3\ell \\ 3\ell & 2\ell^2 & -3\ell & \ell^2 \\ -6 & -3\ell & 6 & -3\ell \\ 3\ell & \ell^2 & -3\ell & 2\ell^2 \end{bmatrix} \qquad (6.20)$$

6.5. Variational Formulation Based on Assumed Displacements

The direct methods of obtaining element stiffness equations are of limited use. A general method of obtaining element equations is based on the principle of virtual work that was presented in Sec. 5.1.5. The virtual work expression that is appropriate for the development of the element stiffness equations is

$$- \int_{V_{o\ell}} \sigma_e^T \; \delta e_e \; dV_{o\ell} + \int_{V_{o\ell}} X_e^T \; \delta v_e \; dV_{o\ell} + \int_A T_e^T \; \delta v_e \; dA + P_e^T \delta u_e = 0 \qquad (6.21)$$

where

P_e Generalized external forces acting at the node points.

σ_e Set of stresses in the element.

e_e Set of strains in the element.

X_e Set of body forces.

T_e Set of surface tractions.

The principle of virtual work then states that among all possible displacements that satisfy the kinematic constraints, the set that satisfies the variational condition (6.21) also satisfies equilibrium.

6.6. Approximate Displacement Function

The true displacement state for the element would lead to a stationary value of the virtual work expression (6.21) and would satisfy the following conditions:

1. Equilibrium conditions in the interior

2. Inter-element equilibrium

3. Continuity of the displacements and displacement derivatives.

The functions that are used to represent the element displacement will be approximate in most cases so that not all the above requirements will be satisfied. We will proceed by choosing approximation functions to represent the element displacement in terms of generalized degrees of freedom.

Allowable displacement functions must satisfy the criteria (Ref. 6-2)

1. The strain energy associated with a rigid body displacement is equal to zero.

2. The strain state must include all the constant strain components.

3. The strains at the element boundaries must be finite.

Consider an axial rod shown in Fig. 6-5 as a simple example. It is assumed that the displacement varies linearly over the length of the rod. The linear displacement function can then be written in terms of the axial displacement of the node points as

$$v_x = (1 - \frac{x}{\ell}) u_1 + \frac{x}{\ell} u_2 \tag{6.22}$$

or in matrix form

$$v_x = N u \tag{6.23}$$

where

$$N = [(1 - \frac{x}{\ell}) \frac{x}{\ell}] \qquad ; \qquad u = [u_{x1} \; u_{x2}]^T \tag{6.24}$$

This approach can be generalized for an arbitrary element by assuming that the displacement of any point in the element is given in the form

$$v_e = N_e \, u_e \tag{6.25}$$

where v_e is the displacement vector for element.

$$v_e = \begin{Bmatrix} v_x\,(x) \\ v_y\,(x) \\ v_z\,(x) \end{Bmatrix} \tag{6.26}$$

and where u_e is the set of all node point degrees of freedom.

The number of degrees of freedom at a node point depends on the type of behavior to be represented. A number of different types of elements are shown in Fig. 6-6 that require from one to six degrees of freedom at a node to describe their behavior.

The number of rows and columns of N is clearly dependent on the type of elemental behavior represented. The number of rows of N is equal to the number of components of the displacement vector, and the number of columns is equal to n times the number of degrees of freedom at each node where n is the number of nodes. The shape functions N may be obtained in a systematic manner using the techniques discussed in Chapter Eight.

At this time we assume that shape functions can be found that are appropriate to the specific element. The representation of displacements throughout the element in terms of nodal displacements is then given by equation (6.25). An equation governing the element behavior is then obtained by using the variational expression (6.21). We proceed by representing the strain-displacement relations in matrix form as

$$e_e = D \, v_e \tag{6.27}$$

where D is a matrix of differential operators.

The linear strain-displacement relations (4.23) are expressed in extended notation as

$$\begin{Bmatrix} e_{xx} \\ e_{yy} \\ e_{zz} \\ e_{xy} \\ e_{yz} \\ e_{zx} \end{Bmatrix} = \begin{bmatrix} \partial/\partial x & 0 & 0 \\ 0 & \partial/\partial y & 0 \\ 0 & 0 & \partial/\partial z \\ \partial/\partial y & \partial/\partial x & 0 \\ 0 & \partial/\partial z & \partial/\partial y \\ \partial/\partial z & 0 & \partial/\partial x \end{bmatrix} \begin{Bmatrix} v_x \\ v_y \\ v_z \end{Bmatrix} \tag{6.28}$$

so the D matrix is, for three-dimensional behavior,

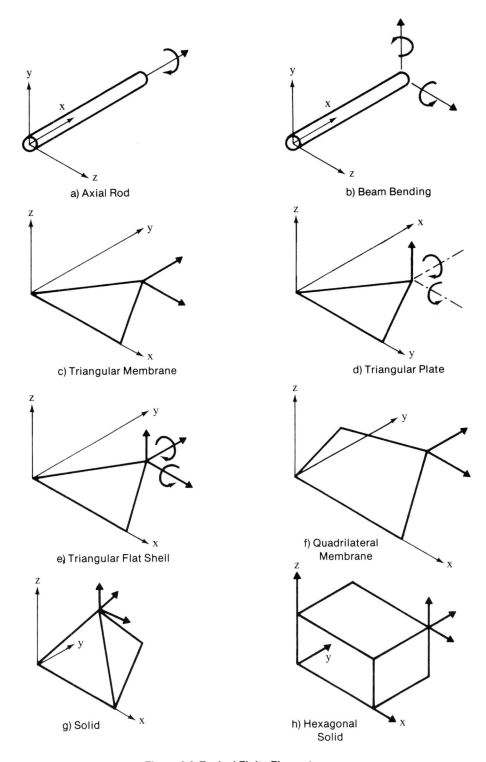

a) Axial Rod

b) Beam Bending

c) Triangular Membrane

d) Triangular Plate

e) Triangular Flat Shell

f) Quadrilateral Membrane

g) Solid

h) Hexagonal Solid

Figure 6-6. Typical Finite Elements

$$D = \begin{bmatrix} \partial/\partial x & 0 & 0 \\ 0 & \partial/\partial y & 0 \\ 0 & 0 & \partial/\partial z \\ \partial/\partial y & \partial/\partial x & 0 \\ 0 & \partial/\partial z & \partial/\partial y \\ \partial/\partial z & 0 & \partial/\partial x \end{bmatrix} \qquad (6.29)$$

The strains can be expressed in terms of the generalized displacements by using the approximate displacement functions (6.25), which leads to

$$e_e = D(N_e u_e) \qquad (6.30)$$

The node point degrees of freedom are not functions of position so that the differential operator operates only on N_e to give

$$e_e = DN_e u_e \qquad (6.31)$$

or

$$e_e = b_e u_e \qquad (6.32)$$

where

$$b_e = D N_e \qquad (6.33)$$

The admissible variations in strain must satisfy the approximate strain-displacement relations so that

$$\delta v_e = N_e \delta u_e \qquad (6.34)$$

and

$$\delta e_e = b_e \delta u_e \qquad (6.35)$$

The use of the approximate displacement function thus allows the variations in displacement and strains to be expressed in terms of the variation of the generalized node point degrees of freedom. In order to complete the variational formulation, the stress must be expressed in terms of the generalized displacements.

The stress-displacement relationship may be obtained by assuming that the material is linearly elastic. The stress-strain relationship is given by equations (4.73) so that

$$\sigma_e = E_e (e_e - e_{eI}) \qquad (6.36)$$

where

E_e is the matrix of elastic constants for the element

and

e_{eI} is the set of initial strains in the element

The substitution of the approximate strain-displacement relation (6.32) into the constitutive relations (6.36) then gives

$$\sigma_e = E_e \, (b_e \, u_e - e_{eI}) \tag{6.37}$$

The equations governing element behavior are then obtained by substituting the expressions for the stress and strain into the variational expression (6.21) to give

$$- \int_{V_{o\ell}} \left[u_e^T b_e^T E_e - e_{el}^T E_e \right] b_e \, \delta u_e \, dV_{o\ell} + \int_{V_{o\ell}} X_e^T N_e \, \delta u_e \, dV_{o\ell} + \int_A T_e^T N_e \, \delta u_e \, dA + P_e^T \delta u_e = 0 \tag{6.38}$$

or

$$\left\{ - u_e^T \int_{V_{o\ell}} b_e^T E_e \, b_e \, dV_{o\ell} + \int_{V_{o\ell}} X_e^T N_e \, dV_{o\ell} + \int_{V_{o\ell}} e_{el}^T E_e \, b_e \, dV_{o\ell} + \int_A T_e^T N_e \, dA + P_e^T \right\} \delta u_e = 0 \tag{6.39}$$

Since the variation of node point displacements is completely arbitrary, it follows that the coefficient matrix must vanish. The equilibrium equations for the element are thus given by

$$k_{ee} \, u_e = P_e + P_{ex} + P_{es} + P_{eI} \tag{6.40}$$

where the stiffness matrix is given by

$$k_{ee} = \int_{V_{o\ell}} b_e^T E_e \, b_e \, dV_{o\ell} \tag{6.41}$$

and where the generalized forces are

$$P_{ex} = \int_{V_{o\ell}} N_e^T X_e \, dV_{o\ell} \tag{6.42}$$

$$P_{es} = \int_A N_e^T T_e \, dA \tag{6.43}$$

$$P_{eI} = \int_{V_{o\ell}} b_e^T E_e \, e_{eI} \, dV_{o\ell} \tag{6.44}$$

The generalized forces defined above are called the work equivalent forces because they will produce the same amount of virtual work as the distributed forces.

6.7. The Elemental Stiffness Matrix

The stiffness matrix for an element is given by equation (6.41). The evaluation of the stiffness is simply a matter of integrating over the volume of the element once the shape functions N have been defined. The technique is illustrated in following sections by considering the rod and beam elements.

6.7.1. The Axial Rod Element

The displacement function of the axial rod shown by Fig. 6-2 is given by the linear interpolation function defined by (6.22). The quantities required in the variational expression are

6.7.2   The Beam Element

$$\sigma = \{\sigma_{xx}\} \qquad ; \qquad e = \{e_{xx}\} \qquad ; \quad E = E$$

and

$$v = \{v_x\}$$

The matrix of differential coefficients is seen to be

$$D = \frac{\partial}{\partial x}$$

so the **b** matrix is then given by

$$b = D N = \frac{\partial}{\partial x} \lfloor (1 - \tfrac{x}{\ell}) \quad \tfrac{x}{\ell} \rfloor$$

or

$$b = \lfloor -\tfrac{1}{\ell} \quad \tfrac{1}{\ell} \rfloor$$

The stiffness matrix is obtained from (6.41) as

$$k_{ee} = AE \int b^T b \, dx$$

or

$$k_{ee} = \frac{AE}{\ell} \begin{bmatrix} 1 & -1 \\ -1 & 1 \end{bmatrix} \tag{6.45}$$

The equilibrium equation for the rod element then becomes

$$\frac{AE}{\ell} \begin{bmatrix} 1 & -1 \\ -1 & 1 \end{bmatrix} \begin{Bmatrix} u_{x1} \\ u_{x2} \end{Bmatrix} = \begin{Bmatrix} P_{x1} \\ P_{x2} \end{Bmatrix}$$

If the rod is constrained by setting u_{x1} equal to zero, then it follows from the equilibrium equations that

$$\frac{AE}{\ell} u_{x2} = P_{x2}$$

which is the well-known expression for the axial displacement of a rod. The stiffness matrix for the rod element is thus seen to lead to the exact solution.

6.7.2.   The Beam Element

The beam element is shown in Fig. 6-7. The principle moments of inertia for the cross-section coincide with the y- and z-axes. The beam is located by concentrated forces and moments at the ends so that bending will take place in only the x,z-plane.

The axial displacement for the beam is assumed to vary linearly over the cross-section so that

$$v_x = z\theta_{yo} \tag{6.46}$$

where θ_{yo} is the slope of the neutral axis of the beam. The slope is defined in terms of the displacement function as

$$\theta_{yo} = -\frac{dv_{zo}}{dx} \tag{6.47}$$

where v_{zo} is the transverse displacement of the neutral axis. The axial strain is then given by

106

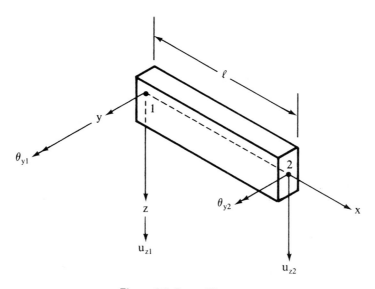

Figure 6-7. Beam Element

$$e_{xx} = -z \frac{d^2 v_{zo}}{dx^2} \tag{6.48}$$

The axial stress and strain are assumed to be the only nonzero components so that the strain energy is given by

$$U = \int_0^\ell EI \left[\frac{d^2 v_{zo}}{dx^2} \right]^2 dx \tag{6.49}$$

where I is the moment of inertia of the cross-section.

The transverse displacement is expressed in terms of the node point degrees of freedom as

$$v_{zo} = N_e u_e$$

so that the strain energy can be expressed by

$$U = \tfrac{1}{2} u_e^T \int_0^\ell b_e^T E \, b_e \, u_e \, dx \tag{6.50}$$

where $E = EI$ and

$$b_e = \frac{d^2}{dx_2} N_e \tag{6.51}$$

The shape functions are obtained by assuming that the transverse displacement is a cubic polynomial:

$$v_{zo} = a_o + a_1 x + a_2 x^2 + a_3 x^3 \tag{6.52}$$

The polynomial coefficients can be expressed in terms of nodal degrees of freedom by noting that

6.7.2 The Beam Element

The polynomial coefficients can be expressed in terms of nodal degrees of freedom by noting that

$$v_z(0) \quad = u_{z1} \quad = a_0$$

$$v_z(\ell) \quad = u_{z2} \quad = a_0 + a_1\ell + a_2\ell^2 + a_3\ell^3$$

(6.53)

$$-\frac{dv_z}{dx}(0) = \theta_{y1} \quad = -a_1$$

$$-\frac{dv_z}{dx}(\ell) = \theta_{y2} \quad = -(a_1 + 2a_2\ell + 3a_3\ell^3)$$

After some algebraic manipulation, the transverse displacement can be expressed in terms of the generalized node point displacements as

$$v_{zo} = \mathbf{N_e}\,\mathbf{u_e}$$

(6.54)

where

$$\mathbf{u_e} = \begin{Bmatrix} u_1 \\ u_2 \\ u_3 \\ u_4 \end{Bmatrix} = \begin{Bmatrix} u_{z1} \\ \theta_{y1} \\ u_{z2} \\ \theta_{y2} \end{Bmatrix}$$

where $\mathbf{N_e}$ is a row matrix of the form

$$\mathbf{N_e} = \lfloor N_1 \quad N_2 \quad N_3 \quad N_4 \rfloor$$

(6.55)

and where the elements are defined by

$$N_1 = \left(1 - \frac{3x^2}{\ell^2} + \frac{2x^3}{\ell^3}\right) \qquad\qquad N_3 = \left(\frac{3x^2}{\ell^2} - \frac{2x^3}{\ell^3}\right)$$

(6.56)

$$N_2 = -x\left(1 - \frac{2x}{\ell} + \frac{x^2}{\ell^2}\right) \qquad\qquad N_4 = x\left(\frac{x}{\ell} - \frac{x^2}{\ell^2}\right)$$

The stiffness matrix can now be obtained by evaluating the **b** matrix, which is

$$b = \left\lfloor \left(-\frac{6}{\ell^2} + \frac{12x}{\ell^3}\right) \quad \left(-\frac{6x}{\ell^2} + \frac{4}{\ell}\right) \quad \left(\frac{6}{\ell^2} - \frac{12x}{\ell^3}\right) \quad \left(\frac{2}{\ell} - \frac{6x}{\ell^2}\right) \right\rfloor$$

(6.57)

The stiffness matrix for a beam with constant area and material properties along the length is then defined in terms of the coefficients of **b** as

$$\mathbf{k_{ee}} = \int_0^\ell EI \begin{bmatrix} b_1^2 & b_1b_2 & b_1b_3 & b_1b_4 \\ b_2b_1 & b_2^2 & b_2b_3 & b_2b_4 \\ b_3b_1 & b_3b_2 & b_3^2 & b_3b_4 \\ b_4b_1 & b_4b_2 & b_4b_3 & b_4^2 \end{bmatrix}$$

(6.58)

108

These expressions are then integrated over the length of the beam to give the stiffness coefficients

$$k_{ee} = \frac{2EI}{\ell^3} \begin{bmatrix} 6 & -3\ell & -6 & -3\ell \\ -3\ell & 2\ell^2 & 3\ell & \ell^2 \\ -6 & 3\ell & 6 & 3\ell \\ -3\ell & \ell^2 & 3\ell & 2\ell^2 \end{bmatrix} \qquad (6.59)$$

This set of stiffness coefficients is defined for the beam bending in the x,z-plane. If bending takes place in the x,y-plane, then the node point degrees of freedom would be u_{yi} and θ_{zi}, and the previous results would have to be modified to account for the fact that the slope of the beam and the rotation have the same sign.

6.8.   Work Equivalent Forces

The distributed forces that act over the surface of the element must be represented as discrete node point forces and moments. The two methods for discretizing the distributed applied loads are

1. The work equivalent formulation

2. Ad hoc lumping

The work equivalent formulation is defined by equations (6.42) through (6.44). The shape functions N_e are employed to obtain the set of concentrated forces that will produce the same amount of virtual work as the distributed forces.

Ad hoc lumping, on the other hand, is associated with the use of simple rules for distributing the total applied load to the node points. It would appear that the work equivalent loads should be used since they are correct from a work and energy point-of-view. In fact, however, in many applications the lumped mass approach is used because it gives adequate results and is less costly.

6.8.1.   Work Equivalent Forces for Beam Element

Consider the beam element with the distributed load shown in Fig. 6-8.

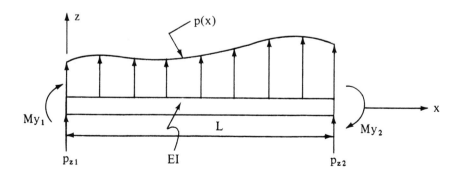

Figure 6-8. Beam Element with Distributed Loading

An ad hoc technique for distributing the load would be that of calculating the nodal forces such that they produce the same moment and force as the actual distributed load. From equilibrium considerations, it follows that

$$P_{z1} + P_{z2} = \int_0^\ell p_z(x)\, dx \qquad (6.60)$$

$$-M_{y1} - M_{y2} + P_{z2}\,\ell = \int_0^\ell x\, p_z(x)\, dx \qquad (6.61)$$

Since there are only two equations that the nodal forces must satisfy, we can choose any criteria that seems to make sense to allow the determination of all the lumped forces. The most expeditious choice is that of setting the nodal moments to zero. This choice would result in the application of one-half the total applied load at each of the grid points for the case of a uniformly distributed load.

The work equivalent forces associated with the distributed load on the beam are calculated by (6.43), which is repeated here:

$$P_{es} = \int_0^\ell N_e^T\, T_e\, dA$$

The shape functions for the beam are given by equations (6.56) so that the work equivalent forces become

$$P_{es} = \int_0^\ell p(x) \begin{Bmatrix} N_1(x) \\ N_2(x) \\ N_3(x) \\ N_4(x) \end{Bmatrix} dx$$

It is interesting to compare the set of lumped forces with the work equivalent forces for the case of a uniformly distributed load. The lumped forces are found to be

$$P_e = \begin{Bmatrix} \dfrac{p_0\ell}{2} \\ 0 \\ \dfrac{p_0\ell}{2} \\ 0 \end{Bmatrix} \qquad (6.63)$$

while the work equivalent forces are given by

$$P_{es} = \begin{Bmatrix} \dfrac{p_0\ell}{2} \\ -\dfrac{p_0\ell^2}{12} \\ \dfrac{p_0\ell}{2} \\ \dfrac{p_0\ell^2}{12} \end{Bmatrix} \qquad (6.64)$$

110

The work equivalent forces for a uniformly loaded beam thus include nodal moments as well as nodal forces. The relative accuracy of the two formulations can be evaluated by comparing the predicted tip deflections for both the lumped and work equivalent formulations with the exact results for a uniformly loaded cantilever beam. The deflections at the tip are obtained using the stiffness matrix for the beam element, which results in the expression

$$\left\{ \begin{array}{c} u_{z2} \\ \theta_{y2} \end{array} \right\} = \frac{\ell}{6EI} \left[\begin{array}{cc} 2\ell^2 & -3\ell \\ -3\ell & 6 \end{array} \right] \left\{ \begin{array}{c} P_{z2} \\ M_{y2} \end{array} \right\}$$

The lumped formulation then gives a tip deflection of

$$\left(u_{z2} \right)_L = \frac{p_0 \ell^4}{6EI}$$

while the work equivalent formulation gives

$$\left(u_{z2} \right)_{WE} = \frac{p_0 \ell^3}{8EI}$$

which is the same as the exact solution for the tip deflection of a uniformly loaded cantilever beam.

We see, then, that the use of work equivalent loads for this particular case leads to the same node point displacements which are predicted by the exact solution. The displacements predicted by the lumped formulation, on the other hand, are 33 percent greater than the exact solution.

We can make two observations based on the comparison of the displacements for the lumped and work equivalent formulations.

1. The displacements for the lumped formulation are too large. At first this may seem surprising because, by definition, an approximate solution based on assumed displacements using an energy-based approach should too stiff. This seems to imply that the approximate displacement should be less than the exact solution. However, this expected convergence characteristic depends on the use of a consistent formulation, i.e. the use of work equivalent forces.

2. The displacements predicted by the work equivalent formulation are closer to the exact result than those predicted by the lumped formulation.

We can generalize these observations to the following rule for good modeling practice.

The work equivalent forces are always to be preferred for *straight* beams and *flat* plates.

Work equivalent forces for uniformly loaded MSC/NASTRAN bend elements are generated by the PLOAD1 Bulk Data card (Sec. 11.3.).

Several authors have noted that when straight beam elements are used to model curved arches and/or when flat plate elements are used to model curved surfaces the use of work equivalent loads leads to significant errors when compared to the lumped formulation (see Ref. 2.1, for example). For these cases the lumped formulation should thus be used.

6.9. The Element Mass Matrix

The stiffness equation for the finite element given by equation (6.40) was derived for static loads. The set of static equations can be extended to include inertial effects by using D'Alembert's principle. D'Alembert recognized the simple fact that the equations of motion for a particle can be written as

6.9 The Element Mass Matrix

$$\mathbf{F} - \mathbf{m}\mathbf{a} = 0 \qquad (6.65)$$

where $\mathbf{a}$ is the acceleration of the particle and m is its mass. The negative inertia force is therefore included in the expression for the distributed body force to obtain the dynamic equilibrium equations. The work of the distributed body forces included in (6.21) is then written as

$$\delta W_x = \int_{V_{o\ell}} \widetilde{\mathbf{X}}_e^T \delta \mathbf{v}_e dV_{o\ell} \qquad (6.66)$$

where

$$\widetilde{\mathbf{X}}_e = \mathbf{X}_e - \rho \frac{d^2\mathbf{v}}{dt^2} \qquad (6.67)$$

$\mathbf{X}$ Time-dependent body forces
ρ Mass density per unit volume
$\frac{d^2\mathbf{v}}{dt^2}$ Acceleration

The substitution of (6.67) into (6.62) then gives

$$\delta W_x = \int_{V_{o\ell}} \mathbf{X}_e^T \delta \mathbf{v}_e dV_{o\ell} - \int_{V_{o\ell}} \rho \frac{d^2\mathbf{v}_e}{dt^2} \qquad (6.68)$$

It is now assumed that the solution for the displacements can be represented in separable form as

$$\frac{d^2}{dt^2}(\mathbf{v}_e) = \mathbf{N}_e(\mathbf{x}) \frac{d^2}{dt^2}\mathbf{u}_e(t) \qquad (6.69)$$

The virtual work of the external forces is then obtained by substituting the approximate displacement functions into the expressions for the work equivalent forces to obtain

$$\delta W_x = \left\{ \int_{V_{o\ell}} \mathbf{X}_e^T \mathbf{N}_e dV_{o\ell} - \frac{d^2}{dt^2}(\mathbf{u}_e^T) \int_{V_{o\ell}} \mathbf{N}_e^T \rho \, \mathbf{N}_e dV_{o\ell} \right\} \delta \mathbf{u}_e \qquad (6.70)$$

or

$$\delta W_x = \left\{ \mathbf{P}_{ex}^T - \ddot{\mathbf{u}}_e^T \, \mathbf{m}_{ee} \right\} \delta \mathbf{u}_e \qquad (6.71)$$

where $\mathbf{P}_{ex}$ is defined by equation (6.42) and where the elemental mass matrix $\mathbf{m}_{ee}$ is given by

$$\mathbf{m}_{ee} = \int_{V_{o\ell}} \mathbf{N}_e^T \rho \mathbf{N}_e \, dV_{o\ell} \qquad (6.72)$$

The equilibrium equation (6.40) then becomes

$$\mathbf{m}_{ee} \, \ddot{\mathbf{u}}_e + \mathbf{k}_{ee} \mathbf{u}_e = \mathbf{P}_e(t) + \mathbf{P}_{ex}(t) + \mathbf{P}_{es}(t) + \mathbf{P}_{eI}(t) \qquad (6.73)$$

The mass matrix defined by (6.72) is called the consistent mass matrix because it is defined using a consistent energy formulation. We see from equation (6.71) that the work done by concentrated inertia forces calculated using the consistent mass matrix is the same as the work done by the distributed inertia forces. The consistent mass matrix in conjunction with node point accelerations thus produce work equivalent inertia forces.

A lumped mass matrix may also be defined using the same ad hoc lumping criteria that were used to lump the distributed forces. The mass formulation to be preferred is by no means obvious. NASTRAN generally allows the user a choice of using either consistent or lumped formulations, with the default being the lumped formulation.

6.10.   References

6-1   Gallagher, R. H., *Finite Element Analysis: Fundamental*, Prentice Hall, 1975, pp. 108-134.

6-2   Zienkiewicz, O. C., *The Finite Element Method in Engineering Science*, Second Edition, McGraw-Hill, 1971, pp. 28-29.

7

Global Analysis Procedures

A structural system is composed of a collection of structural members that are attached to each other in some defined way. The purpose of this chapter is to consider those operations that lead to the global stiffness matrix, together with all operations that are performed on the global stiffness matrix. These operations include the specification of constraints, partitioning, and flexibility-stiffness transformations.

7.1.   The Global Stiffness Matrix

A technique was developed in Chapter Six for obtaining a set of algebraic equations that relate the element degrees of freedom and the element forces in the form

$$\mathbf{k}_{ee}\,\mathbf{u}_e \,=\, \mathbf{P}_e \tag{7.1}$$

where $\mathbf{P}_e$ includes all external forces that act on the element. We now look ahead to Section 7.4 and define $\mathbf{u}_g$ as the set of all displacement degrees of freedom in the structural system. The $\mathbf{u}_g$ set (the g-set) is called the set of all grid point degrees of freedom in NASTRAN. The element e provides connectivity to a subset of the $\mathbf{u}_g$ degrees of freedom so that the element degrees of freedom $\mathbf{u}_e$ can be expressed in terms of $\mathbf{u}_g$ as

$$\mathbf{u}_e \,=\, \mathbf{B}_{eg}\,\mathbf{u}_g \tag{7.2}$$

where $\mathbf{B}_{eg}$ is an e-by-g matrix whose elements are either one or zero.

Consider the structure shown by Fig. 7-1 where the structural system is composed of six triangular elements that connect the seven node points.

If we assume, for purposes of explanation, that there is a single degree of freedom of each node, then the g-set is given by

$$\mathbf{u}_g \,=\, \begin{bmatrix} u_1\,u_2\,u_3\,u_4\,u_5\,u_6\,u_7 \end{bmatrix}^T \tag{7.3}$$

The set of displacement degrees of freedom connected by element one includes displacements at nodes one, two, and seven so that

$$\mathbf{u}_1 \,=\, \left\{ \begin{matrix} u_1 \\ u_2 \\ u_7 \end{matrix} \right\} \,=\, \begin{bmatrix} 1 & 0 & 0 & 0 & 0 & 0 & 0 \\ 0 & 1 & 0 & 0 & 0 & 0 & 0 \\ 0 & 0 & 0 & 0 & 0 & 0 & 1 \end{bmatrix} \mathbf{u}_g$$

7.1.1 Energy-Based Approach

Transformations of this kind are called Boolean Transformations.

The global stiffness may now be defined using either an energy or a direct approach. Both methods will be described in following sections.

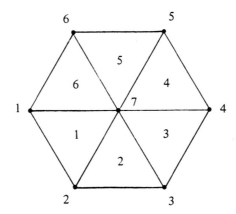

Figure 7-1. Idealized Structure

7.1.1. Energy-Based Approach

The internal energy in the structural system is equal to the sum of the internal energy in each of the elements so that

$$\delta U_g = \delta U_1 + \delta U_2 + \cdots + \delta U_e + \cdots + \delta U_N \tag{7.4}$$

where δU_e (e = 1,2,...,n) is the virtual work of the internal forces in element e and δU_g is the virtual work of the internal forces in the entire system. The virtual work of the internal forces can be expressed in terms of the appropriate stiffness so that (7.4) can be written as

$$\delta u_g^T K_{gg} u_g = \delta u_1^T k_{11} u_1 + \delta u_2^T k_{22} u_2 + \cdots + \delta u_N^T k_{NN} u_N \tag{7.5}$$

The element displacements must satisfy the set of transformations defined by (7.2) so that (7.5) becomes

$$\delta u_g^T K_{gg} u_g = \delta u_g^T \left\{ B_{1g}^T k_{11} B_{1g} + B_{2g}^T k_{22} B_{2g} + \cdots + B_{Ng}^T k_{NN} B_{Ng} \right\} u_g$$

where the global stiffness matrix can be seen by inspection to be

$$k_{gg} = \sum_{e=1}^{N} B_{eg}^T k_{ee} B_{eg} \tag{7.6}$$

116

The effect of the transformation defined by (7.6) is to expand each of the $\mathbf{k}_{ee}$-matrices from e-size (i.e., a packed matrix of order specified by the number of degrees of freedom for the element) to g-size. The stiffness coefficients are not changed. They are just placed in appropriate rows and columns of a matrix of order given by the total number of degrees of freedom. The resulting g-size elemental stiffness matrices are then added to obtain the global stiffness matrix $\mathbf{K}_{gg}$.

Consider the expansion of the stiffness matrix for element two of the structural system shown in Fig. 7-1. The application of the transformation defined by (7.6) leads to

$$\mathbf{B}_{2g}^T\,\mathbf{k}_{22}\,\mathbf{B}_{2g} = \begin{bmatrix} 0 & 0 & 0 & 0 & 0 & 0 & 0 \\ 0 & k_{22} & k_{23} & 0 & 0 & 0 & k_{27} \\ 0 & k_{32} & k_{33} & 0 & 0 & 0 & k_{37} \\ 0 & 0 & 0 & 0 & 0 & 0 & 0 \\ 0 & 0 & 0 & 0 & 0 & 0 & 0 \\ 0 & 0 & 0 & 0 & 0 & 0 & 0 \\ 0 & k_{72} & k_{73} & 0 & 0 & 0 & k_{77} \end{bmatrix}_2$$

where the subscript on the expanded matrix is used to indicate the element number. Now that we have seen the consequences of the transformation (7.6) an algorithm can be defined for generating the global stiffness coefficients without formally performing the matrix multiplications. The procedure is

1. Generate the stiffness coefficients for the element $\mathbf{k}_{ee}$ in terms of element degrees of freedom.

2. Relate element degrees of freedom to global degrees of freedom and identify the rows and columns of the element matrix in terms of global degrees of freedom.

3. Add all elemental stiffness coefficients with the same row and column designations.

7.1.2.   Direct Formulation of Global Stiffness

In the direct approach, we specify that

1. The displacements at a node joined by two or more elements are compatible.

2. The forces at a nodal degree of freedom are in equilibrium.

The use of the transformation (7.2) to represent element degrees of freedom in terms of global degrees of freedom will guarantee that the displacements of all elements with a common node will have the same displacement at that node.

For the equilibrium of the force associated with the jth degree of freedom, we consider the node associated with degree of freedom i as shown by Fig. 7-2.

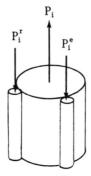

Figure 7-2. Free-Body of Degree of Freedom

117

7.1.2   Direct Formulation of Global Stiffness

The external force P_i acting on the degree of freedom is the ith element of the set of external forces P_g that are associated with the g-set. The forces P_i^e and P_i^r are the element forces acting in the direction of the ith degree of freedom on elements e and r. The element forces produce equal and opposite forces at the node so that the nodal equilibrium equation is

$$P_i = \sum_e P_i^e \tag{7.7}$$

where the summation is taken over all elements that are connected to degree of freedom i.

The equilibrium equation can be written in terms of the stiffness coefficients by noting that

$$P_i^e = \sum_{j=1}^{g} k_{ij}^e \, u_j^g \tag{7.8}$$

where the coefficients of the elemental stiffness matrix are imbedded in a matrix of order g and u_j^g is the jth element of the g-set. The substitution of (7.8) into (7.7) gives

$$P_i^g = \sum_e \left(\sum_{j=1}^{g} k_{ij}^e \, u_j^g \right) \tag{7.9}$$

The order of performing the summations can be interchanged so that (7.9) can be written as

$$P_i^g = \sum_{j=1}^{g} \left(\sum_e k_{ij}^e \, u_j^g \right) \tag{7.10}$$

The relation holds for every degree of freedom so that

$$\mathbf{P}_g = \mathbf{K}_{gg} \, \mathbf{u}_g \tag{7.11}$$

where

$$\mathbf{K}_{gg} = \sum_{e=1}^{N} \mathbf{K}_{gg}^e \tag{7.12}$$

The global stiffness matrices given by (7.12) and (7.6) are equal so that the variational and direct methods are equivalent techniques for generating the global stiffness coefficients for the elemental stiffness coefficients.

7.1.3.   Alternative Computing Strategies

An algorithm for generating the global stiffness matrix may be based on two tables that can be developed using element connectivity data. These tables are the

1. Gridpoint connection table, which defines the grid points that are elastically coupled to a pivotal point, i.e. degrees of freedom on the diagonal of the stiffness matrix through the elements which connect the points.

2. Element connection table, which defines the elements that connect a pivotal point.

Nonzero terms in the global stiffness matrix will occur at the pivotal points and at the grid points that are elastically coupled to the pivotal point. The grid point connection table thus defines the topology of the stiffness matrix.

The algorithm then proceeds by considering each of the pivotal grid points in turn. The element table defines all the elements connected to the grid point. The element stiffness for each degree of freedom is obtained by using the technique described in the previous section.

There are two alternatives for obtaining the element stiffness matrices:

1. Initially calculate each stiffness matrix for retrieval as required.

2. Recalculate the stiffness coefficients as required.

If the cost of recalculating the stiffness matrices is low and the cost of using mass storage is high, it makes sense to recalculate. This was the state of affairs when NASTRAN was developed and is the technique that was adopted in that program. In the intervening years we have seen the almost standard use of higher order elements and the availability of inexpensive high speed mass storage. It is now expensive to calculate the elemental stiffness for many elements but the cost of mass storage is relatively low.

The computing strategy in MSC/NASTRAN and in COSMIC/NASTRAN level 16 has been changed to the calculate-and-store method rather than recalculate as is done in earlier COSMIC releases. The incorporation of higher order elements into COSMIC releases prior to level 16 will lead to high computer costs for stiffness generation unless the stiffness generation and assembly modules are changed to take advantage of high speed random access mass storage.

7.2.   Local and Global Coordinate Systems

The development of the system stiffness matrix in the previous section was based on the assumption that all the element degrees of freedom $\mathbf{u}_e$ were referred to the same set of coordinates. It may be convenient and expedient, on the other hand, to develop the elemental equations in a set of different local coordinates for each element. The same stiffness equations could then be used for each geometrically similar element. The resulting sets of element equations would be transformed to the same global coordinates using the techniques described in the following sections.

7.2.1.   Local-to-Global Transformations

Consider an element of a structural system as shown by Fig. 7-3. The global coordinates are defined as (X, Y, Z), and the local coordinates for a typical element are (x, y, z). The coordinate systems are related by a set of transformation equations that are obtained by considering unit vectors $(\mathbf{I}_1, \mathbf{I}_2, \mathbf{I}_3)$ and $(\mathbf{i}_1, \mathbf{i}_2, \mathbf{i}_3)$ defined in the directions of the global and local coordinates, respectively.

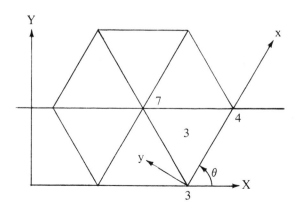

Figure 7-3. Element in Local Coordinate System

119

7.2 Local and Global Coordinate Systems

The two sets of unit vectors are then related by

$$
\begin{aligned}
\mathbf{I}_1 &= c_{11}\,\mathbf{i}_1 + c_{12}\,\mathbf{i}_2 + c_{13}\,\mathbf{i}_3 \\
\mathbf{I}_2 &= c_{21}\,\mathbf{i}_1 + c_{22}\,\mathbf{i}_2 + c_{23}\,\mathbf{i}_3 \\
\mathbf{I}_3 &= c_{31}\,\mathbf{i}_1 + c_{32}\,\mathbf{i}_2 + c_{33}\,\mathbf{i}_3
\end{aligned}
\tag{7.13}
$$

where the coefficient c_{ij} is the direction cosine between the ith-axis in the global coordinate system and the jth-axis in the local coordinate system.

The set of equations can be represented in matrix form as

$$
\mathbf{I} = \mathbf{C}\,\mathbf{i}
\tag{7.14}
$$

where

$$
\mathbf{I} = \begin{Bmatrix} \mathbf{I}_1 \\ \mathbf{I}_2 \\ \mathbf{I}_3 \end{Bmatrix} \quad,\ \mathbf{i} = \begin{Bmatrix} \mathbf{i}_1 \\ \mathbf{i}_2 \\ \mathbf{i}_3 \end{Bmatrix}
\tag{7.15}
$$

and

$$
\mathbf{C} = \begin{bmatrix} c_{11} & c_{12} & c_{13} \\ c_{21} & c_{22} & c_{23} \\ c_{31} & c_{32} & c_{33} \end{bmatrix}
\tag{7.16}
$$

The displacement and rotation vectors are defined with respect to the local coordinate system as

$$
\begin{aligned}
\mathbf{u} &= u_1\,\mathbf{i}_1 + u_2\,\mathbf{i}_2 + u_3\,\mathbf{i}_3 \\
\boldsymbol{\theta} &= \theta_1\,\mathbf{i}_1 + \theta_2\,\mathbf{i}_2 + \theta_3\,\mathbf{i}_3
\end{aligned}
\tag{7.17}
$$

The set of generalized displacements at the grid point is then represented in matrix form by (6.1). The nodal degrees of freedom are then transformed, where u_i and $u_i{'}$ are taken to be global and local coordinates, respectively, to

$$
\begin{Bmatrix} u_1 \\ u_2 \\ u_3 \\ \theta_1 \\ \theta_2 \\ \theta_3 \end{Bmatrix}_i
=
\begin{bmatrix}
c_{11} & c_{12} & c_{13} & & & \\
c_{21} & c_{22} & c_{23} & & \mathbf{0} & \\
c_{31} & c_{32} & c_{33} & & & \\
& & & c_{11} & c_{12} & c_{13} \\
& \mathbf{0} & & c_{21} & c_{22} & c_{23} \\
& & & c_{31} & c_{32} & c_{33}
\end{bmatrix}
\begin{Bmatrix} u_1' \\ u_2' \\ u_3' \\ \theta_1' \\ \theta_2' \\ \theta_3' \end{Bmatrix}_i
\tag{7.18}
$$

The set of element displacements is the union of all connected sets of node point displacements. We can therefore express the set of element displacements in the global system in terms of those referred to the local coordinate system as

$$
\mathbf{u}_e = \mathbf{G}\,\mathbf{u}_e'
\tag{7.19}
$$

where

$\mathbf{u}_e$ Set of displacements referred to global coordinates.

$\mathbf{u}_e'$ Set of element displacements referred to local coordinates.

$\mathbf{G}$ Transformation matrix that is suitably populated with the transformation matrix $\mathbf{C}$.

7.2.2.   Transformation of Stiffness Matrices

The rule for transforming the elemental stiffness matrix under a coordinate transformation defined by (7.19) can be found by using the principle of virtual work. The virtual work for the element is given in terms of quantities defined with respect to local coordinates by (6.40), which can be written as

$$\mathbf{u}_e'^{\mathrm{T}} \mathbf{k}_{ee}' \, \delta \mathbf{u}_e' \; = \; \mathbf{P}_e'^{\mathrm{T}} \, \delta \mathbf{u}_e' \tag{7.20}$$

The element displacements specified in terms of local coordinates can be expressed in terms of global coordinates inverting (7.19) to give

$$\mathbf{u}_e' = \mathbf{G}^{\mathrm{T}} \mathbf{u}_e \tag{7.21}$$

where we note that transpose of the matrix of direction cosines is equal to its inverse. The substitution of (7.21) into (7.20) then leads to

$$\mathbf{u}_e^{\mathrm{T}} \mathbf{G} \, \mathbf{k}_{ee}' \, \mathbf{G}^{\mathrm{T}} \, \delta \mathbf{u}_e - \mathbf{P}_e'^{\mathrm{T}} \mathbf{G}^{\mathrm{T}} \, \delta \mathbf{u}_e = 0 \tag{7.22}$$

or

$$\mathbf{k}_{ee} \, \mathbf{u}_e = \mathbf{P}_e \tag{7.23}$$

where the transformed element stiffness and load are defined to be

$$\mathbf{k}_{ee} = \mathbf{G} \, \mathbf{k}_{ee}' \, \mathbf{G}^{\mathrm{T}} \tag{7.24}$$

and

$$\mathbf{P}_e = \mathbf{G} \, \mathbf{P}_e' \tag{7.25}$$

The transformation of displacements, loads, and stiffness from local to global coordinates is completely automated in finite element programs such as MSC/NASTRAN. In many instances the user may be unconcerned with the local coordinate system, but there are cases that the user must exercise care in their specification. These are

1. The specification of the local axes for the three-dimensional beam

2. The specification of a normal pressure on plate bending elements

3. The interpretation of stress output.

7.3.   Specifying Structural Degrees of Freedom

We saw in Chapter Six that the finite element method allows us to represent a structural system as an assemblage of elements that are connected at discrete points in the structure. The behavior of the structure is characterized by the value of the generalized displacements at these discrete points. The accuracy of the solution is therefore dependent on the number of node points used to describe the system as well as the distribution of the node points throughout the structure. Suitable criteria for choosing the number and the distribution of node points is an area of current research and is beyond the scope of this text.

The node points serve four distinct purposes:

1. The specification of structural topology

2. The specification of degrees of freedom

3. Accurately locate points at which displacements are constrained or at which loads are applied

4. Define locations where behavioral variables are to be calculated

The structural topology is of importance only during the calculation of the stiffness matrix. Since that function is transparent to the user, the fact that degrees of freedom are associated with the node points is of greatest interest.

For structurally oriented finite element models it is convenient to associate six degrees of freedom with a geometric point defined on the structure. These degrees of freedom at the geometric point are shown by Fig. 6-2a and are represented by the set

$$\mathbf{u}_i = \begin{bmatrix} u_1 & u_2 & u_3 & \theta_1 & \theta_2 & \theta_3 \end{bmatrix}_i^T \tag{7.26}$$

A grid point degree of freedom can be identified by the pair (G,C) where

G   Number of a geometric grid point

C   Number from one to six that identifies a degree of freedom using the correspondence table in Sec. 7.3.3.4.

Geometric grid points are defined using GRID Bulk Data cards in NASTRAN as described in Section 7.3.3. The coordinate systems used to define the location of the geometric grid points are described in Section 7.3.2.

Degrees of freedom may be associated with nonstructural behavior such as control voltages, temperatures, and scalar spring mass systems. Some means of defining degrees of freedom without reference to spatial location is therefore desirable. Scalar degrees of freedom may be defined directly in NASTRAN as described in Section 7.3.1.

7.3.1.   Scalar Degrees of Freedom — SPOINT

Scalar degrees of freedom may be defined in two different ways:

1. Implicitly by reference on a scalar element card (i.e. CELAS, CMASS, etc.)

2. Explicitly by an SPOINT Bulk Data card

In either case a single degree of freedom in the g-set for each scalar point. Scalar elements are defined explicitly by using the SPOINT Bulk Data card shown by Card Image 7-1.

1	2	3	4	5	6	7	8	9	10
SPOINT	S_1	S_2	S_3	S_4	S_5	etc.			

*alternatively

SPOINT	S_1	THRU	S_2						

where
S_i Scalar point numbers that must be unique among all grid or scalar point numbers.

Card Image 7-1. Specification of Scalar Point — SPOINT

7.3.2.   Coordinate Systems — CORD

Coordinate systems provide a means of specifying the location of the geometric grid points that are used to describe the topology of the structure. We know from experience that different types of coordinate systems are convenient for different topologies so that we would expect programs such as MSC/NASTRAN to provide the user with some flexibility in specifying coordinate systems.

NASTRAN allows the user to specify any number of rectangular, cylindrical or spherical coordinate systems. These subsidiary coordinate systems are defined relative to the basic coordinate system by CORD-type Bulk Data cards that will be described later in this section. Coordinate systems are identified by a coordinate identification number (CID), which may be any integer that is equal to or greater than zero. The set CID = 0 refers to a special set of rectangular cartesian coordinates which is called the *Basic Coordinates* and which is always taken as the default coordinate system.

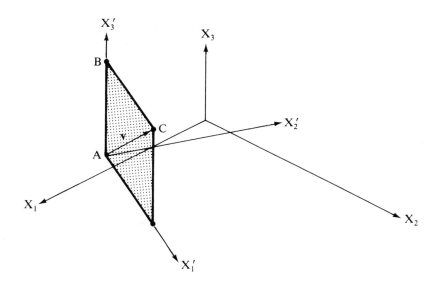

Figure 7-4. Subsidiary Coordinate System

The subsidiary coordinate system (X_1', X_2', X_3') shown by Fig. 7-4 can be defined in terms of the reference system (X_1, X_2, X_3) by specifying the position of three points A, B, and C as follows:

1. Point A is the origin of the transformed coordinates

2. The directed line segment between point A and B defines the transformed X_3'-axis.

3. The point C lies in the X_1', X_3'-plane.

The X_2'-axis is thus given by

$$i_2' = i_3' \times v \tag{7.27}$$

and

$$i_1' = i_2' \times i_3' \tag{7.28}$$

123

7.3.2 Coordinate Systems — CORD

where **v** is the vector from point A to C.

The coordinates of the points A, B, and C can be specified directly by the CORD2-type cards, which are shown in Card Image 7-2, or by specifying three geometric grid points which correspond to points A, B, and C as shown by Card Image 7-3.

*Cylindrical

1	2	3	4	5	6	7	8	9	10
CORD2C +1	CID C_1	RID C_2	A_1 C_3	A_2	A_3	B_1	B_2	B_3	+1

*Rectangular

CORD2R +2	CID C_1	RID C_2	A_1 C_3	A_2	A_3	B_1	B_2	B_3	+2

*Spherical

CORD2S +3	CID C_1	RID C_2	A_1 C_3	A_2	A_3	B_1	B_2	B_3	+3

Card Image 7-2. Coordinate System Defined by Coordinates of Three Points

The logical CORD2-type cards described by Card Image 7-2 require two physical cards. The coordinate definition cards for each type of coordinate system are identical except for the card mnemonic in the first field where CORD2C, CORD2R, and CORD2S specify cylindrical, rectangular, and spherical coordinates, respectively. The other fields of the CORD2-type cards are

CID Coordinate system identification number (integer ≥ 0)

RID The CID of the reference coordinate system. A blank or zero entry in this field indicates that the basic coordinate system is the reference. However, any coordinate system defined in the Bulk Data deck may be used. The coordinates of the points A, B, and C are then interpreted for the various allowable types of coordinate systems as shown by Table 7-1 (integer ≥ 0)

(A_1, A_2, A_3) Coordinates of point A, which defines the origin of coordinate system (real)

(B_1, B_2, B_3) Coordinates of point B, which lies on the X_3'-axis (real)

(C_1, C_2, C_3) Coordinates of point C, which lies in the X_3', X_1'-plane (real)

Coordinate Type	Coordinate Component		
	1	2	3
Rectangular	X	Y	Z
Cylindrical	R	θ(degrees)	Z
Spherical	R	θ(degrees)	φ (degrees)

Table 7-1. Definition of Coordinate Components

*Cylindrical

1	2	3	4	5	6	7	8	9	10
CORD1C	CID	GA	GB	GC	CID	GA	GB	GC	

*Rectangular

CORD1R	CID	GA	GB	GC	CID	GA	GB	GC	

*Spherical

CORD1S	CID	GA	GB	GC	CID	GA	GB	GC	

Card Image 7-3. Coordinate System Defined by Three GRID Points

The coordinate definition cards shown on Card Image 7-3 are identical for each type of coordinate system except for the card mnemonic in the first field where CORD1C, CORD1R, and CORD1S specify cylindrical, rectangular, and spherical coordinates, respectively. The other field designations are

CID   Coordinate system identification number (integer, > 0)

GA,GB,   Three identification numbers (integer, > 0) of three grid points where
GC   GA defines the origin
            GB lies on the X_3'-axis, and
            GC lies in the X_3', X_1'-plane

The cylindrical, rectangular, and spherical coordinate systems that are defined by the CORD-type Bulk Data cards are shown by Figs. 7-5a, 7-5b, and 7-5c, respectively. The components of the points A, B, and C specified on the CORD2-type cards are interpreted in terms of the coordinate system defined by set RID. For example, if a spherical coordinate system is associated with this set identification number, then the components would be the R, θ, and φ coordinates of the point as shown by Fig. 7-5c.

The components of displacement referred to rectangular, cylindrical, and spherical coordinates are also shown by Figs. 7-5a, 7-5b, and 7-5c. MSC/NASTRAN identifies the grid point degrees of freedom in the output by labeling the components of displacement T1, T2, and T3 and the components of the rotation R1, R2, and R3. These components are interpreted using Table 7-1. The user can specify that the displacement coordinate system at each geometric grid point is different from the system used to define the location of the point.

7.3.3.   Geometric Grid Points — GRID

We discussed the concept of defining degrees of freedom in the introduction to this section where we noted that six degrees of freedom are defined at a geometric grid point. The geometric grid point is defined in NASTRAN by the GRID and GRDSET Bulk Data cards shown in Card Image 7-4. The geometric grid point has six degrees of freedom, which include the three components of the displacement vector (u_1, u_2, u_3) and three components of the rotation-vector (θ_1, θ_2, θ_3) as described in Section 6.1. NASTRAN defines six degrees of freedom in the system matrix for each geometric grid point. The associated rows and columns are logically filled with zeros. The system matrix will therefore be singular unless the finite element model or other NASTRAN input data defines nonzero stiffness terms, or the rows and columns containing only zero elements are removed.

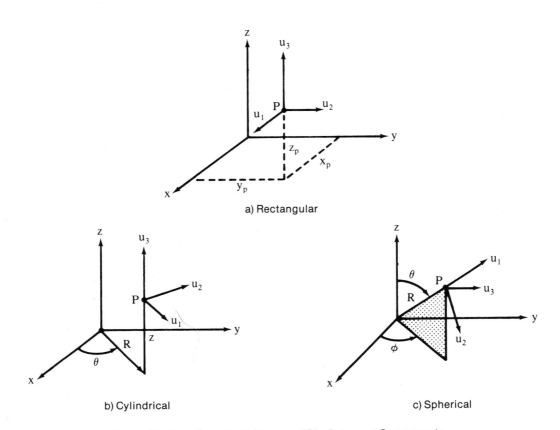

a) Rectangular

b) Cylindrical

c) Spherical

Figure 7-5. Coordinate Definitions and Displacement Components

1	2	3	4	5	6	7	8	9	10
GRDSET		CP				CD	PSPC		
GRID	ID	CP	X_1	X_2	X_3	CD	PSPC		

where

ID   Grid point identification number (integer, >0)

CP   Set identification number of the coordinate system used to define the grid point coordinates (integer, ≥ 0)

(X_1, X_2, X_3) Coordinates of the grid point with respect to the CP-coordinate system (real)

CD   Set identification of the coordinate system with respect to which the displacements are referred (integer, ≥ 0)

PSPC   Permanent single point constraints (integer, >0 or blank)

Card Image 7-4. Geometric Grid Point Definition

7.3.3.1.   Grid Identification

Each grid point must have an identification number that is unique among all point identifica-

126

tion. Since NASTRAN generates an internal sequence for degrees of freedom by starting at the lowest ID and progressing to the highest, the ID's need not form a consecutive numerical sequence. If a structural model were to be represented by three geometric grid points, for example, the sequences (100, 200, 300), (1, 2, 3), or (7, 12, 17) would produce the same internal sequence of equations in NASTRAN and would result in system matrices with the same matrix topology. The user can therefore use grid point number sequences that enhance definition of the model or the interpretation of the results.

7.3.3.2.   Coordinates

The geometric grid point is defined by specifying its coordinates (X_1, X_2, X_3) in terms of the coordinate system identified by the CP parameter, which is a coordinate system identification (CID). If CP is zero, then (X_1, X_2, X_3) are taken to be the location of the point referenced in the basic coordinate system. If CP is the number of a user-defined coordinate system, then the components are interpreted according to Table 7-1.

7.3.3.3.   Displacement Coordinates

The degrees of freedom at the geometric grid point are interpreted as components in the coordinate system specified by the CD parameter on the GRID card. If CD is zero, then the displacement components are taken in terms of the basic coordinate systems. If CD is the CID of a user-defined coordinate system then they are interpreted as the vector components shown by Fig. 7-5 for the various coordinate systems. The rotations $(\theta_1, \theta_2, \theta_3)$ are components of the rotation vector in the directions using the right-hand rule.

7.3.3.4.   Permanent Constraints

Displacement boundary conditions which are specified for individual degrees of freedom are termed single point constraints (SPCs) in NASTRAN. These constraint conditions can be defined by means of the SPC Bulk Data command which is described in Sec. 7.5.2. or by means of the PSPC field on the GRID card.

The PSPC entry is a set of degree of freedom codes that specify degrees of freedom which are to be set equal to zero. The codes for the six displacement at the geometric grid point are given by Table 7-2.

Degree of Freedom	Code
u_1	1
u_2	2
u_3	3
θ_1	4
θ_2	5
θ_3	6

Table 7-2. Degree of Freedom Codes

These degrees of freedom are interpreted as displacement components in the coordinate system specified by the CD specification on the GRID card.

The use and specification of constraints is described in succeeding sections of this chapter. We note at this time that the constraints specified at the GRID card level cannot be changed by other constraint specifications. Permanent constraints provide a convenient means of removing one or more of the six node point degrees of freedom that are automatically defined by NASTRAN, but that do not physically exist in the mathematical model.

7.3.3.5.   Default Value — The GRDSET Card

The GRDSET card, which is also shown by Card Image 7-4, may be used to provide default values for the parameters CP, CD, and PSPC in the GRID card. This is a user convenience and allows the elimination of repetitious data. A word of caution is in order, however, regarding the use of the GRDSET card. The values CP, CD, and PSPC on the GRDSET card are *default* values and are used if the corresponding fields of the GRID card are blank. A default value is overriden only if an integer, including the integer zero, exists in the associated field of the GRID card. A common mistake is that of assuming that permanent single point constraints placed in the GRID card are added to those specified in the GRDSET. On the contrary, a PSPC specified on the GRID card overrides the default value on the GRDSET card. Only one GRDSET card may appear in the Bulk Data deck and at least one of the values, CP, CD, or PSPC must be different from zero. The inclusion of a GRDSET card with only zero entries will result in a fatal error in NASTRAN.

7.3.3.6. Use of Replication, Incrementation, and Repeat Features

The specification of lists of card images, such as GRID cards which define points along a line, where there is a logical relation between each of the cards can be automated in MSC/NASTRAN either by means of the replication feature in free format Bulk Data (Sec. 1.6.) or by MSGMESH. It is therefore instructive to consider both of these techniques. The replication feature is described in this section while MSGMESH is described in Sec. 7.3.3.7.

We recall that the replication feature for Bulk Data is defined by certain symbols

      =   in a field means that the contents of the previous card is to be copied

      = =   in a field means that the contents of all fields beyond and including = = are to be copied

      *(N)   in a field means that the value of the corresponding field in the previous card is to be incremented by N (which can be real or integer depending on the field)

      = (M)   in the *first field* of a card means that the replication and/or incrementation defined on the previous card is to be repeated M times where M is an integer

With these constructions in mind we can represent the set of GRID points, which are equally spaced along the x-axis as shown by Fig. 7-6, as follows where the location of points and displacements are referred to the basic coordinate system.

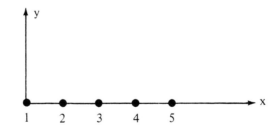

Figure 7-6. Node Point Location Along X-Axis

Card No.	1	2	3	4	5	6	7	8	9	10
1-	GRID	1	0	0.	0.	0.	0			
2-	=	*(1)	=	*(1.)	= =					
3-	= (3)									

where we note that

1. The first card has the form of the GRID Bulk Data card shown by Card Image 7-4.

2. The = in field 1 and 3 of card 2- means that these fields are to be reproduced from the previous card

3. The = = field 5 of card 2- means that fields 5 through 9 are to be reproduced from the previous card

4. The *(1) in field 2 of card 2- means that the value from the previous card is to be incremented by an integer one

5. The *(1.) in field 4 of card 2- means that the value from the previous card is to be incremented by 1.

6. The = (3) in field 1 of card 3- means that the replication and incrementation defined by the previous card is to be repeated three more times.

Cards 1- through 3- of this example will then generate the following GRID Bulk Data

1	2	3	4	5	6	7	8	9	10
GRID	1	0	0.	0.	0.	0			
GRID	2	0	1.	0.	0.	0			
GRID	3	0	2.	0.	0.	0			
GRID	4	0	3.	0.	0.	0			
GRID	5	0	4.	0.	0.	0			

where zeros in fields three and seven indicate that the basic coordinate system will be used. Note that the values in fields four through six are real numbers in a FORTRAN sense. The decimal point must be included, or NASTRAN will detect an input error and will terminate execution after reading the NASTRAN input data.

7.3.3.7   Use of MSGMESH

MSGMESH is an *optional* feature in MSC/NASTRAN that provides a powerful utility for generating several types of Bulk Data sets of grid points in one, two, and three dimensions. A set of points is defined along a line, for example, by specifying the identification number of two existing points which define the ends of the segment, and then by generating the interior set of points with a special MSGMESH command which is called GRIDG.

The MSGMESH commands have the same form as Bulk Data, but are treated as comment cards by the MSC/NASTRAN Bulk Data processor. Only the MSGMESH utility can interpret MSGMESH commands. This optional utility must be activated by specifying the keyword PREFOPT with a value of two on the NASTRAN card (see Sec. 1.9.1.). That is, if MSGMESH is to be used, the very first card in the NASTRAN data deck must be

NASTRAN PREFOPT = 2

MSGMESH can be used to define fields of points on one, two, and three dimensional regions as shown by Fig. 7-7. In each case the user describes the type of region, i.e., LINE, TRIA, QUAD, or HEX by defining its vertices, and the grid spacing by using the MSGMESH GRIDG command which is shown by Card Image 7-5.

The type of region determines the number of vertices to be defined by the GRIDG MSGMESH command. With reference to Fig. 7-5 we see that a LINE is defined by the two vertices A,B whose point identification numbers are to be specified by the two entries GA and GB on the GRIDG card. Similarly the three dimensional HEX region is defined by eight vertices A through H which are specified by the entries GA through GH on the GRIDG card.

129

7.3.3.7   Use of MSGMESH

We now have to consider three questions

1. How to define vertex points
2. How to define the subdivision incrementation
3. How MSGMESH numbers the GRID point

1	2	3	4	5	6	7	8	9	10
GRIDG	FID	CD	PS	L	GA	GB	GC		+ G1
+ G1	M	GD	N	GE	GF	GG	GH	CP	

where

FID   Identification number of region or field of points (Integer, $1 \leq FID \leq 99$)

CD   Displacement coordinated system for all GRID cards which are generated for the field (Integer > 0)

PS   Permanent single point constraints for all GRID cards in the field (Integer ≥ 0)

GA,GB,...   Identification numbers for GRID (or EGRID) points which define the vertices
GH   A,B,... of the region. (Integer)

CP   Coordinate system to which the GRID points are referenced (Integer ≥ 0)

L,M,N   Subdivision Parameters

Card Image 7-5. MSGMESH GRID GENERATION — GRIDG

Vertices are defined either by GRID Bulk Data or by a special MSGMESH command call EGRID which is used specifically for this purpose and which is shown by Card Image 7-6

1	2	3	4	5	6	7	8	9	10
EGRID	ID	CP	X1	X2	X3				

Card Image 7-6. MSGMESH Vertex Definition — EGRID

The entries in the fields two through six are the same as those for the GRID card defined on Card image 7-4. Points which are defined on EGRID cards are known only to MSGMESH and can be used to define the geometric location of vertex points. However, the EGRID cards are ignored by the Bulk Data processor since all MSGMESH cards are treated as comment cards. However, the GRID cards which are generated by MSGMESH do become part of the Bulk Data Deck and are interpreted as such by the Bulk Data processor.

In order to generate a field of GRID points the user must now understand how to define the subdivision incrementation by means of the incrementation parameters L, M, and N which appear on the GRIDG card and which define the number of increments in up to three directions. In order to understand the use of the incrementation parameters and the resulting GRID point numbers let's consider the one dimensional LINE region which is shown by Fig. 7-8.

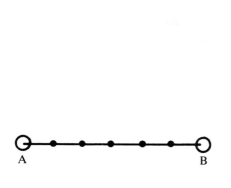

A) LINE, a one-dimensional region

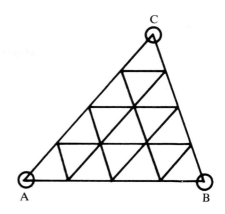

B) TRIA, a two-dimensional region with
three sides

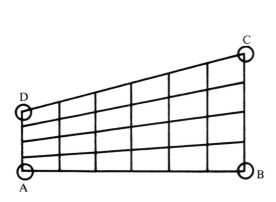

C) QUAD, a two-dimensional region with
four sides

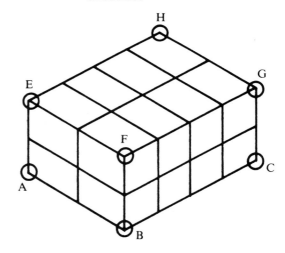

D) HEX, a three-dimensional region with
six faces

Figure 7-7. MSGMESH GRID Point Fields

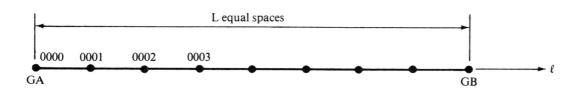

Fig. 7-8 One-Dimensional field

The one dimensional coordinate, ℓ, is the directed line segment from the first vertex, GA, to the second vertex, GB which are defined in fields 6 and 7, respectively of the GRIDG command. The number of increments along the coordinate, ℓ, is then defined by L in field 5 of the GRIDG card.

The MSGMESH processor generates $L + 1$ points associated with this region along the line, ℓ, that are assigned numbers starting with 0000 at end GA and ending with a four digit value of L at end GB where $L \leq 9999$. The GRID number is then formed by concatenating the region identification number, FID, defined in field 2 of the GRIDG card with the point number. Sound confusing? Well, consider the following example. Suppose we want to define 1000 GRID points along the line segment which connects points (0.,0.,0.) and (10.,0.,0.) in Basic coordinates. We could then define the vertices by using the following EGRID MSGMESH commands

1	2	3	4	5	6	7	8	9	10
EGRID	1	0	0.	0.	0.				
EGRID	2	0	10.	0.	0.				

The entire set of GRID cards over the entire region would then be defined by the following GRIDG card

1	2	3	4	5	6	7	8	9	10
GRIDG	7	0	5	999	−1	−2			

which would generate GRID point 70000 through 71000.

The astute observer will note that GA and GB in fields 6 and 7 have been prefaced with a negative (−) sign in this example. The negative sign means that MSGMESH will generate GRID points at the vertices which have identification numbers associated with the region. A positive sign (i.e. an unsigned entry for the vertices) tells MSGMESH *not* to generate GRID points for the vertices. The use of unsigned entries for vertex numbers allows the use of predefined GRID Bulk Data to define the vertices without having MSGMESH generate an additional point at the vertex location.

Now, let's consider defining a mesh over a two dimensional QUAD region which is defined by the two mesh coordinates ℓ and m as shown by Fig. 7-9

A QUAD two dimensional region is defined by specifying the first four vertices on the GRIDG MSGMESH command, i.e. GA, GB, GC, and GD in field 6, 7 and 8 of card 1 − and field 3 of card 2 − together with two mesh parameters L and M in field 5 of card 1 and field 2 of card 2, respectively. The parameter L defines the number of increments in the ℓ direction which is taken as the directed line segment from GA to GB while M is the number of increments in the m direction which is taken as the directed line segment from GA to GD.

The point numbers on the two dimensional field are, as in the case of the LINE, identified by a four digit number starting with 0000 at point GA. However, for two-dimensional fields the last two digits (i.e. least significant digits) are incremented in the ℓ-direction (shown in bold along ℓ-axis) while the first two digits (most significant digits) are incremented in the m-direction. This means that an MSGMESH QUAD region is limited to 99 increments in each the ℓ and m directions which in turn limits the total possible number of points in a square region to $(L + 1)(M + 1) = 10,000$ nodes. We also note in passing that the ℓ-direction is called the primary direction (i.e. the point numbers change most rapidly) while the m-direction is called the secondary direction. (We will make use of this terminology in Chapter 9 where we describe the MSGMESH CGEN command for generated elements over fields of points.)

As an example, suppose we went to define a square mesh over the region shown by Fig. 7-10 which has 4 equal increments in both the x and y directions. In this example we will define the vertices with GRID Bulk Data and request that MSGMESH *not* to generate additional GRID cards at the vertices by using unsigned entries for the vertices.

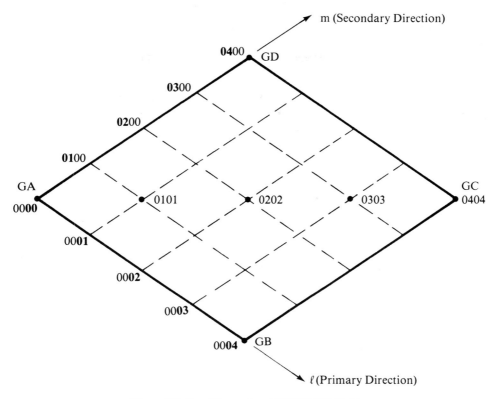

Figure 7-9. Two Dimensional MSGMESH Field

The following GRID Bulk Data and MSGMESH commands can then be used to define the 4 vertices and generate all of the additional GRID cards which define the field of points shown on Fig. 7-10.

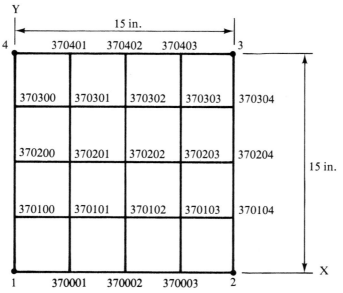

Figure 7-10. Two Dimensional Example

133

7.3.3.7 Use of MSGMESH

1	2	3	4	5	6	7	8	9	10
GRID	1	0	0.	0.	0.	0			
GRID	2	0	15.	0.	0.	0			
GRID	3	0	15.	15.	0.	0			
GRID	4	0	0.	15.	0.	0			
GRIDG	37	0		4	1	2	3		+ G1
+ G1	4	4							

This brief description of MSGMESH will provide us with a powerful utility which we can use to explore the use of MSC/NASTRAN to solve nontrivial example problems. While we will not describe all of MSGMESH's functionality in this book we will look forward in later sections to the use of MSGMESH to

- Generate element connectivity over fields of points (Sec. 9.5.3., 9.6.5., 9.7.3., and 9.9.2.9.)
- Generate boundary displacement constraints (Sec. 7.5.2.3.)

7.3.3.8. Cylindrical Coordinates

Consider the problem of specifying the location of node points that lie along a circular ring as shown by Fig. 7.11. The ring lies in the y,z-plane of the *basic* coordinate system. Since the azimuth angle, θ, is to be measured from the transformed x',z'-plane as shown by Fig. 7-5b this means that we must take care in the specification of the new coordinate system. For the purpose of this example we will make

- The origin of the new coordinate system coincident with the origin of the basic coordinate

- The z'-axis of the new system coincident with the x-axis of the basic coordinate system

- make the x'-axis of the new system coincident with the y-axis of the basic coordinate system

the new coordinate system, for which we will specify CID = 4, is then defined by the following CORD2C Bulk Data card.

1	2	3	4	5	6	7	8	9	10
CORD2C	4	0	0.	0.	0.	1.	0.	0.	+ 2C1
+ 2C1	0.	1.	0.						

where

1. The coordinate set ID is 4. This number can then be referenced as the CP and/or the CD parameter on the GRID card.

2. The reference coordinate system is RID = 0, which means that the components of the points used to define the new coordinate system are specified in terms of the basic coordinate system.

3. The origin is set at A = (0., 0., 0.), which is also the origin of the basic coordinates.

4. The z'-axis is coincident with the basic x since B = (1., 0., 0.)

5. The point C = (0., 1., 0.) implies that azimuth angles are measured from the basic y-axis which is coincident with x'

6. A continuation card is required. The continuation mnemonic is 2C1, and the + on the second card defines a small field continuation card (see Appendix A for description of small

and large fields). Note that the + sign in column 73 of field 10 of the first card is ignored, but its presence aids the user when scanning the cards for possible errors.

The GRID cards required to define the grid points shown by Fig. 7-11 are then as follows:

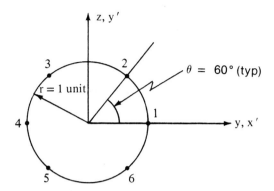

Figure 7-11. Ring in Cylindrical Coordinates

1	2	3	4	5	6	7	8	9	10
GRID	1	4	1.	0.	0.	4			
GRID	2	4	1.	60.	0.	4			
GRID	3	4	1.	120.	0.	4			
GRID	4	4	1.	180.	0.	4			
GRID	5	4	1.	240.	0.	4			
GRID	6	4	1.	300.	0.	4			

where

1. The coordinate identification CP = 4 on each GRID card specifies that the coordinates in fields four through six are to be interpreted as components of the coordinate system whose CID is 4.

2. The radius is equal to one for all grid points.

3. The angular coordinate in field five is specified in degrees.

4. The displacements are to be interpreted with respect to the CD = 4 coordinate system, i.e., the cylindrical system. These displacement degrees of freedom are shown on Fig. 7-5b.

This set of GRID cards could also be defined by using the following replication and repeat features

1	2	3	4	5	6	7	8	9	10
GRID	1	4	1.0	0.0	0.0	4			
=	*(1)	=	=	*(60.)	==				
= (4)									

7.3.4. External and Internal Degrees of Freedom

The program logic is simplified if the degrees of freedom are identified by a set of consecutive numbers starting at one. Since the user is accustomed to thinking about grid point rather than scalar degrees of freedom, NASTRAN converts the external degrees of freedom associated with GRID and

SPOINT points to internal degrees of freedom. The conversion from external to internal degrees of freedom is automatically performed by NASTRAN as follows:
- The lowest point number is found. If it is a SPOINT then the first internal degree of freedom corresponds to the SPOINT; if it is a GRID then the first six internal degrees of freedom correspond to the GRID point.
- The next highest point number is found and one internal degree of freedom is generated if it is an SPOINT and six internal degrees of freedom if it is a GRID, etc.

The set of all GRID point and SPOINT scalar degrees of freedom is called the g-set and is denoted by $\mathbf{u}_g$. The total number of degrees of freedom in the g-set is

$$N_g = 6N + S$$

where N is the number of GRID points and S is the number of SPOINT. The parameter called LUSET is given the value of N_g in the solution sequences.

7.3.5. Control of Matrix Topology

Matrices for structural problems are typically sparse, i.e. contain relatively few nonzero terms in comparison to the number of elements in a full matrix of the same order. Programs such as MSC/NASTRAN thus incorporate matrix packing algorithms to store only the nonzero terms of a matrix so that the storage and I/O costs associated with manipulating large matrices are minimized.

The cost associated with solving a set of equations is influenced not only by the sparseness but also by the distribution of nonzero elements in the matrix. This distribution of nonzero terms is characterized by certain parameters which define the matrix topology. In defining these parameters it is useful to consider the finite element idealization of a simple structure and the associated stiffness matrix as shown by Fig. 7-12 where only the upper triangular half of the matrix is shown. We should also note that there may be more than a single degree of freedom at each node so that the elements of the stiffness matrix $\mathbf{k}_{ij}$ are matrices of order six or less.

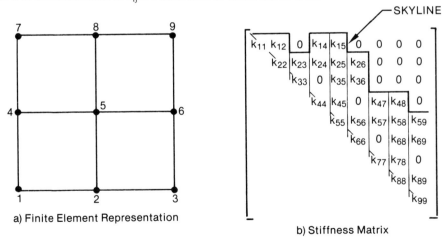

a) Finite Element Representation

b) Stiffness Matrix

Figure 7-12. Finite Element Idealization of Flat Plate and Associated Stiffness Matrix Topology

The time required to perform a matrix decomposition is a complicated function of machine timing constants and matrix topological parameters which is presented by Ref. 7-1. An approximation for the decomposition time is given by

$$T = \tfrac{1}{2}M \sum_{i=1}^{N} c_i^2 \tag{7.29}$$

136

where   M   is an experimentally-determined machine-dependent time for a multiply-add loop. Typical values are given by Table 7-3.

   N   is the order of the matrix

   c_i is the number of active columns in row i

Computer	M (microseconds)
CDC 6400	15.0
6600	2.6
7600	0.4
Cyber 172	11.0
173, 174	8.0
175/100	1.1
175/200	0.6
176	0.4
IBM 360/65,67	16.0
360/195	0.8
370/148	47.0
370/155	16.0
370/158	10.0
370/165,168S	3.0
370/168F	1.8
3031	8.5
3032	2.9
3033	1.1
4331	150.0
4341	9.5
INTEL AS/5	10.0
AS/6	1.2
AMDAHL 470/V5	2.2
470/V6	1.8
470/V7	1.4
470/V8	1.1
UNIVAC 1106	25.0
1108	12.0
1110	6.0
1110/10	18.0
1110/20	13.0
1110/80	5.5
VAX 11/780	12.0

Table 7-3. Multiply-Add Times for Several Computers

A column j is said to be active in row i if for $j \geq i$ there is an entry in the column for any row k where $k \leq i$.*
   Other topological parameters that are of interest in discussing solution costs are matrix

*Active columns may become "passive" in the decomposition process when the diagonal term initiates a new active column. (See Ref. 7-1)

7.3.5 Control of Matrix Topology

wavefront, W, which is defined as

$$W = \max_{i \le N} c_i \tag{7.30}$$

and the average and root-mean-square wave fronts, W_{ave} and W_{rms}, respectively which are defined as

$$W_{ave} = \frac{1}{N} \sum_{i=1}^{N} c_i \tag{7.31}$$

and

$$W_{rms} = \sqrt{\frac{1}{N} \sum_{i=1}^{N} c_i^2} \tag{7.32}$$

The decomposition time (7.29) can be expressed in terms of root-mean-square wavefront by using (7.32) which gives

$$T = \frac{1}{2} \frac{M}{N} W_{rms}^2 \tag{7.33}$$

The extent of the active terms in each column of the stiffness matrix are indicated by outlining the columns in Fig. 7-12. The irregular pattern which encloses all active terms is called the skyline of the matrix. Only terms within the skyline need be considered in the decomposition process.

The topological parameters for the matrix shown in Fig. 7-12 are as follows:

row	c_i	c_i^2
1	4	16
2	5	25
3	4	16
4	5	25
5	5	25
6	4	16
7	3	9
8	2	4
9	1	1
	= 33	= 137

so that

$$W = 5$$

$$W_{ave} = 3.67$$

$$W_{rms} = 3.90$$

In addition to the time required for matrix decomposition there are two additional costs which are associated with solving a set of equations and which are influenced by matrix topology. These are

1. The size of high-speed memory required for matrix decomposition

2. The number of nonzero terms in the decomposed matrix

The first of these, the size of core, is related to the wavefront W. The second, the number of nonzero terms in the decomposed matrix, directly influences the number of multiply-add cycles that must be performed in the forward sweep-backward substitution associated with the solution process.

The analyst thus seems to be confronted with a mind boggling modeling task: descretize the structure in sufficient detail to obtain a solution of acceptable accuracy and numerically sequence the node numbers such that the solution cost is minimized. Fortunately some assistance can be provided to the analyst in choosing a node number sequence. First, general guide lines are presented in Ref. 7-2 for various classes of connectivities. These guide lines are summarized in Sec. 7.3.5.1. In addition, the problem of resequencing a set of node numbers with prescribed connectivity has been considered by a number of researchers who have developed algorithms for obtaining the best node number sequence. The resequencing algorithms which are included in MSC/NASTRAN are described in Sec. 7.3.5.2.

7.3.5.1.   General Guidelines for Node Sequencing

One-Dimensional Systems

Open and closed one dimensional systems are shown by Fig. 7-13. A consecutive node numbering sequence is optimum for the open system shown by Fig. 7-13a. A closed system can be sequenced either as shown by Fig. 7-13b or Fig. 7-13c. For those solution techniques where decomposition time is a function of semibandwidth (see Sec. 2.2.2.4) node number sequence shown by Fig. 7-13b is appropriate. Since the MSC/NASTRAN uses an active-column technique and since the root-mean-square wavefront is the same for both either can be used. Simplicity would seem to favor the consecutive node numbering.

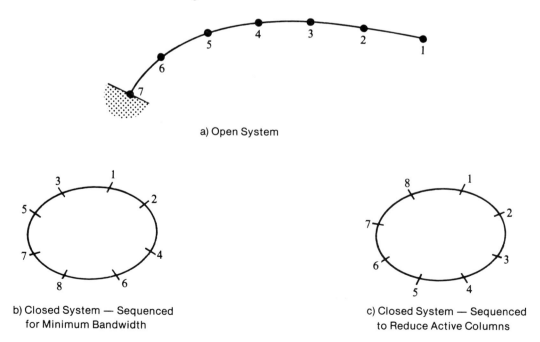

a) Open System

b) Closed System — Sequenced
for Minimum Bandwidth

c) Closed System — Sequenced
to Reduce Active Columns

Figure 7-13. Node Numbering for One Dimensional Systems

Two-Dimensional Systems

Grid point numbering sequences for rectangular and curvilinear two dimensional systems are shown by Fig. 7-14. The sequencing of rectangular patterns such as that shown by Fig. 7-14a will lead to acceptable solution times when the grid points are numbered consecutively along grid lines having the fewest number of grid lines starting at one end. If the rectangular surface is closed to form a cylinder by connecting the lines containing nodes 17 through 20 and 13 through 16 then the most cost effective node numbering sequence is dependent on the ratio of circumferential to axial grid lines. If this ratio is greater than two then the node numbering sequence described above for the rectangular mesh will provide acceptable results. If the ratio is less than two then a sequence of consecutive numbers in the circumferential direction will be better.

The sequencing guide lines for a radial mesh such as that shown in Fig. 7-14b are generally the same as those described above with the exception of a central point. If the mesh contains a central point it should be sequenced last.

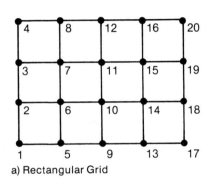

a) Rectangular Grid

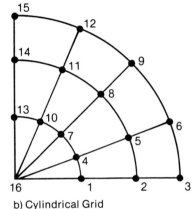

b) Cylindrical Grid

Figure 7-14. Node Numbering for Two Dimensional Systems

7.3.5.2.   Node Point Resequencing — SEQGP

The node numbering sequence that is defined on the GRID Bulk Data cards can be changed by the SEQGP Bulk Data card shown by Card Image 7-7.

1	2	3	4	5	6	7	8	9	10
SEQGP	ID	SEQID	ID	SEQID	ID	SEQID	ID	SEQID	

where

1. ID is any grid or scalar point number whose internal degree of freedom code is to be resequenced. The SEQID is a special number of the form of a four-level Dewey decimal; i.e., xxxx, xxxx.x, xxxx.x.x, and xxxx.x.x.x, where x is a number, are acceptable forms.

2. The SEQID numbers must be unique and cannot be the same as the number of a grid or scalar point that is not being changed.

3. The SEQGP card cannot be continued.

4. From one to four grid or scalar point numbers may be resequenced on a single card.

Card Image 7-7. Grid and Scalar Point Resequencing

The SEQID number is an internal alias for the associated grid point number. If a SEQID alias for a grid point number exists then the alias is used in generating the internal degree of freedom numbers rather than the grid point ID number.

The SEQGP capability thus allows the analyst to insert a node number logically between two consecutive grid point IDs. Suppose, for example, that the user wishes to insert a grid point number between grid points 3 and 4. The new grid point could be defined as 34 on the GRID card. A SEQGP card for inserting 34 between 3 and 4 would then be as follows

1	2	3	4	5	6	7	8	9	10
SEQGP	34	3.5							

The SEQGP Bulk Data can also be used to resequence the entire set of connected node points in order to obtain a more favorable matrix topology from a cost point of view. In this case an appropriate sequence of SEQID numbers would be specified as alias for the original set of node numbers.

Several resequencing algorithms have been proposed for the type of solution process incorporated in NASTRAN. These include

- Cuthill-McKee (Ref. 7-3)

- Gibbs-Poole-Stockmeyer (Ref. 7-4)

- Levy (Ref. 7-5)

These algorithms are reviewed in Ref. 7-6 where it is shown that Levy's wavefront performance is generally best for small problems and that Gibbs-Poole-Stockmeyer is best for large problems.

MSC/NASTRAN includes a general resequencing capability that incorporates both the Levy wavefront and the Gibbs-Poole-Stockmeyer methods as options. The MSC/NASTRAN grid point resequencing processor is included in rigid format 3 for normal mode analysis and available in rigid format 24 as a rigid format alter RF24D74 (see Sec. 1.9.7. for a discussion of rigid format alters).

The resequencing procedure in either case is controlled by means of the following PARAMeter Bulk Data cards.

NEWSEQ   Selects the sequencing option according to the following values of the PARAMeter

- 1 No resequencing

0 Do not add generated SEQGP cards to GEOM1 data block

1 Use active/passive option

2 Use band option

3 Try both options 1 and 2 and take sequence giving lowest root-mean-square wavefront (Default)

MPCX   Controls processing of multipoint constraints (See Sec. 7.5.1) according to PARAMeter values as follows

- 1 Do not include multipoint constraints defined on MPC or constraint elements

0 Process all rigid (constraint) elements (Default)

>0 Process all rigid (constraint) elements and the MPC set associated with the value of the PARAMeter

SEQOUT   Controls the output options according to the following values of the PARAMeter

0 Do not generate printed or punched output (Default)

141

1 Print a correspondence table between new and old sequence in resequenced order

2 Write the SEQGP images on the system punch file

3 Union of options 1 and 2

7.4.   Displacement Sets

It is convenient to consider the displacement degrees of freedom as the elements of a displacement set. The set of all grid point degrees of freedom including scalar degrees of freedom is called the g-set and is of order N_g as described in Section 7.3.4.

The stiffness matrix associated with the g-set is denoted by $\mathbf{K}_{gg}$ and is normally defined by a finite element model. The system matrix associated with the g-set of degrees of freedom may be singular, i.e., the determinant is equal to zero, either because the internal degree of freedom does not physically exist, or because the elements of the g-set are linearly dependent. We recall that six internal degrees of freedom are defined at each geometric grid point so that there are six rows and six columns in the global stiffness matrix that are initially zero. If the finite element model does not define elements in the stiffness matrix associated with a degree of freedom, then the degree of freedom is not connected and must be purged from the g-set. After purging all unconnected degrees of freedom, the resulting subset of $\mathbf{u}_g$ may still include rigid body motion that must be restrained to make $\mathbf{K}_{gg}$ nonsingular.

NASTRAN allows the user to define a number of independent subsets of $\mathbf{u}_g$ by the following types of constraints:

1. Specification of values for specific degrees of freedom, which is termed a single point constraint (SPC)

2. Specification of linear relation between two or more degrees of freedom, which is termed a multipoint constraint (MPC)

3. Specification of reactionless constraints, which are used to model unsupported structures (SUPORT)

NASTRAN also provides the facility for performing matrix reduction using the ASET and OMIT Bulk Data cards.

Each of these constraint and reduction operations acts on a set of displacement degrees of freedom to produce partitioned data sets, one of which is retained in the analysis and one of which is removed. These operations are performed in the sequence shown by Table 7-4, which identifies the data set that is operated on, the data set removed, and the data set retained by the operation.

The data sets that are removed by a constraint or reduction operation are mutually exclusive. A degree of freedom can only exist in one of the mutually exclusive sets so that a degree of freedom specified in any one of the sets cannot be specified in another removed data set.

7.4.1.   Merged Data Sets

The merged data sets are

$\mathbf{u}_g$ Set of all **g**rid point degrees of freedom including extra points.

$\mathbf{u}_n$ Set of all degrees of freedom **n**ot eliminated by multipoint constraints.

$\mathbf{u}_f$ Set of **f**ree degrees of freedom that remain after specification of single point constraints.

$\mathbf{u}_a$ **A**nalysis set is that used in real eigenvalue analysis.

7.4.2.   Mutually Independent Data Sets

The mutually independent displacement sets are identified as removed data sets in Table 7-4. These data sets are

$\mathbf{u}_m$ Set removed by **m**ultipoint constraints

$\mathbf{u}_s$ Set removed by **s**ingle point constraints

$\mathbf{u}_o$ Set **o**mitted by matrix reduction

$\mathbf{u}_r$ Set of forceless degrees of freedom, which remove **r**igid body motion and

$\mathbf{u}_\ell$ Set **l**eft over, which is the solution set in static analysis

NASTRAN Operation	Operates on	Partitioned Data Sets	
		Set Retained	Set Removed
MPC	$\mathbf{u}_g$	$\mathbf{u}_n$	$\mathbf{u}_m$
SPC	$\mathbf{u}_n$	$\mathbf{u}_f$	$\mathbf{u}_s$
OMIT or ASET	$\mathbf{u}_f$	$\mathbf{u}_a$	$\mathbf{u}_o$
SUPORT	$\mathbf{u}_a$	$\mathbf{u}_\ell$	$\mathbf{u}_r$

Table 7-4. Displacement Data Sets for Static Analysis

7.5.   Specification of Constraints

A set of linear relations that describes a set of kinematic constraints between degrees of freedom can be specified directly in NASTRAN by the multipoint constraints, as described in Section 7.5.1.

The prescribed value for a single degree of freedom can be specified by single point constraints, as described in Section 7.5.2. The combined capability of multipoint constraints, single point constraints and scalar degrees of freedom is sufficient to allow the user to specify any linear relationship between degrees of freedom.

7.5.1.   Multipoint Constraints — MPC cards

A multipoint constraint is simply a linear equation that relates the displacement degrees of freedom. Relations of this type can be used to model rigid links between node points or to specify constraints that are a linear combination of grid point displacements. For example, consider the rigid link that connects grid points A and B as shown by Figure 7-15.

Since the link between points A and B is rigid, the following kinematic relations exist between displacement degrees of freedom at A and B:

$$
\begin{aligned}
u_{1B} &= u_{1A} - y_{AB}\, u_{6A} \\
u_{2B} &= u_{2A} + x_{AB}\, u_{6A} \\
u_{6B} &= u_{6A}
\end{aligned}
\tag{7.34}
$$

where x_{AB} and y_{AB} represent the distances along the x and y coordinates from point A to B, respectively.

7.5.1 Multipoint Constraints — MPC cards

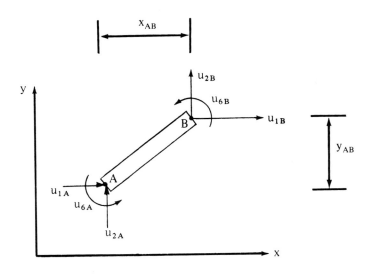

Figure 7-15. Planar Rigid Link

NASTRAN allows the user to express sets of linear relations such as (7.34) in the general form

$$\mathbf{G}_{mg}\,\mathbf{u}_g = \mathbf{O} \tag{7.35}$$

which represents a set of m-constraint equations where $\mathbf{G}_{mg}$ is a matrix of coefficients which is to be specified by the user. The solution set $\mathbf{u}_g$ must, therefore, satisfy (7.35) in addition to the set of equilibrium equations for the g-set

$$\mathbf{K}_{gg}\,\mathbf{u}_g = \mathbf{P}_g + \mathbf{c}_g \tag{7.36}$$

where $\mathbf{P}_g$ are external forces applied to the g-set degrees of freedom and $\mathbf{c}_g$ are forces of constraint.

Generally speaking the constraint equations can be incorporated either by an elimination procedure or by means of Lagrange multipliers. The elimination procedure which is the only procedure in the NASTRAN solution algorithm proceeds by partitioning the g-set into two complimentary sets; the m-set which contains exactly m degrees of freedom where m is the number of constraint equations, and the remaining degrees of freedom which is called the n-set. That is

$$\mathbf{u}_g = \begin{Bmatrix} \mathbf{u}_m \\ \mathbf{u}_n \end{Bmatrix} \tag{7.37}$$

The multipoint constraint specification must, therefore, perform two tasks:

1. Define the matrix of coefficients $\mathbf{G}_{mg}$

2. Specify the degrees of freedom in the m-set

This is done by defining each constraint equation with a logical MPC Bulk Data card as shown by Card Image 7-8 which defines a degree of freedom to be included in the m-set as well as nonzero coefficients of the constraint.

	1	2	3	4	5	6	7	8	9	10
MPC +M1	SID	GM G_2	CM C_2	A_m A_2	G_1 etc.	C_1	A_1		+M1
MPCADD +MX	SID S_8	S_1 etc.	S_2	S_3	S_4	S_5	S_6	S_7	+MX

where

SID Set identification (integer, > 0)

S_1, S_2 MPC set identification numbers (integer, > 0)
etc.

Card Image 7-8. Multipoint Constraint Specification

7.5.1.1. MPC Sets

Sets of relations of the form of (7.35) can be specified in the Bulk Data deck where each is given a set identification number in field two of the MPC card. The particular MPC set that is to be used at execution time is specified by the Case Control Directive

$$MPC = SID$$

where SID is the integer number assigned to MPC set in Bulk Data.

MPC sets can be combined into a single logical set by the MPCADD Bulk Data card. The MPC sets specified by sets S_1, S_2,...,S_N are combined and given an SID on the MPCADD card, which is then specified by a Case Control Directive. All the MPC and MPCADD set identification numbers which appear on the MPCADD Bulk Data card must be unique.

7.5.1.2. Specifying the Dependent Degrees of Freedom

One logical MPC card is required for each degree of freedom to be included in the m-set. The degrees of freedom are identified by the external degree of freedom number, which consists of the pair (G, C) where

G is the identification number of a GRID or SPOINT

and

C is a degree of freedom code at grid point G. If G is a scalar point, then C is either blank or equal to integer zero.

The first degree of freedom, identified by (GM, CM) in fields four and five, is a dependent degree of freedom and is included in the m-set. The coefficient A_m is the associated element of $\mathbf{G}_{mg}$. All subsequent pairs (G_i, C_i) specify degrees of freedom in the constraint equation with nonzero elements A_i in the $\mathbf{G}_{mg}$-matrix. The degrees of freedom specified on the MPC card are defined with respect to the CD coordinate system defined on the GRID Bulk Data card.

7.5.1.3. Reduction to the $\mathbf{u}_n$ Set

In order to reduce the set of equations to the n-set, we proceed by writing the set of constraint equations (7.35) in terms of the m- and n-partitions as follows:

$$\mathbf{R}_{mm}\mathbf{u}_m + \mathbf{R}_{mn}\mathbf{u}_m = 0 \qquad (7.38)$$

145

The dependent displacements $\mathbf{u}_m$ can then be expressed in terms of the independent set $\mathbf{u}_n$ as

$$\mathbf{u}_m = \mathbf{G}_{mn}\,\mathbf{u}_n \qquad (7.39)$$

where

$$\mathbf{G}_{mn} = -\mathbf{R}_{mm}^{-1}\mathbf{R}_{mn} \qquad (7.40)$$

We can now use the constraint relation (7.39) to express the g-set displacements in terms of those of the n-set by writing (7.37) as follows

$$\mathbf{u}_g = \begin{bmatrix} \mathbf{G}_{mn} \\ \mathbf{I}_{nn} \end{bmatrix} \mathbf{u}_n \qquad (7.41)$$

or

$$\mathbf{u}_g = \mathbf{G}_{gn}\,\mathbf{u}_n \qquad (7.42)$$

where $\mathbf{I}_{nn}$ is an identity matrix of n-size.

The reduced stiffness matrix is then found by noting that the constraint forces $\mathbf{c}_g$ perform no work during a virtual displacement $\mathbf{u}_g$ so that the virtual work expression associated with (7.36) is

$$\mathbf{u}_g^T(\mathbf{K}_{gg}\,\mathbf{u}_g - \mathbf{P}_g) = 0 \qquad (7.43)$$

Now, admissable displacements must satisfy (7.42), so (7.43) becomes

$$\mathbf{u}_n^T\mathbf{G}_{gn}^T(\mathbf{K}_{gg}\,\mathbf{G}_{gn}\,\mathbf{u}_n - \mathbf{P}_g) = 0 \qquad (7.44)$$

Since the virtual displacements $\mathbf{u}_n$ are arbitrary the satisfaction of (7.44) requires that

$$\mathbf{G}_{gn}^T\mathbf{K}_{gg}\,\mathbf{G}_{gn}\,\mathbf{u}_n - \mathbf{G}_{gn}^T\mathbf{P}_g = 0 \qquad (7.45)$$

or

$$\mathbf{K}_{nn}\,\mathbf{u}_n = \mathbf{P}_n \qquad (7.46)$$

where the reduced stiffness and load are given by

$$\mathbf{K}_{nn} = \mathbf{G}_{gn}^T\,\mathbf{K}_{gg}\,\mathbf{G}_{gn} \qquad (7.47)$$

$$\mathbf{P}_n = \mathbf{G}_{gn}^T\,\mathbf{P}_g \qquad (7.48)$$

7.5.1.4.   Example: Modeling a Rigid Link with End Fixity

A rigid linkage between grid point degrees of freedom in the structural system is a common modeling problem. One may be tempted to use a stiff beam-type element to connect such points, but an ill-conditioned stiffness matrix may result. Since a kinematic constraint involves a linear relationship between degrees of freedom, the correct approach is that of employing a multipoint constraint.

Consider two grid points $\mathbf{A}$ and $\mathbf{B}$, as shown by Fig. 7-16 with a rigid link connecting the two points. The rotations of the two points are θ_A and θ_B, respectively; and the displacements are $\mathbf{u}_A$ and $\mathbf{u}_B$. The displacement and rotation of B can then be expressed in terms of the displacement at A as

$$\mathbf{u}_B = \mathbf{u}_A + \theta_A \times \ell \qquad (7.49)$$

and

$$\theta_B = \theta_A \tag{7.50}$$

where ℓ is the vector from point A to point B. These vector equations can be written in scalar form as

$$
\begin{aligned}
u_{1B} &= u_{1A} - \ell_y u_{6A} + \ell_z u_{5A} \\
u_{2B} &= u_{2A} - \ell_z u_{4A} + \ell_x u_{6A} \\
u_{3B} &= u_{3A} - \ell_x u_{5A} + \ell_y u_{4A} \\
u_{4B} &= u_{uA} \\
u_{5B} &= u_{5A} \\
u_{6B} &= u_{6A}
\end{aligned}
\tag{7.51}
$$

where ℓ_x, ℓ_y, ℓ_z are the components of ℓ in the x-, y-, and z-directions.

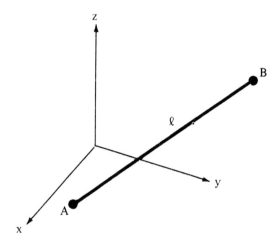

Figure 7-16. General Rigid Link

As a numerical example, let the coordinates of points **A** and **B** be given as

$$
\begin{aligned}
\mathbf{A} &\Rightarrow (1, 2, 3) \\
\mathbf{B} &\Rightarrow (5, 3, 1)
\end{aligned}
$$

which are identified as grid points 363 and 132, respectively. The components of ℓ can then be found to be

$$
\begin{aligned}
\ell_x &= 4 \\
\ell_y &= 1 \\
\ell_z &= 2
\end{aligned}
$$

The multipoint constraints (7.51) can then be written as in the form of (7.35) as follows

147

7.5.2 Single Point Constraints — SPC cards

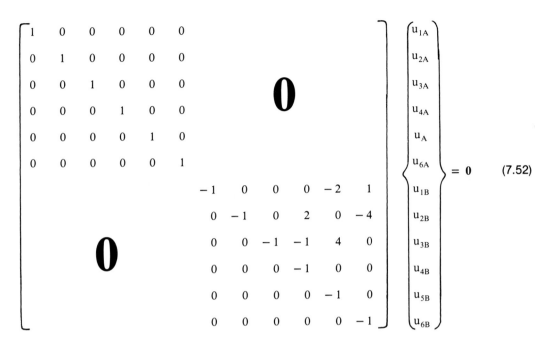

$$\begin{bmatrix} \begin{array}{cccccc} 1 & 0 & 0 & 0 & 0 & 0 \\ 0 & 1 & 0 & 0 & 0 & 0 \\ 0 & 0 & 1 & 0 & 0 & 0 \\ 0 & 0 & 0 & 1 & 0 & 0 \\ 0 & 0 & 0 & 0 & 1 & 0 \\ 0 & 0 & 0 & 0 & 0 & 1 \end{array} & \mathbf{0} \\[2em] \mathbf{0} & \begin{array}{cccccc} -1 & 0 & 0 & 0 & -2 & 1 \\ 0 & -1 & 0 & 2 & 0 & -4 \\ 0 & 0 & -1 & -1 & 4 & 0 \\ 0 & 0 & 0 & -1 & 0 & 0 \\ 0 & 0 & 0 & 0 & -1 & 0 \\ 0 & 0 & 0 & 0 & 0 & -1 \end{array} \end{bmatrix} \begin{Bmatrix} u_{1A} \\ u_{2A} \\ u_{3A} \\ u_{4A} \\ u_{A} \\ u_{6A} \\ u_{1B} \\ u_{2B} \\ u_{3B} \\ u_{4B} \\ u_{5B} \\ u_{6B} \end{Bmatrix} = \mathbf{0} \qquad (7.52)$$

The MPC cards required to specify the rigid link between the points A and B taking the degrees of freedom at B to be in the m-set are then

1	2	3	4	5	6	7	8	9	10
MPC	101	132	1	1.	363	1	− 1.		+ M1
+ M1		363	5	− 2.	363	6	1.		
MPC	101	132	2	1.	363	2	− 1.		+ M2
+ M2		363	4	2.	363	6	− 4.		
MPC	101	132	3	1.	363	3	− 1.		+ M3
+ M3		363	4	− 1.	363	5	4.		
MPC	101	132	4	1.	363	4	− 1.		
MPC	101	132	5	1.	363	5	− 1.		
MPC	101	132	6	1.	363	6	− 1.		

where the MPC set identification SID = 101 has been used in each logical MPC card. The user will note that nine data cards are required to define the simple kinematic constraint defined by the rigid link

The specification of even simple rigid elements connecting two points is a laborious task. Since all of the geometric data required to define the kinematic constraint equations is included on the GRID card it would seem logical to let the program generate the associated MPC set automatically. MSC/NASTRAN includes a library of constraint elements as a convenient alternative to writing MPC Bulk Data. The example described above could have been defined by using an RBAR constraint element where the constraint elements are described in Sec. 9.11 and are summarized in Table 9-10.

7.5.2. Single Point Constraints — SPC cards

The specification of displacement values in the form

$$\mathbf{u}_s = \mathbf{Y}_s \qquad (7.53)$$

where Y_s is prescribed is called a Single Point Constraint (SPC) and is defined by SPC, SPC1, and SPCADD cards as shown in Card Image 7-9.

1	2	3	4	5	6	7	8	9	10
SPC	SID	G	C	D	G	C	D		
SPCADD	SID	S_1	S_2	S_3	S_4	etc.			

*Alternate Forms

1	2	3	4	5	6	7	8	9	10
SPC1	SID	C	G1	G2	G3	G4	G5	G6	+ ABC
+ ABC	G7	G8	etc.						
SPC1	SID	C	GI	THRU	GJ				

where

SID Set identification number (integer, ≥ 0)

(G, C) Pair defining external degree of freedom number. G is the grid or scalar point identification number (integer, > 0) and C is the degree of freedom code. C may be a packed integer number $0 \leq C \leq 6$ to specify all degrees of freedom at G that have the value given by D.

D Value of the prescribed displacement (real).

$S_1, S_2,...$ SPC Set identification numbers

Card Image 7-9. Single Point Constraint Specification

7.5.2.1. SPC Sets

The user may define several sets of single point constraints in Bulk Data where each set is given a unique set identification number. The SPC set that is to be used at execution time is then specified by the Case Control Directive

$$SPC = SID$$

where SID is the integer number assigned to a SPC set in Bulk Data.

SPC sets can be combined into a single logical set by the SPCADD Bulk Data. The SPC sets specified by set identification numbers S_1, S_2,...,etc. are combined and are given a unique SID on the SPCADD Bulk Data card, which is then specified by the above Case Control Directive.

7.5.2.2. Specifying s-set Degrees of Freedom and Constraint Value

The SPC Bulk Data perform two independent functions. These are

1. Purging nonexistent degrees of freedom.
2. Setting displacement boundary conditions.

The form of the SPC card supports these two functions by

1. Defining degrees of freedom to be included in the s-set.
2. Specifying a value for each degree of freedom either implicitly or explicitly.

149

7.5.2.3   Generating SPC Bulk Data with MSGMESH

The SPC card is used to explicitly set the degree(s) of freedom defined by the pair (G, C) to the value D where

   G is a grid or scalar point number.
   C is a packed set of one to six degrees of freedom codes at point G.

All of the C degrees of freedom at grid point G then are set equal to the value D.

  The SPC1 Bulk Data card implicitly defines all degrees of freedom specified to zero. The degrees of freedom specified by the packed code C are set equal to zero at all the grid points listed on the remainder of the card. The SPC1 card can be continued whereas the SPC card cannot. The second form of the SPC1 card allows the user to define an inclusive set of points by use of the literal string THRU. The total set of degrees of freedom included in the s-set is taken to be the union of all degrees of freedom defined on SPC-type Bulk Data and those defined as permanent single point constraints (PSPC) on GRID Bulk Data.

7.5.2.3.   Generating SPC Bulk Data with MSGMESH

  SPC Bulk Data can be generated on fields of GRID points which were originally defined by MSGMESH by means of the SPCG MSGMESH command which is shown by Card Image 7-10.

1	2	3	4	5	6	7	8	9	10
SPCG	SID	FID	C	E1	E2	E3	E4		

Card Image 7-10. Generation of SPC — SPCG

  SPCG is an MSGMESH command so it is only understood by the MSGMESH processor and is treated as a comment card by the Bulk Data processor in MSC/NASTRAN. It is useful for generating displacement boundary conditions on the boundary edges of two-dimensional fields and boundary surfaces of three-dimensional fields that have been generated by means of the GRIDG MSGMESH command (see Sec. 7.3.3.7.). MSGMESH uses the data on the SPCG command to generate SPC1 Bulk Data with set number equal to SID for Grid point field FID. The degrees of freedom specified by the code, C, which can be the packed set of integers one through six, are included in SPC1 Bulk Data for all points which lie along the edge or surface of the field that is identified by entries in the E1, E2, E3, E4 fields. Referring to Fig. 7-7, edges are identified in these fields by specifying pairs of corner, AB, BC, AE, etc., while surfaces on three dimensional fields are identified by the corner symbols of either diagonal on the face, AF, BG, etc.

7.5.2.4.   Reduction to the u_f Set

  We found that the reduced stiffness equation associated with the n-set is given by (7.46). This equation is further reduced by specifying that the n-set is the union of the s- and f- sets so that (7.46) can be written in partitioned form as

$$\begin{bmatrix} \mathbf{K}_{ss} & \mathbf{K}_{sf} \\ \mathbf{K}_{fs} & \mathbf{K}_{ff} \end{bmatrix} \begin{Bmatrix} \mathbf{u}_s \\ \mathbf{u}_f \end{Bmatrix} = \begin{Bmatrix} \mathbf{P}_s \\ \widetilde{\mathbf{P}}_f \end{Bmatrix} \tag{7.54}$$

The set $\mathbf{u}_s$ is prescribed by (7.53) so that the reduced set of equations for the free or f-set becomes

$$\mathbf{K}_{ff}\,\mathbf{u}_f = \mathbf{P}_f \tag{7.55}$$

where

$$\mathbf{P}_f = \widetilde{\mathbf{P}}_f - \mathbf{K}_{fs}\,\mathbf{Y}_s \tag{7.56}$$

7.5.2.5. Purging Degrees of Freedom

It is frequently necessary to purge degrees of freedom from the solution set. Typically these are degrees of freedom that are automatically defined at a GRID point but which are unconnected by the finite element model. Examples would include out of plane behavior for plane problems, the rotational degrees of freedom for membranes and solids, and the normal rotation for plates and shells.

Purging can be accomplished by simply including all unconnected degrees of freedom in the s-set. Suppose, for purpose of argument, that only unconnected degrees of freedom are included in the s-set. Then, since there are no stiffness coefficients associated with these degrees of freedom the partitions of the stiffness matrix associated with the s-set are null. The reduced set of equations is then given by (7.57) where $\mathbf{P}_f$ is equal to $\widetilde{\mathbf{P}}_f$ independent of the prescribed values $\mathbf{Y}_s$ since $\mathbf{K}_{fs}$ is null.

7.5.2.6. Automatic Purging

In large analysis problems it is sometimes a difficult task to identify degrees of freedom which are unconnected in the system stiffness matrix. MSC/NASTRAN thus includes the capability of automatically generating SPC1-type Bulk Data to purge unconnected degrees of freedom.

The process is controlled by user-defined PARAMeters and takes place after the unconstrained stiffness matrix $\mathbf{K}_{gg}$ has been generated including the stiffness defined by finite elements, scalar elements, general elements and direct matrix input but prior to the incorporation of constraints.

The mathematical procedure for detecting potential singularities and a description of the PARAMeters which are used to control automatic purging are described in Sec. 12.4.3.1. In essence the inclusion of a PARAM Bulk Data card whose general form is shown by Card Image 3-2 with the name AUTOSPC and a value of YES will cause MSC/NASTRAN to purge unconnected degrees of freedom. The required PARAMeter card is thus as shown below

1	2	3	4	5	6	7	8	9	10
PARAM	AUTOSPC	YES							

7.5.2.7. Single Point Constraint Forces

The internal forces that are required to enforce the single point constraints are given by

$$\left\{ \begin{array}{c} \mathbf{c}_s \\ \mathbf{c}_f \end{array} \right\} = \left[\begin{array}{cc} \mathbf{K}_{ss} & \mathbf{K}_{sf} \\ \mathbf{K}_{fs} & \mathbf{K}_{ff} \end{array} \right] \left\{ \begin{array}{c} \mathbf{Y}_s \\ \mathbf{u}_f \end{array} \right\} - \left\{ \begin{array}{c} \mathbf{P}_s \\ \mathbf{P}_f \end{array} \right\} \tag{7.57}$$

The forces of reaction associated with $\mathbf{u}_s$ degrees of freedom are found from the first of equations (7.58) to be

$$\mathbf{c}_s = \mathbf{K}_{ss} \mathbf{Y}_s + \mathbf{K}_{sf} \mathbf{u}_f - \mathbf{P}_s \tag{7.58}$$

where $\mathbf{c}_f = 0$ since there are no constraints on the f-set. The single point constraint forces can be recovered by the Case Control Directive.

$$\text{SPCFORCE} = \ <set>$$

where <set> is defined by a SET Ease Control directive and specifies the points at which the forces of constraint are desired.

7.5.2.8. Example: Specification of Single Point Constraints

Consider the cantilever beam in Fig. 7-17.

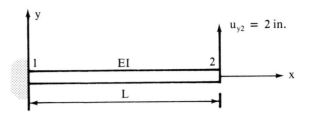

Figure 7-17. Enforced Displacement of a Beam

The beam is constrained to move in the x,y-plane, and where an enforced displacement $u_{y2} = 2$ in. is to be specified at grid point two. The constraints are specified by the following SPC cards:

1	2	3	4	5	6	7	8	9	10
SPC1	1	123456	1						
SPC1	1	1345	2						
SPC	1	2	2	2.					

where the SPC1 cards are used to apply constraints and to purge unconnected degrees of freedom at grid points one and two and the SPC card is used to specify the enforced displacement of grid point two.

7.6. Static Condensation — OMIT and ASET

The set of stiffness equations that relate the u_f degrees of freedom can be partitioned and reduced by the OMIT or ASET Bulk Data as shown by Card Images 7-11 and 7-12 respectively.

1	2	3	4	5	6	7	8	9	10
OMIT	G	C	G	C	G	C	G	C	

*Alternate Forms

1	2	3	4	5	6	7	8	9
OMIT1	C	G1	G2	G3	G4	G5	G6	G7	+ OM1
+ OM1	G8	G9	etc.						
OMIT1	C	GI	THRU	GJ					

where

    G Grid or scalar point identification number (integer, ≥ 0)

    C Degree of freedom code, an integer if G is a geometric point or zero or blank if G is a scalar point.

Card Image 7-11. Matrix Reduction — OMIT

The presence of either OMIT or ASET type cards in the Bulk Data deck indicates that static condensation is to be performed. The OMIT Bulk Data cards specify degrees of freedom to be reduced out of the analysis set while the ASET Bulk Data cards specify degrees of freedom to be retained. Either OMIT or ASET Bulk Data can be used, but not both. Since they represent complementary sets the user should specify that which represents the smaller of the two sets.

1	2	3	4	5	6	7	8	9	10
ASET	G	C	G	C	G	C	G	C	

*Alternate Forms

ASET1	C	G1	G2	G3	G4	G5	G6	G7	+A1
+A1	G8	G9	etc.						
ASET1	C	GI	THRU	GJ					

Card Image 7-12. Matrix Partitioning — ASET

7.6.1. Specifying Degrees of Freedom

The user has two alternate forms of specifying the o-set and a-set by the OMIT or ASET and the OMIT1 or ASET1 cards. The OMIT and ASET cards allow the user to specify a degree of freedom by the external degree of freedom number, which consists of the pair (G,C) where

G   is the grid or scalar point number

and

C   is one or more degree of freedom codes at point G.

Degrees of freedom specified on the OMIT card are placed in the omit-set while those specified on ASET cards are placed in the analysis-set. Note that neither the OMIT nor ASET cards can be continued.

The OMIT1 and ASET1 cards allow the user to define degrees of freedom to be placed in the o- or a-sets, respectively, by specifying first the degree of freedom code C followed by all the grid points at which the degree(s) of freedom are to be omitted or retained. This form of the OMIT1 and ASET1 cards can have continuations.

Finally, both the OMIT1 and ASET1 cards have an alternative form that allows the user to specify an inclusive set of grid and scalar points by use of the literal string THRU in the field separating the first and last grid or scalar point.

7.6.2. Reduction to the u_a Set

The stiffness matrix associated with the u_f set is given by (7.55), which is written in partitioned form as

$$\begin{bmatrix} K_{oo} & K_{oa} \\ K_{ao} & K_{aa} \end{bmatrix} \begin{Bmatrix} u_o \\ u_a \end{Bmatrix} = \begin{Bmatrix} P_o \\ P_a \end{Bmatrix} \tag{7.59}$$

The transformation between the u_o and u_a displacement sets, which is used in the reduction process, is found from the first of (7.59) to be

$$u_o = G_{oa} u_a \tag{7.60}$$

where

$$G_{oa} = -K_{oo}^{-1} K_{oa} \tag{7.61}$$

we note that the term $-K_{oo}^{-1} P_o$ which is associated with the loads on the o-set has been neglected. This contribution will be included during the recovery of the displacement set u_o after the analysis set, u_a, has been found.

153

Proceeding with the reduction process we can express the f-set as the union of the o- and a-sets in matrix form as follows

$$\mathbf{u}_f = \left\{ \begin{matrix} \mathbf{u}_o \\ \mathbf{u}_a \end{matrix} \right\} \tag{7.62}$$

Then, using (7.60) the f-set can be expressed in terms of the a-set as

$$\mathbf{u}_f = \left[\begin{matrix} \mathbf{G}_{oa} \\ \mathbf{I}_{aa} \end{matrix} \right] \mathbf{u}_a \tag{7.63}$$

or

$$\mathbf{u}_f = \mathbf{G}_{fa} \mathbf{u}_a \tag{7.64}$$

where $\mathbf{I}_{aa}$ is an identity matrix of a-size. The reduced set of equations is then given by

$$\mathbf{K}_{aa} \mathbf{u}_a = \mathbf{P}_a \tag{7.65}$$

where

$$\mathbf{K}_{aa} = \mathbf{G}_{fa}^T \mathbf{K}_{ff} \mathbf{G}_{fa} \tag{7.66}$$

and

$$\mathbf{P}_a = \mathbf{G}_{fa}^T \mathbf{P}_f \tag{7.67}$$

7.6.3. Recovery of Omitted Degrees of Freedom

After the displacements in the a-set are determined the degrees of freedom in the o-set are evaluated by augmenting the displacements calculated by means of (7.60) with the displacements produced by the loads $\mathbf{P}_o$. That is, during data recovery the o-set displacements are given by

$$\mathbf{u}_o = \mathbf{G}_{oa} \mathbf{u}_a + \mathbf{u}_o^o \tag{7.68}$$

where

$$\mathbf{u}_o^o = \mathbf{K}_{oo}^{-1} \mathbf{P}_o \tag{7.69}$$

7.6.4. Physical Interpretation of $\mathbf{G}_{oa}$

The transformation matrix $\mathbf{G}_{oa}$ (7.61) which relates the omitted degrees of freedom to those retained in the analysis has a useful physical interpretation. The columns of $\mathbf{G}_{oa}$ are static displacement modes of the structure. That is each column represents the static displacement of the entire o-set for a unit displacement of the a-set degree of freedom associated with that column, with all other a-set degrees of freedom set equal to zero.

7.6.5. Example: Static Condensation

Consider the finite element model shown in Fig. 7-18, in which we wish to place all degrees of freedom associated with the interior grid points in the o-set.

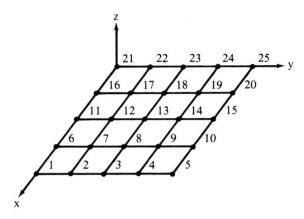

Figure 7-18. Elimination of Internal Degrees of Freedom using OMIT

The structure is that of a plate, and it is assumed that that the rotation about the normal u_6 has been purged by use of single point constraints. The following Bulk Data then reduce the degrees of freedom in the analysis set, u_a, to those associated with the boundary.

1	2	3	4	5	6	7	8	9	10
OMIT1	12345	7	8	9	12	13	14	17	+ 01
+ 01	18	19							

where the number in the second field specifies the degrees of freedom that are to be included in the o-set for each of the grid points listed. Conversely, the following ASET cards could be used

1	2	3	4	5	6	7	8	9	10
ASET1	12345	1	THRU	5					
ASET1	12345	6	10	11	15	16	20		
ASET1	12345	21	THRU	25					

For this example the o-set is smaller than the a-set, and it makes sense to use the OMIT-type card. One could visualize the case where the converse would be true and then the ASET card should be used.

7.7. Support for Free Bodies — SUPORT

An elastic body that is capable of undergoing rigid body motion is termed a free body. Free elastic bodies are capable of motion that produces no internal forces in the body. The stiffness matrix for a free body is singular and a set of constraints must be specified to remove the rigid body motion for static analysis.

The required constraints could be specified by single point or multipoint constraints, or by means of free-body supports. The advantage in using free-body supports is that the rigid body characteristics are calculated and the supports are checked for sufficiency.

The singularity can be removed by restraining sufficient degrees of freedom u_r to eliminate rigid body motion of the structure without introducing redundant reactions. The set of forces associated with the r-set are thus statically determinate.

NASTRAN includes a special Bulk Data card called the SUPORT card that is used to specify the degrees of freedom u_r that will remove rigid body motion. The SUPORT card is shown by Card Image 7-13.

7.7.3 Rigid Body Transformation Matrix

1	2	3	4	5	6	7	8	9	10
SUPORT	G	C	G	C	G	C	G	C	

where

G Grid or scalar point identification (integer, > 0)

C Component number integer $0 \le C \le 6$ or blank if G is a scalar point.

Card Image 7-13. Specification of Statically Determinate Supports.

7.7.1. Specifying Degrees of Freedom

The user specifies the degrees of freedom that will restrain rigid body motion by the external degrees of freedom numbers, which consist of the pair (G,C) where

G is the grid or scalar point number

and

C is one or more degrees of freedom codes at point G.

7.7.2. Reduction to the u_ℓ Set

The stiffness equation for the a-set (7.65) can be written in partitioned form as

$$\begin{bmatrix} \tilde{\mathbf{K}}_{rr} & \mathbf{K}_{r\ell} \\ \mathbf{K}_{\ell r} & \mathbf{K}_{\ell\ell} \end{bmatrix} \begin{Bmatrix} \mathbf{u}_r \\ \mathbf{u}_\ell \end{Bmatrix} = \begin{Bmatrix} \mathbf{P}_r \\ \mathbf{P}_\ell \end{Bmatrix} + \begin{Bmatrix} \mathbf{C}_r \\ 0 \end{Bmatrix} \tag{7.70}$$

where $\mathbf{C}_r$ are constraint forces associated with the r-set and where

$$\mathbf{u}_a = \begin{Bmatrix} \mathbf{u}_r \\ \mathbf{u}_\ell \end{Bmatrix} \tag{7.71}$$

The set of displacements $\mathbf{u}_r$ is specified by the user on the SUPORT card and are set equal to zero. We have then, from the second of (7.70),

$$\mathbf{K}_{\ell\ell}\mathbf{u}_\ell = \mathbf{P}_\ell \tag{7.72}$$

The stiffness matrix $\mathbf{K}_{\ell\ell}$ is nonsingular so that (7.72) can be solved for the $\mathbf{u}_\ell$ set of displacements.

7.7.3. Rigid Body Transformation Matrix

Although the SUPORTed degrees of freedom $\mathbf{u}_r$, are set equal to zero in reducing to the solution set, $\mathbf{u}_\ell$, this operation differs from that associated with the use of SPCs in a very fundamental way — the forces of constraint associated with the r-set are equal to zero. Thus, from the first of (7.70) we find

$$\mathbf{c}_r = 0 = -\mathbf{P}_r + \mathbf{K}_{r\ell}\mathbf{u}_\ell \tag{7.73}$$

The forces applied to the SUPORTed degrees of freedom, $\mathbf{P}_r$, can now be expressed in terms of the loads applied to the solution set, $\mathbf{P}_\ell$, by noting that $\mathbf{u}_\ell$ can be found from (7.72) as

$$\mathbf{U}_\ell = \mathbf{K}_{\ell\ell}^{-1}\,\mathbf{P}_\ell \tag{7.74}$$

so that

$$\mathbf{P}_r = -\mathbf{G}_{r\ell}\mathbf{P}_\ell \tag{7.75}$$

where $\mathbf{G}_{r\ell}$ is called the rigid body transformation matrix and is given by

$$\mathbf{G}_{r\ell} = -\mathbf{K}_{r\ell}\mathbf{K}_{\ell\ell}^{-1} \tag{7.76}$$

It is left as an exercise to show that, in the absence of external loads, the motion of the ℓ-set is related to motion of the r-set through the following relation

$$\mathbf{u}_\ell = \mathbf{G}_{\ell r}\mathbf{u}_r = \mathbf{G}_{r\ell}^T\mathbf{u}_r \tag{7.77}$$

7.7.4. Rigid Body Stiffness Matrix

The SUPORTed degrees of freedom, $\mathbf{u}_r$, define the rigid body motion of the structure. Therefore, the reduced stiffness matrix for the r-set should be completely null. The reduced matrix is found by noting that rigid body motion of the ℓ-set is related to r-set displacements by (7.77) so we can write (7.71) for rigid body motion as

$$\mathbf{u}_a = \mathbf{G}_{ar}\mathbf{u}_r \tag{7.78}$$

where

$$\mathbf{G}_{ar} = \begin{bmatrix} \mathbf{I}_{rr} \\ \mathbf{G}_{\ell r} \end{bmatrix} \tag{7.79}$$

then, the reduced stiffness matrix $\mathbf{K}_{rr}$ is given by

$$\mathbf{K}_{rr} = \mathbf{G}_{ar}^T\mathbf{K}_{aa}\mathbf{G}_{ar} \tag{7.80}$$

The substitution of (7.70) and (7.79) into (7.80) then gives

$$\mathbf{K}_{rr} = \widetilde{\mathbf{K}}_{rr} + \mathbf{K}_{r\ell}\mathbf{G}_{\ell r} \tag{7.81}$$

where $\mathbf{G}_{\ell r}$ is given by (7.76). The reduced matrix $\mathbf{K}_{rr}$ should be completely null at this point. MSC/NASTRAN calculates the rigid body error ratio

$$\epsilon = \frac{\|\mathbf{K}'_{rr}\|}{\|\mathbf{K}_{rr}\|} \tag{7.82}$$

and the strain energy associated with giving the r-set degrees of freedom unit displacements or rotations where the notation $\|\mathbf{K}_{rr}\|$ means the Euclidian norm of the matrix. These quantities are automatically printed after they are calculated. Except for roundoff error the rigid body error ratio and the strain energy should be zero if a compatible set of statically determinate supports have been chosen by the user. These quantities may be nonzero for any of the following reasons.

1. Round-off error accumulation.

2. The $\mathbf{u}_r$ set is overdetermined leading to redundant supports (high strain energy).

3. The $\mathbf{u}_r$ set is underspecified leading to a singular reduced stiffness matrix (high rigid body error ratio).

4. The multipoint constraints are incompatible (high strain energy and high rigid body error ratio).

5. There are too many single point constraints (high strain energy and high rigid body error ratio).

6. K_{rr} is null (unit value for rigid body error but low strain energy). This is an acceptable condition and may occur when generalized dynamic reduction is used.

NASTRAN can not determine the modeling error. The user must review the prescribed constraints to determine possible changes in the finite element model.

The structure could be restrained against rigid body motion by single point constraints, but there are advantages to using the SUPORT option. These are

1. The G_{rf}-matrix is used to calculate the rigid body mass matrix for dynamic analysis and static analysis with inertia relief.

2. The NASTRAN program automatically calculates and prints diagnostic data concerning sufficiency of constraints.

7.8.   Flexibility to Stiffness Transformation

The stiffness equation for an element was found in Chapter Six to be of the form

$$K_{ee}\,u_e = P_e \tag{7.83}$$

There is a complementary approach whereby we find a set of relations in the form

$$F\,P = u \tag{7.84}$$

where F is called the flexibility matrix. We showed in Chapter Six that the stiffness coefficients k_{ij} are the forces at degrees of freedom i due to unit displacement of degree of freedom j, holding all other displacements equal to zero. We may be tempted to use an analogous approach to define the flexibility coefficients, but we recognize that we cannot specify a single force component for an unconstrained element since the equilibrium conditions for the element would not be satisfied in that case. We therefore conclude that the flexibility coefficients cannot be defined for an unsupported element.

We thus consider an element which is supported in such a manner that the support forces can be expressed in terms of the forces at the unsupported degrees of freedom. Structures that are supported in this manner are called statically determinate because the support forces can be evaluated solely by static equilibrium considerations. If we consider the beam element, for example, both the simply supported beam and the cantilever beams are statically determinate.

If the structure is restrained against rigid body motion, then we can proceed. The flexibility equations for a statically determinate beam are

$$\begin{bmatrix} f_{11} & f_{12} \\ f_{12} & f_{22} \end{bmatrix} \begin{Bmatrix} P_1 \\ P_2 \end{Bmatrix} = \begin{Bmatrix} u_1 \\ u_2 \end{Bmatrix} \tag{7.85}$$

The flexibility coefficients are then seen to be the displacements of degree of freedom i due to a unit force at and in the direction of degree of freedom j with all other forces equal to zero.

It is easy to show that the flexibility matrices for the simply supported and cantilevered beam which are shown by Figs. 7-18 and 7-19 are given by (7.86) and (7.87), respectively.

The flexibility coefficients are much easier to obtain by a laboratory test than the stiffness coefficients. All that is required for the flexibility approach is the mounting of the structure in a statically determinate manner. Loads are then applied at each of the selected node points, and the displace-

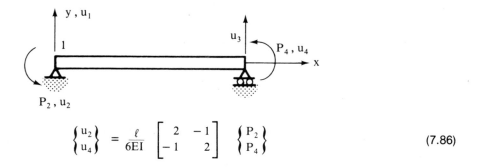

$$\begin{Bmatrix} u_2 \\ u_4 \end{Bmatrix} = \frac{\ell}{6EI} \begin{bmatrix} 2 & -1 \\ -1 & 2 \end{bmatrix} \begin{Bmatrix} P_2 \\ P_4 \end{Bmatrix} \tag{7.86}$$

Figure 7-18. Flexibility equation for simple supported beam

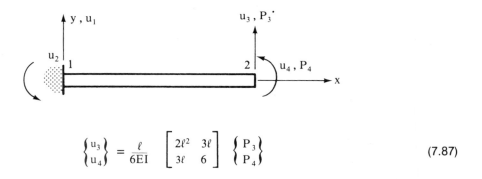

$$\begin{Bmatrix} u_3 \\ u_4 \end{Bmatrix} = \frac{\ell}{6EI} \begin{bmatrix} 2\ell^2 & 3\ell \\ 3\ell & 6 \end{bmatrix} \begin{Bmatrix} P_3 \\ P_4 \end{Bmatrix} \tag{7.87}$$

Figure 7-19. Flexibility equation for cantilevered beam

ments at all node point degrees of freedom are measured using appropriate instrumentation. These measurements are then scaled by the magnitude of the applied load to give the flexibility coefficients.

While the analysis problem can be formulated using a flexibility approach, the stiffness approach has found almost universal acceptance and is the only approach implemented in NASTRAN. A method is therefore required to transform element flexibility coefficients into an equivalent stiffness matrix.

We proceed by first making the observation that

1. The stiffness matrix is singular because the node point displacements include rigid body motion.

2. The flexibility matrix is formed for a structural element that is statically determinate.

These two statements are really equivalent and the transformation of the flexibility coefficients to a set of stiffness coefficients for the elements must include the rigid body degrees of freedom.

Let us consider the set of all grid point displacements for the element as the union of two subsets; the set of degrees of freedom $\mathbf{u}_d$ and $\mathbf{u}_i$ where

7.8 Flexibility to Stiffness Transformation

$\mathbf{u}_d$ are a set of degree of freedoms that would eliminate rigid body motion if constrained.

and

$\mathbf{u}_i$ are unconstrained degrees of freedom that may displace relative to the d-set

The flexibility equations relate the forces and displacements of the i-set so that

$$\mathbf{F}_{ii}\,\mathbf{P}_i = \mathbf{u}_i \tag{7.88}$$

The stiffness equations relate the forces and displacements for both the d- and i-sets. The stiffness equations can thus be represented in partitioned form as

$$\begin{bmatrix} \mathbf{K}_{ii} & \mathbf{K}_{id} \\ \mathbf{K}_{di} & \mathbf{K}_{dd} \end{bmatrix} \begin{Bmatrix} \mathbf{u}_i \\ \mathbf{u}_d \end{Bmatrix} = \begin{Bmatrix} \mathbf{P}_i \\ \mathbf{P}_d \end{Bmatrix} \tag{7.89}$$

Setting the set of displacements $\mathbf{u}_d$ equal to zero then gives

$$\mathbf{K}_{ii}\,\mathbf{u}_i = \mathbf{P}_i \tag{7.90}$$

A comparison of (7.90) with (7.88) shows that the $\mathbf{K}_{ii}$ partition of the stiffness matrix is given by

$$\mathbf{K}_{ii} = \mathbf{F}_{ii}^{-1} \tag{7.91}$$

In order to determine the other partitions of the stiffness matrix we must include information about the relation between the $\mathbf{u}_i$ and $\mathbf{u}_d$ displacement sets, since all the other partitions involve the $\mathbf{u}_d$ set. In the absence of forces $\mathbf{P}_i$, the element may displace as a rigid body so that a relation between the $\mathbf{u}_i$ and the $\mathbf{u}_d$ degrees of freedom must exist in the form

$$\mathbf{u}_i^r = \mathbf{S}_{id}\,\mathbf{u}_d \tag{7.92}$$

If the element is subjected to a set of forces $\mathbf{P}_i$ and the $\mathbf{u}_d$ set is not equal to zero, then the total displacement of the $\mathbf{u}_i$-set is the sum of the displacements given by

$$\mathbf{u}_i = \mathbf{u}_i^f + \mathbf{u}_i^r \tag{7.93}$$

where $\mathbf{u}_i^f$ are the displacements due to structural flexibility and $\mathbf{u}_i^r$ represent rigid body motion relative to the d-set. The substitution of equations (7.88) and (7.92) into (7.93) gives

$$\mathbf{u}_i = \mathbf{F}_{ii}\,\mathbf{P}_i + \mathbf{S}_{id}\,\mathbf{u}_d \tag{7.94}$$

which can be put into the form

$$\mathbf{F}_{ii}^{-1}\,\mathbf{u}_i - \mathbf{F}_{ii}^{-1}\,\mathbf{S}_{id}\,\mathbf{u}_d = \mathbf{P}_i \tag{7.95}$$

Now, by comparing the first of equations (7.89) with equation (7.95) we see that

$$\mathbf{K}_{id} = -\mathbf{F}_{ii}^{-1}\,\mathbf{S}_{id} \tag{7.96}$$

and, since the stiffness matrix and flexibility matrices are symmetric, we have

$$\mathbf{K}_{di} = -\mathbf{S}_{id}^{T}\,\mathbf{F}_{ii}^{-1} \tag{7.97}$$

The final part of the flexibility to stiffness transformation is the determination of the partition $\mathbf{K}_{dd}$, which relates the $\mathbf{u}_d$ displacements to the forces $\mathbf{P}_d$. This can be done by noting that the flexibility relations for an element are obtained by specifying that $\mathbf{u}_d$ are constrained so that the element is statically determinate. This means that the forces $\mathbf{P}_d$ can be determined from the $\mathbf{P}_i$ set by a relation of the form

$$\mathbf{P}_d = \mathbf{R}_{di}\,\mathbf{P}_i \tag{7.98}$$

The substitution of (7.95) into (7.98) then gives

$$\mathbf{P}_d = \mathbf{R}_{di}\,\mathbf{F}_{ii}^{-1}\,\mathbf{u}_i - \mathbf{R}_{di}\,\mathbf{F}_{ii}^{-1}\,\mathbf{S}_{id}\,\mathbf{u}_d \tag{7.99}$$

The $\mathbf{R}_{di}$ and $\mathbf{S}_{id}$ matrices are related. The relation is implicit if we note that $\mathbf{K}_{di}$ is given by (7.97) as a result of symmetry and is also obtained from equation (7.99) as

$$\mathbf{K}_{di} = \mathbf{R}_{di}\,\mathbf{F}_{ii}^{-1} \tag{7.100}$$

A comparison of these two expressions shows that

$$\mathbf{R}_{di} = -\,\mathbf{S}_{id}^{T} \tag{7.101}$$

where we have used equation (7.97) to relate $\mathbf{R}_{di}$ and $\mathbf{S}_{id}$. A more direct way of showing that the relation holds is to note that the virtual work of the external forces must vanish if we allow only rigid body motion.

$$\mathbf{P}_i^{T}\delta\mathbf{u}_i + \mathbf{P}_d^{T}\,\delta\mathbf{u}_d = 0 \tag{7.102}$$

Then we have from (7.98)

$$\mathbf{P}_d^{T} = \mathbf{P}_i^{T}\mathbf{R}_{di}^{T} \tag{7.103}$$

and, from (7.92),

$$\delta\mathbf{u}_i = \mathbf{S}_{id}\,\delta\mathbf{u}_d \tag{7.104}$$

The substitution of (7.103) and (7.104) into (7.102) then gives

$$\mathbf{R}_{di}^{T} = -\,\mathbf{S}_{id}$$

Finally, the coefficients of $\mathbf{u}_d$ are the $\mathbf{K}_{dd}$ partition and are given by

$$\mathbf{K}_{dd} = \mathbf{S}_{id}^{T}\,\mathbf{F}_{ii}^{-1}\,\mathbf{S}_{id} \tag{7.105}$$

We have thus shown that given the element flexibility $\mathbf{F}$ and either $\mathbf{S}$ or $\mathbf{R}$, we can form the associated matrix

$$\mathbf{K} = \begin{bmatrix} \mathbf{K}_{ii} & \mathbf{K}_{id} \\ \mathbf{K}_{id}^{T} & \mathbf{K}_{dd} \end{bmatrix} = \begin{bmatrix} \mathbf{F}^{-1} & -\mathbf{F}^{-1}\mathbf{S} \\ -\mathbf{S}^{T}\mathbf{F}^{-1} & \mathbf{S}^{T}\mathbf{F}\mathbf{S} \end{bmatrix} \tag{7.106}$$

NASTRAN generates the stiffness equations using the flexibility and rigid body transformation matrices specified on a GENEL Bulk Data card, which is described by Card Image 7-14.

The GENEL Bulk Data Card is not as formidable as it might appear. The form of the card includes four logical sections that
   1. Specify flexible degrees of freedom that comprise the i-set. These degrees of freedom must be defined using GRID or SPOINT Bulk Data.
   2. Specify the restrained degrees of freedom.
   3. List the coefficients of the flexibility matrix.
   4. List the coefficients of the rigid body transformation matrix.

7.8 Flexibility to Stiffness Transformation

*Define degrees of freedom in the i-set

1	2	3	4	5	6	7	8	9	10
GENEL +1	EID GI4	CI4	GI1 etc.	CI1	GI2	CI2	GI3	CI3	+1 +2

*Define degrees of freedom in the d-set

+2 +3	UD GD4	CD4	GD1 etc.	CD1	GD2	CD2	GD3	CD3	+3 +4

*Define elements of flexibility matrix by columns

+4 +5 +6	Z etc. etc.	Z_{11} Z_{33}	Z_{21} Z_{43}	Z_{31} Z_{53}	etc. etc.	Z_{22} Z_{44}	Z_{32} Z_{54}	Z_{42} etc.	+5 +6 +7

*Define Rigid Body Transformation Matrix by Rows

+7 +8	S etc.	S_{11} S_{31}	S_{12} S_{32}	S_{13} etc.	etc.	S_{21}	S_{22}	S_{23}	+8

where

EID Unique element number (integer, > 0).

GI,CI Pairs defining the degrees of freedom that comprise the i-set of displacements for the element (integer).

UD Literal string data in field two, which defines the beginning of the list of d-set degrees of freedom.

GD,CD Pairs defining the degrees of freedom that comprise the d-set.

Z Literal value in field two that defines the beginning of flexibility coefficients.

Z_{ij} Elements of the flexibility matrix by columns starting with the diagonal in the order of the list for the i-set.

S Literal value in field two, which defines the beginning of rigid body coefficients.

S_{ij} Elements of the rigid body transformation matrix by rows in the order of the list for the d-set.

Card Image 7-14. Flexibility to Stiffness Transformation — GENEL

7.8.1. Example: Specification of Beam Properties Using GENEL

The stiffness properties for the beam element can be defined by using either (7.86) or (7.87) together with the appropriate rigid body transformation matrix. We therefore consider the problem of determining the response of a beam supported as a cantilever using the flexibility coefficients for the simple supported beam as given by (7.86).

Let the beam properties be given as

$$EI = 1$$

$$\ell = 6$$

Then the flexibility coefficients (7.85) become

$$F = \begin{bmatrix} 2 & -1 \\ -1 & 2 \end{bmatrix}$$

The rigid body transformation matrix is obtained by noting that

$$u_2 = u_4 = \frac{(u_3 - u_1)}{\ell}$$

so that S_{id} is given by

$$S_{id} = \frac{1}{\ell} \begin{bmatrix} -1 & 1 \\ -1 & 1 \end{bmatrix}$$

We will define the degrees of freedom connected by the beam by SPOINT scalar points rather than by geometric grid points using the displacement numbers defined on Fig. 7-18. The bulk data required to define the beam element and the constraints and apply a unit force at the tip are

1	2	3	4	5	6	7	8	9	10
SPOINT	1	THRU	4						
GENEL	1		2	0	4	0			+ G1
+ G1	UD		1	0	3	0			+ G2
+ G2	Z	2.	− 1.	2.					+ G3
+ G3	S	− .1667	1.	− .1667	1.				
SPC	100	1		0.	2		0.		
SLOAD	100	3	1.						

7.8.2.   Direct Specification of Element Stiffness

The GENEL can also be used in an alternative form for specifying the stiffness coefficients associated with the partitioned equations

$$\begin{Bmatrix} F_i \\ F_d \end{Bmatrix} = \begin{bmatrix} K_{ii} & -K_{ii} S_{id} \\ -S_{id}^T K_{ii} & S_{id}^T K_{ii} S_{id} \end{bmatrix} \begin{Bmatrix} u_i \\ u_d \end{Bmatrix} \tag{7.107}$$

The only change to the GENEL card is the replacement of Z by K on continuation card 4 shown in Card Image 7-13. The coefficients are then taken to be the elements of the stiffness partition K_{ii} rather than the flexibility matrix.

The NASTRAN GENEL element thus provides the user with a means of defining elements of the global stiffness matrix directly without using a finite element model. The coefficients can be defined either in terms of stiffness or flexibility.

7.9. References

7-1 NASTRAN *Theoretical Manual, NASA SP-221*, 1976, pp. 2.2-3.

7-2 MSC/NASTRAN *Users Manual*, MacNeal-Schwendler Corp., 1978, pp. 1.2-2 through 1.2-5.

7-3 Cuthill, E. H., and McKee, J. M., "Reducing the Bandwidth of Sparse Symmetric Matrices," *ACM Pub. P69*, New York, 1969, pp. 157-172.

7-4 Gibbs, N. E., Poole, W. G., Jr., and Stockmeyer, P. K., "An Algorithm for Reducing the Bandwidth and Profile of a Sparse Matrix". *SIAM J. Numer. Anal.*, Vol. 13, No. 12, April 1976, pp. 236-250.

7-5 Levy, R. "Structural Stiffness Matrix Wavefront Resequencing Program (WAVEFRONT)", *JPL Tech. Rept.* 32-1526, Vol. XIV, 1972, pp. 50-55.

7-6 Everstine, G. C., "Reduction of Matrix Wavefront", in *Seventh NASTRAN User's Colloquium* NASA CP-2062, Oct. 1978, pp. 111-121.

7-7 MSC/NASTRAN *User's Manual*, Vol. I, Sec. 1.10, 1978.

7-10. Problems

7.1 The Lagrange multiplier approach to the incorporation of linear constraint equation involves the definition of a set of workless constraint forces $\mathbf{G}_m$. Using the fact that the constraint forces produce no virtual work show that the augmented stiffness equations can be written as

$$\begin{bmatrix} \mathbf{K}_{gg} & \mathbf{G}_{mg}^T \\ \mathbf{G}_{mg} & \mathbf{O} \end{bmatrix} \left\{ \begin{array}{c} \mathbf{U} \\ \mathbf{G}_m \end{array} \right\} = \left\{ \begin{array}{c} \mathbf{P}_g \\ \mathbf{O} \end{array} \right\}$$

7.2 Given the augmented set of equations from problem 7.1 show that $\mathbf{G}_m$ can be found as

$$\mathbf{G}_m = \left[\mathbf{G}_{mg} \mathbf{K}_{gg}^{-1} \mathbf{G}_{mg}^T \right]^{-1} \left(\mathbf{G}_{mg} \mathbf{K}_{gg} \mathbf{P}_g \right)$$

7.3 Suppose that a rigid link is to connect node points 1 and 2 as shown below where there is no restraint to rotation θ_{y2}.

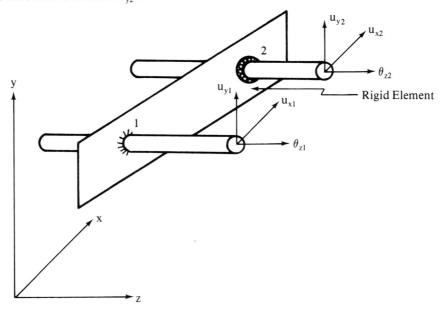

Assuming that the nodes are located the basic coordinate system at $\mathbf{X}_1 = (1.,1.,0.)$ and $\mathbf{X}_2 = (3.,5.,0.)$, write the set of constraint relations which define the motion of point 2 in terms of the displacements at point 1.

7.4 Given the system of axial members shown below show that the augmented set of equations for the constraint condition $u_2 - u_3 = 0$ are as follows

$$\begin{bmatrix} 2k_o & -k_o & 1 \\ -k_o & 2k_o & -1 \\ 1 & -1 & 0 \end{bmatrix} \begin{Bmatrix} u_2 \\ u_3 \\ \lambda \end{Bmatrix} = \begin{Bmatrix} P_2 \\ P_3 \\ 0 \end{Bmatrix}$$

where $k_o = \dfrac{AE}{L}$

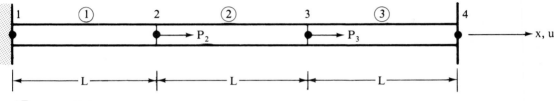

AE = constant

7.5 Show that the Lagrange multiplier for problem 7.4 is $\lambda = \frac{1}{2}(P_2 - P_3)$. What is the physical interpretation of λ?

7.6 Using the stiffness to flexibility relation (7.107) show that the correct element stiffness matrix for the beam as given by (6.59) is obtained when starting from the flexibility for either the simply supported beam (7.86) or the centilevered beam (7.87).

7.7 The stiffness matrix for the beam element (6.59) is singular because the node point displacements include rigid body motion. Show that the reduced stiffness matrix associated with including the transverse displacements at each end of the beam in the r-set is null.

7.8 Verify that (7.77) relates the rigid body displacements of the ℓ-set to rigid body motion of the r-set displacement.

8

Behavioral Functions for Finite Elements

The formulation of the finite element method that we have outlined in previous chapters has been based on a set of assumed displacement fields. In this chapter we turn our attention to the problem of selecting these fields in a rational manner. We begin this section by stating the general conditions that the assumed functions must satisfy. We then consider linear interpolation functions followed by a discussion of functions based on higher order polynomial series.

The use of higher ordered polynomials leads to overconstrained elements that contain internal degrees of freedom. Another polynomial formulation that leads to the so-called serendipity elements is then presented.

The techniques involved in generating the element stiffness for the serendipity elements naturally lead to the use of a set of interpolation functions to represent the element boundaries. The use of the same functional representation for both the displacements and the geometry leads to the isoparametric elements.

8.1.   Requirements on Shape Functions

There are three general requirements that the shape functions must satisfy (Ref. 8-1). These are

1. The shape function must possess continuity of derivatives one order lower than the highest derivative that appears in the variational formulation.

2. The elemental stiffness matrix should give zero internal energy for a rigid body displacement.

3. The strains associated with the assumed displacement functions must include the representation of the constant strain state.

The first requirement is necessary in order to calculate the strain energy since the evaluation of the integral require continuity of the function and all derivatives up to one order lower than the highest derivative in the energy expression. Therefore, only the displacement function must be continuous to represent extensional behavior; but both the displacement and first derivative be continuous to represent bending behavior.

The second requirement is based on the fact that a rigid body displacement produces no strain and, therefore, no strain energy. Since the stiffness approach is based in the representation of strain energy the strain energy associated with rigid body motion should be zero.

The third requirement is based on the observation that as elements become smaller and smaller, the strain state becomes a constant in the element. The shape functions must therefore be capable of representing a constant strain (or constant curvature) state.

8.2.   Polynomial Shape Functions

The finite elements that are of general interest are usually single geometric forms such as triangles or quadrilaterals so that it is appropriate to consider polynomial representations of the shape functions. The polynomial approximation for the displacement of the element is constructed so that the number of arbitrary coefficients in the expansion is equal to the number of degrees of freedom at the nodes of the element.

A general expression for the displacement components is then given by an expression of the form

$$\mathbf{v}_e = \mathbf{p}_e(m)\mathbf{a}_e \tag{8.1}$$

where

$\mathbf{v}_e$ Set displacement components in the element

$\mathbf{p}(m)$ Set of polynomial functions of order m, where the order is the highest power of a variable in the polynomial

$\mathbf{a}_e$ Set of undetermined polynomial coefficients.

In order to relate the polynomial coefficients to the element degrees of freedom, we equate the displacements evaluated at the node points to the node point degrees of freedom.

Let $\mathbf{x}_N$ be the set of all grid point coordinates, then in a symbolic way we can express the grid point displacement in terms of the displacement vector as

$$\mathbf{u}_e = \mathbf{v}_e(\mathbf{x}_N) \tag{8.2}$$

The degrees of freedom at each node can then be expressed in terms of the polynomial coefficients as

$$\mathbf{u}_e = \mathbf{G}_{ee}\,\mathbf{a}_e \tag{8.3}$$

The matrix $\mathbf{G}_{ee}$ is a set of known coefficients whose values depend on $\mathbf{x}$. Since the matrix is square and nonsingular, we can solve the set of equations for the polynomial coefficients by

$$\mathbf{a}_e = \mathbf{G}_{ee}^{-1}\,\mathbf{u}_e \tag{8.4}$$

The substitution of (8.4) into (8.1) then gives

$$\mathbf{v}_e = \mathbf{N}_e\,\mathbf{u}_e \tag{8.5}$$

where

$$\mathbf{N}_e = \mathbf{p}(m)\mathbf{G}_{ee}^{-1} \tag{8.6}$$

8.2.1.   Linear Shape Functions

Shape functions based on the use of linear interpolation functions were among the first type used in the finite element analysis. These functions lead to a constant strain state in the element and satisfy inter-element compatibility of displacements. The constant strain elements continue to be used because of the simplicity of the element stiffness and the associated low cost for generating the stiffness matrix.

8.2.1.1.   One-Dimensional Element

The one-dimensional element connects two grid points as shown by Fig. 8-1, where there is a single degree of freedom at each grid point. The displacement vector consists of a single component that is represented by a linear polynomial as

$$v_x = [\,1 \quad x\,] \begin{Bmatrix} a_1 \\ a_2 \end{Bmatrix} \tag{8.7}$$

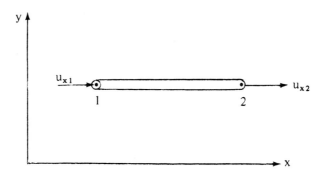

Figure 8-1. Axial Element

The location of the grid points is given by

$$\mathbf{x}_N = \begin{Bmatrix} 0 \\ \ell \end{Bmatrix} \tag{8.8}$$

so that the set of grid point displacements is given by

$$\begin{Bmatrix} v_x(x_1) \\ v_x(x_2) \end{Bmatrix} = \begin{Bmatrix} u_{x1} \\ u_{x2} \end{Bmatrix} = \begin{bmatrix} 1 & 0 \\ 1 & \ell \end{bmatrix} \begin{Bmatrix} a_1 \\ a_2 \end{Bmatrix} \tag{8.9}$$

Then, solving for $\mathbf{a}_e$ gives

$$\begin{Bmatrix} a_1 \\ a_2 \end{Bmatrix} = \frac{1}{\ell} \begin{bmatrix} \ell & 0 \\ -1 & 1 \end{bmatrix} \begin{Bmatrix} u_{x1} \\ u_{x2} \end{Bmatrix} \tag{8.10}$$

The shape functions are then found by using (8.6), which gives

$$\mathbf{N}_e = \left\lfloor (1 - \frac{x}{\ell}) \quad \frac{x}{\ell} \right\rfloor \tag{8.11}$$

which is the same as those used in Chapter Six to obtain the stiffness matrix for the axial element.

8.2.1.2.   Triangular Two-Dimensional Element

Triangular two-dimensional elements are particularly attractive because the number of nodal degrees of freedom is equal to the number of terms in a complete polynomial expansion in terms of two variables. The polynomial representation in this case is

169

8.2.2   Triangular Two-Dimensional Element

$$\begin{Bmatrix} v_x \\ v_y \end{Bmatrix} = \begin{bmatrix} 1 & x & y & 0 & 0 & 0 \\ 0 & 0 & 0 & 1 & x & y \end{bmatrix} \begin{Bmatrix} a_1 \\ a_2 \\ a_3 \\ a_4 \\ a_5 \\ a_6 \end{Bmatrix} \tag{8.12}$$

In order to obtain the shape functions we consider the triangle in local coordinates as shown by Fig. 8-2. The coordinates of the grid points are then

$$\mathbf{x}_N = [\, \mathbf{x}_1 \quad \mathbf{x}_2 \quad \mathbf{x}_3 \,] = \begin{bmatrix} 0 & 0 & x_3 \\ 0 & x_2 & y_3 \end{bmatrix} \tag{8.13}$$

The grid point degrees of freedom are then expressed in terms of the polynomial coefficients by evaluating the displacement functions at the node points to give

$$\mathbf{u}_e = \begin{Bmatrix} u_{x1} \\ u_{y1} \\ u_{x2} \\ u_{y2} \\ u_{x3} \\ u_{y3} \end{Bmatrix} = \begin{bmatrix} 1 & 0 & 0 & 0 & 0 & 0 \\ 0 & 0 & 0 & 1 & 0 & 0 \\ 1 & x_2 & 0 & 0 & 0 & 0 \\ 0 & 0 & 0 & 1 & x_2 & 0 \\ 1 & x_3 & y_3 & 0 & 0 & 0 \\ 0 & 0 & 0 & 1 & x_3 & y_3 \end{bmatrix} \begin{Bmatrix} a_1 \\ a_2 \\ a_3 \\ a_4 \\ a_5 \\ a_6 \end{Bmatrix} \tag{8.14}$$

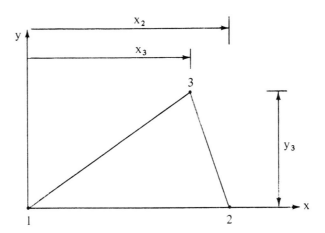

Figure 8-2. Triangular Element

The process of obtaining the inverse relationship and the determination of the shape functions $\mathbf{N}_e$ is straightforward and time consuming. The resulting shape functions are of the matrix form

$$\mathbf{N}_e = \begin{bmatrix} N_1 & N_2 & N_3 & 0 & 0 & 0 \\ 0 & 0 & 0 & N_1 & N_2 & N_3 \end{bmatrix} \tag{8.15}$$

where the shape functions are given by

$$N_1 = \frac{1}{x_2 y_3} \; [x_2 \, y_3 - y_3 \, x + (x_3 - x_2) \, y]$$

$$N_2 = \frac{1}{x_2 y_3} \; [y_3 x - x_3 y] \tag{8.16}$$

$$N_3 = \frac{y}{y_3}$$

8.2.1.3.   Tetrahedronal Three-Dimensional Element

The tetrahedronal element is the three-dimensional element defined by four points as shown by Fig. 8-3.

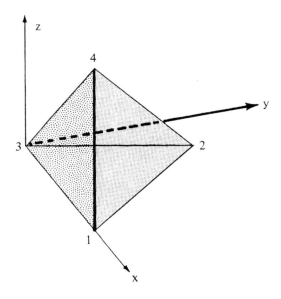

Figure 8-3. Tetrahedronal Element

The tetrahedron is the three-dimensional analogy of the constant strain triangle. The element is characterized by 12 degrees of freedom, which is equal to the number of terms in a complete linear polynomial expansion in terms of three variables. The polynomial representation is

$$\begin{Bmatrix} v_x \\ v_y \\ v_z \end{Bmatrix} = \begin{bmatrix} 1 & x & y & z & 0 & 0 & 0 & 0 & 0 & 0 & 0 & 0 \\ 0 & 0 & 0 & 0 & 1 & x & y & z & 0 & 0 & 0 & 0 \\ 0 & 0 & 0 & 0 & 0 & 0 & 0 & 0 & 1 & x & y & z \end{bmatrix} a_e \tag{8.17}$$

where a_e is a set of 12 coefficients.

We follow the same procedure outlined in the previous section and express the grid point displacements in terms of the polynomial coefficients. For convenience the resulting equations are re-ordered so that the displacements are given by

$$\begin{Bmatrix} u_{x1} \\ u_{x2} \\ u_{x3} \\ u_{x4} \end{Bmatrix} = \begin{bmatrix} 1 & 0 & 0 & 0 \\ 1 & x_2 & 0 & 0 \\ 1 & x_3 & y_3 & 0 \\ 1 & x_4 & y_4 & z_4 \end{bmatrix} \begin{Bmatrix} a_1 \\ a_2 \\ a_3 \\ a_4 \end{Bmatrix} \tag{8.18}$$

where the grid point locations have been taken as

$$\mathbf{x}_N = [\mathbf{x}_1 \quad \mathbf{x}_2 \quad \mathbf{x}_3 \quad \mathbf{x}_4] = \begin{bmatrix} 0 & x_2 & x_3 & x_4 \\ 0 & 0 & y_3 & y_4 \\ 0 & 0 & 0 & z_4 \end{bmatrix} \tag{8.19}$$

The displacement functions can then be represented in the form

$$\begin{Bmatrix} v_x \\ v_y \\ v_z \end{Bmatrix} = \begin{bmatrix} N_1 & N_2 & N_3 & N_4 & 0 & 0 & 0 & 0 & 0 & 0 & 0 & 0 \\ 0 & 0 & 0 & 0 & N_1 & N_2 & N_3 & N_4 & 0 & 0 & 0 & 0 \\ 0 & 0 & 0 & 0 & 0 & 0 & 0 & 0 & N_1 & N_2 & N_3 & N_4 \end{bmatrix} \mathbf{u}_e \tag{8.20}$$

where the shape functions are found by using

$$\begin{bmatrix} 1 & 1 & 1 & 1 \\ 0 & x_1 & x_2 & x_3 \\ 0 & 0 & y_2 & y_3 \\ 0 & 0 & 0 & z_3 \end{bmatrix} \begin{Bmatrix} N_1 \\ N_2 \\ N_3 \\ N_4 \end{Bmatrix} = \begin{Bmatrix} 1 \\ x \\ y \\ z \end{Bmatrix} \tag{8.21}$$

8.3.   Interpolation Functions

The usefulness of the polynomial formulation is limited by the need to transform from the generalized polynomial coefficients to the displacement degrees of freedom as indicated by (8.4). The polynomial formulation has its pedagogical place, but in practice it is much easier to obtain the shape functions directly by interpolation formulas.

Lagrangian interpolation allows us to find the polynomial coefficients that represents a function in terms of values of the function evaluated along a line. The resulting expression is of the form

$$\mathbf{v} = \sum_{i=1}^{m+1} N_i u_i$$

where m is the number of segments along the line. The coefficients N_i, which we identify as the shape functions in the finite element method, are then given by

$$N_i = \frac{\displaystyle\prod_{\substack{j=1 \\ i \neq j}}^{m+1} (x - x_j)}{\displaystyle\prod_{\substack{j=1 \\ j \neq i}}^{m+1} (x_i - x_j)} \tag{8.22}$$

Interpolation between two points then gives

$$N_1 = \frac{(x - x_2)}{(x_1 - x_2)} = 1 - \frac{x}{\ell}$$

$$N_2 = \frac{(x - x_1)}{(x_2 - x_1)} = \frac{x}{\ell}$$

which are seen to be the same as (8.11) if $x_1 = 0$ and $x_2 = \ell$. Higher ordered polynomial expressions can be found with similar ease. For example, for three points on a line we obtain the functions

$$N_1 = \frac{(x - x_2)(x - x_3)}{(x_1 - x_2)(x_1 - x_3)}$$

$$N_2 = \frac{(x - x_1)(x - x_3)}{(x_2 - x_1)(x_2 - x_3)}$$

$$N_3 = \frac{(x - x_1)(x - x_2)}{(x_3 - x_1)(x_3 - x_2)}$$

8.4. Rectangular Elements

The interpolation functions obtained in one dimension by using Lagrange interpolation can be applied to rectangular elements by using the product of one-dimensional shape functions.

8.4.1. Bilinear Element

Consider the element shown in Fig. 8-4.

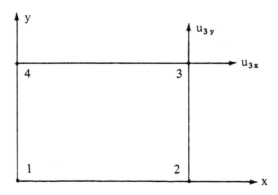

Figure 8-4. Rectangular Bilinear Element

We can obtain the shape functions for this element by noting that the displacement components along the lines $y = 0$ and $y = b$ are given by

$$v_x(x, 0) = N_{1x} u_{1x} + N_{2x} u_{2x}$$

$$v_x(x, b) = N_{4x} u_{4x} + N_{3x} u_{3x}$$

(8.23)

173

8.4.2 Quadratic Element

and the displacements along $x = 0, x = a$ are given by

$$v_x (0, y) = N_{1y} u_{1x} + N_{4y} u_{4x}$$

$$v_x (a, y) = N_{2y} u_{2x} + N_{3y} u_{3x}$$

(8.24)

The displacement $v_x(x,y)$ can then be written in terms of the shape functions as

$$v_x (x, y) = N_{1x} N_{1y} u_{1x} + N_{2x} N_{2y} u_{2x} + N_{3x} N_{3y} u_{3x} + N_{4x} N_{4y} u_{4x}$$

(8.25)

where

$$N_{1x} = N_{4x} = (1 - \frac{x}{a}) \qquad\qquad N_{1y} = N_{2y} = (1 - \frac{y}{b})$$

$$N_{2x} = N_{3x} = \frac{x}{a} \qquad\qquad\qquad N_{3y} = N_{4y} = \frac{y}{b}$$

The displacement component then varies linearly along each of the coordinate edges so that inter-element displacement compatibility is guaranteed.

The shape function N_i has the important property that it is equal to one when evaluated at grid point i and is equal to zero at all other grid points. The displacement function then equals the nodal displacements when evaluated at the nodes.

8.4.2. Quadratic Element

A displacement function for the element shown by Fig. 8-5 can be obtained by using quadratic interpolation. In this case the interpolation expressions for the midside nodes include a center node point. The resulting displacement function is

$$v_x (x, y) = N_{1x} N_{1y} u_{1x} + N_{2x} N_{2y} u_{2x} + N_{3x} N_{3y} u_{3x} +$$

$$N_{4x} N_{4y} u_{4x} + N_{5x} N_{5y} u_{5x} + N_{6x} N_{6y} u_{6x} +$$

(8.26)

$$N_{7x} N_{7y} u_{7x} + N_{8x} N_{8x} u_{8x} + N_{9x} N_{9y} u_{9x}$$

where the one-dimensional shape functions are given by the Lagrange interpolation formula (8.22).

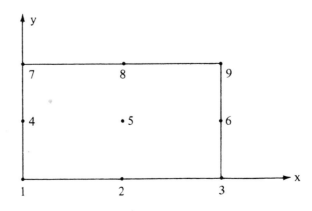

Figure 8-5. Rectangular Biquadratic Element

The use of the simple product of the one-dimensional interpolation functions provides a straightforward method of generating shape functions for two- and three-dimensional elements. When applied to higher ordered interpolation functions along the edges the procedure leads to an internal node point. Internal points pose no real problem from a matrix analysis point of view since the internal degrees of freedom can be removed by static condensation. The real problem is that the displacement function is constrained at the internal node points and will result in a stiffness matrix that is overly stiff.

We can retain the simplicity of the basic approach to the formulation of the shape functions and reduce the number of internal nodes by using a procedure that involves the superposition of ingeniously-derived shape functions. The elements obtained by using this approach are called the serendipity elements.

8.5. Ingenious Functions

Ref. 8-1 describes a set of ingenious functions that allow the representation of element behavior using the node points shown by Figure 8-6.

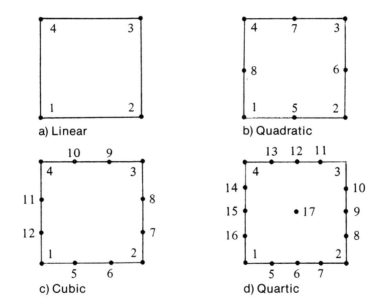

Figure 8-6. Nodal Pattern for Rectangular Ingenious Elements

8.5.1. Bilinear Elements

The bilinear element has four node points as shown by Fig. 8-6a. The element is first transformed to the normalized coordinate system as shown by Fig. 8-7 where the transformation equations for the rectangle are

$$\left.\begin{array}{l} \xi = \dfrac{x}{a} \\[2mm] \eta = \dfrac{y}{b} \end{array}\right\} \qquad (8.27)$$

175

8.5.2   Biquadratic Serendipity Element

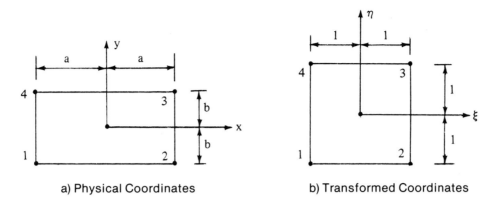

a) Physical Coordinates   b) Transformed Coordinates

Figure 8-7. Transformation of Rectangular Element

The displacement function for the bilinear element that was obtained in the previous section can then be written as

$$v_\xi(\xi, \eta) = \tfrac{1}{4}(1-\xi)(1-\eta)u_{\xi1} + \tfrac{1}{4}(1-\xi)(1+\eta)u_{\xi4} +$$

$$\tfrac{1}{4}(1+\xi)(1+\eta)u_{\xi3} + \tfrac{1}{4}(1+\xi)(1-\eta)u_{\xi2} \qquad (8.28)$$

with a similar expression for the displacement in the η-direction. The evaluation of (8.28) at the node points is seen to give

$$u_{\xi1} = v_\xi(-1, -1) \qquad\qquad u_{\xi3} = v_\xi(1, 1)$$

$$u_{\xi2} = v_\xi(-1, 1) \qquad\qquad u_{\xi4} = v_\xi(1, -1)$$

which then satisfies the requirement that the displacement function must equal the nodal displacement when evaluated at the node point.

The shape function at node i can be expressed in the general form

$$N_i = \tfrac{1}{4}(1+\xi_0)(1+\eta_0) \qquad (8.29)$$

where

$$\left.\begin{array}{l} \xi_0 = \xi\xi_i \\ \eta_0 = \eta\eta_i \end{array}\right\} \qquad (8.30)$$

8.5.2.   Biquadratic Serendipity Element

In order to develop the shape functions for the biquadratic element shown by Fig. 8-6b we first consider the shape functions at the midside nodes. The shape function associated with this node has the property that it is equal to one when evaluated at the coordinates of the node point and zero at all other node points. The functions

$$f(\xi) = (1-\xi^2)$$

$$g(\eta) = (1-\eta^2)$$

176

are then suitable functions for the midpoint nodes when evaluated along the edge containing the node. We see from Fig. 8-6b, for example, that $f(\xi)$ has the value of unity at node five and is zero at nodes one and two. We can then synthesize a shape function for node five:

$$N_5 = \tfrac{1}{2}(1-\eta)(1-\xi^2)$$

where N_5 is equal to unity at node five and is equal to zero at all other nodes. A general relation for the midside nodes of the quadratic element is then given by

$$N_i = \tfrac{1}{2}(1+\eta_0)(1-\xi^2) \qquad \text{for nodes 5 and 7}$$
$$N_i = \tfrac{1}{2}(1+\xi_0)(1-\eta^2) \qquad \text{for nodes 6 and 8}$$

$$(8.31)$$

The shape functions for the corner nodes can now be obtained by modifying the bilinear function (8.29). These bilinear shape functions are equal to unity at the corner points and are zero at all other nodes, except the adjacent midside nodes where the value is one-half. The bilinear functions are thus modified by using the shape function for the adjacent midside nodes:

$$N_1 = \tfrac{1}{4}(1-\xi)(1-\eta) - \frac{N_5}{2} - \frac{N_8}{2}$$

or

$$N_1 = -\tfrac{1}{4}(1-\xi)(1-\eta)(1+\xi+\eta) \qquad (8.32)$$

A general relation for the shape functions at the corner nodes is then given by

$$N_i = -\tfrac{1}{4}(1+\xi_0)(1+\eta_0)(1-\xi_0-\eta_0) \qquad (8.33)$$

8.5.3.   Cubic Serendipity Element

The shape functions for the cubic element that is shown by Fig. 8-6c can be developed by using a similar approach to obtain the following functions at the one-third points:

$$N_i = \frac{9}{32}(1+\xi_0)(1-\eta^2)(1+9\eta_0) \qquad \text{at} \quad \xi_i = \pm 1 , \eta_i = \pm\tfrac{1}{3} \qquad (8.34)$$

$$N_i = \frac{9}{32}(1+\eta_0)(1-\xi^2)(1+9\xi_0) \qquad \text{at} \quad \eta_i = \pm 1 , \xi_i = \pm\tfrac{1}{3} \qquad (8.35)$$

and

$$N_i = \frac{1}{32}(1+\xi_0)(1+\eta_0)\left\{9(\xi^2+\eta^2)-10\right\} \qquad \text{at corners} \qquad (8.36)$$

8.5.4.   Three-Dimensional Serendipity Elements

Ingenious shape functions for three-dimensional elements can be formulated using much the same technique as that used to derive shape functions for two-dimensional elements. Three-dimensional elements with linear, quadratic, and cubic variations of displacement along the edges are shown by Fig. 8-8.

8.5.4 Three-Dimensional Serendipity Elements

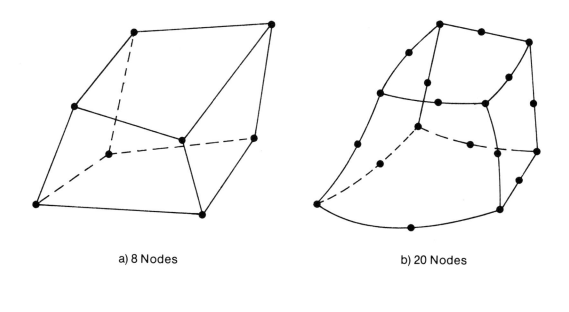

a) 8 Nodes   b) 20 Nodes

c) 32 Nodes

Figure 8-8. Three-Dimensional Serendipity Elements

The shape functions for the three-dimensional prisms are

LINEAR (8 Nodes)

$$N_i = \frac{1}{8}(1 + \xi_0)(1 + \eta_0)(1 + \zeta_0)$$

(8.37)

QUADRATIC (20 Nodes)

at the corners

$$N_i = \frac{1}{8} (1 + \xi_0) (1 + \eta_0) (1 + \zeta_0) (\zeta_0 + \xi_0 + \eta_0 - 2) \qquad (8.38)$$

at $\quad \xi_i = 0, \quad \eta_i = \pm 1, \quad \zeta_i = \pm 1$

$$N_i = \frac{1}{4} (1 - \xi^2) (1 + \eta_0) (1 + \zeta_0) \qquad (8.39)$$

at $\quad \eta_i = 0, \quad \zeta_i = \pm 1, \quad \xi_i = \pm 1$

$$N_i = \frac{1}{4} (1 - \eta^2) (1 + \xi_0) (1 + \eta_0) \qquad (8.40)$$

at $\quad \zeta_i = 0, \quad \xi_i = \pm 1, \quad \eta_i = \pm 1$

$$N_i = \frac{1}{4} (1 - \zeta^2) (1 + \eta_0) (1 + \xi_0) \qquad (8.41)$$

CUBIC (32 Nodes)

at the corners

$$N_i = \frac{1}{64} (1 + \xi_0) (1 + \eta_0) (1 + \zeta_0) \left\{ 9(\xi^2 + \eta^2 + \zeta^2) - 19 \right\} \qquad (8.42)$$

at $\quad \xi_i = \pm \frac{1}{3}, \quad \eta_i = \pm 1, \quad \zeta_i = \pm 1$

$$N_i = \frac{9}{64} (1 - \xi^2) (1 + 9\xi_0) (1 + \eta_0) (1 + \zeta_0) \qquad (8.43)$$

at $\quad \eta_i = \pm \frac{1}{3}, \quad \xi_i = \pm 1, \quad \zeta_i = \pm 1$

$$N_i = \frac{9}{64} (1 - \eta^2) (1 + 9\eta_0) (1 + \zeta_0) (1 + \xi_0) \qquad (8.44)$$

at $\quad \zeta_i = \pm \frac{1}{3}, \quad \xi_i = \pm 1, \quad \eta_i = \pm 1$

$$N_i = \frac{9}{64} (1 - \zeta^2) (1 + 9\zeta_0) (1 + \xi_0) (1 + \eta_0) \qquad (8.45)$$

8.6. Isoparametric Elements

The ingenious shape functions that were described in Sec. 8-5 are defined on a transformed square for two dimensions and on a transformed cube for three dimensions. The set of shape functions defined in the transformed space are valid independent of the shape of the element in physical space. If it is possible to map elements with curved boundaries into the transformed space, then we can represent the displacement field in the transformed space using the ingenious shape functions.

8.6.1. Parametric Mapping

A convenient mapping is provided by using the shape functions used to represent displacement to transform the coordinates. Material points in the physical space are thus related to material points in the transformed space by

$$\begin{aligned} x &= \mathbf{N}\,\mathbf{x} \\ y &= \mathbf{N}\,\mathbf{y} \\ z &= \mathbf{N}\,\mathbf{z} \end{aligned} \qquad (8.46)$$

where x, y, z are the coordinates of node points. If the shape functions **N** are the same functions that are used to represent the displacement, the mapping is called isoparametric. Subparametric and superparametric mappings imply that fewer and more node points, respectively, are used to represent the geometric mapping than are used to represent displacement.

8.6.2.   Evaluation of Stiffness Matrix

The expression for the stiffness matrix for an element was obtained in Chapter Six and is

$$\mathbf{k} = \int_{V_{o\ell}} \mathbf{b}^T \mathbf{E} \mathbf{b} \, dx dy dz \qquad (8.47)$$

where the integration is taken over the volume of the element in physical space. The integration is transformed to the (ξ, η, ζ) coordinates by using the transformation equations (8.46).

The **b** matrix is given by (6.33) as

$$\mathbf{b} = \mathbf{D} \mathbf{N}$$

where **D** represents a set of differential operators in the physical coordinates (x, y, z) and the shape functions are defined in terms of the transformed coordinates. The derivatives of N_i with respect to the physical coordinates are obtained by using the chain rule for differentiation to give

$$\frac{\partial N_i}{\partial \xi} = \frac{\partial N_i}{\partial x}\frac{\partial x}{\partial \xi} + \frac{\partial N_i}{\partial y}\frac{\partial y}{\partial \xi} + \frac{\partial N_i}{\partial z}\frac{\partial z}{\partial \xi} \qquad (8.48)$$

The partial derivatives of the shape functions can then be expressed as

$$\begin{Bmatrix} \frac{\partial N_i}{\partial \xi} \\ \frac{\partial N_i}{\partial \eta} \\ \frac{\partial N_i}{\partial \zeta} \end{Bmatrix} = \begin{bmatrix} \frac{\partial x}{\partial \xi} & \frac{\partial y}{\partial \xi} & \frac{\partial z}{\partial \xi} \\ \frac{\partial x}{\partial \eta} & \frac{\partial y}{\partial \eta} & \frac{\partial z}{\partial \eta} \\ \frac{\partial x}{\partial \zeta} & \frac{\partial y}{\partial \zeta} & \frac{\partial z}{\partial \zeta} \end{bmatrix} \begin{Bmatrix} \frac{\partial N_i}{\partial x} \\ \frac{\partial N_i}{\partial y} \\ \frac{\partial N_i}{\partial z} \end{Bmatrix} = \mathbf{J} \begin{Bmatrix} \frac{\partial N_i}{\partial x} \\ \frac{\partial N_i}{\partial y} \\ \frac{\partial N_i}{\partial z} \end{Bmatrix} \qquad (8.49)$$

where **J** is called the Jacobian of the transformation. Since the Jacobian can be calculated using (8.46) and the terms on the left are known, we can solve for the partials on the right-hand side of the equation of (8.49) by

$$\begin{Bmatrix} \frac{\partial N_i}{\partial x} \\ \frac{\partial N_i}{\partial y} \\ \frac{\partial N_i}{\partial z} \end{Bmatrix} = \mathbf{J}^{-1} \begin{Bmatrix} \frac{\partial N_i}{\partial \xi} \\ \frac{\partial N_i}{\partial \eta} \\ \frac{\partial N_i}{\partial \zeta} \end{Bmatrix} \qquad (8.50)$$

The stiffness matrix can be expressed entirely in terms of the transformed variables as

$$\mathbf{k} = \int_{-1}^{1}\int_{-1}^{1}\int_{-1}^{1} \mathbf{b}^T \mathbf{E} \mathbf{b} \det(\mathbf{J}) \, d\xi d\eta d\zeta \qquad (8.51)$$

where the differential volume in the physical and transformed coordinates are related by

$$dx\,dy\,dz = \det(\mathbf{J})\,d\xi\,d\eta\,d\zeta \tag{8.52}$$

The stiffness for the element can now be found by integrating in the transformed coordinates. Unfortunately the integrand is a complicated form so that numerical quadrature is used to evaluate the stiffness coefficients.

The numerical integration procedure which has found wide acceptance in finite element programs is called Gauss integration. This procedure is used because it requires fewer function evaluations at special integration points, which are termed "Gauss Points," than would be required using procedures such as trapezoidal integration to obtain a specified level of accuracy.

8.7. Reduced Order Parametric Shell Elements

Experience has shown that the standard isoparametric formulation outlined in Sec. 8.5 results in an element that is generally overly stiff. In order to obtain improved accuracy, higher-ordered elements are available that lead to essentially exact results.

On the other hand the lower ordered elements are attractive since the computer cost associated with the generation of the element matrix increases rapidly with element complexity as shown by MacNeal in Ref. 8-2 where he compared generation time for solid elements included in the COSMIC version of NASTRAN. These results show that the time required for a 32 noded element with a $4 \times 4 \times 4$ array of Gauss integration points is on the order of 100 times that of an 8 noded element with a $2 \times 2 \times 2$ array of Gauss points. Since the lower ordered elements are attractive from a cost point of view it is reasonable to ask if the poor performance of the lower order isoparametric elements is an intrinsic characteristic or whether the performance can be improved by relaxing the conformability requirement.

This question has been addressed by several authors (see Refs. 8-3 and 8-4 for example) who have shown that the performance of elements can be improved by using "reduced" integration to represent selected terms in the energy expression. This procedure leads to a better representation for the overall element behavior but the displacements along the boundary between two elements are not the same on each element except at the nodes. This behavior is termed "nonconforming." It is shown in Refs. 8-3 and 8-4 that the solution converges but that it is not monotonic from below as would be the case for a completely consistent formulation without reduced integration.

MacNeal (Ref. 8-5) has used the concept of reduced integration and other clever techniques to formulate a combined membrane/bending element using lower-ordered shape functions. The formulation presented in that reference is the basis for the flat and curved shell elements which are called the QUAD4 and QUAD8, respectively in MSC/NASTRAN.

8.8. References

8-1   Zienkiewicz, O.C., *The Finite Element Method in Engineering Science*, McGraw-Hill, 1971, pp. 107-110.

8-2   MacNeal, R. H., *Higher Order vs. Lower Order Elements, Economics and Accuracy*, presented at 2nd Congress on Finite Elements, Bournmouth, England, Oct., 1978.

8-3   Zienkiewicz, O. C., Taylor, R. L., and Too, J. M., *Reduced Integration Techniques in General Analysis of Plates and Shells*, Int. J. Num. Meth. Engr., Vol. 3, pp. 275-290, 1971.

8-4   Iron, B. N. and Hellen, T. K. *On Reduced Integration in Solid Isoparametric Elements When Used in Shells with Membrane Modes*, Int. J. Num. Meth. Engr., Vol. 10, pp. 1179-1182, 1975-1976.

8-5   MacNeal, R. H., *A Simple Quadrilateral Shell Element*, Computers and Structures, Vol. 8, pp. 175-183, 1978.

9
Structural Elements in MSC/NASTRAN

9.1. Introduction

Large analysis programs such as MSC/NASTRAN include a comprehensive library of finite elements. The stiffness and mass characteristics of these elements are calculated using the variational formulation described in Chapter 6. The behavior of the individual element and therefore of the system being modeled is dependent on the shape functions used (Chapter 8) and, for two and three dimensional elements, on the skillfulness of the finite element developer.

The MSC/NASTRAN element library includes a set of modern isoparametric two and three dimensional elements that have replaced the elements which were available in level 15.5 NASTRAN. The formulation for these modern MSC/NASTRAN includes the differential stiffness, the mass matrix, and nonlinear strain-displacement effects for geometric nonlinearities in addition to the linear stiffness matrix.

The MSC/NASTRAN library includes the following types of elements:

- Elastic springs

- Truss element

- Beam Bending Element having
      Offset neutral and shear axes
      Bending about two planes
      Pinned joints
      Stress recovery at intermediate points

- Pipe Element

- Flat and Curved Isoparametric Shell Elements with
      Membrane-Bending Behavior
      Anisotropic Material
      Material Coupling between extensional and bending behavior

- Isoparametric Solid Elements with Anisotropic Material

- Rigid Elements

- Spline Fit and Weighted Average Elements

The modern MSC/NASTRAN two and three dimensional isoparametric elements provide superior performance at a reduced cost when compared to the earlier NASTRAN elements. A set of recommended elements is described in this chapter by

1. Defining the appropriate Bulk Data cards

183

2. Describing the degrees of freedom for each element

3. Describing special modeling features

4. Describing stress recovery features

The nonisoparametric two and three dimensional elements associated with level 15.5 NASTRAN are not described in this chapter. However, the Bulk Data card images for these elements are included in Appendix C.

9.2.   Defining Element Properties

The element stiffness and mass matrices can be evaluated if the local geometry, the area properties, and the material properties are prescribed. Since the data base required to define a finite element model may include thousands of elements it is important that a minimum set of data be specified for the element definition.

Typical structural systems are generally composed of relatively few materials. Since several parameters may be required to define the properties of a material it makes sense to attach a set number, i.e., a numerical flag, to the data associated with each individual material. Then, instead of repeating the material parameters for each element, the appropriate material can be specified by pointing to the correct material set number. Furthermore, area properties such as plate thickness and beam cross-sectional area moments of inertia tend to be the same over several elements. So once again the concept of attaching a numerical flag to a related set of data is useful in defining a minimum data set.

NASTRAN uses the set concept for the definition of the element data base by defining

• Connectivity information on a "connection" card which points to a set of element properties.

• Element properties on a "property" card which in turn points to a set of material properties.

• Material properties on a "material" card.

The Bulk Data associated with the element "connectivity" and "properties" are described in this chapter. The Bulk Data associated with the definition of material properties are described in Chapter 10.

The form of the "connection" and "property" cards is similar for all the elements. The general characteristics of these Bulk Data and standard notation that will be used throughout this chapter are described in subsequent sections.

9.2.1.   The Connection Card

The finite elements are characterized by a name such as ROD, BAR, or HEXA for truss, beam, and solid hexagonal elements, respectively. The mnemonic for a connection card is characterized by a 'C' preceding the element type. Then CROD, CBAR, and CHEXA specify the connectivity data for the truss, beam, and solid elements.

The type of element is therefore defined by the Bulk Data card name, and the connection card defines the grid or scalar degrees of freedom to be connected.

The connection cards have the following general characteristics:

1. The type of element is specified by the mnemonic in the first field of the card.

2. The second field is the Element Identification Number (EID). The EID must be a unique integer number for each element in the data deck among all element types.

3. The third field is a Property Identification Number (PID). The PID is an integer number that must be unique only among the PID's for a specific type of element and points to an associated Property-type card.

4. The number and the format of additional fields are element-dependent. The datum in these fields includes the grid or scalar points which are connected by the element together with other connectivity-type data such as beam offsets and orientation of material axes.

9.2.2. The Property Card

The mnemonic of the property card is characterized by a P preceding the element mnemonic. For example, PROD, PBAR, and PSOLID are property cards for the truss, beam, and solid hexagonal elements. The property card includes all the properties for an element. A single property card may be referenced by all connection cards that define elements with the same property. The use of the pointer system thus eliminates repetition of data.

The property cards have the following general characteristics:

1. The type of element is specified by the mnemonic in the first field.

2. The second field is the Property Identification, which must be an integer number. The PID must be unique among the property numbers for a specific type of element.

3. The third field is a Material Identification (MID), which is an integer number of the MID of a MAT-type card.

4. The remainder of the property card is dependent on the element type.

There are some elements that have no cross-sectional properties and therefore have no property cards. The property card for isoparametric solid elements includes the specification of integration order and error limits rather than cross-sectional properties.

9.2.3. Standard Notation

NASTRAN input data lines must satisfy specific restrictions on the type of number (real or integer) and permissible range of values. In the remainder of this chapter the following standard notation will be used:

EID   Element identification number. (integer, >0)

PID   Property identification number. (integer, >0)

MID   Material identification number. (integer, >0)

G   Grid or scalar point number. (integer, >0)

C   Degree of freedom (integer, ≥ 0 or blank) code at grid point, equal to zero or blank for a scalar point.

CID   Coordinate identification number. (integer, ≥ 0)

NSM   Nonstructural mass defined per unit length for lineal elements and per unit area for two-dimensional elements. (real)

9.3.   Scalar Elastic Elements

A scalar element defines a single elastic constant that relates the displacements of two degrees of freedom.

9.3 Scalar Elastic Elements

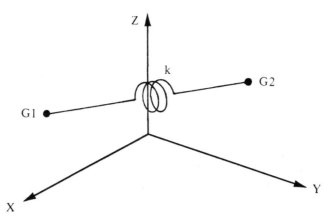

Figure 9-1. Scalar Elastic Element

Scalar elements may be defined between two grid point degrees of freedom by the ELAS1 and ELAS2 elements and between two scalar points by the ELAS3 and ELAS4 elements as shown by Card Image 9-1.

*Spring Connecting Geometric Degrees of Freedom

1	2	3	4	5	6	7	8	9	10
CELAS1	EID	PID	G1	C1	G2	C2			
PELAS	PID	K	GE	S					
CELAS2	EID	K	G1	C1	G2	C2	GE	S	

*Spring Connecting Scalar Points.

CELAS3	EID	PID	S1	S2					
PELAS	PID	K	GE	S					
CELAS4	EID	K	S1	S2					

Card Image 9-1. Elastic Spring

9.3.1. Specification of Connected Degrees of Freedom

The connected degrees of freedom at a grid point are defined on the ELAS1 and ELAS2 cards by specifying the external degree of freedom code using the pair G, C where

G is a grid or scalar point

and

C is a degree of freedom code that may be zero or blank if G is a scalar point. If G is a grid point, then $1 < C < 6$, where the degree of freedom codes are interpreted in terms of the displacement coordinate system of G as specified on the GRID card.

If the entry for one of the degrees of freedom connected by the spring is left completely blank, then the displacement of the spring at that end is taken to be zero and the spring is said to be connected to ground.

If the element is to connect only scalar points, then the ELAS3 and ELAS4-type cards should be used where the degree of freedom is specified by the scalar point number. The presence of a scalar point number on a scalar element specifies that the point exists, and it need not be defined using the SPOINT Bulk Data card.

9.3.2. Properties

The properties associated with the scalar spring may be defined directly on the connection card, if CELAS2 or CELAS4 are used, or on a separate PELAS property card. The properties in either case are defined as

K The spring rate (real)

GE Damping coefficient (real) (Not used in Rigid Formats 3 and 24)

S Stress recovery coefficient (real)

9.3.3. Stress Recovery

The stress recovery factor defined on the PELAS or CELAS card is used to calculate the stress in the scalar element by

$$\sigma = \frac{P}{S} \tag{9.1}$$

where P is the force in the element and S is the stress recovery coefficient. The stress is printed by using the STRESS Case Control Directive discussed in Chapter One.

9.3.4. Modeling with the ELAS Element

The ELAS element can be used to

- Define elastic constraint for generalized coordinates.

- Represent boundary flexibilities.

- Define elastic connections between degrees of freedom.

This general capability would allow the ELAS element to be used to model an axial elastic element between two grid points as shown by Fig. 9-1. However, the ELAS element is not recommended as a substitute for the ROD element, which is described in Sec. 9.4, because even a slight misalignment between the spring and the coordinate axes can lead to serious spurious internal constraints.

In spite of the potential problems involved with the use of the ELAS element to represent ROD behavior we will consider modeling the elastic spring shown on Fig. 9-1 to illustrate the modeling procedures involved in its specification.

The spring has a spring rate of 5000 lb_f/inch and connects the points G1 and G2 which have the following coordinates

$$G1 = (5, 3, 4) \text{ inch}$$

$$G2 = (2, 5, 2) \text{ inch}$$

The most straightforward way of specifying the spring is to define and connect displacement degrees of freedom which are in the direction of the line segment which connects the two grid points. This can be accomplished by

- Defining a new coordinate system which has an axis parallel to the line between the two points.

- Referring the displacement degrees of freedom at the two grid points to the new coordinate system.

This modeling procedure has the advantage that the element and coordinate axes are aligned so that no spurious constraints will be produced. The spring could then be represented by the following Bulk Data.

1	2	3	4	5	6	7	8	9	10
CORD1R	100	1	2	3					
GRID	1	0	5.	3.	4.	100			
GRID	2	0	2.	5.	3.	100			
GRID	3	0	0.	0.	0.		123456		
CELAS1	1	5	1	3	2	3			
PELAS	5	5.E3							

where

1. Coordinate system CID = 100 is a right-handed system whose origin is at point 1, whose X3-axis is along the line joining points 1 and 2.

2. Specification of CD = 100 on the GRID cards means that any reference to the degrees of freedom at these points will be interpreted with respect to the CID = 100 coordinate system.

3. The elastic spring defined by the CELAS1 card defines a scalar spring in the X3-direction of the CID = 100 coordinate system.

The use of a new coordinate system has the disadvantage that the displacement degrees of freedom at the connected node points are defined relative to a different coordinate system than all other degrees of freedom. Another way of representing the elastic spring that does not have this drawback is to connect each of the degrees of freedom which are referred to the basic coordinate system. This procedure, which leads to a full 3×3 stiffness matrix at each point, can be briefly described as follows.

Let u be the *difference* in the displacements at the two connected points, in the sense of the line segment which joins the two points. The total internal strain energy can then be represented in matrix form as

$$U = \tfrac{1}{2}\, u^T k\, u \tag{9.2}$$

where k is the spring rate. The directed relative displacement, u, can then be represented in terms of the element displacements, u_e, referred to basic coordinates as

$$u = G\, u_e \tag{9.3}$$

where the components of u_e are relative displacements as follows

$$u_e = (u_x, u_y, u_z) \tag{9.4}$$

and the transformation matrix, G, is given by

$$G = \lfloor G_x, G_y, G_z \rfloor^{\mathrm{T}} \tag{9.5}$$

where the elements of **G** are direction cosines between the directed line segment and coordinate axes.

The substitution of (9.3) into (9.2) then gives

$$U = \tfrac{1}{2}\, \mathbf{u}_e^T \mathbf{G}^T\, \mathbf{k}\, \mathbf{G}\, \mathbf{u}_e \tag{9.6}$$

So that the stiffness matrix associated with the spring is, by inspection

$$\mathbf{K}_e = k \begin{bmatrix} \mathbf{G}_x^2 & \mathbf{G}_x\mathbf{G}_y & \mathbf{G}_x\mathbf{G}_z \\ & \mathbf{G}_y^2 & \mathbf{G}_y\mathbf{G}_z \\ \text{Sym} & & \mathbf{G}_z^2 \end{bmatrix} \tag{9.7}$$

This is definitely *not* the way to define an elastic spring in a non-coordinate direction. The correct procedure is, of course, that of modeling the elastic element with the ROD element which is described in Sec. 9.4.

9.4.   Truss-Type Elements

A truss element is a lineal structural element whose properties and behavioral variables are continuously distributed along a line that joins two grid points and that provides resistance to axial displacement and torsion, as shown in Fig. 9-2.

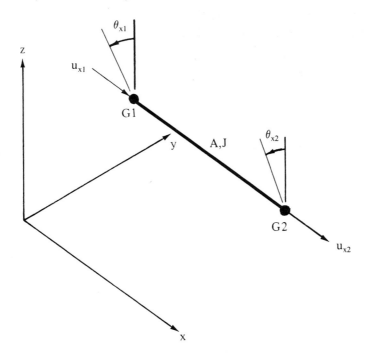

Figure 9-2. Truss-Type Element

The element has a uniform cross-sectional area A and torsional constant J and connects the two grid points G1 and G2, as shown. The local x-axis is defined by the directed line drawn from G1 to G2.

189

The element may be defined either by CONROD, which includes connective as well as property data on one card, or by the pairs CROD-PROD or CTUBE-PTUBE, as shown in Card Image 9-2. The difference between the TUBE and ROD elements is that the cross-section of the tube is assumed to be a circular cylinder of diameter D and thickness T, while the rod has a cross-sectional area A and torsional constant J.

1	2	3	4	5	6	7	8	9	10
CONROD	EID	G1	G2	MID	A	J	C	NSM	
CROD	EID	PID	G1	G2					
PROD	PID	MID	A	J	C	NSM			
CTUBE	EID	PID	G1	G2					
PTUBE	PID	MID	D	T	NSM				

Card Image 9-2. Specification of Truss Element

9.4.1.   Description of Input Data for Truss

The input data items included on the connect and property cards are

EID   Element identification number, which must be unique among all elements defined in Bulk Data. (integer, >0)

G1, G2   Geometric grid point joined by the element. (integer, >0, G1 $\neq$ G2)

MID   Material identification number that points to a set of material properties. (integer, >0)

A   Cross-sectional area. (real)

J   Torsional constant. The torsional constant is equal to the polar moment of inertia only for circular cross-section. In general, J must be determined experimentally, from a handbook such as the American Institute for Steel Construction, or by means of torsion theory. (real)

D   Outside diameter of the tube. (real)

T   Thickness of the tube. (real, $T < \tfrac{1}{2}D$)

C   Stress recovery coefficient, which is the distance from the neutral axis to the point at which the shear stress is desired. (real)

NSM   Nonstructural mass per unit length of the element.

9.4.2.   Stiffness Matrix and Degrees of Freedom

It was pointed out in Chapter Seven that NASTRAN associates six degrees of freedom with each geometric grid point. Thus, in the absence of other members connecting grid points G1 and G2, there are no stiffness coefficients that relate three of the independent degrees of freedom at each point. The analyst must therefore remove the unconnected degrees of freedom, either by defining permanent single point constraints on the GRID card or by a SPC card. The analyst should also note that the absence of a geometric parameter that provides a stiffness for a degree of freedom, such as the torsional stiffness J, will introduce an additional singularity, which must also be removed by one of these two methods, into the elemental stiffness matrix.

The stiffness matrix for the truss element is based on the assumption that the axial displacement and the rotation about the local x-axis vary linearly along the length of the beam. The displacement and rotation are then taken to be

$$\left\{ \begin{array}{c} \mathbf{u} \\ \theta \end{array} \right\} = \left[\begin{array}{cccc} N_1 & N_2 & 0 & 0 \\ 0 & 0 & N_1 & N_2 \end{array} \right] \left\{ \begin{array}{c} u_{x1} \\ u_{x2} \\ \theta_{x1} \\ \theta_{y1} \end{array} \right\} \tag{9.8}$$

where

$$N_1 = (1 - \frac{x}{L}) \qquad N_2 = \frac{x}{L} \tag{9.9}$$

and L is the length of the element between G1 and G2. The resulting stiffness equation for the element is given by

$$\left[\begin{array}{cc} \mathbf{k}_{axial} & \mathbf{0} \\ \mathbf{0} & \mathbf{k}_{tor} \end{array} \right] \left\{ \begin{array}{c} u_{x1} \\ u_{x2} \\ \theta_{x1} \\ \theta_{x2} \end{array} \right\} = \left\{ \begin{array}{c} F_{x2} \\ F_{x2} \\ M_{x1} \\ M_{x2} \end{array} \right\} \tag{9.10}$$

where the stiffness matrices are

$$\mathbf{k}_{axial} = \frac{AE}{L} \left[\begin{array}{cc} 1 & -1 \\ -1 & 1 \end{array} \right] \tag{9.11}$$

$$\mathbf{k}_{tor} = \frac{JG}{L} \left[\begin{array}{cc} 1 & -1 \\ -1 & 1 \end{array} \right] \tag{9.12}$$

9.4.3. Stress Recovery

The axial and shear stress are calculated as

$$\sigma_x = \frac{F}{A} \tag{9.13}$$

$$\sigma_{xy} = \frac{M_x C}{J} \tag{9.14}$$

where A is the cross-sectional area. The stress recovery coefficient, C, is specified directly on the PROD card and is taken to be D/2 for the TUBE. If A or J is omitted in defining the element, then the associated stress recovery is bypassed. Stresses are printed by using a STRESS Case Control Directive.

9.4   Truss-Type Elements

Example 9-2. Plane Truss

Consider the truss shown in Fig. 9-3. The Bulk Data cards required to specify the grid point locations, the element connections, purge of the unconnected degree of freedom, and the specification of geometric constraints using permanent single point constraints are shown below.

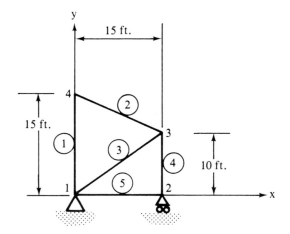

Note:

1. Element numbers are shown in circles.

2. The areas for all elements is 3 in².

3. Only loads in the x, y-plane are considered.

4. Simply supported at nodes 1 and 2.

Figure 9-3. Plane Truss

1	2	3	4	5	6	7	8	9	10
GRDSET		0				0	3456		
GRID	1		0.	0.	0.		123456		
GRID	2		180.	0.	0.		23456		
GRID	3		180.	120.	0.				
GRID	4		0.	180.	0.				
CROD	1	1	1	4					
CROD	2	1	4	3					
CROD	3	1	1	3					
CROD	4	1	3	2					
CROD	5	1	1	2					
PROD	1	100	3.						
MAT1	100	3.E7							

where

1. A GRDSET card has been used to specify default values for permanent single point constraints to purge degrees of freedom 3, 4, 5, and 6 at each grid point. This allows each grid point to move only in the x- and y-directions.

2. The coordinates of the grid points and the area on the PROD card are expressed in consistent units (inches).

192

3. The fields associated with the torsional stiffness, the torsional stress recovery coefficient, and the nonstructural mass have been left blank. These quantities will therefore be interpreted as zero by NASTRAN.

4. The PROD card points to a MAT1 material card (see Sec. 10.1.1.) whose ID is 100. Since only the modulus of elasticity is used to calculate the stiffness for the rod element, the entries for other material coefficients have been omitted.

5. The structure is restrained against rigid body motion by setting the x and y components of displacement at point one and the y component at point two equal to zero by means of the PSPC field. Since any entry in the PSPC field of the GRID card overrides the default value on the GRDSET card, it is necessary to include all the degrees of freedom as shown.

9.5. The BAR Element

A beam is a lineal element whose properties and behavioral variables are continuously distributed along a line segment that joins two grid points. The beam elements in NASTRAN provide resistance to all six degrees of freedom at a geometric grid point, as shown in Fig. 9-4.

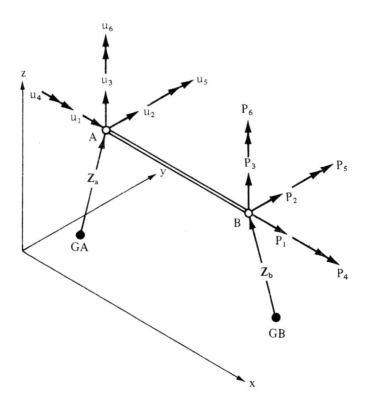

Figure 9-4. The BAR Element

MSC/NASTRAN incorporates two straight beam-type elements, the BAR and the BEAM as well as a curved beam and pipe element called the BEND. The BEAM allows an off-set shear center and axially-varying area properties while the BAR represents a subclass of the BEAM element capability without these features. The BAR element is described in this section while the additional capability of the BEAM is presented in Sec. 9.6. The BEND element is described in Section 9.7.

The Bar element has constant cross-sectional area and material properties along the length of the BAR. The area properties are specified with respect to the local coordinate system for the BAR.

The BAR element may be offset from the grid points to allow the modeling of eccentrically stiffened plates and shells. The BAR element connects the offset ends A and B and the local x-axis is taken as the directed line segment from end A to end B of the beam.

The neutral axis for the BAR element is assumed to coincide with the local x-axis. The assumption precludes the use of the BAR element to model a beam whose neutral axis and shear center do not coincide. The BEAM element described in Sec. 9.6 must be used in this case.

The NASTRAN BAR element has the following modeling features and limitations:

1. The element resists bending behavior about two perpendicular axes in addition to axial and torsional motion.

2. The neutral axis may be offset from the grid points.

3. The neutral axis and shear center coincide.

4. Transverse shear flexibility may be included.

5. Pinned connections may be defined.

6. The area properties are constant.

7. The principal axes of inertia need not coincide with local axes.

8. Stress can be recovered up to four points on the cross-section at each end.

9.5.1.   Description of BAR Input Data

The Bulk Data used to specify the BAR element consists of the CBAR, CBARAO, PBAR, and BAROR cards that are shown in Card Image 9-3, where

CBAR   Defines the connectivity, the beam offset, the local coordinate system, and pinned connections.

CBARAO   Defines a series of points along the BAR element at which stress and/or internal element forces may be recovered.

PBAR   Defines the area properties relative to the local coordinate system, the nonstructural mass, the points at which stresses are to be recovered, and the shear factors.

BAROR   Provides default values for fields three and six through nine of the CBAR card. One BAROR card is allowed in the entire Bulk Data set. Defaults are used if the corresponding field of the CBAR card is left blank.

The contents of the CBAR and PBAR card are described in Section 9.5.1.1 and 9.5.1.2, respectively.

1	2	3	4	5	6	7	8	9	10
BAROR		PID			V_1, GO	V_2	V_3		
CBAR	EID	PID	GA	GB	V_1, GO	V_2	V_3		+C1
+C1	PA	PB	Z_{1A}	Z_{2A}	Z_{3A}	Z_{1B}	Z_{2B}	Z_{3B}	
PBAR	PID	MID	A	I_{zz}	I_{yy}	J	NSM		+P1
+P1	C_y	C_z	D_y	D_z	E_y	E_z	F_y	F_z	+P2
+P2	K_y	K_z	I_{yz}						
CBARAO	EID	SCALE	X_1	X_2	X_3	X_4	X_5	X_6	

*Alternate Form of CBARAO

CBARAO	EID	SCALE	NPTS	X_1	Δx				

Card Image 9-3. Specification of the BAR element

9.5.1.1. Element Connectivity

The connectivity specification for the BAR element, including the definition of the offsets at grid points GA and GB and the specification of the local coordinate system, is made on the CBAR card. The fields of the CBAR card are defined in Table 9-1.

FIELD   DESCRIPTION

GA, GB Grid point identification numbers of connection points. (integer, >0, GA $\neq$ GB)

V_1, V_2, V_3 Components of a free vector at end A defined with respect to the displacement (i.e. CD) coordinate system at GRID GA. The vector is used to determine the orientation of the element coordinate system. (real)

GO Identification number of third grid point to optionally define the free vector. (integer, >0)

PA, PB Pin flags for bar ends A and B. Used to specify forceless degrees of freedom corresponding to the pin flag number at the appropriate end of the bar. (Up to 5 of the unique digits 1-6 can be put anywhere in the field with no imbedded blanks, integer, >0).

(Z_{1A}, Z_{2A}, Z_{3A}) Components of the offset vectors defined with respect to the displacement
(Z_{1B}, Z_{2B}, Z_{3B}) coordinate systems at grid points GA and GB which define the position of the neutral axis relative to the grid points. (real)

Table 9-1. Description of CBAR Data

9.5.1.1.1. Local Coordinate System

The features of beam offset and the three-dimensional behavior of the element complicate the specification of the local coordinate system. The ends of the BAR are at points A and B, which coincide with the geometric grid point only if there are no offsets. With this in mind, the local x,y,z-coordinate system, which is shown in Fig. 9-5, is defined as follows

9.5.1 Description of BAR Input Data

1. The local x-axis is coincident with the line segment between points A and B positive from A to B.

2. The local x,y-plane is determined by defining a vector, **v**, that lies in the local x,y-plane and that has its origin at end A of the BAR. Since the x,y-plane is defined by the x-axis and **v**, the vector may not be coincident with x-axis.

The user may define the vector in either of two ways

1. By specifying the components (V_1, V_2, V_3) of a vector **v**, which are defined in terms of the displacement coordinate system at grid point GA and which has its origin at end A. (Note: The displacement coordinate system is specified by the CD coordinate system in field seven of the GRID card that defines grid point GA.)

2. By specifying a third grid point GO. The vector is then taken to be the directed line from end A of the BAR to point GO. (Note: The program does not do quite what the documentation suggests. If GO is specified the vector is *always* taken as the directed line segment from GA to GO even if offsets are present.)

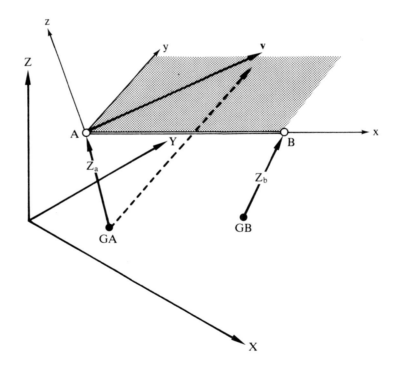

Figure 9-5. Local Coordinates for BAR Element

If a third grid point GO is defined only for the purpose of specifying the vector, then the degrees of freedom at GO are not connected to the structure and must be removed. Otherwise, a singular system matrix will result.

196

The local coordinate system is then defined using the local x-axis and $\mathbf{v}$

$$\mathbf{z} = \mathbf{x} \times \mathbf{v}$$

and   (9.15)

$$\mathbf{y} = \mathbf{z} \times \mathbf{x}$$

9.5.1.1.2.   BAR Offset

The BAR element may be offset from the grid points by specifying offset vectors $\mathbf{Z}_a$ and $\mathbf{Z}_b$ as shown in Fig. 9-5. The position of points A and B is then given by

$$\mathbf{A} = \text{GA} + \mathbf{Z}_a$$
$$\mathbf{B} = \text{GB} + \mathbf{Z}_b$$

(9.16)

where

1. The offset vectors $\mathbf{Z}_a$ and $\mathbf{Z}_b$ are defined by componenets (Z_{1A}, Z_{2A}, Z_{3A}) and (Z_{1B}, Z_{2B}, Z_{3B}) on the CBAR card. These components are interpreted in terms of the displacement coordinate system for the respective points. Thus, if the displacement coordinate systems associated with GA and GB are rectangular and cylindrical, respectively, the components of $\mathbf{Z}_a$ and $\mathbf{Z}_b$ will be interpreted in the sense of unit vectors in the (X, Y, Z) and (R, θ, Z) directions, respectively.

2. The offset vector is a rigid link between the grid points and the associated ends of the bar.

3. The local coordinate system is defined with respect to the offset bar element.

9.5.1.1.3.   Pinned Connections

The user can specify that degrees of freedom at either end of the BAR are to transmit no force by means of the pin flags. The pin flags PA and PB are defined in fields two and three of the optional CBAR continuation card. The pin flag is a packed set of degree of freedom code numbers. The presence of the pin flag indicates that no force or moment associated with the specified degree of freedom is to be transmitted to the element. The degree of freedom specified by the pin flag is defined in terms of the local (i.e. element) coordinates. The pin flag degree of freedom codes are defined as

Pin Flag	Meaning
1	No force in local x-direction
2	No force in local y-direction
3	No force in local z-direction
4	No moment about local x-axis
5	No moment about local y-axis
6	No moment about local z-axis

The specification of a pinned connection actually results in an additional degree of freedom at a grid point, as indicated in Fig. 9-6, which shows two BAR elements that are attached at grid point two.

9.5.1   Description of BAR Input Data

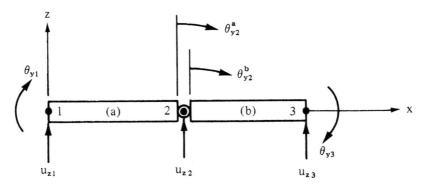

Figure 9-6. Independent Rotations at a Hinge

The specification of a momentless hinge associated with the rotation about the z-axis at grid point two is made by specifying either PB = 5 for element A or PA = 5 for element B.

Since the pin flag defines a forceless degree of freedom, the stiffness for the element in which the pin flag is defined can be reduced by noting that the stiffness equation for the specified degree of freedom is equal to zero. For example, the stiffness equation for element (a) in Fig. 9-6 is given by

$$\begin{bmatrix} k_{11} & k_{12} & k_{13} & k_{14} \\ k_{21} & k_{22} & k_{23} & k_{24} \\ k_{31} & k_{32} & k_{33} & k_{34} \\ k_{41} & k_{42} & k_{43} & k_{44} \end{bmatrix} \begin{Bmatrix} u_{z1} \\ \theta_{y1} \\ u_{z2} \\ \theta_{y2} \end{Bmatrix} = \begin{Bmatrix} F_{z1} \\ M_{y1} \\ F_{z2} \\ M_{y2} \end{Bmatrix} \tag{9.17}$$

Setting the moment M_{y2} equal to zero gives

$$k_{41}\; u_{z1}\; +\; k_{42}\; \theta_{y1}\; +\; k_{43}\; u_{z2}\; +\; k_{44}\; \theta_{y2}\; =\; 0 \tag{9.18}$$

The displacement θ_{y2} associated with the pin flag can now be determined as

$$\theta_{y2}\; =\; -\frac{1}{k_{44}} \Big[k_{41}\; u_{z1}\; +\; k_{42}\;\; \theta_{y1}\; +\; k_{43}\; u_{z2} \Big] \tag{9.19}$$

This equation is of the form of multipoint constraint relation for the pinned degree of freedom in terms of the remaining degrees of freedom which can be used to reduce the order of the stiffness matrix for the element in which the pin connection is specified. The stiffness coefficient for the pinned degree of freedom must therefore be nonzero.

Because the pinned degree of freedom is removed from the stiffness representation of the element we see that the hinge may be specified in either element but not in both. If the same degree of freedom were specified in both elements it would be completely uncoupled (i.e. it would have no stiffness).

NASTRAN does not recover the displacement degree of freedom associated with the pin. This fact may influence the user's choice of the element in which the pin is defined. The displacement may be recovered external to the program only by the appropriate constraint relationship of the form

$$u_i\; =\; -\frac{1}{k_{ii}} \left[\sum_{\substack{k=1 \\ k\neq i}}^{n} k_{ik}\; u_k \right] \tag{9.20}$$

where i is the degree of freedom corresponding to the pin and n is the order of the stiffness matrix. For a beam with six degrees of freedom at each end, n = 12.

9.5.1.2.   Specification of BAR Properties

The properties of the BAR element are specified on the PBAR card, whose fields are defined in

198

Table 9-2.

FIELD	DESCRIPTION
A	Area of bar cross-section. (real)
I_{yy}, I_{zz}, I_{yz}	Area moments of inertia about the local y- and z-axes and the associated cross product of inertia, respectively. (real)
J	Torsional constant. (real)
NSM	Nonstructural mass per unit length. (real)
K_y, K_z	Shear factors in the local y- and z-directions, respectively. The shear factor is dependent on the beam cross-section.
(C_y, C_z) (D_y, D_z) (E_y, E_z) (F_y, F_z)	Local y,z-coordinates of up to four points on beam cross-section at which stresses are to be recovered at each end of the BAR. (real)

Table 9-2. Description of PBAR Card Fields

The area properties which are to be specified on the PBAR card are calculated with respect to the local coordinate system which is defined by means of the v-vector on CBAR Bulk Data. In order to define the area properties we thus consider the cross-section of a general beam element as shown in Figure 9-7.

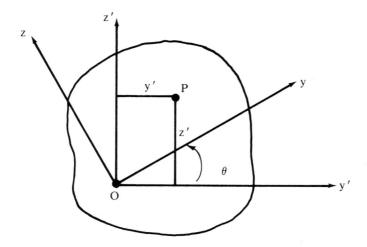

Figure 9-7. General BAR cross section

where

0 is a point which lies on the neutral axis

P is a general point on the cross section with an area dA

199

9.5.1   Description of BAR Input Data

(y', z') is a set of local coordinates for which the area coefficients are defined as

$$I_{y'y'} = \int (z')^2 \, dA \qquad (9.21)$$

$$I_{z'z'} = \int (y')^2 \, dA \qquad (9.22)$$

$$I_{y'x'} = \int y'z' \, dA \qquad (9.23)$$

$$A = \int dA \qquad (9.24)$$

(y,z) is the set of local coordinates which is shown by Fig. 9-5 and which is to be defined on CBAR Bulk Data. The moments of inertia of the cross section relative to (y,z) are defined in terms of those found with respect to (y',z') as follows

$$I_{yy} = I_{y'y'}\cos^2\theta + I_{z'z'}\sin^2\theta - I_{y'z'}\sin 2\theta \qquad (9.25)$$

$$I_{zz} = I_{z'z'}\cos^2\theta + I_{y'y'}\sin^2\theta - I_{y'z'}\sin 2\theta \qquad (9.26)$$

$$I_{yz} = I_{y'z'}\cos^2\theta + \tfrac{1}{2}(I_{y'y'} - I_{z'z'})\sin 2\theta \qquad (9.27)$$

Since the moments of inertia for the cross-section are defined relative to a specific local coordinate system it is vitally important that the analyst define the orientation of the local coordinates with respect to global coordinates on the CBAR card.

The other definitions of cross-sectional properties, J, the torsional constant and the transverse shear coefficients, K_y and K_z, are not as straight forward since both depend on the distribution of area in a more complex way than do the bending moments of inertia and area.

The torsional constant, J, relates the angle of twist, θ_x, to the torsional moment, M_x, the length L, and the shear constant G as follows

$$\theta = \frac{TL}{JG} \qquad (9.28)$$

The torsional constant is equal to the polar moment of inertia only for the case of a circular cross-section. For other cross-sections the analyst should consult handbooks such as Ref. 9-1.

The shear constants K_y and K_z define the shear-effectiveness of the beam. These shear constants define the shear displacements v_{ys} and v_{zs}, respectively. The total displacement of the reference axis is then given by

$$v_y = v_{yb} + v_{ys} \qquad (9.29)$$

and

$$v_z = v_{zb} + v_{zs} \qquad (9.30)$$

where v_{yb} and v_{zb} are bending displacements.

The total shear displacement of a beam of length L in the z-direction is related to the shear strain γ_{xz} as follows

$$v_{zs} = \gamma_{xz}L \qquad (9.31)$$

where the shear strain and shear stress are related by

$$\gamma_{xz} = \frac{\sigma_{xz}}{G} \qquad (9.32)$$

Then, since $\sigma_{xz} = V_z/A$ where V_z is the transverse shear force, we have

$$\gamma_{xz} = \frac{V_z Q}{I_{zz} b}$$

(9.33)

where Q is the static moment of the area beyond that value of z for which the shear stress is to be determined, and b is the width of the cross section at that point. Since $Q/I_{zz}b$ has the units of area we can represent (9.33) as

$$\sigma_{xz} = \frac{V_z}{K_z A}$$

(9.34)

where K_z is a factor which depends on the cross-section and accounts for the of shear distribution over the cross-section. The substitution of (9.34) and (9.32) into (9.31) then gives

$$V_{zs} = \frac{V_z L}{K_z A G}$$

(9.35)

where the factor $1/KAG$ is called the shear flexibility. The shear factor, K, which is the reciprocal of factor, F, defined in Ref. 9-5 is $K = 5/6$ for rectangular cross-sections, $K = 9/10$ for circular cross-sections, $K \approx A_f/1.2A$ and $K \approx A_w/A$ for bending of wide flange I-beam about minor and major axes of inertia, respectively, where A_f is the flange area and A_w is the web area. The analyst should consult handbooks such as Ref. 9-5 for additional material.

9.5.1.2.1 Area Properties

The beam element relates the six grid point displacement degrees of freedom at each end of the beam and the associated stress and moment resultants as indicated by P_1 through P_6 on Fig. 9-4. The components of this force vector are defined as

P_1 Axial force in direction of the local x-axis

P_2 Axial force in direction of the local y-axis

P_3 Axial force in direction of the local z-axis

P_4 Moment about the local x-axis

P_5 Moment about the local y-axis

P_6 Moment about the local z-axis

The following area coefficients relate the element displacement degree of freedom u_e and force resultants P_e.

A Cross-sectional area defines resistance to an axial load P_1.

K_y Shear area coefficient, resists the transverse load P_2.

K_z Shear area coefficient, resists the transverse load P_3.

J Torsional constant, resists the torsional moment P_4.

I_{yy} Area moment of inertia about the local y-axis, resists the bending moment P_5 and the transverse load P_3.

I_{zz} Area moment of inertia about the local z-axis, resists the bending moment P_6 and the transverse load P_2.

I_{yz} Cross product of inertia, nonzero unless the local y- and z-axes are principal axes of the cross section; for non-principal axes, resists all loads except P_1 and P_3.

The area coefficients generate nonzero terms in the stiffness matrix associated with the element degrees of freedom as shown by Table 9-3. The absence of an area coefficient on the PBAR card will result in zero coefficients in the rows and columns of the element stiffness matrix for the associated degrees of freedom.

For example, if I_{yy} is the only nonzero area coefficient specified on the PBAR card, then the stiffness matrix will provide resistance to only the u_3 and u_5 degrees of freedom (the displacement in the z direction and the rotation about the y-axis). Since the grid point has six degrees of freedom, the remaining unconnected degrees of freedom must be purged using single point constraints as described in Chapter Seven.

The shear coefficients K_y and K_z can be utilized only if the local coordinate system coincides with the principal axis for the cross-sectional inertia. If $I_{yz} \neq 0$, the BAR element is assumed to be infinitely rigid to shear deformations.

Area Coefficient Symbol	Description	Nonzero Displacement Degrees Of Freedom					
		u_1	u_2	u_3	u_4	u_5	u_6
A	Area	X					
K_y	Shear Coef.		X				
K_z	Shear Coef.			X			
J	Torsion Const.				X		
I_{yy}	Inertia about y-axis			X		X	
I_{zz}	Inertia about z-axis		X				X
I_{yz}	Inertia cross prod.		X	X		X	X

Table 9-3. Degrees of Freedom Associated with Area Coefficients

9.5.1.2.2.   Nonstructural Mass

The mass of the beam per unit length may be entered by the parameter NSM in field eight of the PBAR card. The calculation of mass properties is discussed in Chapter Thirteen.

9.5.2.   Stress Recovery

The location of up to four points labeled C, D, E, F at which stress is desired in the cross-section at each end of the bar element can be specified relative to the neutral axis as shown by Fig. 9-8. The location of these points is specified by y- and z-coordinates of up to four points on the PBAR card.

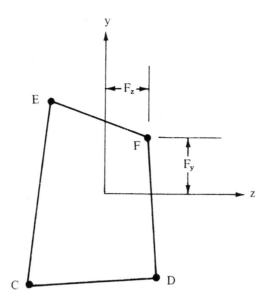

y

E

F_z

F

F_y

z

C   D

Figure 9-8. Stress Recovery Points on the BAR

The following stress output is printed at ends A and B of the BAR element by STRESS Case Control Directives:

1. The bending stress at points C, D, E, and F on the cross-section

2. The axial stress

3. The maximum stress

4. The margins of safety based on stress limits prescribed on a material card.

9.5.3. Generation of BAR Elements with MSGMESH — CGEN

BAR Bulk Data can be generated on a field of GRIDs, which have previously been defined by MSGMESH, by means of the CGEN MSGMESH command which is shown by Card Image 9-4.

Card	1	2	3	4	5	6	7	8	9	10
1-	CGEN	BAR	FEID	PID	FID	DIR	GEOM	EIDL	EIDH	+ G1
2-	+ G1	X_1orG_0	X_2	X_3	PEND	PINT	Z_1	Z_2	Z_3	

Card Image 9-4. Generation of BAR Elements with MSGMESH — CGEN

The purpose of this CGEN MSGMESH command is to generate BAR elements along a LINE-type field or along one of the coordinate directions in two or three dimensional fields where the FID (field 5) identifies the MSGMESH field of GRID points. The direction in which the BARs are to be generated is controlled by the DIR (field 6), where the integer values 1,2, or 3 define the MSGMESH directions. The value 1, which is associated with ℓ-direction is default. This is the only direction for the LINE field and is, with reference to Fig. 7-9, the primary direction for a two dimensional field. The value 2 refers to the secondary direction for the two and three dimensional field, and 3 refers to the 3rd coordinate (which we haven't described in this book) for a three dimensional field.

The orientation vector for the generated BAR elements is defined by the components (X_1, X_2, X_3) as described in Sec. 9.5.1.1.1. and the offset of the neutral axis from the gridpoints is taken to be the same at each end and is specified by the vector components (Z_1, Z_2, Z_3) as described in 9.5.1.1.2.

The pin flag entries, PEND and PINT, do not define pinned (i.e. forceless) degrees of freedom at ends A and B of each generated beam (see sec. 9.5.1.1.2.). Instead PEND specifies the pin flags at each end of a generated string of BARs while PINT specifies the pin flag for the internal nodes in the generated string of elements.

The analyst controls the element number generation by means of FEID, EIDL, and EIDH (fields 3, 8, and 9, respectively) where FEID is the integer number of the first element which is generated, and is positive for incrementation and negative for decrementation. The lowest element ID is then assigned to the element which connects vertex A in the field. However, the corresponding BAR Bulk Data is generated only if (assuming positive incrementation of element identification numbers) the EID is equal to or greater than EIDL, which is the element identification number of lowest numbered element which will be generated. Similarly no BAR elements will be generated which have element identification numbers greater than the upper limit, EIDH.

As an example of the use of this feature, consider the two dimensional field which is shown by Fig. 9-9, where we wish to generate strings of BAR elements which connect GRID points along the edges X = 0 and Y = 0 as shown. The BARs along Y = 0 are to be numbered starting with 1 at vertex A and those along X = 0 are to be numbered starting with 4 at vertex A. The GRID points and elements can then be generated by using the following MSGMESH commands.

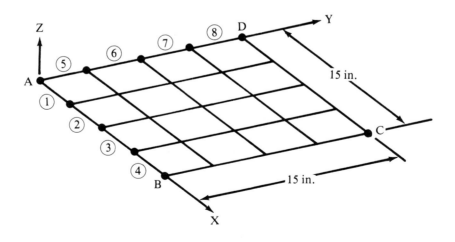

Fig. 9-9. Generation of BAR Elements using MSGMESH-CBARG.

Card	1	2	3	4	5	6	7	8	9	10
1-	EGRID	1	0	0.	0.	0.				
2-	EGRID	2	0	15.	0.	0.				
3-	EGRID	3	0	15.	15.	0.				
4-	EGRID	4	0	0.	15.	0.				
5-	GRIDG	3	0		4	− 1	− 2	− 3		+ G1
6-	+ G1	4	− 4							
7-	CGEN	BAR	1	12	3	1		1	4	+ G2
8-	+ G2	0.	0.	1.				4		
9-	CGEN	BAR	5	12	3	2		5	8	+ G3
10-	+ G3	0.	0.	1.						
11-	PBAR	12	30	etc.						
13-	MAT1	30	etc.							

Card 1- The geometric location of verticies are defined by MSGMESH.
4 EGRID commands.

Card 5- A four-by-four (i.e. L = M = 4) quadrilateral field of points which has FID = 3 is generated with the X-axis being the primary direction (i.e. DIR = 1) of point generation. The negative vertex numbers means that GRID BULK data will be generated at the vertices.

Card 7- Generates BAR elements in the primary direction (DIR = 1) starting with element number 1 on GRID field number 3 with the orientation vector for all elements in the basic z-direction (i.e. local y is normal to the basic X-Y plane).

Card 8- Tells MSGMESH to stop generating BAR Bulk Data after element number 4.

Card 9- Generated BAR elements in the secondary direction (DIR = 2) starting with element number FEID = 5.

Card 10- Terminates element generation with EIDH = 8.

Card 11- Incomplete PBAR with PID = 12.

Card 12- Incomplete MAT1 with MID = 30.

9.5.4.   Element Forces — Use of CBARAO

The CBARAO Bulk Data is an MSC/NASTRAN feature which allows the user to request the recovery of element forces and stresses at intermediate points along the length of the BAR element. The CBARAO card is typically used in conjunction with a nonuniform load distribution defined by a PLOAD1 Bulk Data card. (See Chapt. 11.)

The inclusion of internal data recovery points may lead to some confusion concerning the sign convention used to interpret the element forces since either of the following sign conventions can be used.

- Beam Convention

- Internal Convention

The beam sign convention is shown by Figure 9-10 and is such that positive forces and moments cause positive curvature of the beam element. The internal sign convention on the other hand is such that positive forces and moments are in the direction of positive displacements and rotations, respectively.

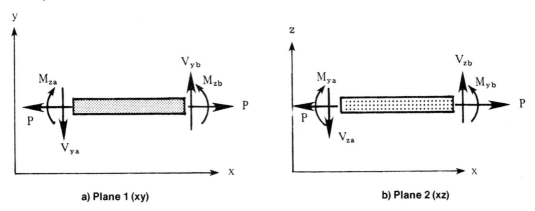

Figure 9-10. Beam Forces and Moments

In earlier versions of NASTRAN, i.e., before internal data recovery points could be specified, the beam sign convention was used for element forces. It is reasonable, however, to use the internal sign convention for element forces associated with the internal data recovery points.

The element forces for the BAR element are thus interpreted as follows

- Internal forces if PLOAD1 and/or CBARAO Bulk Data exist

- External forces otherwise

For other MSC/NASTRAN beam-type elements, i.e., the BEAM and BEND elements the element forces are *always* interpreted as internal forces.

There are two forms of the CBARAO Bulk Data card shown on Card Image 9-3 that provide the user with two different ways of prescribing internal data recovery points.

Form 1-   Allows the user to prescribe up to six unique positions on the BAR

Form 2-   Allows the user to specify positions by means of a length increment and number of increments.

9.5.4.1.   Data Recovery Points — CBARAO Form 1

The data fields on the first form of the CBARAO card allow the user to define internal points by direct specification of up to six interior points along the length of the bar. The data fields shown on Card Image 9-3 are described as follows.

EID   Element identification number of a specific BAR element (Integer > 0)

SCALE A literal parameter that defines how the axial coordinates of interior points are to be scaled as follows

LE - The values x_i are actual distances.

FR - The values x_i are normalized distances where element length is the normalizing factor.

x_i The positions of up to six interior points along the element axis. The end points are not to be included since the forces and stresses are normally recovered at these points. (Real >0.0)

If the literal value 'LE' is supplied for the SCALE field then a PLOAD1 Bulk Data card for the element must be present.

9.5.4.2.   Data Recovery Points — CBARAO Form 2

The second form allows the user to specify a number of equally spaced internal points with a minimum input. The specific form of the card is implied by the type of number in the fourth field as follows

Real - Form 1

Integer - Form 2

The fields of the second form which are different from the first form are as follows

NPTS   Number of interior data recovery points. (Integer $0 < NPTS \le 6$)

x_1 Position of first point. (Real >0.0)

Δx Incremental distance along element axis. (Real >0.0)

The series interior points

$$x_i = x_{i-1} + \Delta x \qquad (i = 1,2,...NPTS) \qquad (9.21)$$

are then generated.

9.5.5.   BAR Element Stiffness Matrix

The 12-by-12 stiffness matrix for the BAR element relates the six displacement degrees of freedom of each end of the BAR to the node point forces. The beam bending coefficients are obtained by modifying the energy expression (6.49) to include the transverse shear stress. The shape functions given by (6.56) are then used to obtain a set of stiffness coefficients that are similar to those given by (6.59) but which include the transverse shear coefficients.

The total stiffness matrix is obtained by adding the beam bending stiffness to the axial and torsional stiffness coefficients for the truss element as given by (9.11) and (9.12). The resulting stiffness matrix, which does not include coupling between axial and bending behavior, is presented in Refs. 9-2 and 9-3.

9.5.6.   BAR-Element Examples

9.5.6.1.   Specifying Local Coordinate System

Consider the structure shown in Fig. 9-11, which consists of two beams at right angles. The structure is fully constrained at grid point one, and may be loaded with arbitrary forces and moments at grid points two and three. Each of the beams has the same cross-sectional inertia properties, but the moments of inertia about the two orthogonal axes are not equal. Assuming that the local axes are principal axes, we wish to orient the local axes of the two beams such that each beam provides maximum resistance to bending in the global X, Y-plane.

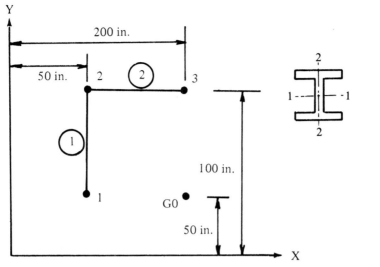

$$I_{12} = 0$$
$$I_{22} = 420 \text{ in}^4$$
$$I_{11} = 1170 \text{ in}^4$$
$$A = 30.3 \text{ in}^2$$
$$k_1 = k_2 = 0$$
$$J = 10 \text{ in}^4$$
$$E = 30 \times 10^6 \text{ psi}$$

Figure 9-11. Example of Specifying Local Axes

The vector **v** must be specified either by using a third geometric grid point or by means of its components in order to define the local, x,y-axes. The vector **v** must lie in the local x,y-plane, and the same vector can be used for both elements if it is not colinear with the local x-axis for either element. The vector can then be specified in terms of components on a BAROR card as

1	2	3	4	5	6	7	8	9	10
BAROR					1.	1.	0.		

where the components define a vector at 45 degrees to the basic x-axis. The local x,y-plane is then coincident with the basic X,Y-plane, since **v** lies in the basic X,Y-plane and by definition also lies in the local x,y-plane.

Alternately, grid points three and one could be used to specify GO for elements one and two, respectively, or an additional grid point GO, as shown, could be defined and be referenced by both elements. Experience has shown that when the new NASTRAN user defines a free point GO to specify **v**, an almost universal error is neglecting to purge the degrees of freedom associated with the unconnected free point GO.

Now that the local coordinates have been defined, it is necessary to specify the element properties by means of the PBAR cards. The data set required to define the grid points, the beam properties, and the constraints is

1	2	3	4	5	6	7	8	9	10
GRID	1		50.	50.	0.		123456		
GRID	2		50.	100.	0.				
GRID	3		200.	100.	0.				
BAROR					1.	1.	0.		
CBAR	1	30	1	2					
CBAR	2	30	2	3					
PBAR	30	700	30.3	1170.	420.	10.			
MAT1	700	3.E7		.3					

where

1. The unconnected degrees of freedom have been purged and geometric constraints at grid points have been specified by means of permanent single point constraints on the GRID card. (The unconnected could also be purged by using the AUTOPC PARAMeter as described in Sec. 12.4.3.1.)

2. The units used in specifying grid point coordinates are consistent with those used in defining the element properties.

3. The BAROR card has been used to define the components of v as a default for each element. Note that the vector lies in the basic X,Y-plane. The local x,y-plane for each element is thus coplanar with the basic X,Y-plane.

4. Each of the CBAR cards points to the same property set 30. Note that the PID's can be any unique integer.

5. The PBAR card points to a MAT1 Bulk Data card which has a material set 700. (The specification of material cards is described in Chapter Ten.)

9.5.5.2. Use of Pin Flags

Consider the structural system shown in Fig. 9-12, which consists of two cantilevered beams loaded in the global X,Y-plane that are attached with a momentless hinge at point A.

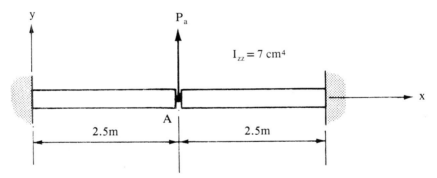

Figure 9-12. Example of Forceless Hinge

The system is modeled using two BAR elements as

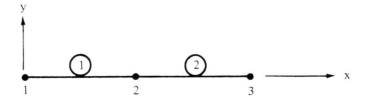

The condition that no moment M_z is transmitted from element one to element two is specified by setting the pin flag in element two at grid point two equal to 6. This modeling specification means that the rotation of element one will be different than the rotation of element two at grid point two. This degree of freedom is not recovered by the NASTRAN output modules. The displacement printed at grid point two will include the rotation of element one and the common displacement u_{y2}. The Bulk Data cards required to describe the system are as follows.

1	2	3	4	5	6	7	8	9	10
GRID	1	0	0.	0.	0.	0	123456		
GRID	2	0	250.	0.	0.	0	1345		
GRID	3	0	500.	0.	0.	0	123456		
CBAR	1	1	1	2	0.	1.	0.		
CBAR	2	1	2	3	0.	1.	0.		+ C1
PBAR	1	1		7.					
MAT1	1	2.E2							
+ C1	6								

where

1. A consistent set of metric units (cgs) has been used so that the load would be specified in a consistent force unit.

2. The constraints are specified on the grid card.

3. The local x,y-axes of the beams have been defined to be coincident with the global X,Y-axes.

4. The pin flag is specified in element two. The pin flag could be specified in either element but not in both. The rotational degree of freedom at grid point two in element two is not recovered since the displacement degree of freedom associated with the pin flag is not recovered.

5. The pin flag is specified in a continuation card whose parent card is the CBAR card for element two. The continuation card has been placed after the MAT1 card to emphasize that the Bulk Data cards may be placed in any order.

9.5.5.3.   Use of Offset Vector

Consider the case of the eccentrically stiffened plate shown in Fig. 9-13 with geometric parameters for the plate and beam given as follows

$$L = 10 \text{ cm} \qquad I_{yy} = 1 \text{ cm}^4$$

$$a = b = 20 \text{ cm} \qquad I_{zz} = .25 \text{ cm}^4$$

$$h = 3 \text{ cm} \qquad J = .5 \text{ cm}^4$$

$$t = .5 \text{ cm} \qquad A = .75 \text{ cm}^2$$

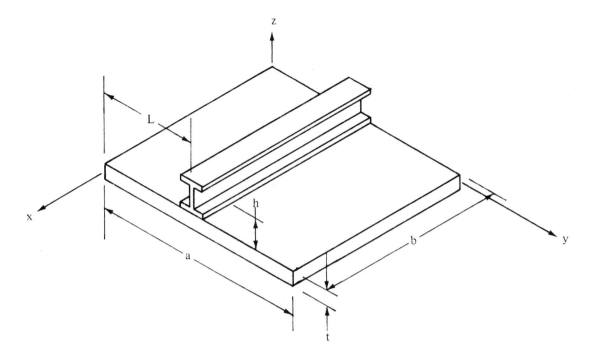

Figure 9-13. Eccentrically Stiffened Plate

The load is assumed to be symmetric so that the system can be modeled by using one-quarter of the structure and appropriate symmetry boundary conditions. The finite element model for the eccentrically stiffened plate is shown in Fig. 9-14, where the quarter panel has been discretized by using nine plate-type elements and three BAR elements as shown. The BAR neutral axis is to be off-set from the neutral surface of the plate through a distance of $(h + t)/2$.

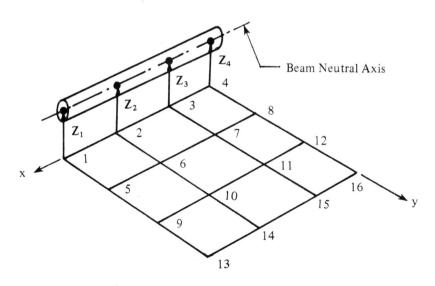

Figure 9-14. Finite Element Model of Stiffened Plate

211

The plate elements must include both bending and membrane action; however, only the input necessary to model the offset beam is included in the data set shown below.

1	2	3	4	5	6	7	8	9	10
CBAR	1	1	1	2	0.	1.	0.		+ C1
CBAR	2	1	2	3	0.	1.	0.		+ C2
CBAR	3	1	3	4	0.	1.	0.		+ C3
+ C1			0.	0.	1.75	0.	0.	1.75	
+ C2			0.	0.	1.75	0.	0.	1.75	
+ C3			0.	0.	1.75	0.	0.	1.75	
PBAR	1	1	.3725	.125	.5	.25			

In this Bulk Data we have defined three BAR elements that include the offset vectors.

1. The offset vector $\mathbf{Z}$ is the same at each point. The vector is the global Z-direction and has a magnitude of $(t+h)/2$.

2. The area properties are one-half those for the physical beam because the other half of the system is accounted for by symmetry conditions.

3. The vector $\mathbf{v}$ is taken as a unit vector in the y-direction for each beam. This vector has its origin at the offset points that lie on the beam neutral axis. The vector thus lies in a plane $z = 1.75$.

4. Consistent metric units have been used.

9.5.6. Modeling Considerations

The stiffness matrix included in NASTRAN is exact, within the context of beam theory, for the case where the beam cross-section is constant and the beam is loaded only by concentrated forces and moments at the ends. More often than not the structural analysis problem involves distributed loads and nonuniform cross-sections, and the question of modeling errors naturally arises.

9.5.6.1. Distributed Loads

Some indication of the number of elements required to model adequately a distributed load acting on a beam can be obtained by considering the cantilevered beam subject to a uniform load as shown in Fig. 9-15.

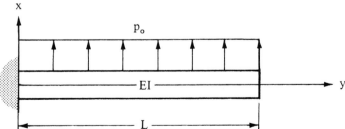

Figure 9-15. Uniformly Loaded Cantilever Beam

The beam is represented as a collection of beam elements where the lumped load at the ends of each element is given by

$$p_i = \tfrac{1}{2} p_o \frac{L}{N}$$

where N is the number of elements used to discretize the beam.

The approximate tip displacement, normalized with respect to the exact solution, is presented as a function of the number of elements in Fig. 9-16. It can be seen that for this particular case of load distribution and boundary conditions that four elements are required to give a reasonable solution for the tip displacement when force lumping is used. One would expect that even more elements would be required to provide adequate resolution to the stress distribution, especially in the area of the base where there are high curvature gradients. The correct solution procedure for this load case is that of using work equivalent loads which leads to the exact solution by using one element. This load, which is called PLOAD1 is described in Sec. 11.3.

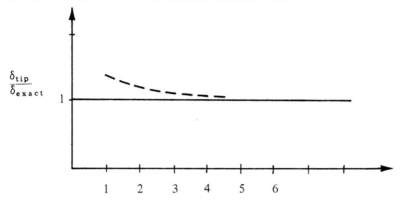

Figure 9-16. Discretization Error in Modeling Uniform Load

9.5.6.2.   Nonuniform Cross-Section

In order to investigate the effect of nonuniform cross-section, a cantilever beam is considered with a variable moment of inertia loaded by a concentrated load in Fig. 9-17.

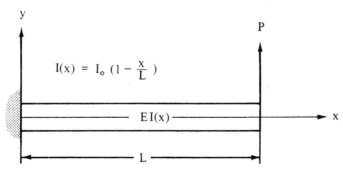

Figure 9-17. Variable Cross-Section Beam

The nondimensional tip displacement is presented as a function of the number of elements in Fig. 9-18. The cross-sectional moment of inertia for each element is taken to be that at the midpoint of the element. It can be seen that for this particular case of element geometry and external loads, approximately four elements are required to obtain reasonable convergence to the exact solution. In MSC/NASTRAN a variable cross-section bending element is more properly defined by using the BEAM element which is described in Sec. 9.6.

Both these examples indicate that the knowledgable user will perform simple analyses of this kind to evaluate the effect of parametric changes on the number and distribution of structural elements.

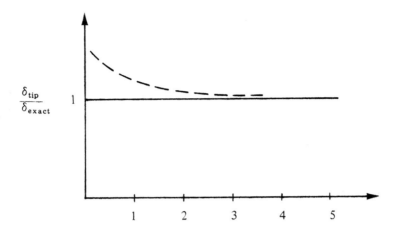

Figure 9-18. Normalized Tip Displacement for Variable Cross-Section Beam

9.6.   BEAM Element

The MSC/NASTRAN BEAM element is a generalization of the BAR element that includes all of the modeling capability of the BAR and the following additional features.

1. The neutral axis, the axis of shear centers, and the axis of center of nonstructural mass may all be different.

2. Section area properties and nonstructural mass may vary arbitrarily along the beam.

3. Contribution of cross-section warping on torsional stiffness may be included.

4. Distribution of mass polar moment of inertia can be specified.

5. Shear relief due to taper can be defined.

9.6.1.   Degrees of Freedom

The degrees of freedom associated with the BEAM element are the three displacements and three rotations, as shown in Fig. 9-4 for the BAR element and one additional degree of freedom at each end, the twist ϕ. The twist is related to the rotation about the axis of the beam as follows

$$\phi = \frac{d\theta_x}{dx} \qquad (9.36)$$

9.6.2.   BEAM Description

The BEAM element connects two offset points A and B as shown by Fig. 9-19. The geometry of the BEAM is thus similar to the BAR element shown by Fig. 9-5 but the local x-axis, which is the line segment drawn between A and B, is now assumed to be coincident with the axis of shear centers rather than the neutral axis.

The BEAM is described by the CBEAM and PBEAM Bulk Data cards shown by Card Image 9-5. The connectivity for the BEAM is defined on a CBEAM Bulk Data card which is similar to the CBAR card except for the specification of scalar degrees of freedom at each end which represent the twist.

The BEAM properties are specified by the PBEAM Bulk Data card. The PBEAM card is similar to the PBAR card but, since variable area properties and internal stress recovery points can be specified, the form of the PBEAM must support these options. Because the BEAM represents an extension of the BAR modeling capability only those BEAM features that are not supported by the BAR element will be described.

	1	2	3	4	5	6	7	8	9	10
1-	CBEAM	EID	PID	GA	GB	V_1, GO	V_2	V_3		+ CB1
2-	+ CB1	PA	PB	Z_{1A}	Z_{2A}	Z_{3A}	Z_{1B}	Z_{2B}	Z_{3B}	+ CB2
3-	+ CB2	SA	SB							

*Beam Properties — PBEAM

	1	2	3	4	5	6	7	8	9	10
1-	PBEAM	PID	MID	A_A	I_{zzA}	I_{yyA}	I_{yzA}	J_A	NSM_A	+ PB1
2-	+ PB1	C_{yA}	C_{zA}	D_{yA}	D_{zA}	E_{yA}	E_{zA}	F_{yA}	F_{zA}	+ PB2
3-	+ PB2	SOPT	x/x_B	A	I_{zz}	I_{yy}	I_{yz}	J	NSM	+ PB3
4-	+ PB3	C_y	C_z	D_y	D_z	E_y	E_z	F_y	F_z	+ PB4
5-	+ PB4	K_y	K_z	S_y	S_z	NSI_A	NSI_B	CW_A	CW_B	+ PB5
6-	+ PB5	M_{yA}	M_{zA}	M_{yB}	M_{zB}	N_{yA}	N_{zA}	N_{yB}	N_{zB}	

Card Image 9-5. Specification of BEAM Element

9.6.3.   CBEAM Description

The CBEAM Bulk Data card includes all of the data described on Table 9-1 for the BAR element and an optional second continuation card (card 3) containing the fields SA and SB where

SA, SB   Scalar or grid point identification numbers for the warping variables at ends A and B, respectively. (Integer ≥ 0 or blank)

The warping degrees of freedom SA and SB must be defined using either SPOINT or GRID cards. If GRID cards are used then the first degree of freedom is considered to be the warpage.

9.6.3.1.   Local Coordinate System for the BEAM

The definition of the local coordinate system for the BEAM element is complicated by the ability to define noncoincident neutral axis, axis of shear centers, and axis of centers of nonstructural mass in addition to defining the orientation of the local beam axes with respect to the global coordinates.

The local coordinate system for the BEAM is shown by Fig. 9-19 where

1. The local x-axis is taken to be along the line from end A to end B.

2. The axis of shear centers coincide with the local x-axis.

3. Ends A and B may be offset from the geometric gridpoints GA and GB by vectors Z_A and Z_B as in the case of the BAR element (Sec. 9.5.1.1.2).

4. The local x,y-plane is defined by the vector **v** as shown by Fig. 9-5 where the vector can be specified in either of two ways.
   a) Components of a free vector (V_1, V_2, V_3) taken from end A

   b) The vector from end A to a third geometric grid point GO

The definition of the local coordinate system is thus the same as that described in Sec. 9.5.1.1.1..

5. The neutral axis is along the line from points A' to B' which are defined relative to A and B by specifying the components of the offset vectors N_A and N_B, respectively. The components of these vectors (N_{yA}, N_{zA}) and (N_{yB}, N_{zB}) are specified in the *local* element coordinates on the PBEAM card.

6. The axis of nonstructural mass centers of gravity is along the line from points A″ to B″ which are defined relative to A and B by the components of the offset vectors M_A and M_B, respectively. The components of these vectors (M_{yA}, M_{zA}) and (M_{yB}, M_{zB}) are specified in the *local* element coordinates on the PBEAM card.

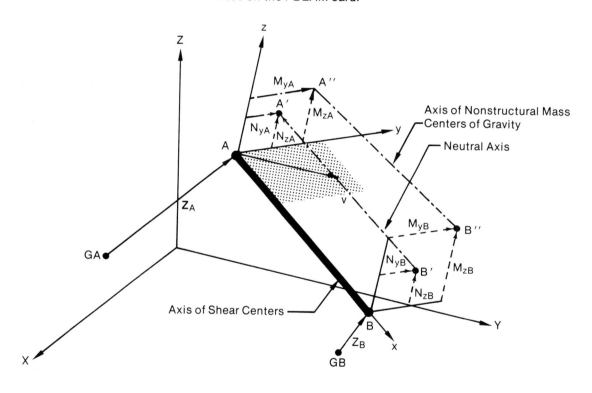

Figure 9-19. Local Coordinate System for the BEAM Element

9.6.4.   PBEAM Description

The properties of the BEAM element are specified on the PBEAM card shown on Card Image 9-5. The PBEAM card is designed to allow the specification of a significant amount of descriptive data for the most general case but for the case where the modeling capability required coincides with the BAR capability the PBEAM data fields are closely related to the PBAR card. The user may thus consider using the BEAM exclusively since it contains the BAR capability as a subset.

The PBEAM together with all of the continuation cards look formidable but is necessary to allow the analyst to use all of the BEAM capability. The purpose of the physical cards which define the entire logical PBEAM Bulk Data are as follows

Card 1- Includes a pointer to a MAT1-type Bulk Data set and specifies the cross-sectional area properties and the non structural mass where the fields are defined as follows

A_A Cross-sectional area at end A (real $>0.$, no default)

(I_{yyA}, I_{zzA}) Cross-sectional moment of inertias about axes parallel to y and z axes which pass through neutral axis (real $>0.$, no default)

Iyz_A Cross product of inertia at end A. (real or blank, default is 0.)

J_A Torsional constant at end A. (real or blank, default is 0.)

NSM_A Nonstructural mass per unit length at end A. (real or blank, default is 0.)

Card 2- An optional card which specifies the location of four stress recovery points (C,D,E,F) on the cross section at end A. The card may be omitted if stress recovery is not required and if data fields on subsequent continuation cards do not require its use.

Card 3- and Card 4- Successive packets of cards having the form of cards 3 and 4 that allow the analyst to specify area properties and nonstructural mass and/or stress recovery points at internal points along the length of the BEAM. The second field, SOPT, of card 3 is a literal string which does two things: it defines a 3-type card and it controls the calculation of stress and internal forces at intermediate points depending on the value of the parameter as follows

'YES'   Calculate stresses at the points defined on the following 4-type card

'YESA'   Calculate stresses at the same points defined at end A by a 2-type card which is then required if this option is specified

'NO'   No intermediate stress output is desired.

The 4-type card is allowed only as a continuation to a 3-type card which has a literal value 'YES' in field 2.

The normalized position along the beam is defined by the x/x_B-field on a 3-type card followed by fields which define the area coefficients and non-structural mass at that position. Up to nine points can be defined but one of them must have a value of 1.0 for x/x_B to define the properties of end B.

Card 5- An optional continuation card which defines

(K_y, K_z) Shear stiffness factor K which appears in the relation KAG in the y and z directions. (real or blank, note that the default is 1, whereas the default is zero for the PBAR)

(S_y, S_z) Shear relief coefficient due to taper in the y and z directions. (real or blank, default is 0.)

(NSI_A, NSI_B) Nonstructural mass moment of inertia per unit length about the nonstructural mass center of gravity at ends A and B. (real or blank, default for NSI_A is 0., that for NSI_B is the value of NSI_A)

(CW_A, CW_B) Warping coefficients at ends A and B. (real or blank, default for CW_A is 0., that for CW_B is the value of CW_A)

Card 6- An optional continuation card which defines the components of the offset vectors

(M_{yA}, M_{zA}) (M_{yB}, M_{zB}) Offset of axis of nonstructural mass center of gravity from the axis of shear centers at end A and B. (real or blank, default for M_y is 0., that for M_z is the value of M_y)

(N_{yA}, N_{zA}) (N_{yB}, N_{zB}) Offset of neutral axis from the axis of shear centers at ends A and B. (real or blank, default for N_y is 0., that for N_z is the value of N_y)

9.6.4.1.   Specifying Non-Coincident Shear and Neutral Axes.

Consider the channel beam shown in Fig. 9-20. The BEAM modeling capability provides a great deal of freedom in defining the shear and neutral axes. By using the various offset vectors we can define either the shear and neutral axes to be coincident with the line segment between two geometric gridpoints. We will proceed to define the BEAM both ways, but first we need to obtain the geometric properties of the cross-section.

The position of the shear center and the neutral axes must be calculated based on the cross-sectional geometric parameters. The position of the shear center relative to the center of the web is given by e. The position of the shear center can be calculated using the techniques outlined in Ref. 9-4 or can be looked up in handbooks such as Ref. 9-5. The neutral axis offset from the center of the web, n, can also be determined from the condition that the first area moment about the neutral axis must be zero. The offset of the neutral axis from the shear center as well as other cross-sectional properties for the channel can then be found and are shown on Fig. 9-20.

Shear Axis on Line Joining Grid Points

The axis of shear centers lies on the line joining offset points A and B as shown by Fig. 9-19. If the offset vectors of each end of the beam are null then the axis of shear centers lies on the line joining the geometric grid points. The channel could be modeled with a single BEAM element which connects the structural degrees of freedom associated with geometric grid points 1 and 2 at each end and two scalar degrees of freedom, points 3 and 4, which represent the twist at the left and right ends, respectively, by the following Bulk Data

Card	1	2	3	4	5	6	7	8	9	10
1-	GRID	1	0	0.	0.	0.				
2-	GRID	2	0	20.	0.	0.				
3-	SPOINT	3	4							
4-	CBEAM	1	2	1	2	0.	1.	0.		+ CB1
5-	+ CB1									+ CB2
6-	+ CB2	3	4							
7-	PBEAM	2	101	0.986	1.58	.259	0.	0.009	0.	+ PB1
8-	+ PB1									+ PB2
9-	+ PB2	0.	0.					0.301	0.301	+ PB3
10-	+ PB3					0.766	0.	0.766	0.	

where cards 1 and 2 define geometric grid points along the X-axis of the basic coordinate system and card 3 defines the two scalar points which are associated with warping. The degrees of freedom associated with these points are connected by the CBEAM, card 4, and its continuation card 5 and 6 where we note

1. Grid points 1 and 2 are associated with ends A and B, respectively

2. The local coordinate system is defined by vector components (0., 1., 0.) on card 4 in terms of the basic coordinate system so that the local coordinates of the BEAM coincide with the coordinate system shown in Fig. 9-20

3. The continuation card having a mnemonic CB1, card 5, is a CBEAM 2-card as shown on Card Image 9-5 and is required even though the fields are null because the twist degrees of freedom are defined on the CBEAM 3-card

4. The continuation card having a mnemonic CB2, card 6, is a CBEAM 3-card as shown on Card Image 9-5 on which scalar degrees of freedom 3 and 4 are associated with the twist at ends A and B, respectively.

218

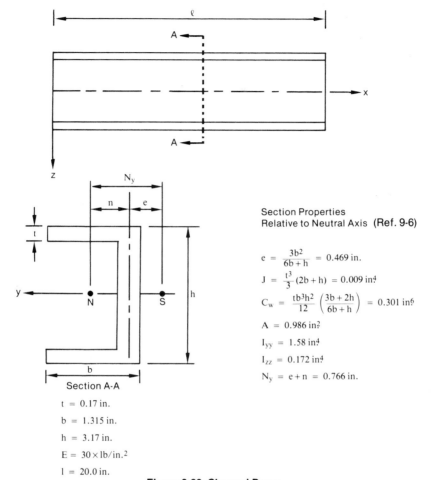

Section Properties
Relative to Neutral Axis (Ref. 9-6)

$$e = \frac{3b^2}{6b+h} = 0.469 \text{ in.}$$

$$J = \frac{t^3}{3}(2b+h) = 0.009 \text{ in}^4$$

$$C_w = \frac{tb^3h^2}{12}\left(\frac{3b+2h}{6b+h}\right) = 0.301 \text{ in}^6$$

$$A = 0.986 \text{ in}^2$$

$$I_{yy} = 1.58 \text{ in}^4$$

$$I_{zz} = 0.172 \text{ in}^4$$

$$N_y = e+n = 0.766 \text{ in.}$$

Section A-A

$t = 0.17 \text{ in.}$

$b = 1.315 \text{ in.}$

$h = 3.17 \text{ in.}$

$E = 30 \times \text{lb/in.}^2$

$l = 20.0 \text{ in.}$

Figure 9-20. Channel Beam

The BEAM properties are defined on the PBEAM, card 7 and its continuation cards 8, 9 and 10 where we note that

1. The specification of moments of inertia is appropriate for the local coordinate system defined by the connection card where I_{zz} has been transferred to the shear axis

2. The continuation card having the continuation mnemonic PB1, Card 8, is a PBEAM 2-card as shown on Card Image 9-5. This card is required in this case even though stress recovery is not desired because data fields in subsequent continuation cards must be defined

3. The continuation card having the continuation mnemonic PB2, Card 9, is a PBEAM 5-card as shown on Card Image 9-5 on which the warping coefficients are specified

4. The continuation card having the continuation mnemonic PB3, Card 10, is a PBEAM 6-card as shown on Card Image 9-5 on which the component of the offset vector from the shear center to the neutral axis are specified. The vector components (0.766, 0.) at each end are interpreted in local coordinates so that the neutral axis is offset 0.766 in along the local y-axis at each end.

9.6.4 PBEAM Description

Neutral Axis on Line Joining Grid Points

The neutral axis can be made coincident with the line joining grid points GA and GB if points A′ and B′ as shown by Fig. 9-19 coincide with GA and GB. This can be accomplished by defining $Z_A = -N_A$ and $Z_B = -N_B$. The channel could then be modeled using the following Bulk Data

Card	1	2	3	4	5	6	7	8	9	10
1-	GRID	1	0	0.	0.	0.				
2-	GRID	2	0	20.	0.	0.				
3-	SPOINT	3	4							
4-	CBEAM	1	2	1	2	0.	1.	0.		+ W1
5-	+ W1			− 0.766	0.	0.	− 0.766	0.	0.	+ W2
6-	+ W2	3	4							
7-	PBEAM	2	101	0.986	1.58	0.172	0.	0.009	0.	+ Z3
8-	+ Z3									+ Z4
9-	+ Z4							0.301	0.301	+ Z5
10-	+ Z5					0.766	0.	0.766	0.	

Card 5 which is a CBEAM 2-card contains the components of the offset vectors Z_A and Z_B. The components (− 0.766, 0., 0.) taken in terms of the basic coordinate system define points A and B to be offset from the geometric grid points GA and GB by 0.766 inch in the negative basic Y-direction. Since the local and basic coordinate systems are coincident the offset defined by card 10 makes points A′ and B′ coincident with GA and GB as desired.

9.6.4.2. Tapered Beam with Shear Relief

Consider the tapered beam with heavy flange shown by Fig. 9-21. The beam is to be modeled using five BEAM elements which connect geometric gridpoints as shown. The element area properties are presented by Table 9-4 where

1. The local element x-axis is taken in the sense of the basic x-axis

2. The cross-sectional area is taken to be equal to the web area

3. The bending moment of inertia about the y-axis is calculated using only the web area

4. The web depth is assumed to vary linearly along the length of the beam

5. The bending moment of inertia about the z-axis is taken to be equal to 1 in⁴.

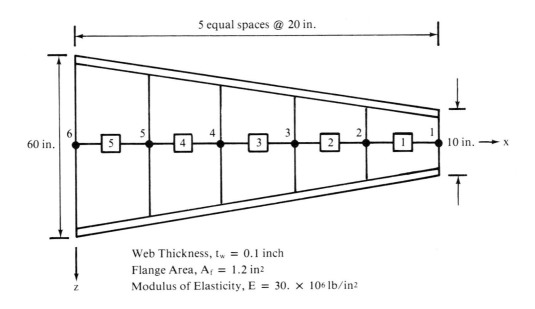

Figure 9-21. Tapered Beam

Web Thickness, t_w = 0.1 inch
Flange Area, A_f = 1.2 in²
Modulus of Elasticity, E = 30. × 10⁶ lb/in²

The shear factors which account for the effect of beam taper can be determined by considering the idealization of the beam element that is shown by Fig. 9-22.

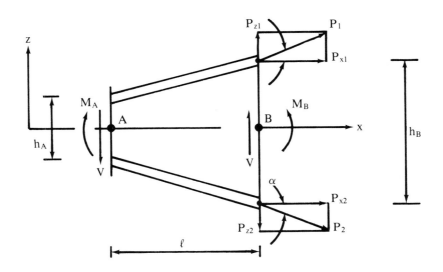

Figure 9-22. Tapered Beam Element

221

9.6.4 PBEAM Description

Element No.	Area properties		
	A_A (in²)	I_{yyA} (in⁴)	I_{zzA} (in⁴)
1	2.	240.	1.
2	3.	540.	1.
3	4.	960.	1.
4	5.	1500.	1.
5	6.	2160.	1.

Table 9-4. Area Properties for Tapered Beam

The shear, Q_B, at cross section B is found to be

$$Q_B = V + \sin \alpha \, (P_1 - P_2) \tag{9.37}$$

where P_1 and P_2 are the forces in upper and lower flanges, respectively. The flange forces are related to the moment M_B by the equilibrium of moments so that

$$P_2 - P_1 = \frac{2M_B}{h_B \cos \alpha} \tag{9.38}$$

The substitution of (9.38) into (9.37) then gives

$$Q_B = V - \frac{2M_B \tan \alpha}{h_B} \tag{9.39}$$

The transverse shear in the element y and z axes can then be written as

$$Q_y = V_y - \frac{S_y}{\ell} M_z \tag{9.40}$$

$$Q_z = V_z - \frac{S_z}{\ell} M_y \tag{9.41}$$

where S_y and S_z are the average shear relief coefficients for taper. The shear coefficient S_z is given by

$$S_z = \frac{2(h_A - h_B)}{(h_A + h_B)} \tag{9.42}$$

The values for the stress relief factors for the tapered beam shown by Fig. 9-21, calculated using (9.42), are presented by Table 9-5.

The tapered beam presented by Fig. 9-21 could be modeled using the following Bulk Data

222

Card	1	2	3	4	5	6	7	8	9	10
1-	GRID	1	0	100.	0.	0.				
2-	GRID	2	0	80.	0.	0.				
3-	GRID	3	0	60.	0.	0.				
4-	GRID	4	0	40.	0.	0.				
5-	GRID	5	0	20.	0.	0.				
6-	GRID	6	0	10.	0.	0.				
7-	CBEAM	1	1	2	1	0.	1.	0.		
8-	CBEAM	2	2	3	2	0.	1.	0.		
9-	CBEAM	3	3	4	3	0.	1.	0.		
10-	CBEAM	4	4	5	4	0.	1.	0.		
11-	CBEAM	5	5	6	5	0.	1.	0.		
12-	PBEAM	1	101	2.	240.	1.				+ PB11
13-	+ PB11	NO	1.	1.	60.	1.				+ PB12
14-	+ PB12	0.	0.	0.	.667	0.				
15-	PBEAM	2	101	3.	540.	1.				+ PB21
16-	+ PB21	NO	1.	2.	240.	1.				+ PB22
17-	+ PB22	0.	0.	0.	.400	0.				
18-	PBEAM	3	101	4.	960.	1.				+ PB31
19-	+ PB31	NO	1.	3.	540.	1.				+ PB32
20-	+ PB32	0.	0.	0.	.286	0.				
21-	PBEAM	4	101	5.	1500.	1.				+ PB41
22-	+ PB41	NO	1.	4.	960.	1.				+ PB42
23-	+ PB42	0.	0.	0.	.222	0.				
24-	PBEAM	5	101	6.	2160.	1.				+ PB51
25-	+ PB51	NO	1.	5.	1500.	1.				+ PB52
26-	+ PB52	0.	0.	0.	.182	0.				

where

1. The grid point sequence and orientation vector defined on CBEAM cards define a local element coordinate system in same sense as the basic coordinate system shown by Fig. 9-21.

2. Since the properties for each element are different, each element connection card must point to a different PBEAM card.

3. A PBEAM 2-card as shown by Card Image 9-5 is not required because a 3-card which requests no stress calculation is included.

Element	Web Depth		S_z
No.	h_A	h_B	
1	20.	10.	0.667
2	30.	20.	0.400
3	40.	30.	0.286
4	50.	40.	0.222
5	60.	50.	0.182

Table 9-5. Shear Coefficients for Tapered Beam

9.6.5.   Generation of BEAM Elements

BEAM Bulk Data can be generated by using the MSGMESH command, CGEN, which is described by Card Image 9-4 in Sec. 9.5.3. where the mnemonic "BAR" in field 2 of the CGEN command is replaced by the mnemonic "BEAM". The PID in field 4 of the CGEN command then, of course, is the property identification number of PBEAM Bulk Data.

9.7.   Curved Beam or Pipe Element

A curved beam element called the BEND element, which is convenient for modeling piping systems, and the element's degrees of freedom are shown by Fig. 9-23. The MSC/NASTRAN BEND element has the following characteristics

1. The area properties and radius of curvature are constant.

2. The local coordinate axes (r,z) must coincide with the principal axes of inertia for the cross section.

3. Flexibility and stress intensification factors can be specified in several ways.

4. Bending about and transverse shear in the direction of two perpendicular axes as well as extension and torsion.

5. Only the consistant mass matrix can be calculated for structural or nonstructural mass.

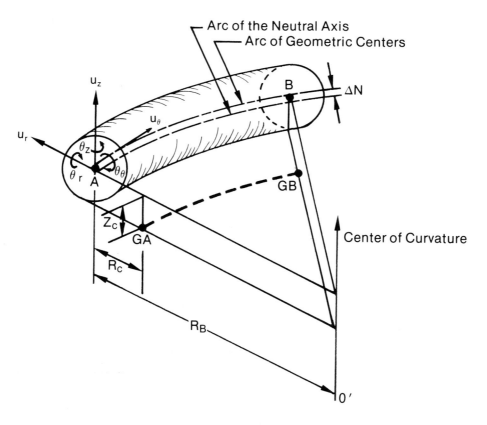

Figure 9-23. Curved Pipe Element — CBEND

6. The arc of geometric centers can be offset from the arc joining the geometric grid points. The offset is the same at both ends.

The Bulk Data cards for determining the connective and properties of the BEND element are shown by Card Image 9-6.

*BEND Connection

1	2	3	4	5	6	7	8	9	10
CBEND	EID	PID	GA	GB	V_1, GO	V_2	V_3	GEOM	

*BEND Property

PBEND	PID	MID	A	I_{zz}	I_{rr}	J	R_B	θ_B	+ PB1
+ PB1	C_r	C_z	D_r	D_z	E_r	E_z	F_r	F_z	+ PB2
+ PB2	K_r	K_z	NSM	R_c	Z_c	ΔN			

*Alternate form of BEND Property for Elbows and Curved Pipes

PBEND	PID	MID	FSI	R	t	P	R_B	θ_B	+ PBA1
+ PBA1			NSM	R_c	Z_c				

Card Image 9-6. Specification of BEND element

9.7.1. Bend Element Connectivity and Geometry

A curved beam or pipe element is specified by

1. Defining the connected grid points, GA and GB.

2. Defining the plane containing the arc from the two connected grid points.

3. Defining the curvature and center of curvature of the BEND element.

4. Defining the position of the arc of geometric centers and the arc of neutral axes relative to the arc connecting the geometric grid points.

In general the geometry of the BEND element cannot be completely defined by the data on the CBEND card. The CBEND element is sufficient only if the following conditions are satisfied.

1. The element is an elbow or curved pipe and is described by the alternate form of the PBEND Bulk Data card. In this case the offset of the arc of the neutral axis is calculated by MSC/NASTRAN.

2. The arc of geometric centers coincide with the arc joining the geometric grid points.

3. The radius and centers of curvatures are defined by
   a) Specifying a line which contains the center of curvature. (GEOM = 1 in field 9)
   b) Specifying a line which is tangent to the arc of the element. (GEOM = 2 in field 9)

For all other cases the additional data which are required to specify the geometry of the BEND element are defined on the PBEND card. These data include

225

9.7.1 Bend Element Connectivity and Geometry

R_B- The radius of the arc of the geometric axis. (real)

θ_B- The arc angle of the element. (real >0.)

R_c- The radial offset of the arc of geometric centers from the arc joining the geometric grid points. (real)

Z_c- Offset of the axis of geometric centroids in a direction perpendicular to plane containing points GA, GB and the vector **v**. (real)

ΔN- Radial offset of the arc of the neutral axis from the geometric centroid, positive toward the center of curvature. (real)

9.7.1.1. BEND Local Coordinate System

The local coordinate system for the BEND element that is shown by Figure 9-24 is defined by one of four methods which is specified by the analyst using the GEOM field on the CBEND card. The GEOM options define

1. How the vector **v** is to be used in determining the orientation element coordinate system.

2. Whether radius of curvature or arc angle for the element are specified on an associated PBEND card.

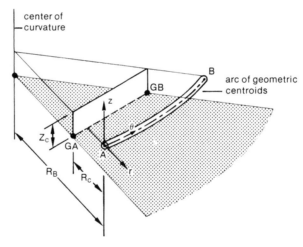

Figure 9-24. Local Coordinate System for the BEND Element

The geometric configurations associated with the GEOM-options are shown by Fig. 9-25 and are described as follows

GEOM (integer >0)	Meaning

1 The center of curvature lies on a line which is coincident with the vector **v** or the line connecting GA and GO.

2 The tangent to the arc of the element at GA is coincident with the vector **v** or the line connecting GA and GO.

3 The BEND radius (R_B) is specified on a PBEND card. The center of curvature lies

in a plane which is parallel to that containing the line connecting GA and GB and the vector **v**, and lies on the opposite side of the line **AB** from GO or the vector **v**.

4 The arc angle is specified on a PBEND card. The center of curvature is then located as described above for GEOM = 3.

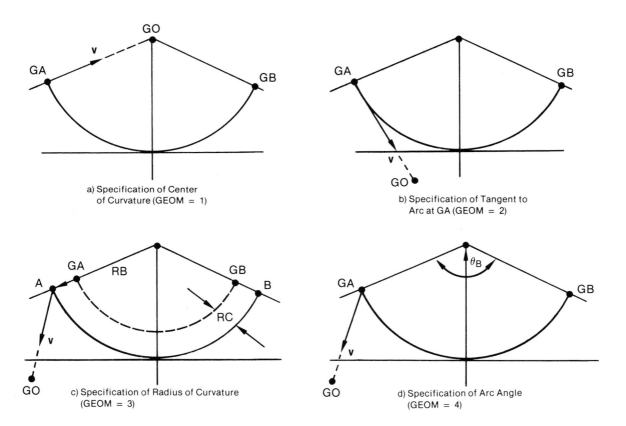

a) Specification of Center of Curvature (GEOM = 1)

b) Specification of Tangent to Arc at GA (GEOM = 2)

c) Specification of Radius of Curvature (GEOM = 3)

d) Specification of Arc Angle (GEOM = 4)

Figure 9-25. Specification of BEND Element Curvature

The positive sense of the local curvilinear element coordinates system (r, θ, z) that is shown on Fig. 9-22 depends on the GEOM option chosen by the analyst. The local z axis is taken in the sense of a vector **z** which is defined by the cross product **AB** × **v** for GEOM = 1 and **v** × **AB** for all other GEOM options, where **AB** is the vector from GA to GB.

The components of the vector **v** can be defined in two ways on the CBEND card

1. Three components of a free vector (V_1, V_2, V_3) originating at GA which are defined in terms of the displacement coordinate system at GA. (real)

2. The directed line segment from GA to a third geometric grid point, GO. (integer)

9.7.1.2. Specification of Arc of Geometric Centroids

The offset of the arc of the axis of geometric centroids is specified with respect to the local element coordinate system by the dimensions R_c and Z_c, using either form of the PBEND Bulk Data as shown by Card Image 9-6. The local (r, θ, z) coordinate system is defined in the offset plane as shown by Fig. 9-23 where

1. The (r, θ) plane is parallel to the plane which contains the vector **v**, and the line joining the geometric gridpoints GA and GB.

2. The element angular coordinate, θ, has its origin at end A of the curved beam or pipe element.

9.7.2. BEND Element Properties

The BEND element properties are defined using one of the two forms for the PBEND Bulk Data card shown by Card Image 9-6. The first of these two alternate forms can be used to define the properties of a curved beam element which has an arbitrary cross section. The second can be used to define elbow or pipe elements which have circular cross sections. For either form, fields two and three of the PBEND card are

PID Property identification number (Integer >0)

MID Identification number of an isotropic material (MAT1) (Integer >0)

9.7.2.1. Geometric Parameters for Curved Beam

A BEND element having an arbitrary cross section can be described by the first form of the PBEND card shown on Card Image 9-6 where the fields are defined as follows

A Cross Sectional area (Real >0.0)

I_{zz}, I_{rr} Area moments about the element z and r axes, respectively (Real $\geq 0.$)

J Torsional constant (Real $\geq 0.$)

The offset of the arc of the neutral axis from the arc of the axis of geometric centroids can be specified by the parameter, ΔN (real or blank) which is positive towards the center of curvature. If the field associated with ΔN is left blank then MSC/NASTRAN will calculate an approximate offset using the relation

$$\Delta N = \frac{I_{zz}}{A R_B} \tag{9.43}$$

where the parameters in (9.43) are defined on PBEND Bulk Data card. The default value is recommended if $(R_B^2 A)/I_{zz} > 15$ in which case the calculated value is within five percent of the exact expression for an element having either a circular or square cross section. Alternatively, the user may choose to calculate the exact value for the offset using the following analytical expression, Ref 9-7

$$\Delta N = \frac{R_B}{1 + \dfrac{R_B^2 A}{Z}} \tag{9.44}$$

where

$$Z = \int_A \frac{r^2 \, dA}{1 + \dfrac{r}{R_B}} \tag{9.45}$$

228

and where the integration is taken over the cross section with r being the radius to a point on the cross section of the element.

9.7.2.2.   Circular Cross Section

An elbow or a pipe element which has a circular cross section as shown by Fig. 9-26 can be described by using the alternate or second form of the PBEND Bulk Data card as shown by Card Image 9-5. The following properties are then calculated by MSC/NASTRAN

1. Cross sectional area and, area moments, and torsional constant

2. Neutral axis offset

3. Shear factors

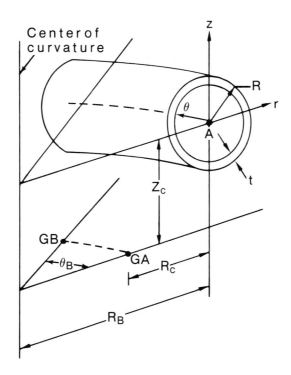

Figure 9-26. Curved Pipe Cross Section

The cross section of the elbow or pipe element is completely defined by the following fields on the alternate form of the PBEND card

R Mean radius of elbow or pipe. (Real > 0.)

t Wall thickness. (Real ≥ 0.; $R + t/2 < R_B$)

If t equals zero then a solid cross-section of radius R is assumed.

The flexibility and stress intensification factors are defined by an integer value for the FSI field on the alternate form of the PBEND as follows

9.7.2   Bend Element Properties

FSI   Meaning

1   The flexibility factors which multiply the bending terms of the flexibility matrix are set to unity. The stress intensification factor for bending about the z-axis is set to unity and that associated with bending about the r-axis is set equal to S_i where

$$S_i = \frac{I_{zz}}{AR_B} \left[\frac{1}{r_i} + \frac{R_B - \Delta N}{\Delta N + (R_B + r_i)} \right] \qquad (9.46)$$

and r_i is the radius of the ith stress recovery point relative to the element coordinate system.

2   ASME Code Section III, NB-3687.2., NB-3685.2., 1977.

3   Empirical factors from Welding Research Council Bulletin 179 by Dodge and Moore.

Finally, an internal pipe pressure can be specified by the P (Real) field on the alternate form of the PBEND card.

9.7.2.3.   Shear Factors

The shear factors are automatically calculated if the alternate form of the PBEND card is used. If the first form is used to describe a curved beam then the shear factors are specified by the fields K_r and K_z (Real) which are terms in the relation KAG. A blank or zero value specifies that shear flexibility is to be set to zero where the factors are calculated automatically for the alternate form.

9.7.2.4.   Stress Recovery Points

The position of four stress recovery points (C,D,E, and F as described in Sec. 9.5.2) can be specified by defining the position of the four points in element coordinates. For example (C_r, C_z) define r and z coordinates of point C relative to the θ-axis. If the alternate form of the PBEND is used then the stress recovery points are automatically located as shown by Fig. 9-27.

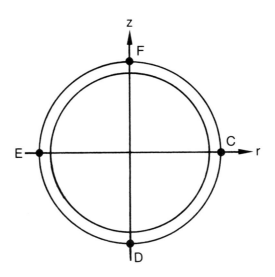

Figure 9-27. Stress Recovery Points for Elbow and Pipe Element

230

9.7.3. Generation of BEND Elements Using MSGMESH

CBEND Bulk Data can be generated with CGEN MSGMESH command which is shown by Card Image 9-4 in Sec. 9.5.3. where the mnemonic "BAR" in field 2 of the CGEN command is replaced by the mnemonic "BEND". The GEOM option for the generated CBEND Bulk Data is specified by the GEOM field (i.e. field 7) of the CGEN MSGMESH command.

9.7.4. BEND Degrees of Freedom and Element Stiffness

The BEND element connects the six structural degrees of freedom at ends GA and GB. The stiffness matrix is formulated by

1. Calculating the flexibility matrix, $\mathbf{F}$, at end B and the rigid body transformation matrix $\mathbf{S}_{id}$ between ends A and B.

2. Calculating the partitions of the stiffness matrix using the flexibility-to-stiffness transformation described in Sec. 7.9.

3. Transforming to Basic Coordinates including the effect of offsets.

The displacement degrees of freedom are recovered at gridpoints GA and GB referred to the displacement coordinate system defined on the appropriate GRID Bulk Data cards.

9.7.5. Element Forces and Stresses

The element forces for the BEND element are interpreted as internal forces at each end of the beam. The positive sign convention for internal forces in the bend element are shown by Figure 9-28 at an arbitrary angular position, θ. The following element forces are requested by an 'ELFORCE' Case Control Directive

1. Bending moments M_z and M_r, (identified as M_1 and M_2, respectively, in the MSC/NASTRAN printout)

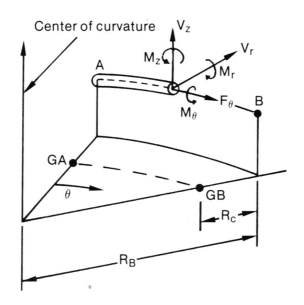

Figure 9-28. Positive Element Forces for BEND Element

2. Shear forces V_r and V_z. (identified as V_1 and V_2, respectively, in the printout)

3. The average axial force, F_θ.

4. The torque about the axis of geometric centroids, M_θ.

The following stresses are requested by a 'STRESS' Case Control Directive.

1. Longitudinal stress at the four stress recovery points at each end.

2. Maximum and minimum longitudinal stress.

3. Margins of safety in tension and compression if stress limits are defined on the MAT1 Bulk Data card.

The stresses are modified if the alternate form of the PBEND is used to account for internal pressure and stress intensification due to curvature as indicated by the FSI field. Tensile stress is considered positive.

9.8.   Shear Panels

The shear panel is an essential element for modeling aircraft as well as other structures which are characterized by very thin elastic sheets and stiffeners. This class of structures *cannot* be modeled properly by shell elements without using an enormous number of elements. This class of structures has been traditionally modeled by a combination of ROD and SHEAR elements where the RODs account for the extential behavior of the stiffeners and the SHEARs account for the shear rigidity of the thin elastic sheets.

The element coordinate system for the shear panel is shown in Fig. 9-29, where the integers 1, 2, 3, and 4 refer to the order in which the connected grid points are specified using the CSHEAR Data card shown by Card Image 9-7.

1	2	3	4	5	6	7	8	9	10
CSHEAR	EID	PID	G1	G2	G3	G4			
PSHEAR	PID	MID	T	NSM	PID	MID	T	NSM	

*Alternate form of PSHEAR

PSHEAR	PID	EID	T	NSM	F1	F2			

Card Image 9-7. Shear Panel

9.8.1.   Description of Shear Panel Input

The Bulk Data for the shear panel description consists of a connection card with a unique element identification number that references an appropriate property card. The shear panel is defined by a CSHEAR card, and its properties, by a PSHEAR card.

9.8.1.1.   Element Connectivity

The shear panel connects four grid points as shown in Fig. 9-29. The grid point numbers must be ordered consecutively around the perimeter of the element, as shown.

9.8.1.2.   Element Properties

The element properties are defined on the PSHEAR Bulk Data card. The material property for the element is defined by reference to a material specification, which must be a MAT1-type Bulk

Data card. The other element properties are

>   T Shear panel thickness. (real, $\neq 0$.)

>   NSM Nonstructural mass per unit area. (real)

The alternate form of the PSHEAR allows the user to define equivalent axial RODs on the periphery of the element by means of the fields F1 and F2 which are area effectiveness parameters. Field F1 defines RODs along edges 1-2 and 3-4 while F2 is associated with edges 1-4 and 2-3. Real entries in these fields will cause the generation of an effective extensional area as follows

> $F_i < 1.01$ Set effective ROD areas equal to $\frac{1}{2} F_i (T w_i)$ where w_i is the effective width in the i-direction and T is the panel thickness.

> $F_i > 1.01$ Set effective ROD areas equal to $\frac{1}{2} F_i T^2$.

9.8.2. Recovery of Forces

The element forces may be output by the Case Control Directive

$$\text{ELFORCE} = <\text{set}>$$

where $<\text{set}>$ is a set of elements defined in Case Control. The shear panel forces consist of the force applied to the element at the node points, kick forces at the corners in a direction normal to the plane formed by the two adjacent sides, and shear flows (force per unit length) along the four edges as shown by Fig. 9-29

The element stresses consist of the average of the shear stress calculated at the corners and the maximum stress. The shear stresses as well as margin of safety may be output by the Case Control Directive

$$\text{STRESS} = <\text{set}>$$

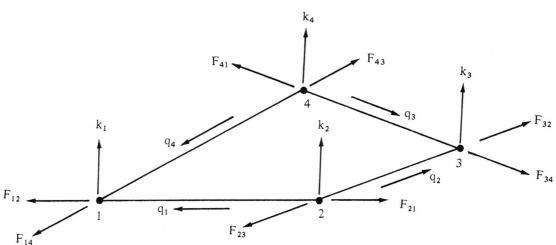

Figure 9-29. Shear Panel Showing Corner Forces and Shear Flows

9.8.3. Shear Panel Elemental Matrices

The stiffness matrix for the shear element is obtained in a rather ad hoc way by assuming that the only nonzero component of stress is the inplane shear stress q. The strain energy can then be expressed as

$$U = \tfrac{1}{2} z q^2 \qquad (9.47)$$

where z is an undetermined coefficient. The energy can also be expressed in terms of node point displacements as

$$U = \tfrac{1}{2} \mathbf{u}_e^T \mathbf{k}_{ee} \mathbf{u}_e \qquad (9.48)$$

where the nodal displacements and forces are related through the stiffness matrix as

$$\mathbf{k}_{ee} \mathbf{u}_e = \mathbf{f}_e \qquad (9.49)$$

The elemental forces are taken to be the force resultants shown in Fig. 9-30, and the element displacements act at and in the direction of the element forces. The elemental forces are assumed to be the average of the adjacent edge force at each corner so that the corner forces can be related to the shear stress in the element as

$$\mathbf{f}_e = \mathbf{C} \, q \qquad (9.50)$$

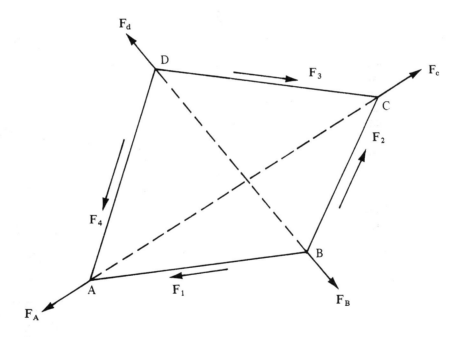

Figure 9-30. Element Corner Forces for Shear Panel

We assume that the shear strain γ is related to the shear stress as

$$\gamma = z q \qquad (9.51)$$

so that the complementary form of (9.47) is

$$U^* = \tfrac{1}{2} z \gamma^2 \qquad (9.52)$$

The substitution of (9.50) and (9.51) into (9.52) and some algebraic manipulation then leads to the following expression for the elemental stiffness:

$$\mathbf{k}_{ee} = \frac{1}{z} \, \mathbf{C} \, \mathbf{C}^{T} \tag{9.53}$$

The elemental stiffness matrix is transformed to the g-set by means of the geometric transformation

$$\mathbf{u}_e = \mathbf{T} \mathbf{u}_g$$

so that the stiffness matrix referred to the basic coordinates is given by

$$\mathbf{k}_{gg} = \mathbf{T}^{T} \mathbf{K}_{ee} \, \mathbf{T} \tag{9.54}$$

The coefficient z appearing in (9.47) is evaluated by equating the strain energy to the work done by the average shear flows. Assuming that the panel is rectangular,

$$z = \frac{A}{Gt} \tag{9.55}$$

where A is the surface area, G is the shear modulus and t is the thickness. If the panel is a parallelogram, then

$$z = \frac{A}{Gt} \, (1 + \frac{2\tan^2\theta}{1+\nu}) \tag{9.56}$$

where θ is the complement of the smallest interior angle and ν is Poisson's ratio.

To obtain expressions for z for nonrectangular elements, it is assumed that the tangential forces do not couple elastically with the normal forces. This assumption is not valid for nonrectangular elements and can lead to erroneous results for panels with nonrectangular shapes.

Thermal expansion is not included in the element formulation for shear panels but it is included in the effective RODs. The user should exercise extreme care in using this element in thermal stress analysis.

The mass matrix is obtained by dividing the panel into four triangles by each of the diagonals. One sixth of the mass for each triangle is then distributed to the nodes of the triangle.

9.9.   Shell Elements

The MSC/NASTRAN element library includes both flat and curved shell elements which support membrane and bending behavior. The form of the element specification allows the analyst to control the generation of stiffness coefficients for

- Membrane-only behavior

- Bending-only behavior

- Bending and membrane behavior

- Materially-coupled bending-membrane behavior

The modern shell elements in the MSC/NASTRAN include

- TRIA3   A three noded isoparametric flat element

- QUAD4   A four noded isoparametric flat element

- TRIA6   A six noded triangular isoparametric curved thin shell element

- QUAD8   An eight noded isoparametric quadrilateral curved thin shell element

235

where the quadrilateral "flat" shell element may be defined by four grid points which do not lie in a "flat" plane.

9.9.1. Flat Shell Elements — QUAD4 and TRIA3

The triangular and quadrilateral flat shell elements are shown by Fig. 9.31a and Fig. 9.31b, respectively, and are defined using the Bulk Data cards shown on Card Image 9-8.

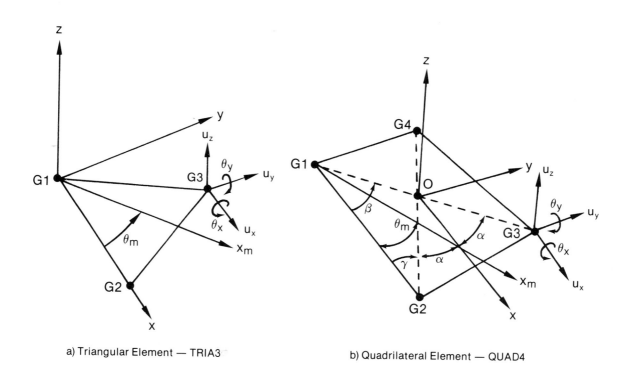

a) Triangular Element — TRIA3   b) Quadrilateral Element — QUAD4

Figure 9-31. Isoparametric Flat Thin Shell Elements

*Three-noded Isoparametric Triangular Element — TRIA3

1	2	3	4	5	6	7	8	9	10
CTRIA3 +T3	EID	PID	G1 T1	G2 T2	G3 T3	θ_m			+T3
PSHELL +P3	PID Z1	MID1 Z2	T MID4	MID2	R_I	MID3	R_T	NSM	+P3

*Four-noded Isoparametric Quadrilateral Element — QUAD4

1	2	3	4	5	6	7	8	9	10
CQUAD4 +Q4	EID	PID	G1 T1	G2 T2	G3 T3	G4 T4	θ_m		+Q4
PSHELL +P4	PID Z1	MID1 Z2	T MID4	MID2	R_l	MID3	R_T	NSM	+P4

Card Image 9-8. Specification of Flat Shell Elements — QUAD4 and TRIA3

The general capabilities of the TRIA3 and QUAD4 are

1. Thickness may vary isoparametrically over the surface of the element.

2. The element formulation allows both coupled and lumped mass matrices but the coupled mass matrix does not include inertias associated with rotational degrees of freedom.

3. The anisotropic elastic coefficients associated with inplane, bending, transverse shear, and coupling between in-plane and bending behavior may be defined independently. These elements can thus be used to model unbalanced composite materials or plates offset from node points.

9.9.1.1.   Element Connectivity

The triangular and quadrilateral elements connect three and four grid points, respectively, as shown by Figs. 9-31a and 9-31b. The grid point numbers associated with the fields G1, G2, G3, (and G4) must be unique for either element and must be ordered consecutively around the perimeter of the QUAD4 such that all interior angles are less than 180 degrees.

The flat shell elements connect the five degrees of freedom in element coordinates including the two inplane displacements u_x, and u_y, the normal displacement u_z, and the two bending rotations, θ_x and θ_y. There is no rotational degree of freedom about the normal for these elements so that there will be a row and column of zeros in the six-by-six stiffness matrix associated with each connected grid point. The system stiffness matrix will thus be singular unless the normal rotation is connected by another type of element such as a BAR or if the flat plates joining at the grid point do not lie in a plane so that there is a geometry-related stiffness. It is the responsibility of the analyst to purge unconnected degrees of freedom either directly by using a single point constraint (Sec. 7.5) or by using the automatic purge capability associated with the AUTOSPC PARAMeter (Appendix B).

9.9.1.1.1.   Local Coordinate System

The definition of the local element coordinate system is of interest to the analyst in determining the direction and positive sense of the normal to the surface. The positive normal direction then defines the sense of positive normal pressure on the PLOAD2 and PLOAD4 Bulk Data (Chapt. 11) and the positive element face for stress recovery. The local coordinate systems for the triangular and quadrilateral flat shell elements are shown by Figs. 9-31a and 9-31b, respectively.

The local system for the TRIA3 is defined such that

1. The local x-axis coincides with the line drawn from grid point G1 to G2.

2. The three gridpoints define the local x-y plane

3. The local z-direction is normal to the plane containing the three geometric grid points and

is positive in the sense of the right hand rule when applied to the order of grid point specification.

The local coordinate system for the QUAD4 element, shown by Fig. 9-31b, has the desirable properties of

1. Being uniquely defined, independent of the starting grid point number within even multiples of 90 degrees.

2. Being continuous with respect to changes in element shape.

3. Being parallel to the edges for a rectangular element.

4. Having the x-axis nearly parallel to the longest bisector of opposite sides in the general case.

The local z-axis is perpendicular to the local x-y plane and is positive in the sense of the right hand rule applied to the grid point numbering scheme.

9.9.1.1.2. Material Coordinate

The MSC/NASTRAN shell elements support anisotropic material behavior. Since nonisotropic material properties are defined relative to a set of material coordinates the analyst must specify the orientation of one of the material axes relative to a reference axis in the element. The field θ_m (Real), on the connection cards is the orientation angle, in degrees, between the reference line between G1 and G2 and the x_m material axis.

9.9.1.2. Element Properties

The element properties are defined using the PSHELL card for all thin shell elements. The fields on the property card for isoparametric shell elements are defined as follows

MID1 Material identification number for membrane behavior (Integer >0 or blank)

T Membrane Thickness (Real)

MID2 Material identification number for bending behavior (Integer >0 or blank)

R_I Normalized bending inertia per unit length. $R_I = I/I_o$ where $I_o = T^3/12$ and I is the bending moment of inertia. (Real or blank, default = 1.)

MID3 Material identification number for transverse shear behavior. (Integer >0 or blank)

R_T Normalized shear thickness. $R_T = TS/T$ where TS is the shear thickness and T is the membrane thickness. (Real or blank, default = 0.833333)

NSM Nonstructural mass per unit area (Real)

Z1, Z2 Stress recovery distances for bending (Real, default Z1 = Z2 = T/2 thickness)

MID4 Material identification number for membrane-bending coupling (Integer >0 or blank)

9.9.1.2.1. Selecting Element Mechanical Behavior

The shell elements provide inplane, bending and transverse shear behavior. The presence or absence of the corresponding material identification number in the appropriate field then defines the type of mechanical behavior that is desired while the type of constitutive relation is defined by the specific material card associated with the material identification. The presence of material identification numbers defines the following type of behavior

Material Field	Type of Behavior
MID1	Membrane (MAT1 or MAT2)
MID2	Bending (MAT1 or MAT2)
MID3	Transverse shear (MAT1 or MAT2)
MID4	Bending-Membrane Coupling (MAT2 only)

Material fields are not exclusive so that entries for MID1 and MID2, and MID4 would specify that coupled membrane-bending behavior without transverse shear is desired, while entries in only MID1 would specify membrane-only behavior.

9.9.1.2.2. Element Constitutive Relations

In order to clarify what is meant by the various mechanical behaviors and their associated material identification numbers it is worthwhile to consider the constitutive relations that are supported by the MSC/NASTRAN shell elements. The general form of the constitutive relation is

$$\left\{ \begin{array}{c} \mathbf{N} \\ \mathbf{M} \\ \mathbf{Q} \end{array} \right\} = \left[\begin{array}{ccc} T\mathbf{G}_1 & T^2\mathbf{G}_4 & 0 \\ T^2\mathbf{G}_4^T & I\mathbf{G}_2 & 0 \\ 0 & 0 & T_s\mathbf{G}_3 \end{array} \right] \left\{ \begin{array}{c} \mathbf{e}^\circ - \mathbf{e}_I^\circ \\ \kappa^\circ - \kappa_I^\circ \\ \gamma^\circ \end{array} \right\} \tag{9.57}$$

where $\mathbf{M}$ and $\mathbf{N}$ are given by (4.82) and (4.83), respectively, $\mathbf{e}^\circ$ are reference surface strains given by (4.80), κ° are reference surface curvatures given by (4.81), $\mathbf{e}_I^\circ$, κ_I° are initial strains and curvatures, and $\mathbf{Q}$ and γ° are defined as

$$\mathbf{Q} = \left\{ \begin{array}{c} Q_x \\ Q_y \end{array} \right\} \tag{9.58}$$

$$\gamma^\circ = \left\{ \begin{array}{c} \gamma_{xz}^\circ \\ \gamma_{yz}^\circ \end{array} \right\} \tag{9.59}$$

The quantities Q_x and Q_y are the transverse shear forces shown by Fig. 4-10 and γ_{xz}°, γ_{yz}° are the corresponding transverse shear strains of the reference surface. The cross section properties T, I, and T_s are the membrane thickness, second area moment for the cross section and shear thickness respectively, referred to the reference surface. The matrices $\mathbf{G}_1$, $\mathbf{G}_2$, $\mathbf{G}_3$, and $\mathbf{G}_4$ are elastic constants which are defined by material sets MID1, MID2, MID3, and MID4, respectively.

The form of the relation (9.57) allows for the coupling of bending and membrane action through the coupling terms $T^2\mathbf{G}_4$. *The coupling terms do not exist for symmetric cross-sections when the middle surface is taken as the reference surface but have been included in the element formulation to allow the analyst to model composite materials having unsymmetric layups and to model offset plates.* In the usual case of a solid homogeneous plate the field associated with coupling, MID4, would be blank and the cross sectional properties would be evaluated with respect to the middle surface.

9.9.1.2.3. Solid Homogeneous Symmetric Cross-Section

The desired mechanical behavior is specified by entries in the material identification fields, as appropriate. We can define, for example, uncoupled membrane or bending behavior and include transverse shear effects by using the MID1, MID2, and MID3 fields. Since there is no material coupling of bending and membrane behavior for a solid homogeneous symmetric cross section if the middle surface is used as the reference surface, it follows that MID4 is to be blank.

The membrane thickness can vary isoparametrically over the surface of the element. The fields T1, T2, T3, (and T4) on the CTRIA3 and CQUAD4 Bulk Data cards define the membrane thickness at the associated grid points. The T-field on the property card defines the default value for membrane thickness.

The bending moment of inertia per unit length of the edge and the transverse shear thickness are defined in a manner such that the default values are correct for solid plates. The bending moment of inertia is specified as the quantity R_I which is equal to 1. if the mid surface is taken as the reference for a solid homogeneous cross section. If bending behavior is requested (i.e. an entry in the MID2-field which points to a MAT-type card) and if the plate has a solid homogeneous cross section then the R_I-field can be left blank since the default is 1.0.

Transverse shear behavior is specified by an entry in the MID3 field that points to a MAT-type card which defines the shear material constants. If the entry R_T is blank then the default value $R_T = 0.833333$ is taken. If a MAT2 card is used to define transverse shear mate coefficients only supply G_{11}, G_{12}, and G_{22}.

A membrane having a uniform thickness of 0.5 in. could be defined by the following property card

1	2	3	4	5	6	7	8	9	10
PSHELL	1	10	0.5						

where the material membrane behavior is defined by material set number 10. An element having membrane, bending and transverse shear behavior could be defined by the following

1	2	3	4	5	6	7	8	9	10
PSHELL	1	10	0.5	10		10			

where material set 10, which we suppose is a MAT1 card, has been specified in the fields associated with membrane, bending, and shear behavior and where the default values for the fields R_I and R_T have been taken.

9.9.1.2.4. Sandwich Type Cross-Section

A sandwich plate is constructed of a core and two face sheets as shown by Fig. 9-32. The core is typically a light-weight material such as metal or paper honeycomb, or wood, whose purpose is to separate the facesheets in order to obtain a desired bending moment of inertia. The core is assumed to exhibit only shear behavior while the facesheets provide membrane and bending behavior. Generally the shear modulus of the core is an order-of-magnitude smaller than the elastic constants for the facesheets so that appreciable shear deformation can be expected.

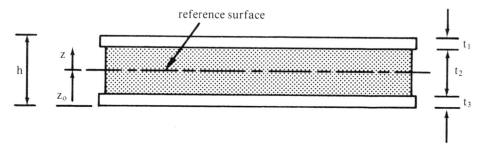

Figure 9-32. Sandwich Plate

240

The constitutive relations for the sandwich plate are then formulated by noting that the moment and force resultants are defined by (4.82) and (4.83). The components of stress in these equations can then be written in terms of strains and curvatures of a reference surface located at a distance z_0 from the bottom of the cross section as follows

$$\sigma = \mathbf{E}\,(e - z\kappa) \tag{9.60}$$

where z is the distance from the reference surface. The substitution of (9.60) into (4.82) and (4.83) then gives the following expressions for moment and force resultants.

$$\mathbf{M} = -\int z\mathbf{E}\,(e° - z\kappa°)\,dz \tag{9.61}$$

$$\mathbf{N} = \int \mathbf{E}\,(e° - z\kappa°)\,dz \tag{9.62}$$

where the integration is taken through the thickness of the plate.

In general, the elastic modulae are piecewise constant functions of the shell depth. In the present case the elastic coefficients are constant over the core depth, t_2, and may be different but constant over the cover plate thicknesses t_1 and t_3. The force resultants can then be found by piecewise integration provided that we are careful to define $e°$ and $\kappa°$ to be the strains and curvatures of the reference surface, which is defined at a distance z_0 from the bottom of the cross section. The expression for the force resultants for the sandwich plate shown by Fig. 9-32 then becomes

$$\mathbf{N} = \int_{h - z_0 - t_1}^{h - z_0} \mathbf{E}_1\,(e° + z\kappa°)\,dz + \int_{h - z_0 - t_1 - t_2}^{h - z_0 - t_1} \mathbf{E}_2\,(e° + z\kappa°)\,dz + \int_{h - z_0 - t_1 - t_2 - t_3}^{h - z_0 - t_1 - t_2} \mathbf{E}_3\,(e° + z\kappa°)\,dz \tag{9.63}$$

For a symmetric cross section we have

$$t_1 = t_3 = t$$

$$\mathbf{E}_1 = \mathbf{E}_3 = \mathbf{E}_f$$

$$t_2 = c$$

$$\mathbf{E}_2 = \mathbf{E}_c$$

So that the integration of (9.63) leads to the following expression.

$$\mathbf{N} = e°\,[2t\mathbf{E}_f + c\mathbf{E}_c] - \frac{\kappa°}{2}\,[(2th\mathbf{E}_f + ch\mathbf{E}_c)\,(1 - 2a)] \tag{9.64}$$

where we have set $z_0 = ah$ where a is a parameter that can be chosen by the analyst.

Inspection of the coefficient of the curvature term shows that the inplane forces can be made independent of the curvature if a is set equal to one-half. The strains and curvatures are then associated with the reference surface located at $h/2$ which is the middle surface for a symmetric layup. However, the MSC/NASTRAN shell elements allow for the coupling terms so that the analyst has the freedom to choose any convenient reference surface.

The force and moment resultants associated with a reference surface at the middle of a symmetric cross section can now be determined by using (9.61) and (9.62) and by noting that the strains and curvatures are defined at the middle surface. The coupling term in the moment relation then disappears so that the moment and force resultants are the moment given by

241

9.9.1.2   Element Properties

$$N = 2tE_f\, e° = TG_1 e° \qquad (9.65)$$

$$M = E_f[c^2t + ct^2 + \frac{t^3}{3}]\kappa° = IG_2\,\kappa° \qquad (9.66)$$

where we have assumed that the core does not carry membrane forces.

As a specific example consider the case where $t = 0.25$ in. and $c = 0.50$ in. The face sheets are isotropic aluminum and the core has a shear modulus of 300,000 psi. The element properties could then be defined using the following Bulk Data.

1	2	3	4	5	6	7	8	9	10
PSHELL	1	101	0.5	101	9.5	102	1.		
MAT1	101	10. + 6		0.3					
MAT1	102		3. + 5	0.3					

where the bending moment of inertia and shear thickness have been scaled appropriately by the membrane thickness.

The subject of unsymmetric sandwich construction and composite materials is beyond the scope of the present text. The interested reader should consult Refs. 9-8 and 9-9 for more details.

9.9.1.2.5.   Layered Composite Materials

A general capability for modeling layered composite structures is available for the thin shell elements. The purpose of this capability is to allow the analyst to define orthotropic lamina properties on an appropriate material card (called the MAT8 which is described in Chapter 10) and to define the laminate properties by means of a special property card called PCOMP which is shown by Card Image 9-9.

1	2	3	4	5	6	7	8	9	10
PCOMP	PID	Z_o	NSM	S_b	FT	T_{ref}	GE		+ P1
+ P1	MID_1	T_1	θ_1	$SOUT_1$	MID_2	T_2	θ_2	$SOUT_2$	+ P2
+ P2	MID_3	T_3	θ_3	$SOUT_3$	etc.				

Card Image 9-9. Laminate Properties for Thin Shell Elements — PCOMP

The PCOMP card defines general element properties in the first card including

Z_o The distance from the reference surface to the bottom of the first lamina. (real)

NSM   The nonstructural mass per unit area. (real)

S_b The allowable shear stress for the matrix (i.e. bond) material. (real)

FT   The theory to be used to predict lamina failure is specified by one of the following literal strings

   HILL − Hill Theory

   HOFF − Hoffman Theory

   TSAI − Tsai-wu Theory

T_{ref} The reference termperature, T_o, for calculating thermal strains

GE   The structural damping coefficient (used for dynamics).

Then each lamina is specified by defining

MID_i The identification of a MAT1, MAT2, or MAT8 material set which defines the material properties for the ith lamina

T_i The thickness of the ith lamina

θ_i The orientation angle for the ith lamina

$SOUT_i$ A literal string (i.e. YES or NO) which requests stress output for the ith lamina with NO being the default

The lamina data are specified for each lamina starting at the bottom (i.e. MID_i = MID1, etc.). The number of lamina is then determined by the number of sets of lamina properties that are defined.

The material properties for any lamina can be defined on MAT1, MAT2, or MAT8 material cards. The orientation of the specific ply relative to the material axes for the element is then defined by θ_i in degrees. If the orientation angle for the element material axes is not defined on the element connection card then the X-material axis is assumed to be parallel to the line joining vertices 1 and 2 of the element.

9.9.1.3. Effect of Warping

The QUAD4 element connects four grid points which might not lie in a plane if the element is used to model a doubly-curved shell surface. The elemental matrices for a flat element are modified in this case by appropriate pre- and post-multiplications in order to satisfy rigid body properties. The procedure which is used is described by Ref. 9-10 and is only satisfactory for small deviations from flatness and accounts for nodal forces.

9.9.1.4. Effect of Aspect Ratio

Aspect ratio studies reported in Ref. 9-10 show that the QUAD4 is accurate to within 1.5 percent for aspect ratios up to 20 for torsion and up to 11 for bending-torsion.

9.9.1.5. Effect of Nonrectangular Mesh

Tests have been performed which suggest that the element performance is degraded if the element is nonrectangular. The user should use caution when using nonrectangular elements even though the results from Ref. 9-10 show a maximum error of only 5.94 percent in the transverse central displacement for a 4×4 mesh of a square simply supported plate using the nonrectangular mesh shown by Fig. 9-33. Additional testing and refinement has been done to reduce the maximum

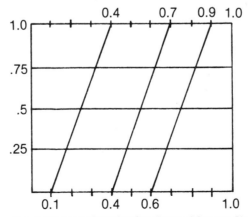

Figure 9-33. Nonrectangular 4×4 Mesh for Quadrant of Square Simply Supported Plate

error for this configuration to 1.16 percent. General good results are obtained for skew angles up to 45°. For larger angles the results deteriorate rapidly.

9.9.1.6.   Modeling Curved Shell Structures

It is common practice to use flat shell elements such as the QUAD4 to model cylindrical shell structures. The performance of the QUAD4 was compared to two COSMIC NASTRAN elements, the QUAD2 and TRIA2 in Ref. 9-10 by analyzing the cylinder shown by Fig. 9-34. The results show that the QUAD4 provides superior performance over the older elements for all mesh sizes and converges from above rather then below.

In order to shed some light on the reason for the excess flexibility of the QUAD4 one of the 2 × 2 mesh cases was rerun where each of the original flat elements was replaced by 4 flat elements. The results were identical to those obtained for the coarser mesh and imply that the flexibility is due primarily to the use of flat elements to model curved surfaces. A tentative rule, based on the results of this numerical test, is that the included angle per element should be 10 degrees or less to obtain errors of 4 percent or less in deflections. Even smaller included angles may be required to give adequate results for normal modes and frequencies.

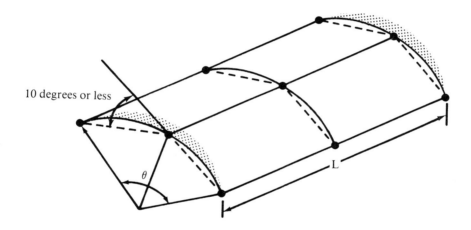

Figure 9-34. Modeling Cylindrical Arch with Flat Elements

9.9.1.7.   Elastic Stiffness Matrices

Both the TRIA3 and the QUAD4 use the shape functions which are used to interpolate displacements to transform the element geometry from physical to parametric space. The basic theory is straight-forward and follows the isoparametric development outlined in Chapter 8.

The formulation of the shear stiffness is handled quite differently than the extensional stiffness in the MSC/NASTRAN isoparametric elements. The extensional strains are calculated at the usual Gauss points but the shear strains are evaluated at special points as described in Ref. 9-10 for the QUAD4 element. A reduced integration scheme is therefore employed for the shear strains that generally results in improved element performance over a broad spectrum of loads.

9.9.1.8.   Mass Matrix

Lumped and consistent mass matrices are calculated at user option. The default is lumped while consistent mass is requested by a PARAMeter called COUPMASS in Bulk Data (see Appendix B). Mass coefficients are calculated for only translational degrees of freedom for both the lumped and consistent formulations.

The structural mass is calculated using the density defined on the *membrane material* property Bulk Data card. Therefore, even if bending-only behavior is desired for dynamics the membrane properties must be specified in order to generate the structural mass matrix. The nonstructural mass is calculated using the value for NSM on the property card. If bending-only behavior is desired the mass matrix for transverse displacements can be calculated by using NSM without specifying membrane action.

9.9.1.9.   Stress and Element Force Recovery

The stresses are computed at distances z_1 and z_2 from the reference plane along a line perpendicular to the reference plane at the centroid of the element. The stress is given by

$$\sigma^1 = -\frac{z_1}{I}\mathbf{M} + \sigma^\circ + \Delta\sigma \qquad (9.67)$$

where the membrane stress is given by

$$\sigma^\circ = \mathbf{G}_1(\mathbf{e}^\circ - \mathbf{e}_1^\circ) + T\mathbf{G}_4(\kappa^\circ - \kappa_1^\circ) \qquad (9.68)$$

and where $\Delta\sigma$ is the thermal stress which results from the difference between the fiber temperature and a linear fit between the temperatures at the plate surfaces.

In addition to the stresses, the force resultants $\mathbf{M}$, $\mathbf{N}$, and $\mathbf{Q}$ are calculated at the node points using (9.57). The user may request stress and force output by the 'STRESS' and 'ELFORCE' Case Control Directives, respectively.

9.9.2.   Curved Shell Elements

The QUAD8 and TRIA6 curved shell elements which are included in the MSC/NASTRAN library have all of the general modeling capability associated with the flat shell elements described in Sec. 9.9.1. including

1. Isoparametric thickness variation over the element

2. Element thermal field

3. Anisotropic temperature-dependent material properties

4. Elastic coupling of membrane and bending behavior

The major differences between the curved and the flat shell elements are

1. The shape functions used for the QUAD8 and TRIA6 for displacements and geometry are of a higher order than those used for the QUAD4 and TRIA3.

2. The QUAD8 and TRIA6 may connect up to eight and six node points, respectively.

The TRIA6 and QUAD8 elements are shown by Figs. 9-35a and 9-35b, respectively, where it can be seen that the elements connect all degrees of freedom except the normal rotation in intrinsic element coordinates at the node point. If the element is flat there will thus be only five elastically coupled degrees of freedom.

The connectivity for the elements is defined by the CQUAD8 and the CTRIA6 Bulk Data which are shown in Card Image 9-10. The PSHELL property card which is shown on Card Image 9-8 and which was described in Sec. 9.9.1. is used to define the element property for the QUAD8 and TRIA6 as well as the TRIA3 and QUAD4.

9.9.2 Curved Shell Elements

*Six-Noded Curved Element — TRIA6

1	2	3	4	5	6	7	8	9	10
CTRIA6	EID	PID	G1	G2	G3	G4	G5	G6	+ CT1
+ CT1	θ		T1	T2	T3				

*Eight-Noded Curved Element — QUAD8

CQUAD8	EID	PID	G1	G2	G3	G4	G5	G6	+ CQ1
+ CQ1	G7	G8	T1	T2	T3	T4	θ		

Card Image 9-10. Specification of Curved Thin Shell Elements

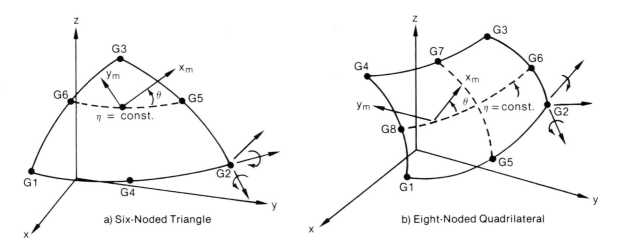

a) Six-Noded Triangle

b) Eight-Noded Quadrilateral

Figure 9-35. Isoparametric Curved Thick Shell Elements

9.9.2.1. Element Connectivity

The TRIA6 and QUAD8 element connect up to six and eight nodes as shown by Figs. 9-35a and 9-35b, respectively. The midside nodes may be selectively deleted so that the TRIA6 can connect from 3 to 6 nodes and the QUAD8 can connect from 4 to 8 nodes.

The connected node points are defined by the fields G1 through G6 on the TRIA6 and G1 through G8 on the QUAD8. The entries in these fields are integer grid point numbers and must be ordered as shown on Fig. 9-35a and 9-35b for the TRIA6 and QUAD8 elements, respectively.

All of the corner node points must be defined. The midside nodes should be at or near the center of the edges but any of the midside nodes can be deleted by leaving the appropriate field blank. For example, a blank in the G6-field of the CTRIA6 card would imply that there is no midside point on the edge connecting nodes G1 and G3. Geometrically-speaking the corresponding edge would then be taken to be a straight line connecting the geometric grid points but the displacements would still be represented using cubic interpolation along the edge.

9.9.2.2. Element Coordinate Systems

The local coordinate system for the curved shell elements is taken to be an orthogonal curvilinear system in geometric space as shown by Figs. 9-35a and 9-35b for the TRIA6 and QUAD8 elements, respectively. The normal coordinate is taken to be perpendicular to the surface with a positive sense determined by applying the right hand rule to the corner node numbers.

9.9.2.3. Material Orientation

The orientation of the material coordinate system relative to the element coordinates is defined by the θ-field on the appropriate connection. The angle θ (real) in degrees is taken to be constant over the element and is used at each Gauss integration point to define the orientation of the x_m material axis as a line in the plane tangent to the surface of the element and at an angle θ to the intrinsic element coordinate η = constant as shown by Figs. 9-35a and 9-35b for the TRIA6 and QUAD8, respectively.

9.9.2.4. Element Thickness

The membrane thickness can be defined as a constant over the element using the T-field on the PSHELL card or by defining the thickness at the corner node points on the appropriate connection card using the fields T1, T2, T3, (and T4) (Real). If the thickness fields on the connection card are left blank the thickness on the PSHELL card is used.

9.9.2.5. Selecting Element Mechanical Behavior

The TRIA6 and QUAD8 are capable of selectively representing membrane, bending, or coupled membrane-bending behavior depending on the entries in the MID-type fields of the PSHELL as described in Sec. 9.9.1.2.1 for the flat shell elements. The resulting constitutive equations are then defined by (9.57).

9.9.2.6. Element Stiffness Matrices

The TRIA6 and QUAD8 are isoparametric elements which use quadratic interpolation for displacement as well as geometric mapping. The stiffness (and mass) matrices are then formulated in parametric space using the techniques described in Chapter 8.

Both the TRIA6 and QUAD8 use reduced integration to represent shear effects. As we have noted in Chapter 8, reduced integration generally results in a more flexible element which has superior convergence characteristics over the standard approach of evaluating all strain components at the appropriate Gauss integration points. The resulting element is nonconformable in the sense that the displacement fields do not match along common element edges and the behavior does not converge monotonically to actual solution, but it does converge.

9.9.2.7. Element Mass Matrices

The lumped mass formulation is the default for both the TRIA6 and QUAD8 but the analyst can request the consistent mass by means of the COUPMASS PARAMeter Bulk Data card which is described in Appendix B. Mass coefficients for rotational degrees of freedom are not calculated in either case so that the elemental mass matrix associated with bending behavior is singular.

9.9.2.8. Stress Recovery

The element strains and curvatures, and therefore the stress components, are calculated in element coordinates. The stress is computed using (9.67) at distances z_1 and z_2 from the reference surface where z_1 and z_2 are defined on the PSHELL property card. The stresses are recovered at the vertices and the centroid for each element.

9.9.2.9. Use of MSGMESH to Generate Thin Shell Elements

The optional MSGMESH preprocessor can be used to connect GRID points which are generated by using the GRIDG MSGMESH Command (see Sec. 7.7.3.7.). The CGEN MSGMESH Command which is shown by Card Image 9-11 can then be used to define connectivity over the entire field.

9.10   Solid Elements

1	2	3	4	5	6	7	8	9	10
CGEN + CG1	TYPE TA	FEID TB	PID TC	FID TD	DIR	TH	EIDL	EIDH	+ CG1

where

TYPE   One of the element mnemonics

QUAD4   for quadrilaterial fields
QUAD8

TRIA3   for triangular fields
TRIA6

FEID   The EID for the lowest element number which is to be generated for the field of points

PID   The property number for the generated connection cards

FID   The identification number for the field of points over which connection cards are to be generated

DIR   Elements are numbered starting at vertex A of the field in one of two directions in a QUAD field, as shown by Fig. 7-9, depending on the value of DIR

1 — proceed in the primary direction

2 — proceed in the secondary direction

TH   Material orientation angle (degrees)

EIDL   The element IDs below which (EIDL) and above

EIDH   which (EIDH) no element connection Bulk Data will be generated

TA, TB   Thickness of vertices of the QUAD MSGMESH
TC, TD   field

Card Image 9-11. MSGMESH Command for Generating Thin Shell Elements — CGEN

9.10.   Solid Elements

The MSC/NASTRAN solid elements include a five-sided element called the PENTA and a six-sided element called the HEXA. These elements are shown by Figs. 9-36 and 9-37, respectively, and are defined by the Bulk Data cards shown by Card Image 9-12.

The PENTA and HEXA are recommended over the older MSC/NASTRAN solid elements which include the WEDGE, HEXA1, HEXA2, HEX8, and HEX20. The PENTA and HEXA use isoparametric representation of element geometry as well as displacement field. These elements were developed to

1. Support Anisotropic material coefficients

2. Improve stress output

3. Improve performance in representation of curved shell behavior

4. Improve treatment of differential stiffness

In order to effectively model using the solid elements the analyst may have a requirement for a 4-noded TETRA element. This element, which is a three dimensional analogy of the constant strain membrane element, is not described in this section but is listed in Appendix C.

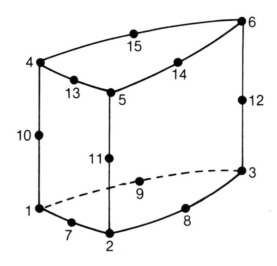

Figure 9-36. Five-Sided Isoparametric Solid Element — PENTA

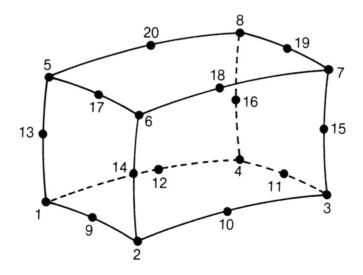

Figure 9-37. Six-Sided Isoparametric Element — HEXA

*PENTA — Five Sided Solid Isoparametric Element

1	2	3	4	5	6	7	8	9	10
CPENTA	EID	PID	G1	G2	G3	G4	G5	G6	+ CP1
+ CP1	G7	G8	G9	G10	G11	G12	G13	G14	+ CP2
+ CP2	G15								

*HEXA — Six Sided Solid Isoparametric Element

CHEXA	EID	PID	G1	G2	G3	G4	G5	G6	+ CH1
+ CH1	G7	G8	G9	G10	G11	G12	G13	G14	+ CH2
+ CH2	G15	G16	G17	G18	G19	G20			

*PSOLID — Common Property Card

PSOLID	PID	MID	CORDM	IN					

Card Image 9-12. Isoparametric Solids; PENTA and HEXA

9.10.1.   Element Connectivity

The PENTA and HEXA elements provide connectivity for three displacement degrees of freedom at each node point on the element. The PENTA and HEXA provide connection of up to 15 and 20 node points, respectively. The node points to be connected are identified by G1 through G15 on the CPENTA and G1 through G20 on the CHEXA Bulk Data cards shown by Card Image 9-12. The property field, PID, refers to a common property card, the PSOLID.

9.10.1.1.   The PENTA Element

The PENTA element has six corner nodes and nine edge nodes. The node number sequence shown on Fig. 9-36 must be preserved, i.e. nodes G1 through G3 must define the vertices of a triangular face such that the normal to the surface, according to the right hand rule, is directed into the solid. Nodes G4 through G6 must then define the opposite triangular face with G4, G5, and G6 on the edges connecting G1, G2, and G3, respectively. The normal to the second surface is then directed outward from the surface, again using the right hand rule.

The edge nodes G7 through G15 are optional any or all of which are positionally defined. That is G7 is the node on the edge between G1 and G2, G8 is the node on the edge between G2 and G3, etc. If the element is to be modeled without the midside note G7 then the field associated with that node (field 2 on the first continuation card) contains no entry and is thus blank. The continuation cards are not required if all of the midside nodes are omitted.

9.10.1.2.   The HEXA Element

The HEXA element has eight corner nodes and twelve edge nodes. The node number sequence shown on Fig. 9-37 must be preserved, i.e. nodes G1 through G4 must define a face having an inward normal, using the right hand rule. Nodes G5 through G8 must then define the opposite face with G5 lying on the edge connecting G1 and whose sequence defines an outward normal to the element, using the right hand rule.

The edge nodes G9 through G20 are optional and any or all may be defined. As in the case of the PENTA element the edge nodes are positionally defined with node G9 on the line segment connecting G1 and G2 and G17 on the line segment between G5 and G6, for example. The absence of an entry for G9 (field 4 of the first continuation card) then specifies that there is no node on the edge connecting G1 and G2. If no edge nodes are defined then the second continuation card is not required.

9.10.2.   Properties of PENTA and HEXA Solid Element

The properties of the PENTA and HEXA solid elements are defined by a common property card, the PSOLID, as shown on Card Image 9-12. The material identification refers to either an isotropic or an anisotropic material defined by a MAT1 or MAT9 material card, respectively. If the material is anisotropic then the orientation of the material axis relative to local element coordinates must be defined by an entry in the CORDM field as follows

CORDM	Meaning
Blank or −1	Align material coordinates with local element coordinates.
0	Material axes are aligned with basic coordinates.
>0	Material axes are aligned with coordinates defined by coordinate identification number appearing in the field.

9.10.2.1.   Element Coordinate System

The orientation of the element coordinate system is of importance to the analyst if anisotropic material axes are to be aligned with the element axes. The element coordinates for the HEXA element are chosen using the following procedure.

1. Let a_1, a_2, and a_3 be the directed line segments joining the centroids of faces 1 and 2, faces 3 and 4, and faces 5 and 6, respectively where the faces contain nodes as follows

Face	Nodes
1	1, 2, 3, 4
2	5, 6, 7, 8
3	1, 2, 6, 5
4	4, 3, 7, 8
5	1, 5, 8, 4
6	2, 6, 7, 3

2. Choose the unit vector **i** such that $|a_i|$ (i = 1, 2, 3) is a maximum.

3. Among the remaining directed line segments choose the unit vector **v** in the direction of the next longest directed line segment.

4. Find the unit vector **k** perpendicular to the plane containing (**i**, **v**) by forming the cross product $k = i \times v$.

5. Define the unit vector **j** to be perpendicular to the plane containing (**i**, **k**) by forming the cross product $j = k \times i$.

6. Permute the directions (**i**, **j**, **k**) so that **i**′ is approximately parallel to the line segment from G1 to G2 and **j**′ is approximately parallel to the line segment joining G1 and G4.

Consider the example shown by Fig. 9-38.

251

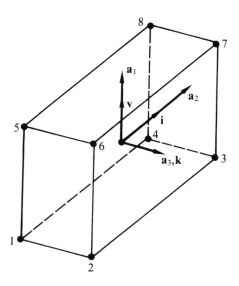

Figure 9-38. Orientation of Local Coordinates for HEXA Element

Apparently, $\mathbf{a}_2$ is the longest segment so that the unit vector $\mathbf{i}$ is in that direction. The line segment $\mathbf{a}_1$ is the next longest segment so that $\mathbf{v}$ is a unit vector in this direction. The unit vector $\mathbf{k}$ (assumed to be coincident with $\mathbf{a}_3$) is then perpendicular to the plane containing $\mathbf{i}$ and $\mathbf{v}$ while $\mathbf{j}$ (here assumed to be coincident with $\mathbf{v}$) is perpendicular to the plane containing ($\mathbf{i}$ and $\mathbf{k}$). The direction $\mathbf{k}$ is seen to be approximately parallel to the edge 1-2 while $\mathbf{i}$ is approximately parallel to the edge 1-4. The local coordinate system is then taken to be $\mathbf{x} = \mathbf{k}$, $\mathbf{y} = \mathbf{i}$, and $\mathbf{z} = \mathbf{j}$.

The local coordinate system for the PENTA element is formed as shown by Fig. 9-39 which shows only the vertices.

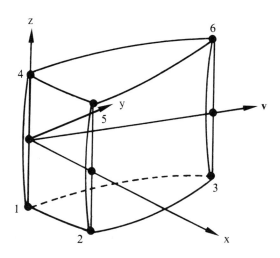

Figure 9-39. PENTA Local Coordinate System

The local x-axis is taken to be the line segment that joins the centroids of the straight line segments which join vertices 1-4 and 2-5, respectively. A vector $\mathbf{v}$ is then defined by the directed line segment that joins the centroids of the straight line segments which join vertices 1-4 and 3-6. The vector $\mathbf{v}$ is then taken to be in the local xy plane so that $z = x \times v$ and $y = z \times x$.

9.10.2.2. Integration Order

Two sets of integration points are provided for each element as described in the next section. The user can specify either of the sets by including an integer value for the IN field on the PSOLID card or the default can be taken by specifying either a zero or a blank in the field.

The allowable numerical values for IN and the associate number of integration points to be used in Gauss integration are presented by Table 9-9. The default values are IN = 2 if only vertex nodes are defined and IN = 3 if only midside nodes are defined.

IN	Element Type	
	HEXA	PENTA
2	8 points	6 points
3	27 points	9 points

Table 9-9. Specification of Number of Gauss Integration Points for HEXA and PENTA Solid Elements

9.10.3. Elastic Stiffness Matrix

HEXA and PENTA elements may have any or all of the edge nodes deleted. The calculation of the stiffness matrix is then formulated by taking the deleted nodes into account.

9.10.3.1. The HEXA Element

The element is transformed to parametric space as described in Sec. 8.5.4. The stiffness matrix is then calculated using Gaussian integration with either of two integration schemes which correspond to the 8- and 20-noded elements.

The 8-noded element is the three dimensional analogy of the two dimensional bilinear quadratic element. The same type of shear correction is thus used in the three dimensional element that is used to improve the membrane shear behavior of the QUAD4 element. Thus, for the 8-noded element the extensional strains are evaluated at a $2 \times 2 \times 2$ array of Gauss points but the shear strain is evaluated at a reduced number of special points.

The second integration scheme corresponds to elements having one or more undeleted edge nodes. The extensional strains are evaluated at a $3 \times 3 \times 3$ array of Gauss points with reduced integration at special points for shear strains.

9.10.3.2. The PENTA Element

The PENTA element is transformed to a right isoceles prism in parameter space as shown on Fig. 9-40 by using appropriate shape functions. Two integration schemes are provided that use six or nine integration points. The six point scheme is the default when all edge nodes are deleted. In all other cases the nine node scheme is the default. Reduced integration is used for shear strains in either integration scheme.

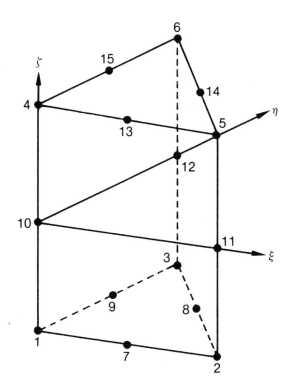

Figure 9-40. PENTA in Parameter Space

9.10.4. Mass

The PENTA and HEXA elements support both the coupled and lumped mass formulations. The lumped formulation is default only for the six node PENTA and the eight node HEXA elements. If the elements have midside points the coupled formulation is used. The coupled formulation can be specified independent of the default by including a COUPMASS PARAMeter card in Bulk Data (See Appendix B).

9.10.5. Stress Recovery

The components of stress are calculated in the material coordinate system (i.e. that system specified by the CORDM field on the associated PSOLID Bulk Data card). The components of stress are recovered at the center of each element and at the six corner nodes for the PENTA and the eight corner nodes for the HEXA elements.

9.11. Constraint Elements

The multipoint constraint (MPC) capability is a useful but cumbersome way of defining sets of linear relations between degrees of freedom. We saw in Sec. 7.5.1., for example, that a rigid link could be represented by six equations (7.51) and could be modeled using the set of MPC Bulk Data cards presented in that section.

MSC/NASTRAN incorporates a number of constraint elements which allow the user to specify the following types of relations between degrees of freedom directly by means of appropriate Bulk Data

- Rigid Elements

- Elastic Spline Fit

- Weighted Average

The MSC/NASTRAN constraint elements which provide these capabilities are summarized by Table 9-10 where the element names such as RROD are the mnemonics for the associated Bulk Data cards.

    The MSC/NASTRAN rigid elements, i.e. elements that represent kinematic constraints between degrees of freedom based on rigid body motion between connected degrees of freedom include the RROD, RBAR, RTRPLT, RBE1 and RBE2. The other two elements, the RSPLINE and the RBE3 are more correctly termed constraint elements because the relationship between degrees of freedom is based on assumptions other than rigid body motion. The RSPLINE assumes an elastic curve fit and the RBE3 assumes a weighted average between specified degrees of freedom.

Constraint Element Name	Description	Number of Constraint Equations Generated — m
RROD	Defines extensional constraint in the direction of a line segment between two geometric grid points.	$m = 1$
RBAR	Defines a rigid linkage between two geometric grid points that relates the six degrees of freedom at each end.	$1 \leq m \leq 6$
RTRPLT	A rigid connection between three geometric grid points.	$1 \leq m \leq 12$
RBE1	A rigid connection of an arbitrary number of grid points. Dependent and independent degrees of freedom are selected by user.	$m \geq 1$
RBE2	A rigid element connecting an arbitrary number of grid points. The independent degrees of freedom are associated with a single grid point.	$m \geq 6$
RBE3	A constraint element with reference degrees of freedom set equal to the weighted average of the connected degrees of freedom.	$1 \leq m \leq 6$
RSPLINE	Elastic constraint element with degrees of freedom related by hermitian polynomial passing through connected points.	$m \geq 1$

Table 9-10. MSC/NASTRAN Constraint Elements

9.11.1 RROD — Extensional Constraint

The specification of constraint elements requires an understanding of the form and function of the linear constraint equations which can be defined in MSC/NASTRAN. The MPC operation partitions the g-set into two subsets, the m-set and the n-set which are related by a set of linear constraint equations given by (7.38) where the m-set is identified as m degrees of freedom which are related by m constraint equations to the n-set degrees of freedom. The g-set of equations is reduced to n-size by using the formulation presented in Sec. 7.5.1.3.

The purpose of the MSC/NASTRAN constraint elements is to provide an efficient means of generating constraint equations in the form of (7.38). We would anticipate, therefore, that the associated constraint element Bulk Data cards must provide a mechanism for specifying the set membership of the connected degrees of freedom. Furthermore, since the constraint elements in effect define MPCs, the user must follow all of the rules associated with MPCs including

1. A degree of freedom specified in the m-set cannot be included in any of the other removed sets. If the user attempts to do so a fatal error message will be issued from the MSC/NASTRAN module which defines and checks set membership.

2. A degree of freedom can be specified in the m-set only once. A fatal error will be issued if the same degree of freedom is designated as dependent on two constraint elements.

3. The user-selected degrees of freedom in the n-set for all rigid elements except the RROD must be sufficient to represent rigid body motion.

9.11.1. RROD — Extensional Constraint

The RROD constraint element is shown by Fig. 9-41 and is defined by the RROD Bulk Data shown on Card Image 9-13.

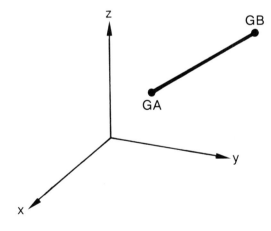

Figure 9-41. RROD Constraint Element

1	2	3	4	5	6	7	8	9	10
RROD	EID	GA	GB	CMA	CMB				

where

GA, GB   are grid point identification numbers (Integer > 0)

CMA, CMB   component number of one translational degree of freedom at either end A or at end B

256

that is to be included in the m-set. One of the two fields contains the integer code for the m-set degree of freedom while the other field is blank.

Card Image 9-13. Extensional Constraint Element — RROD

The extensional constraint condition implies that the relative displacement in the direction of the line segment joining the connected geometric grid points must be zero. Thus we have

$$\mathbf{d}_A = \mathbf{d}_B \tag{9.69}$$

where $\mathbf{d}$ is the displacement in the direction of the line segment from grid point A to grid point B. Expressing $\mathbf{d}$ in terms of displacement components at A and B gives

$$u_{xA}\alpha_x + u_{yA}\alpha_y + u_{zA}\alpha_z = u_{xB}\alpha_x + u_{yB}\alpha_y + u_{zB}\alpha_z \tag{9.70}$$

where $(\alpha_x, \alpha_y, \alpha_z)$ are direction cosines between the directed line segment between the points and the coordinate axes. The RROD thus defines a single equation which can be put into the form of the MPC equation (7.38) provided that the dependent degree of freedom, i.e. the m-set degree of freedom, is specified. This specification is made by identifying one of the six degrees of freedom in (9.70) as an m-set degree of freedom and entering the associate degree of freedom code in field 5 or field 6 of the RROD depending on whether the m-set degree of freedom is at end A or B, respectively. Finally, with reference to (9.70) it is apparent that the direction cosine associated with the m-set degree of freedom must be nonzero. This implies that the m-set degree of freedom cannot be perpendicular to the line segment joining A and B.

9.11.2.   RBAR — Rigid Link with End Fixity

The RBAR element provides the capability of modeling the rigid link shown by Fig. 7-12 by using the single Bulk Data card shown on Card Image 9-14 rather than a set of MPC cards necessary to specify the associated constraint equations (7.51).

1	2	3	4	5	6	7	8	9	10
RBAR	EID	GA	GB	CNA	CNB	CMA	CMB		

where

CNA, CNB are codes for n-set degrees of freedom at ends A and B, respectively (Integer ≥ 0 or blank)

CMA, CMB are codes for m-set degrees of freedom at ends A and B, respectively (Integer ≥ 0 or blank)

Card Image 9-14. Specification Rigid Link Constraint Element — RBAR

The RBAR element defines a rigid connection for up to six degrees of freedom at each of two geometric grid points. The associated kinematic conditions can then be expressed as the six equations (7.51). In order to formulate the associated MPC relationships in the form of (7.38) the user must specify the set membership for the connected degrees of freedom such that the degrees of freedom in the n-set are capable of representing rigid body motion for the rigid element.

The six rigid body degrees of freedom are defined by the CNA and CNB fields which contain codes associated with degrees of freedom at grid points GA and GB, respectively that are to be included in the n-set. Since the m- and n-sets are complementary the six remaining degrees of freedom are included in the m-set. These m-set degrees of freedom can be specified explicitly by means of the CMA and CMB fields which contain codes for m-set degrees of freedom at grid points GA and

GB, respectively or implicitly by leaving the CMA and CMB fields blank. It is not necessary to include all remaining degrees of freedom in the m-set. Those not specified are unconnected by the rigid rod and are equivalent to the forceless degrees of freedom, which can be specified by pin flags on the elastic BAR element.

9.11.2.1. Example — Rigid Link Connecting Two Points

Suppose that two grid points, 363 and 132, are connected by a member which is extremely stiff compared to other elements in the structure. The correct modeling procedure in this case is to define a set of constraint equations using a RBAR rather than using an extremely stiff elastic beam element.

The set of MPC Bulk Data required to model this rigid body constraint equations is given in Sec. 7.5.1.5. The RBAR can be used as an alternative in which case the rigid link is defined by the following single Bulk Data

1	2	3	4	5	6	7	8	9	10
RBAR	153	363	132	123456					

where the six degrees of freedom at point 363 have been included in the n-set implying that the six degrees of freedom at point 132 are in the m-set in agreement with the MPC Specification in Sec. 7.5.1.5.

9.11.3. RTRPLT — Rigid Triangular Constraint Element

A constraint element which connects three geometric grid points is shown by Fig. 9-42 and is described using the RTRPLT Bulk Data card shown on Card Image 9-15.

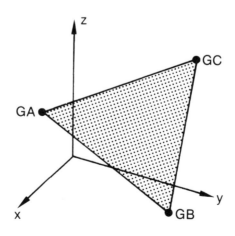

Figure 9-42. Triangular Constraint Element

258

1	2	3	4	5	6	7	8	9	10
RTRPLT + R1	EID CMA	GA CMB	GB CMC	GC	CNA	CNB	CNC		+ R1

where

CNA, CNB, CNC are codes for n-set degrees of freedom at points A, B, and C, respectively (integer ≥ 0 or blank)

CMA, CMB, CMC are codes for m-set degrees of freedom at A, B, and C, respectively. (Integer ≥ 0 or blank)

Card Image 9-15. Rigid Triangular Constraint Element — RTRPLT

There are six rigid body degrees of freedom for the rigid element that are to be represented by the n-set degrees of freedom. The user must therefore specify six degrees of freedom at the connected grid points which are to be included in the n-set by means of the CNA, CNB, and CNC fields which contain codes associated with degrees of freedom at grid points GA, GB, and GC, respectively that are to be included in the n-set. The remaining degrees of freedom may be defined to be members of the m-set if the associated degree of freedom codes are left blank, in which case the continuation card is not required. The m-set can be specified to be some subset of the remaining degrees of freedom by entering explicit codes on the continuation; those not included are uncoupled and are effectively pinned degrees of freedom.

9.11.3.1.   Example — Bell Crank

Consider the structural system shown by Fig. 9-43.

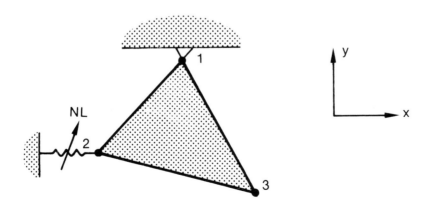

Figure 9-43. Structural Model Including TRPLT Rigid Element

where the rigid triangular element is free to rotate about point 1 in a plane containing the three points and where the spring is to be modeled using the MSC/NASTRAN NOLIN-type capability. The constraint elements and single point constraints required to model the system are shown below

1	2	3	4	5	6	7	8	9	10
RTRPLT	156	1	2	3	12345	1			+R1
+R1	6	26	126						
SPC1	100	345	1	THRU	3				
SPC1	100	12	1						

where

1. Degree of freedom 1 at node 2 is included in the n-set because nonlinear springs cannot be attached to m-set degrees of freedom.

2. Degrees of freedom 12345 at node 1 are additional degrees of freedom in the n-set which in conjunction with those at node 2 represent six rigid body degrees of freedom.

3. Degrees of freedom 3, 4, and 5 are purged at all grid points to restrict the problem to one of planar motion.

4. Degrees of freedom 1 and 2 are constrained at point 1 to model the physical constraint at this point.

9.11.4.   General Rigid Constraint Element — RBE1 and RBE2

The RBE1 and RBE2 constraint elements are generalizations of the RBAR and RTRPLT elements that allow connection of an arbitrary number of geometric grid points. These rigid constraint elements have six rigid body degrees of freedom in the n-set which the user must define. The form of the RBE1 and RBE2 rigid elements is shown on Card Image 9-16.

1	2	3	4	5	6	7	8	9	10
RBE1	EID	GN_1	CN_1	GN_2	CN_2	GN_3	CN_3		+RB1
+RB1		GN_4	CN_4	GN_5	CN_5	GN_6	CN_6		+RB2
+RB2	UM	GM_1	CM_1	GM_2	CM_2	GM_3	CM_3		+RB3
+RB3		GM_4	CM_4	etc.					

*Alternate Form of General Rigid Body Element

RBE2	EID	GN	CM	GM_1	GM_2	GM_3	GM_4	GM_5	+RB4
+RB4	GM_6	GM_7	GM_8	etc.					

where

GN_i are grid points at which n-set degrees of freedom are defined

CN_i are codes for degrees of freedom at grid point GN that are to be included in the n-set

UM   is a literal string which terminates the specification of the n-set

GM_i are grid points at which m-set degrees of freedom are specified

CM_i are codes for degrees of freedom which are to be included in the m-set.

Card Image 9-16. General Rigid Body Constraint Elements — RBE1 and RBE2

The RBE1 and RBE2 perform the same function but have the following differences

1. The RBE1 allows the user to define the six degrees of freedom in the n-set that are capable of representing rigid body motion. The number of degree of freedom codes must total six and may be defined at up to six grid points. If the n-set is defined at three or less grid points then the first continuation card is not required. The dependent degrees of freedom are then defined after the UM field by pairs (GM_i, CM_i) where GM is the grid point number and CM is a degree of freedom code.

2. The RBE2 takes the six degrees of freedom at the grid point defined in the GN-field to be in the n-set. The CM-field then contains the code for up to six degrees of freedom at the grid points GM_i that are then to be included in the m-set.

9.11.4.1.   Example — Rigid Inclusion

It may be necessary to model a rigid inclusion as a structure such as a tightly fitting bolt in a bolt hole. The grid points on the circumference of the bolt hole shown by Fig. 9-44 can thus have no relative motion

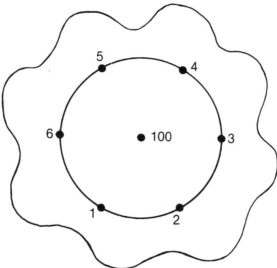

Figure 9-44. Rigid Circular Inclusion.

The equations that specify the desired constraint condition can be defined by using either the RBE1 or RBE2 rigid element, both of which are shown below.

1	2	3	4	5	6	7	8	9	10
RBE1	156	100	123456						+R1
+R1	UM	1	123456	2	123456	3	123456		+R2
+R2		4	123456	5	123456	6	123456		

or

1	2	3	4	5	6	7	8	9	10
RBE2	156	100	123456	1	2	3	4	5	+R3
+R3	6								

In both cases the six degrees of freedom at the center of the hole are included in the n-set while the six degrees of freedom at each point around the circumference are included in the m-set.

9.11.5.   Elastic Constraint Element — RSPLINE

The constraint elements which have been described in the previous sections are rigid elements. For those elements the constraint equations result from the kinematic condition that there is no relative motion between specified degrees of freedom. The RSPLINE element described in this section and the RBE3 element described in the next section define relationships between degrees of freedom that are based on assumptions other than rigidity. The RSPLINE uses an elastic fit and the RBE3 uses a weighted average to relate degrees of freedom. In either case, since the concept of rigidity is not employed, it is no longer appropriate to specify six degrees of freedom which are capable of representing rigid body motion in the n-set. On the contrary, for both of these elements an arbitrary number of degrees of freedom can be put in the n-set. However, there must be at least six.

The elastic interpolation element is shown by Fig. 9-45 and is defined by the RSPLINE Bulk Data shown on Card Image 9-17.

1	2	3	4	5	6	7	8	9	10
RSPLINE	EID	D/L	G1	G2	C2	G3	C3	G4	+RS1
+RS1	C4	G5	C5	G6	etc.				

where

D/L   is the ratio of elastic tube diameter to total tube length. (Real ≥ 0. Default = 0.1)

G   are grid point numbers. (Integer >0)

C   are degree of freedom codes. (Integer >0 or blank)

Card Image 9-17. Specification of Elastic Interpolation Element — RSPLINE

The elastic interpolation element connects two end points (identified by solid circles) and user-specified interior points (identified as solid triangle).

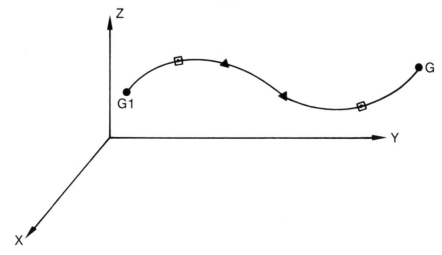

Figure 9-45. Elastic Interpolation Element — RSPLINE

The RSPLINE element uses straight beam-like segments to represent a curve which has the property of matching the displacement and slope at the end points and at the user-specified 'primary' interior points. The displacements at user-designated 'secondary' interior points (indicated by the open squares) can then be determined by using the equation for the elastic curve which matches displacement at the primary designated points. The values of the displacement at the secondary points (open squares) are thus dependent on the displacements of the primary points which determine the equation of the spline. The displacement degrees of freedom at the secondary points are thus included in the m-set while the degrees of freedom associated with the end points and primary interior points are independent and are included in the n-set.

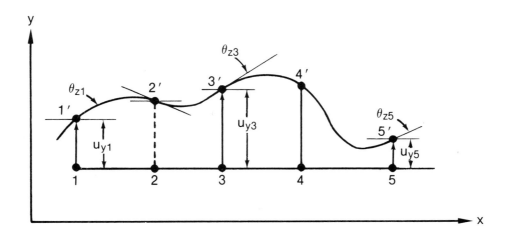

Figure 9-46. Elastic Spline Fit Passing Through Displaced Points

Consider the case shown by Fig. 9-46 where we wish to connect the grid points which lie along the line y = constant using an elastic spline. The elastic curve is to be determined by the displacement u_y and rotation θ_z at end points 1 and 5 and a primary interior point 3. The displacements at secondary points 2 and 4 are then to be evaluated from the equation of the elastic curve which passes through points 1, 3, and 5. The RSPLINE constraint element in effect uses the straight elastic beam equation (6.54) to provide a relation between specified and interpolated degrees of freedom.

The RSPLINE Bulk Data card allows the user to define the elastic interpolation function as follows

1. The first and last grid points are taken to be the ends of the spline and, by definition, all of the degrees of freedom at these points are members of the n-set.

2. An arbitrary number of interior points can be defined which may be either primary points which define the elastic curve such as point 3 in Fig. 9-46, or secondary points at which interpolated values are to be determined such as points 2 and 4 in Fig. 9-46. The interior degrees of freedom are defined by a pair of fields such as (G2, C2) where G2 is the grid point number. The presence or absence of the associated degree of freedom code field then determines whether the points are primary or secondary as follows.

Value of
C-field   Meaning

Blank   The associated grid point is primary and the degrees of freedom at the grid point are used to determine the equation for the elastic curve and are thus to be included in the n-set.

263

Integer >0 A secondary grid point. The degrees of freedom associated with the packed degree of freedom code are to be evaluated from the equation for the elastic curve and are thus to be included in the m-set. All other degrees of freedom at the grid point (if any) are to be used to define elastic behavior and are thus in the n-set.

3. The ratio D/L defines the ratio of bending "stiffness" to torsional "stiffness" for the elastic tube which connects the independent (primary) degrees of freedom. A value for this parameter can be specified or the default value D/L = 0.1 will be taken if the field is blank. The value is of interest only if the RSPLINE connects grid points which do not lie on a straight line. In that case bending and torsional moments are coupled and some difference in the behavior of the RSPLINE element will be observed if D/L is changed. The default is recommended unless the user has a specific reason to use another value.

9.11.5.1.   Example — Change of Mesh Size Using RSPLINE

Finite element meshes should be relatively fine (i.e. many elements) in regions of high strain gradient and may be relatively coarse in other regions of the structure. The use of a transition region as shown by Fig. 9-47a is a traditional technique for changing mesh size.

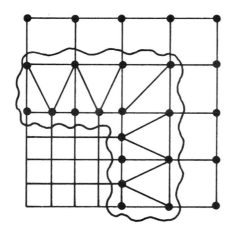

a) Change of Mesh Size using Transition Region

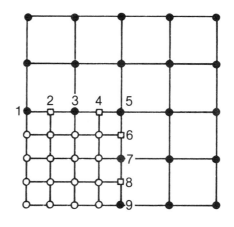

b) Change of Mesh Size using RSPLINE Interpolation

Figure 9-47. Use of RSPLINE to Change Mesh Size

The RSPLINE elastic interpolation element provides the analyst with an alternate approach as shown by Fig. 9-47b which eliminates the complicated model associated with the transition in Fig. 9-47a. The RSPLINE element in this case is passed through primary points 1, 3, 5, 7, and 9 and the displacement degrees of freedom at secondary points 2, 4, 6, and 8 are interpolated from the spline fit. The RSPLINE elastic interpolation element required to model the mesh transition shown by Fig. 9-47b could be defined by the following Bulk Data.

1	2	3	4	5	6	7	8	9	10
RSPLINE	151		1	2	123456	3		4	+RS1
+RS1	123456	5		6	123456	7		8	+RS2
+RS2	123456	9							

where

1. The default value for D/L has been taken since the D/L field is blank

2. The G1 field specifies the grid point 1 is at one end of the RSPLINE element

3. The C-field associated with primary grid points 3, 5, 7, and 9 are blank so that the degrees of freedom at these points are used to define the elastic spline fit.

4. The C-field associated with secondary grid points 2, 4, and 6 contain the packed code 123456 so that all six degrees of freedom at these points are to be interpolated by using the equation for the spline fit.

5. Grid point 9 is the last entry and is thus taken to be at the last point on the RSPLINE element.

9.11.6. Weighted Average Constraint Element — RBE3

The RBE3 constraint element which is described by the Bulk Data shown on Card Image 9-18 provides a means of specifying that the value of selected degrees of freedom is to be a weighted average of displacement of the other degrees of freedom

1	2	3	4	5	6	7	8	9	10
RBE3	EID		GREF	CREF	W_i	C_i	$G1_i$	$G2_i$	+1
+1	$G3_i$	W_j	C_j	$G1_j$	$G2_j$	W_k	C_k	$G1_k$	+2
+2	...								+3
+3	UM	GM1	CM1	GM2	CM2	GM3	CM3		+4
+4		GM4	CM4	GM5	CM5	GM6	CM6		

Card Image 9-18. Weighted Average Constraint Element — RBE3

The form of the RBE3 constraint element allows the user to define the motion of a reference point by

1. Specifying the reference point using the fields
   GREF — the reference grid point
   CREF — the degrees of freedom at the reference grid point.

2. Specifying weighting factors, W_i.

3. Specifying degrees of freedoms associated with the weighting factors by first specifying the degree of freedom code, C_i, followed by the grid point identification numbers of which the degree of freedom, C_i, are to be given the weight W_i.

4. Specifying up to six degrees of freedom which are to be placed in the m-set. These (the m-set) degrees of freedom may be specified as follows

   a. The default m-set includes the degrees of freedom specified at the reference point.

   b. The m-set can be explicitly defined by placing the literal string UM in field two of a continuation card after the definition of the weighting factors and associated degrees of freedom. The literal string (UM) is then followed by pairs (GM, CM) which specify one or more degrees of freedom (CM) at the grid point (GM) that are to be included in the m-set.

265

A set of linear equations is then formed by taking the displacement of the reference point to be the weighted average of the set of independent displacements. The m-set is then taken to be the reference set by default or those degrees of freedom explicitly defined as the m-set. If the m-set is explicitly defined then

a. The total number of degrees of freedom in the m-set must be the same as the number of degrees of freedom defined at the reference point.
b. The degrees of freedom must be a subset of those at the reference and the weighted grid points.
c. The coefficient matrix of the m-set, $\mathbf{R}_{mm}$, must be nonsingular.

9.11.6.1.   Example — "Beaming" Loads and Masses

The user will often have to "transfer" loads and masses from a reference node, which may not be part of the structural model, to nodes which are part of the model. Consider the cross-section of a cylindrical shell as shown by Fig. 9-48 where the total mass of the adjacent structure and the associated center of gravity is at node 100 which lies on the axis of the cylinder. This mass and inertia must be distributed to the structural nodes 1 through 6. The following RBE3 element will properly distribute the mass *equally* to the six nodes on the shell.

1	2	3	4	5	6	7	8	9	10
RBE3	74		100	123456	1.	123	1	2	+ BC

1	2	3	4	5	6	7	8	9	10
+ BC	3	4	5	6					

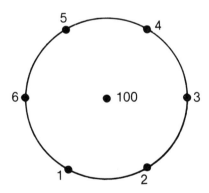

Figure 9-48. Circular Cross-Section

The mass could be defined by means of a CONM2 Bulk Data card which references point 100. Note that degrees of freedom 1 through 6 of point 100 are dependent while all components at nodes 1 through 6 are independent. The displacements of node 100 represent the weighted average motions at nodes 1 through 6.

We might also consider the case where the mass is to be distributed to the nodes on the cylinder but where 2/3 of the total mass is to be equally distributed to nodes 2 through 4 and that 1/3 of the total mass is to be equally distributed to points 1, 5, and 6. The associated RBE3 bulk data is then

1	2	3	4	5	6	7	8	9	10
RBE3	75		100	123456	2.	123	2	3	+ EF

1	2	3	4	5	6	7	8	9	10
+ EF	4	1.	123	1	5	6			

Applied static or dynamic loads can be distributed to structural degrees of freedom by means of the same technique. For example, if loads are defined at point 100 then the first RBE3 which was defined in this section would equally distribute the loads to points 1 through 6.

The degrees of freedom at the reference point are generally included in the m-set. In some modeling situations the degrees of freedom at the reference point must be included in the n-set. In these cases the user can explicitly define the degrees of freedom in the m-set. For example, the following RBE3 element will evenly distribute loads at the reference point to the structure

1	2	3	4	5	6	7	8	9	10
RBE3	74		100	123	1.	123	1	2	+ EF

1	2	3	4	5	6	7	8	9	10
+ EF	3	4	5	6					+ HI

1	2	3	4	5	6	7	8	9	10
+ HI	UM	6	123						

In this case the first two physical cards are similar to the first example discussed above except that here the RBE3 element is connected to only the three translational degrees of freedom of the reference grid point. The last card has been added to define components 123 of node 6 as dependent. Now components 123 of node 100 are included in the n-set and can thus be included in a removed data set or if not removed will be included in the analysis set.

Any of the digits 1-6 may be used in the REFC field. Omission of any of these digits merely indicates that the RBE3 element is not connected to that degree of freedom. The recommended values for the C fields are the digits 1-3. While the digits 4-6 may be used in these fields, determination of proper weighting factors is much more difficult as the ratios between translation and rotational weighting factors are related to the dimensions of the structure which is connected by the RBE3 element.

9.12. Congruent Elements

Congruent elements can be defined to designate secondary elements that are identical to a primary element. The congruent elements are defined using the CNGRNT Bulk Data card, which is shown in Card Image 9-19.

1	2	3	4	5	6	7	8	9	10
CNGRNT	PRID	SECID1	SECID2	SECID3	SECID4	SECID5	SECID6	SECID7	+C1
+C1	SECID8	SECID9	etc.						

*Alternate Form

1	2	3	4	5	6	7	8	9	10
CNGRNT	PRID	SECID1	THRU	SECID2					

Card Image 9-19. Specification of Identical Elements

9.13. References

where the fields are defined as

PRID Identification number of the primary element for which elemental properties will be calculated

SECIDi Element identification numbers of secondary elements whose elemental properties will be identical to the primary element

9.13. References

9-1   Roark, R.J., *Formulas for Stress and Strain*, McGraw-Hill, Third Edition, 1954, pp. 119-121.
9-2   Przemieniecki, J.S., *Theory of Matrix Structural Analysis*, McGraw-Hill, 1965, pp. 79.
9-3   *NASTRAN Programmers Manual*, NASA SP-223(01) pp. 4.87-21 through -23.
9-4   Rivello, R.M., *Theory and Analysis of Flight Structures*, McGraw-Hill, 1969, pp. 241-246.
9-5   Roark, R.J., *Formulas for Stress and Strain*, McGraw-Hill, Third Edition 1954, pp. 129-130.
9-6   *MSC/NASTRAN Application Manual*, MacNeal-Schwendler Corp., 1977, p. 2.6-19.
9-7   Seeley, F.B., and Smith, J.O., *Advanced Mechanics of Materials*, Wiley & Sons, 2nd Edition, 1952, pp. 139-144.
9-8   Ashton, J.E., Halpin, J.C., and Petit, P.H., *Primer on Composite Materials: Analysis*, Technomic, 1969, pp. 37-45.
9-9   Jones, R.M., *Mechanics of Composite Material*, McGraw-Hill, 1975, pp. 147-173.
9-10   MacNeal, R.H., "A Simple Quadrilateral Shell Element", Computers & Structures, Vol. 8, pp. 175-183, Pergamon 1978.

10
Material Properties

The constitutive equations as well as other material properties are described in this chapter. Constitutive relations may be of the following types in MSC/NASTRAN:

1. Isotropic temperature-dependent material

2. Anisotropic temperature-dependent material for two- and three-dimensional elements.

Temperature-independent properties are defined using MATi Bulk Data cards. Temperature dependence of properties is then prescribed by MATTi Bulk Data, which define pointers to appropriate material tables on which the temperature dependence is defined.

The MSC/NASTRAN Bulk Data cards that are used to specify material properties are summarized in Table 10-1.

CARD NAME	DESCRIPTION
MAT1	Linear, temperature-independent, isotropic material
MAT2	Linear, temperature-independent, anisotropic material for two-dimensional elements
MAT8	Linear, temperature-independent, orthotrophic material for two-dimensional elements
MAT9	Linear, temperature-independent, anisotropic material for three-dimensional elements
MATT1	Specifies table references for temperature-dependent material properties in conjunction with MAT1
MATT2	Specifies temperature-dependent material properties in conjunction with MAT2
MATT9	Specifies temperature-dependent material properties in conjunction with MAT9

Table 10-1. Material Specifications for Structural Analysis

The allowable material relations for the recommended MSC/NASTRAN elements are summarized in Table 10-2.

Element type	Material Type		
	MAT1	MAT2	MAT9
BAR	X		
BEAM	X		
BEND	X		
HEXA	X		X
PENTA	X		X
QUAD4	X	X	
QUAD8	X	X	
ROD	X		
SHEAR	X		
TRIA3	X	X	
TRIA6	X	X	
TUBE	X		

Table 10-2. Allowable Material Relations for Structural Elements in MSC/NASTRAN.

10.1. Isotropic Material

Material properties for a linear, temperature-independent isotropic material are specified on a MAT1 card, which is shown in Card Image 10-1.

1	2	3	4	5	6	7	8	9	10
MAT1	MID	E	G	NU	RH	A	TREF	GE	+ AB
+ AB	ST	SC	SS	MCSID					

where

MID Material identification number (integer, >0)

E Modulus of elasticity (real, >0. or blank)

G Shear modulus (real, >0. or blank)

NU Poisson's ratio (− 1.0<NU≤0.5, real or blank)

RH Mass density (real)

A Coefficient of thermal expansion (real)

TREF Reference temperature for thermal expansion (real)

GE Structural element damping coefficient (real)

ST, SC, SS Stress limits for tension, compression, and shear (real). Used to compute margins of safety in certain elements and have no effect on computational procedures.

MCSID Coordinate System with respect to which material properties are defined

Card Image 10-1. Isotropic Material Property Definition

Features of the MAT1 card are

1. The MID must be unique among all MATi-type cards.

2. The mass density RH is used to calculate the structural mass matrix for all elements with a defined volume. Alternatively, the weight density may be specified and is converted to mass density by means of a PARAM card whose parameter name is WTMASS, which has the value 1/g where g is the acceleration of gravity (see Appendix B for parameters).

3. If E and NU, or G and NU, are both blank, they will be set equal to zero. If two of the three coefficients are defined, the remaining coefficient is calculated using the isotropic relation (see Eq. 10.4).

10.1.1. One-Dimensional Elements

The constitutive relations for the one-dimensional element is of the form

$$\sigma_{xx} = E\,(e_{xx} - \alpha\,\Delta T) \tag{10.1}$$

where E is the modulus of elasticity, α is the coefficient of thermal expansion, and $\Delta T = T - T_{ref}$. The only elastic constant that needs to be specified for the ROD and BAR elements is the modulus E. The shear modulus and Poisson's ratio may be left blank.

10.1.2. Two-Dimensional Elements — Plane Stress

The isotropic constitutive relations for the plane stress formulation are of the form

$$\sigma = E\,(e - \alpha\,\Delta T) \tag{10.2}$$

where

$$\sigma = [\,\sigma_{xx}\ \sigma_{yy}\ \sigma_{xy}\,]^T$$

$$e = [\,e_{xx}\ e_{yy}\ e_{xy}\,]^T$$

$$\alpha = [\,\alpha\ \alpha\ 0]^T$$

$$E = \begin{bmatrix} \dfrac{E}{(1-\nu^2)} & \dfrac{\nu E}{(1-\nu^2)} & 0 \\[2ex] \dfrac{\nu E}{(1-\nu^2)} & \dfrac{E}{(1-\nu^2)} & 0 \\[2ex] 0 & 0 & G \end{bmatrix} \tag{10.3}$$

and

E Modulus of Elasticity

ν Poisson's ratio

G Shear modulus

α Coefficient of thermal expansion

ΔT Temperature change, $T - T_{ref}$

10.1   Isotropic Material

For an isotropic material, only two of the three material coefficients are independent since

$$G = \frac{E}{2(1+\nu)} \tag{10.4}$$

10.1.3.   Two-Dimensional Elements — Plane Strain

The isotropic constitutive relations for the plane strain formulation are of the form

$$\sigma = E' (e - \alpha' \Delta T) \tag{10.5}$$

where

$$E' = \frac{E}{(1+\nu)(1-2\nu)} \begin{bmatrix} (1-\nu) & \nu & 0 \\ \nu & (1-\nu) & 0 \\ 0 & 0 & \frac{(1-2\nu)}{2} \end{bmatrix} \tag{10.6}$$

$$\alpha' = (1+\nu) [\, \alpha \;\; \alpha \;\; 0 \,]$$

The material properties for plane strain can be specified by using the MAT1 Bulk Data card if E, ν, and α are replaced by E', ν', and α' where

$$E' = \frac{E}{(1 - \nu^2)}$$

$$\nu' = \frac{\nu}{(1-\nu)} \tag{10.7}$$

$$\alpha' = (1+\nu)\,\alpha$$

10.1.4.   Three-Dimensional Elements

The constitutive relations for the three-dimensional case are

$$\sigma = E(e - \alpha \Delta T) \tag{10.8}$$

$$\sigma = [\, \sigma_{xx} \;\; \sigma_{yy} \;\; \sigma_{zz} \;\; \sigma_{xy} \;\; \sigma_{yz} \;\; \sigma_{zx} \,]^{T}$$

where

$$e = [\, e_{xx} \;\; e_{yy} \;\; e_{zz} \;\; e_{xy} \;\; e_{yz} \;\; e_{zx} \,]^{T}$$

$$\alpha = [\, \alpha \;\; \alpha \;\; \alpha \;\; 0 \;\; 0 \;\; 0 \,]^{T}$$

272

$$E = -\frac{1}{(1-\nu^2)}\begin{bmatrix} 1 & \nu & \nu & 0 & 0 & 0 \\ \nu & 1 & \nu & 0 & 0 & 0 \\ \nu & \nu & 1 & 0 & 0 & 0 \\ 0 & 0 & 0 & \frac{(1-\nu)}{2} & 0 & 0 \\ 0 & 0 & 0 & 0 & \frac{(1-\nu)}{2} & 0 \\ 0 & 0 & 0 & 0 & 0 & \frac{(1-\nu)}{2} \end{bmatrix} \qquad (10.9)$$

10.2. Anisotropic Material for Two-Dimensional Elements

The material coefficients for a linear temperature-independent anisotropic material are shown in Card Image 10-2.

1	2	3	4	5	6	7	8	9	10
MAT2 + ABC + CDE	MID A_1 MCSID	G_{11} A_2	G_{12} A_{12}	G_{13} TREF	G_{22} GE	G_{23} ST	G_{33} SC	RH SS	+ ABC + CDE

where

    G_{ij} Elements of elasticity matrix

    A_i Elements of thermal expansion vector

Card Image 10-2. Anisotropic Material for Two-Dimensional Elements

The general anisotropic relationship is of the form

$$\sigma = E\,(e - \alpha\Delta T) \qquad (10.10)$$

where

$$\sigma = [\,\sigma_{xx}\ \ \sigma_{yy}\ \ \sigma_{xy}\,]^T$$
$$e = [\,e_{xx}\ \ e_{yy}\ \ e_{xy}\,]^T$$
$$\alpha = [\,\alpha_1\ \ \alpha_2\ \ \alpha_3\,]^T$$

$$E = \begin{bmatrix} G_{11} & G_{12} & G_{13} \\ G_{21} & G_{22} & G_{23} \\ G_{31} & G_{32} & G_{33} \end{bmatrix} \qquad (10.11)$$

and where E is a symmetric matrix.

273

10.2 Anisotropic Material for Two-Dimensional Elements

10.2.1. Orthotropic Material Properties

The orthotropic relations for two-dimensional behavior are given by

$$
\begin{Bmatrix} \sigma_{xx} \\ \sigma_{yy} \\ \sigma_{xy} \end{Bmatrix}
=
\begin{bmatrix} G_{11} & G_{12} & 0 \\ G_{12} & G_{22} & 0 \\ 0 & 0 & G_{33} \end{bmatrix}
\left(\begin{Bmatrix} e_{xx} \\ e_{yy} \\ e_{xy} \end{Bmatrix} - \Delta T \begin{Bmatrix} \alpha_1 \\ \alpha_2 \\ 0 \end{Bmatrix} \right)
\tag{10.12}
$$

The orthotropic material coefficients are defined relative to a specific set of axes which are called the material axes in MSC/NASTRAN. The elastic coefficients are given in terms of engineering constants as

$$
G_{11} = \frac{E_x}{(1-\nu_{xy}\,\nu_{yx})}
$$

$$
G_{12} = \frac{\nu_{xy}\,E_y}{(1-\nu_{xy}\,\nu_{yx})} = \frac{\nu_{yx}\,E_x}{(1-\nu_{xy}\,\nu_{yx})}
\tag{10.13}
$$

$$
G_{22} = \frac{E_y}{(1-\nu_{xy}\,\nu_{yx})}
$$

where

E_x Elastic modulus in the direction of the x material axis.

E_y Elastic modulus in the direction of the y material axis.

ν_{xy} Poisson's ratio for transverse strain in the y-direction when stress is applied in the x-direction.

ν_{yx} Poisson's ratio for transverse strain in the x-direction when stress is applied in the y-direction.

G_{33} Shear modulus

α_1 Coefficient of thermal expansion in the x-direction

α_2 Thermal expansion coefficient in the y-direction

10.2.1.1. Example: Orthotropic Material

The properties of an E-glass epoxy lamina are

$$E_x = 7.8 \times 10^6 \text{ psi} \qquad E_y = 2.6 \times 10^6 \text{ psi}$$

$$\nu_{xy} = 0.25 \qquad G_{33} = 1.25 \times 10^6 \text{ psi}$$

$$\alpha_1 = 3.5 \times 10^{-6} \text{ in./in.} -°F \qquad \alpha_2 = 11.4 \times 10^{-6} \text{ in./in.} -°F$$

274

The stress limits for a composite material are generally vastly different in the directions of the material axes since one axis is aligned parallel to the fiber direction and one axis is transverse to the fiber direction. Typical values for the lamina strengths in strength of E-glass are

$$X_T = X_c = 150 \times 10^3 \text{ psi}$$

$$Y_T = 4 \times 10^3 \text{ psi}$$

$$Y_c = 20 \times 10^3 \text{ psi}$$

$$S = 6 \times 10^3 \text{ psi}$$

where

(X_T, X_c) Tensile and compressive strengths in the fiber direction

(Y_T, Y_c) Tensile and compressive strengths transverse to fiber direction

S Shear strength

For the purpose of this example, we will assume that the longitudinal stress is of interest, and we will therefore take the following stress limits:

$$ST = 150 \times 10^3 \text{ psi}$$

$$SC = 150 \times 10^3 \text{ psi}$$

$$SS = 6 \times 10^3 \text{ psi}$$

The elastic constants are calculated by first noting that the missing Poisson's ratio can be calculated using the second of (10.13) to give

$$\nu_{yx} = \frac{\nu_{xy} E_y}{E_x} = 0.083$$

We then find

$$G_{11} = 7.965 \times 10^6 \text{ psi}$$

$$G_{12} = 0.664 \times 10^6 \text{ psi}$$

$$G_{22} = 2.655 \times 10^6 \text{ psi}$$

These material properties can be defined on a MAT2 Bulk Data card as follows:

1	2	3	4	5	6	7	8	9	10
MAT2	101	7.965E6	0.664E6	0.	2.655E6	0.	1.25E6	0.	+M1
+M1	3.5E-6	11.4E-6	0.	72.		1.5E5	1.5E5	6.0E3	

10.3   Orthotropic Material for Two-Dimensional Component Elements

The calculation of the coefficients of the elastic matrix using (10.13) can be eliminated if we use the MAT8 Bulk Data, as shown by Card Image 10-3, which allows us to specify engineering material constants.

1	2	3	4	5	6	7	8	9	10
MAT8	MID	E_1	E_2	ν_{12}	G_{12}	G_{1z}	G_{2z}	RHO	+ M1
+ M1	α_1	α_2	T_{ref}	X_t	X_c	Y_t	Y_c	S	+ M2
+ M2	G_e	F_{12}							

Card Image 10.3. Orthotropic Two-Dimensional Material Properties

The MAT8 material specification is used in conjunction with the PCOMP property card, which is described in Sec. 9.9.1.2.5, for thin shell elements to define the lamina properties with respect to a set of principal material axes (X_1, X_2). The elastic constants with respect to the material coordinates are then defined by (10.11) and are transformed by using the lamina orientation angle θ, which is defined on PCOMP Bulk Data, by using appropriate transformation equations (see Ref 10-1, for example).

The material coefficients that are specified by MAT8 Bulk Data are described as follows

E_1, E_2 Modulus of Elasticity along and normal to the fiber direction, respectively (real $\neq 0$)

ν_{12} Poisson's ratio (e_2 / e_1, for loading in the 1-direction). The poisson's ratio ν_{21} is related to ν_{12} by the equation $\nu_{12}E_2 = \nu_2E_1$. (real)

G_{12} Inplane shear modulus. (real $\neq 0$.)

G_{1z},G_{2z} Transverse shear modulae (real or blank)

RHO Mass Density (real or blank)

α_1,α_2 Coefficients of thermal expansion in 1− and 2− directions. (real or blank)

T_{ref} Reference temperature for calculation of thermal expansion

X_t,X_c Allowable stress in tension and compression, respectively, in the fiber direction. (real or blank)

Y_t,Y_c Allowable stress in tension and compression, respectively, normal to fiber direction. (real or blank)

S Allowable Shear stress (real or blank)

G_e Structural damping coefficient. (real or blank)

F_{12} Interaction term in tensor polynomial for Tsai-Wu. (real or blank)

10.4.   Anisotropic Material for Three-Dimensional Elements

The material coefficients for a linear temperature-independent three dimensional material are defined using the MAT9 Bulk Data card shown on Card Image 10-4. The only elements that can reference this material formulation are the PENTA and HEXA three-dimensional isoparametric elements.

1	2	3	4	5	6	7	8	9	10
MAT9	MID	C_{11}	C_{12}	C_{13}	C_{14}	C_{15}	C_{16}	C_{22}	+ M1
+ M1	C_{23}	C_{24}	C_{25}	C_{26}	C_{33}	C_{34}	C_{35}	C_{36}	+ M2
+ M2	C_{44}	C_{45}	C_{46}	C_{55}	C_{56}	C_{66}	RH	A_1	+ M3
+ M3	A_2	A_3	A_4	A_5	A_6	TREF	GE		

Card Image 10-4. Anisotropic Material for Three-Dimensional Elements

The general form of the elastic relationshhip for three-dimensional elements in a three-dimensional stress state is given by

$$\sigma = \mathbf{E}\,(\mathbf{e} - \alpha \Delta T) \tag{10.14}$$

where

$$\sigma = \lfloor \sigma_{xx} \ \sigma_{yy} \ \sigma_{zz} \ \sigma_{xy} \ \sigma_{yz} \ \sigma_{zx} \rfloor^T$$

$$\mathbf{e} = \lfloor e_{xx} \ e_{yy} \ e_{zz} \ e_{xy} \ e_{yz} \ e_{zx} \rfloor^T$$

and where the elastic constants, $\mathbf{E}$, and the coefficients of thermal expansion, α, are full arrays as shown below

$$\mathbf{E} = \begin{bmatrix} C_{11} & C_{12} & C_{13} & C_{14} & C_{15} & C_{16} \\ C_{21} & C_{22} & C_{23} & C_{24} & C_{25} & C_{26} \\ C_{31} & C_{32} & C_{33} & C_{34} & C_{35} & C_{36} \\ C_{41} & C_{42} & C_{43} & C_{44} & C_{45} & C_{46} \\ C_{51} & C_{52} & C_{53} & C_{54} & C_{55} & C_{56} \\ C_{61} & C_{62} & C_{63} & C_{64} & C_{65} & C_{66} \end{bmatrix} \tag{10.15}$$

and

$$\alpha = \begin{bmatrix} \alpha_1 & \alpha_2 & \alpha_3 & \alpha_4 & \alpha_5 & \alpha_6 \end{bmatrix}^T \tag{10.16}$$

The upper triangular half of the $\mathbf{E}$ matrix, which is symmetric, is specified on the MAT9 Bulk Data Card by the fields C_{11}, C_{12}, C_{13},..., C_{66} and the elements of the thermal coefficient vector are defined by the fields A_1, A_2, A_3,..., A_6. The elastic constants for orthotropic materials are defined in terms of elastic modulae and Poisson's ratio in Sec. 10.4.1.

The form of the MAT9 Bulk Data card thus allows the user to define an anisotropic material having twenty-one independent material coefficients. The inclusion of the six components of the thermal expansion vector allows the definition of transformed material coefficients.

10.4.1.   Orthotropic Constants for Three-Dimensional Elements

Engineering materials having orthotropic properties are finding increased application in the design of structural systems. An orthotropic material is completely defined by nine independent elastic constants. The most common elastic constants are the following

- Elastic modulae, E_1, E_2, E_3 in three orthogonal directions
- Poisson's ratios, ν_{ij}, for transverse strain in the j-directions due to stress in i-direction.
- Shear moduli, G_{12}, G_{23}, G_{31} in the 1-2, 2-3, and 3-1 planes, respectively.

The inverse of the elastic matrix which is called the compliance matrix, S, is then given by

$$
S = E^{-1} = \begin{bmatrix}
\frac{1}{E_1} & -\frac{\nu_{21}}{E_2} & -\frac{\nu_{31}}{E_3} & 0 & 0 & 0 \\
-\frac{\nu_{12}}{E_1} & \frac{1}{E_2} & -\frac{\nu_{32}}{E_3} & 0 & 0 & 0 \\
-\frac{\nu_{13}}{E_1} & -\frac{\nu_{23}}{E_2} & \frac{1}{E_3} & 0 & 0 & 0 \\
0 & 0 & 0 & \frac{1}{G_{12}} & 0 & 0 \\
0 & 0 & 0 & 0 & \frac{1}{G_{23}} & 0 \\
0 & 0 & 0 & 0 & 0 & \frac{1}{G_{31}}
\end{bmatrix}
\tag{10.17}
$$

The compliance matrix is symmetric so that the following symmetry relations must hold

$$\nu_{12}E_2 = \nu_{21}E_1$$

$$\nu_{23}E_3 = \nu_{32}E_2 \tag{10.18}$$

$$\nu_{31}E_1 = \nu_{13}E_3$$

The nonzero stiffness coefficients, C_{ij}, are found by inverting the compliance matrix (10.17) and are

$$C_{11} = \frac{1-\nu_{23}\nu_{32}}{C\,E_2E_3} \qquad C_{22} = \frac{1-\nu_{31}\nu_{13}}{C\,E_3E_1} \qquad C_{44} = G_{12}$$

$$C_{12} = \frac{\nu_{12}+\nu_{32}\nu_{13}}{C\,E_1E_3} \qquad C_{23} = \frac{\nu_{23}+\nu_{21}\nu_{13}}{C\,E_1E_2} \qquad C_{55} = G_{23} \tag{10.19}$$

$$C_{13} = \frac{\nu_{13}+\nu_{12}\nu_{23}}{C\,E_1E_2} \qquad C_{33} = \frac{1-\nu_{12}\nu_{21}}{C\,E_1E_2} \qquad C_{66} = G_{31}$$

where

$$C = \frac{1 - \nu_{12}\nu_{21} - \nu_{23}\nu_{32} - \nu_{31}\nu_{13} - 2\nu_{21}\nu_{32}\nu_{13}}{E_1 E_2 E_3} \qquad (10.20)$$

10.4.2. Transformation of Elastic Constants

The elastic constants for non-isotropic materials must be defined with respect to a specific set of coordinates. The user then specifies both a material set identification number and the coordinate identification number associated with the material coefficients on a PSOLID Bulk Data card as shown by Card Image 9-12. The capability of specifying coordinate systems using the CORD-type Bulk Data and the reference system used on the PSOLID relieves the analyst from the burden of transforming elastic constants from one coordinate system to another.

10.5 Temperature-Dependent Materials

10.5.1. MATTi Cards

Any of the temperature-independent material property fields specifed on the MAT1, MAT2, or MAT9 cards can be made temperature dependent by means of MATTi cards, as shown in Card Image 10-5.

1	2	3	4	5	6	7	8	9	10
MATT1	MID	R1	R2	R3	R4	R5	R6	R7	+ M1
+ M1	R8	R9	R10						
MATT2	MID	R1	R2	R3	R4	R5	R6	R7	+ M2
+ M2	R8	R9	R10	R11	R12	R13	R14	R15	
MATT9	MID	R1	R2	R3	R4	R5	R6	R7	+ M3
+ M3	R8	R9	R10	R11	R12	R13	R14	R15	+ M4
+ M4	R16	R17	R18	R19	R20	R21	R22	R23	+ M5
+ M5	R24	R25	R26	R27	R28		R30		

where

> MID   Matches the MID on an appropriate MAT1, MAT2, or MAT9 Bulk Data card (integer, > 0)

> Rj   Set number of a TABLEMi-type Bulk Data card on which the temperature dependence of the material property in the corresponding field of the appropriate MAT-type card is defined. (integer, > 0)

Card Image 10-5. Specification of Temperature-Dependent Material Properties

The form of all three MATTi cards is the same. The MID of the MATTi card must match the MID on the corresponding MATi card whose properties are to be made temperature dependent. The temperature-dependence of a specific property is then defined by reference to an appropriate table in the field of the MATTi card associated with the temperature-dependent property. Blank or zero entries in the table reference field of MATTi are taken to mean that the property on the associated MATi card is temperature independent.

10.5.2. Material Property Table

The temperature dependence of material properties is defined by means of material property tables. Each of the four types of TABLEMi cards that are shown in Card Image 10-6 uses a different table look-up algorithm. The algorithms are defined in Table 10-3.

10.5 Temperature-Dependent Materials

1	2	3	4	5	6	7	8	9	10
TABLEM1	ID								+M1
+M1	T_1	P_1	T_2	P_2	T_3	P_3	ENDT		
TABLEM2	ID	T_a							+M2
+M2	T_1	P_1	T_2	P_2	T_3	P_3	ENDT		
TABLEM3	ID	T_a	T_b						+M3
+M3	T_1	P_1	T_2	P_2	T_3	P_3	ENDT		
TABLEM4	ID	T_a	T_b	T_L	T_u				+M4
+M4	A_0	A_1	A_2	A_3	etc.	ENDT			

where

ID Table set number (integer, >0)

T_i, P_i Table entries

T_a, T_b, T_u, T_L Table parameters (real, $T_b \neq 0.$, $T_L < T_u$)

$A_i (i = 0,1,...,n)$ Power series coefficients (real)

Card Image 10-6. Temperature-Dependent Material Property Tables

TABLE TYPE	ALGORITHM
TABLEM1	$P = Y_T (T)$
TABLEM2	$P = P_o\ Y_T (T - T_a)$
TABLEM3	$P = P_o\ Y_T \left(\dfrac{T - T_a}{T_b} \right)$
TABLEM4	$P = P_o \displaystyle\sum_{i=0}^{N} A_i \left(\dfrac{T - T_a}{T_b} \right)^i$

Table 10-3. Algorithms Used for Material Tables

Features of the TABLEMi cards are

1. At least two entries must exist for tables TABLEMi ($i = 1,2,3$).

2. At least one entry must exist for TABLEM4.

3. Tables must be terminated with the alphabetic string 'ENDT' in the field following the last entry.

4. The table temperatures must define either an ascending or descending sequence.

TABLEM1 provides a simple tabular look-up. The pairs (T_i, P_i) are specified where T is the temperature and P is the associated material property. The table look-up evaluates the property P at temperature T by using linear interpolation within the table and linear extrapolation outside the table based on the last two points at the end of the table. A discontinuous material property may be defined at a specific temperature, as indicated in Fig. 10-1.

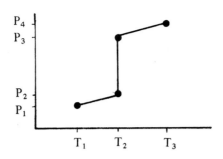

Figure 10-1. Allowable Variation in Material Property

Discontinuities may not be defined at the endpoints of the table and the average value of the property is taken at the jump. For example, at $T = T_2$

$$P(T_2) = \frac{P_3 + P_2}{2}$$

TABLEM2 is similar to TABLEM1 except that tabulated values are used to scale the basic property value P_o defined on the MATi card that is referenced on the MATTi card. The inclusion of a reference temperature T_a is an added convenience since many material properties are defined relative to room temperature. TABLEM3 card is similar to the TABLEM2 card, except that the temperature is normalized with respect to the parameter T_b.

TABLEM4 allows the analyst to define the temperature-dependent property using a power series in the normalized independent variable $t = (T - T_a)/T_b$. As in TABLEM2 and TABLEM3, the reference value of the property P_o is defined on the appropriate field of the MATi card. However, in using the TABLEM4 card to define the property, the analyst must supply the coefficients of a power series expansion on continuation cards if the coefficients are positionally dependent. That is, the first coefficient A_o must appear in the second field of the continuation card, followed by $A_1, A_2,...,A_n$. If one of the coefficients is zero, then a zero entry must be included in the corresponding field. The parameters T_L and T_u are upper and lower temperature limits that are defined as

$$T = \begin{array}{l} T_L \text{ if } T < T_L \\ T_u \text{ if } T > T_u \end{array}$$

10.5.3. Example: Temperature-Dependent Modulus of Elasticity

Consider the temperature-dependent modulus of elasticity that is shown in Fig. 10-2. The isotropic room temperature properties are

$$E = 10 \times 10^6 \text{ psi}$$

$$\nu = 0.3$$

$$\alpha = 7 \times 10^{-6} \text{ in./in.} - {}^\circ F$$

$$\gamma = 0.1 \text{ lb}_f/\text{in.}^3$$

$$T_{ref} = 72^\circ$$

281

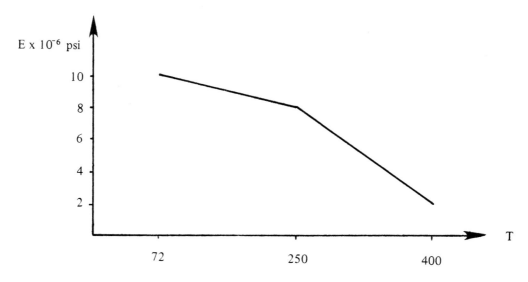

Figure 10-2. Temperature-Dependent Elastic Modulus

The data set required to specify this material with temperature dependence of E is

1	2	3	4	5	6	7	8	9	10
MAT1	1	1.E7	0.	.3	.1	7.E-6	72.		
MATT1	1	37							
TABLEM1	37								+ TM1
+ TM1	72.	1.E7	250.	.8E7	400.	2.E6	ENDT		

where

1. The MATT1 card has the same MID as the MAT1 card.

2. The temperature table number is entered in the field of MATT1 that corresponds to the modulus of elasticity E and points to a TABLEM1 card whose identification number is 37.

3. The table must be terminated by the alphabetic string 'ENDT' in the field following the last entry.

The temperature-dependent modulus could have been defined using a TABLEM2 card:

1	2	3	4	5	6	7	8	9	10
TABLEM2	37	72.							+ TM2
+ TM2	0.	1.	178.	.8	328.	.2	ENDT		

where the table temperatures have been reduced by the value of the reference temperature and the property entries have been normalized with respect to the value on the MAT1 card.

282

10.6. References

10-1 Jones, R. M., *Mechanics of Composite Materials*, McGraw-Hill, 1975, pp. 147-164.

10-2 Isakson, G., Pardo, H., and Letner, E., "ASOP-3: A Program for Optimum Design of Metallic and Composite Structures Subjected to Strength and Deflection Constraints," Paper 77-378, presented at AIAA/ASME 18th Structures, Structural Dynamics, and Materials Conference, San Diego, California 1977.

11

Static External Loads

The loads that are applied to a structure may result from a variety of effects, including

1. Concentrated contact forces

2. Applied surface forces

3. Distributed body forces

4. Enforced grid point displacement

5. Enforced element deformation

6. Thermal fields

The total load applied to each element is shown in Chapter Six to be the superposition of all these various loading terms so that the total element load is given by

$$P_{eT} = P_e + P_{eX} + P_{eS} + P_{eI} \tag{11.1}$$

where P_e are the concentrated loads applied to the grid points and where P_{eX}, P_{eS}, and P_{eI} are the work equivalent grid point forces associated with body forces, surface tractions and initial strains as given by (6.42), (6.43), and (6.44), respectively.

The MSC/NASTRAN Bulk Data for specifying loads are summarized by Table 11-1. These Bulk Data cards allow the user to specify concentrated forces and moments at the grid points, scalar forces, distributed body forces due to gravity and centrifugal acceleration fields, enforced grid point displacements, enforced element deformations, and temperature fields. These various types of structural loading are described in subsequent sections of this chapter.

11.1.   Concentrated External Forces at Grid Points

Concentrated force and moment vectors can be defined at geometric grid points in the following alternative ways:

1. Specification of the grid point G at which the vector acts and the vector components, as shown in Fig. 11-1a.

2. Specification of the grid point G at which the vector acts and the sense of the vector using two geometric grid points, as shown in Fig. 11-1b.

3. Specification of the geometric grid point G at which the vector acts with the vector direction specified as the cross product of two vectors, as shown in Fig. 11-1c.

11.1   Concentrated External Forces at Grid Points

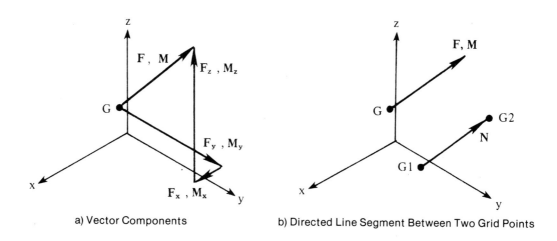

a) Vector Components   b) Directed Line Segment Between Two Grid Points

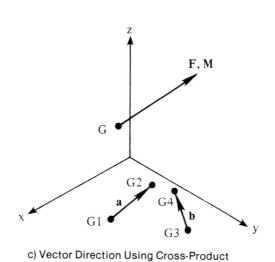

c) Vector Direction Using Cross-Product

Figure 11-1. Definition of Concentrated Force and Moments

LOAD TYPE	DESCRIPTION
FORCE MOMENT	Defines a static load, applied to a geometric grid point in terms of vector components which are defined with respect to a specified coordinate system.
FORCE1 MOMENT1	Defines a static load by specifying a magnitude and two grid points which determine the direction
FORCE2 MOMENT2	Defines a static load by specifying a magnitude and a direction determined by the cross product of two vectors.
SLOAD	Static load at scalar point

PLOAD1   Defines concentrated and uniform or linearly varying distributed loads along the length of BAR, BEAM, and BEND elements

PLOAD2   Defines a uniform normal pressure load on two-dimensional elements

PLOAD4   Defines surface traction for HEXA, PENTA, QUAD4, QUAD8, TRIA3, and TRIA6 elements

GRAV   Gravity load specified by defining gravity vector in any defined coordinate system

RFORCE   Static load due to centrifugal force field

SPCD   Defines an enforced grid point displacement

DEFORM   Enforced axial deformation for one-dimensional elements

TEMP   Grid point temperature field

TEMPD   Grid point temperature default

TEMPRB   One-dimensional element temperature field

TEMPP1   Plate element temperature field

Table 11-1. Load Specification for Statics

11.1.1.   Force Vector Defined by Components

The force or moment vector can be defined by specifying the magnitude A and the components of a free vector (N_1, N_2, N_3) that acts in the direction of the force by means of the FORCE and MOMENT Bulk Data described by Card Image 11-1.

1	2	3	4	5	6	7	8	9	10
FORCE	SID	G	CID	A	N_1	N_2	N_3		
MOMENT	SID	G	CID	A	N_1	N_2	N_3		

where

SID   Load set identification number. Load sets must be specified at run-time by a LOAD = SID card in Case Control. (integer, >0)

G   Grid point at which load is to be applied. (integer, >0)

A   Magnitudes of force or moment. (real $\neq 0.$)

N_1, N_2, N_3 Components of a free vector defined with respect to the CID coordinate system. (real)

CID   Coordinate identification number. (integer)

Card Image 11-1. Static Force and Moment Using Vector Components.

The vector components (N_1, N_2, N_3) define a vector

$$\mathbf{N} = N_1\mathbf{i}_1 + N_2\mathbf{i}_2 + N_3\mathbf{i}_3 \tag{11.2}$$

where the unit vectors are taken in the sense of the displacement degrees of freedom for the CID co-ordinate system, as shown on Fig. 7-5. The resulting vector is then given by

$$F = A\ N \tag{11.3}$$

so that the magnitude of the force is given by

$$|F| = A\ |N| \tag{11.4}$$

The magnitude of the force (or moment) is thus equal to the magnitude A specified on the FORCE or MOMENT Bulk Data card only if the magnitude of N is equal to one.

11.1.2.   Static Force and Moment Direction Defined by Two Points

The force or moment vector can be defined by specifying a magnitude A and a direction determined by the directed line segment between two grid points by means of the FORCE1 and MOMENT1 Bulk Data cards shown in Card Image 11-2.

1	2	3	4	5	6	7	8	9	10
FORCE1	SID	G	A	G_1	G_2				
MOMENT1	SID	G	A	G_1	G_2				

where

   SID   Load set identification number. (integer, > 0)

   G   Grid point at which the load is to be applied. (integer, > 0)

   A   Magnitude of the force or moment. (real)

   G_1, G_2 Two noncoincident grid points that define the sense of the load vector as the unit vector N along the directed line segment from G_1 to G_2. (integers, > 0, $G_1 \neq G_2$)

Card Image 11-2. Direction of Force Defined by Two Points

The force or moment is defined as

$$F = A N \tag{11.5}$$

where N is a unit vector in the direction of the line segment drawn between geometric grid points G_1, G_2.

11.1.3.   Vector Direction Determined by Vector Cross Product

The force or moment vector can be defined by specifying a magnitude A and a direction determined by the vector product of two vectors by using the FORCE2 and MOMENT2 Bulk Data shown in Card Image 11-3.

1	2	3	4	5	6	7	8	9	10
FORCE2	SID	G	A	G_1	G_2	G_3	G_4		
MOMENT2	SID	G	A	G_1	G_2	G_3	G_4		

where

SID Load set identification number. (integer, >0)

G Grid point at which the load is to be applied. (integer, >0)

A Magnitude of the load. (real)

G_1, G_2, G_3, G_4 Pairs of grid points that define the vectors **a** and **b**, respectively as shown on Fig. 11-1c. $G_1 \neq G_2, G_3 \neq G_4$. (integers, >0)

Card Image 11-3. Direction of Force Defined by Vector Cross Product

The force or moment is defined as $\mathbf{F} = A\mathbf{N}$

where **N** is a unit vector defined by the cross product

$$\mathbf{N} = \frac{\mathbf{a} \times \mathbf{b}}{|\mathbf{a} \times \mathbf{b}|} \qquad (11.6)$$

and where

a is the vector from geometric grid point G_1 to G_2

and

b is the vector from geometric grid point G_3 to G_4

The force then acts at grid point G, which may be the same as points G_1 and/or G_3. This form of force specification is useful when defining a force vector that is perpendicular to the surface of an element, such as that shown in Fig. 11-2, where a force is to be defined at grid point one in the direction of the outward normal.

The force can be most conveniently specified by means of the FORCE2 Bulk Data card as shown below.

1	2	3	4	5	6	7	8	9	10
FORCE2	101	1	10.	1	2	1	3		

We note that **a** is defined from point one to two and **b** is defined from one to three. Since three points define a plane, it follows that the cross product defines a vector normal to the plane as desired.

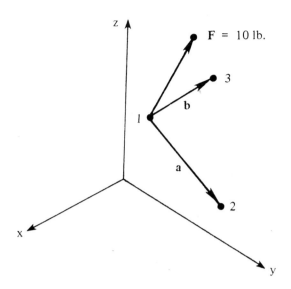

Figure 11-2. Force Acting Normal to a Surface.

11.2.   Scalar Loads

A static load can be applied to a scalar degree of freedom by the SLOAD Bulk Data, which is shown in Card Image 11-4.

1	2	3	4	5	6	7	8	9	10
SLOAD	SID	S	F	S	F	S	F		

where

SID   Load identification number. (integer, >0)

S   Scalar point identification number. (integer, >0)

F   Magnitude of the force. (real)

Card Image 11-4. Specification of Force at Scalar Points.

11.3.   Distributed Load on Beam-bending Elements — PLOAD1

The user can define distributed and/or concentrated loads along the BAR, BEAM, and BEND elements by means of the PLOAD1 Bulk Data card which is shown by Card Image 11-5.

1	2	3	4	5	6	7	8	9	10
PLOAD1	SID	EID	TYPE	SCALE	X_1	P_1	X_2	P_2	

Card Image 11-5. Specification of Concentrated and/or Distributed Loads on Beams-Bending Elements-PLOAD1

11.3.1.   Load Type and Direction

The type of load, i.e., force or moment, and the vector sense of the load with respect to either local element or basic coordinates is specified by an appropriate literal value in the TYPE field. The allowable entries are as follows

   FX, FY, FZ   Force in the X, Y, or Z directions in basic coordinates, respectively

   MX, MY, MZ   Moment about the X, Y, or Z axes in basic coordinates, respectively

   FXE, FYE, FZE   Force in the local x, y, or z directions, respectively

   MXE, MYE, MZE   Moment about the local x, y, or z axes, respectively.

11.3.2.   Load Definition

The load distribution is described by

1. Specifying the region over which the load is to be distributed using the fields X_1, X_2 (real) where X_1 defines the start of the loaded region and X_2 defines the end. If a concentrated load at X_1 is desired then X_2 must either be blank or equal to X_1.

2. Specifying whether the length is defined as the actual element length or is scaled by either actual length or projected length by using the following literal values for the SCALE field.

   LE   Distance is actual length along the neutral axis. If $X_2 > X_1$ the load is a force per unit length.

   FR   Distances are normalized with respect to total element length. If $X_2 > X_1$ the load is a force per unit length.

   LEPR   Same as LE except loads are defined in terms of projected lengths of the neutral axis on the basic coordinate axes.

   FRPR   Same as FR except loads are defined in terms of normalized projected length of the neutral axis on the basic coordinate axes.

3. Specifying the load intensity using the P_1, P_2 fields (real) where

   • A concentrated load is defined by a real value for P_1 with P_2 blank

   • A uniform load between X_1 and X_2 is defined by setting $P_2 = P_1$

   • A linearly varying load is defined between X_1 an X_2 if $P_2 \neq P_1$.

11.3.3.   Example — Load Distribution on Beam Elements

Consider the specification of the loads applied to the structural system as shown by Figure 11-3 where the loads are as follows

1. A uniform load $\mathbf{p}_a$ of magnitude 20 lb/in. applied to element 2 in the negative x-direction in basic coordinates.

2. A concentrated load P_b applied to element 2 at a distance of 10 inches from node 2 (taken to be the A-end of the element) having a magnitude of 30 lb.

3. A concentrated force P_c of 20 lb. and a concentrated moment M_d of 60 in.-lb. at the mid-

11.4.1 Uniform Normal Pressure — PLOAD2

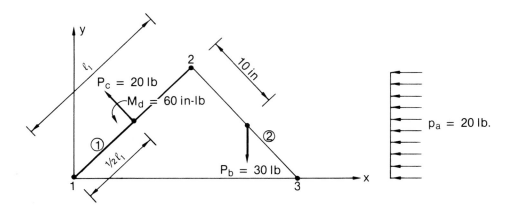

Figure 11-3. Distributed and Concentrated Forces Along Beam-Type Elements

point of element 1.

If we assume that the local z-axis is normal to the basic X-Y plane these loads could be described by using the following PLOAD1 Bulk Data cards.

1	2	3	4	5	6	7	8	9	10
PLOAD1	101	2	FX	FRPR	0.	− 20.	1.	− 20.	
PLOAD1	101	2	FY	LE	10.	− 30.			
PLOAD1	101	1	FYE	FR	0.5	20.			
PLOAD1	101	1	MZE	FR	0.5	60.			

where cards 1 thru 4 define p_a, P_b, P_c, and M_d, respectively.

11.4. Distributed Surface Tractions

A uniform normal pressure load as well as a more general nonuniform surface traction in an arbitrary direction can be specified by appropriate MSC/NASTRAN Bulk Data. The PLOAD4, which is described in Sec. 11.4.2, defines a nonuniform surface traction on both two and three dimensional elements. The PLOAD2, which is described in Sec. 11.4.1, defines a uniform pressure load on two dimensional elements.

11.4.1. Uniform Normal Pressure — PLOAD2

The PLOAD2 Bulk Data shown by Card Image 11-6 allows the analyst to define a uniform normal pressure on the surface of the two dimensional shell elements including the QUAD4, QUAD8, TRIA3, and TRIA6.

1	2	3	4	5	6	7	8	9	10
PLOAD2	SID	P	EID_1	EID_2	EID_3				

*Alternative form for PLOAD2 card

PLOAD2	SID	P	EID_1	THRU	EID_2				

where

SID   Load set identification number. (integer, > 0)

P   Magnitude of the pressure. (real)

EID$_i$ Element identification numbers. All elements referenced must exist and must be two-dimensional. When using the alternate form of EID$_1$ THRU EID$_2$, all elements must exist. (Integer)

Card Image 11-6. Normal Pressure for Bending Elements

11.4.1.1.   Sign Convention for Positive Pressure on Shell Elements

The positive sense of the pressure is determined by the grid number sequence specified on the appropriate element connection Bulk Data. The sense of positive pressure is found by applying the right hand rule to the numbering sequence for the element vertices. When viewed from above the element a counter-clockwise sequence defines positive pressure in the sense of a vector towards the viewer, i.e., a positive pressure acting on bottom surface.

Since the node numbering sequence defines the sense of positive pressure it is important that a consistent numbering sequence be used. If the element connections are defined by a preprocessor program the analyst should verify that a consistent node numbering sequence has been defined.

11.4.2.   Nonuniform Surface Tractions — PLOAD4

A nonuniform surface traction can be applied to the surface of the two dimensional shell elements or any face of three dimensional HEXA or PENTA elements by the PLOAD4 Bulk Data shown by Card Image 11-7.

1	2	3	4	5	6	7	8	9	10
PLOAD4	SID	EID	P_1	P_2	P_3	P_4	G_1	G_3	+P1
+P1	CID	N_1	N_2	N_3					

*Alternate form for two-dimensional elements

PLOAD4	SID	EID$_1$	P_1	P_2	P_3	P_4	THRU	EID$_n$	+P1
+P1	CID	N_1	N_2	N_3					

Card Image 11-7. Nonuniform Surface Traction — PLOAD4

The alternate form can be used to define a surface traction over a set of TRIA3, QUAD4, TRIA6, and QUAD8 elements by using the THRU option in field 8.

11.4.2.1.   Direction of Surface Traction

The direction of the surface traction can be defined by specifying the three real components of a vector (N_1, N_2, N_3) with respect to the CID (integer) coordinate system on the optional continuation card. If the continuation card is not present then the traction is taken to be normal to the surface using the following sign convention.

1. For two dimensional elements positive pressure is the direction determined by applying the right hand rule to the node number sequence as described in Sec. 11.4.1.1.

2. For three-dimensional elements positive pressure is in the direction of the inward normal to the face.

11.4.2.2. Specifying Load Intensity

The fields P_1, P_2, P_3, P_4 (real) are interpreted as

1. The values of the surface traction at grid points G_1, G_2, G_3, and G_4 as defined on the connection card for a two dimensional element where P_4 is blank if the element is triangular.

2. The values of surface traction at grid points on the face of a three dimensional element. The face is identified by specifying two grid points, G_1 and G_3, which define a diagonal on the face. The field P_1 is then taken to be the traction at G_1 and P_2, P_3, (and P_4) are tractions at the other vertices in a sequence determined by applying the right hand rule to the outward normal to the face.

11.4.2.3. Example — Surface Traction on Three Dimensional Element

Consider the specification of the surface traction applied to the eight-noded HEXA element shown by Figure 11-4.

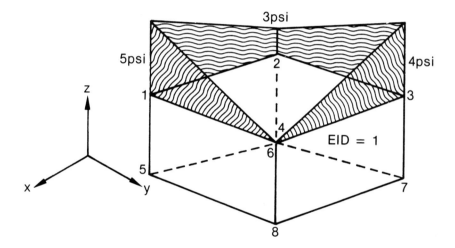

Figure 11-4. Surface Traction on Three Dimensional Element

The magnitude on the surface traction is taken to be

5 psi at node 1
3 psi at node 2
4 psi at node 3
0 psi at node 4

and varies linearly along the edge of the element. A surface traction of this magnitude can be specified in the direction of the basic X-axis by means of the following PLOAD4 card

1	2	3	4	5	6	7	8	9	10
PLOAD4	101	1	5.	0.	4.	3.	1	3	+P1
+P1	0	1.	0.	0.					

where the face is identified by grid points 1 and three in fields 8 and 9 and P_1, P_2, P_3, and P_4 are associated with grid points 1, 4, 3, and 2, respectively.

294

11.5. Gravity Loads

A uniform gravity load can be applied to the structure by specifying an acceleration vector using the GRAV Bulk Data card, which is shown in Card Image 11-8.

1	2	3	4	5	6	7	8	9	10
GRAV	SID	CID	G	N_1	N_2	N_3			

where

SID Load set identification number. The SID cannot be the same as any other static load sets. Load sets in Bulk Data can be combined using the LOAD card (see section 11.7). (integer, >0)

CID Set identification of the coordinate system in which the vector components N_1, N_2, and N_3 are defined. (integer, >0)

N_1, N_2, N_3 Components of a vector taken in the sense of the displacement degrees of freedom shown by Fig. 7-5 for the coordinate type specified by CID. (real)

G Scale factor such that the desired acceleration is given by

$$\mathbf{a} = G\mathbf{N}$$

where $\mathbf{N}$ need not be a unit vector. (real $\neq 0$.)

Card Image 11-8. Specification of Gravity Vector

The acceleration vector is transformed to the basic coordinate system and expanded to a set of vectors acting on the g-set. Letting $\mathbf{a_g}$ be the set of node point accelerations, the gravity loads are calculated using the structural mass matrix as

$$\mathbf{P_g} = \mathbf{M_{gg}}\ \mathbf{a_g} \qquad (11.7)$$

where

$\mathbf{M}_{gg}$ is the system mass matrix. (See Sec. 13.1).

The inclusion of the GRAV loads in the analysis implies that the mass matrix must be calculated. The user must therefore insure that the mass for all elements is defined as described in Section 13.4 of the text.

Sets of gravity loads may be specified by giving each set an identification number that is unique among all load set identifications. The gravity load to be used as execution time is then specified by the Case Control Directive

$$\text{LOAD} = \text{SID}$$

It is important to note that MSC/NASTRAN does not allow GRAV loads to have the same set number as the applied external loads described in previous sections. If both gravity and applied external loads are desired they must be combined using the LOAD Bulk Data card, which is described in Section 11.7.

11.6. Static Loads Due to Centripetal Acceleration

The centrifugal force field due to rotation about a geometric grid point, seen in Fig. 11-5, is specified by the RFORCE Bulk Data card, shown in Card Image 11-9. The structure is assumed to rotate such that point G_0 lies on the axis of rotation. If field three of the RFORCE card is left blank, then the spin axis passes through the origin of the basic coordinate system. The angular rotation vector is defined as

$$\Omega = A\,N \tag{11.8}$$

The angular velocity in radians per unit time is then given by

$$\omega = 2\,\pi\,\Omega \tag{11.9}$$

The centripetal acceleration at a point i in the structure is then given by

$$\mathbf{a_i} = \omega \times (\omega \times \mathbf{r_i}) \tag{11.10}$$

where we see from Fig. 11-5 that

$$\mathbf{r_i} = \mathbf{R_o} - \mathbf{R_i} \tag{11.11}$$

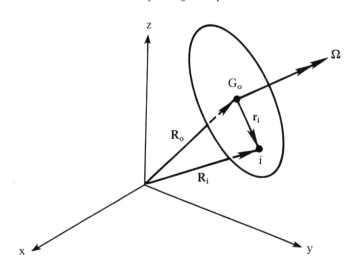

Figure 11-5. Angular Rotation Vector for Centrifugal Forces

where $\mathbf{R_o}$ is the radius vector from the origin of the basic coordinate system to point G_0.

Denoting the set of accelerations associated with all geometric grid point degrees of freedom as $\mathbf{a_g}$, the centrifugal forces are then calculated to be

$$\mathbf{P_g} = -\,\mathbf{M_{gg}}\,\mathbf{a_g} \tag{11.12}$$

1	2	3	4	5	6	7	8	9	10
RFORCE	SID	G_0	CID	A	N_1	N_2	N_3	METHOD	

where

SID   Load set identification number. Centrifugal forces can be combined with other static loads only by means of LOAD card. (integer, >0)

G_0 Grid point through which the rotation vector acts. If $G_0 = 0$ then acts through origin of basic coordinate system.

296

CID   Identification of the coordinate system used to define the components of the rotation vector.

N_1, N_2, N_3 Components of a vector N defined in the sense of displacement degrees of freedom as shown in Fig. 7-5 for the CID coordinate system.

A   Magnitude in revolutions per unit time.

METHOD   Method used to compute centrifugal force vector. (Integer = 1 or 2, or blank)

Card Image 11-9. Specification of Angular Velocity Vector

The inclusion of centrifugal forces in the analysis implies that the system mass matrix must be calculated. The user must therefore insure that the mass for all structural elements as described in Section 13-4 of the text is defined. The user is also cautioned that the use of consistent mass may lead to erroneous centrifugal forces if the default for METHOD (i.e. METHOD = 1) is taken. The METHOD field on RFORCE Bulk Data gives the analyst a means of correctly incorporating the effect of off-diagonal mass terms which are associated with the consistent mass formulation by using a value of 2 for this field. Even for METHOD = 2 the mass terms which are due to mass offsets on CONM2 Bulk Data (Card Image 13-2) are not correctly calculated.

Centrifugal forces can be combined with other types of loads by means of the LOAD Bulk Data card, which is described in the next section.

11.7.   Combined Loading

The loads defined in the previous sections are identified by means of a set number. The load to be used at execution time is then specified by means of the following Case Control Directive

$$LOAD = SID$$

Combinations of loads may be required and can be specified by means of the LOAD Bulk Data card shown by Card Image 11-10. The LOAD card is used to combine sets of static loads as well as to combine RFORCE and GRAV loads with other static loads.

1	2	3	4	5	6	7	8	9	10
LOAD	SID	S_0	S_1	L_1	S_2	L_2	S_3	L_3	+L1
+L1	S_4	L_4	etc						

where

SID   Set identification of the combined load set. The magnitude of entire load is given by

$$L = S_o \sum_{i=1}^{N} S_i L_i$$

S_i (i = 0, 1, 2, ..N) are scale factors. (real)

L_i (i = 1, 2, ..N) are LOAD set identification numbers of any load set which can be specified by a LOAD = SID Case Control Directive.

Card Image 11-10. Specification of Combined Load Sets.

The static load vector specified by the set of loads used at execution time can be displayed by the Case Control Directive.

$$OLOAD = <set>$$

where $<set>$ is a set of grid and scalar points defined using a SET Case Control Directive.

11.8.   Enforced Value for Displacements — SPCD

The SPCD Bulk Data card shown by Card Image 11-11 provides the user with the capability of defining a constraint that will be treated as load associated with a degree of freedom in the s-set. The use of the SPCD Bulk Data avoids the decomposition of the stiffness matrix when only the magnitudes of enforced displacements are changed

1	2	3	4	5	6	7	8	9	10
SPCD	SID	G	C	D	G	C	D		

Card Image 11-11. Enforced Displacement in Load Set

The SPCD is similar to the SPC Bulk Data described in Sec. 7.5.2 except that the SID associated with the SPCD refers to a load set and is thus included in the analysis by a LOAD Case Control Directive. The following rules must be followed in using the load-set enforced displacement.

1. The degrees of freedom specified on the SPCD card must also be specified in the s-set by SPC or SPC1 Bulk Data.

2. The value D overrides the value on the constraint which is defined by the SPC or SPC1 Bulk Data only if the appropriate load set is selected in Case Control.

3. The Bulk Data LOAD combination capability (Sec. 11.7) can not be used to select SPCD sets.

4. At least one external load specification (FORCE, MOMENT, etc.) must be present in the Bulk Data, however, the load may be zero.

The SPCD capability assists the analyst in performing rigid body checks for large structural models. The SPCD allows the specification of displacement boundary conditions as loading conditions and so that rigid body checks can be performed in a single solution with only one matrix decomposition.

11.9.   Enforced Deformation

An enforced axial deformation can be specified for the ROD-type and BAR-type elements by means of the DEFORM Bulk Data card shown by Card Image 11-12.

1	2	3	4	5	6	7	8	9	10
DEFORM	SID	EID	D	EID	D	EID	D		

where

SID   Load set identification. (integer, >0)

EID   Element number of a ROD, TUBE, CONROD, BAR, or BEAM element. (integer, >0)

D   Enforced axial deformation, plus for elongation. (real)

Card Image 11-12. Specification of Enforced Axial Displacement

The set of enforced displacements that is to be used at execution time is specified by means of the Case Control Directive

$$\text{DEFORM} = \text{SID}$$

where SID is the identification number of a DEFORM set in Bulk Data.

11.10. Specification of Structural Temperature

Element and grid point temperatures are specified by Bulk Data cards for the determination of

1. Thermal loading

2. Temperature-dependent material properties

3. Stress-recovery

The analyst selects a specific set of temperature data and specifies whether the temperatures are to be used to determine temperature-dependent material properties or to define equivalent thermal loads by the TEMPERATURE Case Control Directive, which has the format

$$\text{TEMPERATURE} \left(\begin{array}{l} \text{MATERIAL} \\ \text{LOAD} \\ \text{BOTH} \end{array} \right) = \text{SID}$$

where BOTH is the default option. For example,

$$\text{TEMP(LOAD)} = 30$$

specifies that temperature set 30 is to be used to calculate thermal loads and

$$\text{TEMP(MATERIAL)} = 20$$

specifies that temperature set 20 is to be used to calculate temperature-dependent material properties. These specifications are mutually exclusive; i.e. temperature-dependent material properties will not be calculated if LOAD is specified, and thermal loads will not be calculated if MATERIAL is specified. Both thermal loads and material-dependent properties are specified by either of the equivalent forms

$$\text{TEMP(BOTH)} = \text{SID}$$

or

$$\text{TEMP} = \text{SID}$$

If the thermal effects are specified, then all elements must have a temperature field defined either directly by an element temperature field or indirectly by grid point temperatures. If both are given then precedence is always given to element temperatures.

The equivalent concentrated thermal loads are calculated by means of (6.44), which is

$$\mathbf{P}_{eI} = \int_{V_{o\ell}} \mathbf{b}_e^T \mathbf{E}_e \, \mathbf{e}_{eI} \, dV_{o\ell}$$

where the initial strains are due to thermal effects and are taken in the form

$$\mathbf{e}_{eI} = \Delta T \, (x,y,z) \, \alpha \tag{11.13}$$

where α is the set of thermal coefficients that is defined on an appropriate MATi Bulk Data card, as described in Chapter 10.

If node point temperatures are used to calculate the thermal strains, then the element temperature is assumed to be the average of the temperature of the connected node points for the lineal elements. In this case the thermal strains for an element are constant over the element and are given by

$$\mathbf{e}_{el} = T_{ave}\, \alpha \tag{11.14}$$

The effective thermal loads are then given by

$$\mathbf{P}_{el}^T = T_{ave}\, \alpha^T \int_{V_{o\ell}} \mathbf{E}\, \mathbf{b}_e\, dV_{o\ell} \tag{11.15}$$

The temperature at interior points of the isoparametric elements is found by interpolation of the temperatures at the corner nodes.

11.11.   Specification of Grid Point Temperatures

The grid point temperature can be specified by means of the TEMP and TEMPD Bulk Data cards, which are shown in Card Image 11-13. The TEMP card specifies a scalar value of temperature at grid points, and the TEMPD card specifies a default temperature for all grid points whose temperatures are not defined by a TEMP card.

1	2	3	4	5	6	7	8	9	10
TEMP	SID	G	T	G	T	G	T		
TEMPD	SID	T	SID	T	SID	T	SID	T	

where

SID Identification number of the temperature set.

G, T Pairs that define the temperature T at grid point G.

SID, T Pairs on the TEMPD card that define default values for grid point temperatures which have not been specified on a TEMP card for temperature set SID.

Card Image 11-13. Specification of Grid Point Temperatures

The grid point temperatures may be calculated in a separate execution of MSC/NASTRAN by specifying the HEAT approach in the Executive Control Deck. This feature is especially attractive since the grid point temperatures are calculated using basically the same finite element model as that used for the structural analysis.

11.12.   Specification of Temperature Field for Axial Elements

The temperature is assumed to vary linearly over the length of an axial element. If only axial thermal strains are of interest then it may be reasonable to define grid point temperatures using the TEMP Bulk Data card described in the previous section.

For elements that exhibit bending behavior the situation is not quite so simple since the temperature gradients through the thickness give rise to thermal moments. The effective thermal gradients in the bending elements are calculated using the following relations

$$T_y = \frac{1}{I_y} \int_A z\, T\,(y, z)\ dA$$

(11.16)

and

$$T_z = \frac{1}{I_z} \int_A y\, T\,(y, z)\ dA$$

(11.17)

where $T(y,z)$ is the temperature distribution over the plane normal to the neutral axis, and I_y and I_z are the area moments of inertia of the cross-section about the local y- and z-axes, respectively. In this case the temperature field is defined using the TEMPRB Bulk Data card, which is shown in Card Image 11-14.

1	2	3	4	5	6	7	8	9	10
TEMPRB	SID	EID_1	T_a	T_b	T_{ya}	T_{yb}	T_{za}	T_{zb}	+T1
+T1	TC_a	TD_a	TE_a	TF_a	TC_b	TD_b	TE_b	TF_b	+T2
+T2	EID_2	EID_3	etc.						

*Alternate form for second continuation card

+T2	EID_2	THRU	EID_i	EID_j	THRU	EID_k			

where

    SID Temperature set identification. (integer, >0)

    EID_i Unique element identification numbers of elements with specified temperature field. (integer, >0)

    T_a, T_b Average temperature at ends a and b, respectively. (real)

    $T_{ya}, T_{yb}, T_{za}, T_{zb}$ Effective thermal gradient for calculation of thermal moment in a bending element. (real)

    TC_i, TD_i, TE_i, TF_i Temperatures at points C, D, E, and F at end i (i = a, b) at which stresses are to be recovered in a bending element. (real)

Card Image 11-14. Specification of Temperature Field for Axial Elements

The bending stresses in a BEAM-type element that result from the mechanical loads are modified by the element temperatures if at least one of the temperatures TC_a, TD_a, etc. are different from zero. The thermal stresses at end a are then given by

301

$$\Delta\,\sigma_c \;=\; -\,E\,\alpha\,\,(TC_a - T_{ya}\,CY_a \;-\; T_{za}\,CZ_a \;-\; T_a)$$

$$\Delta\,\sigma_d \;=\; -\,E\,\alpha\,\,(TD_a - T_{ya}\,DY_a \;-\; T_{za}\,DZ_a \;-\; T_a)$$

$$\Delta\,\sigma_e \;=\; -\,E\,\alpha\,\,(TE_a - T_{ya}\,EY_a \;-\; T_{za}\,EZ_a \;-\; T_a)$$

$$\Delta\,\sigma_f \;=\; -\,E\,\alpha\,\,(TF_a - T_{ya}\,FY_a \;-\; T_{za}\,FZ_a \;-\; T_a)$$

(11.18)

where the material properties are defined on a MAT1 Bulk Data card and where the distances to the four points C, D, E and F on the cross-section are specified on an appropriate property card. The thermal stress at end b of the element are given by a set of equations that are similar in form to (11.18).

11.13.   Specification of Temperature Field for Two-Dimensional Elements.

For two-dimensional elements that have bending behavior, a thermal moment will result if the temperature distribution through the thickness is an odd function of the thickness relative to the plate neutral surface. The user may specify the effect of the temperature variation through the thickness by specifying the effective gradient:

$$T' = \frac{1}{I}\int_z z\,T\,(z)\,dz$$

(11.19)

on a TEMPP1 card as shown by Card Image 11-15.

1	2	3	4	5	6	7	8	9	10
TEMPP1	SID	EID_1	T	T'	T_1	T_2			+T1
+T1	EID_2	EID_3	EID_4	etc.					

*Alternate form of continuation card

+T1	EID_2	THRU	EID_i	EID_j	THRU	EID_k	etc.		

where

      SID Load set identification. (integer, >0)

      EID_i Element identification numbers. (integer, >0)

      T Average temperature of the element. (real)

      T_1, T_2 Temperatures at the upper and lower surfaces used only for stress recovery. (real)

      T' Effective gradient defined on the TEMPP1 card. (real)

Card Image 11-15. Plate Thermal Field Using Thermal Gradients

303

12

Static Analysis with MSC/NASTRAN

The MSC/NASTRAN rigid format 24 is recommended for linear static analysis based on the finite element method. Rigid format 24 supports all of the modern MSC/NASTRAN features including

- Modern element library

- Constraint and rigid elements

- Automatic purging of unconnected degrees of freedom

- Distributed surface tractions on two and three dimensional elements

- Inertia relief

The other MSC/NASTRAN rigid formats for static analysis include nonlinear strain displacement relations or nonlinear material behavior and are therefore beyond the scope of the present text.

The MSC/NASTRAN algorithm for each of the standard analysis sequences is defined by a set of DMAP instructions. This preprogrammed DMAP sequence is selected by a SOL card in the Executive Control deck and can be optionally printed by the DIAG 14 card in Executive Control.

12.1.   Static Analysis Capability

12.1.1.   Specification of System Matrices

The system matrices may include the mass matrix $\mathbf{M}_{gg}$ as well as the stiffness matrix $\mathbf{K}_{gg}$. These matrices can be

- Calculated using finite element model

- Defined using, Direct Matrix Input (DMIG)

where the specification of the mass matrix by the finite element model is described in Sec. 13.1. The user has the additional option of defining the stiffness matrix for all or part of the structure by means of stiffness or flexibility coefficients on the GENEL general element.

The system matrices associated with the finite element model can be defined and calculated by MSC/NASTRAN by

- Defining grid point locations using GRID cards.

- Defining structural element connectivity and properties using the recommended elements described in Chapter 9.

- Defining element properties using MAT-type cards described in Chapter 10.

12.1.1 Specification of System Matrices

- Defining inertia properties (if required).

12.1.1.1. Direct Specification of System Matrices

MSC/NASTRAN assumes that the stiffness and mass matrices associated with g-set of displacements are of the following form

$$\mathbf{K}_{gg} = \mathbf{K}^1_{gg} + \mathbf{K}^2_{gg} \tag{12.1}$$

$$\mathbf{M}_{gg} = \mathbf{M}^1_{gg} + \mathbf{M}^2_{gg} \tag{12.2}$$

where $\mathbf{K}^1_{gg}$ and $\mathbf{M}^1_{gg}$ are the stiffness and mass matrices which are generated using the finite element model and where $\mathbf{K}^2_{gg}$ and $\mathbf{M}^2_{gg}$ are stiffness and mass coefficients which can be defined directly by using DMIG Bulk Data which is shown by Card Image 12-1.

*Header card

1	2	3	4	5	6	7	8	9	10
DMIG	NAME	0	FORM	TIN	TOUT				

*Column card

DMIG	NAME	G_j	C_j		G_i	C_i	$X_{i,j}$		+D1
+D1	G_m	C_m	$X_{m,j}$		G_k	C_k	$X_{k,j}$		+D2
+D2	G_l	C_l	$X_{l,j}$	-etc.-					

Card Image 12-1. Direct Matrix Input Using External (Grid Point) Degree of Freedom Codes — DMIG

The form of the DMIG Bulk Data is similar to the DMI Bulk Data card which is described in Sec. 3-4. The basic difference between the two is that external degree of freedom codes are used to define matrix elements on DMIG while internal degrees of freedom are used on DMI.

The matrix data is associated with a NAME which is a literal string which must begin with an alphabetic character. The matrix is then defined by

- A header card which must have a zero, (0), in field 3 and where

    FORM -Matrix form defined by Table 3-2 in Section 3.4. (Integer >0)
      (Must be 6 for solution 24 and 3)

    TIN -Type of matrix defined by Table 3-3 in Section 3.4. (Integer >0)
    TOUT

- A column card for each non-null column where

    G_j, C_j -Defines the jth column in terms of the external degrees of freedom code where G_j is the grid point number and C_j is the code for *one* degree of freedom at the grid point.

    G_i, C_i -Defines the ith row in the jth column.

    $X_{i,j}$ -Defines matrix element in ith row of the jth column. (real)

306

Each nonzero element in the jth column must be specified by defining the row associated with the element followed by the value of the matrix element. DMIG has the general capability of defining complex symmetric matrices so that the row designation is followed by two fields, the first, X_{ij}, is the real part. Since only real matrices are used in static and normal modes analysis the second field must be left blank. The more general capability for defining complex matrices is described in Ref. 12-1.

The matrices defined on DMIG Bulk Data can be selected as $\mathbf{M}_{gg}^2$ or $\mathbf{K}_{gg}^2$ type input by the following Case Control Directives

- M2GG = <name> for $\mathbf{M}_{gg}^2$ input

- K2GG = <name> for $\mathbf{K}_{gg}^2$ input

where <name> is the NAME associated with the matrix on DMIG Bulk Data.

Consider the specification of the stiffness matrix for the cantilevered beam shown by Fig. 12-1, for example

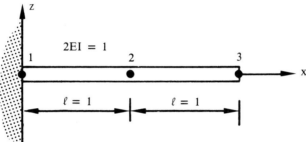

Fig. 12-1. Cantilevered Beam Defined by DMIG

The stiffness matrix for the beam is then given by (6.59) so that the stiffness matrix for each element is

$$
\mathbf{k}_{ee} = \begin{bmatrix} 6 & -3 & -6 & -3 \\ -3 & 2 & 3 & 1 \\ -6 & 3 & 6 & 3 \\ -3 & 1 & 3 & 2 \end{bmatrix} \tag{12.3}
$$

The system stiffness matrix, which is of order 4×4 is then given by

$$
\mathbf{K}_{gg} = \begin{bmatrix} 12 & 0 & -6 & -3 \\ 0 & 4 & 3 & 1 \\ -6 & 3 & 6 & 3 \\ -3 & 1 & 3 & 2 \end{bmatrix} \tag{12.4}
$$

where for the purpose of this example the g-set includes the following physical degrees of freedom

$$
\mathbf{u}_g = [u_{z2}, \theta_{y2}, u_{z3}, \theta_{y3}]^T \tag{12.5}
$$

The stiffness matrix (12.4) could then be defined by the following Bulk Data.

12.1.2   Constraint and Static Condensation

1	2	3	4	5	6	7	8	9	10
DMIG	BEAM	0	6	1	0				
DMIG	BEAM	2	3		2	3	12.		+ B1
+B1	2	5	0.		3	3	− 6.		+ B2
+B2	3	5	− 3.						
DMIG	BEAM	2	5		2	5	4.		+B3
+ B3	3	3	3.		3	5	1.		
DMIG	BEAM	3	3		3	3	6.		+ B4
+B4	3	5	3.						
DMIG	BEAM	3	5		3	5	2.		

where the matrix name is BEAM and

1. The first card is the header card which specifies that the matrix will be symmetric (FORM = 6), will be input as real single precision (TIN = 1) but is to be redefined within MSC/NASTRAN as appropriate for the type of computer (TOUT = 0).

2. The specification of symmetric matrix on DMIG implies that a given off-diagonal element can be input either above or below the diagonal, but not both. Thus, in counterdistinction to the DMI Bulk Data, only the diagonal and either upper or lower off-diagonal elements are to be entered for a symmetric matrix.

3. The external column and row codes represent the non-null degrees of freedom in the displacement set defined by (12.5).

4. The stiffness matrix would be selected by the following Case Control Directive

$$K2GG = BEAM$$

12.1.2.   Constraint and Static Condensation

The stiffness matrix associated with the set of all grid and scalar degrees of freedom can be modified by means of various constraint and partitioning operations. These include

1. Specification of multipoint constraints (Section 7.5.1)

2. Specification of single point constraints (Section 7.5.2)

3. Static Condensation (Section 7.6)

4. Support of free bodies (Section 7.7)

5. Specification of matrix elements using GENEL (Section 7.8)

The set of displacements remaining after these operations is called the ℓ-set which is the solution set for static analysis.

12.1.3.   Static Loads

The set of static loads that is applied to the grid and scalar points can result from a variety of sources, including

1. Concentrated forces and moments applied directly to the grid points (Section 11.1.)

2. Concentrated loads applied to scalar points (Section 11.2.)

308

3. Distributed pressure load on one-, two-, and three-dimensional elements (Section 11.3. and 11.4.)

4. Gravity loads (Section 11.5.)

5. Centripetal acceleration (Section 11.6.)

6. Enforced boundary displacement (Section 11.8.)

7. Enforced axial deformation (Section 11.9.)

8. Temperature field (Sections 11.10., 11.11., 11.12., and 11.13.)

The set of node point forces from all these effects is reduced to that associated with the ℓ-set of displacements by using the transformation defined by the constraints and partitioning specifications. The resulting set of equations is of the form

$$\mathbf{K}_{\ell\ell}\mathbf{u}_\ell = \mathbf{P}_\ell \tag{12.6}$$

This set of equations is solved by first decomposing the stiffness matrix into its lower and upper triangular factors. A forward-backward substitution is then performed for all load subcases which have the same set of constraints.

12.1.4. Inertia Relief

A free body may be subject to a set of external forces which are not in static equilibrium and which therefore produce rigid body accelerations. If the rate of change of the external forces is sufficiently small compared to the lowest natural frequency, we may consider the external forces to be in equilibrium with inertia forces.

The analyst may choose to apply a set of forces that represents a nonequilibrium set. The analyst may be interested in the effect of the inertia forces. In this case, a condition must be defined in which the effects of the inertia forces are not present, hence the term "inertia relief."

The general procedure for removing the effects of inertia is

1. Select a set of determinate support points, e.g., the r-set, which is defined using a SUPORT Bulk Data card (Section 7.7)

2. Determine the rigid body acceleration of the r-set from the loads applied to the a-set of degrees of freedom

3. Calculate the rigid body accelerations of the ℓ-set of degrees of freedom

4. Subtract the inertia forces that result from accelerations of the ℓ-set from the external load $\mathbf{P}_\ell$, and solve for the set of displacements obtained by constraining the r-set. The forces of reaction of the r-set of degrees of freedom will be zero.

The equations of motion that include inertia relief are obtained by noting that the a-set is partitioned into the ℓ- and r-sets where the degrees of freedom in the r-set are just sufficient to remove rigid body motion. The ℓ- and r-sets are then related by the rigid body transformation matrix defined by (7.76). The reduced mass matrix which is obtained by applying the same set of transformations that were used to reduce the stiffness is then obtained by partitioning the a-set of equations into the ℓ- and r-sets as

$$\mathbf{M}_{aa} = \begin{bmatrix} \mathbf{M}_{\ell\ell} & \mathbf{M}_{\ell r} \\ \mathbf{M}_{r\ell} & \tilde{\mathbf{M}}_{rr} \end{bmatrix} \tag{12.7}$$

309

12.1.4   Inertia Relief

The reduced mass matrix is obtained by means of the transformation

$$\mathbf{M}_{rr} = \mathbf{G}_{ar}^{T} \mathbf{M}_{aa} \mathbf{G}_{ar} \tag{12.8}$$

The transformation matrix relates the a- and r-sets and is expressed in terms of the rigid body transformation matrix (7.76) as

$$\mathbf{u}_a = \begin{bmatrix} \mathbf{G}_{\ell r} \\ \mathbf{I}_{rr} \end{bmatrix} \mathbf{u}_r = \mathbf{G}_{ar} \mathbf{u}_r \tag{12.9}$$

The reduced mass matrix then becomes

$$\mathbf{M}_{rr} = \tilde{\mathbf{M}}_{rr} + \mathbf{M}_{\ell r}^{T} \mathbf{G}_{\ell r} + \mathbf{G}_{r\ell} \mathbf{M}_{\ell r} + \mathbf{G}_{r\ell} \mathbf{M}_{\ell\ell} \mathbf{G}_{\ell r} \tag{12.10}$$

The set of forces associated with the r-set is reduced in a similar way to give

$$\mathbf{P}_r = \mathbf{G}_{ar}^{T} \mathbf{P}_a \tag{12.11}$$

or

$$\mathbf{P}_r = \tilde{\mathbf{P}}_r + \mathbf{G}_{r\ell} \mathbf{P}_\ell \tag{12.12}$$

The equations of motion can be written as

$$\mathbf{M}_{rr} \ddot{\mathbf{u}}_r = \mathbf{P}_r \tag{12.13}$$

The accelerations of the r-set can now be determined as

$$\ddot{\mathbf{u}}_r = -\mathbf{M}_{rr}^{-1} \mathbf{P}_r \tag{12.14}$$

and by using (7.76), the accelerations of the ℓ-set become

$$\ddot{\mathbf{u}}_\ell = \mathbf{G}_{\ell r} \ddot{\mathbf{u}}_r \tag{12.15}$$

The inertia forces associated with the ℓ-set can now be determined in terms of the partitions of the matrix as

$$\mathbf{q}_\ell = -\mathbf{M}_{\ell\ell} \mathbf{u}_\ell - \mathbf{M}_{\ell r} \mathbf{u}_r \tag{12.16}$$

where $\mathbf{q}_\ell$ are the inertia forces. These forces can be expressed by using (12.14) and (12.15) as

$$\mathbf{q}_\ell = -[\mathbf{M}_{\ell\ell} \mathbf{G}_{\ell r} + \mathbf{M}_{\ell r}] \mathbf{M}_{rr}^{-1} \mathbf{P}_r \tag{12.17}$$

The inertia forces are then added to the set of applied loads when inertia refllief effects are desired.

It is important that the analyst realize that the presence of SUPORT Bulk Data results in the inertia relief calculation in the MSC/NASTRAN static analysis algorithm. The analyst must, therefore, include Bulk Data that defines the system mass matrix (see Sec. 13.4.) since it is required for the calculation of the inertia forces.

12.1.5.   Data Recovery

The displacement sets associated with the various constraint and static condensation operations are recovered to obtain the set of all grid point displacements. The details concerning this recovery process are described in Chapter 7.

Once the displacements have been recovered, the element forces, stresses, forces of constraint, and strain energy are selectively calculated based on user-supplied Case Control Directives, which are described in Section 1.8.

12.2.   Input Specifications for Rigid Formats

12.2.1.   Executive Control Deck

The Executive Control deck is described in Section 1.9. The user specifies static analysis by means of the SOL card. A minimum Executive Control deck includes

```
ID       A1,A2
TIME     <minutes>
SOL      24
CEND
```

12.2.2.   Case Control Deck

The Case Control decks for static analysis and static analysis with inertia relief are similar. The Case Control specifications that apply to both are

1. A separate subcase must be defined for each unique combination of constraints and static loads

2. A static load must be defined above the subcase level with a LOAD, TEMPERATURE (LOAD), DEFORM, or SPC Case Control Directive. Loads defined within a subcase supersede the load defined above the subcase level. If loading results from SPC sets, then at least one specified displacement degree of freedom must be nonzero.

3. An SPC set must be specified for each subcase unless the body is a properly supported free body, or all constraints are specified on GRID cards, scalar connections (i.e., springs to ground) or with the general element.

4. Loading conditions associated with same set of constraints should be contiguous subcases to eliminate looping in the DMAP instructions.

5. The REPCASE directive may be used to allow multiple sets of the same output.

6. A single set of direct input matrices may be selected with K2GG and/or M2GG Case Control directives above the subcase level.

For inertia relief, a SUPORT card must be selected to remove at least one rigid body degree of freedom. The remaining constraints can be used to remove some, but not all, of the free body degrees of freedom. If the SUPORT card is present then the mass matrix is required. An error condition exists if the mass matrix is null.

12.2.3.   Parameters

The parameters which are useful for static analysis are described in Appendix B. These parameters include

- GRDPNT — Turns on the weight generator.

- WTMASS — Conversion factor applied to mass matrix.

- AUTOSPC — Automatically purges unconnected degrees of freedom.

- COUPMASS — Optionally calculates consistent rather than lumped mass.

- NEWSEQ — Controls resequence of node point numbers.

12.3.   Rigid Format Output

The major part of the output from the execution of any one of the rigid formats is associated with data recovery and plot modules and is selectively controlled by Case Control Directives. However, a part of the output is automatically printed or, if requested, is the same for all rigid formats. The output that falls into these latter categories is described in following sections.

12.4.   Solution Sequence Output

Although most of the solution sequence output which describes the structural behavior is optional and is requested in the Case Control Deck, some of the printer output is automatic or under control of DIAG cards in the Executive Control Deck. The printer output is designed for 132 characters per line, with the lines per page controlled by the LINE card in the Case Control Deck. The default is LINE = 50 for 11-inch paper. Optional titles which are defined by TITLE, SUBTITLE, and LABEL Case Control Directives are printed at the top of each page. Titling directives may be defined at the subcase level. The pages are automatically dated and numbered, and the NASTRAN generation date is specified.

All of the output from data recovery and plot modules is optional, and its selection is controlled by appropriate Case Control directives. The details of making printer selections in the Case Control Deck are described in Section 1.8 for printer and punch output. Detailed information on the force and stress output available for each element type is given in Chapter 9.

A few printer output items are under the control of PARAM Bulk Data cards. The use of PARAM cards is described in Appendix B. The DIAG Executive Control directive is used to control the printing of diagnostic output. The available output under DIAG control is given in the description of the executive control cards in Section 1.9.

12.4.1.   Automatic Output

The first part of the output for a NASTRAN run is prepared during the execution of the Preface, prior to the beginning of the DMAP sequence. The following output is either automatically or optionally provided during the execution of the Preface:

1. NASTRAN title page — automatic

2. Executive Control Deck echo — automatic

3. Case Control Deck echo — automatic

4. Unsorted Bulk Data Deck echo — optional, selected in Case Control Deck

5. Sorted Bulk Data Deck echo — automatic, unless suppressed in the Case Control Deck

6. Checkpoint Dictionary — automatic, when operating in checkpoint mode. A printed echo and an entry on the system punch file are prepared for additions to the checkpoint dictionary after the execution of each checkpoint.

When making restarts with rigid formats, the following additional output is automatically prepared during the execution of the Preface if DIAG 14 is set in the Executive Control Deck:

1. Asterisks are placed beside the DMAP statement numbers of all instructions marked for execution by the Card Name Table in the case of modified restarts, and by the Rigid Format Change Table in the case of restarts on different rigid formats.

2. Message indicating the bit position activated by a rigid format change.

3. Table indicating, among other things, the card names and the associated "packed bit positions" activated by modifications in the NASTRAN Data Deck. The reader is referred to the Programmer's Manual for the interpretation of the rest of this table.

4. A list of data blocks, along with the DMAP instructions that were marked for execution by the File Name Table.

5. List of data blocks from the Old Problem Tape, including purged data blocks, used to initiate the restart.

The Grid Point Singularity Table is automatically output following the execution of the Grid Point Singularity Processor (GPSP1) if singularities remain in the stiffness matrix at the grid point level. This table lists singular degrees of freedom in the global coordinate system. These singular degrees of freedom may be automatically purged at user option, using the AUTOSPC PARAMeter.

Any of the matrices or tables that are prepared by the functional modules can be printed by using selected DMAP utility modules such as TABPRT and MATPRN. These utility modules can be scheduled at any point in the rigid format by using the ALTER feature. In general, they should be scheduled immediately after the functional module that generates the table or matrix to be printed. However, the user is cautioned to check the calling sequence for the utility module in order to be certain that all required inputs have been generated prior to this point.

12.4.2. Output of System Response Variables

MSC/NASTRAN is designed to solve problems of several thousand variables and can produce a very large amount of data. Data recovery and its printout is therefore performed under user control. The output options provided as a part of the static rigid format include the following Case Control directives

1. Displacements at selected GRID points — DISP

2. Nonzero components of applied loads — OLOAD

3. Nonzero components of single point constraint forces — SPCF

4. Gridpoint force balance of selected points — GPFO

5. Element forces in selected elements — ELFO

6. Stress in selected elements — STRESS

7. Strain energy in selected elements — ESE

12.5. Fatal Errors

There are two classes of fatal errors in MSC/NASTRAN:

1. Those that occur during the execution of a DMAP module

2. Those which are associated with a logical inconsistancies during execution of the DMAP instructions

12.4.1 Automatic Output

The first type of fatal error is identified with a message in the printout and is associated with a message number. The message numbers are assigned in groups as follows

1-1000	Errors found in the form of data deck (termed Preface Errors)
1001-2000	Errors found by the executive DMAP modules
2001-8999	Errors found by the functional modules
9000-9499	Errors found by MSGMESH

For example, the message

$$* * *\text{USER FATAL ERROR 2025, UNDEFINED COORDINATE SYSTEM 102}$$

means that the user has made an error. A reference has been made to coordinate system 102 but that coordinate system has not been defined on CORDinate Bulk Data.

All user and system errors are tabulated by message number in Ref. 12-2. In most cases the description of the errors in the reference is more informative than the terse message which is printed in the output.

The other class of error is associated with logical errors in the DMAP Solution Sequence which sets the values of certain variable PARAMeters to cause a jump to an error condition in the DMAP sequence. The contents of the variable parameter table, which includes the values of all variable parameters, is then printed and MSC/NASTRAN terminates normally. In these cases the fact that the variable parameter table has been printed is the clue which tells us that an error condition has been found. The variable parameters which control this action, and the associated logical error are described by Table 12-1.

PARAMeter Name	Meaning
NOL	There are no independent degrees of freedom in the ℓ-set
NOMGG	The mass matrix has not been generated and is required
NOKGG	The stiffness matrix has not been generated
SING	Matrix decomposition of a singular matrix has been attempted
NOGPDT	No grid or scalar points have been defined
TEST	An incompability exists between a SOL subset and the Case Control looping directives

Table 12.1. Variable Parameters Used for Error Exit in Statics

The NASTRAN diagnostic messages may be either user or program diagnostics that contain warnings, information, or indication of fatal errors. These messages are usually identified by number and are documented in Ref. 12-2. These diagnostic messages are identified by three asterisks that precede the message. The messages are self-explanatory and are thus not included in this text.

In addition to the numbered diagnostic messages there are a few self-explanatory messages, such as the time required for matrix decomposition and the grid point singularity table if potential singularities are found.

314

12.6.   Grid Point Singularity Processing

The stiffness and constraint set membership data are inspected prior to the actual constraint and reduction processing in order to identify singular degrees of freedom. Several necessary but not sufficient tests are performed to identify potential singularities. Those degrees of freedom which are identified as potentially singular are then added to the s-set at user's option by using the AUTOSPC PARAMeter which is described below. The $\mathbf{K}_{gg}$ stiffness matrix which includes all terms due to GENEL-type elements and matrix coefficients defined on DMI or DMIG Bulk Data is considered together with the multipoint constraint equations and the set membership tables.

12.6.1.   Identification of Singularities

The most common modeling situation which leads to singular degrees of freedom occurs when the elements chosen to represent the structure do not connect all of the structural degrees of freedom at a grid point. The criteria which are used to identify singular degrees of freedom are thus bias toward that situation. The user should carefully review the list of singularities which are identified before removing them from the analysis set. The user is encouraged to use special caution when using the option for automatically placing the singular degrees of freedom in the s-set.

The logic used to identify singular degrees of freedom is not universally applicable to all modeling situations. Those which will cause difficulty include

1.   A local singularity will not be identified for a degree of freedom which is connected by a multipoint constraint equation (i.e., an MPC or constraint element)

2.   Singularities which involve more than a single degree of freedom such as rigid body motion or a mechanism

The local grid point singularities are identified by examining the stiffness matrix $\mathbf{K}_{gg}$ by the following procedure.

1.   Calculate the principal stiffness, K_i, and principal direction of stiffness, $\mathbf{d}_i$, for each 3×3 partition of $\mathbf{K}_{gg}$.

2.   Normalize the three principal stiffness as follows

$$R_i = \frac{K_i}{K_{max}} \qquad \text{if } K_{max} > 0, i = 1, 2, 3$$

$$R_i = 0 \qquad \qquad \text{if } K_{max} = 0$$

3.   Compare the ration, R_i, to a small positive number EPZERO which is defined by a PARAMeter

If $R_i < $ EPZERO then a potential singularity exists and can be removed by including the degree of freedom having a direction closest to the principal direction, $\mathbf{d}_i$, in the s-set. The list of potentially singular degrees of freedom is then compared with the displacement set membership as defined by MPCs and SPCs. A potentially singular degree of freedom which is not included in either the m- or s-sets is then identified as a true singularity. The user can request that these singular degrees of freedom be purged by appending them to the user-defined s-set by means of the AUTOSPC PARAMeter as described in the next section.

12.6.2.   User Control

The user can exercise control over the identification of potential singularities as well as their removal by means of the following PARAMeters in Bulk Data.

AUTOSPC   Controls automatic purging of true singularities

        YES   Automatic purge (i.e. append identified singularities to the s-set)

        NO   No purge (Default)

EPZERO   Singularity test value

        $10.^{-8}$ (Default)

PRGPST   Controls the printout of singularity messages

        YES   Print messages (Default)

        NO   No messages

SPCGEN   Controls SPC card generation

        >0   Generate SPC card images on the system PUNCH file for all user defined and internally generated SPC cards

        0   No cards generated (Default)

12.6.3.   Automatic Output

The grid point singularity table is automatically printed if the associated control parameter PRGPST is YES. An example of the table which could result due to the definition of a planar bending problem is as follows

GRID POINT SINGULARITY TABLE

Point ID	Type	Failed Direction	Stiffness Ratio	Old USET	NEW USET
1	G	1	0.	L	S
1	G	2	0.	L	S
1	G	4	0.	L	S
1	G	6	0.	L	S
2	G	1	0.	L	S
2	G	2	0.	L	S
2	G	4	0.	L	S
2	G	6	0.	L	S
3	G	1	0.	L	S
3	G	2	0.	L	S
3	G	4	0.	L	S
3	G	6	0.	L	S

This table contains one line for each degree of freedom which is unconnected and which has not been explicitly purged by SPC-type input. Degrees of freedom which have been purged by the action of PARAM, AUTOSPC, YES are identified by an asterisk following the last "New Uset" entry. The list can be lengthy if, for example, AUTOSPC is used to purge unconnected degree of freedom for a solid element model.

12.6.4. Displacement Set Membership

It is often necessary for the analyst to know the displacement set membership of each degree of freedom and the internal equation number associated with each degree of freedom in a specific set. For example, it is inconsistent and improper to define a degree of freedom in more than one of the removed displacement sets. That is, with reference to Table 7-4, a degree of freedom cannot be defined in more than one of the m-, s-, o-, or r-sets. If the analyst attempts to do so the following error message will be printed

   USER FATAL MESSAGE 2101A, GRID POINT*COMPONENT****ILLEGALLY DEFINED IN SETS****

The set membership tables are printed by the TABPRT DMAP module which is incorporated in Rigid Format 3 for Normal Modes but which must be incorporated into rigid format 24 either by including rigid format alter RF24D80 (see Sec.12.9) or by including the following alter

   ALTER 99

   TABPRT   USET, EQXEXIN//USET/C,Y,USETPRT = 0/C,Y,USETSEL $

where the user can optionally select the type and number of tables to be printed by means of the parameters USETPRT and USETSEL as follows

PARAMETER NAME	PARAMETER VALUE	ACTION
USETPRT	0 (Default)	Membership of each degree of freedom
	1	Degrees of freedom for specific sets
	>1	Both of the above
USETSEL	1	M-set
	2	S-set
	4	O-set
	8	R-set
	16	G-set
	32	N-set
	64	F-set
	128	L-set
	512	SG-set (SPCs on GRID cards)
	1024	SB-set (SPCs on SPC cards)
	1048576	C-SET
	2097152	B-SET
	4194304	Q-SET
	8388608	T-SET
	647 (Default)	Union of SG-, SB-, M-, S-, O-, and A-sets

12.7. Grid Point Weight Generator

Weight and balance information can be calculated in any of the rigid formats for structural analysis. The calculation is requested by the inclusion of a PARAM Bulk Data card that has the parameter name GRDPNT. The value of the parameter defines the reference GRID point with a value of zero (0) specifying the origin of basic coordinates. A blank field for the value is not allowed.

The grid point weight generator calculates the mass, center of gravity and moments of inertia for the finite element model of the structure. These data are calculated from the system mass matrix by a rigid body transformation about a reference point that is specified on the PARAM Bulk Data card.

12.7.1.   Rigid Body Transformation Matrix

Let $\mathbf{u}_o$ represent the six degrees of freedom associated with a reference point. Then using the geometry of the grid points, a rigid body transformation matrix is obtained that relates the displacement of the set of all grid point displacements to displacements of the reference point:

$$\mathbf{u}_g = \mathbf{D}_{go}\, \mathbf{u}_o \tag{12.18}$$

where $\mathbf{D}_{go}$ is a g-by-6 matrix.

12.7.2.   Rigid Body Mass Matrix

The rigid body mass matrix is calculated with respect to the reference point by the transformation

$$\mathbf{M}_o = \mathbf{D}_{go}^T\, \mathbf{M}_{gg}\, \mathbf{D}_{go} \tag{12.19}$$

which results in a 6-by-6 rigid body mass matrix. The mass matrix may have directional properties because of scalar mass effects.

12.7.3.   Principal Mass Axes

The set of grid point displacements is partitioned into translational (subscript t) and rotational degrees of freedom (subscript r) so that the mass matrix can be partitioned as

$$\mathbf{M}_o = \begin{bmatrix} \overline{\mathbf{M}}_{tt} & \overline{\mathbf{M}}_{tr} \\ \overline{\mathbf{M}}_{tr}^T & \overline{\mathbf{M}}_{rr} \end{bmatrix} \tag{12.20}$$

If the $\overline{\mathbf{M}}_{tt}$ matrix is not diagonal (i.e. if the elements of the off-diagonal terms are larger than some preassigned small value) then the principal masses and associated principal axes of the translational mass matrix are calculated. The transformation $\mathbf{S}$ from basic coordinates to principal directions is defined in terms of the normalized eigenvectors as

$$\mathbf{S} = [\, \mathbf{e}_1\, \mathbf{e}_2\, \mathbf{e}_3\,] \tag{12.21}$$

Each of the partitions of $\mathbf{M}_o$ is then transformed to the principal axes of $\overline{\mathbf{M}}_{tt}$ as

$$\mathbf{M}_{tr} = \mathbf{S}^T\, \overline{\mathbf{M}}_{tr}\, \mathbf{S}$$

$$\overline{\mathbf{M}}_{rr} = \mathbf{S}^T\, \overline{\mathbf{M}}_{rr}\, \mathbf{S} \tag{12.22}$$

$$\mathbf{M}_{tt} = \mathbf{S}^T\, \overline{\mathbf{M}}_{tt}\, \mathbf{S}$$

12.7.4.   Centroid

The position of the center of gravity may be different when taken with respect to different mass directions since the diagonal elements of the translational mass elements may be different if scalar masses are specified (see Sec. 13.4.). The location of the center of mass is therefore calculated with respect to the reference point for each mass direction.

12.7.5.   Moments of Inertia

The moments of inertia with respect to the principal mass axes at the center of gravity are determined using the parallel axis theorem for each of the mass systems. The resulting inertia tensor is then labeled $\mathbf{I}(S)$.

The set of principal directions **Q** is then found so that the principal moments of inertia are given by

$$\mathbf{I}(Q) = \mathbf{Q}^T \mathbf{I}(S) \mathbf{Q} \qquad (12.23)$$

12.8. Example Problems

General purpose finite element programs such as MSC/NASTRAN are designed to provide computational horsepower for the solution of large problems which are represented by several thousand degrees of freedom. However, it is always a good idea to build up a base of experience and confidence in our computational tool by exploring all of its features and capabilities for the solution of relatively simple problems before moving to the complex world of real-life structures.

We will, therefore, use MSC/NASTRAN to solve several problems for which solutions are known including:

1. A uniformly loaded cantilever beam

2. A simply supported rectangular plate with uniform load

These problems will allow us to use several of the elements and modeling features together with data recovery features in MSC/NASTRAN including

- Use of BAR, BEAM, and QUAD4, elements

- Use of single point constraints (SPC)

- Use of PLOAD1 and PLOAD2, loads

- Complete data deck

- Grid point weight generator

- Printing displacement set membership tables

- Data recovery including

    - Node point displacements

    - Element forces and stresses

    - Element strains and curvatures

    - Single point Constraint forces

While no one example problem will incorporate all of these features, each will be included in at least one of the examples which are described in the following sections.

12.8.1. Cantilevered Beam with Uniform Load

The structural element for this example is shown by Figure 12.2.

12.8.1 Cantilevered Beam with Uniform Load

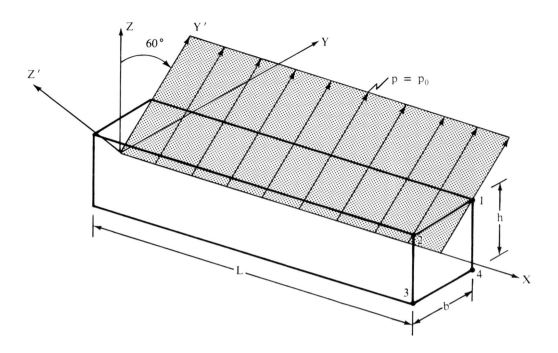

Figure 12-2. Beam Element

Where the beam has the following geometric and elastic properties

$E = 30 \times 10^6\,\text{psi}$

$\nu = 0.3$

$K_y = K_y = 0.833$

$L = 10\,\text{in.}$

$h = 0.5\,\text{in.}$

$\gamma = 0.281\,\text{lb}_f/\text{in.}^3$

$b = 0.25\,\text{in.}$

$p_o = 10\,\text{lb/in.}$

The pressure loading acts in a plane which is rotated 60 degrees from the X-Y plane as shown.

We now have to make a choice concerning the orientation of the local coordinate system. If we choose to define the local coordinates of the cross section (i.e., local yz coordinates shown by Fig. 9-5) so that they coincide with the basic coordinates (YZ) then we must represent the load in terms of its components in the Y and Z directions. If, on the other hand, we choose the local coordinate system such that one of the local axes coincides with the plane of the loading then we must calculate the cross-sectional moments of inertia with respect to a set of non-principal axes. For the purpose of this example we will describe the local coordinates and loads both ways. Specifically we will perform two analyses in which we

320

a) Define the local y-axis to be parallel with (actually lie in the plane of) the distributed load. The load will then be defined by PLOAD1 Bulk Data using the local coordinate option (i.e., TYPE = FYE).

b) Define the local coordinate (xyz) to be coincident with the basic coordinate (XYZ). Three load subcases will then be specified by suitable SUBCASE directives

    1. Uniform load of magnitude $p_o\cos\theta$ in basic Y-Direction using PLOAD1 with basic coordinate option (i.e., TYPE = FY).

    2. Uniform load of magnitude $p_o\sin\theta$ in basic z-direction using PLOAD1 with basic coordinate option (i.e., TYPE = FZ).

    3. Combination of two previous subcases to obtain response to actual load vector; results should correspond with those from example (a).

12.8.1a.   Non-Principal Local Coordinates

We will use (9.25) through (9.27) to calculate the moments of inertia with respect to the non-principal axes (y,z) which are shown by Fig. 9-5. We will then specify the coefficients I_{yy}, I_{zz}, and I_{yz} on PBAR Bulk Data and align the local coordinates as appropriate by means of the orientation vector on the CBAR card.

The moments of inertia about the principal axes of the cross-section are first found, using (9.21) through (9.24), to be

$$I_{y'y'} = 0.002604 \text{ in}^4$$

$$I_{z'z'} = 0.000651 \text{ in}^4$$

$$I_{y'z'} = 0 \tag{12.24}$$

$$A = 0.125 \text{ in}^2$$

The substitution of these coefficients into (9.25) through (9.27), noting that $0 = 60$ degrees, then leads to the following values for the non-principal moments of inertia for the cross-section

$$I_{yy} = 0.001139 \text{ in}^4$$

$$I_{zz} = 0.002116 \text{ in}^4 \tag{12.25}$$

$$I_{yz} = 0.00846 \text{ in}^4$$

The orientation vector is now defined so that the local y-axis for the BAR coincides with the plane of the load. One possible way of defining this orientation is by means of components of v. These components are defined relative to basic coordinates so that the vector lies in the YZ plane relative to basic coordinates at an angle of sixty degrees to the basic Y-axis giving v as

$$v = (0, \cos60°, \sin60°) = (0., \quad 0.5, \quad 0.86603)$$

We will now define the complete MSC/NASTRAN data deck which will

- Request static analysis, Rigid Format 24

- Include an Alter sequence to print displacement set membership tables

- Request SPC set 23 which will define geometric boundary conditions at X = 0.

12.8.1a Non-Principal Local Coordinates

- Purge unconnected degrees of freedom using AUTOSPC

- Select static load set 101 which defines a uniform load by means of PLOAD1 Bulk Data

- Requests displacements, SPC forces, element forces, and stresses at corner points as output

- Generates weight and balance information using GRDPNT parameter

The MSC/NASTRAN Data Deck is then as follows

Card	1	2	3	4	5	6	7	8	9	10
1-	ID	PROBLEM	121A							
2-	SOL	24	$REQUEST STATIC ANALYSIS							
3-	TIME	2	$SET SOLUTION TIME TO TWO MINUTES							
4-	ALTER	99	$ALTER IN TABLE PRINTER							
5-	TABPRT	USET, EQEXIN // USET / C,Y,USETPRT = 0 / C,Y,USETSEL $								
6-	CEND									
7-	TITLE = UNIFORMLY LOADED CANTILEVERED BEAM									
8-	SUBTITLE = NON-PRINCIPAL LOCAL COORDINATES									
9-	SPC = 23									
10-	LOAD = 101									
11-	DISP = ALL									
12-	SPCFORCE = ALL									
13-	ELFORCE = ALL									
14-	STRESS = ALL									
15-	BEGIN BULK									
16-	GRID	1	0	10.	0.	0.				
17-	GRID	2	0	0.	0.	0.				
18-	CBAR	1	129	2	1	0.	0.5	.86603		
19-	PBAR	129	30		2.116-3	1.139-3		3.537-2		+ P1
20-	+ P1	.279	.0167	.154	.233	− .279	− .0167	− .154	− .233	+ P2
21-	+ P2			8.457-4						
22-	MAT1	30	3. + 7		0.3					
23-	SPC	23	2	2356						
24-	PLOAD1	101	1	FYE	FR	0.	10.	1.	10.	
25-	PARAM	AUTOSPC	YES							
26-	PARAM	GRDPNT	0							
27-	PARAM	USETPRT	2							
28-	PARAM	USETSEL	210							
29-	ENDDATA									

With reference to the card numbers:

Card 1- Required Executive Control card

Card 2- Requests Rigid Format 24, Static analysis

Card 3- Requests two minutes of cpu time for MSC/NASTRAN execution

Card 4- Requests that Card 5 be merged in DMAP sequence for Rigid Format 24 following
Card 5   DMAP statement 99.

322

Card 6- Required to terminate Executive Control

Card 7- optional titling directives
Card 8

Card 9- Requests that SPC set 23 be used

Card 10- Requests that LOAD set 101 be used

Card 11- output requests
 thru
Card 14

Card 15- Required to terminate Case Control

Card 16- Defines GRID points 1 and 2, with the lowest GRID number located at the free end of
Card 17   the structure in order to minimize matrix ill conditioning.

Card 18- Connects GRID points 1 and 2 with a BAR bending element and aligns local y axis at
          60 degrees to the basic Y-axis. Points to PBAR with PID = 129

Card 19- Points to MAT1 with MID = 30. Defines $I_{yy} = 1.139 \times 10^{-3}$ in⁴, $I_{zz} = 2.116 \times 10^{-3}$ in⁴,
          and NSM = 0.035375 lb/in.

Card 20- Defines the four stress recovery points, as shown by Fig. 12-2 in *local* coordinates

Card 21- Defines $I_{yz} = 0.008457$; transverse shear flexibility for non-principal axes can not be
          defined

Card 22- Defines isotropic material with E = 30 × 10⁶ psi and $\nu = 0.3$

Card 23- Specifies constraints to physical degrees of freedom at node 2 (u_{x2} and θ_{x2} are not con-
          nected since A = 0 and J = 0 on PBAR card). All unconnected degrees of freedom
          will be purged using AUTOSPC.

Card 24- Defines uniform pressure load of 10 lb/in. in the local y-direction along length of the
          BAR

Card 25- Requests that unconnected degrees of freedom be automatically purged

Card 26- Requests that weight and balance information be with respect to Grid point 0, which is
          a nonexistant GRID point, causing the origin of basic coordinates to be used.

Card 27- Requests two forms of set membership tables (overrides the default)

Card 28- Request only membership tables for S-, G-, F-, and A-sets using sum of appropriate
          USETSEL values defined in Sec. 12.6.4. (i.e., USETSEL = 2 + 8 + 64 + 128 = 210)

Card 29- Required to terminate BULK DATA

12.8.1a.1.   Executive Control Deck
The echo of the Executive Control deck is presented by Fig. 12-3.

12.8.1a.1   Executive Control Deck

```
              N A S T R A N    E X E C U T I V E    C O N T R O L    D E C K    E C H O



ID PRIMER PROB121A
SOL 24      $REQUEST STATIC ANALYSIS
TIME 4      $SET SOLUTION TIME TO FOUR MINUTES
ALTER 99    $ALTER IN TABLE PRINTER
TABPRT USET , EQEXIN // USET / C,Y,USETPRT=0 / C,Y,USETSEL $
CEND
```

Figure 12-3. Executive Control Deck Echo

12.8.1a.2.   Case Control Deck

The echo of the Case Control deck is presented by Fig. 12-4.

```
                               C A S E    C O N T R O L    D E C K    E C H O
CARD
COUNT
  1        TITLE = UNIFORMLY LOADED CANTILEVERED BEAM
  2        SUBTITLE = NON-PRINCIPAL LOCAL COORDINATES
  3        SPC = 23
  4        LOAD = 101
  5            DISP = ALL
  6            SPCFORCE = ALL
  7            ELFORCE = ALL
  8            STRESS = ALL
  9        BEGIN BULK

           INPUT BULK DATA CARD COUNT =       14
```

Figure 12-4. Case Control Echo

12.8.1a.3.   Sorted Bulk Data Deck

The echo of the Sorted Bulk Data Deck is shown by Fig. 12-5.

```
                               S O R T E D    B U L K    D A T A    E C H O
CARD
COUNT        .   1   ..   2   ..   3   ..   4   ..   5   ..   6   ..   7   ..   8   ..   9   ..  10  .
  1-        CBAR      1        129       2        1        0.        .5       .86603
  2-        GRID      1        0        10.       0.       0.
  3-        GRID      2        0        0.        0.       0.
  4-        MAT1      30       3.+7              .3
  5-        PARAM     AUTOSPC  YES
  6-        PARAM     GRDPNT   0
  7-        PARAM     USETPRT  2
  8-        PARAM     USETSEL  210
  9-        PBAR      129      30                2.116-3  1.139-3            3.5375-2          +P1
 10-        +P1       .279     .0167    .154     .233     -.279    -.0167   -.154    -.233    +P2
 11-        +P2                         8.457-4
 12-        PLOAD1    101      1        FYE      FR       0.       10.      1.       10.
 13-        SPC       23       2        2356
            ENDDATA

       TOTAL COUNT=    14
```

Figure 12-5.

324

12.8.1a.4.   Grid Point Weight Table

The weight and balance information requested by the inclusion of the GRDPNT parameter card is shown by Fig. 12-6. The units of the coefficients of the mass and inertia matrices are in terms of weight units because the weight per unit length was specified on the PBAR-card. The weight of the structure is the same in the three coordinate directions and is equal to 0.35375 lb.

```
     O U T P U T    F R O M    G R I D    P O I N T    W E I G H T    G E N E R A T O R

                         REFERENCE POINT =        0
                                      M O
  *  3.537500E-01   0.000000E+00   0.000000E+00   0.000000E+00   0.000000E+00   0.000000E+00 *
  *  0.000000E+00   3.537500E-01   0.000000E+00   0.000000E+00   0.000000E+00   1.768750E+00 *
  *  0.000000E+00   0.000000E+00   3.537500E-01   0.000000E+00  -1.768750E+00   0.000000E+00 *
  *  0.000000E+00   0.000000E+00   0.000000E+00   0.000000E+00   0.000000E+00   0.000000E+00 *
  *  0.000000E+00   0.000000E+00  -1.768750E+00   0.000000E+00   1.768750E+01   0.000000E+00 *
  *  0.000000E+00   1.768750E+00   0.000000E+00   0.000000E+00   0.000000E+00   1.768750E+01 *
                                       S
                    *  1.000000E+00   0.000000E+00   0.000000E+00 *
                    *  0.000000E+00   1.000000E+00   0.000000E+00 *
                    *  0.000000E+00   0.000000E+00   1.000000E+00 *
          DIRECTION
  MASS AXIS SYSTEM (S)        MASS           X-C.G.         Y-C.G.         Z-C.G.
          X              3.537500E-01     0.000000E+00   0.000000E+00   0.000000E+00
          Y              3.537500E-01     5.000000E+00   0.000000E+00   0.000000E+00
          Z              3.537500E-01     5.000000E+00   0.000000E+00   0.000000E+00
                                      I(S)
                    *  0.000000E+00   0.000000E+00   0.000000E+00 *
                    *  0.000000E+00   8.843750E+00   0.000000E+00 *
                    *  0.000000E+00   0.000000E+00   8.843750E+00 *
                                      I(Q)
                    *  0.000000E+00                                 *
                    *                  8.843750E+00                 *
                    *                                 8.843750E+00  *
                                       Q
                    *  1.000000E+00   0.000000E+00   0.000000E+00 *
                    *  0.000000E+00   1.000000E+00   0.000000E+00 *
                    *  0.000000E+00   0.000000E+00   1.000000E+00 *
```

Figure 12-6. Grid Point Weight Table

12.8.1a.5.   Displacement Set Membership Tables

The displacement set memberships can be defined for each degree of freedom as shown by Fig. 12-7, or the degrees of freedom in logical displacement sets can be printed as shown by Fig. 12-8. The printout of these sets was requested by ALTERing the TABPRT DMAP module into Rigid Format 24 as indicated in the Executive Control Deck Echo, Fig. 12-3. The type of tables to be printed is controlled by the USETPRT PARAMeter, while the specific displacement sets for which membership is desired are specified by the USETSEL PARAMeter.

INT DOF	INT GP.	EXT GP. DOF	SB	SG	L	A	F	N	G	R	O	S	M	E	INT DOF
1-	1 G	1 - 1	1					1	1			1		-	1
2-		- 2			1	1	1	2	2					-	2
3-		- 3			2	2	2	3	3					-	3
4-		- 4	2					4	4			2		-	4
5-		- 5			3	3	3	5	5					-	5
6-		- 6			4	4	4	6	6					-	6
7-	2 G	2 - 1	3					7	7			3		-	7
8-		- 2	4					8	8			4		-	8
9-		- 3	5					9	9			5		-	9
10-		- 4	6					10	10			6		-	10
11-		- 5	7					11	11			7		-	11
12-		- 6	8					12	12			8		-	12
INT DOF	INT GP.	EXT GP. DOF	SB	SG	L	A	F	N	G	R	O	S	M	E	INT DOF
---- C O L U M N T O T A L S ----			8	0	4	4	4	12	12	0	0	8	0	0	

Figure 12-7. Correspondence Between Internal and External Degrees of Freedom

325

12.8.1a.5   Displacement Set Membership Tables

The columns of this table are

INT DOF The internal number for the degree of freedom

EXT. GP. DOF The external degree of freedom code. The first number is the grid or scalar point number, and the second is the degree of freedom code at the grid or scalar point.

SB Single point constraints specified on SPC cards

SG Single point constraints specified on GRID Bulk Data cards

L Degrees of freedom in the ℓ-set

A Degrees of freedom in the a-set

F Degrees of freedom in the f-set

N Degrees of freedom in the n-set

G Degrees of freedom in the g-set

M Degrees of freedom in the m-set

R Degrees of freedom in the r-set

O Degrees of freedom in the o-set

S Degrees of freedom specified in SG and SB sets

```
                                          A     DISPLACEMENT SET
              -1-      -2-      -3-     -4-      -5-       -6-       -7-       -8-       -9-      -10-
      1=       1-2      1-3      1-5     1-6


                                          F     DISPLACEMENT SET
              -1-      -2-      -3-     -4-      -5-       -6-       -7-       -8-       -9-      -10-
      1=       1-2      1-3      1-5     1-6


                                          S     DISPLACEMENT SET
              -1-      -2-      -3-     -4-      -5-       -6-       -7-       -8-       -9-      -10-
      1=       1-1      1-4      2-1     2-2      2-3       2-4       2-5       2-6


                                          G     DISPLACEMENT SET
              -1-      -2-      -3-     -4-      -5-       -6-       -7-       -8-       -9-      -10-
      1=       1-1      1-2      1-3     1-4      1-5       1-6       2-1       2-2       2-3       2-4 =    10
     11=       2-5      2-6
```

Figure 12-8. Definition of Displacement Sets

The information contained in these tables are extremely valuable, especially when the user is attempting to find the cause of a singular stiffness or mass matrix. These data should therefore be requested for every structural analysis when using NASTRAN.

12.8.1a.6. Selected Output

The displacements, forces of constraint, forces in the BAR element, and the stress in the BAR element are shown below. The GRID point-oriented printout such as displacements and SPC forces are sorted by GRID point number. The components are then printed under the headings T1, T2, T3 for displacement or force components and R1, R2, R3 for rotation or moment components. The components are interpreted with respect to the displacement coordinate systems which is associated with grid point displacements.

The headings under Force Distribution in BAR Elements are

1. The Element ID

2. The normalized distance from the end of the element at which the forces are calculated

3. The bending moments about the local z-axis (i.e., normal to the local xy-plane) which is identified as PLANE1, and the bending moment about the local y-axis which is normal to the xz-plane (identified as PLANE2)

4. Shear Force —

   PLANE1 — in local y-direction

   PLANE2 — in local z-direction

5. Axial Force

6. Torque

The headings under Stress Distribution are:

1. SXC   Bending stress at the four stress recovery points identified as points C, D, E,
   SXD   and F
   SXE
   SXF

2. AXIAL   Axial stress, P/A

3. S-MAX   The maximum combined stress at the four stress recovery points

4. S-MIN   The minimum combined stress at the four stress recovery points

5. M.S   The margin of safety for stress based on stress limit defined by MAT1 Bulk DATA for the element

```
                          D I S P L A C E M E N T    V E C T O R

POINT ID.   TYPE        T1              T2              T3            R1            R2              R3
    1        G       0.0         3.200494E-01   1.385408E-01     0.0      -1.847211E-02   4.267326E-02
    2        G       0.0         0.0            0.0              0.0       0.0             0.0


               F O R C E S    O F    S I N G L E - P O I N T    C O N S T R A I N T

POINT ID.   TYPE        T1              T2              T3            R1            R2              R3
    2        G       0.0        -4.999980E+01  -8.660265E+01     0.0       4.330132E+02   -2.499990E+02


            F O R C E    D I S T R I B U T I O N    I N    B A R    E L E M E N T S       ( C B A R )

ELEMENT  STATION        BEND-MOMENT                     SHEAR FORCE                 AXIAL
   ID.    (PCT)    PLANE 1       PLANE 2          PLANE 1        PLANE 2            FORCE               TORQUE
    1     0.000  5.000000E+02  1.395373E-05    1.000000E+02   1.781405E-06        0.0                 0.0
    1     1.000 -7.629395E-06 -3.860315E-06   -3.814697E-06   1.781405E-06        0.0                 0.0


            S T R E S S    D I S T R I B U T I O N    I N    B A R    E L E M E N T S    ( C B A R )

ELEMENT  STATION    SXC           SXD           SXE           SXF           AXIAL        S-MAX          S-MIN        M.S.
   ID.    (PCT)
    1     0.000 -8.957904E+04  6.384410E+03  8.957904E+04  -6.384410E+03    0.0     8.957904E+04   -8.957904E+04
    1     1.000  9.099543E-04  7.288672E-04 -9.099543E-04  -7.288672E-04    0.0     9.099543E-04   -9.099543E-04
```

12.8.1b.   Use of Principal Axes

The moments of inertia for the cross section were found in the previous section (12.24.). Now, since the principal axes coincide with the basic axes we must represent the load in terms of its vector components as shown by Fig. 12-9.

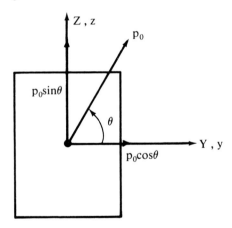

Figure 12-9. Components of Distributed Pressure Load

We will now define the complete MSC/NASTRAN data deck for the beam referred to principal axes by

- Requesting static analysis, Rigid Format 24

- Including an ALTER sequence to print displacement set membership

- Requesting SPC set 23 which will define constraints to physical degrees of freedom using PSPC on GRDSET Bulk Data

- Selecting static load set 100 in SUBCASE one which defines a uniform load in the basic Y — direction

- Selecting static load set 200 in Subcase two which defines a uniform load in the basic Z — direction

- Combining the results from the two previous subcases

- Requesting displacement, SPC.force, element force and stress output

The MSC/NASTRAN Data Deck is as follows

Card	1	2	3	4	5	6	7	8	9	10
1-	ID PROBLEM 121B									
2-	SOL 24									
3-	TIME 2									
4-	ALTER 99									
5-	TABPRT USET,EQEXIN // USET / C,Y,USETPRT = 0 / C,Y,USETSEL $									
6-	CEND									
7-	TITLE = UNIFORMLY LOADED CANTILEVERED BEAM									
8-	SUBTITLE = PRINCIPAL LOCAL COORDINATES									
9-	SPC = 23									
10-	DISP = ALL									
11-	SPCFORCE = ALL									
12-	ELFORCE = ALL									
13-	STRESS = ALL									
14-	SUBCASE 1									
15-	LABEL = LOAD COMPONENT P COS60 IN BASIC Y									
16-	LOAD = 100									
17-	SUBCASE 2									
18-	LABEL = LOAD COMPONENT P SIN60 IN BASIC Z									
19-	LOAD = 200									
20-	SUBCOM 3									
21-	SUBSEQ = 1.,1.									
22-	LABEL = COMBINED RESULTS FOR LOAD AT 60 DEGREES									
23-	BEGIN BULK									
24-	GRDSET							14		
25-	GRID	1	0	10.	0.	0.				
26-	GRID	2	0	0.	0.	0.				
27-	CBAR	1	229	2	1	0.	1.	0.		
28-	PBAR	229	30		6.5104-4	2.604-3				+ P21
29-	+ P21	.125	.25	− .125	.25	− .125	− .25	.125	− .25	
30-	MAT1	30	30. + 6		.3					+ M1
31-	+ M1	1. + 4	1. + 4	.5 + 4						
32-	SPC	23	2	2356	0.					
33-	PLOAD1	100	1	FY	FR	0.	5.	1.	5.	
34-	PLOAD1	200	1	FZ	FR	0.	8.6603	1.	8.6603	
35-	PARAM	USETSEL	1746							
36-	PARAM	AUTOSPC	YES							
37-	ENDDATA									

12.8.1b Use of Principal Axes

With reference to the card numbers in the previous data listing:

Card 1- Required Executive Control Card

Card 2- Requests static solution

Card 3- Request MSC/NASTRAN cpu time of two minutes

Card 4- Defines change to DMAP sequence which prints out set membership tables
Card 5

Card 6- Required to terminate Executive Control

Card 7- Titling information
Card 8

Card 9- Requests SPC set 23 which defines constraints to physical degrees of freedom

Card 10- Output requests above the SUBCASE level which will be honored by each subcase
Card 13

Card 14- Defines the start of SUBCASE 1

Card 15- Titling information for the SUBCASE

Card 16- Requests the static loads associated with set 100 from Bulk Data

Card 17- Defines start of SUBCASE 2

Card 18- Titling information for second SUBCASE

Card 19- Requests the static loads associated with set 200 from Bulk Data

Card 20- Defines a combination of the previous two SUBCASES. This is a data recovery operation and does not require an additional forward-backward substitution

Card 21- Defines the factors which are to be used to multiply the results from two previous SUBCASES

Card 22- Titling information for combination SUBCASE

Card 23- Required to terminate Case Control

Card 24- Defines default PSPC to purge u_x and θ_x for all GRID points

Card 25- Defines two GRID points with point number 1 at the flexible end
Card 26

Card 27- Defines the BAR connection between nodes 2 and 1, specifies the components of v such that it is parallel to the basic Y-axis, and points to PBAR Bulk Data with PID = 229

Card 28- Specifies the moments of inertia with respect to the local coordinate system which is defined by the v-vector on card 27- and points to a material card which has a MID = 30

Card 29- Defines stress recovery points in local coordinates

Card 30- Defines elastic constants for isotropic material

Card 31- Defines stress limits for material

Card 32- Defines constraints to physical degrees of freedom at x = 0.

Card 33- Defines the load component $p_y = p_o \cos 60$

Card 34- Defines the load component $p_z = p_o \sin 60$

Card 35- Request that tables, of S-, G-, F-, A-, SG-, and SB-sets of degrees of freedom be printed. We have requested SG and SB to show the degrees of freedom which are included on PSPC field on the GRID-card (the SG-set) as well as those which are specified by SPC Bulk Data (the SB-set). The S- set is that the union of both the SG- and SB-sets. The integer value of USETSEL is the sum of the integers 2, 16, 64, 128, 512, and 1024 which request the S-, G-, F-, A-, SG-, and SB-sets, respectively.

Card 36- Automatic purge of unconnected degrees of freedom

Card 37- Required termination of Bulk Data

12.8.1b.1.   Selected Output

The displacements, SPC forces, Forces in BAR elements, and stress in BAR element for each of the three SUBCASES is shown below. The combined output is presented by SUBCOM 3 which should agree with the results for the previous problem. A comparison of the two sets of results will verify that, within roundoff error limits, the results are the same.

```
              N A S T R A N   E X E C U T I V E   C O N T R O L   D E C K   E C H O


ID PRIMER PROB121B
SOL 24     $REQUEST STATIC ANALYSIS
TIME 4     $SET SOLUTION TIME TO FOUR MINUTES
ALTER 99   $ALTER IN TABLE PRINTER
TABPRT USET , EQEXIN // USET / C,Y,USETPRT=0 / C,Y,USETSEL $
CEND


                          C A S E   C O N T R O L   D E C K   E C H O
              CARD
              COUNT
                1       TITLE = UNIFORMLY LOADED CANTILEVERED BEAM
                2       SUBTITLE = PRINCIPAL LOCAL COORDINATES
                3       SPC = 23
                4           DISP = ALL
                5           SPCFORCE = ALL
                6           ELFORCE = ALL
                7           STRESS = ALL
                8       SUBCASE 1           (
                9           LABEL = LOAD COMPONENT P COS60 IN BASIC Y DIRECTION
               10           LOAD = 100
               11       SUBCASE 2
               12           LABEL = LOAD COMPONENT P SIN60 IN BASIC Z
               13           LOAD = 200
               14       SUBCOM 3
               15           LABEL = COMBINED RESULTS FOR LOAD AT 60 DEGREES
               16           SUBSEQ = 1.,1.
               17       BEGIN BULK

                   INPUT BULK DATA CARD COUNT =      14


                          S O R T E D   B U L K   D A T A   E C H O
              CARD
              COUNT     .  1  ..  2  ..  3  ..  4  ..  5  ..  6  ..  7  ..  8  ..  9  .. 10  .
                1-      CBAR     1       229     2       1       0.      1.      0.
                2-      GRDSET                                                  14
                3-      GRID     1       0       10.     0.      0.
                4-      GRID     2       0       0.      0.      0.
                5-      MAT1     30      3.+7            .3                              +M1
                6-      +M1      1.+5    1.+5    .5+5
                7-      PARAM    AUTOSPC YES
                8-      PARAM    USETSEL 1746
                9-      PBAR     229     30              6.5104-42.604-3                 +P21
```

12.8.1b.1 Selected Output

```
10-      +P21     .125    .25     -.125   .25     -.125   -.25    .125    -.25
11-      PLOAD1   100     1       FY      FR      0.      5.      1.      5.
12-      PLOAD1   200     1       FZ      FR      0.      8.6603  1.      8.6603
13-      SPC      23      2       2356
         ENDDATA

    TOTAL COUNT=    14
```

```
                              SG   DISPLACEMENT SET

        -1-      -2-      -3-      -4-     -5-      -6-      -7-      -8-      -9-      -10-

1=      1-1      1-4      2-1      2-4
```

```
                              SB   DISPLACEMENT SET

        -1-      -2-      -3-      -4-     -5-      -6-      -7-      -8-      -9-      -10-

1=      2-2      2-3      2-5      2-6
```

```
                              A    DISPLACEMENT SET

        -1-      -2-      -3-      -4-     -5-      -6-      -7-      -8-      -9-      -10-

1=      1-2      1-3      1-5      1-6
```

```
                              F    DISPLACEMENT SET

        -1-      -2-      -3-      -4-     -5-      -6-      -7-      -8-      -9-      -10-

1=      1-2      1-3      1-5      1-6
```

```
                              S    DISPLACEMENT SET

        -1-      -2-      -3-      -4-     -5-      -6-      -7-      -8-      -9-      -10-

1=      1-1      1-4      2-1      2-2     2-3      2-4      2-5      2-6
```

```
                              G    DISPLACEMENT SET

        -1-      -2-      -3-      -4-     -5-      -6-      -7-      -8-      -9-      -10-

1=      1-1      1-2      1-3      1-4     1-5      1-6      2-1      2-2      2-3      2-4 =   10
11=     2-5      2-6
```

```
*** USER INFORMATION MESSAGE 3035 FOR DATA BLOCK   KLL

    LOAD SEQ. NO.          EPSILON          STRAIN  ENERGY     EPSILONS LARGER THAN0.001 ARE FLAGGED WITH ASTERISKS
         1            0.0000000E+00        3.1111190E+00
         2            5.2743835E-17        2.3335078E+00
```

```
                                                                                SUBCASE 1

                     D I S P L A C E M E N T   V E C T O R

POINT ID.   TYPE       T1            T2           T3            R1            R2            R3
    1       G       0.0        3.200008E-01    0.0          0.0           0.0        4.266677E-02
    2       G       0.0        0.0             0.0          0.0           0.0        0.0
```

```
                                                                                SUBCASE 2

                     D I S P L A C E M E N T   V E C T O R

POINT ID.   TYPE       T1            T2           T3            R1            R2            R3
    1       G       0.0        0.0          1.385737E-01    0.0       -1.847649E-02    0.0
    2       G       0.0        0.0          0.0             0.0        0.0             0.0
```

```
                                                                                SUBCOM 3

                     D I S P L A C E M E N T   V E C T O R

POINT ID.   TYPE       T1            T2           T3            R1            R2            R3
    1       G       0.0        3.200008E-01 1.385737E-01    0.0       -1.847649E-02 4.266677E-02
    2       G       0.0        0.0          0.0             0.0        0.0          0.0
```

```
                                                                                SUBCASE 1

               F O R C E S   O F   S I N G L E - P O I N T   C O N S T R A I N T

POINT ID.   TYPE       T1            T2           T3            R1            R2            R3
    2       G       0.0       -5.000000E+01    0.0          0.0           0.0       -2.500000E+02
```

SUBCASE 2

F O R C E S   O F   S I N G L E - P O I N T   C O N S T R A I N T

POINT ID.	TYPE	T1	T2	T3	R1	R2	R3
2	G	0.0	0.0	-8.660300E+01	0.0	4.330150E+02	0.0

SUBCOM 3

F O R C E S   O F   S I N G L E - P O I N T   C O N S T R A I N T

POINT ID.	TYPE	T1	T2	T3	R1	R2	R3
2	G	0.0	-5.000000E+01	-8.660300E+01	0.0	4.330150E+02	-2.500000E+02

SUBCASE 1

F O R C E   D I S T R I B U T I O N   I N   B A R   E L E M E N T S   (C B A R)

ELEMENT ID.	STATION (PCT)	BEND-MOMENT PLANE 1	PLANE 2	SHEAR FORCE PLANE 1	PLANE 2	AXIAL FORCE	TORQUE
1	0.000	2.500000E+02	0.0	5.000000E+01	0.0	0.0	0.0
1	1.000	-3.814697E-06	0.0	0.0	0.0	0.0	0.0

SUBCASE 2

F O R C E   D I S T R I B U T I O N   I N   B A R   E L E M E N T S   (C B A R)

ELEMENT ID.	STATION (PCT)	BEND-MOMENT PLANE 1	PLANE 2	SHEAR FORCE PLANE 1	PLANE 2	AXIAL FORCE	TORQUE
1	0.000	0.0	4.330150E+02	0.0	8.660300E+01	0.0	0.0
1	1.000	0.0	0.0	0.0	0.0	0.0	0.0

SUBCOM 3

F O R C E   D I S T R I B U T I O N   I N   B A R   E L E M E N T S   (C B A R)

ELEMENT ID.	STATION (PCT)	BEND-MOMENT PLANE 1	PLANE 2	SHEAR FORCE PLANE 1	PLANE 2	AXIAL FORCE	TORQUE
1	0.000	2.500000E+02	4.330150E+02	5.000000E+01	8.660300E+01	0.0	0.0
1	1.000	-3.814697E-06	0.0	0.0	0.0	0.0	0.0

SUBCASE 1

S T R E S S   D I S T R I B U T I O N   I N   B A R   E L E M E N T S   (C B A R)

ELEMENT ID.	STATION (PCT)	SXC	SXD	SXE	SXF	AXIAL	S-MAX	S-MIN	M.S.
1	0.000	-4.800012E+04	4.800012E+04	4.800012E+04	-4.800012E+04	0.0	4.800012E+04	-4.800012E+04	1.1E+00
1	1.000	7.324237E-04	-7.324237E-04	-7.324237E-04	7.324237E-04	0.0	7.324237E-04	-7.324237E-04	1.4E+08

SUBCASE 2

S T R E S S   D I S T R I B U T I O N   I N   B A R   E L E M E N T S   (C B A R)

ELEMENT ID.	STATION (PCT)	SXC	SXD	SXE	SXF	AXIAL	S-MAX	S-MIN	M.S.
1	0.000	-4.157210E+04	-4.157210E+04	4.157210E+04	4.157210E+04	0.0	4.157210E+04	-4.157210E+04	1.4E+00
1	1.000	0.0	0.0	0.0	0.0	0.0	0.0	0.0	

SUBCOM 3

S T R E S S   D I S T R I B U T I O N   I N   B A R   E L E M E N T S   (C B A R)

ELEMENT ID.	STATION (PCT)	SXC	SXD	SXE	SXF	AXIAL	S-MAX	S-MIN	M.S.
1	0.000	-8.957223E+04	6.428020E+03	8.957223E+04	-6.428020E+03	0.0	8.957223E+04	-8.957223E+04	1.2E-01
1	1.000	7.324237E-04	-7.324237E-04	-7.324237E-04	7.324237E-04	0.0	7.324237E-04	-7.324237E-04	1.4E+08

12.8.2.   Simply-Supported Plate

The next example, which is a stiffened flat plate shown by Fig. 12-10, will allow us to explore the use of the MSC/NASTRAN shell elements for modeling. With reference to Fig. 12-10, we will consider the following solutions

   a) A simply supported flat plate subject to uniform pressure load without stiffeners using appropriate symmetry conditions to model ¼ of the plate

b) A simply supported plate with BEAM stiffeners where the middle of the plate is used as the reference surface and where the stiffener is modeled with an offset BEAM element.

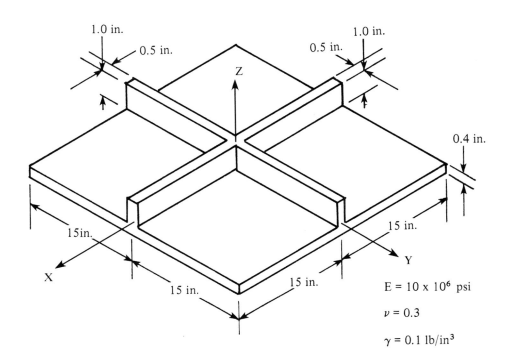

Figure 12-10. Eccentrically Stiffened Plate

12.8.2a. Simply Supported Plate without Stiffeners

We consider the square plate (a = c) shown by Fig. 12-10 with no stiffeners (i.e., h = b = 0), with simple supports on all edges, and with a uniform pressure load, p_o = 1.5 lb/in², which acts in the basic z-direction. The response of the plate in this case will only involve bending behavior so that we will use only the MID2 field on the PSHELL Card (Card Image 9-7) to select a material set for bending behavior.

The plate geometry and the loads are both symmetric so that we can use symmetry conditions along the X = 0, Y = 0 planes. The quarter panel, which is shown by Fig. 12-11, also has a plane of symmetry along the line x = y. However, we intend to use the MSC/NASTRAN preprocessor, MSGMESH (Sec. 7.3.3.7.) to generate a quadrilateral field of GRID points so that quarter symmetry satisfies our modeling objectives. The points A,B,C,D which are shown on Figure 12.11 are the vertex points for the generation of the field of GRID points, and the associated GRID numbers are those which will be generated by MSGMESH.

The displacement conditions along a plane of symmetry specify that points on the plane do not displace out of the plane. With reference to Fig. 12-12 the general set of conditions to be applied to degrees of freedom for a point P which lies on a plane of symmetry such as the X-Z plane are then:

$$u_y = 0$$

$$\theta_z = 0 \qquad\qquad (12.26)$$

$$\theta_x = 0$$

334

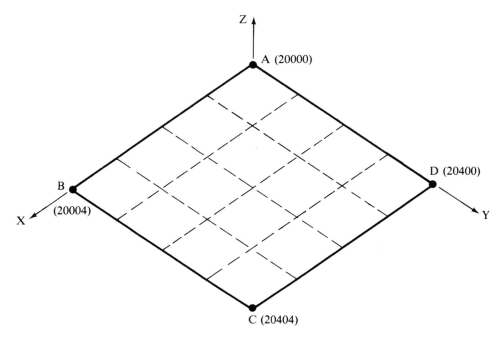

Figure 12-11. Quarter of Square Plate

with similar conditions for other planes of symmetry. There is also a complementary set of boundary conditions for a point P which lies on a plane of antisymmetry. These conditions impose the complementary condition that points which lie on a plane of antisymmetry must displace out of the plane i.e., again referring to the X-Z plane in Fig. 12-12, the antisymmetry conditions are:

$$u_z = 0$$

$$u_x = 0 \tag{12.27}$$

$$\theta_{xy} = 0$$

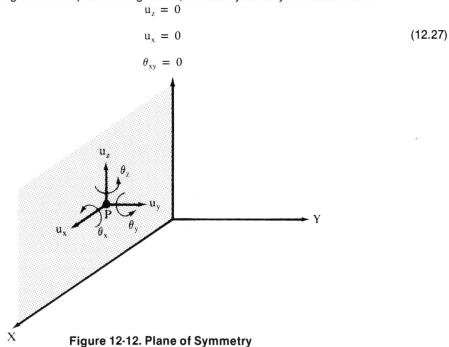

Figure 12-12. Plane of Symmetry

335

12.8.2a   Simply Supported Plate without Stiffeners

For the present example the symmetry conditions (12.26) are appropriate along the planes of symmetry $X = 0, Y = 0$.

We will now define the complete MSC/NASTRAN data deck which will

- Request static analysis, Rigid Format 24

- Include an ALTER to print displacement set membership tables

- Purge unconnected degrees of freedom by means of the PSPC field on GRDSET Bulk Data

- Request SPC set 124 which will define constraints to physical degrees of freedom and symmetry conditions

- Select a LOAD set 51 which defines the static pressure load that is specified by PLOAD2 Bulk Data

- Uses MSGMESH to generate

    - A quadrilateral field of GRID points

    - The connectivity for the thin shell element

    - Displacement boundary conditions

- Requests displacements, element forces, SPC forces, and stresses

The MSC/NASTRAN Data Deck is then as follows

Card	1	2	3	4	5	6	7	8	9	10
1-	NASTRAN PREFOPT = 2 $ REQUESTS MSGMESH PROCESSOR									
2-	ID PRIMER PROB122A									
3-	SOL 24									
4-	TIME 4									
5-	ALTER 99 $ PRINT SET MEMBERSHIP TABLES									
6-	TABPRT USET, EQEXIN // USET / C,Y,USETPRT = 0 / C,Y,USETSEL $									
7-	CEND									
8-	TITLE = SQUARE SIMPLY SUPPORTED PLATE WITHOUT STIFFENER									
9-	SUBTITLE = UNIFORM PRESSURE LOAD									
10-	LABEL = MODELLED USING QUARTER-SYMMETRY									
11-	SPC = 124									
12-	LOAD = 51									
13-	DISP = ALL									
14-	SPCF = ALL									
15-	OLOAD = ALL									
16-	EFFO = ALL									
17-	STRESS = ALL									
18-	BEGIN BULK									
19-	GRDSET							126		
20-	$GENERATE A 4-BY-FOUR FIELD OF POINTS USING MSGMESH									
21-	EGRID	1	0	0.	0.	0.				
22-	EGRID	2	0	15.	0.	0.				
23-	EGRID	3	0	15.	15.	0.				

24-	EGRID	4	0	0.	15.	0.				
25-	GRIDG	2	0		4	− 1	− 2	− 3		+ G1
26-	+ G1	4	− 4							
27-	$CONNECT GRIDS IN FID = 2 WITH QUAD 4 ELEMENTS									
28-	CGEN	QUAD4	1	11	2					
29-	$GENERATE SPCS FOR SYMMETRY ALONG X = 0									
30-	SPCG	1241	2	156	DA					
31-	$GENERATE SPCS FOR SYMMETRY ALONG Y = 0									
32-	SPCG	1242	2	246	AB					
33-	$GENERATE SIMPLE SUPPORT CONSTRAINT ALONG X = 15									
34-	SPCG	1243	2	35	CD					
35-	$GENERATE SIMPLE SUPPORT CONSTRAINT ALONG Y = 15									
36-	SPCG	1244	2	34	BC					
37-	$ADD SPC SETS USING SPCADD									
38-	SPCADD	124	1241	1242	1243	1244				
39-	PLOAD2	51	1.5	1	THRU	16				
40-	PSHELL	11		.4	10					
41-	MAT1	10	10. + 6		.3					
42-	PARAM	USETSEL	1746							
43-	ENDDATA									

The input cards in the NASTRAN data deck are described, with reference to the card number as follows

Card 1- The NASTRAN card contains the keyword PREFOPT = 2 which requests that MSGMESH be used to generate input data

Card 2- Typical Executive Control deck as described in Sec. 12.8.1.
Card 7

Card 8- Titling directives
Card 10

Card 11- Requests SPC set 124 which is defined by SPCADD in Bulk Data

Card 12- Request the set of static loads that is defined by PLOAD2 Bulk Data with SID = 51

Card 13- Output requests
Card 17

Card 18- Required termination card

Card 21- Define vertices of quadrilateral field using MSGMESH EGRID command
Card 24

Card 25- MSGMESH Command which generates a 4-by-4 field of GRID points which is identified as FID = 2 by MSGMESH. The negative signs associated with the EGRID points specifies that GRID points are to be generated at the vertices.

Card 28- MSGMESH Command which connects all the GRIDS generated in FID = 2 by QUAD4 elements. The PID for each CQUAD4 Bulk Data card is set to 11.

Card 30- MSGMESH Commands which generate SPC cards along each of the boundaries. The
Card 36 second field specifies FID = 2, the third field defines the constrained degrees of freedom (i.e., 156 in Card 30), and the fifth field specifies the MSGMESH field boundary
along which SPC Bulk Data are to be generated (the edge connecting vertices D and A
in Card 30).

Card 38- Creates the union of SPC sets and gives the union SID = 124

Card 39- Defines a uniform pressure load of 1.5 psi which is applied to elements 1 thru 16

Card 40- Specifies the plate thickness to be 0.4 in., and the entry in field 5 points to the MAT1-
card

12.8.2a.2.   Solution Output

The printout for this problem includes the automatic output which is described in Sec. 12.4. and
which will not be repeated here. The output which is of interest is the SORTED BULK DATA Deck
which includes the Bulk Data cards which were generated by MSGMESH as well as those which
were included in the input data deck. The Sorted Bulk Data, the set membership in SG, SB, A, F, S,
and G sets, and the requested DISPLACEMENTS, LOAD VECTOR, FORCES OF SINGLE POINT
CONSTRAINT, FORCES IN QUADRILATERAL ELEMENTS, and STRESSES IN QUADRILATERAL
ELEMENTS are shown below.

In this printout we will note that

1. The maximum displacement is $u_o = 0.08475$ which occurs at GRID point 20000 which is at
the center of the plate. The theoretical center displacement for a uniformly loaded square
plate can be found in Ref. 12-3, for example, to be

$$y_{max} = \frac{0.1422 \, p_o a^4}{Et^3 (1 + 2.21)} \tag{12.28}$$

The substitution of the appropriate values for this problem then gives $y_{max} = 0.0841$ in. The
resulting displacement error in the finite element solution is then 0.76 percent.

2. The bending moments and transverse shears are sorted by element number. The positive
sense of the element forces is shown by Figs. 4-9 and 4-10. The membrane forces are zero
because only bending behavior was selected on the PSHELL Bulk Data Card.

3. The stresses in QUAD4 elements are sorted by element number and contains two lines of
output for each element. The stress at the top and the bottom of the plate, where the outer
fiber distance has been taken to be 0.2 in. which is one half the plate thickness. The stresses are referenced to the element coordinate system and are calculated at the center of the
element. (Stresses at the node points can be obtained by using Rigid Format Alter
RF24D40 which is described in Ref. 12-4.) In addition to the components of stress, the principal stresses, the associated angle and the maximum shear are printed.

```
 N A S T R A N    E X E C U T I V E    C O N T R O L    D E C K    E C H O


ID PRIMER PROB122A
SOL 24
TIME 4
ALTER 99
TABPRT USET , EQEXIN // USET / C,Y USETPRT= 0 / C,Y,USETSEL $
CEND
```

```
                    C A S E   C O N T R O L   D E C K   E C H O
CARD
COUNT
  1        TITLE = SQUARE SIMPLY SUPPORTED PLATE WITHOUT STIFFENER
  2        SUBTITLE = UNIFORM PRESSURE LOAD
  3        LABEL = MODELLED USING QUARTER-SYMMETRY
  4        SPC = 124
  5        LOAD = 51
  6          DISP = ALL
  7          SPCF = ALL
  8          OLOAD = ALL
  9          ELFO = ALL
 10          STRESS = ALL
 11        BEGIN BULK

          INPUT BULK DATA CARD COUNT =      70
```

```
                    S O R T E D   B U L K   D A T A   E C H O
CARD
COUNT        .   1  ..  2  ..  3  ..  4  ..  5  ..  6  ..  7  ..  8  ..  9  .. 10  .
  1-        CQUAD4    1       11      20000    20001    20101    20100
  2-        CQUAD4    2       11      20001    20002    20102    20101
  3-        CQUAD4    3       11      20002    20003    20103    20102
  4-        CQUAD4    4       11      20003    20004    20104    20103
  5-        CQUAD4    5       11      20100    20101    20201    20200
  6-        CQUAD4    6       11      20101    20102    20202    20201
  7-        CQUAD4    7       11      20102    20103    20203    20202
  8-        CQUAD4    8       11      20103    20104    20204    20203
  9-        CQUAD4    9       11      20200    20201    20301    20300
 10-        CQUAD4   10       11      20201    20202    20302    20301
 11-        CQUAD4   11       11      20202    20203    20303    20302
 12-        CQUAD4   12       11      20203    20204    20304    20303
 13-        CQUAD4   13       11      20300    20301    20401    20400
 14-        CQUAD4   14       11      20301    20302    20402    20401
 15-        CQUAD4   15       11      20302    20303    20403    20402
 16-        CQUAD4   16       11      20303    20304    20404    20403
 17-        GRDSET                                                          126
 18-        GRID    20000    0     0.0      0.0      0.0       0
 19-        GRID    20001    0     3.75     0.0      0.0       0
 20-        GRID    20002    0     7.5      0.0      0.0       0
 21-        GRID    20003    0    11.25     0.0      0.0       0
 22-        GRID    20004    0    15.      0.0      0.0       0
 23-        GRID    20100    0     0.0      3.75     0.0       0
 24-        GRID    20101    0     3.75     3.75     0.0       0
 25-        GRID    20102    0     7.5      3.75     0.0       0
 26-        GRID    20103    0    11.25     3.75     0.0       0
 27-        GRID    20104    0    15.       3.75     0.0       0
 28-        GRID    20200    0     0.0      7.5      0.0       0
 29-        GRID    20201    0     3.75     7.5      0.0       0
 30-        GRID    20202    0     7.5      7.5      0.0       0
 31-        GRID    20203    0    11.25     7.5      0.0       0
 32-        GRID    20204    0    15.       7.5      0.0       0
 33-        GRID    20300    0     0.0     11.25     0.0       0
 34-        GRID    20301    0     3.75    11.25     0.0       0
 35-        GRID    20302    0     7.5     11.25     0.0       0
 36-        GRID    20303    0    11.25    11.25     0.0       0
 37-        GRID    20304    0    15.      11.25     0.0       0
 38-        GRID    20400    0     0.0     15.       0.0       0
 39-        GRID    20401    0     3.75    15.       0.0       0
 40-        GRID    20402    0     7.5     15.       0.0       0
 41-        GRID    20403    0    11.25    15.       0.0       0
 42-        GRID    20404    0    15.      15.       0.0       0
 43-        MAT1     10     10.+6              .3
 44-        PARAM   USETSEL 1746
 45-        PLOAD2   51     1.5     1       THRU     16
 46-        PSHELL   11             .4      10                          .04
 47-        SPC1    1241    156     20000    20100    20200    20300    20400
 48-        SPC1    1242    246     20000    20001    20002    20003    20004
 49-        SPC1    1243    35      20400    20401    20402    20403    20404
 50-        SPC1    1244    34      20004    20104    20204    20304    20404
 51-        SPCADD   124    1241    1242     1243     1244
            ENDDATA
          TOTAL COUNT=      52
```

```
                              SG   DISPLACEMENT SET

            -1-        -2-        -3-        -4-        -5-        -6-        -7-        -8-        -9-        -10-

  1=     20000-1    20000-2    20000-6    20001-1    20001-2    20001-6    20002-1    20002-2    20002-6    20003-1 =    10
 11=     20003-2    20004-1    20004-2    20102-6    20004-6    20100-1    20100-2    20100-6    20101-1    20101-2 =    20
 21=     20101-6    20102-1    20102-2    20102-6    20103-1    20103-2    20103-6    20104-1    20104-2    20104-6 =    30
 31=     20200-1    20200-2    20200-6    20201-1    20201-2    20201-6    20202-1    20202-2    20202-6    20203-1 =    40
 41=     20203-2    20203-6    20204-1    20204-2    20204-6    20300-1    20300-2    20300-6    20301-1    20301-2 =    50
 51=     20301-6    20302-1    20302-2    20302-6    20303-1    20303-2    20303-6    20304-1    20304-2    20304-6 =    60
 61=     20400-1    20400-2    20400-6    20401-1    20401-2    20401-6    20402-1    20402-2    20402-6    20403-1 =    70
 71=     20403-2    20403-6    20404-1    20404-2    20404-6
```

```
                              SB   DISPLACEMENT SET

            -1-        -2-        -3-        -4-        -5-        -6-        -7-        -8-        -9-        -10-

  1=     20000-1    20000-2    20000-4    20000-5    20000-6    20001-2    20001-4    20001-6    20002-2    20002-4 =    10
 11=     20002-6    20003-2    20003-4    20003-6    20004-2    20004-3    20004-4    20004-6    20100-1    20100-5 =    20
 21=     20100-6    20104-3    20104-4    20200-1    20200-5    20200-6    20204-3    20204-4    20300-1    20300-5 =    30
 31=     20300-6    20304-3    20304-4    20400-1    20400-3    20400-5    20400-6    20401-3    20401-5    20402-3 =    40
 41=     20402-5    20403-3    20403-5    20404-3    20404-4    20404-5
```

339

12.8.2a.2 Solution Output

A   DISPLACEMENT SET

	-1-	-2-	-3-	-4-	-5-	-6-	-7-	-8-	-9-	-10-	
1=	20000-3	20001-3	20001-5	20002-3	20002-5	20003-3	20003-5	20004-5	20100-3	20100-4	= 10
11=	20101-3	20101-4	20101-5	20102-3	20102-4	20102-5	20103-3	20103-4	20103-5	20104-5	= 20
21=	20200-3	20200-4	20201-3	20201-4	20201-5	20202-3	20202-4	20202-5	20203-3	20203-4	= 30
31=	20203-5	20204-5	20300-3	20300-4	20301-3	20301-4	20301-5	20302-3	20302-4	20302-5	= 40
41=	20303-3	20303-4	20303-5	20304-5	20400-4	20401-4	20402-4	20403-4			

F   DISPLACEMENT SET

	-1-	-2-	-3-	-4-	-5-	-6-	-7-	-8-	-9-	-10-	
1=	20000-3	20001-3	20001-5	20002-3	20002-5	20003-3	20003-5	20004-5	20100-3	20100-4	= 10
11=	20101-3	20101-4	20101-5	20102-3	20102-4	20102-5	20103-3	20103-4	20103-5	20104-5	= 20
21=	20200-3	20200-4	20201-3	20201-4	20201-5	20202-3	20202-4	20202-5	20203-3	20203-4	= 30
31=	20203-5	20204-5	20300-3	20300-4	20301-3	20301-4	20301-5	20302-3	20302-4	20302-5	= 40
41=	20303-3	20303-4	20303-5	20304-5	20400-4	20401-4	20402-4	20403-4			

S   DISPLACEMENT SET

	-1-	-2-	-3-	-4-	-5-	-6-	-7-	-8-	-9-	-10-	
1=	20000-1	20000-2	20000-4	20000-5	20000-6	20001-1	20001-2	20001-4	20001-6	20002-1	= 10
11=	20002-2	20002-4	20002-6	20003-1	20003-2	20003-4	20003-6	20004-1	20004-2	20004-3	= 20
21=	20004-4	20004-6	20100-1	20100-2	20100-5	20100-6	20101-1	20101-2	20101-6	20102-1	= 30
31=	20102-2	20102-6	20103-1	20103-2	20103-6	20104-1	20104-2	20104-3	20104-4	20104-6	= 40
41=	20200-1	20200-2	20200-5	20200-6	20201-1	20201-2	20201-6	20202-1	20202-2	20202-6	= 50
51=	20203-1	20203-2	20203-6	20204-1	20204-2	20204-4	20204-6	20300-1	20300-2	20300-3	= 60
61=	20300-5	20300-6	20301-1	20301-2	20301-6	20302-1	20302-2	20302-6	20303-1	20303-2	= 70
71=	20303-6	20304-1	20304-2	20304-3	20304-4	20304-6	20400-1	20400-2	20400-3	20400-5	= 80
81=	20400-6	20401-1	20401-2	20401-3	20401-5	20401-6	20402-1	20402-2	20402-3	20402-5	= 90
91=	20402-6	20403-1	20403-2	20403-3	20403-5	20403-6	20404-1	20404-2	20404-3	20404-4	= 100
101=	20404-5	20404-6									

G   DISPLACEMENT SET

	-1-	-2-	-3-	-4-	-5-	-6-	-7-	-8-	-9-	-10-	
1=	20000-1	20000-2	20000-3	20000-4	20000-5	20000-6	20001-1	20001-2	20001-3	20001-4	= 10
11=	20001-5	20001-6	20002-1	20002-2	20002-3	20002-4	20002-5	20002-6	20003-1	20003-2	= 20
21=	20003-3	20003-4	20003-5	20003-6	20004-1	20004-2	20004-3	20004-4	20004-5	20004-6	= 30
31=	20100-1	20100-2	20100-3	20100-4	20100-5	20100-6	20101-1	20101-2	20101-3	20101-4	= 40
41=	20101-5	20101-6	20102-1	20102-2	20102-3	20102-4	20102-5	20102-6	20103-1	20103-2	= 50
51=	20103-3	20103-4	20103-5	20103-6	20104-1	20104-2	20104-3	20104-4	20104-5	20104-6	= 60
61=	20200-1	20200-2	20200-3	20200-4	20200-5	20200-6	20201-1	20201-2	20201-3	20201-4	= 70
71=	20201-5	20201-6	20202-1	20202-2	20202-3	20202-4	20202-5	20202-6	20203-1	20203-2	= 80
81=	20203-3	20203-4	20203-5	20203-6	20204-1	20204-2	20204-3	20204-4	20204-5	20204-6	= 90
91=	20300-1	20300-2	20300-3	20300-4	20300-5	20300-6	20301-1	20301-2	20301-3	20301-4	= 100
101=	20301-5	20301-6	20302-1	20302-2	20302-3	20302-4	20302-5	20302-6	20303-1	20303-2	= 110
111=	20303-3	20303-4	20303-5	20303-6	20304-1	20304-2	20304-3	20304-4	20304-5	20304-6	= 120
121=	20400-1	20400-2	20400-3	20400-4	20400-5	20400-6	20401-1	20401-2	20401-3	20401-4	= 130
131=	20401-5	20401-6	20402-1	20402-2	20402-3	20402-4	20402-5	20402-6	20403-1	20403-2	= 140
141=	20403-3	20403-4	20403-5	20403-6	20404-1	20404-2	20404-3	20404-4	20404-5	20404-6	= 150

*** USER INFORMATION MESSAGE 3035 FOR DATA BLOCK   KLL

LOAD SEQ. NO.	EPSILON	STRAIN ENERGY	EPSILONS LARGER THAN0.001 ARE FLAGGED WITH ASTERISKS
1	2.0755546E-14	5.8140559E+00	

DISPLACEMENT VECTOR

POINT ID.	TYPE	T1	T2	T3	R1	R2	R3
20000	G	0.0	0.0	8.475222E-02	0.0	0.0	0.0
20001	G	0.0	0.0	7.874262E-02	0.0	3.161035E-03	0.0
20002	G	0.0	0.0	6.116964E-02	0.0	6.071973E-03	0.0
20003	G	0.0	0.0	3.368807E-02	0.0	8.329205E-03	0.0
20004	G	0.0	0.0	0.0	0.0	9.229645E-03	0.0
20100	G	0.0	0.0	7.874262E-02	-3.161035E-03	0.0	0.0
20101	G	0.0	0.0	7.317635E-02	-2.927911E-03	2.927911E-03	0.0
20102	G	0.0	0.0	5.688222E-02	-2.255311E-03	5.633364E-03	0.0
20103	G	0.0	0.0	3.135117E-02	-1.229351E-03	7.745520E-03	0.0
20104	G	0.0	0.0	0.0	0.0	8.592794E-03	0.0
20200	G	0.0	0.0	6.116964E-02	-6.071973E-03	0.0	0.0
20201	G	0.0	0.0	5.688222E-02	-5.633364E-03	2.255311E-03	0.0
20202	G	0.0	0.0	4.430025E-02	-4.355887E-03	4.355887E-03	0.0
20203	G	0.0	0.0	2.447714E-02	-2.382759E-03	6.031956E-03	0.0
20204	G	0.0	0.0	0.0	0.0	6.718618E-03	0.0
20300	G	0.0	0.0	3.368807E-02	-8.329205E-03	0.0	0.0
20301	G	0.0	0.0	3.135117E-02	-7.745520E-03	1.229351E-03	0.0
20302	G	0.0	0.0	2.447714E-02	-6.031956E-03	2.382759E-03	0.0
20303	G	0.0	0.0	1.357256E-02	-3.331975E-03	3.331975E-03	0.0
20304	G	0.0	0.0	0.0	0.0	3.734659E-03	0.0
20400	G	0.0	0.0	0.0	-9.229645E-03	0.0	0.0
20401	G	0.0	0.0	0.0	-8.592794E-03	0.0	0.0
20402	G	0.0	0.0	0.0	-6.718618E-03	0.0	0.0
20403	G	0.0	0.0	0.0	-3.734659E-03	0.0	0.0
20404	G	0.0	0.0	0.0	0.0	0.0	0.0

L O A D   V E C T O R

POINT ID.	TYPE	T1	T2	T3	R1	R2	R3
20000	G	0.0	0.0	5.273438E+00	0.0	0.0	0.0
20001	G	0.0	0.0	1.054688E+01	0.0	0.0	0.0
20002	G	0.0	0.0	1.054688E+01	0.0	0.0	0.0
20003	G	0.0	0.0	1.054688E+01	0.0	0.0	0.0
20004	G	0.0	0.0	5.273438E+00	0.0	0.0	0.0
20100	G	0.0	0.0	1.054688E+01	0.0	0.0	0.0
20101	G	0.0	0.0	2.109375E+01	0.0	0.0	0.0
20102	G	0.0	0.0	2.109375E+01	0.0	0.0	0.0
20103	G	0.0	0.0	2.109375E+01	0.0	0.0	0.0
20104	G	0.0	0.0	1.054688E+01	0.0	0.0	0.0
20200	G	0.0	0.0	1.054688E+01	0.0	0.0	0.0
20201	G	0.0	0.0	2.109375E+01	0.0	0.0	0.0
20202	G	0.0	0.0	2.109375E+01	0.0	0.0	0.0
20203	G	0.0	0.0	2.109375E+01	0.0	0.0	0.0
20204	G	0.0	0.0	1.054688E+01	0.0	0.0	0.0
20300	G	0.0	0.0	1.054688E+01	0.0	0.0	0.0
20301	G	0.0	0.0	2.109375E+01	0.0	0.0	0.0
20302	G	0.0	0.0	2.109375E+01	0.0	0.0	0.0
20303	G	0.0	0.0	2.109375E+01	0.0	0.0	0.0
20304	G	0.0	0.0	1.054688E+01	0.0	0.0	0.0
20400	G	0.0	0.0	5.273438E+00	0.0	0.0	0.0
20401	G	0.0	0.0	1.054688E+01	0.0	0.0	0.0
20402	G	0.0	0.0	1.054688E+01	0.0	0.0	0.0
20403	G	0.0	0.0	1.054688E+01	0.0	0.0	0.0
20404	G	0.0	0.0	5.273438E+00	0.0	0.0	0.0

F O R C E S   O F   S I N G L E – P O I N T   C O N S T R A I N T

POINT ID.	TYPE	T1	T2	T3	R1	R2	R3
20000	G	0.0	0.0	0.0	1.212654E+02	-1.212654E+02	0.0
20001	G	0.0	0.0	0.0	2.264094E+02	0.0	0.0
20002	G	0.0	0.0	0.0	1.785002E+02	0.0	0.0
20003	G	0.0	0.0	0.0	1.001330E+02	0.0	0.0
20004	G	0.0	0.0	-3.176732E+01	1.837024E+01	0.0	0.0
20100	G	0.0	0.0	0.0	0.0	-2.264094E+02	0.0
20104	G	0.0	0.0	-6.180846E+01	2.542675E+01	0.0	0.0
20200	G	0.0	0.0	0.0	0.0	-1.785002E+02	0.0
20204	G	0.0	0.0	-5.631221E+01	4.283396E+01	0.0	0.0
20300	G	0.0	0.0	0.0	0.0	-1.001330E+02	0.0
20304	G	0.0	0.0	-4.580593E+01	3.827784E+01	0.0	0.0
20400	G	0.0	0.0	-3.176732E+01	0.0	-1.837024E+01	0.0
20401	G	0.0	0.0	-6.180846E+01	0.0	-2.542675E+01	0.0
20402	G	0.0	0.0	-5.631221E+01	0.0	-4.283396E+01	0.0
20403	G	0.0	0.0	-4.580593E+01	0.0	-3.827784E+01	0.0
20404	G	0.0	0.0	5.388783E+01	1.406454E+01	-1.406454E+01	0.0

F O R C E S   I N   Q U A D R I L A T E R A L   E L E M E N T S   (Q U A D 4)

ELEMENT ID	FX	– MEMBRANE FORCES – FY	FXY	MX	– BENDING MOMENTS – MY	MXY	– TRANSVERSE SHEAR FORCES – QX	QY
1	0.0	0.0	0.0	-6.185596E+01	-6.185596E+01	1.275206E+00	-1.060963E+00	-1.060963E+00
2	0.0	0.0	0.0	-5.603991E+01	-5.367044E+01	3.676807E+00	-3.352968E+00	-9.012766E-01
3	0.0	0.0	0.0	-4.231335E+01	-3.747382E+01	5.602062E+00	-6.168253E+00	-6.039940E-01
4	0.0	0.0	0.0	-1.653935E+01	-1.370386E+01	6.700547E+00	-9.882811E+00	-2.124815E-01
5	0.0	0.0	0.0	-5.367044E+01	-5.603991E+01	3.676807E+00	-9.012766E-01	-3.352968E+00
6	0.0	0.0	0.0	-4.882316E+01	-4.882316E+01	1.066709E+01	-2.852072E+00	-2.852072E+00
7	0.0	0.0	0.0	-3.723112E+01	-3.430878E+01	1.638326E+01	-5.278270E+00	-1.915780E+00
8	0.0	0.0	0.0	-1.469077E+01	-1.260924E+01	1.969190E+01	-8.579784E+00	-6.756390E-01
9	0.0	0.0	0.0	-3.747382E+01	-4.231335E+01	5.602062E+00	-6.039940E-01	-6.168253E+00
10	0.0	0.0	0.0	-3.430878E+01	-3.723112E+01	1.638326E+01	-1.915780E+00	-5.278270E+00
11	0.0	0.0	0.0	-2.666956E+01	-2.666956E+01	2.556231E+01	-3.569960E+00	-3.569960E+00
12	0.0	0.0	0.0	-1.073787E+01	-9.971341E+00	3.117586E+01	-5.951042E+00	-1.263386E+00
13	0.0	0.0	0.0	-1.370386E+01	-1.653935E+01	6.700547E+00	-2.124815E-01	-9.882811E+00
14	0.0	0.0	0.0	-1.260924E+01	-1.469077E+01	1.969190E+01	-6.756390E-01	-8.579784E+00
15	0.0	0.0	0.0	-9.971341E+00	-1.073787E+01	3.117586E+01	-1.263386E+00	-5.951042E+00
16	0.0	0.0	0.0	-4.090765E+00	-4.090765E+00	3.865509E+01	-2.151319E+00	-2.151319E+00

S T R E S S E S   I N   Q U A D R I L A T E R A L   E L E M E N T S   (Q U A D 4)

ELEMENT ID.	FIBRE DISTANCE	STRESSES IN ELEMENT COORD SYSTEM NORMAL-X	NORMAL-Y	SHEAR-XY	PRINCIPAL STRESSES (ZERO SHEAR) ANGLE	MAJOR	MINOR	MAX SHEAR
1	-2.000000E-01	-2.319598E+03	-2.319598E+03	4.782024E+01	45.0000	-2.271778E+03	-2.367419E+03	4.782024E+01
	2.000000E-01	2.319598E+03	2.319598E+03	-4.782024E+01	-45.0000	2.367419E+03	2.271778E+03	4.782024E+01
2	-2.000000E-01	-2.101497E+03	-2.012641E+03	1.378803E+02	53.9300	-1.912208E+03	-2.201930E+03	1.448612E+02
	2.000000E-01	2.101497E+03	2.012641E+03	-1.378803E+02	-36.0700	2.201930E+03	1.912208E+03	1.448612E+02
3	-2.000000E-01	-1.586751E+03	-1.405268E+03	2.100773E+02	56.6808	-1.267172E+03	-1.724847E+03	2.288371E+02
	2.000000E-01	1.586751E+03	1.405268E+03	-2.100773E+02	-33.3192	1.724847E+03	1.267172E+03	2.288371E+02
4	-2.000000E-01	-6.202255E+02	-5.138946E+02	2.512705E+02	50.9734	-3.102266E+02	-8.238936E+02	2.568335E+02
	2.000000E-01	6.202255E+02	5.138946E+02	-2.512705E+02	-39.0266	8.238936E+02	3.102266E+02	2.568335E+02
5	-2.000000E-01	-2.012641E+03	-2.101497E+03	1.378803E+02	36.0700	-1.912208E+03	-2.201930E+03	1.448612E+02
	2.000000E-01	2.012641E+03	2.101497E+03	-1.378803E+02	-53.9300	2.201930E+03	1.912208E+03	1.448612E+02
6	-2.000000E-01	-1.830868E+03	-1.830868E+03	4.000158E+02	45.0000	-1.430853E+03	-2.230884E+03	4.000158E+02
	2.000000E-01	1.830868E+03	1.830868E+03	-4.000158E+02	-45.0000	2.230884E+03	1.430853E+03	4.000158E+02
7	-2.000000E-01	-1.396167E+03	-1.286579E+03	6.143721E+02	47.5483	-7.245624E+02	-1.958184E+03	6.168107E+02
	2.000000E-01	1.396167E+03	1.286579E+03	-6.143721E+02	-42.4517	1.958184E+03	7.245624E+02	6.168107E+02

8	-2.000000E-01	-5.509037E+02	-4.728466E+02	7.384461E+02	46.5127	2.276016E+02	-1.251352E+03	7.394767E+02
	2.000000E-01	5.509037E+02	4.728466E+02	-7.384461E+02	-43.4873	1.251352E+03	-2.276016E+02	7.394767E+02
9	-2.000000E-01	-1.405268E+03	-1.586751E+03	2.100773E+02	33.3192	-1.267172E+03	-1.724847E+03	2.288371E+02
	2.000000E-01	1.405268E+03	1.586751E+03	-2.100773E+02	-56.6808	1.724847E+03	1.267172E+03	2.288371E+02
10	-2.000000E-01	-1.286579E+03	-1.396167E+03	6.143721E+02	42.4517	-7.245624E+02	-1.958184E+03	6.168107E+02
	2.000000E-01	1.286579E+03	1.396167E+03	-6.143721E+02	-47.5483	1.958184E+03	7.245624E+02	6.168107E+02
11	-2.000000E-01	-1.000108E+03	-1.000108E+03	9.585865E+02	45.0000	-4.152185E+01	-1.958695E+03	9.585865E+02
	2.000000E-01	1.000108E+03	1.000108E+03	-9.585865E+02	-45.0000	1.958695E+03	4.152185E+01	9.585865E+02
12	-2.000000E-01	-4.026701E+02	-3.739253E+02	1.169095E+03	45.3522	7.808854E+02	-1.557481E+03	1.169183E+03
	2.000000E-01	4.026701E+02	3.739253E+02	-1.169095E+03	-44.6478	1.557481E+03	-7.808854E+02	1.169183E+03
13	-2.000000E-01	-5.138946E+02	-6.202255E+02	2.512705E+02	39.0266	-3.102266E+02	-8.238936E+02	2.568335E+02
	2.000000E-01	5.138946E+02	6.202255E+02	-2.512705E+02	-50.9734	8.238936E+02	3.102266E+02	2.568335E+02
14	-2.000000E-01	-4.728466E+02	-5.509037E+02	7.384461E+02	43.4873	2.276016E+02	-1.251352E+03	7.394767E+02
	2.000000E-01	4.728466E+02	5.509037E+02	-7.384461E+02	-46.5127	1.251352E+03	-2.276016E+02	7.394767E+02
15	-2.000000E-01	-3.739253E+02	-4.026701E+02	1.169095E+03	44.6478	7.808854E+02	-1.557481E+03	1.169183E+03
	2.000000E-01	3.739253E+02	4.026701E+02	-1.169095E+03	-45.3522	1.557481E+03	-7.808854E+02	1.169183E+03
16	-2.000000E-01	-1.534037E+02	-1.534037E+02	1.449566E+03	45.0000	1.296162E+03	-1.602970E+03	1.449566E+03
	2.000000E-01	1.534037E+02	1.534037E+02	-1.449566E+03	-45.0000	1.602970E+03	-1.296162E+03	1.449566E+03

12.8.2b.   Stiffened Plate with Reference Surface at Middle of Plate

We will now modify the problem which we considered in example 12.8.2a. to include beam elements which represent the eccentric stiffeners along the center of the plate. With reference to Fig. 12-10 we will again specify that the plate is square having dimensions a = c = 15 in, and that, in addition, the cross sectional dimensions of the stiffener are h = 1 in, b = 0.5 in. The pressure load p_o = 1.5 lb/in^2 acts in the basic z-direction and the plate is simply supported.

The model of the stiffened plate is described relative to a reference surface which coincides with the midsurface of the plate as shown by Fig. 12-13. As in the previous example we will use the QUAD4 element, but we must recognize that the response of plate-beam configuration will include

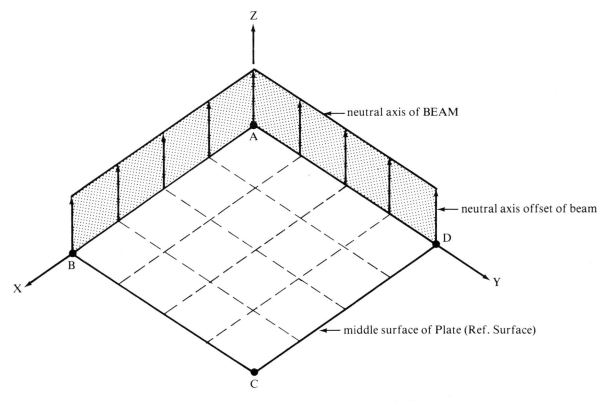

Figure 12-13. Quarter Panel of Eccentrically Stiffened Plate

membrane behavior in the plate elements and axial forces in the stiffener as well as bending behavior. We must specify this behavior by including entries in both the MID1 and MID2 fields of the PSHELL card.

We will use the BEAM element to model the effect of the stiffener. The local coordinate system will be taken to coincide with the principal axes of inertia of cross section so that $I_{yz} = 0$, and we will neglect the effect of transverse shear flexibility by setting the coefficients K_z and K_y to zero. We also note that, because we are using symmetry in our model, the cross-sectional area properties must be divided by two so that the stiffness of the BEAM is one-half of the actual stiffeners.

With these thoughts in mind, the complete MSC/NASTRAN data deck for this example which will perform all the functions of the data deck for the previous problem and, in addition will

- Include Rigid Format Alter RF24D40 to calculate stresses at the vertices of the QUAD4 elements

- Include BEAM elements to model the stiffeners

- Use the off-set feature of the BEAM to model the eccentricity of the BEAM neutral axis from the reference surface, which is taken to be the middle surface of the plate

- Request that intermediate results be saved for later use using the checkpoint/restart feature. (Restart is described in Sec. 13.9.)

is as follows

12.8.2b   Stiffened Plate with Reference Surface at Middle of Plate

Card	1	2	3	4	5	6	7	8	9	10
1-	NASTRAN PREFOPT = 2									
2-	ID PRIMER PROB122B									
3-	SOL 24									
4-	CHKPNT YES									
5-	TIME 4									
6-	READ 9 $ MERGE IN RF24D40									
7-	ALTER 99									
8-	TABPRT USET, EQEXIN // USET / C,Y,USETPRT = 0 / C,Y,USETSEL $									
9-	CEND									
10-	TITLE = SQUARE SIMPLY SUPPORTED PLATE WITH STIFFENER									
11-	SUBTITLE = UNIFORM PRESSURE LOAD									
12-	LABEL = MODELLED USING QUARTER-SYMMETRY									
13-	SPC = 124									
14-	LOAD = 51									
15-	DISP = ALL									
16-	SPCF = ALL									
17-	OLOAD = ALL									
18-	ELFO = ALL									
19-	STRESS = ALL									
20-	BEGIN BULK									
21-	GRDSET							6		
22-	EGRID	1	0	0.	0.	0.				
23-	EGRID	2	0	15.	0.	0.				
24-	EGRID	3	0	15.	15.	0.				
25-	EGRID	4	0	0.	15.	0.				
26-	GRIDG	2	0		4	− 1	− 2	− 3		+ G1
27-	+ G1	4	− 4							
28-	CGEN	QUAD4	1	12	2					
29-	SPCG	1241	2	156	DA					
30-	SPCG	1242	2	246	AB					
31-	SPCG	1243	2	35	CD					
32-	SPCG	1244	2	34	BC					
33-	SPCADD	124	1241	1242	1243	1244				
34-	PLOAD2	51	1.5	1	THRU	16				
35-	PSHELL	12	10	.4	10				.25	
36-	MAT1	10	10.+6		.3					+ M1
37-	+ M1	50.+3	50.+3	25.+3	101					
38-	CORD2R	101	0	0.	0.	0.	0.	0.	1.	+ CD1
39-	+ CD1	1.	0.	0.						
40-	PARAM	USETSEL	1746							
41-	PARAM	S1G	1							
42-	PARAM	S1AG	1							
43-	CGEN	BEAM	101	30	2	1		101	104	+ CG1
44-	+ CG1	0.	0.	1.			0.	0.	.7	
45-	CGEN	BEAM	105	30	2	2		105	108	+ CG2
46-	+ CG2	0.	0.	1.			0.	0.	.7	
47-	PBEAM	30	10	.25	.02085	.00521			.4	+ PB1
48-	+ PB1	0.	.5	0.	− .5					+ PB2
49-	+ PB2	YESA	1.							+ PB3
50-	+ PB2	0.	0.							
51-	ENDDATA									

Most of the input data items for this example are the same as those which were described in Sec. 12.8.2a. The additions or changes are described as follows

Card 4- Requests that intermediate results be saved on the New Problem Take (a NASTRAN file whose name is NPTP). This file must be defined and cataloged by suitable machine-dependent operating system commands. A directory of the files on the NPTP is also written on the system PUNCH file. These two files (i.e., NPTP and the PUNCH-file) must be saved for a later restart (see page 406 for restart).

Card 35- Nonstructural mass defined for calculation of the mass matrix for the shell elements

Card 38- A continuation to the MAT1 card is included to specify the material coordinate system (MCSID = 101) as required by RF24D40.

Card 38- Define the material coordinates to be coincident with the Basic coordinate system
Card-39

Card 41- PARAMeter S1G requests that the stresses be calculated with respect to coordinate system 101 at the node points

Card 42- PARAMeter S1AG requests that the strains and curvatures be calculated with respect to coordinate system 101 at the mode points

Card 43- MSGMESH Commands to generate the BEAM elements to model the eccentric
Card 45   stiffeners.

Card 47- PBEAM defines cross-sectional properties A, I_{zz}, and I_{yy} as well as the nonstructural mass

Card 48- defines stress recovery points at end A of the BEAM

Card 49- requests stress output at end B using the same stress recovery points as A

Card 50- Specifies that the shear flexibility is to be set equal to zero

12.8.2b.1. Selected Output

The printout for the stiffened plate is shown below where the reader should note

1. The rigid format alter, RF24D40 is printed as a part of the Executive Control Deck Echo.

2. The Sorted Bulk Data Deck Echo includes the Bulk Data which has been generated by MSGMESH Commands

3. The user message 3035 tells us that the error in solving the set of equations for the ℓ-set is small (i.e., 7.97×10^{-15}). We should find a value of EPSILON and strain energy for each load case. (Strangely, if the EPSILON should turn out to be zero, implying that no numerical errors exist, then the program incorrectly tells us that the strain energy is also equal to zero. Perhaps this bug will be fixed in one of the later releases of MSC/NASTRAN).

12.8.2b.1 Selected Output

```
ID PRIMER PROB122B
SOL 24
TIME 4
CHKPNT YES
READ 9 $MERGE IN RF24D40 TO CALCULATE NODAL STRESSES
$ BEGINNING OF RF ALTER 24$40
$ + + + + + + + + + + + +           23 JUNE 1976           + + + +          + + + +
$ GENERATE STRAINS AND CURVATURES FOR QUAD4, TRIA1, TRIA2, QUAD1, AND
$         QUAD2 ELEMENTS.  THESE QUANTITIES AS WELL AS STRESSES FOR THESE
$         ELEMENTS MAY BE COMPUTED IN ELEMENT COORDINATE SYSTEMS AT THE
$         ELEMENT CENTERS OR THEY MAY BE COMPUTED IN USER DEFINED
$         MATERIAL COORDINATE SYSTEMS AT THE ELEMENT CENTERS OR AT THE
$         GRID POINTS TO WHICH THE ELEMENTS CONNECT.
$
$ 03/24/76     R I G I D   F O R M A T   24   /
$
$ EXECUTIVE DECK INPUT--
$      1. RF24$40
$
$ CASE CONTROL DECK INPUT--
$      1. ALL STANDARD OPTIONS AVAILABLE
$      2. ELEMENT STRESS AND/OR STRAIN-CURVATURE OUTPUT IS REQUESTED
$         THROUGH THE STANDARD OPTIONS
$                        STRESS = ALL
$                             OR
$                        STRESS = N
$
$ BULK DATA DECK INPUT--
$      1. THE FOLLOWING PARAMETERS ARE USED TO DEFINE THE TYPE OF DATA
$         DESIRED.
$
$      S1  =0  FOR STRESSES COMPUTED IN ELEMENT COORDINATE SYSTEMS
$                 AT THE ELEMENT CENTERS
$      S1M =0  FOR STRESSES COMPUTED IN USER-DEFINED MATERIAL
$                 COORDINATE SYSTEMS AT THE ELEMENT CENTERS
$      S1G =0  FOR STRESSES COMPUTED IN USER-DEFINED MATERIAL
$                 COORDINATE SYSTEMS AT THE GRID POINTS TO WHICH THE
$                 ELEMENTS ARE CONNECTED
$      S1A =0  FOR STRAIN/CURV. DATA COMPUTED IN ELEMENT COORDINATE
$                 SYSTEMS AT THE ELEMENT CENTERS
$      S1AM=0  FOR STRAIN/CURV. DATA COMPUTED IN USER-DEFINED MATERIAL
$                 COORDINATE SYSTEMS AT THE ELEMENT CENTERS.
$      S1AG=0  FOR STRAIN/CURV. DATA COMPUTED IN USER-DEFINED MATERIAL
$                 COORDINATE SYSTEMS AT THE GRID POINTS TO WHICH THE
$                 ELEMENTS ARE CONNECTED.
$
$      2. THE PARAMETER OUTOPT MAY BE SET TO SELECT PRINT, PUNCH AND/OR
$         PLOTTER OUTPUT FOR ANY QUANTITIES COMPUTED IN USER-DEFINED
$         MATERIAL COORDINATE SYSTEMS.
$         OUTOPT=0, DEFAULT-STANDARD NASTRAN DEVICE CODES ARE USED.
$          OUTOPT=1  PRINT ONLY
$         OUTOPT=2    PLOT ONLY
$          OUTOPT=4  PUNCH ONLY
$          THE ABOVE CODES MAY BE COMBINED, FOR EXAMPLE, OUTOPT=6 WOULD
$          ALLOW FOR PLOT AND PUNCH OUTPUT
$
$      3. THE PARAMETER OG HAS A DEFAULT VALUE OF 0 THAT ALLOWS STRESSES
$         AND/OR STRAIN/CURV TO BE CALCULATED AT GRIDPOINTS. IF OG IS
$         SET TO OTHER THAN ZERO, THE CALCULATION OF STRESSES AND STRAIN/
$         CURV AT GRID POINTS WILL NOT BE PERFORMED.
$         CURV WILL NOT BE PERFORMED.
$
$      4. THE PARAMETER NINTPTS HAS A DEFAULT VALUE OF 0 THAT REQUESTS
$         GRIDPOINT STRESSES AND/OR STRAIN/CURV DATA AT GRIDPOINTS BE
$         OBTAINED THROUGH INTERPOLATION OVER ALL ELEMENTS. IF NINTPTS=N,
$         THE INTERPOLATION IS PERFORMED ONLY OVER THE N ELEMENTS CLOSEST
$         TO THE GRIDPOINT IN QUESTION.
$
$      5. THE PARAMETER Z1Z2 HAS A DEFAULT VALUE OF ZERO THAT REQUESTS
$         STRAIN/CURV DATA AT THE MIDDLE SURFACE OF THE ELEMENT. IF Z1Z2
$         EQUALS -1 THE STRAIN DATA IS COMPUTED AT FIBER DISTANCES
$         Z1 AND Z2.
$
$ REMARKS--
$      1. USER-DEFINED MATERIAL COORDINATE SYSTEMS ARE SPECIFIED OM MAT1
$         AND/OR MAT2 BULK DATA CARDS.
$
$      2. THE OUTPUT FORMAT FOR STRAIN/CURV DATA IS THE SAME AS FOR
$         STRESS DATA. DIFFERENTIATION BETWEEN THE SEVERAL TYPES OF OUTPUT
$         PRESENTED UNDER THE SAME FORMAT IS MADE THROUGH REFERENCE TO
$         THE COLUMN OF OUTPUT ENTITLED FIBER DISTANCE.
$
$         ELEMENT STRESSES IN ELEMENT COORD. SYS.-Z1 AND Z2 AS GIVEN ON
$                                          ELEMENT PROP. CARD
$         ELEMENT STRESSES IN MATERIAL COORD. SYS.-Z1 MATERIAL COORD.
$                                          SYS. ID.
$                                          Z2=1.0 IF MATERIAL X-
$                                                 AXIS IS MORE
$                                                 NEARLY NORMAL
$                                                 TO ELEMENT
$                                                 NORMAL
$                                          Z2=2.0 IF MATERIAL Y-
$                                                 AXIS IS MORE
$                                                 NEARLY NORMAL
$                                                 TO ELEMENT
$                                                 NORMAL
```

```
$
$            GRID POINT STRESSES IN MAT. COORD. SYS. -Z1=MATERIAL COORD.
$                                                       SYS. ID.
$                                                    Z2=A+10*N, WHERE N IS
$                                                       THE NUMBER OF ELEM
$                                                       USED IN THE INTER-
$                                                       POLATION AND A IS
$                                                       1.0,2.0 OR 3.0
$                                                       DEPENDENT UPON
$                                                       WHETHER THE X-, Y-
$                                                       OR Z-AXIS OF THE
$                                                       MATERIAL COORD. IS
$                                                       NORMAL TO PLANE ON
$                                                       WHICH THESE STRESS
$                                                       VALUES ARE PRO-
$                                                       JECTED.
$            ELEM. STRAIN/CURV IN ELEM. COORD. SYS.  -Z1=0.0
$                                                     Z2=-1.0
$            ELEM. STRAIN/CURV IN MATERIAL COORD. SYS-SAME AS ELEM. STRESS
$                                                       VALUES IN MAT. STRESS
$                                                       SYS.
$            GRID PT. STRAIN/CURV IN MAT. COORD. SYS. -SAME AS GRID PT
$                                                       STRESSES IN MAT
$                                                       COORD. SYS.
$----------------------------------------------------------------------
ALTER    176,188
PARAM //NOP/V,Y,S1  =-1 $ ELEMENT STRESSES IN ELT. C.S.
PARAM //NOP/V,Y,S1M =-1 $ ELEMENT STRESSES IN MAT. C.S.
PARAM //NOP/V,Y,S1G =-1 $ GRID PT STRESSES IN MAT. C.S.
PARAM // AND / V,N,S1MG / V,Y,S1M / V,Y,S1G $
PARAM // AND / V,N,S1MGX / V,N,S1MG / V,Y,S1 $
PARAM //NOP/V,Y,S1A =-1 $ ELEMENT STRAIN/CURVATURES IN ELT. C.S.
PARAM //NOP/V,Y,S1AM=-1 $ ELEMENT STRAIN/CURVATURES IN MAT. C.S.
PARAM //NOP/V,Y,S1AG=-1 $ GRID PT STRAIN/CURVATURES IN MAT. C.S.
PARAM // AND / V,N,S1AMG / V,Y,S1AM / V,Y,S1AG $
PARAM // AND / V,N,S1AMGX / V,Y,S1AMG / V,Y,S1A $
SDR2 CASECC,CSTM,MPT,DIT,EQEXIN,SIL,ETT,EDT,BGPDT,PGG,QG,UGV,EST,/
        OPG1,OQG1,OUGV1,,OEF1,PUGV1/STATICS $
OFP OUGV1,OPG1,OQG1,OEF1,, // S,N,CARDNO $
$
$                GENERATE STRESS OUTPUT.
$
COND LS1MGX,S1MGX $
PARAM // C,N,SSST / C,N,-23 $ TURN DIAG 23 OFF.
SDR2 CASECC,CSTM,MPT,DIT,EQEXIN,SIL,ETT,EDT,BGPDT,,,UGV,EST, /
                    ,,,OES1,, / C,N,STATICS $
COND LS1,S1 $
OFP OES1,,,,, // S,N,CARDNO $
LABEL LS1 $
COND LS1MG,S1MG $
PARAM // C,N,SSST / C,N,-23 $ TURN DIAG 23 OFF.
CURV OES1 ,MPT,CSTM,EST,SIL,GPL / OES1M,OES1G /
        C,Y,OUTOPT / C,Y,OG / C,Y,NINTPTS $
COND LS1M,S1M $
OFP OES1M,,,,, // S,N,CARDNO $
LABEL LS1M $
COND LS1G,S1G $
OFP OES1G,,,,, // S,N,CARDNO $
LABEL LS1G $
LABEL LS1MG $
LABEL LS1MGX $
$
$                GENERATE STRAIN/CURVATURE OUTPUT .
$
PARAM // STSR / V,Y,Z1Z2=0 / -74 $
COND LS1AMGX,S1AMGX $
PARAM // C,N,SSST / C,N,+23 $ TURN DIAG 23 ON.
SDR2 CASECC,CSTM,MPT,DIT,EQEXIN,SIL,ETT,EDT,BGPDT,,,UGV,EST, /
                    ,,,OES1A,, / C,N,STATICS $
PARAM // C,N,SSST / C,N,-23 $ TURN DIAG 23 OFF.
COND LS1A,S1A $
OFP OES1A,,,,, // S,N,CARDNO $
LABEL LS1A $
COND LS1AMG,S1AMG $
PARAM // C,N,SSST / C,N,+23 $ TURN DIAG 23 ON.
CURV OES1A,MPT,CSTM,EST,SIL,GPL / OES1AM,OES1AG /
        C,Y,OUTOPT / C,Y,OG / C,Y,NINTPTS $
PARAM // C,N,SSST / C,N,-23 $ TURN DIAG 23 OFF.
COND LS1AM,S1AM $
OFP OES1AM,,,,, // S,N,CARDNO $
LABEL LS1AM $
COND LS1AG,S1AG $
OFP OES1AG,,,,, // S,N,CARDNO $
LABEL LS1AG $
LABEL LS1AMG $
LABEL LS1AMGX $
$ END OF RFALTER 24$40
ALTER 99
TABPRT USET , EQEXIN // USET / C,Y USETPRT= 0 / C,Y,USETSEL $
CEND

ECHO OF FIRST CARD IN CHECKPOINT DICTIONARY TO BE PUNCHED OUT FOR THIS PROBLEM

  RESTART  PRIMER  ,PROB122B, 7/25/81,   42872,
```

347

12.8.2b.1 Selected Output

```
                        C A S E   C O N T R O L   D E C K   E C H O
CARD
COUNT
  1       TITLE = SQUARE SIMPLY SUPPORTED PLATE WITH STIFFENER
  2       SUBTITLE = UNIFORM PRESSURE LOAD
  3       LABEL = MODELLED USING QUARTER-SYMMETRY
  4       SPC = 124
  5       LOAD = 51
  6          DISP = ALL
  7          SPCF = ALL
  8          OLOAD = ALL
  9          ELFO = ALL
 10          STRESS = ALL
 11       BEGIN BULK

            INPUT BULK DATA CARD COUNT =    101


                        S O R T E D   B U L K   D A T A   E C H O

CARD
COUNT   .  1  ..  2  ..  3  ..  4  ..  5  ..  6  ..  7  ..  8  ..  9  ..  10  .
  1-    CBEAM    101    30     20000   20001   0.0     0.0     1.             +M00000
  2-    +M00000                0.0     0.0     .7      0.0     0.0     .7
  3-    CBEAM    102    30     20001   20002   0.0     0.0     1.             +M00001
  4-    +M00001                0.0     0.0     .7      0.0     0.0     .7
  5-    CBEAM    103    30     20002   20003   0.0     0.0     1.             +M00002
  6-    +M00002                0.0     0.0     .7      0.0     0.0     .7
  7-    CBEAM    104    30     20003   20004   0.0     0.0     1.             +M00003
  8-    +M00003                0.0     0.0     .7      0.0     0.0     .7
  9-    CBEAM    105    30     20000   20100   0.0     0.0     1.             +M00004
 10-    +M00004                0.0     0.0     .7      0.0     0.0     .7
 11-    CBEAM    106    30     20100   20200   0.0     0.0     1.             +M00005
 12-    +M00005                0.0     0.0     .7      0.0     0.0     .7
 13-    CBEAM    107    30     20200   20300   0.0     0.0     1.             +M00006
 14-    +M00006                0.0     0.0     .7      0.0     0.0     .7
 15-    CBEAM    108    30     20300   20400   0.0     0.0     1.             +M00007
 16-    +M00007                0.0     0.0     .7      0.0     0.0     .7
 17-    CORD2R   101    0      0.      0.      0.      0.      0.      1.      +CD1
 18-    +CD1     1.     0.     0.
 19-    CQUAD4   1      12     20000   20001   20101   20100
 20-    CQUAD4   2      12     20001   20002   20102   20101
 21-    CQUAD4   3      12     20002   20003   20103   20102
 22-    CQUAD4   4      12     20003   20004   20104   20103
 23-    CQUAD4   5      12     20100   20101   20201   20200
 24-    CQUAD4   6      12     20101   20102   20202   20201
 25-    CQUAD4   7      12     20102   20103   20203   20202
 26-    CQUAD4   8      12     20103   20104   20204   20203
 27-    CQUAD4   9      12     20200   20201   20301   20300
 28-    CQUAD4   10     12     20201   20202   20302   20301
 29-    CQUAD4   11     12     20202   20203   20303   20302
 30-    CQUAD4   12     12     20203   20204   20304   20303
 31-    CQUAD4   13     12     20300   20301   20401   20400
 32-    CQUAD4   14     12     20301   20302   20402   20401
 33-    CQUAD4   15     12     20302   20303   20403   20402
 34-    CQUAD4   16     12     20303   20304   20404   20403
 35-    GRDSET                                                6
 36-    GRID     20000  0      0.0     0.0     0.0     0
 37-    GRID     20001  0      3.75    0.0     0.0     0
 38-    GRID     20002  0      7.5     0.0     0.0     0
 39-    GRID     20003  0      11.25   0.0     0.0     0
 40-    GRID     20004  0      15.     0.0     0.0     0
 41-    GRID     20100  0      0.0     3.75    0.0     0
 42-    GRID     20101  0      3.75    3.75    0.0     0
 43-    GRID     20102  0      7.5     3.75    0.0     0
 44-    GRID     20103  0      11.25   3.75    0.0     0
 45-    GRID     20104  0      15.     3.75    0.0     0
 46-    GRID     20200  0      0.0     7.5     0.0     0
 47-    GRID     20201  0      3.75    7.5     0.0     0
 48-    GRID     20202  0      7.5     7.5     0.0     0
 49-    GRID     20203  0      11.25   7.5     0.0     0
 50-    GRID     20204  0      15.     7.5     0.0     0
 51-    GRID     20300  0      0.0     11.25   0.0     0
 52-    GRID     20301  0      3.75    11.25   0.0     0
 53-    GRID     20302  0      7.5     11.25   0.0     0
 54-    GRID     20303  0      11.25   11.25   0.0     0
 55-    GRID     20304  0      15.     11.25   0.0     0
 56-    GRID     20400  0      0.0     15.     0.0     0
 57-    GRID     20401  0      3.75    15.     0.0     0
 58-    GRID     20402  0      7.5     15.     0.0     0
 59-    GRID     20403  0      11.25   15.     0.0     0
 60-    GRID     20404  0      15.     15.     0.0     0
 61-    MAT1     10     10.+6          .3                             +M1
 62-    +M1      50.+3  50.+3  25.+3   101
 63-    PARAM    S1AG   1
 64-    PARAM    S1G    1
 65-    PARAM    USETSEL 1746
 66-    PBEAM    30     10     .25     .02085  .00521          .4     +PB1
 67-    +PB1     0.     .5     0.      -.5                            +PB2
 68-    +PB2     YESA   1.                                            +PB3
 69-    +PB3     0.     0.
 70-    PLOAD2   51     1.5    1       THRU    16
 71-    PSHELL   12     10     .4      10                      .25
 72-    SPC1     1241   156    20000   20100   20200   20300   20400
 73-    SPC1     1242   246    20000   20001   20002   20003   20004
 74-    SPC1     1243   35     20400   20401   20402   20403   20404
 75-    SPC1     1244   34     20004   20104   20204   20304   20404
 76-    SPCADD   124    1241   1242    1243    1244
        ENDDATA
     TOTAL COUNT=    77
```

348

```
                                    SG    DISPLACEMENT SET

            -1-       -2-       -3-       -4-       -5-       -6-       -7-       -8-       -9-      -10-

     1=  20000-6   20001-6   20002-6   20003-6   20004-6   20100-6   20101-6   20102-6   20103-6   20104-6 =    10
    11=  20200-6   20201-6   20202-6   20203-6   20204-6   20300-6   20301-6   20302-6   20303-6   20304-6 =    20
    21=  20400-6   20401-6   20402-6   20403-6   20404-6


                                    SB    DISPLACEMENT SET

            -1-       -2-       -3-       -4-       -5-       -6-       -7-       -8-       -9-      -10-

     1=  20000-1   20000-2   20000-4   20000-5   20000-6   20001-2   20001-4   20001-6   20002-2   20002-4 =    10
    11=  20002-6   20003-2   20003-4   20003-6   20004-2   20004-3   20004-4   20004-6   20100-1   20100-5 =    20
    21=  20100-6   20104-3   20104-4   20200-1   20200-5   20200-6   20204-3   20204-4   20300-1   20300-5 =    30
    31=  20300-6   20304-3   20304-4   20400-1   20400-3   20400-5   20400-6   20401-3   20401-5   20402-3 =    40
    41=  20402-5   20403-3   20403-5   20404-3   20404-4   20404-5


                                    A    DISPLACEMENT SET

            -1-       -2-       -3-       -4-       -5-       -6-       -7-       -8-       -9-      -10-

     1=  20000-3   20001-1   20001-3   20001-5   20002-1   20002-3   20002-5   20003-1   20003-3   20003-5 =    10
    11=  20004-1   20004-5   20100-2   20100-3   20100-4   20101-1   20101-2   20101-3   20101-4   20101-5 =    20
    21=  20102-1   20102-2   20102-3   20102-4   20102-5   20103-1   20103-2   20103-3   20103-4   20103-5 =    30
    31=  20104-1   20104-2   20104-5   20200-2   20200-3   20200-4   20201-1   20201-2   20201-3   20201-4 =    40
    41=  20201-5   20202-1   20202-2   20202-3   20202-4   20202-5   20203-1   20203-2   20203-3   20203-4 =    50
    51=  20203-5   20204-1   20204-2   20204-5   20300-2   20300-3   20300-4   20301-1   20301-2   20301-3 =    60
    61=  20301-4   20301-5   20302-1   20302-2   20302-3   20302-4   20302-5   20303-1   20303-2   20303-3 =    70
    71=  20303-4   20303-5   20304-1   20304-2   20304-5   20400-2   20400-4   20401-1   20401-2   20401-4 =    80
    81=  20402-1   20402-2   20402-4   20403-1   20403-2   20403-4   20404-1   20404-2


                                    F    DISPLACEMENT SET

            -1-       -2-       -3-       -4-       -5-       -6-       -7-       -8-       -9-      -10-

     1=  20000-3   20001-1   20001-3   20001-5   20002-1   20002-3   20002-5   20003-1   20003-3   20003-5 =    10
    11=  20004-1   20004-5   20100-2   20100-3   20100-4   20101-1   20101-2   20101-3   20101-4   20101-5 =    20
    21=  20102-1   20102-2   20102-3   20102-4   20102-5   20103-1   20103-2   20103-3   20103-4   20103-5 =    30
    31=  20104-1   20104-2   20104-5   20200-2   20200-3   20200-4   20201-1   20201-2   20201-3   20201-4 =    40
    41=  20201-5   20202-1   20202-2   20202-3   20202-4   20202-5   20203-1   20203-2   20203-3   20203-4 =    50
    51=  20203-5   20204-1   20204-2   20204-5   20300-2   20300-3   20300-4   20301-1   20301-2   20301-3 =    60
    61=  20301-4   20301-5   20302-1   20302-2   20302-3   20302-4   20302-5   20303-1   20303-2   20303-3 =    70
    71=  20303-4   20303-5   20304-1   20304-2   20304-5   20400-2   20400-4   20401-1   20401-2   20401-4 =    80
    81=  20402-1   20402-2   20402-4   20403-1   20403-2   20403-4   20404-1   20404-2


                                    S    DISPLACEMENT SET

            -1-       -2-       -3-       -4-       -5-       -6-       -7-       -8-       -9-      -10-

     1=  20000-1   20000-2   20000-4   20000-5   20000-6   20001-2   20001-4   20001-6   20002-2   20002-4 =    10
    11=  20002-6   20003-2   20003-4   20003-6   20004-2   20004-3   20004-4   20004-6   20100-1   20100-5 =    20
    21=  20100-6   20101-6   20102-6   20103-6   20104-3   20104-4   20104-6   20200-1   20200-5   20200-6 =    30
    31=  20201-6   20202-6   20203-6   20204-3   20204-4   20204-6   20300-1   20300-5   20300-6   20301-6 =    40
    41=  20302-6   20303-6   20304-3   20304-4   20400-1   20400-3   20400-5   20400-6   20401-3   20401-4 =    50
    51=  20401-5   20401-6   20402-3   20402-5   20402-6   20403-3   20403-5   20403-6   20404-3   20404-4 =    60
    61=  20404-5   20404-6


                                    G    DISPLACEMENT SET

            -1-       -2-       -3-       -4-       -5-       -6-       -7-       -8-       -9-      -10-

     1=  20000-1   20000-2   20000-3   20000-4   20000-5   20000-6   20001-1   20001-2   20001-3   20001-4 =    10
    11=  20001-5   20001-6   20002-1   20002-2   20002-3   20002-4   20002-5   20002-6   20003-1   20003-2 =    20
    21=  20003-3   20003-4   20003-5   20003-6   20004-1   20004-2   20004-3   20004-4   20004-5   20004-6 =    30
    31=  20100-1   20100-2   20100-3   20100-4   20100-5   20100-6   20101-1   20101-2   20101-3   20101-4 =    40
    41=  20101-5   20101-6   20102-1   20102-2   20102-3   20102-4   20102-5   20102-6   20103-1   20103-2 =    50
    51=  20103-3   20103-4   20103-5   20103-6   20104-1   20104-2   20104-3   20104-4   20104-5   20104-6 =    60
    61=  20200-1   20200-2   20200-3   20200-4   20200-5   20200-6   20201-1   20201-2   20201-3   20201-4 =    70
    71=  20201-5   20201-6   20202-1   20202-2   20202-3   20202-4   20202-5   20202-6   20203-1   20203-2 =    80
    81=  20203-3   20203-4   20203-5   20203-6   20204-1   20204-2   20204-3   20204-4   20204-5   20204-6 =    90
    91=  20300-1   20300-2   20300-3   20300-4   20300-5   20300-6   20301-1   20301-2   20301-3   20301-4 =   100
   101=  20301-5   20301-6   20302-1   20302-2   20302-3   20302-4   20302-5   20302-6   20303-1   20303-2 =   110
   111=  20303-3   20303-4   20303-5   20303-6   20304-1   20304-2   20304-3   20304-4   20304-5   20304-6 =   120
   121=  20400-1   20400-2   20400-3   20400-4   20400-5   20400-6   20401-1   20401-2   20401-3   20401-4 =   130
   131=  20401-5   20401-6   20402-1   20402-2   20402-3   20402-4   20402-5   20402-6   20403-1   20403-2 =   140
   141=  20403-3   20403-4   20403-5   20403-6   20404-1   20404-2   20404-3   20404-4   20404-5   20404-6 =   150
```

*** USER INFORMATION MESSAGE 3035 FOR DATA BLOCK   KLL

```
LOAD SEQ. NO.           EPSILON          STRAIN   ENERGY    EPSILONS LARGER THAN 0.001 ARE FLAGGED WITH ASTERISKS
        1            7.9722622E-15       2.4188459E+00
```

12.8.2b.1   Selected Output

D I S P L A C E M E N T   V E C T O R

POINT ID.	TYPE	T1	T2	T3	R1	R2	R3
20000	G	0.0	0.0	3.357303E-02	0.0	0.0	0.0
20001	G	-5.026594E-05	0.0	3.135407E-02	0.0	1.204342E-03	0.0
20002	G	-1.247074E-04	0.0	2.449893E-02	0.0	2.358252E-03	0.0
20003	G	-2.036451E-04	0.0	1.353859E-02	0.0	3.252859E-03	0.0
20004	G	-2.303921E-04	0.0	0.0	0.0	3.589568E-03	0.0
20100	G	0.0	-5.026594E-05	3.135407E-02	-1.204342E-03	0.0	0.0
20101	G	-2.217033E-05	-2.217033E-05	2.961528E-02	-9.801023E-04	9.801023E-04	0.0
20102	G	-5.602421E-05	-4.191995E-07	2.359256E-02	-5.628090E-04	2.175302E-03	0.0
20103	G	-8.466114E-05	2.145853E-06	1.324477E-02	-2.188077E-04	3.183177E-03	0.0
20104	G	-9.245333E-05	-5.246765E-05	0.0	0.0	3.603040E-03	0.0
20200	G	0.0	-1.247074E-04	2.449893E-02	-2.358252E-03	0.0	0.0
20201	G	-4.191995E-07	-5.602421E-05	2.359256E-02	-2.175302E-03	5.628090E-04	0.0
20202	G	-1.528429E-05	-1.528429E-05	1.941434E-02	-1.642096E-03	1.642096E-03	0.0
20203	G	-2.569039E-05	-1.156513E-05	1.116363E-02	-8.849135E-04	2.650511E-03	0.0
20204	G	-3.110561E-05	-3.853151E-05	0.0	0.0	3.092433E-03	0.0
20300	G	0.0	-2.036451E-04	1.353859E-02	-3.252859E-03	0.0	0.0
20301	G	2.145853E-06	-8.466114E-05	1.324477E-02	-3.183177E-03	2.188077E-04	0.0
20302	G	-1.156513E-05	-2.569039E-05	1.116363E-02	-2.650511E-03	8.849135E-04	0.0
20303	G	-1.629947E-05	-1.629947E-05	6.526025E-03	-1.532661E-03	1.532661E-03	0.0
20304	G	-1.806531E-05	-2.329844E-05	0.0	0.0	1.827422E-03	0.0
20400	G	0.0	-2.303921E-04	0.0	-3.589568E-03	0.0	0.0
20401	G	-5.246765E-05	-9.245333E-05	0.0	-3.603040E-03	0.0	0.0
20402	G	-3.853151E-05	-3.110561E-05	0.0	-3.092433E-03	0.0	0.0
20403	G	-2.329844E-05	-1.806531E-05	0.0	-1.827422E-03	0.0	0.0
20404	G	-1.889725E-05	-1.889725E-05	0.0	0.0	0.0	0.0

L O A D   V E C T O R

POINT ID.	TYPE	T1	T2	T3	R1	R2	R3
20000	G	0.0	0.0	5.273438E+00	0.0	0.0	0.0
20001	G	0.0	0.0	1.054688E+01	0.0	0.0	0.0
20002	G	0.0	0.0	1.054688E+01	0.0	0.0	0.0
20003	G	0.0	0.0	1.054688E+01	0.0	0.0	0.0
20004	G	0.0	0.0	5.273438E+00	0.0	0.0	0.0
20100	G	0.0	0.0	1.054688E+01	0.0	0.0	0.0
20101	G	0.0	0.0	2.109375E+01	0.0	0.0	0.0
20102	G	0.0	0.0	2.109375E+01	0.0	0.0	0.0
20103	G	0.0	0.0	2.109375E+01	0.0	0.0	0.0
20104	G	0.0	0.0	1.054688E+01	0.0	0.0	0.0
20200	G	0.0	0.0	1.054688E+01	0.0	0.0	0.0
20201	G	0.0	0.0	2.109375E+01	0.0	0.0	0.0
20202	G	0.0	0.0	2.109375E+01	0.0	0.0	0.0
20203	G	0.0	0.0	2.109375E+01	0.0	0.0	0.0
20204	G	0.0	0.0	1.054688E+01	0.0	0.0	0.0
20300	G	0.0	0.0	1.054688E+01	0.0	0.0	0.0
20301	G	0.0	0.0	2.109375E+01	0.0	0.0	0.0
20302	G	0.0	0.0	2.109375E+01	0.0	0.0	0.0
20303	G	0.0	0.0	2.109375E+01	0.0	0.0	0.0
20304	G	0.0	0.0	1.054688E+01	0.0	0.0	0.0
20400	G	0.0	0.0	5.273438E+00	0.0	0.0	0.0
20401	G	0.0	0.0	1.054688E+01	0.0	0.0	0.0
20402	G	0.0	0.0	1.054688E+01	0.0	0.0	0.0
20403	G	0.0	0.0	1.054688E+01	0.0	0.0	0.0
20404	G	0.0	0.0	5.273438E+00	0.0	0.0	0.0

F O R C E S   O F   S I N G L E - P O I N T   C O N S T R A I N T

POINT ID.	TYPE	T1	T2	T3	R1	R2	R3
20000	G	-4.363558E+02	-4.363558E+02	0.0	4.838032E+02	-4.838032E+02	0.0
20001	G		1.377054E+02	0.0	6.393059E+01	0.0	0.0
20002	G		5.948650E+01	0.0	2.491817E+01	0.0	0.0
20003	G		7.466244E+01	0.0	1.168610E+00	0.0	0.0
20004	G		1.645014E+02	-6.324347E+01	2.539656E+01	0.0	0.0
20100	G	1.377054E+02	0.0	0.0	0.0	-6.393059E+01	0.0
20104	G		0.0	-4.251658E+01	3.220742E+01	0.0	0.0
20200	G	5.948650E+01	0.0	0.0	0.0	-2.491817E+01	0.0
20204	G		0.0	-4.295871E+01	1.502720E+01	0.0	0.0
20300	G	7.466244E+01	0.0	0.0	0.0	-1.168610E+00	0.0
20304	G		0.0	-3.810430E+01	-7.188506E-01	0.0	0.0
20400	G	1.645014E+02		-6.324347E+01	0.0	-2.539656E+01	0.0
20401	G		0.0	-4.251658E+01	0.0	-3.220742E+01	0.0
20402	G		0.0	-4.295871E+01	0.0	-1.502720E+01	0.0
20403	G		0.0	-3.810430E+01	0.0	7.188506E-01	0.0
20404	G		0.0	3.614611E+01	-6.527850E+00	6.527850E+00	0.0

F O R C E S   I N   B E A M   E L E M E N T S   (C B E A M)

ELEMENT-ID	GRID	STAT DIST/ LENGTH	- BENDING MOMENTS - PLANE 1	PLANE 2	- WEB SHEARS - PLANE 1	PLANE 2	AXIAL FORCE	TOTAL TORQUE	WARPING TORQUE
101									
	20000	0.000	-6.347569E+01	0.0	1.859051E+00	0.0	5.285156E+02	0.0	0.0
	20001	1.000	-7.044714E+01	0.0	1.859051E+00	0.0	5.285156E+02	0.0	0.0
102									
	20001	0.000	-7.975031E+01	0.0	-8.316226E+00	0.0	4.888636E+02	0.0	0.0
	20002	1.000	-4.856446E+01	0.0	-8.316226E+00	0.0	4.888636E+02	0.0	0.0
103									
	20002	0.000	-8.883862E+01	0.0	-2.085250E+01	0.0	3.648585E+02	0.0	0.0
	20003	1.000	-1.064176E+01	0.0	-2.085250E+01	0.0	3.648585E+02	0.0	0.0
104									
	20003	0.000	-8.179704E+01	0.0	-3.364055E+01	0.0	1.392993E+02	0.0	0.0
	20004	1.000	4.435504E+01	0.0	-3.364055E+01	0.0	1.392993E+02	0.0	0.0
105									
	20000	0.000	-6.347569E+01	0.0	1.859051E+00	0.0	5.285156E+02	0.0	0.0
	20100	1.000	-7.044714E+01	0.0	1.859051E+00	0.0	5.285156E+02	0.0	0.0
106									
	20100	0.000	-7.975031E+01	0.0	-8.316226E+00	0.0	4.888636E+02	0.0	0.0
	20200	1.000	-4.856446E+01	0.0	-8.316226E+00	0.0	4.888636E+02	0.0	0.0
107									
	20200	0.000	-8.883862E+01	0.0	-2.085250E+01	0.0	3.648585E+02	0.0	0.0
	20300	1.000	-1.064176E+01	0.0	-2.085250E+01	0.0	3.648585E+02	0.0	0.0
108									
	20300	0.000	-8.179704E+01	0.0	-3.364055E+01	0.0	1.392993E+02	0.0	0.0
	20400	1.000	4.435504E+01	0.0	-3.364055E+01	0.0	1.392993E+02	0.0	0.0

F O R C E S   I N   Q U A D R I L A T E R A L   E L E M E N T S   (Q U A D 4)

ELEMENT ID	FX	FY	FXY	MX	MY	MXY	QX	QY
	- MEMBRANE FORCES -			- BENDING MOMENTS -			- TRANSVERSE SHEAR FORCES -	
1	-5.518954E+01	-5.518954E+01	1.152640E+01	-2.219118E+01	-2.219118E+01	1.226610E+00	9.207919E-01	9.207919E-01
2	-6.744158E+01	-3.228022E+01	2.431383E+01	-2.197398E+01	-1.756401E+01	2.254994E+00	-1.877882E+00	1.652436E+00
3	-6.274379E+01	-1.790226E+01	3.902198E+01	-1.669913E+01	-1.056790E+01	1.631817E+00	-4.935527E+00	1.769439E+00
4	-2.909059E+01	-3.556547E+01	4.149932E+01	-6.425119E+00	-3.483502E+00	7.521861E-01	-8.199698E+00	7.765110E-01
5	-3.228022E+01	-6.744158E+01	2.431383E+01	-1.756401E+01	-2.197398E+01	2.254994E+00	1.652436E+00	-1.877882E+00
6	-3.711922E+01	-3.711922E+01	2.563735E+01	-2.310590E+01	-2.310590E+01	5.199316E+00	-1.002619E+00	-1.002619E+00
7	-2.790673E+01	-2.361259E+01	2.174254E+01	-1.984787E+01	-1.836604E+01	5.926990E+00	-3.352285E+00	-3.713582E-01
8	-7.701023E+00	-2.190222E+00	7.946379E+00	-8.295909E+00	-7.225526E+00	5.872119E+00	-6.109650E+00	-7.780136E-02
9	-1.790226E+01	-6.274379E+01	3.902198E+01	-1.056790E+01	-1.669913E+01	1.631817E+00	1.769439E+00	-4.935527E+00
10	-2.361259E+01	-2.790673E+01	2.174254E+01	-1.836604E+01	-1.984787E+01	5.926990E+00	-3.713582E-01	-3.352285E+00
11	-1.153557E+01	-1.153557E+01	5.378489E+00	-1.682452E+01	-1.682452E+01	1.025659E+01	-2.045349E+00	-2.045349E+00
12	-2.362749E+01	4.890497E+00	-2.365974E+00	-7.275265E+00	-6.788786E+00	1.312940E+01	-4.144192E+00	-6.978379E-01
13	-3.556547E+01	-2.909059E+01	4.149932E+01	-3.483502E+00	-6.425119E+00	7.521861E-01	7.765110E-01	-8.199698E+00
14	-2.190222E+00	-7.701023E+00	7.946379E+00	-7.225526E+00	-8.295909E+00	5.872119E+00	-7.780136E-02	-6.109650E+00
15	4.890497E+00	-2.362749E+00	-2.365974E+00	-6.788786E+00	-7.275265E+00	1.312940E+01	-6.978379E-01	-4.144192E+00
16	2.007889E+00	2.007889E+00	-3.212680E+00	-2.994392E+00	-2.994392E+00	1.837994E+01	-1.506165E+00	-1.506165E+00

S T R E S S E S   A T   G R I D   P O I N T S

GRID ID.	MAT-COORD-ID PROJ-CODE	NORMAL-X	NORMAL-Y	SHEAR-XY	ANGLE	MAJOR	MINOR	MAXIMUM SHEAR
		STRESSES AT FIBRE DISTANCES (Z1 / Z2)			PRINCIPAL STRESSES (ZERO SHEAR)			
20000	101	-1.010056E+03	-1.010056E+03	-2.359819E+01	-45.0000	-9.864578E+02	-1.033654E+03	2.359819E+01
	163	6.838461E+02	6.838463E+02	7.908218E+01	45.0000	7.629283E+02	6.047640E+02	7.908218E+01
20001	101	-1.028597E+03	-8.022081E+02	5.848453E+01	76.3379	-7.879921E+02	-1.042813E+03	1.274106E+02
	163	6.638206E+02	5.882371E+02	3.001493E+01	19.2286	6.742897E+02	5.777680E+02	4.826088E+01
20002	101	-9.044111E+02	-5.091900E+02	9.773799E+01	76.8415	-4.863405E+02	-9.272606E+02	2.204601E+02
	163	5.136682E+02	3.780195E+02	8.015481E+01	24.8816	5.508435E+02	3.408441E+02	1.049997E+02
20003	101	-5.556064E+02	-2.679566E+02	9.272864E+01	73.5944	-2.406552E+02	-5.829078E+02	1.711263E+02
	163	2.661513E+02	1.034874E+02	1.495874E+02	30.7334	3.550876E+02	1.455110E+01	1.702683E+02
20004	101	-1.620069E+02	-6.404278E+01	1.013537E+02	57.8967	-4.556503E-01	-2.255941E+02	1.125692E+02
	163	1.724841E+01	-1.542599E+02	1.384444E+02	29.1127	9.434578E+01	-2.313573E+02	1.628515E+02
20100	101	-8.022080E+02	-1.028597E+03	5.848454E+01	13.6621	-7.879920E+02	-1.042813E+03	1.274105E+02
	163	5.882369E+02	6.638204E+02	3.001490E+01	70.7714	6.742896E+02	5.777678E+02	4.826086E+01
20101	101	-9.466137E+02	-9.466138E+02	1.693250E+02	45.0000	-7.772888E+02	-1.115939E+03	1.693250E+02
	163	7.080412E+02	7.080412E+02	-7.039150E+01	-45.0000	7.784327E+02	6.376497E+02	7.039150E+01
20102	101	-9.460861E+02	-7.511503E+02	2.229560E+02	56.8066	-6.052885E+02	-1.091948E+03	2.433298E+02
	163	6.883455E+02	6.224686E+02	-7.776692E+01	-33.5224	7.398621E+02	5.709521E+02	8.445493E+01
20103	101	-5.743922E+02	-4.326441E+02	1.909479E+02	55.1817	-2.998414E+02	-7.071949E+02	2.036768E+02
	163	4.165288E+02	3.383161E+02	-4.913618E+01	-25.7423	4.402211E+02	3.146238E+02	6.279865E+01
20104	101	-1.202885E+02	-9.585992E+01	1.978066E+02	46.7667	9.010917E+01	-3.062576E+02	1.981834E+02
	163	8.190357E+01	3.337006E+00	-8.334446E+01	-32.3819	1.347586E+02	-4.951806E+01	9.213835E+01
20200	101	-5.091897E+02	-9.044108E+02	9.773795E+01	13.1585	-4.863402E+02	-9.272603E+02	2.204600E+02
	163	3.780194E+02	5.136680E+02	8.015483E+01	65.1184	5.508434E+02	3.408440E+02	1.049997E+02
20201	101	-7.511505E+02	-9.460863E+02	2.229560E+02	33.1934	-6.052887E+02	-1.091948E+03	2.433297E+02
	163	6.224686E+02	6.883458E+02	-7.776689E+01	-56.4777	7.398622E+02	5.709523E+02	8.445495E+01
20202	101	-8.832332E+02	-8.832332E+02	3.168277E+02	45.0000	-5.664055E+02	-1.200061E+03	3.168277E+02
	163	7.547968E+02	7.547968E+02	-2.208172E+02	-45.0000	9.756140E+02	5.339795E+02	2.208172E+02
20203	101	-5.591436E+02	-5.247626E+02	3.471005E+02	46.4177	-1.944272E+02	-8.894791E+02	3.475259E+02
	163	5.045917E+02	4.923853E+02	-3.185845E+02	-44.4513	8.171314E+02	1.798456E+02	3.186429E+02

12.8.2b.1 Selected Output

GRID ID.	MAT-COORD-ID PROJ-CODE	NORMAL-X	NORMAL-Y	SHEAR-XY	ANGLE	MAJOR	MINOR	MAXIMUM SHEAR
20204	101	-1.177955E+02	-8.694693E+01	3.896850E+02	46.1333	2.876190E+02	-4.923614E+02	3.899902E+02
	163	1.286971E+02	1.148516E+02	-3.886201E+02	-44.4897	5.104561E+02	-2.669074E+02	3.886818E+02
20300	101	-2.679566E+02	-5.556064E+02	9.272866E+01	16.4056	-2.406552E+02	-5.829078E+02	1.711263E+02
	163	1.034874E+02	2.661513E+02	1.495874E+02	59.2667	3.550876E+02	1.455112E+01	1.702682E+02

S T R E S S E S   A T   G R I D   P O I N T S

GRID ID.	MAT-COORD-ID PROJ-CODE	STRESSES AT FIBRE DISTANCES (Z1 / Z2) NORMAL-X	NORMAL-Y	SHEAR-XY	PRINCIPAL STRESSES (ZERO SHEAR) ANGLE	MAJOR	MINOR	MAXIMUM SHEAR
20301	101	-4.326443E+02	-5.743923E+02	1.909480E+02	34.8183	-2.998415E+02	-7.071951E+02	2.036768E+02
	163	3.383163E+02	4.165289E+02	-4.913618E+01	-64.2577	4.402212E+02	3.146239E+02	6.279864E+01
20302	101	-5.247628E+02	-5.591438E+02	3.471003E+02	43.5823	-1.944275E+02	-8.894791E+02	3.475258E+02
	163	4.923854E+02	5.045919E+02	-3.185844E+02	-45.5488	8.171315E+02	1.798459E+02	3.186428E+02
20303	101	-3.511645E+02	-3.511644E+02	5.308886E+02	45.0000	1.797242E+02	-8.820531E+02	5.308886E+02
	163	3.423259E+02	3.423259E+02	-5.410394E+02	-45.0000	8.833652E+02	-1.987135E+02	5.410394E+02
20304	101	-5.041730E+01	-3.015026E+01	6.362927E+02	45.4562	5.960896E+02	-6.766572E+02	6.363734E+02
	163	6.855756E+01	6.576968E+01	-6.567148E+02	-44.9392	7.238799E+02	-5.895526E+02	6.567162E+02
20400	101	-6.404268E+01	-1.620067E+02	1.013537E+02	32.1033	-4.555359E-01	-2.255939E+02	1.125692E+02
	163	-1.542600E+02	1.724835E+01	1.384444E+02	60.8873	9.434576E+01	-2.313574E+02	1.628516E+02
20401	101	-9.585976E+01	-1.202882E+02	1.978067E+02	43.2333	9.010944E+01	-3.062574E+02	1.981834E+02
	163	3.336850E+00	8.190342E+01	-8.334449E+01	-57.6181	1.347585E+02	-4.951824E+01	9.213837E+01
20402	101	-8.694693E+01	-1.177955E+02	3.896851E+02	43.8667	2.876190E+02	-4.923614E+02	3.899902E+02
	163	1.148516E+02	1.286970E+02	-3.886201E+02	-45.5103	5.104561E+02	-2.669075E+02	3.886818E+02
20403	101	-3.015038E+01	-5.041740E+01	6.362926E+02	44.5438	5.960894E+02	-6.766572E+02	6.363733E+02
	163	6.576974E+01	6.855766E+01	-6.567147E+02	-45.0608	7.238799E+02	-5.895525E+02	6.567162E+02
20404	101	1.314621E+02	1.314622E+02	7.907836E+02	45.0000	9.222458E+02	-6.593215E+02	7.907836E+02
	163	-8.581239E+01	-8.581239E+01	-8.180652E+02	-45.0000	7.322528E+02	-9.038776E+02	8.180652E+02

S T R A I N S   A N D   C U R V A T U R E S   A T   G R I D   P O I N T S

GRID ID.	MAT-COORD-ID PROJ-CODE	STRAINS / CURVATURES NORMAL-X	NORMAL-Y	SHEAR-XY	PRINCIPAL STRAINS / CURVATURES ANGLE	MAJOR	MINOR	MAXIMUM SHEAR
20000	101	-1.141735E-05	-1.141735E-05	7.212919E-06	45.0000	-7.810890E-06	-1.502381E-05	7.212919E-06
	163	-2.964329E-04	-2.964329E-04	-6.674225E-05	-45.0000	-2.630618E-04	-3.298040E-04	6.674225E-05
20001	101	-1.502926E-05	-5.226907E-06	1.150493E-05	65.2157	-2.570811E-06	-1.768536E-05	1.511455E-05
	163	-3.188210E-04	-2.206800E-04	1.850521E-05	84.6609	-2.198153E-04	-3.196857E-04	9.987048E-05
20002	101	-1.756959E-05	-6.973737E-07	2.312606E-05	63.0568	5.179854E-06	-2.344682E-05	2.862667E-05
	163	-2.879791E-04	-1.154464E-04	1.142906E-05	88.1051	-1.152573E-04	-2.881681E-04	1.729108E-04
20003	101	-1.200572E-05	-3.881629E-06	3.150109E-05	52.2307	8.322241E-06	-2.420959E-05	3.253183E-05
	163	-1.775811E-04	-3.122917E-05	-3.695823E-05	-82.9137	-2.893192E-05	-1.798783E-04	1.509464E-04
20004	101	-3.963381E-06	-8.743753E-06	3.117376E-05	40.6409	9.415512E-06	-2.212265E-05	3.153816E-05
	163	-5.158013E-05	3.599844E-05	-2.410893E-05	-82.3043	3.762735E-05	-5.320903E-05	9.083637E-05
20100	101	-5.226905E-06	-1.502926E-05	1.150492E-05	24.7843	-2.570810E-06	-1.768535E-05	1.511454E-05
	163	-2.206799E-04	-3.188209E-04	1.850525E-05	5.3391	-2.198152E-04	-3.196856E-04	9.987044E-05
20101	101	-8.350036E-06	-8.350037E-06	1.286136E-05	45.0000	-1.919359E-06	-1.478072E-05	1.286136E-05
	163	-2.895646E-04	-2.895646E-04	1.558157E-04	45.0000	-2.116568E-04	-3.674725E-04	1.558157E-04
20102	101	-1.095680E-05	-2.567983E-06	1.887458E-05	56.9814	3.565023E-06	-1.708981E-05	2.065483E-05
	163	-3.055865E-04	-2.208223E-04	1.954699E-04	56.7218	-1.566757E-04	-3.697331E-04	2.130574E-04
20103	101	-6.478247E-06	-2.348449E-06	1.843553E-05	51.3133	5.032869E-06	-1.385957E-05	1.889244E-05
	163	-1.899082E-04	-1.184210E-04	1.560547E-04	57.3060	-6.833249E-05	-2.399893E-04	1.716493E-04
20104	101	-5.314013E-07	-4.050371E-06	1.488009E-05	38.3473	5.354376E-06	-9.936148E-06	1.529052E-05
	163	-4.310824E-05	-9.634826E-06	1.827482E-05	50.1898	6.652274E-05	-1.192658E-04	1.857886E-04
20200	101	-6.973719E-07	-1.756959E-05	2.312606E-05	26.9432	5.179857E-06	-2.344682E-05	2.862667E-05
	163	-1.154463E-04	-2.879790E-04	1.142903E-05	1.8949	-1.152573E-04	-2.881681E-04	1.729108E-04
20201	101	-2.567983E-06	-1.095681E-05	1.887458E-05	33.0186	3.565024E-06	-1.708981E-05	2.065484E-05
	163	-2.208223E-04	-3.055865E-04	1.954699E-04	33.2782	-1.566758E-04	-3.697331E-04	2.130573E-04
20202	101	-4.495275E-06	-4.495275E-06	1.248136E-05	45.0000	1.745404E-06	-1.073595E-05	1.248136E-05
	163	-2.866553E-04	-2.866553E-04	3.494692E-04	45.0000	-1.119207E-04	-4.613899E-04	3.494692E-04
20203	101	-2.241932E-06	-8.005894E-07	3.707080E-06	55.6232	4.674520E-07	-3.509974E-06	3.977426E-06
	163	-1.896478E-04	-1.745068E-04	4.326952E-04	46.0020	3.440269E-04	-3.985573E-04	4.329600E-04
20204	101	1.265072E-07	1.231713E-06	1.384386E-07	86.4302	1.236032E-06	1.221889E-07	1.113843E-06
	163	-4.648824E-05	-3.196271E-05	5.058983E-04	45.8223	2.138279E-04	-2.922789E-04	5.061068E-04
20300	101	-3.881629E-06	-1.200572E-05	3.150109E-05	37.7693	8.322239E-06	-2.420959E-05	3.253183E-05
	163	-3.122916E-05	-1.775811E-04	-3.695820E-05	-7.0863	-2.893196E-05	-1.798783E-04	1.509464E-04

352

STRAINS   AND   CURVATURES   AT   GRID   POINTS

| GRID ID. | MAT-COORD-ID PROJ-CODE | STRAINS / CURVATURES | | | PRINCIPAL STRAINS / CURVATURES | | | MAXIMUM SHEAR |
		NORMAL-X	NORMAL-Y	SHEAR-XY	ANGLE	MAJOR	MINOR	
20301	101	-2.348450E-06	-6.478247E-06	1.843553E-05	38.6867	5.032867E-06	-1.385956E-05	1.889243E-05
	163	-1.184210E-04	-1.899082E-04	1.560547E-04	32.6940	-6.833996E-05	-2.399893E-04	1.716493E-04
20302	101	-8.005903E-07	-2.241934E-06	3.707083E-06	34.3768	4.674519E-07	-3.509976E-06	3.977428E-06
	163	-1.745069E-04	-1.896478E-04	4.326951E-04	43.9980	3.440263E-05	-3.985573E-04	4.329600E-04
20303	101	-3.093492E-07	-3.093492E-07	-1.319596E-06	-45.0000	3.504490E-07	-9.691474E-07	1.319596E-06
	163	-1.213608E-04	-1.213608E-04	6.967532E-04	45.0000	2.270158E-04	-4.697374E-04	6.967532E-04
20304	101	3.727213E-07	1.508867E-06	-2.654871E-06	-56.5842	2.384675E-06	-5.030865E-07	2.887761E-06
	163	-2.254971E-05	-1.505687E-05	8.404548E-06	45.2554	4.014408E-04	-4.390474E-04	8.404882E-04
20400	101	-8.743756E-06	-3.963377E-06	3.117376E-05	49.3591	9.415511E-06	-2.212264E-05	3.153815E-05
	163	3.599847E-05	-5.158006E-05	-2.410895E-05	-7.6957	3.762738E-05	-5.320897E-05	9.083634E-05
20401	101	-4.050372E-06	-5.313969E-07	1.488009E-05	51.6527	5.354377E-06	-9.936146E-06	1.529052E-05
	163	-9.634769E-06	-4.310816E-05	1.827483E-04	39.8102	6.652283E-05	-1.192658E-04	1.857886E-04
20402	101	1.231712E-06	1.265064E-06	1.384446E-07	3.5700	1.236030E-06	1.221877E-07	1.113843E-06
	163	-3.196269E-05	-4.648823E-05	5.058984E-04	44.1777	2.138280E-04	-2.922789E-04	5.061069E-04
20403	101	1.508866E-06	3.727210E-07	-2.654870E-06	-33.4158	2.384673E-06	-5.030868E-07	2.887760E-06
	163	-1.505690E-05	-2.254974E-05	8.404548E-06	44.7446	4.014408E-04	-4.390474E-04	8.404882E-04
20404	101	1.597740E-06	1.597744E-06	-3.546580E-06	-45.0000	3.371032E-06	-1.755481E-07	3.546580E-06
	163	3.802304E-05	3.802306E-05	1.045752E-03	45.0000	5.608989E-04	-4.848528E-04	1.045752E-03

12.9.   Rigid Format Alters for Static Analysis

The concepts of altering rigid formats and the RFALTER library were described in Sec. 1.9.7. and 1.9.8. respectively. The RFALTERS which are appropriate for Rigid Format 24 are summarized below and are described in detail in Ref. 12-4.

RFALTER No.	Description
RF24D13A	Static analyses which involve multiple subcases and two or more sets of boundary conditions may currently be performed in a single execution with NASTRAN. A typical example of such an analysis is the use of symmetric and anti-symmetric boundary conditions with structures that are characterized by one or more planes of reflective symmetry. Unfortunately, these types of analyses are more difficult to handle if the user desires to RESTART his problem with additional load cases. These difficulties arise because, on RESTART, there is no provision for associating additional loading conditions with the appropriate boundary conditions.

Now, MSC/NASTRAN provides the user with the capability to handle additional loading conditions with standard RESTART procedures. This ALTER is incorporated into the CHECKPOINT run and a companion ALTER, RF24D13B, is incorporated in all subsequent RESTARTs that involve only new loading conditions. The results of matrix decomposition and other data that were computed during the CHECKPOINT run are utilized in the subsequent RESTART and are *not* recomputed. |
| RF24D13B | Standard RESTART procedures may now be utilized in those instances when the original CHECKPOINT run involved multiple subcases and two or more boundary conditions and, in addition, the subsequent RESTART involves only a definition of new loading conditions. The original CHECKPOINT run must include, ALTER RF24D13A, and the RESTART must include this companion ALTER RF24D13B. |
| RF24D32 | Enables the user to check input data for GRID, element connection and property cards, structure mass properties, constraints, loads, and temperature data for *all* subcases. In addition, formatted tables which contain data on grid point geometry, coordinate systems, constrained degrees of freedom, and element connec- |

tions may be requested.

RF24D40   Allows specification of strains, and curvature as well as stress output for two-dimensional plate elements. Both stresses and strains for these elements may be output in element coordinate systems at the element centers or they may be output in user-defined material coordinate systems at the element centers or at the grid points to which the elements connect. The user-defined material coordinate system identification numbers are defined on MAT1 and MAT2 Bulk Data cards.

RF24D41   Sorts stress output on the basis of magnitude, and prints the N largest stresses or those stresses that exceed a value specified by the user.

RF24D67   Provides a method for diverting punched output to a different unit than the one to which the checkpoint dictionary is directed. This option provides a means to avoid sorting the checkpoint dictionary from user requested punched output when they are both directed to the same unit.

RF24D79   Provides for stress recovery and evaluation of failure indices for individual plies of laminated composites.

RF24D80   Provides for printout of displacement set membership tables.

12.10.   References

12-1   MSC/NASTRAN User's Manual, p. 2.4-159.
12-2   Ibid, Sec. 6.2.
12-3   Roark, R. J., Formulas for Stress and Strain, McGraw-Hill, 3rd Edition, 1954, p. 203.
12-4   MSC/NASTRAN Application Manual, Sec. 4.1.

12.11.   Problems

12-1.   Verify, using the results from solving the beam equation, that the displacements of the beam bending element at the free end of the BAR element in Sec. 12.8.1a. and 12.8.1b. are correct.

12-2.   Verify, using the results calculated for example 12.8.1a., that the BAR element is in equilibrium.

12-3.   Verify that the combined results for example problem 12.8.1b. agree with the corresponding results for example problem 12.8.1a.

12-4.   Verify that the margin of safety (i.e., M.S.) values which are calculated for example problem 12.8.1b. are correct.

13

Normal Modes Analysis Using MSC/NASTRAN

Real eigenvalue analyses can be performed using rigid format 3 in MSC/NASTRAN. Normal modes and frequencies are important in their own right since the natural frequencies of structures are of interest for a variety of reasons. Normal modes also serve as a set of modal coordinates that can be used to reduce the number of dynamic degrees of freedom for transient and frequency response analysis.

The general problem of dynamic analysis is beyond the scope of the present text (see refs. 1-3, for example). We will restrict our attention in this chapter to the real eigenvalue problem. In succeeding sections we will present the equations of motion for dynamic systems and define the eigenvalue problem. We will then describe the important properties of normal modes. Finally, the various eigenvalue extraction techniques which are available in MSC/NASTRAN will be described.

13.1. Dynamic Motion

The motion of dynamic systems is described by a set of equations which represents the balance of forces acting on the system. For a structural system these forces are: the inertial forces, f_I, the damping or dissapative forces, f_d, the internal elastic forces, f_e, and the external time-dependent forces, P. Since the external forces must balance all internal forces we can write a force balance as

$$f_I + f_d + f_e = P(t) \tag{13.1}$$

where the internal forces can be expressed in terms of displacements and derivatives of displacements as follows

$$f_I = M\ddot{u} \tag{13.2}$$

$$f_d = C\dot{u} \tag{13.3}$$

$$f_e = Ku \tag{13.4}$$

using these definitions for internal forces we can then write (13.1) as

$$M\ddot{u} + C\dot{u} + Ku + P(t) \tag{13.5}$$

where the stiffness matrix, K, is the same as that for the static case, and we should note that (13.5) reduces to the static equilibrium equation when the time derivatives of displacements, $\dot{u}$ and $\ddot{u}$, are zero. The additional system matrices which are necessary to define the equilibrium for a dynamic system are M, the system mass matrix and C, the system damping matrix.

The solution of (13.5) is beyond the scope of this text. However it is worthwhile to at least describe the solution methods which can be used in order to provide motivation for the topic of normal modes and frequencies. In our discussion we will assume that the dynamic model is based on the structural model used for a static analysis. This implies that the number of degrees of freedom can be large so that cost will be a factor in solving the set of dynamic equations.

Again, just thinking the problem through for a moment, we recognize that if cost is a factor (and it is) then we should be able to reduce this solution cost by reducing the number of degrees of freedom. A question then arises as to how the system of equations can be reduced from some large number which was used for statics to a fairly small number for dynamics.

Let's be a little more specific. Without worrying at the present time about how $\mathbf{M}$ and $\mathbf{C}$ are defined (see Sec. 13.4.), let's assume that MPCs and SPCs have been applied so that the solution set is reduced to the f-set (see Sec. 7.4.1.) so that (13.5) can be written as

$$\mathbf{M}_{ff}\,\ddot{\mathbf{u}}_f + \mathbf{C}_{ff}\,\dot{\mathbf{u}}_f + \mathbf{K}_{ff}\,\mathbf{u}_f = \mathbf{P}_f \tag{13.6}$$

Now let us suppose that we can find a transformation $\mathbf{G}_{fh}$ which relates $\mathbf{u}_f$ to a greatly reduced set of degrees of freedom $\mathbf{u}_h$. That is

$$\mathbf{u}_f = \mathbf{G}_{fh}\,\mathbf{u}_h \tag{13.7}$$

We can then use this transformation to reduce (13.6) to the h-set as follows

$$\mathbf{M}_{hh}\,\ddot{\mathbf{u}}_h + \mathbf{C}_{hh}\,\dot{\mathbf{u}}_h + \mathbf{K}_{hh}\,\mathbf{u}_h = \mathbf{P}_h(t) \tag{13.8}$$

where

$$\mathbf{M}_{hh} = \mathbf{G}_{fh}^{T}\,\mathbf{M}_{ff}\,\mathbf{G}_{fh} \tag{13.9}$$

$$\mathbf{C}_{hh} = \mathbf{G}_{fh}^{T}\,\mathbf{C}_{ff}\,\mathbf{G}_{fh} \tag{13.10}$$

$$\mathbf{K}_{hh} = \mathbf{G}_{fh}^{T}\,\mathbf{K}_{ff}\,\mathbf{G}_{fh} \tag{13.11}$$

$$\mathbf{P}_{n} = \mathbf{G}_{fh}^{T}\,\mathbf{P}_{f} \tag{13.12}$$

There isn't any question about our being able to define the transformation (13.7). The real question is really what are reasonable transformations which could be used. A particularly attractive one would be such that the reduced system matrices $\mathbf{M}_{hh}$, $\mathbf{C}_{hh}$, and $\mathbf{K}_{hh}$ are diagonal. The resulting set of equations (13.8) would be completely decoupled and their solution would be reduced to quadrature (ref. 13-4). We will see in the next section that the eigenvectors for the real eigenvalue problem transform the mass and stiffness matrices to diagonal forms.

The study of and solution for eigenvectors is thus of great importance because of their magical properties in transforming large highly-coupled dynamic problems to small uncoupled dynamic problems. The calculation of the eigenvalues and eigenvectors is also of importance in its own right, of course, because they define the undamped free vibrational modes and frequencies of the system.

13.2.   The Eigenvalue Problem

The eigenvalue problem is associated with the solutions of the undamped (i.e., $\mathbf{C} = 0$) unforced (i.e., $\mathbf{P} = 0$) system of equations. We have then, from (13.5)

$$\mathbf{M}\,\ddot{\mathbf{u}} + \mathbf{K}\,\mathbf{u} = 0 \tag{13.13}$$

For nontivial solutions we assume a solution of the following form

$$\mathbf{u} = \mathbf{a}\,e^{i\omega t} \tag{13.14}$$

where $\mathbf{a}$ is a vector of displacement amplitudes that is the same order as $\mathbf{u}$, ω is the frequency of vibration (radians per unit time), and t is the time. The substitution of $\mathbf{u}$ and $\ddot{\mathbf{u}}$ into (13.13) then gives the following equation which relates **a** and ω

$$\mathbf{K\,a} - \omega^2 \mathbf{M\,a} = 0 \tag{13.15}$$

This equation can then be rearranged as follows

$$(\mathbf{K} - \lambda \mathbf{M})\,\mathbf{a} = 0 \tag{13.16}$$

where

$$\lambda = \omega^2 \tag{13.17}$$

Equation (13.16) has nontrivial solutions (i.e., **a** nonnull) only if the determinant of the coefficient matrix is zero; i.e.

$$\det(\mathbf{K} - \lambda \mathbf{M}) = 0 \tag{13.18}$$

The expansion of (13.18) represents a polynomial expression in terms of λ where the highest power of λ is the same as the order of matrices **M** and **K**. The values of λ which satisfy this characteristic equation are termed the eigenvalues and since an nth order polynomial has n roots there are exactly n eigenvalues.

Each one of the roots, λ_i (i = 1,2,....,n), then satisfies (13.16) so that we have

$$(\mathbf{K} - \lambda_i \mathbf{M})\,\mathbf{a}_i = 0 \tag{13.19}$$

where $\mathbf{a}_i$ is the vector of displacement amplitudes, i.e., the eigenvector, associated with the eigenvalue λ_i. The procedure for determining eigenvalues and the associated eigenvector is quite straightforward. An eigenvalue is obtained by solving (13.18) and then the eigenvector is determined by solving (13.19) with that value of λ.

As an example, let's consider a system with

$$\mathbf{K} = \begin{bmatrix} 6 & -2 \\ -2 & 4 \end{bmatrix}, \quad \mathbf{M} = \begin{bmatrix} 2 & 0 \\ 0 & 1 \end{bmatrix}$$

the characteristic equation (13.17) then becomes

$$\det \begin{bmatrix} (6-2\lambda) & -2 \\ -2 & (4-\lambda) \end{bmatrix} = 0$$

which has two distinct roots

$$\lambda_1 = 2$$

$$\lambda_2 = 5$$

The substitution of these two roots and the given **K** and **M** matrices into (13.19) then leads to the following eigenvectors

$$\lambda_1 = 2\ ;\ \mathbf{a}_1 = \alpha_1 \begin{Bmatrix} 1 \\ 1 \end{Bmatrix}$$

$$\lambda_2 = 5\ ;\ \mathbf{a}_2 = \alpha_2 \begin{Bmatrix} 2 \\ -1 \end{Bmatrix}$$

where the coefficients, α_i, indicate that we can only determine the relative values for the amplitudes of the eigenvectors. We can generalize this last statement to say that if $\mathbf{a}_i$ is an eigenvector, i.e., it satisfies (13.19), then $\alpha_i \mathbf{a}_i$ is also an eigenvector.

Now that we know how to calculate eigenvalues and eigenvectors we can consider some of their important properties and in the process see that the eigenvectors do have the magical property that we alluded to in the last section, i.e., they transform the mass and stiffness matrices to diagonal form. Let's suppose that we have two distinct eigenvalues and their associated eigenvectors $(\lambda_i, \mathbf{a}_i)$ and $(\lambda_j, \mathbf{a}_j)$. Each of their pairs satisfy (13.19) so that we have

$$(\mathbf{K} - \lambda_i \mathbf{M}) \, \mathbf{a}_i = 0 \tag{13.20}$$

$$(\mathbf{K} - \lambda_j \mathbf{M}) \, \mathbf{a}_j = 0 \tag{13.21}$$

The premultiplication of (13.20) by $\mathbf{a}_j^T$ and (13.21) by $\mathbf{a}_i^T$ followed by the transposition of (13.21) then leads to

$$\mathbf{a}_j^T (\mathbf{K} - \lambda_i \mathbf{M}) \, \mathbf{a}_i = 0 \tag{13.22}$$

$$\mathbf{a}_j^T (\mathbf{K} - \lambda_j \mathbf{M}) \, \mathbf{a}_i = 0 \tag{13.23}$$

where we have used the fact that $\mathbf{K}$ and $\mathbf{M}$ are symmetric matrices in writing (13.23).

The subtraction of (13.23) from (13.22) then leads to

$$(\lambda_j - \lambda_i) \, \mathbf{a}_j^T \mathbf{M} \, \mathbf{a}_i = 0 \tag{13.24}$$

from which it follows that

$$\mathbf{a}_j^T \mathbf{M} \, \mathbf{a}_i = 0 \qquad i \neq j \tag{13.25}$$

since λ_i and λ_j are distinct. This relation can be generalized as

$$\tag{13.26}$$

$$\mathbf{a}_j^T \mathbf{M} \, \mathbf{a}_i = \begin{cases} M_{ii} & \text{for} \quad i = j \\ 0 & \text{for} \quad i \neq j \end{cases}$$

This relation shows that the real eigenvectors are orthonormal with respect to the mass matrix. It is a simple matter to show that the eigenvectors are also orthonormal with respect to the stiffness matrix, $\mathbf{K}$

$$\mathbf{a}_j^T \mathbf{K} \, \mathbf{a}_i = \begin{cases} K_{ii} & \text{for} \quad i = j \\ 0 & \text{for} \quad i \neq j \end{cases} \tag{13.27}$$

and that the modal mass, M_{ii} and modal stiffness K_{ii} are related to the eigenvalue as follows

$$\lambda_i = \frac{K_{ii}}{M_{ii}} \tag{13.28}$$

Returning briefly to the transformation (13.7), let us suppose that we have found h eigenvectors which are of order f. We can then define the transformation $\mathbf{G}_{fh}$ to be the ordered set of h eigenvectors, i.e.,

$$\mathbf{G}_{fh} = \begin{bmatrix} \mathbf{a}_1 \, \mathbf{a}_2 \, \mathbf{a}_3 \dots \mathbf{a}_h \end{bmatrix} \tag{13.29}$$

Then, since each of the eigenvectors is orthonormal with respect to the mass and stiffness matrices, it follows that the use of a transformation of the form (13.29) will lead to reduced mass and stiffness matrices which are diagonal. The use of real eigenvectors for the transformation from physical (i.e., u_f) to modal (i.e., u_h) coordinates results in the so-called modal formulation in MSC/NASTRAN.

We noted earlier in this section that if a_i is an eigenvector which satisfies (13.16) then $\alpha_i a_i$ also satisfies (13.16). The choice of α_i depends on how we choose to normalize the eigenvector. Two popular methods are MASS normalization where the eigenvectors are scaled to make the modal mass, $M_{ii} = 1$, and MAX normalization where the scale factor is such that the largest element of the eigenvector is equal to one.

13.3. Standard Form of Eigenvalue Problem

The standard form of the eigenvalue problem is

$$(\mathbf{J} - \lambda \mathbf{I})\mathbf{w} = \mathbf{0} \tag{13.30}$$

where $\mathbf{J}$ is real and symmetric. The set (13.16) can be transformed to the form (13.30) by first decomposing the mass matrix into Choleski factors $\mathbf{C}$ such that

$$\mathbf{M} = \mathbf{C}\,\mathbf{C}^{\mathrm{T}} \tag{13.31}$$

The substitution of (13.31) into (13.16) then gives

$$(-\lambda\,\mathbf{C}\,\mathbf{C}^{\mathrm{T}} + \mathbf{K})\,\mathbf{a} = \mathbf{0} \tag{13.32}$$

A set of transformed variables is then defined as

$$\mathbf{w} = \mathbf{C}^{\mathrm{T}}\mathbf{a} \tag{13.33}$$

The substitution of (13.33) into (13.32) and subsequent premultiplication by $\mathbf{C}^{-1}$ then leads to the form of equations (13.30) where

$$\mathbf{J} = \mathbf{C}^{-1}\,\mathbf{K}\,\mathbf{C}^{-\mathrm{T}} \tag{13.34}$$

The transformation (13.34) is called a similarity transformation. This type of transformation preserves the character of the matrix $\mathbf{K}$ so that if it is real and symmetric $\mathbf{J}$ will also have those characteristics.

It is important to note that the Choleski factors may be singular if $\mathbf{M}$ is singular. This transformation is used for the Givens method for eigenvalue extraction in NASTRAN so that the mass matrix associated with the analysis set must be nonsingular for standard Givens method. Special procedures are available in MSC/NASTRAN to remove these singularities.

13.4. Specification of Element Inertia Properties

Element inertia properties may be defined by means of structural mass, nonstructural mass or by the mass elements. The mass matrix will be calculated:

1. For all dynamic rigid formats.

2. If the structural weight is requested using the parameter GRDPNT in any of the static rigid formats.

3. For the generation of external loads due to GRAV and RFORCE load specifications.

359

13.4.1.   Structural Mass

The structural mass is defined by means of the mass density specification on a MAT-type card. This coefficient is used to calculate the mass matrix for all elements for which a volume can be calculated.

13.4.2.   Nonstructural Mass

The ability to define nonstructural mass (NSM) provides a simple means of specifying a distributed mass on a structural element that is not associated with the geometric coefficients which are associated with structural stiffness. By its very nature the NSM is meant to augment the mass associated with the volume of the element. Thus, if both structural and NSM are specified, NASTRAN will calculate a mass matrix for each and will add the results to obtain the total mass matrix.

Since the NSM is an element property, it is defined on a property card. Nonstructural mass is associated with the strength-of-material elements and is therefore only available for the one- and two-dimensional elements. The NSM is defined as mass per unit length for the lineal elements and as mass per unit area for the two-dimensional elements.

13.4.3.   Consistent and Lumped Formulations

The masses associated with the structural metric elements can be calculated by two methods in NASTRAN using either the lumped or the consistent mass formulations. The lumped formulation is generally used by NASTRAN unless the user requests the consistent formulation by means of a PARAM COUPMASS Bulk Data card.

In the lumped mass method mass properties are only associated with the translational degrees of freedom. The total mass of the element is determined using both the structural and nonstructural mass. The total mass is then distributed to the node points in some ad hoc way, depending on the particular element. The resulting mass fraction is assigned to each of the translational degrees of freedom at each node. In the consistent approach the mass matrix is calculated using the method which is described in Sec. 6.9.

13.4.4.   Mass Elements

Mass can be associated with scalar and geometric grid-points by means of the CMASSi and the CONM1 and CONM2 Bulk Data cards, which are shown in Card Images 13-1 and 13-2, respectively.

The CONM1 Bulk Data allows the user to define a full six by six partition of the mass matrix, $\mathbf{M}_j$, at grid point G referred to the CID coordinate system. The CONM2 can be used to define a concentrated mass which may be offset from the associated geometric grid point.

The components of the offset coordinates (X_1, X_2, X_3) of the concentrated mass, M, and the components of the inertia tensor $\mathbf{I}$ are defined with respect to the CID coordinate system unless CID $= -1$ in which case they are defined with respect to the basic coordinate system. If CID $= -1$ the offsets are taken to be the difference between the grid point location and the position defined by the offset coordinates.

The form of the mass matrix associated with the six degrees of freedom at grid point G_j for the CONM2 specification is as follows

$$\mathbf{M}_j = \begin{bmatrix} M & & & & & \\ 0 & M & & & & \\ 0 & 0 & M & & \text{Sym} & \\ 0 & 0 & 0 & I_{11} & & \\ 0 & 0 & 0 & -I_{21} & I_{22} & \\ 0 & 0 & 0 & -I_{31} & -I_{32} & I_{33} \end{bmatrix} \tag{13.35}$$

where

$$M = \int \rho \, dV \qquad (13.36)$$

$$I_{11} = \int \rho \, (X_2^2 + X_3^2) \, dV$$
$$I_{22} = \int \rho \, (X_3^2 + X_1^2) \, dV \qquad (13.37)$$
$$I_{33} = \int \rho \, (X_1^2 + X_2^2) \, dV$$

$$I_{21} = \int \rho \, X_1 X_2 \, dV$$
$$I_{32} = \int \rho \, X_3 X_2 \, dV \qquad (13.38)$$
$$I_{13} = \int \rho \, X_1 X_3 \, dV$$

*Scalar Mass Connection Between Grid Points

1	2	3	4	5	6	7	8	9	10
CMASS1	EID	PID	G1	C1	G2	C2			
PMASS	PID	M	PID	M	PID	M	PID	M	
CMASS2	EID	M	G1	C1	G2	C2			

*Scalar Mass Connection Between Two Points

CMASS3	EID	PID	S1	S2	EID	PID	S1	S2	
PMASS	PID	M	etc.						
CMASS4	EID	M	S1	S2	EID	M	S1	S2	

where

    M Mass coefficient. (real)

  Gi, Ci Define degrees of freedom connected by the mass where Gi is a grid or scalar point number and Ci is a degree of freedom code.

    Si Defines scalar points connected by mass.

Card Image 13-1. Specification of Scalar Mass

361

*Specification of Mass Matrix Coefficients

1	2	3	4	5	6	7	8	9	10
CONM1	EID	G	CID	M_{11}	M_{21}	M_{22}	M_{31}	M_{32}	+ M1
+ M1	M_{33}	M_{41}	M_{42}	M_{43}	M_{44}	M_{51}	M_{52}	M_{53}	+ M2
+ M2	M_{54}	M_{55}	M_{61}	M_{62}	M_{63}	M_{64}	M_{65}	M_{66}	

*Specification of Mass Properties

CONM2	EID	G	CID	M	X_1	X_2	X_3		+ M1
+ M1	I_{11}	I_{21}	I_{22}	I_{31}	I_{32}	I_{33}			

Card Image 13-2. Specification of Mass at Geometric Grid Point

13.5.   Real Eigenvalue Extraction Techniques

The eigenvalue problem in NASTRAN is defined for the a-set of degrees of freedom. The a-set has a broader meaning for dynamics than it had for statics and may include generalized degrees of freedom as well as physical degrees of freedom, as described in Sec. 13.6. Deferring a discussion of topics such as Guyan Reduction and Generalized Dynamic Reduction until Sec. 13.6., we can write the eigenvalue problem in NASTRAN set notation as

$$(-\lambda \mathbf{M}_{aa} + \mathbf{K}_{aa})\, \mathbf{a}_a = 0 \qquad (13.39)$$

There are three algorithms that can be used for evaluation of real eigenvalues in MSC/NAS-TRAN. An algorithm together with its associated parameters is selected by means of the EIGR-Bulk Data card. The EIGR card and the associated parameters will be described for the three following methods:

- The inverse power method with shifts

- Givens triangularization method

- Modified Givens method

The first method is a root-tracking technique, which finds one eigenvalue and an associated eigenvector at a time. The transformation techniques find all the eigenvalues by transforming the eigenvalue problem.

The relative efficiency of the methods is dependent on the matrix topology, the order of the system matrices, and the number of eigenvalues and eigenvectors to be extracted. Numerical studies have shown that the tridiagonal method in conjunction with a reduction of the degrees of freedom in the a-set as described in Sec. 13-8 is most cost efficient if a significant number of eigenvectors are to be extracted for large problems.

The Givens method requires that the eigenvalue problem be cast in standard form as defined by (13.30). Since $\mathbf{J}$ in this form must be real and symmetric and since $\mathbf{J}$ is obtained from the stiffness matrix $\mathbf{K}$ by the similarity transformation (13.34), this implies that the mass matrix must be positive definite. Thus, the Givens method cannot be used for the buckling problem or for the case where the damping matrix is present.

The following general observations can be made about the choice of eigenvalue extraction technique

1. The inverse power method (INV) is best suited for obtaining only a few eigenvectors for large systems with sparce matrices

2. The tridiagonal methods (GIV and MGIV) are best suited for those cases where several eigenvectors are required. The size of the a-set should be reasonably small so that extensive static and/or dynamic reduction (See Sec. 13.6) may be required before performing the eigensolution.

13.5.1. The Inverse Power Method

The inverse power method seeks solutions to (13.39) using an iterative technique, where (13.39) is rewritten in the following form:

$$\mathbf{a} = \lambda \mathbf{K}^{-1} \mathbf{M} \mathbf{a} \qquad (13.40)$$

If $(\lambda_i, \mathbf{a}_i)$ is an eigenvalue and an associated eigenvector, then the substitution of $(\lambda_i, \mathbf{a}_i)$ into the right-hand side of equation (13.40) would result in a vector $\mathbf{a}_i$ on the left-hand side that is identical to the vector used on the right-hand side. The form of (13.40) can be used to define an iterative technique which converges to the pair $(\lambda_i, \mathbf{a}_i)$.

Let $\mathbf{a}_n$ be the current estimate of the eigenvector after n iterations, where the subscript defines the iteration number. The next estimate is then obtained by first substituting $\mathbf{a}_n$ into (13.40) to obtain

$$\mathbf{w}_{n+1} = \mathbf{K}^{-1} \mathbf{M} \mathbf{a}_n \qquad (13.41)$$

with the next estimate given by

$$\mathbf{a}_{n+1} = \frac{\mathbf{w}_{n+1}}{c_{n+1}} \qquad (13.42)$$

and where c_{n+1} is the largest element in $\mathbf{w}_{n+1}$. The process defined by (13.41) and (13.42) is described by the following algorithm:

1. Decompose $\mathbf{K}$ into its $\mathbf{LU}$ factors

2. Choose a starting vector $\mathbf{a}_1$ and solve for $\mathbf{w}_2$ using (13.41)

3. Calculate $\mathbf{a}_2$ using (13.42)

4. Compare the absolute magnitude of $\mathbf{a}_2$ to $\mathbf{a}_1$. When the difference between the magnitude is less than some preassigned small number, then the process is stopped. Otherwise steps two through four are repeated using the last estimate of the eigenvector as the new starting vector.

The parameter, c_n, converges to the lowest eigenvalue and $\mathbf{a}_n$ converges to the associated eigenvector.

There are several disadvantages of the standard inverse iteration procedure, including

1. Difficulty in handling rigid body modes

2. Slow convergence for closely spaced roots

3. Deterioration of accuracy as more roots are found

All these disadvantages are eliminated by means of a simple modification to the method by which roots are evaluated relative to a shift point. The modified algorithm is posed by representing the eigenvalue as

$$\lambda = \lambda_0 + \Lambda \qquad (13.43)$$

363

where

λ_0 is the shift point

Λ is the shifted eigenvalue

The substitution of (13.43) into (13.39) then gives

$$[-(\lambda_0 + \Lambda)\,\mathbf{M} + \mathbf{K}]\,\mathbf{a} = \mathbf{0} \tag{13.44}$$

The iteration algorithm is then similar to the standard inverse iteration method except that the iteration equation (13.41) becomes

$$\mathbf{w}_{n+1} = (\mathbf{K} - \lambda_0\mathbf{M})^{-1}\,\mathbf{M}\,\mathbf{a}_n \tag{13.45}$$

where

$$\mathbf{a}_{n+1} = \frac{\mathbf{w}_{n+1}}{c_{n+1}} \tag{13.46}$$

As n becomes large, $\mathbf{a}_{n+1}$ converges to the ith eigenvector and c_{n+1} converges to the shifted eigenvalue that is closest to the shift point.

The following observations can be made about the inverse iteration with shifts procedure.

1. A triangular decomposition of $(\mathbf{K} - \lambda_0\mathbf{M})$ is required to calculate $\mathbf{w}_{n+1}$. The effort required to perform a matrix decomposition is a function of the square of the root mean square wavefront and is therefore sensitive to the number of active columns.

2. The stiffness matrix can be singular (provided λ_0 is nonzero) so that rigid body modes offer no special difficulty. Tests of this algorithm suggest that repeated rigid body modes are evaluated with no difficulty.

3. The shift point, λ_0, may be changed at any stage in the solution to improve convergence or to improve accuracy and convergence rate after several roots have been extracted. A change in starting point requires that an additional matrix decomposition be performed.

4. The shift point can be specified so that eigenvalues can be obtained within a specified frequency band rather than obtaining the smallest eigenvalue.

13.5.1.1.   Specification of EIGR for Inverse Power with Shifts

The format for the EIGR-Bulk Data card for the inverse power with shifts is shown by Card Image 13-3.

The data specified on the EIGR card are used to control the inverse iteration method in the following manner:

1. The maximum and minimum frequencies of interest f_{max} and f_{min} are converted to maximum and minimum values of the eigenvalue λ_{max} and λ_{min} where

$$\lambda = (2\,\pi\,f)^2$$

2. The number of roots estimated in the range, N_e, is used to determine the number of starting points, N_s, which is chosen to satisfy the inequality.

$$N_s - 1 < \frac{N_e}{6} \le N_s$$

The starting points are then distributed, as shown in Fig. 13-1 where the increment in the eigenvalue is found from

$$\Delta\lambda = \lambda_{max} - \lambda_{min} \tag{13.47}$$

and the position of the nth starting point is given by

$$\lambda_{sn} = \lambda_{min} + \frac{(n - \frac{1}{2})}{N_s} \Delta\lambda \qquad (13.48)$$

1	2	3	4	5	6	7	8	9	10
EIGR	SID	INV	F1	F2	NE	ND		E	+ E1
+ E1	NORM	G	C						

where

    SID Set identification number (integer) that must be specified by the Case Control Directive

$$\text{METHOD} = \text{SID}$$

    INV Literal string which specifies the inverse power method.

  F1, F2 Frequency range specification of interest $(0. \leq F1 < F2, F2 > 0.)$, cycles per unit time. (real)

     NE Number of roots estimated in frequency range. (integer, > 0)

    ND Number of roots desired. (integer, ≥ 0, default is $ND = 3NE$ if set equal to zero)

      E Convergence test parameter. (Real, default 10^{-4})

  NORM Method of normalizing the eigenvector. One of the literal strings MASS, POINT, or MAX.

    G, C Degree of freedom if POINT is specified where G is the grid or scalar point and C is a degree of freedom code. (integers)

Card Image 13-3. Specification of Inverse Power Method

The NASTRAN algorithm assumes that approximately six good eigenvalues and associated eigenvectors can be found from a single starting point. Thus, if the estimate number of roots is six or less, the algorithm will use only one starting point, which is located in the middle of the eigenvalue range of interest.

The eigenvalue analysis is terminated after ND roots are found. If the user does not specify ND, the algorithm will terminate after finding three times the number of roots estimated.

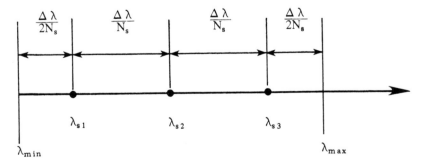

Figure 13-1. Distribution of Starting Points for Inverse Power

13.5.1.2.   NASTRAN Eigenvalue Summary for the Inverse Iteration Method

The NASTRAN program prints a summary of several variables after the execution of the Normal Modes analysis when the inverse power method is specified. To interpret this summary, the user must have some understanding of the inverse iteration algorithm.

First of all, there is a difference between the starting point and the shift point. The algorithm starts the eigenvalue search at a starting point and then may shift to another point (indeed the same concept as a starting point) in order to speed convergence. If, for example, the ratio of the first two shifted eigenvalues relative to the current starting point is approximately equal to unity, the rate of convergence will be very slow. Since the value of the closest eigenvalue and the time required to converge from both the current starting point and the shifted point can be estimated (ref. 13-5), a decision to either shift or continue to iterate can be made.

The algorithms will continue to search for eigenvalues relative to the current starting point until an eigenvalue is found in the range of the next starting point, where a certain overlap between range of starting points is allowed. The algorithm finds successive eigenvalues, the first of which is the closest to the starting point. The eigenvalues then increase in absolute magnitude from the starting point. This means that one cannot be certain that the lowest root has been found in a specified range unless all the roots in the range have been found. The summary of the parameters associated with the algorithm and reasons for termination are as follows.

1. Number of eigenvalues extracted

2. Number of starting points used

3. Number of starting points moves

4. Number of matrix decompositions

5. Number of iterations

6. Reason for termination

    1) Two consecutive singularities encountered while performing matrix decompositions.

        If two successive singularities in $K - \lambda_0 M$ are found, this implies that there may be something abnormal about the problem or (perhaps) there may be a software error. Check the input to insure that the mass matrix has been specified.

    2) Four shift points used while tracking a single root.

        If four shifts are required to track a single root, this implies that the first root is a long way from the first starting point and that the user did not exercise proper care in specifying the frequency range of interest. A preliminary estimate of the lowest root should be made with changes to the frequency range, and perhaps, the number of roots estimated in the range.

    3) All eigenvalues found in the frequency range specified.

        All the roots in the range have been found. An excellent reason for terminating.

    4) Three times the number of estimated eigenvalues have been found.

        If the user has not specified the number of roots desired, the algorithm will terminate after finding $3N_e$ roots. Generally speaking, this is not a good reason for terminating.

5) All the eigenvalues that exist in the problem have been found.

> A valid reason for termination, but one that the user should not receive except for those cases where there are a very few degrees of freedom. If the user desires all the roots, Givens method should be specified since it is more economical than the inverse method if several roots and associated vectors are desired.

6) The number of roots desired have been found.

> same comment as reason 4

7) One or more eigenvalues have been found outside the specified frequency range.

> If one or more eigenvalues have been found outside the range, then either all eigenvalues in the range have been found or there are no roots in the range. A good reason for terminating, especially if only one root is desired.

8) Insufficient time to find another root.

> A bad reason for terminating. Re-execute the problem taking advantage of current results, if possible, by restricting the range of interest.

9) Unable to converge.

> A bad reason for termination because the algorithm can be shown to converge if $\mathbf{M}$ and $\mathbf{K}$ are symmetric. Since the algorithm uses system matrices generated by the finite element model, there should be no convergence problem unless the user has modified the $\mathbf{M}_{aa}$ and/or $\mathbf{K}_{aa}$ matrices by some nonstandard technique.

7. Largest off-diagonal modal mass term and the numbers of the eigenvector pairs that fail the criteria.

13.5.1.3. Finding Lowest Eigenvalue with Inverse Method

The inverse power method is frequently used to determine the lowest eigenvalue, i.e, the lowest natural frequency for a normal mode solution or the lowest buckling load for the buckling problem which is governed by the equation $(\mathbf{K} - \lambda \mathbf{K}^D)\mathbf{u} = 0$ where $\mathbf{K}^D$ is the differential stiffness matrix. If one has no knowledge of the value for the eigenvalue then one is on the horns of a dilemma because

1. The specification of a large frequency range (for normal modes) may lead to the determination of several eigenvalue-eigenvalue pairs at great cost.

2. Even if all roots are found in the range there is always a possibility of having a root below f_{min} if $f_{min} > 0$.

There isn't any magic prescription in NASTRAN that in essence says "find the lowest root." All we can do is give some rather general guidelines which may help reduce the solution costs and which will guarantee that the lowest root is found.

The suggested technique for finding the lowest (positive) eigenvalue is to specify a small frequency range using f_{min} and f_{max} which is so small that the root will be outside the range. Then specify that $N_e = 1$, which will generate one starting point in the middle of the range, and that $N_D = 1$, which will cause the algorithm to terminate after the extraction of one eigenvalue and associated eigenvector. If we were successful in choosing the frequency range correctly then the root is outside the range and is closest to the starting point, which is at the center of the specified frequency range.

13.5.2.   The Tridiagonal (Givens) Method

In order to guarantee that there are no roots below that calculated we can request that parameters which are calculated within the eigenvalue extraction module be printed by using a DIAG 16 Executive Control Command. While this data includes much which will either be incomprehensible or useless it does include the number of roots below the current starting point λ_0. If this number is zero then we can be assured that the one root which was calculated is indeed the lowest. A description of the data which is printed by DIAG 16 in Rigid Format 3 is included in Sec. 13.9.

13.5.2.   The Tridiagonal (Givens) Method

MSC/NASTRAN incorporates Givens (GIV) as well as modified Givens (MGIV) tridiagonal methods. Both of these methods are based on the standard form of the eigenvalue problem given by (13.30). The difference between the two methods is that the traditional Givens method uses the Choleski factors of the mass matrix as shown by (13.31) while the modified Givens reformulates the eigenvalue problem by defining the eigenvalue, λ, as

$$\lambda = \frac{1}{\Lambda'} - \lambda_0 \tag{13.49}$$

where λ_0 is a shift point. The substitution of (13.49) into (13.39) then gives

$$(-\Lambda'(\mathbf{K}_{aa} + \lambda_0 \mathbf{M}_{aa}) + \mathbf{M}_{aa})\mathbf{a}_a = 0 \tag{13.50}$$

The modified eigenvalue problem is thus reduced to standard form by finding the Choleski factors of $(\mathbf{K}_{aa} + \lambda_0 \mathbf{M}_{aa})$ which will ordinarily be nonsingular even if the a-set contains massless degrees of freedom. A user-friendly feature is available for removing null columns which exist in both $\mathbf{K}_{aa}$ and $\mathbf{M}_{aa}$ that is controlled by the ASING PARAMeter which is described in Sec. 13.7.

MSC/NASTRAN uses a modification of the Givens method to reduce the $\mathbf{J}$ matrix in equation (13.30) to tridiagonal form and then uses the Q-R method (ref. 13-6) to obtain a diagonal matrix whose elements are the eigenvalues. The eigenvectors associated with a specific eigenvalue are then determined by the tridiagonal form of the eigenvalue problem to be

$$(\mathbf{A} - \lambda_i \mathbf{I})\mathbf{w}_i = 0 \tag{13.51}$$

The tridiagonal matrix $[\mathbf{A} - \lambda_i \mathbf{I}]$ is decomposed into its $\mathbf{L}_i\mathbf{U}_i$ factors. In this decomposition, partial pivoting is used, which means that the pivotal row at each stage is selected so that it has the largest coefficient of the variable being eliminated. Since the $\mathbf{U}_i$ is tridiagonal, there are only two equations containing that variable. The eigenvector $\mathbf{a}_i$ is then obtained by means of an iterated solution of

$$\mathbf{U}_i\mathbf{a}_i = \mathbf{C} \tag{13.52}$$

where $\mathbf{C}$ is arbitrary. After evaluating $\mathbf{a}_i^{(1)}$ by means of (13.52) the vector $\mathbf{C}$ is replaced by $\mathbf{a}_i^{(1)}$ so that, after the first calculation, equation (13.52) becomes:

$$\mathbf{U}_i\mathbf{a}_i^{(n+1)} = \mathbf{a}_i^n \tag{13.53}$$

It is shown in ref. 13-5 that if the computed eigenvalue is an accurate estimate of the true eigenvalue, then convergence is so rapid that more than two iterations are seldom required. NASTRAN uses an initial $\mathbf{C}$-vector whose elements are unity. In the case of repeated roots, the initial vector for the second root is chosen to be orthogonal to the first.

13.5.2.1.   Specification of EIGR for the Tridiagonalization Method

The EIGR Bulk Data cards for the GIV and MGIV methods are shown by Card Image 13-4. The data specified on the EIGR card is the same for both the Givens and Modified Givens methods. Both of these methods find all of the eigenvalues in the a-set simultaneously. The recovery of eigenvectors is then controlled by specifying

- A frequency range (F_1, F_2) where F_1 is the lowest and F_2 is the highest frequency, in Hertz.

- The number of lowest frequencies for which eigenvectors are to be recovered — ND

The ND field is an integer number which defines the number of eigenvectors starting with that associated with the lowest eigenvalue for either the GIV or MGIV methods. The ND request takes precedence over the frequency range for the GIV method.

The presence of a real number in the E field requests that the mass orthogonality test be performed over all of the eigenvectors which are extracted, with the value of the entry taken to be the test value. The NORM field contains one of the literal strings MASS, MAX, or POINT which define how the eigenvectors are to be normalized. If POINT is specified then the eigenvectors are normalized with respect to the displacement associated with the degree of freedom defined by the pair (G, C) where G is a gridpoint identification number and C is a degree of freedom code. The entry in field 3 contains one of the literal strings GIV or MGIV to request Givens and Modified Givens, respectively. In either case the SID field is an integer set identification number. The particular eigenvalue algorithm which is to be incorporated in the analysis is then specified by the following Case Control Directive.

$$\text{METHOD} = <\text{SID}>$$

*GIV — Givens Method

1	2	3	4	5	6	7	8	9	10
EIGR	SID	GIV	F_1	F_2		ND		E	+ E1
+ E1	NORM	G	C						

*MGIV — Modified Givens Method

EIGR	SID	MGIV	F_1	F_2		ND		E	+ E2
+ E2	NORM	G	C						

Card Image 13-4. Specification of GIV and MGIV Eigenvalue Extraction

13.6. Procedures for Reducing Dynamic Degrees of Freedom

MSC/NASTRAN can be used to model an almost unlimited variety of modern structures. It is not uncommon to use several thousand grid points, with tens of thousands of degrees of freedom in the static analysis of ships, aircraft, automobiles or nuclear reactors to name a few. It is clearly impractical and unnecessary to perform dynamic analyses using the detailed representation which is required for statics. Realistic procedures for reducing the number of degrees of freedom prior to performing dynamic analyses must therefore be formulated.

A number of techniques for reducing the dynamic degrees of freedom have been presented in the literature including the Guyan Reduction (ref. 13-8), the use of static deflection shapes (ref. 13-9), and Generalized Dynamic Reduction (ref. 13-10) to name a few. Generally speaking any reduction technique can be implemented in MSC/NASTRAN by using Direct Matrix Abstract Programming but the Guyan and Generalized Dynamic Reduction procedures can be specified by means of appropriate Bulk Data and are described below.

13.6.1. Static Condensation in Dynamics — The Guyan Reduction

Static condensation is associated with the OMIT feature in NASTRAN which is described in

13.6.1 Static Condensation in Dynamics — The Guyan Reduction

Sec. 7.6 where it is shown that the o- and a-set displacements are related by

$$\mathbf{u}_o = \mathbf{G}_{oa}\mathbf{u}_{oa} \tag{13.54}$$

where

$$\mathbf{G}_{oa} = -\mathbf{K}_{oo}^{-1}\mathbf{K}_{oa} \tag{13.55}$$

The f-set is then related to the a-set by the transformation

$$\mathbf{u}_f = \mathbf{G}_{fa}\mathbf{u}_a \tag{13.56}$$

where

$$\mathbf{G}_{fa} = \begin{bmatrix} \mathbf{G}_{oa} \\ \mathbf{I}_{aa} \end{bmatrix} \tag{13.57}$$

If we were to attempt to use the static condensation technique for the dynamic equations we would run into certain difficulties. As an illustration consider the following equations for normal modes analysis written in partitioned form

$$\left(-\omega^2 \begin{bmatrix} \mathbf{M}_{oo} & \mathbf{M}_{oa} \\ \mathbf{M}_{ao} & \widetilde{\mathbf{M}}_{aa} \end{bmatrix} + \begin{bmatrix} \mathbf{K}_{oo} & \mathbf{K}_{oa} \\ \mathbf{K}_{ao} & \widetilde{\mathbf{K}}_{aa} \end{bmatrix} \right) \begin{Bmatrix} \mathbf{u}_o \\ \mathbf{u}_a \end{Bmatrix} = \begin{Bmatrix} 0 \\ 0 \end{Bmatrix} \tag{13.58}$$

If we attempt to solve for $\mathbf{u}_o$ using the upper partition of (13.58) as was done in the static case we find that the frequency appears in the transformation matrix whch relates $\mathbf{u}_o$ and $\mathbf{u}_a$. An iterative procedure would therefore be required to find the transformation associated with each natural frequency. An approximate technique which is independent of frequency is therefore desirable. The approximate approach associated with the Guyan Reduction is to use the static condensation transformation (13.57) for dynamics so that the reduced mass matrix becomes

$$\mathbf{M}_{aa} = \mathbf{G}_{fa}^T \mathbf{M}_{ff} \mathbf{G}_{fa} \tag{13.59}$$

or in expanded form

$$\mathbf{M}_{aa} = \widetilde{\mathbf{M}}_{aa} + \mathbf{M}_{ao}\mathbf{G}_{oa} + \mathbf{G}_{oa}^T\mathbf{M}_{oa} + \mathbf{G}_{oa}^T\mathbf{M}_{oo}\mathbf{G}_{oa} \tag{13.60}$$

If the mass coefficients associated with the o-set are null then $\mathbf{M}_{aa} = \widetilde{\mathbf{M}}_{aa}$ and the transformation (13.56) is exact.

In order to assess the approximation which is associated with the use of the static relation (13.55) in dynamics it is reasonable to consider the consequences of using (13.56) to define a relation between the o- and a-sets. From the upper partition of (13.58) we find that

$$\mathbf{u}_o = -(\omega^2 \mathbf{M}_{oo} + \mathbf{K}_{oo})^{-1}(-\omega^2 \mathbf{M}_{oa} + \mathbf{K}_{oa})\mathbf{u}_a \tag{13.61}$$

The substitution of (13.61) into the lower partition of (13.58) then gives the following reduced equation

$$-\omega^2 \mathbf{M}_{aa} + \mathbf{K}_{aa} + (-\omega^2 \mathbf{M}_{ao} + \mathbf{K}_{ao})(-\omega^2 \mathbf{M}_{oo} + \mathbf{K}_{oo})^{-1}(-\omega^2 \mathbf{M}_{oa} + \mathbf{K}_{oa})\mathbf{u}_a = 0 \tag{13.62}$$

The inverse term, $(-\omega^2 \mathbf{M}_{oo} + \mathbf{K}_{oo})^{-1}$, can be represented using a series of expansion as follows

$$(-\omega^2 \mathbf{M}_{oo} + \mathbf{K}_{oo})^{-1} = \mathbf{K}_{oo}^{-1} + \omega^2 \mathbf{K}_{oo}^{-1}\mathbf{M}_{oo}\mathbf{K}_{oo}^{-1} + \cdots \tag{13.63}$$

The substitution of (13.63) into (13.62) then leads to the same reduced stiffness matrix (7.66) and reduced mass matrix (13.60) as those obtained by using static condensation when only terms through ω^2 are retained.

The exact solution of the reduced problem is thus seen to involve an interated procedure. Such a procedure is not automated in the normal modes analysis solution algorithm so that some means of selecting the OMITed degrees of freedom to minimize the frequency-dependent error in the reduced mass matrix is required. Unfortunately, there is no automated procedure for selecting those degrees of freedom to be OMITed. There are some guidelines, however, that have appeared in the literature (ref. 13-11, for example), which suggest

1. Retain degrees of freedom with large inertia.

2. Retain degrees of freedom with large accelerations (i.e., large relative displacements for normal mode analysis).

3. Retain approximately 3.5 times as many well-chosen degrees of freedom as the number of accurate modes desired in the solution.

4. Retain displacement degrees of freedom for bending problems.

These suggestions almost presuppose that the user knows the solution to the eigenvalue problem in order to make an intelligent choice of retained physical degrees of freedom in the a-set. While Guyan Reduction (i.e., the use of the OMIT feature) is inexpensive and is therefore popular it requires user prescience to obtain accurate solutions. Another technique which overcomes the need to make hard modeling decisions, and which can lead to a significant reduction in the number of degrees of freedom in the analysis set has been incorporated in MSC/NASTRAN. This procedure which is called generalized dynamic reduction is described in the following section.

13.6.2. Generalized Dynamic Reduction

Guyan reduction is seen to have a number of limitations including

* User effort required in selecting the a-set

* Accuracy is dependent on users skill in selecting the a-set

* High accuracy requires a large number of a-set degrees of freedom regardless of user skill

An alternative technique called generalized dynamic reduction is available as an integral part of Rigid Format 3 in MSC/NASTRAN that does not have these limitations and that provides superior results for fewer degrees of freedom in the a-set.

Generalized Dynamic Reduction is a procedure in MSC/NASTRAN for producing a set of displacement vectors which are "rich" in the lowest eigenvectors for the problem. In this procedure an inverse iteration method is used to generate a set of displacement sets $\mathbf{u}_i^*$ which are themselves a linear combination of the true eigenvectors, $\mathbf{a}_j$, i.e.,

$$\mathbf{u}_i^* = \sum_{j=1}^{q} \alpha_{ij} \mathbf{a}_j \quad i = 1, 2, \ldots q \tag{13.64}$$

The set of q displacement sets is used to define a transformation between the physical displacement degrees of freedom and a set of q modal coordinates $\mathbf{u}_q$. The eigenvalue problem is then defined in the reduced vector space and the eigenvalues and eigenvectors are determined using one of the real eigenvalue extraction routines, Givens, Modified Givens, or inverse power with shifts.

The procedure for determining the set of displacement vectors which is used for the transformation is presented in ref. 13-10. In the following we will discuss the associated MSC/NASTRAN displacement sets and will define the transformation involved in the reduction process.

We start by defining the f-set to be the union of the a- and o-sets in Sec. 7-6 for the static case

$$\mathbf{u}_f = \left\{ \begin{array}{c} \mathbf{u}_o \\ \mathbf{u}_a \end{array} \right\} \tag{13.65}$$

However, in dynamics we will extend our concept of the a-set to be the union of the q-set which includes the q independent modal degrees of freedom and the t-set which includes physical degrees of freedom which are to be retained in the normal mode solution. Thus for normal modes and frequencies the a-set is the union of two sets

$$\mathbf{u}_a = \left\{ \begin{array}{c} \mathbf{u}_q \\ \mathbf{u}_t \end{array} \right\} \tag{13.66}$$

The f-set can now be written using (13.65) and (13.66) as

$$\mathbf{u}_f = \left\{ \begin{array}{c} \mathbf{u}_q \\ \mathbf{u}_o \\ \mathbf{u}_t \end{array} \right\} \tag{13.67}$$

The generalized dynamic reduction procedure is then applied to determine q displacement vectors which relate all of the *physical* degrees of freedom in the f-set as follows

$$\left\{ \begin{array}{c} \mathbf{u}_o \\ \mathbf{u}_t \end{array} \right\} = \left\{ \begin{array}{c} \mathbf{G}_{oq}^\star \\ \mathbf{G}_{tq}^\star \end{array} \right\} \mathbf{u}_q \tag{13.68}$$

The q-columns of $\mathbf{G}_{oq}^\star$ and $\mathbf{G}_{tq}^\star$ are the displacement vectors from the generalized dynamic reduction procedure.

We now define a transformation between the o-set and the a-set components in the following form

$$\mathbf{u}_o = [\ \mathbf{G}_{oq} \quad \mathbf{G}_{ot}\ ] \left\{ \begin{array}{c} \mathbf{u}_q \\ \mathbf{u}_t \end{array} \right\} \tag{13.69}$$

where $\mathbf{G}_{ot}$ is the set of static displacement modes which are defined by Guyan Reduction that is related to the partition of the system stiffness matrix as follows

$$\mathbf{G}_{ot} = -\mathbf{K}_{oo}^{-1}\mathbf{K}_{ot} \tag{13.70}$$

We note from this relation (13.70) that the $\mathbf{K}_{oo}$ partition must be non-singular. This implies that all rigid body motion must be represented by the t-set if the structure is a free body. The rigid body motion could be SUPORTed (see Sec. 7.7) to define a statically determinant set of reference coordinates.

It now remains to determine the transformation matrix $\mathbf{G}_{oq}$. This is done by using (13.68) to rewrite (13.69) as

$$\mathbf{G}^\star_{oq}\, \mathbf{u}_q \;=\; \mathbf{G}_{oq}\, \mathbf{u}_q \;+\; \mathbf{G}_{ot}\, \mathbf{G}^\star_{tq}\, \mathbf{u}_q \tag{13.71}$$

Where we emphasize that $\mathbf{G}^\star_{oq}$ and $\mathbf{G}^\star_{tq}$ are obtained by the generalized dynamic reduction procedure. By inspection we see that, for non-trivial $\mathbf{u}_q$, $\mathbf{G}_{oq}$ is given by

$$\mathbf{G}_{oq} \;=\; \mathbf{G}^\star_{oq} - \mathbf{G}_{ot}\, \mathbf{G}^\star_{tq} \tag{13.72}$$

For the case where there is no static condensation (i.e. the t-set is null) then $\mathbf{G}_{oq} = \mathbf{G}^\star_{oq}$.

13.6.2.1.   Reduction to Solution Set

The solution set for normal modes analysis is the a-set which, as we have seen in the previous section, is the union of the q- and t-sets. The reduction to the a-set thus proceeds by representing the f-set (13.65) in terms of the q- and t-set displacements as

$$\mathbf{u}_f \;=\; \begin{bmatrix} \mathbf{I}_{qq} & \mathbf{0} \\ \mathbf{G}_{oq} & \mathbf{G}_{ot} \\ \mathbf{0} & \mathbf{I}_{tt} \end{bmatrix} \begin{Bmatrix} \mathbf{u}_q \\ \mathbf{u}_t \end{Bmatrix} \;=\; \mathbf{G}_{fa}\, \mathbf{u}_a \tag{13.73}$$

where

$$\mathbf{G}_{fa} \;=\; \begin{bmatrix} \mathbf{I}_{qq} & \mathbf{0} \\ \mathbf{G}_{oq} & \mathbf{G}_{ot} \\ \mathbf{0} & \mathbf{I}_{tt} \end{bmatrix} \tag{13.74}$$

The reduced stiffness and mass matices are then given by

$$\mathbf{K}_{aa} \;=\; \mathbf{G}^T_{fa}\, \mathbf{K}_{ff}\, \mathbf{G}_{fa} \tag{13.75}$$

$$\mathbf{M}_{aa} \;=\; \mathbf{G}^T_{fa}\, \mathbf{M}_{ff}\, \mathbf{G}_{fa} \tag{13.76}$$

Performing these operations the stiffness and mass matrices can be expressed in partitioned form as

$$\mathbf{K}_{aa} \;=\; \begin{bmatrix} \mathbf{G}^T_{oq}\, \mathbf{K}_{oo}\, \mathbf{G}_{oq} & \mathbf{0} \\ \mathbf{0} & \mathbf{K}_{tt} + \mathbf{K}_{to}\, \mathbf{G}_{ot} \end{bmatrix} \tag{13.77}$$

and

$$\mathbf{M}_{aa} \;=\; \begin{bmatrix} \mathbf{G}^T_{oq}\, \mathbf{M}_{oo}\, \mathbf{G}_{oq} & \vdots & \mathbf{G}^T_{oq}\, (\mathbf{M}^T_{to} + \mathbf{M}_{oo}\, \mathbf{G}_{ot}) \\ \cdots & \vdots & \cdots \\ (\mathbf{M}_{to} + \mathbf{G}^T_{ot}\, \mathbf{M}_{oo})\, \mathbf{G}_{oq} & \vdots & \mathbf{M}_{tt} + \mathbf{M}_{to}\, \mathbf{G}_{ot} + \mathbf{G}^T_{ot}\, (\mathbf{M}_{ot} + \mathbf{M}_{oo}\, \mathbf{G}_{ot}) \end{bmatrix} \tag{13.78}$$

where the matrices $\mathbf{K}_{oo}$, $\mathbf{M}_{oo}$, etc. are partitions of the stiffness and mass matrices, $\mathbf{K}_{ff}$ and $\mathbf{M}_{ff}$.

13.6.2.2.   Defining the Generalized Dynamic Reduction Procedure

The Bulk Data required to define the generalized dynamic reduction is shown by Card Image 13-5 and includes

- An SPOINT card which defines the modal coordinates.

- An ASET card which includes the generalized coordinates (modal coordinates) as well as physical degrees of freedom in the a-set.

- A DYNRED card which controls the extraction of the q lowest approximate eigenvectors.

- A QSET card which includes the generalized coordinates in the q-set

1	2	3	4	5	6	7	8	9	10
SPOINT	S_1	THRU	S_n						
ASET1	C	S_1	THRU	S_n					
QSET1	C	S_1	THRU	S_n					
DYNRED	SID	FMAX	NIRV	NIT	IDIR	QDOF			

Card Image 13-5. Bulk Data for Definition of Generalized Dynamic Reduction

Generalized dynamic reduction is then specified by a Case Control Directive

$$\text{DYNRED} = <\text{SID}>$$

where <SID> is the set number on the DYNRED Bulk Data card.

13.6.2.3.   Defining Dynamic Degrees of Freedom

The generalilized dynamic reduction procedure will determine the q sets of displacement vectors which are rich in the eigenvectors at and below the frequency FMAX, in Hertz, specified on the DYNRED card. The associated q modal degrees of freedom must be defined by the analyst by using the SPOINT card and then included in the a-set by ASET or ASET1, and in the q-set by QSET or QSET1 Bulk Data cards. The user is faced with the problem that the number of natural frequencies below FMAX is generally not known. However, this number can be found automatically by MSC/NASTRAN through a Sturm sequence technique in which the number of sign changes on the diagonal of the upper triangular factor of $\mathbf{K} - \mu \mathbf{M}$ defines the number of roots below μ. The number of modal coordinates to be used will be calculated automatically by MSC/NASTRAN if the QDOF field is left blank on DYNRED Bulk Data. If QDOF is blank then the number of modal coordinates is taken to be approximately 1.5 times the number of roots below FMAX. The user may explicitly specify the number of generalized coordinates by entering an integer value for QDOF.

Independent of the option chosen for specifying the number of generalized coordinates on DYNRED Bulk Data the generalized coordinates must be

- Defined as scalar degrees of freedom using SPOINT

- Included in the a-set by using ASET or ASET1 Bulk Data

- Included in the q-set by using QSET or QSET1 Bulk Data

If the number of generalized coordinate, QDOF, is explicitly entered on DYNRED then that number must be less than or equal to the number of generalized degrees of freedom included in the q-set. If

374

the analyst chooses to let the generalized dynamic reduction procedure calculate the number of generalized degrees of freedom by leaving the QDOF field on DYNRED blank then the user must pre-allocate sufficient degrees of freedom in the q-set. In either case if the number of degrees of freedom in the q-set is less than the number required a fatal error message will be written to that effect and the execution of the program will be terminated.

Let us suppose that we have correctly defined the DYNRED Bulk Data, that we have defined "sufficient" degrees of freedom on SPOINT, and have included them in both the a-set and the g-set by using ASET and QSET Bulk Data. Let us also suppose that we have defined FMAX and left QDOF blank on DYNRED and that the number of transformation vectors to be calculated, which we will define to be N_x, is less than the number of generalized degrees of freedom allocated to the g-set, N_q. Since we have no way of guaranteeing that we were clairvoyant in our choice of N_q we suspect that N_q is greater than N_x so that the difference, N_w which represents the number of degrees of freedom in the q-set that will not be used by the generalized dynamic reduction procedure will be greater than zero. This implies that there will be N_w null columns in the transformation matrix G_{og} (13.72) and that the resulting reduced stiffness and mass matrices will be singular. A user-friendly option is thus built into rigid format 3 that is controlled by the ASING PARAMeter that will remove any unconnected degrees of freedom in the g-set (see Sec. 13.7).

13.6.2.4. Control of the Procedure

The remaining entries on the DYNRED Bulk Data card control the algorithm for extraction of the q-set vectors. These parameters

- Control the number of iterations (NIT)
- Define the number of random starting vectors (NIRV)
- Select starting point for random vector generation (IDIR)

All of these parameters have assigned default values. The specification of values for these parameters requires a detailed knowledge of the inverse power procedure that is beyond the scope of the Primer. The interested user should consult ref. 13-10 for a complete description of the inverse power procedure which is used for generalized dynamic reduction.

The NIT, NIRV, and IDIR fields of the DYNRED Bulk Data card are as follows

NIT An integer parameter which specifies the number of iterations where $0 < NIT < 100$. The default is set to a value of 10.

NIRV An integer parameter which specifies the number of initial random vectors, N_r, to be used. The default results in at least 6 random vectors which is sufficient if multiple or closely spaced roots occur in groups of two or three. However, $N_r = 6$ is insufficient if six or more rigid body modes exist in the analysis set. The user should use a SUPORT Bulk Data card in this case to define the rigid body modes.

The user is provided the option of controlling the number of random vectors by explicit specification NIRV through the following algorithm

if, $QDOF \geq NIRV \geq \left\{ \dfrac{QDOF}{NIT} \right\}$, then $N_r = NIRV$

if, $NIRV > QDOF$, then $N_r = NCDES$

if, $NIRV < \left\{ \dfrac{QDOF}{NIT} \right\}$, then $\left\{ \dfrac{QDOF}{NIT} \right\} \leq N_r < \left\{ \dfrac{QDOF}{NIT} \right\} + 1$

where the terms in the braces are rounded to the next highest integer value

IDIR   An integer value used to select a starting point for generation of random starting vectors. The elements of the N_r initial vectors are repeatable quasi-random numbers which have a uniform distribution over the range $-1.$ to $+1.$ Ten different configurations are available with $0 \leq IDIR \leq 9$.

13.7.   Removing Matrix Singularities

All of the eigenvalue extraction techniques perform a decomposition of the stiffness or mass matrix or a linear combination of the two. The matrices which are decomposed by the various methods are as follows:

- INV $\mathbf{K} - \lambda_o \mathbf{M}$

- GIV $\mathbf{M}$

- MGIV $\mathbf{K} + \lambda_0 \mathbf{M}$

Any degree of freedom which is unconnected in both matrices is undefined, and its presence in the analysis set will lead to a singular matrix which, by definition, has no inverse. A singularity check is made in the matrix decomposition modules in MSC/NASTRAN so that a fatal error will be issued and program execution will be terminated.

The unconnected degrees of freedom in the stiffness matrix can be purged either explicitly by single point constraints or implicitly by means of the AUTOSPC PARAMeter (See Sec. 12.4.3. and Appendix B). A singular mass matrix is the analyst's real concern then, especially in the GIV method.

The mass matrix associated with the a-set can be made nonsingular by using static condensation (see Sec. 13.8) to remove all massless degrees of freedom from the analysis set. This procedure leads to a positive definite mass matrix which is required for GIV method and while a positive definite mass matrix is not required by the MGIV method the algorithm is generally faster if massless degrees of freedom are 'OMIT'ed. However, the use of static condensation leads to matrices with greater density and increased active columns so that the INV generally runs slower if static condensation is performed on massless degrees of freedom.

MSC/NASTRAN provides a user option which can be used to detect singularities in the stiffness and mass matrices and to then perform matrix operations which are appropriate for the eigensolution method to remove the singularity. This action is controlled by the integer PARAMeter ASING which provides three options for dealing with the singularity. The parameter values and the associated actions are described below.

13.7.1.   Detect Singularities and Exit — ASING $= -1$

If the PARAMeter is set to -1 then all degrees of freedom with null columns in both the stiffness and mass matrix are identified and a fatal error exit is taken. This is the proper option to use to assure that no modeling errors exist prior to performing an expensive eigensolution.

13.7.2.   Remove Massless Degrees of Freedom Using Static Condensation — ASING $= 0$ (DEFAULT)

If the PARAMeter is set to zero (0) then all degrees of freedom with null columns are identified and placed in the w-set where

$$\mathbf{u}_a = \left\{ \begin{array}{c} \mathbf{u}_x \\ \mathbf{u}_w \end{array} \right\} \tag{13.79}$$

the mass and stiffness matrices are then partitioned so that

$$\left(-\omega^2 \begin{bmatrix} \mathbf{M}_{xx} & \mathbf{M}_{xw} \\ \mathbf{M}_{wx} & \mathbf{M}_{ww} \end{bmatrix} + \begin{bmatrix} \widetilde{\mathbf{K}}_{xx} & \mathbf{K}_{xw} \\ \mathbf{K}_{wx} & \mathbf{K}_{ww} \end{bmatrix} \right) \begin{Bmatrix} \mathbf{u}_x \\ \mathbf{u}_w \end{Bmatrix} = \begin{Bmatrix} 0 \\ 0 \end{Bmatrix} \tag{13.80}$$

where $\mathbf{M}_{xw}$, $\mathbf{M}_{wx}$, and $\mathbf{M}_{ww}$ are null by definition. All zero diagonal terms in $\mathbf{K}_{ww}$ are replaced with unit diagonal terms so that we have from the second of (13.80)

$$\mathbf{K}_{wx}\mathbf{u}_x + \mathbf{K}_{ww}\mathbf{u}_w = 0 \tag{13.81}$$

The inverse of $\mathbf{K}_{ww}$ now exists because former null columns have been replaced with unit diagonals so that we can solve for $\mathbf{u}_w$ by using (13.81) to obtain

$$\mathbf{u}_w = G_{wx}\mathbf{u}_x \tag{13.82}$$

where

$$G_{wx} = -\mathbf{K}_{ww}^{-1}\mathbf{K}_{wx} \tag{13.83}$$

The reduced set of equations for the x-set (i.e. the solution set for eigensolution) is then found to be

$$(-\omega^2\mathbf{M}_{xx} + \mathbf{K}_{xx})\mathbf{u}_x = 0 \tag{13.84}$$

where

$$\mathbf{K}_{xx} = \widetilde{\mathbf{K}}_{xx} + \mathbf{K}_{wx}^T G_{wx} \tag{13.85}$$

This formulation, which is associated with ASING = 0, is appropriate for the GIV and MGIV methods. It will prevent fatal errors which are due to a singular mass matrix in the GIV method if the singularity is caused by null columns in $\mathbf{M}_{ww}$. Mechanisms cannot be detected, however, so that this type of singularity does not necessarily prevent eigensolutions but can cause poor numerical stability.

The MGIV method does not suffer from numerical stability due to singular or nearly singular mass matrices so that it is more reliable than the GIV method. The removal of the massless degrees of freedom by static reduction will reduce solution costs and will also eliminate the calculation of the eigenvalues for high frequency "noise".

The static reduction of massless degrees of freedom does not introduce any of the approximations which are associated with the Guyan Reduction (Sec. 13.6.). The expediency of replacing the null columns of the stiffness matrix by unit diagonals is proper because the associated columns of G_{wx} are null. The same result could be achieved by first purging the unconnected degrees of freedom of $\mathbf{K}_{gg}$ followed by an OMIT of massless degrees of freedom, but at a higher cost.

If the INV method is specified then there is no mass reduction. However, all degrees of freedom having null columns in both mass and stiffness matrices are removed before performing the eigensolution.

13.8.   NASTRAN Data Deck for Normal Modes Analysis

13.8.1.   Executive Control Deck

The executive control deck must specify that the normal modes and frequency analysis, rigid format number 3, is to be executed by means of the following Executive Control Directive.

SOL   3

All other required cards described in Chapter One must be present so that the minimum Executive Control Deck for normal modes analysis includes the following

ID   A1, A2

TIME   <minutes>

SOL   3

CEND

13.8.2.   Case Control Deck

The following items relate to the selection of Bulk Data and subcase definitions for normal modes.

1. A METHOD = SID Case Control Directive must be included to select an EIGR Bulk Data card that defines an eigenvalue extraction technique in Bulk Data.

2. An SPC set must be selected unless the model is a free body or if the constraints are specified as permanent constraints on a GRID card or by means of general elements.

3. Multiple subcases may be used only for output requests. A single subcase is sufficient if the same output requests are appropriate for all modes. The use of multiple subcases is discussed in Chapter One.

All of the output Case Control Directives which are associated with static analysis can be specified for Normal Modes analysis.

13.8.3.   Parameters

The following optional parameters may be used in normal modes analysis. (See Appendix B of the Primer for the form of the PARAM Bulk Data card and additional discussion of use of parameters)

1. AUTOSPC   Purges unconnected degrees of freedom.
2. COUPMASS   Causes the generation of consistent rather than lumped mass.

Other parameters of interest are described in Appendix B.

13.8.4.   NASTRAN Input and Output for Normal Modes Analysis

The input data deck for a normal modes analysis is similar to that for static analysis except that the rigid format is changed from 24 to 3 in the Executive Control deck. In Case Control, the LOAD card is replaced by a METHOD card which references a real eigenvalue extraction technique. The eigenvalue algorithm is then specified in Bulk Data by means of an EIGR card.

The program input and output associated with an example problem is discussed in 13.9.

13.9.   Example Problems

We will consider several example problems whose purpose is to show how to employ the new capability which we have described in this chapter. We will thus use relatively simple structural topologies to solve several eigenvalue problems including

1. An unsupported vibrating beam using

   a) Modified Givens

   b) Guyan reduction followed by Modified Givens

   c) Generalized dynamic reduction followed by Givens

2. A simply supported rectangular plate using

   a) Givens methods with no reduction

   b) Guyan reduction followed by Givens method

   c) Generalized dynamic reduction followed by Givens method

   d) Inverse power with shifts

3. A simply supported eccentrically-stiffened plate using the checkpointed results from Sec. 12.8.2b. and modified Givens method.

These problems will use several of the elements and modeling features in addition to those described in Chapter 12 including:

- Use of GIV, MGIV, and INV methods for eigenvalue extraction

- Use of ASET to define Guyan Reduction

- Use of SPOINT, ASET, QSET, and DYNRED to define generalized dynamic reduction

- Use of Restart from static solution

- Data recovery including

    - Summary of INV statistics (DIAG 16)

    - Eigenvalues and Eigenvectors

13.9.1. Free-Free-Beam

The structural element for this example is shown by Fig. 13-2.

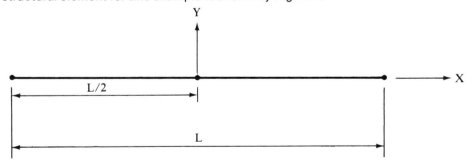

Figure 13-2. Free-Free Beam

where we assume that the beam has the same properties as those defined in Sec. 12.8.1.

In defining the finite element model we recognize that the mesh refinement is dictated by the number of mode shapes that we wish to be adequately represented. We will therefore suppose that we want to be capable of representing the fourth symmetric mode, and that approximately 10 equally spaced increments are required to represent a mode, which we recognize to be sine functions for this problem. The number of grid points is thus 41 for the entire beam. We also note that the vibration modes are symmetric about $X = 0$ so that we will model the right half of the beam using 21 node points.

There are two sets of boundary conditions to be imposed at $X = 0$, those associated with symmetry ($\theta_y = \theta_z = 0$); and, antisymmetry ($u_y = u_z = 0$). We would thus need to perform two analyses; one for symmetric boundary conditions and one for antisymmetric boundary conditions to find all the vibration modes for this problem. However, we will concern ourselves with only symmetric modes for this example.

The eigenvalue problem for the free-free beam model will be solved by using modified Givens method for three cases of solution-set degrees of freedom: no reduction, Guyan Reduction, and Generalized Dynamic Reduction. The input and output for each of these cases is described in the following section.

13.9.1a.   No Reduction

The MSC/NASTRAN data deck for the case where the MGIV method is used with no reduction is as follows

Card	1	2	3	4	5	6	7	8	9	10
1-	ID PRIMER, PROB131A									
2-	SOL 3									
3-	TIME 4									
4-	CEND									
5-	TITLE = NORMAL MODES SOLUTION FOR FREE FREE BEAM									
6-	SUBTITLE = NO REDUCTION									
7-	LABEL = SYMMETRIC MODES									
8-	SPC = 1									
9-	METHOD = 13									
10-	ECHO = BOTH									
11-	SUBCASE 1									
12-	VECTOR = NONE									
13-	MODES = 2									
14-	SUBCASE 3									
15-	SVECTOR = ALL									
16-	BEGIN BULK									
17-	GRID	1	0	0.	0.					
18-	=	*(1)	=	*(.25)	==					
19-	= (19)									
20-	CBAR	1	1	1	2	0.	1.	0.		
21-	=	*(1)	=	*(1)	*(1)	==				
22-	= (18)									
23-	SPC	100	1	56	0.					
24-	SPC	200	1	23	0.					
25-	SPC1	1000	14	1	THRU	21				
26-	SPCADD	1	100	1000						
27-	SPCADD	2	200	1000						
28-	PBAR	1	30		6.5104-4	2.604-3		.035375		
29-	PARAM	WTMASS	.002591							
30-	MAT1	30	3. + 7		.3					
31-	EIGR	13	MGIV				3			+ E1
32-	+ E1	MASS								
33-	ENDDATA									

380

The NASTRAN input data items which are unique for this problem are identified by card number and are as follows

Card 2- SOL Executive Control directive selects Rigid Format 3.

Card 9- The METHOD Case Control Directive selects EIGR Bulk Data with SID = 13

Card 10- Requests that both the sorted and unsorted data be printed

Card 11- Since the first two eigenvectors are rigid body modes we have defined a SUBCASE
Card 13- structure which will suppress their output. Card 11 explicitly defines SUBCASE 1 for which VECTOR = NONE requests no displacement output. The MODES command defines an iteration count for the number of times the SUBCASE structure is to be used. MODES increments the SUBCASE number so that this defines SUBCASES 1 and 2.

Card 14- Defines the subcase for which we desire output

Card 15- Requests the displacements for the solution (i.e., a-) set.

Card 17- Generate 21 equally spaced grid points
Card 19-

Card 20- Generate 20 BAR Elements
Card 22-

Card 23- SPC set 100 defines symmetry conditions at middle (i.e., origin) of the beam.

Card 24- SPC set 200 defines antisymmetry conditions at middle (not used in this analysis).

Card 25- Purges unconnected degrees of freedom at all GRID points

Card 26- Union of purged degrees of freedom and symmetry conditions which is selected by the SPC = 1 Case Control Directive

Card 27- Union of purged degrees of freedom and antisymmetry conditions

Card 28- Defines principal moments of inertia and weight per unit length. (NSM is used because structural weight requires cross sectional area which is not defined)

Card 29- Defines WTMASS parameter to be $1/g$ where $g = 386$ in./sec^2 (WTMASS = .002591)

Card 31- EIGR selects MGIV eigenvalue method and specifies that 3 eigenvectors are to be
Card 32- calculated and are to normalized such that the modal mass is equal to one. The first two eigenvalues are rigid body modes (i.e., the frequency is zero) so that Case Control directives are used to print the first elastic mode which is, in this case, the third eigenvector.

13.9.1a.1. Selected Output

The output data for this example problem is shown below where we note

1. The INPUT DATA DECK ECHO, which was requested by ECHO = BOTH in Case Control prints the input Bulk Data deck exactly as it is read by MSC/NASTRAN. In this case we have used free-field input together with generation and repeat features

2. Sequence Processor Output. The node number resequencer is automatically called in rigid format number 3. The sequence processor summarizes the number of points and elements and estimates the assembly time. The fields are

13.9.1a.1 Selected Output

SUPER(GROUP)ID	— Superelement number
NO. GRIDS	— Number of GRID points
AV. CONNECTIVITY	— The average number of degrees of freedom which are connected
C-AVERAGE	— The average number of active columns
C-RMS	— Root mean square wavefront
C-MAXIMUM	— Maximum number of active columns
DECOMP TIME	— Estimated decomposition

3. VAXW — A partitioning vector which is used to remove the massless degrees of freedom from the solution set by means of static condensation. This is the default action of the control PARAMeter ASING

4. REAL EIGENVALUES. The table of eigenvalues is automatically printed for normal modes. The eigenvalues are sorted in increasing value in the 3rd column and are converted to radians/second and cycles/second in columns 4 and 5. The generalized mass is only determinable for calculated eigenvectors (three in this case) and is equal to 1. because we requested MASS normalization. The generalized stiffness for this case is seen to be equal to the eigenvalue for modes for which modes were calculated.

5. REAL EIGENVECTOR — The displacements in the a-set for the first elastic mode (i.e., the third mode) is printed as a result of SVECTOR = ALL

```
N A S T R A N   E X E C U T I V E   C O N T R O L   D E C K   E C H O


ID PRIMER,PROB131A
SOL 3    $SELECT NORMAL MODES RIGID FORMAT
TIME 4   $SET SOLUTION TIME TO FOUR MINUTES
CEND
                              C A S E   C O N T R O L   D E C K   E C H O
         CARD
         COUNT
           1      TITLE = NORMAL MODES SOLUTION FOR FREE FREE BEAM
           2      SUBTITLE = NO REDUCTION
           3      LABEL = SYMMETRIC MODES
           4      SPC = 1
           5      METHOD = 13
           6      ECHO = BOTH
           7      SUBCASE 1
           8      VECTOR = NONE
           9      MODES = 2
          10      SUBCASE 3
          11      SVECTOR = ALL
          12      BEGIN BULK

                         I N P U T   B U L K   D A T A   D E C K   E C H O

          .   1  ..   2  ..   3  ..   4  ..   5  ..   6  ..   7  ..   8  ..   9  ..  10  .
          GRID,1,0,0.,,0.,,0.
          =,*(1),=,*(.25),==
          =(19)
          CBAR,1,1,1,2,0.,,1.,,0.
          =,*(1),=,*(1),*(1),==
          =(18)
          SPC,100,1,56,0.
          SPC,200,1,23,0.
          SPC1,1000,14,1,THRU,21
          SPCADD,1,100,1000
          SPCADD,2,200,1000
          PBAR,1,30,,6.5104-4,2.604-3,,,3.5375-2
          PARAM,WTMASS,,.002591
          MAT1,30,3.+7,,,.3
          EIGR,13,MGIV,,,,3,,,+E1
          +E1,MASS
          ENDDATA
          INPUT BULK DATA CARD COUNT =      17
```

```
                          S O R T E D   B U L K   D A T A   E C H O
        CARD
        COUNT        .  1  ..  2  ..  3  ..  4  ..  5  ..  6  ..  7  ..  8  ..  9  .. 10  .
         1-     CBAR    1      1      1      2      0.     1.     0.
         2-     CBAR    2      1      2      3      0.     1.     0.
         3-     CBAR    3      1      3      4      0.     1.     0.
         4-     CBAR    4      1      4      5      0.     1.     0.
         5-     CBAR    5      1      5      6      0.     1.     0.
         6-     CBAR    6      1      6      7      0.     1.     0.
         7-     CBAR    7      1      7      8      0.     1.     0.
         8-     CBAR    8      1      8      9      0.     1.     0.
         9-     CBAR    9      1      9     10      0.     1.     0.
        10-     CBAR   10      1     10     11      0.     1.     0.
        11-     CBAR   11      1     11     12      0.     1.     0.
        12-     CBAR   12      1     12     13      0.     1.     0.
        13-     CBAR   13      1     13     14      0.     1.     0.
        14-     CBAR   14      1     14     15      0.     1.     0.
        15-     CBAR   15      1     15     16      0.     1.     0.
        16-     CBAR   16      1     16     17      0.     1.     0.
        17-     CBAR   17      1     17     18      0.     1.     0.
        18-     CBAR   18      1     18     19      0.     1.     0.
        19-     CBAR   19      1     19     20      0.     1.     0.
        20-     CBAR   20      1     20     21      0.     1.     0.
        21-     EIGR   13     MGIV                         3                    +E1
        22-     +E1    MASS
        23-     GRID    1      0     0.      0.     0.
        24-     GRID    2      0     .25     0.     0.
        25-     GRID    3      0     .5      0.     0.
        26-     GRID    4      0     .75     0.     0.
        27-     GRID    5      0     1.0     0.     0.
        28-     GRID    6      0     1.25    0.     0.
        29-     GRID    7      0     1.5     0.     0.
        30-     GRID    8      0     1.75    0.     0.
        31-     GRID    9      0     2.      0.     0.
        32-     GRID   10      0     2.25    0.     0.
        33-     GRID   11      0     2.5     0.     0.
        34-     GRID   12      0     2.75    0.     0.
        35-     GRID   13      0     3.      0.     0.
        36-     GRID   14      0     3.25    0.     0.
        37-     GRID   15      0     3.5     0.     0.
        38-     GRID   16      0     3.75    0.     0.
        39-     GRID   17      0     4.      0.     0.
        40-     GRID   18      0     4.25    0.     0.
        41-     GRID   19      0     4.5     0.     0.
        42-     GRID   20      0     4.75    0.     0.
        43-     GRID   21      0     5.      0.     0.
        44-     MAT1   30     3.+7            .3
        45-     PARAM  WTMASS  .002591
        46-     PBAR    1     30            6.5104-42.604-3      3.5375-2
        47-     SPC    100     1     56      0.
        48-     SPC    200     1     23      0.
        49-     SPC1  1000    14      1     THRU    21
        50-     SPCADD   1    100   1000
        51-     SPCADD   2    200   1000
                ENDDATA
        TOTAL COUNT=    52
```

```
        SEQUENCE PROCESSOR OUTPUT

THERE ARE        21 POINTS DIVIDED INTO    1 GROUP(S).
                 CONNECTION DATA
ELEMENT TYPE       NUMBER    ASSEMBLY TIME(SEC)


  BAR             20         2.80
---------------------------------------------------------
TOTAL MATRIX ASSEMBLY TIME FOR      20 ELEMENTS IS     2.80 SECONDS.
ORIGINAL PERFORMANCE DATA
SUPER(GROUP) ID   NO. GRIDS  AV. CONNECTIVITY   C-AVERAGE   C-RMS   C-MAXIMUM  P-GROUPS  P-AVERAGE   DECOMP TIME(SECS)
                                                                                                     (6.0 DOF/GRID )
          0          21          2.90             1.95      1.96        2          0       0.00          0.105
RESEQUENCED PERFORMANCE DATA
SUPER(GROUP) ID   NO. GRIDS  AV. CONNECTIVITY   C-AVERAGE   C-RMS   C-MAXIMUM  P-GROUPS  P-AVERAGE   DECOMP TIME(SECS)
                                                                                                     (6.0 DOF/GRID )
          0          21          2.90             1.95      1.96        2          0       0.00          0.105
```

```
          VAXW
      POINT     VALUE      POINT     VALUE      POINT     VALUE      POINT     VALUE      POINT     VALUE

COLUMN    1
        2 R2  1.00000E+00     2 R3  1.00000E+00     3 R2  1.00000E+00     3 R3  1.00000E+00     4 R2  1.00000E+00
        4 R3  1.00000E+00     5 R2  1.00000E+00     5 R3  1.00000E+00     6 R2  1.00000E+00     6 R3  1.00000E+00
        7 R2  1.00000E+00     7 R3  1.00000E+00     8 R2  1.00000E+00     8 R3  1.00000E+00     9 R2  1.00000E+00
        9 R3  1.00000E+00    10 R2  1.00000E+00    10 R3  1.00000E+00    11 R2  1.00000E+00    11 R3  1.00000E+00
       12 R2  1.00000E+00    12 R3  1.00000E+00    13 R2  1.00000E+00    13 R3  1.00000E+00    14 R2  1.00000E+00
       14 R3  1.00000E+00    15 R2  1.00000E+00    15 R3  1.00000E+00    16 R2  1.00000E+00    16 R3  1.00000E+00
       17 R2  1.00000E+00    17 R3  1.00000E+00    18 R2  1.00000E+00    18 R3  1.00000E+00    19 R2  1.00000E+00
       19 R3  1.00000E+00    20 R2  1.00000E+00    20 R3  1.00000E+00    21 R2  1.00000E+00    21 R3  1.00000E+00
```

```
                               R E A L   E I G E N V A L U E S
    MODE    EXTRACTION     EIGENVALUE       RADIANS         CYCLES        GENERALIZED      GENERALIZED
    NO.       ORDER                                                          MASS          STIFFNESS
      1         22       2.300954E-01     4.796827E-01    7.634386E-02    1.000000E+00     2.300954E-01
      2          3       9.220734E-01     9.602465E-01    1.528280E-01    1.000000E+00     9.220734E-01
      3          4       1.062539E+07     3.259661E+03    5.187912E+02    1.000000E+00     1.062539E+07
```

383

4	23	4.249896E+07	6.519123E+03	1.037551E+03	0.0	0.0
5	1	3.086549E+08	1.756858E+04	2.796126E+03	0.0	0.0
6	24	1.234544E+09	3.513608E+04	5.592081E+03	0.0	0.0
7	2	1.872308E+09	4.327018E+04	6.886663E+03	0.0	0.0
8	5	6.439972E+09	8.024944E+04	1.277209E+04	0.0	0.0
9	25	7.488774E+09	8.653770E+04	1.377290E+04	0.0	0.0
10	6	1.648935E+10	1.284109E+05	2.043722E+04	0.0	0.0
11	26	2.575831E+10	1.604939E+05	2.554340E+04	0.0	0.0
12	7	3.521233E+10	1.876495E+05	2.986534E+04	0.0	0.0
13	27	6.595337E+10	2.568139E+05	4.087320E+04	0.0	0.0
14	8	6.648174E+10	2.578405E+05	4.103659E+04	0.0	0.0
15	9	1.148005E+11	3.388223E+05	5.392524E+04	0.0	0.0
16	28	1.408407E+11	3.752874E+05	5.972885E+04	0.0	0.0
17	10	1.852113E+11	4.303618E+05	6.849420E+04	0.0	0.0
18	29	2.659104E+11	5.156650E+05	8.207063E+04	0.0	0.0
19	11	2.831286E+11	5.320983E+05	8.468608E+04	0.0	0.0
20	12	4.141043E+11	6.435094E+05	1.024177E+05	0.0	0.0
21	30	4.591739E+11	6.776238E+05	1.078472E+05	0.0	0.0
22	13	5.863568E+11	7.657394E+05	1.218712E+05	0.0	0.0
23	31	7.408045E+11	8.607000E+05	1.369847E+05	0.0	0.0
24	14	8.344247E+11	9.134685E+05	1.453830E+05	0.0	0.0
25	32	1.133992E+12	1.064891E+06	1.694826E+05	0.0	0.0
26	17	1.245781E+12	1.116145E+06	1.776400E+05	0.0	0.0
27	18	1.252757E+12	1.119266E+06	1.781368E+05	0.0	0.0
28	19	1.566322E+12	1.251528E+06	1.991868E+05	0.0	0.0
29	33	1.673059E+12	1.293468E+06	2.058618E+05	0.0	0.0
30	16	1.883350E+12	1.372352E+06	2.184166E+05	0.0	0.0
31	20	1.918441E+12	1.385078E+06	2.204420E+05	0.0	0.0
32	21	2.305253E+12	1.518306E+06	2.416459E+05	0.0	0.0
33	15	2.511840E+12	1.584879E+06	2.522412E+05	0.0	0.0
34	35	3.020659E+12	1.738004E+06	2.766120E+05	0.0	0.0
35	37	3.081687E+12	1.755473E+06	2.793923E+05	0.0	0.0
36	38	4.455430E+12	2.110789E+06	3.359425E+05	0.0	0.0
37	39	4.689470E+12	2.165519E+06	3.446530E+05	0.0	0.0
38	36	5.538469E+12	2.353395E+06	3.745545E+05	0.0	0.0
39	42	7.002527E+12	2.646229E+06	4.211604E+05	0.0	0.0
40	40	7.911116E+12	2.812671E+06	4.476504E+05	0.0	0.0
41	41	8.601729E+12	2.932871E+06	4.667808E+05	0.0	0.0
42	34	9.527947E+12	3.086737E+06	4.912695E+05	0.0	0.0

SUBCASE 3

EIGENVALUE =   1.062539E+07
CYCLES =   5.187912E+02   R E A L   E I G E N V E C T O R   N O .   3

POINT ID.	TYPE	T1	T2	T3	R1	R2	R3
1	G		5.670846E+01	0.0			
2	G		5.619162E+01	0.0		0.0	-4.131061E+00
3	G		5.464659E+01	0.0		0.0	-8.218140E+00
4	G		5.208981E+01	0.0		0.0	-1.221806E+01
5	G		4.854829E+01	0.0		0.0	-1.608924E+01
6	G		4.405918E+01	0.0		0.0	-1.979248E+01
7	G		3.866905E+01	0.0		0.0	-2.329170E+01
8	G		3.243302E+01	0.0		0.0	-2.655468E+01
9	G		2.541371E+01	0.0		0.0	-2.955371E+01
10	G		1.768003E+01	0.0		0.0	-3.226627E+01
11	G		9.305845E+00	0.0		0.0	-3.467555E+01
12	G		3.684061E-01	0.0		0.0	-3.677106E+01
13	G		-9.053224E+00	0.0		0.0	-3.854902E+01
14	G		-1.887992E+01	0.0		0.0	-4.001282E+01
15	G		-2.903436E+01	0.0		0.0	-4.117334E+01
16	G		-3.944287E+01	0.0		0.0	-4.204924E+01
17	G		-5.003748E+01	0.0		0.0	-4.266719E+01
18	G		-6.075788E+01	0.0		0.0	-4.306207E+01
19	G		-7.155352E+01	0.0		0.0	-4.327702E+01
20	G		-8.238570E+01	0.0		0.0	-4.336359E+01
21	G		-9.322961E+01	0.0		0.0	-4.338175E+01

13.9.1b.   Guyan Reduction

It was shown in Sec. 13.6.1. that the number of degrees of freedom in the solution set could be reduced by using Guyan Reduction. The input data deck from the previous example is therefore modified by

- Replacing Card 10 – with

ECHO = SORT(EIGR, ASET1, PARAM)

which prints only Bulk Data with names in parentheses.

- Adding an ASET1 Bulk Data card which retains degrees of freedom at every other GRID starting at point number 1

13.9.1b.1.   Selected Output

The output data for this example problem is shown below where we note

1. The ECHO Case Control directive requests that only ASET1, EIGR, and PARAM Bulk Data items be printed.

384

2. The SORTED BULK DATA only contains a listing of the requested cards.

3. The first natural frequency of system including Guyan reduction is the same as that for the unreduced system.

```
N A S T R A N    E X E C U T I V E    C O N T R O L    D E C K    E C H O


ID PRIMER,PROB131B
SOL 3    $SELECT NORMAL MODES RIGID FORMAT
TIME 4   $SET SOLUTION TIME TO FOUR MINUTES
CEND
```

```
                           C A S E    C O N T R O L    D E C K    E C H O
        CARD
        COUNT
          1       TITLE = NORMAL MODES SOLUTION FOR FREE FREE BEAM
          2       SUBTITLE = USING GUYAN REDUCTION
          3       LABEL = SYMMETRIC MODES
          4       METHOD = 13
          5       SPC = 1
          6       ECHO = SORT(EIGR,ASET1,PARAM)
          7       SUBCASE 1
          8       VECTOR = NONE
          9       MODES = 2
         10       SUBCASE 3
         11       SVECTOR = ALL
         12       BEGIN BULK
                     INPUT BULK DATA CARD COUNT =        20
```

```
                            S O R T E D    B U L K    D A T A    E C H O
        CARD
        COUNT      .   1  ..   2  ..   3  ..   4  ..   5  ..   6  ..   7  ..   8  ..   9  .. 10  .
          1-      ASET1   23      1       3       5       7       9      11      13      +A1
          2-      +A1     15      17      19      21
         23-      EIGR    13      MGIV                            3                       +E1
         24-      +E1     MASS
         47-      PARAM   NEWSEQ  -1
         48-      PARAM   WTMASS  .002591
                  ENDDATA
        TOTAL COUNT =     55
```

```
                                R E A L    E I G E N V A L U E S
MODE    EXTRACTION      EIGENVALUE          RADIANS           CYCLES         GENERALIZED      GENERALIZED
NO.      ORDER                                                                  MASS          STIFFNESS
  1         1        -2.175570E-06       1.474981E-03      2.347505E-04    1.000000E+00     -2.175570E-06
  2        12         7.912517E-06       2.812920E-03      4.476901E-04    1.000000E+00      7.912517E-06
  3         2         1.062545E+07       3.259670E+03      5.187927E+02    1.000000E+00      1.062545E+07
  4        13         4.249919E+07       6.519141E+03      1.037553E+03    0.0               0.0
  5         3         3.087030E+08       1.756995E+04      2.796344E+03    0.0               0.0
  6        14         1.234736E+09       3.513881E+04      5.592516E+03    0.0               0.0
  7         4         1.874150E+09       4.329146E+04      6.890049E+03    0.0               0.0
  8         5         6.463540E+09       8.039615E+04      1.279544E+04    0.0               0.0
  9        15         7.496141E+09       8.658026E+04      1.377968E+04    0.0               0.0
 10         6         1.666242E+10       1.290830E+05      2.054420E+04    0.0               0.0
 11        16         2.585257E+10       1.607873E+05      2.559010E+04    0.0               0.0
 12         7         3.612005E+10       1.900528E+05      3.024783E+04    0.0               0.0
 13        17         6.664558E+10       2.581581E+05      4.108713E+04    0.0               0.0
 14         8         7.023300E+10       2.650151E+05      4.217846E+04    0.0               0.0
 15         9         1.272917E+11       3.567797E+05      5.678325E+04    0.0               0.0
 16        18         1.445061E+11       3.801396E+05      6.050109E+04    0.0               0.0
 17        11         2.155653E+11       4.642901E+05      7.389405E+04    0.0               0.0
 18        19         2.811565E+11       5.302419E+05      8.439061E+04    0.0               0.0
 19        10         3.100105E+11       5.567859E+05      8.861522E+04    0.0               0.0
 20        22         5.524961E+11       7.433008E+05      1.183000E+05    0.0               0.0
 21        21         7.953829E+11       8.918424E+05      1.419411E+05    0.0               0.0
 22        20         1.152469E+12       1.073531E+06      1.708578E+05    0.0               0.0
```

```
SYMMETRIC MODES                                                                          SUBCASE 3
EIGENVALUE =   1.062545E+07
     CYCLES =   5.187927E+02      R E A L    E I G E N V E C T O R    N O.          3

POINT ID.   TYPE      T1            T2            T3           R1           R2           R3
        1     G                -5.670873E+01   0.0
        3     G                -5.464686E+01   0.0
        5     G                -4.854852E+01   0.0
        7     G                -3.866923E+01   0.0
        9     G                -2.541381E+01   0.0
       11     G                -9.305863E+00   0.0
       13     G                 9.053304E+00   0.0
       15     G                 2.903455E+01   0.0
       17     G                 5.003778E+01   0.0
       19     G                 7.155393E+01   0.0
       21     G                 9.323014E+01   0.0
```

13.9.1c.   Generalized Dynamic Reduction

Another technique which we discussed in Sec. 13.6.2. for reducing the number of degrees of freedom in the solution set was called Generalized Dynamic Reduction. The input data deck for the problem described in Sec. 13.9.1a. is therefore modified by

- Replacing card 10 – with

  ECHO = SORT (EIGR, SPOINT, ASET1, QSET1, DYNRED, PARAM)

  which prints out the EIGR card as well as the changes and modifications

- Defining six generalized coordinates using SPOINT

- Including the six generalized coordinates in the a-set by means of ASET1

- Including the six generalized coordinates in the q- set by means of QSET1

- Defining Generalized Dynamic Reduction by means of the DYNRED Bulk Data where the QDOF field (field number 7) is explicitly set equal to six. (If this field were left blank — and it could be for this example — then MSC/NASTRAN would automatically determine the number of q-set degrees of freedom required to represent the eigenmodes for frequencies at and below 500 hz (i.e., FMAX in field 3)

- Selecting the DYNRED Bulk Data by means of a Case Control Directive

  DYNRED = 21

13.9.1c.1.   Selected Output

The output data for this example problem is shown below where we note

1. The Sorted Bulk Data contains a listing of only those Bulk Data card types that were selected by the ECHO Case Control Directive.

2. The GRID POINT SINGULARITY TABLE tells us that, at the time MSC/NASTRAN checks for singularities, the generalized coordinates which were defined by SPOINT Bulk Data are singular. Since these degrees of freedom are explicitly included in the solution set by the ASET1 and QSET1 Bulk Data they are not removed from the analysis set.

3. User Message 4158 tells us that the maximum conditioning number is associated with degree of freedom number 80 in the v-set. In order to identify the associated external degree of freedom we would have to print the set membership table for the v-set, which in this case would be equivalent to the f-set.

4. REAL EIGENVALUES. Only six real eigenvalues, those associated with the six generalized coordinates in the q-set, exist in this analysis. We again note, as in Sec. 13.9.1a.1., that the first two eigenvalues are essentially zero since these represent the rigid body modes.

5. REAL EIGENVECTOR. The displacement components of the real eigenvector includes all degrees of freedom in the g-set. Only the values of the G-type (i.e., GRID) degrees of freedom have physical significance. The values of the generalized coordinates which are defined six per line starting with point 101, indicate the amount of each generalized vector participates is the 3rd real eigenvector. Here we see that the response is almost totally due to the 3rd generalized vector since the associated generalized coordinate (SPOINT number 103) is equal to 1.0 while all other coordinates are orders of magnitude smaller.

N A S T R A N   E X E C U T I V E   C O N T R O L   D E C K   E C H O

```
ID PRIMER,PROB131C
SOL 3   $SELECT NORMAL MODES RIGID FORMAT
TIME 4  $SET SOLUTION TIME TO FOUR MINUTES
CEND
```

C A S E   C O N T R O L   D E C K   E C H O

```
CARD
COUNT
  1     TITLE = NORMAL MODES SOLUTION FOR FREE FREE BEAM
  2     SUBTITLE = USING GENERALIZED DYNAMIC REDUCTION
  3     LABEL = SYMMETRIC MODES
  4     METHOD = 13
  5     DYNRED = 21
  6     ECHO = SORT(EIGR,SPOINT,ASET1,QSET1,DYNRED,PARAM)
  7     SPC =1
  8     SUBCASE 1
  9     VECTOR = NONE
 10     MODES = 2
 11     SUBCASE 3
 12     VECTOR = ALL
 13     BEGIN BULK
           INPUT BULK DATA CARD COUNT =      22
```

S O R T E D   B U L K   D A T A   E C H O

```
CARD
COUNT     . 1 .. 2 .. 3 .. 4 .. 5 .. 6 .. 7 .. 8 .. 9 .. 10 .
  1-      ASET1   0       101     THRU    106
 22-      DYNRED  21      500.                    6
 23-      EIGR    13      GIV                      3                    +E1
 24-      +E1     MASS
 47-      PARAM   NEWSEQ  -1
 48-      PARAM   WTMASS  .002591
 50-      QSET1   0       101     THRU    106
 56-      SPOINT  101     THRU    106
          ENDDATA
     TOTAL COUNT=    57
```

G R I D   P O I N T   S I N G U L A R I T Y   T A B L E

POINT ID	TYPE	FAILED DIRECTION	STIFFNESS RATIO	OLD USET	NEW USET
101	S	0	0.00E+00	L	L
102	S	0	0.00E+00	L	L
103	S	0	0.00E+00	L	L
104	S	0	0.00E+00	L	L
105	S	0	0.00E+00	L	L
106	S	0	0.00E+00	L	L

*** USER INFORMATION MESSAGE 4158---STATISTICS FOR SYMMETRIC DECOMPOSITION OF DATA BLOCK AVV   FOLLOW
MAXIMUM RATIO OF MATRIX DIAGONAL TO FACTOR DIAGONAL = 7.3E+04 AT ROW NUMBER   80

R E A L   E I G E N V A L U E S

MODE NO.	EXTRACTION ORDER	EIGENVALUE	RADIANS	CYCLES	GENERALIZED MASS	GENERALIZED STIFFNESS
1	6	-2.094093E-06	1.447098E-03	2.303128E-04	1.000000E+00	-2.094093E-06
2	5	2.081584E-05	4.562438E-03	7.261345E-04	1.000000E+00	2.081584E-05
3	3	1.062539E+07	3.259662E+03	5.187913E+02	1.000000E+00	1.062539E+07
4	4	4.249896E+07	6.519123E+03	1.037551E+03	0.0	0.0
5	2	4.892393E+08	2.211875E+04	3.520309E+03	0.0	0.0
6	1	1.313765E+12	1.146196E+06	1.824227E+05	0.0	0.0

SUBCASE 3

```
EIGENVALUE =  1.062539E+07
    CYCLES =  5.187913E+02    R E A L   E I G E N V E C T O R   N O .      3
```

POINT ID.	TYPE	T1	T2	T3	R1	R2	R3
1	G	0.0	5.670846E+01	5.891671E-08	0.0	0.0	0.0
2	G	0.0	5.619162E+01	3.567195E-08	0.0	1.247500E-09	-4.131061E+00
3	G	0.0	5.464660E+01	2.396184E-08	0.0	2.480908E-09	-8.218141E+00
4	G	0.0	5.208981E+01	-2.126271E-08	0.0	3.685087E-09	-1.221806E+01
5	G	0.0	4.854829E+01	-2.203352E-08	0.0	4.840324E-09	-1.608924E+01
6	G	0.0	4.405918E+01	-2.868014E-08	0.0	5.938868E-09	-1.979248E+01
7	G	0.0	3.866905E+01	-2.453539E-08	0.0	6.971068E-09	-2.329171E+01
8	G	0.0	3.243302E+01	-2.023460E-08	0.0	7.921823E-09	-2.655468E+01
9	G	0.0	2.541371E+01	3.569470E-09	0.0	8.784959E-09	-2.955371E+01
10	G	0.0	1.768003E+01	-9.880772E-09	0.0	9.563170E-09	-3.226627E+01
11	G	0.0	9.305843E+00	7.478823E-11	0.0	1.022553E-08	-3.467555E+01
12	G	0.0	3.684042E-01	8.995775E-09	0.0	1.079607E-08	-3.677106E+01
13	G	0.0	-9.053225E+00	7.531217E-09	0.0	1.121709E-08	-3.854902E+01
14	G	0.0	-1.887993E+01	2.612051E-08	0.0	1.160888E-08	-4.001282E+01
15	G	0.0	-2.903436E+01	-5.442351E-09	0.0	1.184914E-08	-4.117334E+01
16	G	0.0	-3.944288E+01	4.976447E-10	0.0	1.200745E-08	-4.204923E+01
17	G	0.0	-5.003748E+01	-9.353829E-10	0.0	1.214042E-08	-4.266719E+01

18	G	0.0	-6.075788E+01	-6.710909E-09	0.0	1.218297E-08	-4.306207E+01
19	G	0.0	-7.155352E+01	1.483947E-08	0.0	1.219572E-08	-4.327702E+01
20	G	0.0	-8.238569E+01	-1.256414E-08	0.0	1.220019E-08	-4.336359E+01
21	G	0.0	-9.322961E+01	3.127655E-09	0.0	1.219144E-08	-4.338174E+01
101	S	-1.015144E-10	2.634664E-09	1.000000E+00	-8.558625E-06	-8.617482E-08	2.870511E-08

13.9.2. Simply Supported Plate

The beam example in the previous section allowed us to apply the eigenvalue extraction tools in MSC/NASTRAN to a fairly simple problem. We will now consider the simply-supported rectangular plate shown by Fig. 13-3 which will allow us to develop a fairly large analysis to evaluate the cost of the various options for extracting eigenvalues and eigenvectors.

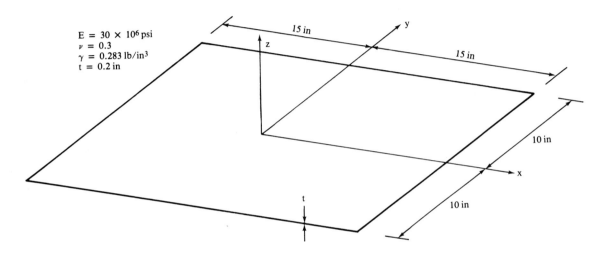

$E = 30 \times 10^6$ psi
$\nu = 0.3$
$\gamma = 0.283$ lb/in³
$t = 0.2$ in

Figure 13-3. Simply Supported Rectangular Plate.

The plate shown by Fig. 13-3 will be modelled using a uniform 20 by 20 mesh over a quarter panel which is connected by the QUAD4 element with only bending behavior. The symmetric modes will be determined by defining the following symmetry boundary conditions

- Along x = 0

  $$\theta_x = \theta_z = 0$$

- Along y = 0

  $$\theta_y = \theta_z = 0$$

We will extract four eigenvectors for this physical problem for each of four different solution techniques which will provide us with some basis for judging their relative cost and accuracy for a non-trivial problem. These solution techniques are

1. Use Givens method for the entire set of physical degrees of freedom with no reduction

2. Use Inverse power with shifts for the entire set of physical degrees of freedom with no reduction

3. Use Guyan Reduction to retain the physical degrees of freedom at every fourth grid point followed by Givens method

4. Use Generalized Dynamic Reduction to transform the eigenvalue problem to sixteen (16) generalized degrees of freedom

13.9.2a.   Givens Method With No Reduction

The quarter section will be modeled by

- Using MSGMESH to generate a field of points with 20 equal subdivisions in both the x and y-directions

- Using MSGMESH to connect the points in the field by QUAD4 elements

- Defining bending behavior by including an entry for only the material set to be used for bending on PSHELL Bulk Data

- Defining the mass properties using the NSM field on the PSHELL because structural mass is calculated for inplane displacements for the QUAD4 and these displacements do not exist in this formulation.

- Using MSGMESH to generate all symmetry and constraint boundary conditions

- Using Givens method and requesting that four eigenvectors be calculated

The associated MSC/NASTRAN input data deck is then as follows

Card	1	2	3	4	5	6	7	8	9	10
1-	NASTRAN	PREFOPT = 2		$REQUESTS MSGMESH						
2-	ID PRIMER, PROB132A									
3-	SOL	3								
4-	TIME	200								
5-	CEND									
6-	TITLE = RECTANGULAR PLATE WITH SIMPLY SUPPORED EDGES									
7-	SUBTITLE = SYMMETRIC MODES FOR ONE-QUARTER MODEL									
8-	LABEL = NO REDUCTION USING GIV METHOD									
9-	METHOD = 29									
10-	SPC = 156									
11-	SET 1 = 130000 THRU 130020, 130100, 130200, 130300,									
12-	130400, 130500, 130600, 130700, 130800, 130900,									
13-	131000, 131100, 131200, 131300, 131400, 131500,									
14-	131600, 131700, 131800, 131900, 132000									
15-	ECHO = BOTH									
16-	SUBCASE 1									
17-	VECTOR = 1									
18-	SUBCASE 2									
19-	VECTOR = NONE									
20-	MODES = 3									
21-	BEGIN BULK									
22-	EGRID	1	0	0.	0.	0.				
23-	EGRID	2	0	15.	0.	0.				
24-	EGRID	3		15.	10.	0.				
25-	EGRID	4		0.	10.	0.				

26-	GRIDG	13	0	126	20	−1	−2	−3		+G1
27-	+G1	20	−4							
28-	CGEN	QUAD4	1	15	13					
29-	PSHELL	15		.2	30				.0566	
30-	MAT1	30	30.+6		.3					
31-	SPCG	12	13	24	AB					
32-	SPCG	23	13	13	BC					
33-	SPCG	34	13	23	CD					
34-	SPCG	41	13	15	DA					
35-	SPCADD	156	12	23	34	41				
36-	PARAM	WTMASS	.002591							
37-	EIGR	29	GIV				4			+E1
38-	+E1	MASS								
39-	PARAM	AUTOSPC	YES							
40-	PARAM	PRGPST	NO							
41-	PARAM	NEWSEQ	−1							
42-	ENDDATA									

The NASTRAN data deck is described, with reference to the card numbers, as follows

Card 1- The NASTRAN card is required to tell MSC/NASTRAN that we will use MSGMESH commands to generate MSC/NASTRAN Bulk Data. The keyword and value are

$$PREFOPT = 2$$

Card 9- Selects EIGR Bulk Data with SID = 29

Card 10- Points to SPC set 156 in Bulk Data (an SPCADD Card in this case)

Card 11- Defines a set of GRID points at which displacements will be printed. This set of points
Card 14- lies on the x and y axes of the quarter panel and, at least for the fundamental mode, are points at which the displacement will be maximum

Card 15- Requests both sorted and unsorted bulk data

Card 16- Although we are calculating four eigenvectors in order to evaluate relative solution time
Card 20- for several methods we will only print the first eigenvector. This subcase construction suppresses the print of the three other eigenvectors.

Card 22- The EGRID MSGMESH commands define the location of the four vertex points, A, B, C,
Card 25- and D, respectively of the quadrilateral field

Card 26- The GRIDG MSGMESH command defines field 13 which has vertex points 1, 2, 3, and 4.
Card 27- A uniform mesh of 20 increments is to be defined along each coordinate, GRID points at the vertex are to be generated (because of the minus signs associated with the point numbers), and permanent single point constraints are to be generated in the PSPC field of all GRID points to purge the inplane displacements and normal rotation (i.e., PSPC = 126).

Card 28- The CGEN MSGMESH Command generates CQUAD4 connection cards having PID = 15 over MSGMESH field 13.

Card 29- The PSHELL card specifies bending-only behavior for the element so that no in-plane

390

stiffness or structural mass is calculated. The nonstructural mass is then used to calculate the mass associated with bending behavior.

Card 31- SPCG MSGMESH command generates SPC1 Bulk data which define symmetry conditions along the x-axis.

Card 32- SPCG MSGMESH command generates SPC1 Bulk Data which define a simple support along x = 15. A better boundary condition might also set the in-plane rotation normal to the boundary equal to zero (i.e., $\theta_x = 0$).

Card 33- SPCG MSGMESH command generates SPC1 Bulk Data which define a simple support along y = 10.

Card 34- SPCG MSGMESH command generates symmetry conditions along the y-axis.

Card 35- Forms the union of SPC sets

Card 36- Defines the conversion factor, $1/g$, from weight to mass units where g is the acceleration of gravity

Card 37- Specifies Givens method with extraction of four eigenvectors
Card 38-

Card 39- Requests that unconnected degrees of freedom be purged (there aren't any since we explicitly purged these degrees of freedom by means of PSPC on GRID Bulk Data)

Card 40- Suppresses the printing of the Grid Point Singularity Tabel

Card 41- Suppresses the execution of the resequencing algorithm

13.9.2a.1. Selected Output

The output for this problem is shown below where we note

1. The MSC/NASTRAN execution summary tells us the resources that have been used in this solution. The entries under MODULE are the names DMAP sequence numbers of the modules which have been executed. The amount of time required for any module can then be found by subtracting the times on succeeding lines. For example, the time required for Element Matrix Generation (EMG), at DMAP statement 52 is 23.11 cpu sec. and 5.3 I/O seconds. The total computer resource required for this solution is then seen to be 1166 I/O sec. and 1880 cpu seconds. We also note that user message 2016 estimates that approximately 2000 cpu seconds will be required for Givens method and that READ (the real eigenvalue module actually required 1262 cpu seconds). (The working set limit on the VAX 11/780 computer was set to 2000 pages for this problem).

2. Executive Control Deck — The TIME card specifies 2000 cpu minutes

3. Input Bulk Data Echo

   The MSGMESH Command are preceeded by a $-sign which means that they are treated as comment cards. We also note that the generated Bulk Data immediately follows the associated MSGMESH command. (Note that not all the GRID and CQUAD4 Bulk Data has been included here.)

13.9.2a.1 Selected Output

4. VAXW — The partitioning vector which is created to condense out massless degrees of freedom. This action is controlled by the ASING PARAMeter which default action is appropriate for Givens method

5. Real Eigenvalue Summary Givens method finds all the eigenvalues (approximately 400 in this case). Not all the eigenvalues are listed here.

6. Real Eigenvector. Although four eigenvectors were calculated only the first was selected for output.

```
                M S C / N A S T R A N   V A X   E X E C U T I O N   S U M M A R Y

DAY TIME   ELAPSED   I/O SEC   CPU SEC   MODULE
12:47:13    0: 0      0.00      0.00     SEM1BEGN
                                                    LOGICAL  ASSIGNMENT TABLE
                                                      NAME    FILE-SPEC
                                                      NPTP    _DRB1:[SCHAEFFER]PROB132A.NPT;
                                                      DB01    _DRB1:[SCHAEFFER]PROB132A.D01;

12:47:37    0:24      1.75      11.18    XSOR
12:48: 9    0:56      4.25      28.74    IFP
12:48:20    1: 7      6.55      33.86    XGPI
12:48:52    1:39      9.10      46.62    24  GP1      BEGN
12:48:57    1:44     10.45      47.83    26  GP2      BEGN
12:48:59    1:46     11.05      48.41    42  GP3      BEGN
12:48:59    1:46     11.10      48.45    43  TA1      BEGN
12:49:14    2: 1     16.55      54.58    52  EMG      BEGN
12:50: 4    2:51     21.85      77.69    54  EMA      BEGN
12:51:28    4:15     32.55     128.80    57  EMA      BEGN
12:51:57    4:44     36.20     146.93    59  EMG      BEGN
12:51:59    4:46     37.15     147.70    66  MTRXIN   BEGN
12:52: 1    4:48     37.65     148.80    95  GP4      BEGN
12:52:10    4:57     38.80     151.99    96  GPSP1    BEGN
12:52:23    5:10     43.05     159.90   125  SCE1     BEGN
12:52:55    5:42     50.30     178.27   220  SCE1     BEGN
12:53: 2    5:49     51.95     182.87   341  MGEN     BEGN
12:53: 3    5:50     52.10     183.11   356  LCGEN    BEGN
12:53: 3    5:50     52.35     183.39   357  SSG1     BEGN
12:53: 6    5:53     52.85     183.90   358  MTRXIN   BEGN
12:53: 7    5:54     53.25     184.82   364  DPD      BEGN
12:53:12    5:59     54.30     186.58   384  MATMOD   BEGN
12:53:13    6: 0     54.45     186.66   388  MATMOD   BEGN
12:53:15    6: 2     55.05     188.56   398  MATGPR   BEGN
12:53:19    6: 6     55.35     191.12   400  PARTN    BEGN
12:53:22    6: 9     55.85     192.70   401  PARTN    BEGN
12:53:40    6:27     60.95     205.11   407  DECOMP   BEGN
12:54:13    7: 0     67.35     226.90   408  FBS      BEGN

*** USER INFORMATION MESSAGE 4153. FBS METHOD 1 TIME ESTIMATE TO FORM GWX1    - CPU=   295, I/O=   64, TOTAL=   553, PASSES=   7
12:54:14    7: 1     67.95     227.21    FBS BEGN
12:55:58    8:45     77.30     279.65    FBS PASS NO 1
12:57:26   10:13     86.80     329.22    FBS PASS NO 2
12:58:51   11:38     96.25     374.76    FBS PASS NO 3
13: 0: 2   12:49    105.75     416.37    FBS PASS NO 4
13: 1: 5   13:52    115.25     453.43    FBS PASS NO 5
13: 2: 1   14:48    124.70     487.19    FBS PASS NO 6
13: 2:30   15:17    132.50     504.51    FBS END
13: 2:30   15:17    132.50     504.53   408  FBS      END
13: 2:30   15:17    132.55     504.59   409  MPYAD    BEGN
13: 4:20   17: 7    199.20     565.13   416  READ     BEGN

*** USER INFORMATION MESSAGE 2016, GIVENS TIME ESTIMATE IS    1973 SECONDS.
                                     PROBLEM SIZE IS       400, SPILL WILL OCCUR FOR THIS CORE AT A PROBLEM SIZE OF    447 .
14:15:52   88:39   1136.10    1827.78   416  READ     END
14:15:56   88:43   1136.20    1828.31   417  OFP      BEGN
14:16: 6   88:53   1136.45    1835.73   423  MPYAD    BEGN
14:17:41   90:28   1161.15    1855.47   425  MERGE    BEGN
14:17:46   90:33   1162.15    1857.29   428  VDR      BEGN
14:21:50   94:37   1163.15    1873.28   441  CASE     BEGN
14:23:10   95:57   1163.35    1873.55   448  SDR1     BEGN
14:23:28   96:15   1165.65    1878.71   450  SDR2     BEGN
14:23:30   96:17   1166.55    1879.44   455  OFP      BEGN
14:23:32   96:19   1166.70    1880.31   510  EXIT     BEGN


            N A S T R A N   E X E C U T I V E   C O N T R O L   D E C K   E C H O


    ID PRIMER PROB132A
    SOL 3
    TIME 200
    CEND
```

```
                        C A S E   C O N T R O L   D E C K   E C H O
CARD
COUNT
  1     TITLE = RECTANGULAR PLATE WITH SIMPLY SUPPORTED EDGES
  2     SUBTITLE = SYMMETRIC MODES FOR ONE-QUARTER MODEL
  3     LABEL = NO REDUCTION USING GIV METHOD
  4     METHOD = 29
  5     SPC = 156
  6     SET 1 = 130000 THRU 130020,130100,130200,130300,130400,
  7             130500,130600,130700,130800,130900,131000,
  8             131100,131200,131300,131400,131500,131600,131700,
  9             131800,131900,132000
 10     ECHO = BOTH
 11     SUBCASE 1
 12     VECTOR = 1
 13     SUBCASE 2
 14     VECTOR = NONE
 15     MODES = 3
 16     BEGIN BULK


                   I N P U T   B U L K   D A T A   D E C K   E C H O

        .  1  ..  2  ..  3  ..  4  ..  5  ..  6  ..  7  ..  8  ..  9  .. 10  .
        $EGRID   1      0      0.     0.     0.
        $EGRID   2      0      15.    0.     0.
        $EGRID   3      0      15.    10.    0.
        $EGRID   4      0      0.     10.    0.
        $GRIDG  13      0      126    20     -1     -2     -3              +G1
        $+G1    20     -4
        GRID    130000  0      0.0    0.0    0.0    0      126
        GRID    130001  0      .75    0.0    0.0    0      126
        GRID    130002  0      1.5    0.0    0.0    0      126
        GRID    130003  0      2.25   0.0    0.0    0      126
          :
          :
        GRID    132020  0      15.    10.    0.0    0      126
        $CGEN   QUAD4   1      15     13
        CQUAD4  1       15     130000 130001 130101 130100
        CQUAD4  2       15     130001 130002 130102 130101
        CQUAD4  3       15     130002 130003 130103 130102
          :
          :
        CQUAD4  400     15     131919 131920 132020 132019
        PSHELL  15             .2     30                           .0566
        MAT1    30      30.+6         .3
        $SPCG   12      13     24     AB
        SPC1    12      24     130000 130001 130002 130003 130004 130005 +M00000
        +M00000 130006 130007 130008 130009 130010 130011 130012 130013 +M00001
        +M00001 130014 130015 130016 130017 130018 130019 130020
        $SPCG   23      13     13     BC
        SPC1    23      13     130020 130120 130220 130320 130420 130520 +M00002
        +M00002 130620 130720 130820 130920 131020 131120 131220 131320 +M00003
        +M00003 131420 131520 131620 131720 131820 131920 132020
        $SPCG   34      13     23     CD
        SPC1    34      23     132000 132001 132002 132003 132004 132005 +M00004
        +M00004 132006 132007 132008 132009 132010 132011 132012 132013 +M00005
        +M00005 132014 132015 132016 132017 132018 132019 132020
        $SPCG   41      13     15     DA
        SPC1    41      15     130000 130100 130200 130300 130400 130500 +M00006
        +M00006 130600 130700 130800 130900 131000 131100 131200 131300 +M00007
        +M00007 131400 131500 131600 131700 131800 131900 132000
        SPCADD  156     12     23     34     41
        PARAM   WTMASS  .002591
        EIGR    29      GIV                         4                     +E1
        +E1     MASS
        PARAM   AUTOSPC YES
        PARAM   PRGPST  NO
        PARAM   NEWSEQ  -1
        ENDDATA
        INPUT BULK DATA CARD COUNT =      874


                   S O R T E D   B U L K   D A T A   E C H O
CARD
COUNT   .  1  ..  2  ..  3  ..  4  ..  5  ..  6  ..  7  ..  8  ..  9  .. 10  .
  1-    CQUAD4  1       15     130000 130001 130101 130100
  2-    CQUAD4  2       15     130001 130002 130102 130101
  3-    CQUAD4  3       15     130002 130003 130103 130102
    :
    :
400-    CQUAD4  400     15     131919 131920 132020 132019
401-    EIGR    29      GIV                         4                     +E1
402-    +E1     MASS
403-    GRID    130000  0      0.0    0.0    0.0    0      126
404-    GRID    130001  0      .75    0.0    0.0    0      126
    :
    :
843-    GRID    132020  0      15.    10.    0.0    0      126
844-    MAT1    30      30.+6         .3
845-    PARAM   AUTOSPC YES
846-    PARAM   NEWSEQ  -1
847-    PARAM   PRGPST  NO
848-    PARAM   WTMASS  .002591
849-    PSHELL  15             .2     30                           .0566
850-    SPC1    12      24     130000 130001 130002 130003 130004 130005 +M00000
```

393

```
851-        +M00000 130006  130007  130008  130009  130010  130011  130012  130013  +M00001
852-        +M00001 130014  130015  130016  130017  130018  130019  130020
853-        SPC1    23      13      130020  130120  130220  130320  130420  130520  +M00002
854-        +M00002 130620  130720  130820  130920  131020  131120  131220  131320  +M00003
855-        +M00003 131420  131520  131620  131720  131820  131920  132020
856-        SPC1    34      23      132000  132001  132002  132003  132004  132005  +M00004
857-        +M00004 132006  132007  132008  132009  132010  132011  132012  132013  +M00005
858-        +M00005 132014  132015  132016  132017  132018  132019  132020
859-        SPC1    41      15      130000  130100  130200  130300  130400  130500  +M00006
860-        +M00006 130600  130700  130800  130900  131000  131100  131200  131300  +M00007
861-        +M00007 131400  131500  131600  131700  131800  131900  132000
862-        SPCADD  156     12      23      34      41
            ENDDATA
   TOTAL COUNT=   863
```

VAXW

	POINT	VALUE	POINT	VALUE	POINT	VALUE	POINT	VALUE	POINT	VALUE
COLUMN	1									
	130001 R2	1.00000E+00	130002 R2	1.00000E+00	130003 R2	1.00000E+00	130004 R2	1.00000E+00	130005 R2	1.00000E+00
	130006 R2	1.00000E+00	130007 R2	1.00000E+00	130008 R2	1.00000E+00	130009 R2	1.00000E+00	130010 R2	1.00000E+00
	132018 R2	1.00000E+00	132019 R1	1.00000E+00	132019 R2	1.00000E+00	132020 R1	1.00000E+00	132020 R2	1.00000E+00

REAL EIGENVALUES

MODE NO.	EXTRACTION ORDER	EIGENVALUE	RADIANS	CYCLES	GENERALIZED MASS	GENERALIZED STIFFNESS
1	369	1.898671E+05	4.357375E+02	6.934977E+01	1.000000E+00	1.898671E+05
2	370	2.271379E+06	1.507109E+03	2.398639E+02	1.000000E+00	2.271379E+06
3	371	8.121678E+06	2.849856E+03	4.535686E+02	1.000000E+00	8.121678E+06
4	372	1.332969E+07	3.650984E+03	5.810721E+02	1.000000E+00	1.332969E+07
5	373	1.522782E+07	3.902284E+03	6.210677E+02	0.0	0.0
6	374	3.615544E+07	6.012939E+03	9.569890E+02	0.0	0.0
7	375	4.716241E+07	6.867489E+03	1.092995E+03	0.0	0.0
8	376	5.896054E+07	7.678577E+03	1.222083E+03	0.0	0.0
9	377	7.566100E+07	8.698333E+03	1.384383E+03	0.0	0.0
10	378	8.441657E+07	9.187849E+03	1.462292E+03	0.0	0.0
11	379	1.154964E+08	1.074693E+04	1.710427E+03	0.0	0.0
12	380	1.244714E+08	1.115688E+04	1.775640E+03	0.0	0.0
13	381	1.804729E+08	1.343402E+04	2.138091E+03	0.0	0.0
14	382	1.915131E+08	1.383883E+04	2.202518E+03	0.0	0.0
15	383	2.226567E+08	1.492169E+04	2.374860E+03	0.0	0.0
16	384	2.527541E+08	1.589824E+04	2.530284E+03	0.0	0.0
17	385	2.728302E+08	1.651757E+04	2.628854E+03	0.0	0.0
18	387	3.190762E+08	1.786270E+04	2.842938E+03	0.0	0.0
19	388	3.237238E+08	1.799233E+04	2.863568E+03	0.0	0.0
20	386	3.519432E+08	1.876015E+04	2.985771E+03	0.0	0.0
21	389	4.341298E+08	2.083578E+04	3.316118E+03	0.0	0.0
22	395					

```
NO REDUCTION USING GIV METHOD                                              SUBCASE 1
EIGENVALUE =  1.898671E+05
CYCLES =  6.934977E+01       REAL  EIGENVECTOR  NO.          1
```

POINT ID.	TYPE	T1	T2	T3	R1	R2	R3
130000	G	0.0	0.0	-1.348318E+01	0.0	0.0	0.0
130001	G	0.0	0.0	-1.344163E+01	0.0	-1.106094E-01	0.0
130002	G	0.0	0.0	-1.331725E+01	0.0	-2.205379E-01	0.0
130003	G	0.0	0.0	-1.311080E+01	0.0	-3.291087E-01	0.0
130004	G	0.0	0.0	-1.282354E+01	0.0	-4.356537E-01	0.0
130005	G	0.0	0.0	-1.245726E+01	0.0	-5.395169E-01	0.0
130006	G	0.0	0.0	-1.201420E+01	0.0	-6.400594E-01	0.0
130007	G	0.0	0.0	-1.149709E+01	0.0	-7.366625E-01	0.0
130008	G	0.0	0.0	-1.090911E+01	0.0	-8.287321E-01	0.0
130009	G	0.0	0.0	-1.025388E+01	0.0	-9.157022E-01	0.0
130010	G	0.0	0.0	-9.535440E+00	0.0	-9.970385E-01	0.0
130011	G	0.0	0.0	-8.758199E+00	0.0	-1.072242E+00	0.0
130012	G	0.0	0.0	-7.926940E+00	0.0	-1.140850E+00	0.0
130013	G	0.0	0.0	-7.046776E+00	0.0	-1.202445E+00	0.0
130014	G	0.0	0.0	-6.123117E+00	0.0	-1.256647E+00	0.0
130015	G	0.0	0.0	-5.161642E+00	0.0	-1.303128E+00	0.0
130016	G	0.0	0.0	-4.168255E+00	0.0	-1.341604E+00	0.0
130017	G	0.0	0.0	-3.149062E+00	0.0	-1.371836E+00	0.0
130018	G	0.0	0.0	-2.110327E+00	0.0	-1.393629E+00	0.0
130019	G	0.0	0.0	-1.058455E+00	0.0	-1.406807E+00	0.0
130020	G	0.0	0.0	0.0	0.0	-1.411145E+00	0.0
130100	G	0.0	0.0	-1.344162E+01	1.660934E-01	0.0	0.0
130200	G	0.0	0.0	-1.331722E+01	3.311639E-01	0.0	0.0
130300	G	0.0	0.0	-1.311072E+01	4.941953E-01	0.0	0.0
130400	G	0.0	0.0	-1.282342E+01	6.541835E-01	0.0	0.0
130500	G	0.0	0.0	-1.245707E+01	8.101434E-01	0.0	0.0
130600	G	0.0	0.0	-1.201392E+01	9.611148E-01	0.0	0.0
130700	G	0.0	0.0	-1.149672E+01	1.106168E+00	0.0	0.0
130800	G	0.0	0.0	-1.090864E+01	1.244410E+00	0.0	0.0
130900	G	0.0	0.0	-1.025331E+01	1.374990E+00	0.0	0.0
131000	G	0.0	0.0	-9.534757E+00	1.497103E+00	0.0	0.0
131100	G	0.0	0.0	-8.757407E+00	1.609998E+00	0.0	0.0
131200	G	0.0	0.0	-7.926050E+00	1.712980E+00	0.0	0.0
131300	G	0.0	0.0	-7.045803E+00	1.805412E+00	0.0	0.0
131400	G	0.0	0.0	-6.122086E+00	1.886726E+00	0.0	0.0
131500	G	0.0	0.0	-5.160591E+00	1.956418E+00	0.0	0.0
131600	G	0.0	0.0	-4.167240E+00	2.014053E+00	0.0	0.0
131700	G	0.0	0.0	-3.148158E+00	2.059269E+00	0.0	0.0
131800	G	0.0	0.0	-2.109630E+00	2.091774E+00	0.0	0.0
131900	G	0.0	0.0	-1.058074E+00	2.111345E+00	0.0	0.0
132000	G	0.0	0.0	0.0	2.117823E+00	0.0	0.0

13.9.2b.   Inverse Power With No Reduction

The physical problem for this case is exactly the same as the solution using Givens method. The only differences in the solution are

- Selection of the inverse power EIGR specification by means of METHOD = 30

- Specification of the inverse power method in Bulk Data. (We have cheated a little and used our knowledge from the previous solution to specify the frequency range which contains the first four eigenvalues.)

- Request INV power summary information by including DIAG 16 in Executive Control.

13.9.2b.1.   Selected Output

The output data for this example is shown below where we note

1. MSC/NASTRAN Execution Summary.
   The total computational resources required to find four eigenvectors using INV was 580 I/O seconds and 664 cpu seconds.

2. Sorted Bulk Data. Only the EIGR and PARAM cards were printed because we included an ECHO card in Case Control with these card names.

3. User information message 4158 tells us that there are two roots below the current shift point. The DIAG 16 output which follows this message tells us that the shift point is 7.155×10^6 and the REAL EIGENVALUE summary confirms that two eigenvalues exist below the shift point. One eigenvalue is found at 8.12×10^6. The next user message 4158 then tells us that there is one root below this value which we can again verify from the eigenvalue summary.

4. User Warning Message 3034 tells us that mode pairs 1 and 2 give an off-diagonal modal mass which is greater than the default test value. The value 1.8×10^{-9} is quite small and is not cause for alarm in this case.

5. Eigenvalue Analysis Summary
   Provides a summary of the INV power method. The reason for termination is number 3 which, according to Sec. 13.5.2.2. means that all the eigenvalues in the range specified have been found.

13.9.2b.1 Selected Output

```
                 M S C / N A S T R A N   V A X   E X E C U T I O N   S U M M A R Y

DAY TIME   ELAPSED  I/O SEC  CPU SEC   MODULE
22:36:36    0: 0     0.00     0.00     SEM1BEGN
                                                   LOGICAL ASSIGNMENT TABLE
                                                      NAME    FILE-SPEC
                                                      NPTP    _DRB1:[SCHAEFFER]PROB132B.NPT;
                                                      DB01    _DRB1:[SCHAEFFER]PROB132B.D01;

22:36:54    0:18     1.75     12.12    XSOR
22:37: 5    0:29     4.25     19.77    IFP
22:37:12    0:36     6.55     24.62    XGPI
22:37:33    0:57     9.10     37.94     24 GP1     BEGN
22:37:37    1: 1    10.45     39.18     26 GP2     BEGN
22:37:38    1: 2    11.05     39.77     42 GP3     BEGN
22:37:38    1: 2    11.10     39.86     43 TA1     BEGN
22:37:49    1:13    16.55     45.76     52 EMG     BEGN
22:38:18    1:42    21.85     69.26     54 EMA     BEGN
22:39:17    2:41    32.55    117.07     57 EMA     BEGN
22:39:37    3: 1    36.20    134.69     59 EMG     BEGN
22:39:39    3: 3    37.15    135.47     66 MTRXIN  BEGN
22:39:41    3: 5    37.65    136.54     95 GP4     BEGN
22:39:46    3:10    38.80    139.62     96 GPSP1   BEGN
22:39:56    3:20    43.05    147.25    125 SCE1    BEGN
22:40:20    3:44    50.30    164.34    220 SCE1    BEGN
22:40:26    3:50    51.95    168.95    341 MGEN    BEGN
22:40:26    3:50    52.10    169.16    356 LCGEN   BEGN
22:40:27    3:51    52.35    169.44    357 SSG1    BEGN
22:40:29    3:53    52.85    169.98    358 MTRXIN  BEGN
22:40:30    3:54    53.25    170.82    364 DPD     BEGN
22:40:35    3:59    54.30    172.54    384 MATMOD  BEGN
22:40:35    3:59    54.45    172.61    388 MATMOD  BEGN
22:40:39    4: 3    57.70    174.64    416 READ    BEGN
22:52:19   15:43   576.65    641.63    416 READ    END
22:52:20   15:44   576.75    641.90    417 OFP     BEGN
22:52:22   15:46   577.15    642.79    428 VDR     BEGN
22:52:38   16: 2   578.05    657.74    441 CASE    BEGN
22:52:39   16: 3   578.25    657.94    448 SDR1    BEGN
22:52:46   16:10   580.55    662.65    450 SDR2    BEGN
22:52:48   16:12   581.45    663.30    455 OFP     BEGN
22:52:50   16:14   581.60    664.10    510 EXIT    BEGN
```

N A S T R A N   E X E C U T I V E   C O N T R O L   D E C K   E C H O

```
ID PRIMER PROB132B
SOL 3
TIME 200
DIAG 16
CEND
```

C A S E   C O N T R O L   D E C K   E C H O

```
CARD
COUNT
   1     TITLE = RECTANGULAR PLATE WITH SIMPLY SUPPORTED EDGES
   2     SUBTITLE = SYMMETRIC MODES FOR ONE-QUARTER MODEL
   3     LABEL = NO REDUCTION USING INV METHOD
   4     METHOD = 30
   5     ECHO = SORT(EIGR,PARAM)
   6     SPC = 156
   7     SET 1 = 130000 THRU 130020,130100,130200,130300,130400,
   8              130500,130600,130700,130800,130900,131000,
   9              131100,131200,131300,131400,131500,131600,131700,
  10              131800,131900,132000
  11     SUBCASE 1
  12     VECTOR = 1
  13     SUBCASE 2
  14     VECTOR = NONE
  15     MODES = 3
  16     BEGIN BULK

          INPUT BULK DATA CARD COUNT =     874
```

```
                         S O R T E D   B U L K   D A T A   E C H O
         CARD
         COUNT            . 1 .. 2 .. 3 .. 4 .. 5 .. 6 .. 7 .. 8 .. 9 .. 10 .
         401-       EIGR   30    INV    50.   600.    4    4                +E1
         402-       +E1    MASS
         845-       PARAM  AUTOSPC YES
         846-       PARAM  NEWSEQ  -1
         847-       PARAM  PRGPST  NO
         848-       PARAM  WTMASS  .002591
                    ENDDATA

             TOTAL COUNT=   863
```

*** USER INFORMATION MESSAGE 4158---STATISTICS FOR SYMMETRIC DECOMPOSITION OF DATA BLOCK LAMA   FOLLOW
          NUMBER OF NEGATIVE TERMS ON FACTOR DIAGONAL =   2

D I A G   16   O U T P U T   F R O M   R O U T I N E   I N V P 3   F O L L O W S .
     SEE SECTION 10.4.2 OF THEORETICAL MANUAL FOR EXPLANATION OF SYMBOLS.
     K = 0 UNTIL ESP1 TEST PASSES.

  RZERO = 7.76244E+06   EPS = 1.00000E-04   GAMMA = 1.00000E-02   A = 1.00000E-01
  EPS1 = 3.00000E-03   EPS2= 2.00000E-02   EPS3 = 5.00000E-02

ITER	START POINT	SHIFT POINT	LAMBDA 1	LAMBDA 2	ETA	DELTA	K	H2N BAR	LAMBDA 1 DIFF.
1	7.15546D+06	7.15546D+06	6.01319D+06	0.00000D+00	1.57631D+00	0.00000D+00	0	0.00000D+00	0.00000D+00
2	7.15546D+06	7.15546D+06	1.19003D+06	-1.62157D+06	7.14418D-01	9.14357D-02	0	-2.26619D-01	0.00000D+00
3	7.15546D+06	7.15546D+06	9.71838D+05	-4.99488D+06	1.24440D-01	1.54853D-03	0	-4.71432D-01	0.00000D+00
4	7.15546D+06	7.15546D+06	9.66353D+05	-5.67166D+06	1.97686D-02	3.90797D-05	4	-9.45821D-02	6.75398D-04
5	7.15546D+06	7.15546D+06	9.66218D+05	-5.39001D+06	3.32139D-03	1.10316D-06	3	3.93611D-02	1.65834D-05
6	7.15546D+06	7.15546D+06	9.66215D+05	-5.15270D+06	5.90701D-04	3.48928D-08	2	3.31655D-02	4.55585D-07
7	7.15546D+06	7.15546D+06	9.66214D+05	-5.00561D+06	1.09746D-04	1.20442D-09	1	2.05558D-02	1.40488D-08
8	7.15546D+06	7.15546D+06	9.66214D+05	-4.92913D+06	2.09740D-05	4.39909D-11	1	1.06887D-02	1.40488D-08

CONVERGENCE ACHIEVED AND EIGENVALUE =   8.12168D+06   FREQ. = 4.53569D+02

8	7.15546D+06	7.15546D+06	8.12168D+06	0.00000D+00	2.09740D-05	0.00000D+00	0	0.00000D+00	0.00000D+00
10	7.15546D+06	7.15546D+06	-4.93033D+06	4.24860D+06	1.40682D-01	5.71015D-03	0	5.93756D-01	0.00000D+00
11	7.15546D+06	7.15546D+06	-4.90775D+06	4.59469D+06	1.10397D-01	3.25094D-03	0	4.83668D-02	0.00000D+00
12	7.15546D+06	7.15546D+06	-4.89620D+06	4.89400D+06	8.65417D-02	1.87321D-03	0	4.18306D-02	9.57948D-04
13	7.15546D+06	7.15546D+06	-4.89032D+06	5.14477D+06	6.78765D-02	1.09413D-03	160	3.50460D-02	4.88328D-04

NEW SHIFT POINT =   2.26514D+06

*** USER INFORMATION MESSAGE 4158---STATISTICS FOR SYMMETRIC DECOMPOSITION OF DATA BLOCK LAMA   FOLLOW
          NUMBER OF NEGATIVE TERMS ON FACTOR DIAGONAL =   1

D I A G   16   O U T P U T   F R O M   R O U T I N E   I N V P 3   F O L L O W S .
     SEE SECTION 10.4.2 OF THEORETICAL MANUAL FOR EXPLANATION OF SYMBOLS.
     K = 0 UNTIL ESP1 TEST PASSES.

  RZERO = 7.76244E+06   EPS = 1.00000E-04   GAMMA = 1.00000E-02   A = 1.00000E-01
  EPS1 = 3.00000E-03   EPS2= 2.00000E-02   EPS3 = 5.00000E-02

ITER	START POINT	SHIFT POINT	LAMBDA 1	LAMBDA 2	ETA	DELTA	K	H2N BAR	LAMBDA 1 DIFF.
14	7.15546D+06	2.26514D+06	6.24475D+03	0.00000D+00	5.32339D-02	0.00000D+00	0	0.00000D+00	0.00000D+00
15	7.15546D+06	2.26514D+06	6.23594D+03	-1.88415D+06	1.35655D-04	1.84024D-09	0	-8.31800D-01	0.00000D+00
16	7.15546D+06	2.26514D+06	6.23594D+03	-1.88415D+06	4.04797D-07	1.84024D-09	0	-8.31800D-01	0.00000D+00
17	7.15546D+06	2.26514D+06	6.23594D+03	-1.88415D+06	4.04797D-07	1.84024D-09	0	-8.31800D-01	0.00000D+00

CONVERGENCE ACHIEVED AND EIGENVALUE =   2.27138D+06   FREQ. = 2.39864D+02

17	7.15546D+06	7.15546D+06	2.27138D+06	0.00000D+00	4.04797D-07	0.00000D+00	0	0.00000D+00	0.00000D+00
19	7.15546D+06	7.15546D+06	6.65809D+06	2.72553D+05	1.58176D+00	2.72011D+00	0	3.80902D-02	0.00000D+00
20	7.15546D+06	7.15546D+06	-6.61175D+06	4.69040D+05	1.31510D+00	1.50795D+00	0	2.74596D-02	0.00000D+00
21	7.15546D+06	7.15546D+06	6.56422D+06	3.63051D+05	1.42528D+00	2.27625D+00	0	-1.48123D-02	9.60370D-01
22	7.15546D+06	7.15546D+06	6.51686D+06	-6.92713D+06	1.33845D+00	4.20942D-01	0	-1.32419D-04	3.46399D-03
23	7.15546D+06	7.15546D+06	6.47100D+06	-6.92808D+06	1.24794D+00	3.63229D-01	0	-1.32419D-04	3.36562D-03
24	7.15546D+06	7.15546D+06	6.42781D+06	-6.92808D+06	1.15557D+00	3.09296D-01	0	-2.70172D-04	3.17987D-03
25	7.15546D+06	7.15546D+06	6.38818D+06	-6.92808D+06	1.06316D+00	2.60129D-01	134	-2.70172D-04	2.92595D-03

NEW SHIFT POINT =   1.35436D+07

*** USER INFORMATION MESSAGE 4158---STATISTICS FOR SYMMETRIC DECOMPOSITION OF DATA BLOCK LAMA   FOLLOW
          NUMBER OF NEGATIVE TERMS ON FACTOR DIAGONAL =   4

D I A G   16   O U T P U T   F R O M   R O U T I N E   I N V P 3   F O L L O W S .
     SEE SECTION 10.4.2 OF THEORETICAL MANUAL FOR EXPLANATION OF SYMBOLS.
     K = 0 UNTIL ESP1 TEST PASSES.

  RZERO = 7.76244E+06   EPS = 1.00000E-04   GAMMA = 1.00000E-02   A = 1.00000E-01
  EPS1 = 3.00000E-03   EPS2= 2.00000E-02   EPS3 = 5.00000E-02

13.9.2b.1 Selected Output

ITER	START POINT	SHIFT POINT	LAMBDA 1	LAMBDA 2	ETA	DELTA	K	H2N BAR	LAMBDA 1 DIFF.
26	7.15546D+06	1.35436D+07	-2.48456D+05	0.00000D+00	5.17908D-01	0.00000D+00	0	0.00000D+00	0.00000D+00
27	7.15546D+06	1.35436D+07	-2.13968D+05	-1.14785D+07	9.31017D-03	8.66792D-06	0	-8.47517D-01	0.00000D+00
28	7.15546D+06	1.35436D+07	-2.13959D+05	-1.28869D+07	1.51505D-04	2.29538D-09	0	-1.03992D-01	0.00000D+00
29	7.15546D+06	1.35436D+07	-2.13959D+05	-3.30884D+06	4.14692D-06	1.71969D-12	0	7.07200D-01	0.00000D+00

CONVERGENCE ACHIEVED AND EIGENVALUE = 1.33297D+07   FREQ. = 5.81072D+02

ITER	START POINT	SHIFT POINT	LAMBDA 1	LAMBDA 2	ETA	DELTA	K	H2N BAR	LAMBDA 1 DIFF.
29	7.15546D+06	7.15546D+06	1.33297D+07	0.00000D+00	4.14692D-06	0.00000D+00	0	0.00000D+00	0.00000D+00
31	7.15546D+06	7.15546D+06	-6.96560D+06	8.07236D+06	3.99227D-03	3.41962D-06	0	1.12814D+00	0.00000D+00
32	7.15546D+06	7.15546D+06	-6.96560D+06	8.07236D+06	3.44491D-03	2.54621D-06	0	4.45452D-08	0.00000D+00
33	7.15546D+06	7.15546D+06	-6.96560D+06	8.07236D+06	2.97259D-03	1.89588D-06	34	3.31669D-08	5.50202D-08

NEW SHIFT POINT = 1.89865D+05

```
D I A G   1 6   O U T P U T   F R O M   R O U T I N E   I N V P 3   F O L L O W S .
    SEE SECTION 10.4.2 OF THEORETICAL MANUAL FOR EXPLANATION OF SYMBOLS.
    K = 0 UNTIL ESP1 TEST PASSES.
```

```
RZERO =  7.76244E+06     EPS = 1.00000E-04   GAMMA = 1.00000E-02   A = 1.00000E-01
EPS1 = 3.00000E-03     EPS2= 2.00000E-02   EPS3 = 5.00000E-02
```

ITER	START POINT	SHIFT POINT	LAMBDA 1	LAMBDA 2	ETA	DELTA	K	H2N BAR	LAMBDA 1 DIFF.
34	7.15546D+06	1.89865D+05	2.26501D+00	0.00000D+00	1.37691D-03	0.00000D+00	0	0.00000D+00	0.00000D+00
35	7.15546D+06	1.89865D+05	2.26501D+00	0.00000D+00	1.37691D-03	0.00000D+00	0	0.00000D+00	0.00000D+00

CONVERGENCE ACHIEVED AND EIGENVALUE = 1.89867D+05   FREQ. = 6.93498D+01

*** USER WARNING MESSAGE 3034, ORTHOGONALITY TEST FAILED. LARGEST TERM = 1.87E-09 ,NUMBER FAILED = 5
                                 PAIR =   2,   1 , EPSILON =   1.00E-10

REAL EIGENVALUES

MODE NO.	EXTRACTION ORDER	EIGENVALUE	RADIANS	CYCLES	GENERALIZED MASS	GENERALIZED STIFFNESS
1	4	1.898671E+05	4.357375E+02	6.934977E+01	1.000000E+00	1.898671E+05
2	2	2.271379E+06	1.507109E+03	2.398639E+02	1.000000E+00	2.271379E+06
3	1	8.121678E+06	2.849856E+03	4.535686E+02	1.000000E+00	8.121678E+06
4	3	1.332969E+07	3.650984E+03	5.810721E+02	1.000000E+00	1.332969E+07

EIGENVALUE ANALYSIS SUMMARY   (INVERSE POWER)

NUMBER OF EIGENVALUES EXTRACTED	4
NUMBER OF STARTING POINTS USED	1
NUMBER OF STARTING POINT MOVES	0
NUMBER OF TRIANGULAR DECOMPOSITIONS	4
TOTAL NUMBER OF VECTOR ITERATIONS	35
REASON FOR TERMINATION	3
LARGEST OFF-DIAGONAL MODAL MASS TERM	0.19E-08
MODE PAIR	2
	1
NUMBER OF OFF-DIAGONAL MODAL MASS TERMS FAILING CRITERION	5

```
NO REDUCTION USING INV METHOD                                                    SUBCASE 1
    EIGENVALUE = 1.898671E+05
    CYCLES = 6.934977E+01          R E A L   E I G E N V E C T O R   N O .        1
```

POINT ID.	TYPE		T1		T2		T3		R1		R2		R3
130000	G	0.0		0.0		-1.348317E+01		0.0		0.0		0.0	
130001	G	0.0		0.0		-1.344162E+01		0.0		-1.106092E-01		0.0	
130002	G	0.0		0.0		-1.331724E+01		0.0		-2.205376E-01		0.0	
130003	G	0.0		0.0		-1.311079E+01		0.0		-3.291083E-01		0.0	
130004	G	0.0		0.0		-1.282354E+01		0.0		-4.356531E-01		0.0	
130005	G	0.0		0.0		-1.245725E+01		0.0		-5.395163E-01		0.0	
130006	G	0.0		0.0		-1.201419E+01		0.0		-6.400588E-01		0.0	
130007	G	0.0		0.0		-1.149708E+01		0.0		-7.366619E-01		0.0	
130008	G	0.0		0.0		-1.090910E+01		0.0		-8.287316E-01		0.0	
130009	G	0.0		0.0		-1.025388E+01		0.0		-9.157018E-01		0.0	
130010	G	0.0		0.0		-9.535435E+00		0.0		-9.970381E-01		0.0	
130011	G	0.0		0.0		-8.758193E+00		0.0		-1.072241E+00		0.0	
130012	G	0.0		0.0		-7.926935E+00		0.0		-1.140850E+00		0.0	
130013	G	0.0		0.0		-7.046772E+00		0.0		-1.202444E+00		0.0	

130014	G	0.0	0.0	-6.123114E+00	0.0	-1.256647E+00	0.0
130015	G	0.0	0.0	-5.161637E+00	0.0	-1.303128E+00	0.0
130016	G	0.0	0.0	-4.168252E+00	0.0	-1.341603E+00	0.0
130017	G	0.0	0.0	-3.149059E+00	0.0	-1.371835E+00	0.0
130018	G	0.0	0.0	-2.110325E+00	0.0	-1.393628E+00	0.0
130019	G	0.0	0.0	-1.058454E+00	0.0	-1.406806E+00	0.0
130020	G	0.0	0.0	0.0	0.0	-1.411144E+00	0.0
130100	G	0.0	0.0	-1.344161E+01	1.660924E-01	0.0	0.0
130200	G	0.0	0.0	-1.331721E+01	3.311620E-01	0.0	0.0
130300	G	0.0	0.0	-1.311072E+01	4.941926E-01	0.0	0.0
130400	G	0.0	0.0	-1.282341E+01	6.541801E-01	0.0	0.0
130500	G	0.0	0.0	-1.245706E+01	8.101396E-01	0.0	0.0
130600	G	0.0	0.0	-1.201392E+01	9.611107E-01	0.0	0.0
130700	G	0.0	0.0	-1.149672E+01	1.106164E+00	0.0	0.0
130800	G	0.0	0.0	-1.090864E+01	1.244406E+00	0.0	0.0
130900	G	0.0	0.0	-1.025331E+01	1.374986E+00	0.0	0.0
131000	G	0.0	0.0	-9.534761E+00	1.497100E+00	0.0	0.0
131100	G	0.0	0.0	-8.757414E+00	1.609996E+00	0.0	0.0
131200	G	0.0	0.0	-7.926058E+00	1.712978E+00	0.0	0.0
131300	G	0.0	0.0	-7.045811E+00	1.805412E+00	0.0	0.0
131400	G	0.0	0.0	-6.122095E+00	1.886727E+00	0.0	0.0
131500	G	0.0	0.0	-5.160599E+00	1.956419E+00	0.0	0.0
131600	G	0.0	0.0	-4.167247E+00	2.014055E+00	0.0	0.0
131700	G	0.0	0.0	-3.148163E+00	2.059272E+00	0.0	0.0
131800	G	0.0	0.0	-2.109634E+00	2.091778E+00	0.0	0.0
131900	G	0.0	0.0	-1.058076E+00	2.111348E+00	0.0	0.0
132000	G	0.0	0.0	0.0	2.117826E+00	0.0	0.0

13.9.2c.   Guyan Reduction with Givens Method

The physical problem is the same as the solution using Givens method which is described in Sec. 13.9.2a. but now we will use Guyan Reduction (Sec. 13.6.1.) to reduce the number of degrees of freedom in the solution set — and thereby hopefully reduce the overall solution cost. The difference between the data deck for the solution presented in Sec. 13.9.2a. and the present solution is

- ASET1 Bulk Data is used to define degrees of freedom to be retained in the solution set. We have made a fairly substantial reduction by including only the transverse displacement at every fourth free GRID point which gives us 25 degrees of freedom in the a-set as compared to some 400 degrees of freedom for the case of no reduction.

13.9.2c.1.   Selected Output

The output is shown below where we note that

1. MSC/NASTRAN Execution Summary. The total computational resources required for this solution are 111 I/O seconds annd 312 cpu seconds

```
                    M S C / N A S T R A N    V A X    E X E C U T I O N    S U M M A R Y

DAY TIME   ELAPSED   I/O SEC   CPU SEC   MODULE
21:27:17    0: 0      0.00      0.00     SEM1BEGN
                                                  LOGICAL ASSIGNMENT TABLE
                                                    NAME    FILE-SPEC
                                                    NPTP    _DRB1:[SCHAEFFER]PROB132C.NPT;
                                                    DB01    _DRB1:[SCHAEFFER]PROB132C.D01;
21:27:35    0:18      1.75     12.27     XSOR
21:27:45    0:28      4.25     20.01     IFP
21:27:52    0:35      6.65     24.85     XGPI
21:28:14    0:57      9.20     38.17      24  GP1     BEGN
21:28:17    1: 0     10.55     39.45      26  GP2     BEGN
21:28:18    1: 1     11.15     40.06      42  GP3     BEGN
21:28:18    1: 1     11.20     40.14      43  TA1     BEGN
21:28:28    1:11     16.65     46.03      52  EMG     BEGN
21:29: 0    1:43     21.95     69.42      54  EMA     BEGN
21:30:18    3: 1     32.65    118.18      57  EMA     BEGN
21:30:55    3:38     36.30    135.79      59  EMG     BEGN
21:30:57    3:40     37.25    136.57      66  MTRXIN  BEGN
21:31: 0    3:43     37.75    137.68      95  GP4     BEGN
21:31: 7    3:50     38.80    140.66      96  GPSP1   BEGN
21:31:21    4: 4     43.15    148.86     125  SCE1    BEGN
21:31:54    4:37     50.05    165.63     129  UPARTN  BEGN
21:32:20    5: 3     55.95    177.07     152  DECOMP  BEGN
21:34:13    6:56     68.10    227.81     173  FBS     BEGN
21:35:34    8:17     81.85    263.72     174  MPYAD   BEGN
21:35:38    8:21     84.35    264.88     220  SCE1    BEGN
21:35:46    8:29     85.60    268.81     224  UPARTN  BEGN
21:35:55    8:38     86.80    272.25     243  MPYAD   BEGN
21:36:12    8:55     91.15    278.58     244  MPYAD   BEGN
21:36:13    8:56     91.30    278.70     245  MPYAD   BEGN
```

13.9.2c.1 Selected Output

```
21:36:40      9:23      95.45     290.66    341 MGEN     BEGN
21:36:43      9:26      95.90     291.52    356 LCGEN    BEGN
21:36:44      9:27      96.15     291.81    357 SSG1     BEGN
21:36:47      9:30      96.65     292.31    358 MTRXIN   BEGN
21:36:51      9:34      97.05     293.21    364 DPD      BEGN
21:36:57      9:40      98.10     294.94    384 MATMOD   BEGN
21:36:57      9:40      98.25     295.03    388 MATMOD   BEGN
21:37: 1      9:44      98.75     295.91    416 READ     BEGN
21:37:14      9:57     103.15     299.26    417 OFP      BEGN
21:37:17     10: 0     103.50     300.48    428 VDR      BEGN
21:37:19     10: 2     104.05     301.53    441 CASE     BEGN
21:37:20     10: 3     104.25     301.72    448 SDR1     BEGN
21:37:45     10:28     110.25     310.73    450 SDR2     BEGN
21:37:48     10:31     111.15     311.38    455 OFP      BEGN
21:37:50     10:33     111.30     312.19    510 EXIT     BEGN
```

N A S T R A N   E X E C U T I V E   C O N T R O L   D E C K   E C H O

```
ID PRIMER PROB132C
SOL 3
TIME 10
CEND
```

C A S E   C O N T R O L   D E C K   E C H O

CARD COUNT	
1	TITLE = RECTANGULAR PLATE WITH SIMPLY SUPPORTED EDGES
2	SUBTITLE = SYMMETRIC MODES FOR ONE-QUARTER MODEL
3	LABEL = GUYAN REDUCTION FOLLOWED BY GIV METHOD
4	ECHO = SORT(ASET1,EIGR,PARAM)
5	METHOD = 29
6	SPC = 156
7	SET 1 = 130000,THRU,130020,
8	130100,130200,130300,130400,130500,
9	130600,130700,130800,130900,131000,
10	131100,131200,131300,131400,131500,131600,
11	131700,131800,131900,132000
12	SUBCASE 1
13	VECTOR = 1
14	SUBCASE 2
15	VECTOR = NONE
16	MODES = 3
17	BEGIN BULK

```
                INPUT BULK DATA CARD COUNT =      879
```

S O R T E D   B U L K   D A T A   E C H O

CARD COUNT	1 ..	2 ..	3 ..	4 ..	5 ..	6 ..	7 ..	8 ..	9 ..	10 .
1-	ASET1	3	130000	130004	130008	130012	130016			
2-	ASET1	3	130400	130404	130408	130412	130416			
3-	ASET1	3	130800	130804	130808	130812	130816			
4-	ASET1	3	131200	131204	131208	131212	131216			
5-	ASET1	3	131600	131604	131608	131612	131616			
406-	EIGR	29	GIV			4				+E1
407-	+E1	MASS								
850-	PARAM	AUTOSPC YES								
851-	PARAM	NEWSEQ	-1							
852-	PARAM	PRGPST	NO							
853-	PARAM	WTMASS	.002591							
	ENDDATA									

```
        TOTAL COUNT=    868
```

R E A L   E I G E N V A L U E S

MODE NO.	EXTRACTION ORDER	EIGENVALUE	RADIANS	CYCLES	GENERALIZED MASS	GENERALIZED STIFFNESS
1	21	1.899063E+05	4.357823E+02	6.935691E+01	1.000000E+00	1.899063E+05
2	22	2.277745E+06	1.509220E+03	2.401998E+02	1.000000E+00	2.277745E+06
3	23	8.191082E+06	2.862007E+03	4.555025E+02	1.000000E+00	8.191082E+06
4	25	1.361196E+07	3.689438E+03	5.871924E+02	1.000000E+00	1.361196E+07
5	24	1.550015E+07	3.937022E+03	6.265966E+02	0.0	0.0
6	20	3.804927E+07	6.168409E+03	9.817327E+02	0.0	0.0
7	19	5.206847E+07	7.215849E+03	1.148438E+03	0.0	0.0
8	18	6.255652E+07	7.909268E+03	1.258799E+03	0.0	0.0
9	17	8.203676E+07	9.057415E+03	1.441532E+03	0.0	0.0
10	16	9.761358E+07	9.879959E+03	1.572444E+03	0.0	0.0
11	15	1.324305E+08	1.150784E+04	1.831530E+03	0.0	0.0
12	14	1.561602E+08	1.249641E+04	1.988865E+03	0.0	0.0
13	13	2.290798E+08	1.513538E+04	2.408871E+03	0.0	0.0

14	12	2.431240E+08	1.559243E+04	2.481613E+03	0.0	0.0
15	11	2.755805E+08	1.660062E+04	2.642071E+03	0.0	0.0
16	10	3.227938E+08	1.796646E+04	2.859451E+03	0.0	0.0
17	9	4.240285E+08	2.059195E+04	3.277311E+03	0.0	0.0
18	8	4.341260E+08	2.083569E+04	3.316103E+03	0.0	0.0
19	7	6.353108E+08	2.520537E+04	4.011560E+03	0.0	0.0
20	6	8.704413E+08	2.950324E+04	4.695587E+03	0.0	0.0
21	5	9.188998E+08	3.031336E+04	4.824521E+03	0.0	0.0
22	4	1.006213E+09	3.172086E+04	5.048532E+03	0.0	0.0
23	3	1.186587E+09	3.444688E+04	5.482390E+03	0.0	0.0
24	2	1.442294E+09	3.797754E+04	6.044313E+03	0.0	0.0
25	1	1.662283E+09	4.077110E+04	6.488922E+03	0.0	0.0

```
GUYAN REDUCTION FOLLOWED BY GIV METHOD                                              SUBCASE 1
EIGENVALUE =  1.899063E+05
      CYCLES =  6.935691E+01          R E A L   E I G E N V E C T O R   N O .          1

POINT ID.    TYPE         T1              T2              T3            R1              R2            R3
 130000       G        0.0             0.0          1.348595E+01     0.0           0.0             0.0
 130001       G        0.0             0.0          1.344191E+01     0.0        1.153030E-01       0.0
 130002       G        0.0             0.0          1.331554E+01     0.0        2.206129E-01       0.0
 130003       G        0.0             0.0          1.311095E+01     0.0        3.245746E-01       0.0
 130004       G        0.0             0.0          1.282619E+01     0.0        4.354666E-01       0.0
 130005       G        0.0             0.0          1.245764E+01     0.0        5.439106E-01       0.0
 130006       G        0.0             0.0          1.201266E+01     0.0        6.402772E-01       0.0
 130007       G        0.0             0.0          1.149711E+01     0.0        7.327313E-01       0.0
 130008       G        0.0             0.0          1.091136E+01     0.0        8.283762E-01       0.0
 130009       G        0.0             0.0          1.025432E+01     0.0        9.193662E-01       0.0
 130010       G        0.0             0.0          9.534217E+00     0.0        9.973778E-01       0.0
 130011       G        0.0             0.0          8.758076E+00     0.0        1.069298E+00       0.0
 130012       G        0.0             0.0          7.928573E+00     0.0        1.140360E+00       0.0
 130013       G        0.0             0.0          7.047228E+00     0.0        1.205020E+00       0.0
 130014       G        0.0             0.0          6.122332E+00     0.0        1.257075E+00       0.0
 130015       G        0.0             0.0          5.161390E+00     0.0        1.301461E+00       0.0
 130016       G        0.0             0.0          4.169114E+00     0.0        1.341027E+00       0.0
 130017       G        0.0             0.0          3.149486E+00     0.0        1.373071E+00       0.0
 130018       G        0.0             0.0          2.110056E+00     0.0        1.394103E+00       0.0
 130019       G        0.0             0.0          1.058100E+00     0.0        1.406579E+00       0.0
 130020       G        0.0             0.0          0.0              0.0        1.410540E+00       0.0
 130100       G        0.0             0.0          1.344352E+01  -1.687299E-01    0.0             0.0
 130200       G        0.0             0.0          1.331838E+01  -3.312468E-01    0.0             0.0
 130300       G        0.0             0.0          1.311253E+01  -4.917299E-01    0.0             0.0
 130400       G        0.0             0.0          1.282606E+01  -6.541741E-01    0.0             0.0
 130500       G        0.0             0.0          1.245886E+01  -8.126932E-01    0.0             0.0
 130600       G        0.0             0.0          1.201497E+01  -9.613553E-01    0.0             0.0
 130700       G        0.0             0.0          1.149826E+01  -1.104115E+00    0.0             0.0
 130800       G        0.0             0.0          1.091089E+01  -1.244392E+00    0.0             0.0
 130900       G        0.0             0.0          1.025483E+01  -1.377203E+00    0.0             0.0
 131000       G        0.0             0.0          9.535586E+00  -1.497477E+00    0.0             0.0
 131100       G        0.0             0.0          8.758535E+00  -1.608559E+00    0.0             0.0
 131200       G        0.0             0.0          7.927682E+00  -1.712956E+00    0.0             0.0
 131300       G        0.0             0.0          7.046899E+00  -1.807075E+00    0.0             0.0
 131400       G        0.0             0.0          6.122617E+00  -1.887199E+00    0.0             0.0
 131500       G        0.0             0.0          5.161192E+00  -1.955731E+00    0.0             0.0
 131600       G        0.0             0.0          4.168098E+00  -2.014019E+00    0.0             0.0
 131700       G        0.0             0.0          3.148729E+00  -2.060205E+00    0.0             0.0
 131800       G        0.0             0.0          2.109822E+00  -2.092289E+00    0.0             0.0
 131900       G        0.0             0.0          1.058101E+00  -2.111485E+00    0.0             0.0
 132000       G        0.0             0.0          0.0           -2.117822E+00    0.0             0.0
```

13.9.2d. Generalized Dynamic Reduction With Givens Method

The last problem in this series is exactly the same as the problem presented in Sec. 13.9.2a. but now we will investigate the use of Generalized Dynamic Reduction as a means of reducing solution costs. The input data is exactly the same as that presented in Sec. 13.9.2c. except

- Sixteen generalized degrees of freedom are defined by SPOINT Bulk Data

- These degrees of freedom are included in the a- and q-sets by means of ASET1 and QSET1 Bulk Data

- Generalized dynamic reduction is defined by DYNRED Bulk Data where the sixteen degrees of freedom are all included in the reduced set by setting the QDOF field equal to sixteen.

13.9.2d.1.   Selected Output

The output data for this example is shown below where we note

1. MSC/NASTRAN Execution Summary — The total compute resources required for this example is 405 I/O seconds and 535 cpu seconds.

```
              M S C / N A S T R A N   V A X   E X E C U T I O N   S U M M A R Y

DAY TIME  ELAPSED  I/O SEC  CPU SEC   MODULE
21:29:45    0: 0    0.00     0.00     SEM1BEGN
                                               LOGICAL ASSIGNMENT TABLE
                                                 NAME    FILE-SPEC
                                                 NPTP    _DRB1:[SCHAEFFER]PROB132D.NPT;
                                                 DB01    _DRB1:[SCHAEFFER]PROB132D.D01;

21:30:27    0:42    1.75    12.45     XSOR
21:30:47    1: 2    4.25    20.32     IFP
21:30:59    1:14    6.75    25.29     XGPI
21:31:42    1:57    9.30    38.76      24 GP1      BEGN
21:31:48    2: 3   11.00    40.12      26 GP2      BEGN
21:31:50    2: 5   11.60    40.82      42 GP3      BEGN
21:31:51    2: 6   11.65    40.92      43 TA1      BEGN
21:32: 8    2:23   17.10    46.92      52 EMG      BEGN
21:33: 3    3:18   22.40    70.88      54 EMA      BEGN
21:34:59    5:14   33.30   119.88      57 EMA      BEGN
21:35:39    5:54   37.15   137.35      59 EMG      BEGN
21:35:42    5:57   38.10   138.11      66 MTRXIN   BEGN
21:35:45    6: 0   38.60   139.21      95 GP4      BEGN
21:35:52    6: 7   39.65   142.38      96 GPSP1    BEGN
21:36: 8    6:23   44.00   150.65     125 SCE1     BEGN
21:36:59    7:14   50.90   167.52     129 UPARTN   BEGN
21:37:33    7:48   57.05   180.08     220 SCE1     BEGN
21:37:43    7:58   58.30   183.96     224 UPARTN   BEGN
21:37:51    8: 6   59.60   187.40     243 MPYAD    BEGN
21:37:52    8: 7   59.65   187.44     244 MPYAD    BEGN
21:37:52    8: 7   59.70   187.47     245 MPYAD    BEGN
21:37:52    8: 7   59.75   187.55     280 DYCNTRL  BEGN
21:37:53    8: 8   59.90   187.61     282 ADD      BEGN
21:38:20    8:35   65.40   202.34     283 DECOMP   BEGN
21:39:33    9:48   77.85   256.43     302 DYNREDU  BEGN
21:46: 1   16:16  372.50   483.92     302 DYNREDU  END
21:46: 2   16:17  372.55   484.06     303 MATGPR   BEGN
21:46: 2   16:17  372.60   484.10     306 MATGEN   BEGN
21:46: 3   16:18  372.75   484.20     325 MATGEN   BEGN
21:46: 3   16:18  372.85   484.27     326 ADD      BEGN
21:46:13   16:28  376.25   490.10     327 SMPYAD   BEGN
21:46:33   16:48  384.75   505.54     328 DIAGONAL BEGN
21:46:33   16:48  384.90   505.67     329 ADD      BEGN
21:46:34   16:49  385.05   505.75     330 MATGPR   BEGN
21:46:34   16:49  385.10   505.78     331 MPYAD    BEGN
21:46:34   16:49  385.15   505.82     332 TRNSP    BEGN
21:46:34   16:49  385.20   505.89     333 SMPYAD   BEGN
21:46:48   17: 3  390.70   516.42     341 MGEN     BEGN
21:46:50   17: 5  391.15   517.34     356 LCGEN    BEGN
21:46:50   17: 5  391.40   517.62     357 SSG1     BEGN
21:46:52   17: 7  391.90   518.11     358 MTRXIN   BEGN
21:46:53   17: 8  392.30   519.07     364 DPD      BEGN
21:46:58   17:13  393.35   520.86     384 MATMOD   BEGN
21:46:58   17:13  393.50   520.94     388 MATMOD   BEGN
21:46:59   17:14  393.95   521.78     416 READ     BEGN
21:47: 9   17:24  397.75   524.16     417 OFP      BEGN
21:47:10   17:25  397.90   524.73     428 VDR      BEGN
21:47:10   17:25  398.45   525.10     441 CASE     BEGN
21:47:11   17:26  398.65   525.31     448 SDR1     BEGN
21:47:26   17:41  404.10   534.07     450 SDR2     BEGN
21:47:28   17:43  405.00   534.68     455 OFP      BEGN
21:47:29   17:44  405.15   535.51     510 EXIT     BEGN


     N A S T R A N   E X E C U T I V E   C O N T R O L   D E C K   E C H O


ID PRIMER PROB132D
SOL 3
TIME 100
CEND
```

```
                              C A S E    C O N T R O L    D E C K    E C H O
            CARD
            COUNT
             1        TITLE = RECTANGULAR PLATE WITH SIMPLY SUPPORTED EDGES
             2        SUBTITLE = SYMMETRIC MODES FOR ONE-QUARTER MODEL
             3        LABEL = GENERALIZED DYNAMIC REDUCTION FOLLOWED BY GIV METHOD
             4        METHOD = 29
             5        ECHO=SORT(ASET1,QSET1,DYNRED,EIGR,PARAM,SPOINT)
             6        DYNRED = 27
             7        SPC = 156
             8        SET 1 = 130000 THRU 130020,
             9              130100,130200,130300,130400,130500,130600,130700,
            10              130800,130900,131000,131100,131200,131300,131400,
            11              131500,131600,131700,131800,131900,132000
            12        SUBCASE 1
            13        VECTOR = 1
            14        SUBCASE 2
            15        VECTOR = NONE
            16        MODES = 3
            17        BEGIN BULK

                    INPUT BULK DATA CARD COUNT =      878


                          S O R T E D    B U L K    D A T A    E C H O
            CARD
            COUNT       .   1  ..   2  ..   3  ..   4  ..   5  ..   6  ..   7  ..   8  ..   9  ..  10  .
             1-      ASET1          1001     THRU      1016
            402-     DYNRED    27    50.                                16
            403-     EIGR      29    GIV                                4                      +E1
            404-     +E1       MASS
            847-     PARAM     AUTOSPC  YES
            848-     PARAM     NEWSEQ   -1
            849-     PARAM     PRGPST   NO
            850-     PARAM     WTMASS   .002591
            852-     QSET1          1001     THRU      1016
            866-     SPOINT    1001     THRU      1016
                     ENDDATA

                    TOTAL COUNT=     867
```

```
                                  R E A L    E I G E N V A L U E S
 MODE    EXTRACTION       EIGENVALUE          RADIANS           CYCLES         GENERALIZED      GENERALIZED
 NO.      ORDER                                                                   MASS          STIFFNESS
   1        1           1.898671E+05       4.357375E+02      6.934977E+01      1.000000E+00     1.898671E+05
   2       10           2.271379E+06       1.507109E+03      2.398639E+02      1.000000E+00     2.271379E+06
   3       13           8.121678E+06       2.849856E+03      4.535686E+02      1.000000E+00     8.121678E+06
   4       14           1.332969E+07       3.650984E+03      5.810721E+02      1.000000E+00     1.332969E+07
   5       15           1.522782E+07       3.902284E+03      6.210677E+02      0.0              0.0
   6       16           3.615618E+07       6.013001E+03      9.569988E+02      0.0              0.0
   7       12           4.717053E+07       6.868081E+03      1.093089E+03      0.0              0.0
   8       11           5.899722E+07       7.680965E+03      1.222464E+03      0.0              0.0
   9        9           7.618789E+07       8.728567E+03      1.389195E+03      0.0              0.0
  10        8           8.471827E+07       9.204253E+03      1.464902E+03      0.0              0.0
  11        7           1.230638E+08       1.109341E+04      1.765571E+03      0.0              0.0
  12        6           1.769827E+08       1.330348E+04      2.117315E+03      0.0              0.0
  13        5           2.210487E+08       1.486771E+04      2.366269E+03      0.0              0.0
  14        4           1.894732E+09       4.352852E+04      6.927779E+03      0.0              0.0
  15        3           3.868097E+10       1.966748E+05      3.130177E+04      0.0              0.0
  16        2           4.965930E+10       2.228437E+05      3.546667E+04      0.0              0.0
```

```
 GENERALIZED DYNAMIC REDUCTION FOLLOWED BY GIV METHOD                                     SUBCASE 1
 EIGENVALUE =   1.898671E+05
      CYCLES =   6.934977E+01         R E A L    E I G E N V E C T O R    N O .        1

 POINT ID.   TYPE       T1             T2             T3            R1             R2             R3
  130000     G       0.0            0.0           1.348318E+01    0.0           0.0            0.0
  130001     G       0.0            0.0           1.344163E+01    0.0           1.106094E-01   0.0
  130002     G       0.0            0.0           1.331725E+01    0.0           2.205379E-01   0.0
  130003     G       0.0            0.0           1.311080E+01    0.0           3.291087E-01   0.0
  130004     G       0.0            0.0           1.282354E+01    0.0           4.356537E-01   0.0
  130005     G       0.0            0.0           1.245726E+01    0.0           5.395169E-01   0.0
  130006     G       0.0            0.0           1.201420E+01    0.0           6.400594E-01   0.0
  130007     G       0.0            0.0           1.149709E+01    0.0           7.366625E-01   0.0
  130008     G       0.0            0.0           1.090911E+01    0.0           8.287321E-01   0.0
  130009     G       0.0            0.0           1.025388E+01    0.0           9.157022E-01   0.0
  130010     G       0.0            0.0           9.535440E+00    0.0           9.970385E-01   0.0
  130011     G       0.0            0.0           8.758199E+00    0.0           1.072242E+00   0.0
  130012     G       0.0            0.0           7.926940E+00    0.0           1.140850E+00   0.0
  130013     G       0.0            0.0           7.046776E+00    0.0           1.202445E+00   0.0
  130014     G       0.0            0.0           6.123117E+00    0.0           1.256647E+00   0.0
  130015     G       0.0            0.0           5.161642E+00    0.0           1.303128E+00   0.0
  130016     G       0.0            0.0           4.168255E+00    0.0           1.341604E+00   0.0
  130017     G       0.0            0.0           3.149062E+00    0.0           1.371836E+00   0.0
  130018     G       0.0            0.0           2.110327E+00    0.0           1.393629E+00   0.0
  130019     G       0.0            0.0           1.058455E+00    0.0           1.406807E+00   0.0
  130020     G       0.0            0.0           0.0             0.0           1.411145E+00   0.0
```

130100	G	0.0	0.0	1.344162E+01	-1.660934E-01	0.0	0.0
130200	G	0.0	0.0	1.331722E+01	-3.311639E-01	0.0	0.0
130300	G	0.0	0.0	1.311072E+01	-4.941953E-01	0.0	0.0
130400	G	0.0	0.0	1.282342E+01	-6.541835E-01	0.0	0.0
130500	G	0.0	0.0	1.245707E+01	-8.101434E-01	0.0	0.0
130600	G	0.0	0.0	1.201392E+01	-9.611148E-01	0.0	0.0
130700	G	0.0	0.0	1.149672E+01	-1.106168E+00	0.0	0.0
130800	G	0.0	0.0	1.090864E+01	-1.244410E+00	0.0	0.0
130900	G	0.0	0.0	1.025331E+01	-1.374990E+00	0.0	0.0
131000	G	0.0	0.0	9.534757E+00	-1.497103E+00	0.0	0.0
131100	G	0.0	0.0	8.757407E+00	-1.609998E+00	0.0	0.0
131200	G	0.0	0.0	7.926050E+00	-1.712980E+00	0.0	0.0
131300	G	0.0	0.0	7.045803E+00	-1.805412E+00	0.0	0.0
131400	G	0.0	0.0	6.122086E+00	-1.886726E+00	0.0	0.0
131500	G	0.0	0.0	5.160591E+00	-1.956418E+00	0.0	0.0
131600	G	0.0	0.0	4.167240E+00	-2.014053E+00	0.0	0.0
131700	G	0.0	0.0	3.148158E+00	-2.059269E+00	0.0	0.0
131800	G	0.0	0.0	2.109630E+00	-2.091774E+00	0.0	0.0
131900	G	0.0	0.0	1.058074E+00	-2.111345E+00	0.0	0.0
132000	G	0.0	0.0	0.0	-2.117823E+00	0.0	0.0

13.9.2.2.   Comparison of Solution Times

The physical problem which we considered for all four examples is exactly the same, we only modified the way that we solved it. The computer resources required for the various methods is presented by Table 13-1.

Method	IO	Cpu
Givens, No Reduction	1166	1880
Inverse, No Reduction	581	664
Givens, Guyan	111	312
Givens, GDR	405	535

Table 13-1. Comparison of Computer Resources for Several Eigenvalue Extraction Strategies

The results of this study indicate that

1. Givens method should never be used for large problems without some sort of reduction

2. Inverse power should be used to extract only a very few modes and frequencies (one or two)

3. Guyan reduction requires the least computational resources but is least accurate

4. Generalized Dynamic Reduction is less expensive than Givens with no reduction however it is significantly more costly than Guyan reduction

13.9.3.   Stiffened Plate Using Restart

Our final example is the calculation of normal modes and frequencies of the checkpointed static solution for the stiffened plate which was described in SEC. 12.8.2b. The data deck for restarted solution, which is shown below, consists of

1. An executive control deck which

   • Requests solution 3

   • Incorporates the restart directory from Section 12.8.2b.

2. A Case Control Deck which

- Requests an eigenvalue method

- Makes other input and output requests as appropriate

3. A Bulk Data Deck which

- Includes only changes to the checkpointed run

Card	1	2	3	4	5	6	7	8	9	10
1-	ID PRIMER, PROB133									
2-	SOL 3									
3-	TIME 4									
4-	READ 10 $ MERGES CHECKPOINT DIRECTORY									
5-	CEND									
6-	TITLE = SQUARE SIMPLY SUPPORTED PLATE WITH STIFFENER									
7-	SUBTITLE = NORMAL MODES SOLUTION USING MGIV									
8-	LABEL = RESTART FROM RF24									
9-	SPC = 124									
10-	METHOD = 101									
11-	DISP = ALL									
12-	BEGIN NORMAL MODES									
13-	EIGR	101	MGIV	0.	50.	1	1			+ E1
14-	+ E1	MASS								
15-	PARAM	WTMASS	.002591							
16-	ENDDATA									

The NASTRAN data deck is described, with reference to the card numbers, as follows

Card 4- A machine dependent command that merges the checkpoint directory into the Executive Control Deck. Machine Job Control Cards may be required to assign and catalog the file on the system

Card 13- Requests MGIV method with one eigenvector
Card 14-

13.9.3.1. Selected Output

The output data for this problem is listed below where we note

1. NASTRAN Executive Control Deck — Lists the entire contents of the restart directory. There are two types of entries, a file description such as 1, and a REENTER such as 2,. The file description defines the data block name (XVPS) as the 6th file on the Old Problem Tape (OPTP). The REENTER statement tells NASTRAN to reenter at DMAP Statement 10 using files defined after the REENTER statement (i.e., GPL, EQEXIN, etc.) to be read from the OPTP. (Not all of the directory entries are included here)

2. Sorted Bulk Data — The EIGR card in the present Bulk Data deck is merged with the Sorted Bulk Data on the OPTP to form the entire Bulk Data deck

3. List of Modified Cards — Describes cards which have been modified or added

13.9.3.1 Selected Output

4. **TO REGENERATE** . . . Describes the modules which must be executed to perform the restart

5. **VAXW** — Partitioning vector to condense out massless degrees of freedom

```
        N A S T R A N   E X E C U T I V E   C O N T R O L   D E C K   E C H O


ID PRIMER PROB133
SOL 3 $ NORMAL MODES
TIME 4
READ 10 $MERGE IN CHECKPOINT DIRECTORY
RESTART  PRIMER  ,PROB122B, 7/25/81,    46371,
        1,   XVPS   ,   FLAGS = 0,   REEL =  1,   FILE =      6
        2,   REENTER AT DMAP SEQUENCE NUMBER    10
        3,   GPL    ,   FLAGS = 0,   REEL =  1,   FILE =      7
        4,   EQEXIN ,   FLAGS = 0,   REEL =  1,   FILE =      8
        5,   GPDT   ,   FLAGS = 0,   REEL =  1,   FILE =      9
        6,   CSTM   ,   FLAGS = 0,   REEL =  1,   FILE =     10
        7,   BGPDT  ,   FLAGS = 0,   REEL =  1,   FILE =     11
        8,   SIL    ,   FLAGS = 0,   REEL =  1,   FILE =     12
        9,   XVPS   ,   FLAGS = 0,   REEL =  1,   FILE =     13
       10,   REENTER AT DMAP SEQUENCE NUMBER    12
       11,   ECT    ,   FLAGS = 0,   REEL =  1,   FILE =     14
       12,   XVPS   ,   FLAGS = 0,   REEL =  1,   FILE =     15
        :
        :
      127,   REENTER AT DMAP SEQUENCE NUMBER   161
      128,   UGV    ,   FLAGS = 0,   REEL =  1,   FILE =     64
      129,   PGG    ,   FLAGS = 0,   REEL =  1,   FILE =     65
      130,   QG     ,   FLAGS = 0,   REEL =  1,   FILE =     66
      131,   XVPS   ,   FLAGS = 0,   REEL =  1,   FILE =     67
      132,   REENTER AT DMAP SEQUENCE NUMBER   169
      133,   CSTM   ,   FLAGS = 0,   REEL =  1,   FILE =     68
      134,   XVPS   ,   FLAGS = 0,   REEL =  1,   FILE =     69
$ END OF CHECKPOINT DICTIONARY
CEND

*** SWITCHED SOLUTION FOR RESTART - OLD SOLUTION = 24, NEW SOLUTION = 3, BIT NUMBER = 86


                    C A S E   C O N T R O L   D E C K   E C H O
  CARD
  COUNT
    1       TITLE = SQUARE SIMPLY SUPPORTED PLATE WITH STIFFENER
    2       SUBTITLE = NORMAL MODES SOLUTION USING MGIV METHOD
    3       LABEL = RESTART FROM STATIC SOL RF 24
    4       SPC = 124
    5       METHOD = 101
    6           DISP = ALL
    7       BEGIN NORMAL MODES SOLUTION

          INPUT BULK DATA CARD COUNT =        4


                    S O R T E D   B U L K   D A T A   E C H O
  CARD
  COUNT     .   1  ..   2  ..   3  ..   4  ..   5  ..   6  ..   7  ..   8  ..   9  ..  10  .
    1-      CBEAM    101     30     20000    20001    0.0      0.0      1.                 +M00000
    2-      +M00000                          0.0      .7       0.0      0.0      .7
    3-      CBEAM    102     30     20001    20002    0.0      0.0      1.                 +M00001
    4-      +M00001                          0.0      .7       0.0      0.0      .7
    5-      CBEAM    103     30     20002    20003    0.0      0.0      1.                 +M00002
    6-      +M00002                          0.0      .7       0.0      0.0      .7
    7-      CBEAM    104     30     20003    20004    0.0      0.0      1.                 +M00003
    8-      +M00003                          0.0      .7       0.0      0.0      .7
    9-      CBEAM    105     30     20000    20100    0.0      0.0      1.                 +M00004
   10-      +M00004                          0.0      .7       0.0      0.0      .7
   11-      CBEAM    106     30     20100    20200    0.0      0.0      1.                 +M00005
   12-      +M00005                          0.0      .7       0.0      0.0      .7
   13-      CBEAM    107     30     20200    20300    0.0      0.0      1.                 +M00006
   14-      +M00006                          0.0      .7       0.0      0.0      .7
   15-      CBEAM    108     30     20300    20400    0.0      0.0      1.                 +M00007
   16-      +M00007                          0.0      .7       0.0      0.0      .7
   17-      CORD2R   101      0     0.       0.       0.       0.       0.       1.        +CD1
   18-      +CD1     1.       0.    0.
   19-      CQUAD4   1       12     20000    20001    20101    20100
   20-      CQUAD4   2       12     20001    20002    20102    20101
   21-      CQUAD4   3       12     20002    20003    20103    20102
   22-      CQUAD4   4       12     20003    20004    20104    20103
   23-      CQUAD4   5       12     20100    20101    20201    20200
   24-      CQUAD4   6       12     20101    20102    20202    20201
   25-      CQUAD4   7       12     20102    20103    20203    20202
   26-      CQUAD4   8       12     20103    20104    20204    20203
   27-      CQUAD4   9       12     20200    20201    20301    20300
   28-      CQUAD4   10      12     20201    20202    20302    20301
   29-      CQUAD4   11      12     20202    20203    20303    20302
   30-      CQUAD4   12      12     20203    20204    20304    20303
   31-      CQUAD4   13      12     20300    20301    20401    20400
   32-      CQUAD4   14      12     20301    20302    20402    20401
   33-      CQUAD4   15      12     20302    20303    20403    20402
   34-      CQUAD4   16      12     20303    20304    20404    20403
   35-      EIGR     101     MGIV   0.       50.      1        1                          +E1
   36-      +E1      MASS
   37-      GRDSET                                                     6
```

38-	GRID	20000	0	0.0	0.0	0.0	0
39-	GRID	20001	0	3.75	0.0	0.0	0
40-	GRID	20002	0	7.5	0.0	0.0	0
41-	GRID	20003	0	11.25	0.0	0.0	0
42-	GRID	20004	0	15.	0.0	0.0	0
43-	GRID	20100	0	0.0	3.75	0.0	0
44-	GRID	20101	0	3.75	3.75	0.0	0
45-	GRID	20102	0	7.5	3.75	0.0	0
46-	GRID	20103	0	11.25	3.75	0.0	0
47-	GRID	20104	0	15.	3.75	0.0	0
48-	GRID	20200	0	0.0	7.5	0.0	0
49-	GRID	20201	0	3.75	7.5	0.0	0
50-	GRID	20202	0	7.5	7.5	0.0	0
51-	GRID	20203	0	11.25	7.5	0.0	0
52-	GRID	20204	0	15.	7.5	0.0	0
53-	GRID	20300	0	0.0	11.25	0.0	0
54-	GRID	20301	0	3.75	11.25	0.0	0
55-	GRID	20302	0	7.5	11.25	0.0	0
56-	GRID	20303	0	11.25	11.25	0.0	0
57-	GRID	20304	0	15.	11.25	0.0	0
58-	GRID	20400	0	0.0	15.	0.0	0
59-	GRID	20401	0	3.75	15.	0.0	0
60-	GRID	20402	0	7.5	15.	0.0	0
61-	GRID	20403	0	11.25	15.	0.0	0
62-	GRID	20404	0	15.	15.	0.0	0

```
63-      MAT1      10      10.+6             .3                                      +M1
64-      +M1       50.+3   50.+3   25.+3    101
65-      PARAM     S1AG    1
66-      PARAM     S1G     1
67-      PARAM     USETSEL 1746
68-      PARAM     WTMASS  .00259
69-      PBEAM     30      10      .25      .02085   .00521                  .4      +PB1
70-      +PB1      0.      .5      0.       -.5                                      +PB2
71-      +PB2      YESA    1.                                                        +PB3
72-      +PB3      0.      0.
73-      PLOAD2    51      1.5     1        THRU     16                      .25
74-      PSHELL    12      10      .4       10
75-      SPC1      1241    156     20000    20100    20200    20300    20400
76-      SPC1      1242    246     20000    20001    20002    20003    20004
77-      SPC1      1243    35      20400    20401    20402    20403    20404
78-      SPC1      1244    34      20004    20104    20204    20304    20404
79-      SPCADD    124     1241    1242     1243     1244
         ENDDATA

         TOTAL COUNT=    80
```

LIST OF MODIFIED CARDS

MASK WORD - BIT POSITION - CARD NAME - PACKED BIT POSITION

```
   1
   2
   3
                23       EIGR             57

   4
   5
   6
   7
   8
   9
  10
  11
  12
                23       WTMASS            5

  13
  14
                 3       LOAD$            59
                 4       METHOD$          58
                17       POUT$            19
                31       NOLOOP$

  15
```

TO REGENERATE DATA BLOCK NAMED VAQT   - EXECUTE THE FOLLOWING DMAP INSTRUCTIONS
```
128  COND
129  UPARTN
130  XEQUIV
131  COND
132  XEQUIV
133  SETVAL
134  COND
135  VEC
136  PARTN
137  UPARTN
138  PARAML
140  PARAM
141  PARAML
142  PARAM
143  PARAML
144  PARAM
145  PARAM
146  SETVAL
147  COND
```

TO REGENERATE DATA BLOCK NAMED KTT   - EXECUTE THE FOLLOWING DMAP INSTRUCTIONS
```
127  XEQUIV
149  PARAML
150  XEQUIV
151  COND
174  MPYAD
```

13.10 References

```
                VAXW
       POINT        VALUE       POINT        VALUE       POINT        VALUE       POINT        VALUE       POINT        VALUE

COLUMN      1
       20101 R1  1.00000E+00    20101 R2  1.00000E+00    20102 R1  1.00000E+00    20102 R2  1.00000E+00    20103 R1  1.00000E+00
       20103 R2  1.00000E+00    20104 R2  1.00000E+00    20201 R1  1.00000E+00    20201 R2  1.00000E+00    20202 R1  1.00000E+00
       20202 R2  1.00000E+00    20203 R1  1.00000E+00    20203 R2  1.00000E+00    20204 R2  1.00000E+00    20301 R1  1.00000E+00
       20301 R2  1.00000E+00    20302 R1  1.00000E+00    20302 R2  1.00000E+00    20303 R1  1.00000E+00    20303 R2  1.00000E+00
       20304 R2  1.00000E+00    20401 R1  1.00000E+00    20402 R1  1.00000E+00    20403 R1  1.00000E+00
```

```
                                  REAL  EIGENVALUES
MODE    EXTRACTION      EIGENVALUE              RADIANS          CYCLES            GENERALIZED         GENERALIZED
NO.      ORDER                                                                       MASS              STIFFNESS
  1         1          7.361953E+04           2.713292E+02     4.318338E+01        1.000000E+00        7.361953E+04
  2         2          1.360244E+06           1.166295E+03     1.856216E+02        0.0                 0.0
  3         3          1.877518E+06           1.370226E+03     2.180782E+02        0.0                 0.0
  4         4          4.771977E+06           2.184485E+03     3.476716E+02        0.0                 0.0
  5         5          7.939844E+06           2.817773E+03     4.484624E+02        0.0                 0.0
  6         7          8.018627E+06           2.831718E+03     4.506819E+02        0.0                 0.0
  7         6          1.414806E+07           3.761391E+03     5.986439E+02        0.0                 0.0
  8        10          1.701749E+07           4.125226E+03     6.565501E+02        0.0                 0.0
  9        11          2.407014E+07           4.906132E+03     7.808352E+02        0.0                 0.0
 10         8          2.431145E+07           4.930665E+03     7.847396E+02        0.0                 0.0
 11         9          3.103711E+07           5.571096E+03     8.866675E+02        0.0                 0.0
 12        16          4.522216E+07           6.724743E+03     1.070276E+03        0.0                 0.0
 13        15          4.768716E+07           6.905589E+03     1.099059E+03        0.0                 0.0
 14        12          4.843974E+07           6.959867E+03     1.107697E+03        0.0                 0.0
 15        19          6.077880E+07           7.796076E+03     1.240784E+03        0.0                 0.0
 16        20          7.990788E+07           8.939121E+03     1.422705E+03        0.0                 0.0
  .
  .
  .
 60        32          1.808157E+09           4.252243E+04     6.767655E+03        0.0                 0.0
 61        58          1.837740E+09           4.286887E+04     6.822792E+03        0.0                 0.0
 62        29          1.867768E+09           4.321768E+04     6.878308E+03        0.0                 0.0
 63        57          1.903810E+09           4.363267E+04     6.944355E+03        0.0                 0.0
 64        28          1.924959E+09           4.387436E+04     6.982820E+03        0.0                 0.0
```

```
RESTART FROM STATIC SOL RF 24
EIGENVALUE =  7.361953E+04
    CYCLES =  4.318338E+01        REAL  EIGENVECTOR  NO.          1

POINT ID.  TYPE       T1              T2              T3              R1              R2              R3
 20000      G      0.0             0.0             4.322013E+00    0.0             0.0             0.0
 20001      G     -7.699554E-03    0.0             4.010321E+00    0.0             1.631044E-01    0.0
 20002      G     -1.705079E-02    0.0             3.089581E+00    0.0             3.085255E-01    0.0
 20003      G     -2.504887E-02    0.0             1.680275E+00    0.0             4.101799E-01    0.0
 20004      G     -2.717401E-02    0.0             0.0             0.0             4.455396E-01    0.0
 20100      G      0.0            -7.699554E-03    4.010321E+00   -1.631044E-01    0.0             0.0
 20101      G     -2.775918E-03   -2.775918E-03    3.736145E+00   -1.463232E-01    1.463232E-01    0.0
 20102      G     -7.120501E-03   -2.963328E-04    2.893574E+00   -1.065361E-01    2.898314E-01    0.0
 20103      G     -1.070301E-02   -1.437557E-04    1.577873E+00   -5.624472E-02    3.890291E-01    0.0
 20104      G     -1.166108E-02   -6.446684E-03    0.0             0.0             4.244479E-01    0.0
 20200      G      0.0            -1.705079E-02    3.089581E+00   -3.085255E-01    0.0             0.0
 20201      G     -2.963328E-04   -7.120501E-03    2.893574E+00   -2.898314E-01    1.065361E-01    0.0
 20202      G     -2.098761E-03   -2.098761E-03    2.259234E+00   -2.234742E-01    2.234742E-01    0.0
 20203      G     -3.442198E-03   -1.681728E-03    1.237802E+00   -1.211268E-01    3.059662E-01    0.0
 20204      G     -4.136870E-03   -4.969796E-03    0.0             0.0             3.352392E-01    0.0
 20300      G      0.0            -2.504887E-02    1.680275E+00   -4.101799E-01    0.0             0.0
 20301      G     -1.437557E-04   -1.070301E-02    1.577873E+00   -3.890291E-01    5.624472E-02    0.0
 20302      G     -1.681728E-03   -3.442198E-03    1.237802E+00   -3.059662E-01    1.211268E-01    0.0
 20303      G     -2.249402E-03   -2.249402E-03    6.806228E-01   -1.682019E-01    1.682019E-01    0.0
 20304      G     -2.476112E-03   -3.120863E-03    0.0             0.0             1.850154E-01    0.0
 20400      G      0.0            -2.717401E-02    0.0            -4.455396E-01    0.0             0.0
 20401      G     -6.446684E-03   -1.166108E-02    0.0            -4.244479E-01    0.0             0.0
 20402      G     -4.969796E-03   -4.136870E-03    0.0            -3.352392E-01    0.0             0.0
 20403      G     -3.120863E-03   -2.476112E-03    0.0            -1.850154E-01    0.0             0.0
 20404      G     -2.572245E-03   -2.572245E-03    0.0             0.0             0.0             0.0
```

13.10. References

13-1 Bathe, K.-J., and Wilson, E.L., *Numerical Methods in Finite Element Analysis*, Englewood Cliffs, N. J., Prentice-Hall, 1976.

13-2 Hurty, W. C., and Rubinstein, M.K., *Dynamics of Structures*, Englewood Cliffs, N. J., Prentice-Hall, 1964.

13-3 Przemieniecki, J.S., *Theory of Matrix Structural Analysis*, New York, McGraw-Hill, 1968.

13-4 Meirovitch, L., *Elements of Vibration Analysis*, New York, McGraw-Hill, 1975, pp. 85-86.

13-5 *NASTRAN Theoretical Manual*, NASA SP-221, Section 5.5.3.

13-6 Wilkinson, J. H., *The Algebraic Eigenvalue Problem*, London, Oxford Press, 1965.

13-7 Wilkinson, J. H., "The Calculation of the Eigenvectors of Co-Diagonal Matrices," *The Computer Journal*, Vol. 1, 1958, pp. 90.

13-8 Guyan, R., "Reduction of Stiffness and Mass Matrices," *AIAA J.*, V. 3, No. 2, February, 1965, pp. 380.

13-9 Dong, S.B., Wolf, J. A., and Peterson, F. E., "On a Direct-Iterative Eigensolution Technique," *Int. J. for Num. Methods in Engr.*, 4, No. 2, pp. 155-161.

13-10 *MSC/NASTRAN Applications Manual*, Sec. 2.4.

13-11 Levy, R., "Guyan Reduction Solutions Recycled for Improved Accuracy," *NASTRAN User Experiences*, NASA TM X-2378, September, 1971, pp. 201-220.

13.11. Problems

13-1. Verify that the first two symmetric elastic frequencies and mode shapes for the free-free beam in Sec. 13.9.1. agree with theoretical results.

13-2. Modify the problem in Sec. 13.9.1. to determine the antisymmetric modes for the free-free beam using SUPORT Bulk Data to define the rigid body modes. Verify that the first two antisymmetric elastic frequencies and mode shapes agree with theoretical results.

13-3. Verify that the first two symmetrical elastic modes and frequencies for the simply-supported plate in Sec. 13.9.2. agree with theoretical results.

13-4. Modify the input data for the problem in Sec. 13.9.2. to obtain the first two antisymmetric elastic modes and frequencies. Verify that the results agree with theoretical results.

Appendix A,

Bulk Data Format

The NASTRAN Bulk Data cards have fixed lengths of either 8 or 16 columns. Either field length, termed small and large field data cards, respectively, may be used. The small field data card should be adequate for the specification of data that define a physical structure. However, the situation may arise when the eight column field will not provide sufficient numerical significance. In these cases the large field data card may be used.

A.1. Small Field Data Card

The small field data card consists of 10 fields of 8 columns each as shown:

1	2	3	4	5	6	7	8	9	10
1-8	9-16	17-24	25-32	33-40	41-48	49-56	57-64	65-72	73-80

A card mnemonic is inserted in field 1. Fields 2 thorugh 9 are for data items. The limitations on data items are that they must lie completely within the designated field, have no imbedded blanks, and be of the proper type, i.e., blank, integer, real, double precision, or literal, as indicated on the appropriate Bulk Data card description. Real numbers can be encoded in various ways. For example, the real number "7" may be encoded as 7.0, .7E1, 0.7E + 1, 70. − 1, .70E + 1, etc. A double precision number must contain an exponent with the character D such as 7.0D0. Double precision data values are only allowed in a few situations.

Normally, the contents of field 10 are not used by NASTRAN and may be used for any purpose. However, in the case where a logical card consists of more than one physical card, field 10 of the parent card is used in conjunction with field 1 of the continuation card as an identifier and hence must contain a unique entry.

Continuation cards contain the symbols + or * in column 1 for a small or large field continuation, respectively, followed by the same characters that appeared in column 74 through 80 of the card that is being continued. The use of continuation mnemonics allows the Bulk Data to be submitted as an unsorted deck. It should be emphasized that all continuation mnemonics must be unique in the data deck.

A.2. Large Field Bulk Data Card

1A	2	3	4	5	10A
1-8	9-24	25-40	41-56	57-72	73-80

1B	2	3	4	5	10B
1-8	9-24	25-40	41-56	57-72	73-80

A large field card is defined by placing the symbol < * > after a Bulk Data mnemonic in field 1A and some unique continuation mnemonic in the last 7 columns of field 10A. The second physical card contains the symbol < * > in column 1 followed by the same continuation mnemonic that appeared in columns 74 through 80 of field 10A in the first card. The second card may in turn be used to point to an either large or small field continuation card. The use of multiple small and large field cards is illustrated by the following examples.

1. Small field with small continuation

TYPE								+ EA
+ EA								

2. Large field card

TYPE*				*ED1
*ED1				

3. Large field card with large field continuation card

TYPE*				*ED21
*ED21				*ED22
*ED22				*ED23
*ED23				

4. Large field card followed by small and large field continuation cards

TYPE*						*ED31
*ED31						+ ED32
+ ED32						*ED33
*ED33						*ED34
*ED34						

Appendix B,

Use of Parameters

Parameters may be specified by the user by means of a PARAM-card in Bulk Data. The PARAM-card is as shown by Card Image B-1.

1	2	3	4	5	6	7	8	9	10
PARAM	N	V1	V2						

where:

N   Parameter name

V1, V2   Parameter value depending on the parameter type as follows:

TYPE	V1	V2
Integer	Integer	Blank
Real, single-precision	Real	Blank
Literal	Literal	Blank
Real, double-precision	D.P.	Blank
Complex, single-precision	Real	Real
Complex, double-precision	D.P.	D.P.

The PARAM Bulk Data Card Image B-1

The allowable PARAMeters which are defined in the MSC/NASTRAN rigid formats are described in Sec. 3.1.3 of the MSC/NASTRAN User's Manual. The PARAMeters which may be useful for rigid formats 24 and 3 are summarized below.

ASING   Automatic elimination of matrix singularities for normal modes analysis (Sec. 13.7)

AUTOSPC   Automatic purge of unconnected degrees of freedom (Sec. 7.5.2.4 and Sec. 12.4.3.2). Associated PARAMeters include

> EPPRT
> EPZERO
> PRGPST
> SPCGEN
> USETPRT
> USETSEL

COUPMASS   A positive value (default is -1) requests the coupled rather than the lumped mass formulation.

GRDPNT   A positive value (default is -1) requests the weight and balance information described in Sec. 12.5 to be calculated and displayed using the grid point number, defined as the value of the PARAMeter as the reference point.

IRES   A positive value (default is -1) requests that the residual for the - and o-sets be displayed.

MAXRATIO   The presence of this parameter will cause the conditioning numbers for each degree of freedom to be compared to the value of the PARAMeter (default is 10^5). If they are greater than MAXRATIO the matrix is considered to include a mechanism. The conditioning numbers and the external degree of freedom codes are printed and execution is terminated.

NEWSEQ   An integer value ≥ 0 requests grid point number resequencing to improve the matrix topology. (Sec. 7.3.5). Related PARAMeters include

> FACTOR
> MPCX
> SEQOUT
> START

NOELOF   A positive integer value (default is -1) requests that grid point forces be aligned with the edges of two-dimensional elements.

NOELOP   A positive integer value (default is -1) requests the printout of the sum of forces parallel to edges of adjacent elements.

NOGPF   A positive integer value (default is -1) requests that grid point forces be printed in the global coordinate system associated with the point.

TINY   A real parameter (default is 1.E-3) which defines a lower bound for controlling strain energy printout. Elements having strain energy less than 'TINY' percent of the total strain energy will not be printed. (See Sec. 1.8.2.5).

WTMASS   The mass matrix is multiplied by the value of this parameter (default is 1.) prior to dynamic analysis. The use of this PARAMeter allows the analyst to define the density and nonstructural mass in terms of weight units which are then multiplied by a value of 1/g which is specified as the WTMASS PARAMeter value.

Appendix C,

Summary of Bulk Data

For Static and Normal Mode Analyis

C.1. Defining Scalar Degrees of Freedom — SPOINT

1	2	3	4	5	6	7	8	9	10
SPOINT	S_1	S_2	S_3	etc.					
SPOINT	S_1	THRU	S_n						

C.2. Defining Global Coordinate Systems

1	2	3	4	5	6	7	8	9	10
CORD1C	CID	GA	GB	GC					
CORD1R	CID	GA	GB	GC					
CORD1S	CID	GA	GB	GC					
CORD2C + C1	CID C_1	RID C_2	A_1 C_3	A_2	A_3	B_1	B_2	B_3	+ C1
CORD2R + C2	CID C_1	RID C_2	A_1 C_3	A_2	A_3	B_1	B_2	B_3	+ C2
CORD2S + C3	CID C_1	RID C_2	A_1 C_3	A_2	A_3	B_1	B_2	B_3	+ C3

C.3. Defining Geometric Grid Points (7.3.3)

1	2	3	4	5	6	7	8	9	10
GRDSET		CP				CD	PSPC		
GRID	ID	CP	X_1	X_2	X_3	CD	PSPC		

C.4. Grid Point Resequencing (7.3.5)

1	2	3	4	5	6	7	8	9	10
SEQGP	ID	SEQID	ID	SEQID	etc.				

C.5. Multipoint Constraints (7.5.1)

1	2	3	4	5	6	7	8	9	10
MPC	SID	GM	CM	A_m	G_1	C_1	A_1		+ M1
+ M1		G_2	C_2	A_2	etc.				
MPCADD	SID	S_1	S_2	S_3	etc.				

C.6. Single Point Constraints (7.5.2)

1	2	3	4	5	6	7	8	9	10
SPC	SID	G	C	D	G	C	D		
SPC1	SID	C	G_1	G_2	G_3	G_4	G_5	G_6	+ S1
+ S1	G_7	etc.							
SPC1	SID	C	S_i	THRU	G_j				
SPCADD	SID	S_1	S_2	S_3	etc.				

C.7. Static Condensation (7.6)

1	2	3	4	5	6	7	8	9	10
OMIT	G	C	G	C	G	C	G	C	
OMIT1	C	G_1	G_2	G_3	G_4	G_5	G_6	G_7	+ 01
+ 01	G_8	etc.							
OMIT1	C	G_i	THRU	G_j					
ASET	G	C	G	C	etc.				
ASET1	C	G_1	G_2	etc.					
ASET1	C	G_i	THRU	G_j					

C.8. Support of Free Bodies

(7.7)

1	2	3	4	5	6	7	8	9	10
SUPORT	G	C	G	C	G	C	G	C	

C.9. General Element

(7.9)

1	2	3	4	5	6	7	8	9	10
GENEL	EID		GI_1	CI_1	GI_2	CI_2	etc.		+1
+1	UD		GD_1	CD_1	GD_2	CD_2	etc.		+2
+2	Z		Z_{11}	Z_{21}	Z_{31}	etc.			+3
+3	S		S_{11}	S_{12}	S_{13}	etc.			

C.10. Scalar Elastic Elements

(9.3)

1	2	3	4	5	6	7	8	9	10
CELAS1	EID	PID	G1	C1	G2	C2			
PELAS	PID	K	GE	S					
CELAS2	EID	K	G1	C1	G2	C2	GE	S	

C.11. Truss Elements

(9.4)

1	2	3	4	5	6	7	8	9	10
CONROD	EID	G1	G2	MID	A	J	C	NSM	
CROD	EID	PID	G1	G2					
PROD	PID	A	J	C	NSM				
CTUBE	EID	PID	G1	G2					
PTUBE	PID	D	T	NSM					

C.12. Uniform Beam

(9.5)

1	2	3	4	5	6	7	8	9	10
BAROR		PID			V_1,GO	V_2	V_3		
CBAR	EID	PID	GA	GB	V_1,GO	V_2	V_3		+C1
+C1	PA	PB	Z_{1A}	Z_{2A}	Z_{3A}	Z_{1B}	Z_{2B}	Z_{3B}	
PBAR	PID	MID	A	I_{zz}	I_{yy}	J	NSM		+P1
+P1	C_y	C_z	D_y	D_z	E_y	E_z	F_y	F_z	+P2
+P2	K_y	K_z	I_{yz}						
CBARAO	EID	SCALE	x_1	x_2	x_3	x_4	x_5	x_6	+C1
CBARAO	EID	SCALE	NPTS	x_1	Δx				

417

C.13. Tapered Beam

(9.6)

1	2	3	4	5	6	7	8	9	10
CBEAM	EID	PID	GA	GB	V_1,GO	V_2	V_3		+ C1
+ C1	PA	PB	Z_{1A}	Z_{2A}	Z_{3A}	Z_{1B}	Z_{2B}	Z_{3B}	+ C2
+ C2	SA	SB							
PBEAM	PID	MID	A_A	I_{zzA}	I_{yyA}	I_{yzA}	J_A	NSM_A	+ P1
+ P1	C_{yA}	C_{zA}	D_{yA}	D_{zA}	E_{yA}	E_{zA}	F_{yA}	F_{zA}	+ P2
+ P2	SOPT	x/x_B	A	I_{zz}	I_{yy}	I_{yz}	J	NSM	+ P3
+ P3	C_y	C_z	D_y	D_z	E_y	E_z	F_y	F_z	+ P4
+ P4	K_y	K_z	S_y	S_z	NSI_A	NSI_B	CW_A	CW_B	+ P5
+ P5	M_{yA}	M_{zA}	M_{yB}	M_{zB}	N_{yA}	N_{zA}	N_{yB}	N_{zB}	

C.14. Curved Beam

(9.7)

1	2	3	4	5	6	7	8	9	10
CBEND	EID	PID	GA	GB	V_1,GO	V_2	V_3	GEOM	
PBEND	PID	MID	A	I_{zz}	I_{rr}	J	R_B	θ_B	+ P1
+ P1	C_r	C_z	D_r	D_z	E_r	E_z	F_r	F_z	+ P2
+ P2	K_r	K_z	NSM	R_c	Z_c	ΔN			
PBEND	PID	MID	FSI	R	t	P	R_B	θ_B	+ P3
+ P3			NSM	R_c	Z_c				

C.15. Shear Panel

(9.8)

1	2	3	4	5	6	7	8	9	10
CSHEAR	EID	PID	G1	G2	G3	G4			
PSHEAR	PID	EID	T	NSM					
PSHEAR	PID	EID	T	NSM	F1	F2			

C.16. Isoparametric Shell Elements
(9.9)

1	2	3	4	5	6	7	8	9	10
CTRIA3 + T3	EID	PID	G1 T1	G2 T2	G3 T3	θ_m			+ T3
CQUAD4 + Q4	EID	PID	G1 T1	G2 T2	G3 T3	G4 T4	θ_m		+ Q4
CTRIA6 + T6	EID	PID θ_m	G1 T1	G2 T2	G3 T3	G4	G5	G6	+ T6
CQUAD8 + Q8	EID G7	PID G8	G1 T1	G2 T2	G3 T3	G4 T4	G5 θ_m	G6	+ Q8
PSHELL + P1	PID Z1	MID1 Z2	T MID4	MID2	R_I	MID3	R_T	NSM	+ P1
PCOMP + P2 + P3	PID MID_1 MID_3	Z_o T_1 T_3	NSM θ_1 θ_3	S_b $SOUT_1$ $SOUT_3$	FT MID_2 etc.	T_{ref} T_2	GE θ_2	$SOUT_2$	+ P2 + P3

C.17. Isoparametric Solids
(9.10)

1	2	3	4	5	6	7	8	9	10
CPENTA + P1 + P2	EID G7 G15	PID G8	G1 G9	G2 G10	G3 G11	G4 G12	G5 G13	G6 G14	+ P1 + P2
CHEXA + H1 + H2	EID G7 G15	PID G8 G16	G1 G9 G17	G2 G10 G18	G3 G11 G19	G4 G12 G20	G5 G13	G6 G14	+ H1 + H2
PSOLID	PID	MID	CORDM	IN					

C.18. Congruent Elements
(9.12)

1	2	3	4	5	6	7	8	9	10
CNGRNT	PRID	$SECID_1$	$SECID_2$	etc.					

C.19. Constraint Elements

1	2	3	4	5	6	7	8	9	
RROD	EID	GA	GB	CMA	CMB				
RBAR	EID	GA	GB	CNA	CNB	CMA	CMB		
RTRPLT	EID	GA	GB	GC	CNA	CNB	CNC		+ R1
+ R1	CMA	CMB	CMC						
RBE1	EID	GN_1	CN_1	GN_2	CN_2	GN_3	CN_3		+ R2
+ R2		GN_4	CN_4	etc.					+ R3
+ R3	UM	GM_1	CM_1	GM_2	CM_2	GM_3	CM_3		+ R4
+ R4		GM_4	CM_4	etc.					
RBE2	EID	GN	CM	GM_1	GM_2	GM_3	GM_4	GM_5	+ R5
+ R5	GM_6	etc.							
RBE3	EID		REFGR	REFC	WT_1	C_1	$G1_1$	$G2_1$	+ R6
+ R6	$G3_1$	WT_2	C_2	$G1_2$	$G2_2$	. . .	WT_3	C_3	+ R7
+ R7	$G1_3$	etc.							+ R8
+ R8	UM	GM_1	CM_1	GM_2	CM_2	GM_3	CM_3		+ R9
+ R9		GM_4	CM_4	etc.					
RSPLINE	EID	D/L	G1	G2	C2	G3	C3	G4	+ R10
+ R10	C4	etc.							

1	2	3	4	5	6	7	8	9	
MAT1	MID	E	G	NU	RH	A	T_{ref}	GE	+ M1
+ M1	ST	SC	SS	MCSID					
MAT2	MID	G_{11}	G_{12}	G_{13}	G_{22}	G_{23}	G_{33}	RH	+ M2
+ M2	A_1	A_2	A_{12}	T_{ref}	GE	ST	SC	SS	+ MM2
+ MM2	MCSID								
MAT8	MID	E_1	E_2	ν_{12}	G_{12}	G_{1Z}	G_{2Z}	RHO	+ 1
+ 1	A_1	A_2	T_{ref}	X_t	X_c	Y_t	Y_c	S	+ 2
+ 2	GE	F_{12}							
MAT9	MID	G_{11}	G_{12}	G_{13}	G_{14}	G_{15}	G_{16}	G_{22}	+ M3
+ M3	G_{23}	G_{24}	G_{25}	G_{26}	G_{33}	G_{34}	G_{35}	G_{36}	+ M4
+ M4	G_{44}	G_{45}	G_{46}	G_{55}	G_{56}	G_{66}	RH	A_1	+ M5
+ M5	A_2	A_3	A_4	A_5	A_6	T_{ref}	GE		
MATT1	MID	R1	R2	R3	R4	R5	R6	R7	+ T1
+ T1	R8	R9	R10						
MATT2	MID	R1	R2	R3	R4	R5	R6	R7	+ T2
+ T2	R8	R9	R10		R12	R13	R14	R15	
MATT9	MID	R1	R2	R3	R4	R5	R6	R7	+ T3
+ T3	R8	R9	R10	R11	R12	R13	R14	R15	+ T4
+ T4	R16	R17	R18	R19	R20	R21	R22	R23	+ T5
+ T5	R24	R25	R26	R27	R28		R30		
TABLEM1	ID								+ TM1
+ TM1	x_1	y_1	x_2	y_2	ENDT				
TABLEM2	ID	T_a							+ TM2
+ TM2	x_1	y_1	x_2	y_2	ENDT				
TABLEM3	ID	T_a	T_b						+ TM3
+ TM3	x_1	y_1	x_2	y_2	ENDT				
TABLEM4	ID	T_a	T_b	T_L	T_u				+ TM4
+ TM4	A_0	A_1	A_2	ENDT					

C.21. Defining Applied Loads

1	2	3	4	5	6	7	8	9	10
FORCE	SID	G	CID	A	N_1	N_2	N_3		
MOMENT	SID	G	CID	A	N_1	N_2	N_3		
FORCE1	SID	G	A	G1	G2				
MOMENT1	SID	G	A	G1	G2				
FORCE2	SID	G	A	G1	G2	G3	G4		
MOMENT2	SID	G	A	G1	G2	G3	G4		
SLOAD	SID	S	F						
PLOAD1	SID	EID	TYPE	SCALE	X_1	P_1	X_2	P_2	
PLOAD2	SID	P	EID_1	EID_2	etc.				
PLOAD2	SID	P	EID_i	THRU	EID_j				
PLOAD4	SID	EID	P_1	P_2	P3	P4	G_1	G_3	+ P1
+ P1	CID	N_1	N_2	N_3					
GRAV	SID	CID	G	N_1	N_2	N_3			
RFORCE	SID	G_0	CID	A	N_1	N_2	N_3	METHOD	
LOAD	SID	S_0	S_1	L_1	S_2	L_2	etc.		
SPCD	SID	G	C	D	G	C	D		
DEFORM	SID	EID	D						
TEMP	SID	G	T	G	T	G	T		
TEMPD	SID	T	SID	T	SID				
TEMPRB	SID	EID1	T_a	T_b	T_{ya}	T_{yb}	T_{za}	T_{zb}	+ T1
+ T1	TC_a	TD_a	TE_a	TF_a	TC_b	TD_b	TE_b	TF_b	+ T2
+ T2	EID2	etc.							
TEMPP1	SID	EID1	T	T'	T_1	T_2			+ TP1
+ TP1	EID2	etc.							

422

C.22. Defining Concentrated Mass (13.4.3)

1	2	3	4	5	6	7	8	9	10
CMASS1	EID	PID	G1	C1	G2	C2			
PMASS	PID	M							
CMASS2	EID	M	G1	C1	G2	C2			
CONM1	EID	G	CID	M_{11}	M_{21}	M_{22}	M_{31}	M_{32}	+ C1
+ C1	M_{33}	M_{41}	M_{42}	M_{43}	M_{44}	M_{51}	M_{52}	M_{53}	+ C2
+ C2	M_{54}	M_{55}	M_{61}	M_{62}	M_{63}	M_{64}	M_{65}	M_{66}	
CONM2	EID	G	CID	M	X_1	X_2	X_3		+ C3
+ C3	I_{11}	I_{21}	I_{22}	I_{31}	I_{32}	I_{33}			

C.23. Defining Real Eigenvalue Method (13.5)

1	2	3	4	5	6	7	8	9	10
EIGR	SID	METHOD	F1	F2	NE	ND	NZ	E	+ E1
+ E1	NORM	G	C						

C.24. Defining Generalized Dynamic Reduction (13.8)

1	2	3	4	5	6	7	8	9	10
DYNRED	SID	FMAX				QDOF			
SPOINT	S_1	THRU	S_n						
ASET1	0	S_1	THRU	S_n					
QSET1	0	S_1	THRU	S_n					

C.25. Defining Direct Matrix Input (3.5)

1	2	3	4	5	6	7	8	9	10
DMI	NAME	0	FORM	TIN	TOUT		M	N	
DMI	NAME	J	I	$A_{i,j}$	$A_{i+1,j}$	etc.			

*DMIG (12.1.1.)

1	2	3	4	5	6	7	8	9	10
DMIG	NAME	0	FORM	TIN	TOUT				
DMIG	NAME	GJ	CJ		GI	CI	X_{ij}	Y_{ij}	

C.26. Obsolete Capability (See COSMIC/NASTRAN User's Manual for description)

	1	2	3	4	5	6	7	8	9	10
CTRMEM	EID	PID	G1	G2	G3	θ_m			
PTRMEM	PID	MID	T	NSM					
CQDMEM	EID	PID	G1	G2	G3	G4	θ_m		
PQDMEM	PID	MID	T	NSM					
CQDMEM1	EID	PID	G1	G2	G3	G4	θ_m		
PQDMEM1	PID	MID	T	NSM					
CQDMEM2	EID	PID	G1	G2	G3	G4	θ_m		
PQDMEM2	PID	MID	T	NSM					
CTRTLT	EID	PID	G1	G2	G3	θ_m			
PTRPLT	PID	MID1	I	MID2	T	NSM	Z1	Z2	
CQDPLT	EID	PID	G1	G2	G3	G4	θ_m		
PQDPLT	PID	MID1	I	MID2	T	NSM	Z1	Z2	
CTRIA1	EID	PID	G1	G2	G3	θ_m			
PTRIA1	PID	MID1	T1	MID2	I	MID3	T2	NSM	+ P1
+ P1	Z1	Z2							
CQUAD1	EID	PID	G1	G2	G3	G4	θ_m		
PQUAD1	PID	MID1	T1	MID2	I	MID3	T2	NSM	+ Q1
+ Q1	Z1	Z2							
CTRIA2	EID	PID	G1	G2	G3	θ_m			
PTRIA2	PID	MID	T	NSM					
CQUAD2	EID	PID	G1	G2	G3	G4	θ_m		
PQUAD2	PID	MID	T	NSM					
CTETRA	EID	MID	G1	G2	G3	G4			
CWEDGE	EID	MID	G1	G2	G3	G4	G5	G6	
CHEXA1	EID	MID	G1	G2	G3	G4	G5	G6	+ H1
+ H1	G7	G8							
CHEXA2	EID	MID	G1	G2	G3	G4	G5	G6	+ H2
+ H2	G7	G8							
CHEX8	EID	PID	G1	G2	G3	G4	G5	G6	+ C1
+ C1	G7	G8							
CHEX20	EID	PID	G1	G2	G3	G4	G5	G6	+ C2
+ C2	G7	G8	G9	G10	G11	G12	G13	G14	+ C3
+ C3	G15	G16	G17	G18	G19	G20			
PHEX	PID	MID		NGP					

Index

426

427